LOEB CLASSICAL LIBRARY
FOUNDED BY JAMES LOEB 1911

EDITED BY
JEFFREY HENDERSON

CICERO

VI

LCL 240

CICERO

PRO QUINCTIO
PRO ROSCIO AMERINO
PRO ROSCIO COMOEDO
PRO TULLIO
DE LEGE AGRARIA

EDITED AND TRANSLATED BY

ANDREW R. DYCK

HARVARD UNIVERSITY PRESS
CAMBRIDGE, MASSACHUSETTS
LONDON, ENGLAND
2025

Copyright © 2025 by the President and Fellows
of Harvard College
All rights reserved

First published 2025

LOEB CLASSICAL LIBRARY® is a registered trademark
of the President and Fellows of Harvard College

Library of Congress Control Number 2024043437
CIP data available from the Library of Congress

ISBN 978-0-674-99767-7

*Composed in ZephGreek and ZephText by
Technologies 'N Typography, Merrimac, Massachusetts.
Printed on acid-free paper and bound by
Maple Press, York, Pennsylvania*

CONTENTS

PREFACE	ix
ABBREVIATIONS	xi
GENERAL BIBLIOGRAPHY	xv

IN DEFENSE OF PUBLIUS QUINCTIUS
Introduction	2
Text and Translation	10

IN DEFENSE OF SEXTUS ROSCIUS OF AMERIA
Introduction	110
Text and Translation	120

IN DEFENSE OF QUINTUS ROSCIUS THE COMIC ACTOR
Introduction	264
Text and Translation	274

IN DEFENSE OF MARCUS TULLIUS
Introduction	328
Text and Translation	336

CONTENTS

ON THE AGRARIAN LAW

Introduction	382
First Speech	400
Second Speech	432
Third Speech	554

INDEX OF PERSONAL NAMES 571

For Janis

PREFACE

In the mid-nineteenth century the English statesman Thomas Babington Macaulay wrote in his journal, "Read Cicero's Pro P. Quinctio Pro Rosc Amer and Pro Rosc Com skipping here and there—Liked the three speeches much. They are inferior in magnificence, no doubt, but superior, I think, in force and sharpness to the more celebrated orations of his manhood. They are capital speeches to juries."[1] These three fine speeches of the young Cicero are here presented along with a fourth, *Pro Tullio*, not previously issued in the Loeb Classical Library, as well as the speeches *On the Agrarian Law*, reedited with refurbished translations and a new set of notes, replacing the 1930 edition prepared by J. H. Freese. I am grateful to General Editor Jeffrey Henderson, Managing Editor Michael B. Sullivan, and the Foundation's Executive Trustee Richard Thomas for their support and encouragement. My greatest debt is acknowledged in the dedication.

[1] Macaulay 2008, 2:233 (April 12, 1850). Of the three speeches, however, only *Rosc. Am.* was pleaded before a jury; the other two were each tried by a single judge.

ABBREVIATIONS

Calboli Montefusco	See Bibliography.
Castelli Montanari	Castelli Montanari, A. L., ed., trans. *Iulii Severiani Praecepta artis rhetoricae*. Bologna, 1995.
Cr.-D.	Crawford, J. W., and A. R. Dyck, eds., trans. *Cicero's Fragmentary Speeches*. Cambridge, MA, 2024.
Dangel	Dangel, J., ed., trans., comm. *Accius: Oeuvres (fragments)*. Paris, 1995.
Elice	Elice, M., ed. *Romani Aquilae De figuris*. Hildesheim, 2007.
FRL	Goldberg, S. M., and G. Manuwald, eds., trans. *Fragmentary Republic Latin: Ennius*. Cambridge, MA, 2018.
FRLO	Manuwald, G., ed., trans. *Fragmentary Republican Latin: Oratory*. 3 vols. Cambridge, MA, 2019.
fr. orat.	fragmenta oratoria
Giomini-Celentano	Giomini, R., and M. S. Celentano, eds. *C. Iulii Victoris Ars rhetorica*. Leipzig, 1980.
GL	Keil, H., ed. *Grammatici Latini*. 7 vols. Leipzig, 1857–1880.

ABBREVIATIONS

HS	sesterces
Jakobi	Jakobi, R., ed. *Grillius: Commentum in Ciceronis Rhetorica.* Munich, 2002.
K–S	Kühner, R., and C. Stegmann. *Ausführliche Grammatik der lateinischen Sprache, 2: Satzlehre.* Edited by A. Thierfelder. 2 vols. 4th ed. Darmstadt, 1966.
L	Lindsay, W. M., ed. *Nonii Marcelli De conpendiosa doctrina libri XX.* 3 vols. Leipzig, 1903.
LPPR	Rotondi, G. *Leges publicae populi Romani.* Milan, 1912. Reprint with supplement, Hildesheim, 1966.
LTUR	Steinby, E. M., ed. *Lexicon topographicum urbis Romae.* 6 vols. Rome, 1993–2000.
MRR	Broughton, T. R. S. *Magistrates of the Roman Republic.* 3 vols. New York-Atlanta, 1951–1986.
OCD	Hornblower, S., A. Spawforth, and E. Eidinow, eds. *The Oxford Classical Dictionary.* 4th ed. Oxford, 2012.
OLD	Glare, P. G. W., ed. *Oxford Latin Dictionary.* Oxford, 1982.
R.	Ramsey, J. T., ed., trans. *Sallust: Fragments of the Histories, Letters to Caesar.* Cambridge, MA, 2015.

ABBREVIATIONS

RAC	Klauser, T., et al., eds. *Reallexikon für Antike und Christentum*. Stuttgart, 1950–.
RE	Wissowa, G., K. Mittelhaus, and K. Ziegler, eds. *Paulys Realencyclopädie der classischen Altertumswissenschaft*. 83 vols. Stuttgart, 1893–1980.
Riesenweber	Riesenweber, T., ed. *C. Marius Victorinus: Commenta in Ciceronis Rhetorica*. Berlin, 2013.
RLM	Halm, C., ed. *Rhetores Latini minores*. Leipzig, 1863.
RS	Crawford, M. H. *Roman Statutes*. Bulletin of the Institute of Classical Studies Suppl. 64. 2 vols. London, 1996.
St	Stangl, T. *Ciceronis orationum scholiastae: Asconius, scholia Bobiensia, scholia Pseudasconii Sangallensia, scholia Cluniacensia et recentiora Ambrosiana ac Vaticana, scholia Lugdunensia sive Gronoviana et eorum excerpta Lugdunensia. Commentarii*. Leipzig, 1912. Reprint, Hildesheim, 1964.
TLL	*Thesaurus linguae Latinae*. Leipzig, 1900–.
TLRR	Alexander, M. C. *Trials of the Late Roman Republic, 149 BC to 50 BC*. Toronto, 1990.

ABBREVIATIONS

trag.	Ribbeck, O., ed. *Tragicorum Romanorum fragmenta*. 3rd ed. Leipzig, 1898.
W.	Warmington, E. H., ed., trans. *Remains of Old Latin*. 4 vols. Cambridge, MA, 1935.
Willis	Willis, J., ed. *Martianus Capella*. Leipzig, 1983.

BRACKETS AND SYMBOLS

In Latin Text

[ ] deletions by modern scholars (unless introduced with sc., in which case, editor's insertion)
⟨ ⟩ additions by modern scholars

In English Text

[ ] editor's insertions

NOTES TO THE TEXT

Readings are cited according to the edition indicated at the end of the Introduction to the given speech. Peculiar errors of individual witnesses and orthographical variants are generally ignored.

GENERAL BIBLIOGRAPHY

Achard, G. 1981. *Pratique rhétorique et idéologie politique dans les discours "optimates" de Cicéron*. Leiden.

———. 2000. "L'influence des jeunes lecteurs sur la rédaction des discours cicéroniens." In Achard and Ledentu, 75–88.

Achard, G., and M. Ledentu, eds. 2000. *Orateur, auditeurs, lecteurs: à propos de l'éloquence romaine à la fin de la République et au début du Principat*. Lyon.

Adams, J. N. 1973. "Two Latin Words for 'Kill.'" *Glotta* 51:280–92.

———. 1978. "Conventions of Naming in Cicero." *Classical Quarterly* 28:145–66.

Afzelius, A. 1940. "Das Ackerverteilungsgesetz des P. Servilius Rullus." *Classica & Mediaevalia* 3:214–35.

Alexander, M. C. 1985. "*Praemia* in the *quaestiones* of the Late Republic." *Classical Philology* 80:20–32.

———. 2002. *The Case for the Prosecution in the Ciceronian Era*. Ann Arbor.

Arena, V. 2012. *Libertas and the Practice of Politics in the Late Roman Republic*. Cambridge.

Arweiler, A. 2008. "Frauen vor Kultlandschaft: Kleinasiatische Geographie in den Reden Ciceros." In *Vom Euphrat bis zum Bosporus: Kleinasien in der Antike. Fest-*

GENERAL BIBLIOGRAPHY

schrift für Elmar Schwertheim zum 65. Geburtstag, edited by E. Winter, 19–38. Bonn.

Axer, J., ed. 1976. *M. Tullius Cicero: Oratio pro Q. Roscio*. Leipzig.

———. 1977a. "Notes on Cicero's *Pro Q. Roscio Comoedo*." *Eos* 65:231–44.

———. 1977b. "Selected Notes on Cicero's *Pro Q. Roscio Comoedo*." *Philologus* 121:226–40.

———. 1980. *The Style and the Composition of Cicero's Speech "Pro Q. Roscio Comoedo."* Warsaw.

———. 1989. "Tribunal—Stage—Arena: Modelling of the Communication Situation in M. Tullius Cicero's Judicial Speeches." *Rhetorica* 7:299–311.

Badian, E. 1967. "The Testament of Ptolemy Alexander." *Rheinisches Museum* 110:178–92.

Balzarini, M. 1968. "Cicerone Pro Tullio e l'editto di Lucullo." In *Studi in onore di Giuseppe Grosso*, 1:323–82. Turin.

Bannon, C. J. 2000. "Self-help and Social Status in Cicero's *Pro Quinctio*." *Ancient Society* 30:71–94.

Beard, M. 2014. *Laughter in Ancient Rome: On Joking, Tickling, and Cracking Up*. Berkeley.

Benferhat, Y. 2003–2004. "*Vita rustica*: un idéal politique et moral? Réflexions sur le *Pro Roscio Amerino*." In *Rus amoenum. Les agréments de la vie rurale en Gaule romaine et dans les régions voisines*, *Caesarodunum*, edited by R. Bedon and N. Dupré, 37–38:259–87.

Berger, A. 1953. *Encyclopedic Dictionary of Roman Law*. Philadelphia.

Blandenet, M. 2017. "Stratégie discursive et valorisation de la *vita rustica* dans le *Pro Roscio Amerino* de Cicéron." In *Tours et détours de la parole dans la littérature*

GENERAL BIBLIOGRAPHY

antique, edited by C. Hunzinger, G. Mérot, and G. Vassiliadès, 189–202. Bordeaux.

Bleicken, J. 1995. *Cicero und die Ritter*. Abhandlungen der Akademie der Wissenschaften in Göttingen, Philologisch-historische Klasse, 3:213. Göttingen.

Bond, S. E. 2016. *Trade and Taboo: Disreputable Professions in the Roman Mediterranean*. Ann Arbor.

Bonnefond-Coudry, M. 1989. *Le Sénat de la république romaine*. Rome.

Bonnet, M. 1906. "Le dilemme de C. Gracchus." *Revue des Études Anciennes* 8:40–46.

Brunt, P. A. 1971. *Italian Manpower, 225 B.C.–A.D. 14*. Oxford.

Bücher, F. 2009. "Die Erinnerung an Krisenjahre. Das Exemplum der Gracchen im politischen Diskurs der späten Republik." In *Eine politische Kultur (in) der Krise. Die "letzte Generation" der römischen Republik*, edited by K.-J. Hölkeskamp, 99–114. Munich.

Buchheit, V. 1975. "Chrysogonus als Tyrann in Ciceros Rede für Roscius aus Ameria." *Chiron* 5:193–211.

Buongiorno, P. 2010. *"Teukris*. Alle radici di uno pseudonimo dell'epistolario ciceroniano." *Latomus* 69:29–37.

Calboli Montefusco, L., ed., comm. 1979. *Consulti Fortunatiani Ars rhetorica*. Bologna.

Canter, H. V. 1931. *"Digressio* in the Orations of Cicero." *American Journal of Philology* 52:351–61.

Carney, T. F. 1961. *A Biography of C. Marius*. Assen.

Casamento, A. 2013. "Quando non c'è altro da dire: forza della parola e forza della legge nella *pro Archia* di Cicerone." *Bollettino di Studi Latini* 43:1–15.

Centola, D. A. 1999. *Il crimen calumniae. Contributo allo studio del processo criminale romano*. Naples.

GENERAL BIBLIOGRAPHY

Charrier, S. 2003. "Les Anneés 90–80 dans le *Brutus* de Cicéron (§§304–312): la formation d'un orateur au temps des guerres civiles." *Revue des Études Latines* 81:79–96.

Churchill, J. B. 1999. "*Ex qua quod vellent facerent*: Roman Magistrates' Authority over *praeda* and *manubiae*." *Transactions of the American Philological Association* 129:85–116.

Clark, A. C. 1905. *The vetus Cluniacensis of Poggio*. Anecdota Oxoniensia 10. Oxford.

Classen, C. J. 1985. *Recht—Rhetorik—Politik. Untersuchungen zu Ciceros rhetorischer Strategie*. Darmstadt.

Cloud, J. D. 1968. "How Did Sulla Style His Law *de sicariis*?" *Classical Review* 18:140–43.

———. 1969. "The Primary Purpose of the *lex Cornelia de sicariis*." *Zeitschrift der Savigny-Stiftung für Rechtsgeschichte, Romanistische Abteilung* 86:258–86.

Coarelli, F. 1981. *Ditorni di Roma*. Rome-Bari.

Corbett, P. 1986. *The* scurra. Edinburgh.

Costa, E. 1927. *Cicerone giureconsulto*. 2nd ed. 2 vols. Bologna.

Craig, C. P. 1985. "The Structural Pedigree of Cicero's Speeches *Pro Archia*, *Pro Milone*, and *Pro Quinctio*." *Classical Philology* 80:136–37.

———. 1993. *Form as Argument in Cicero's Speeches: A Study of Dilemma*. Atlanta.

Crawford, J. W. 1984. *M. Tullius Cicero: The Lost and Unpublished Orations*. Göttingen.

Crook, J. A. 1955. Consilium principis: *Imperial Councils and Counsellors from Augustus to Diocletian*. Cambridge.

———. 1976. "*Sponsione provocare*: Its Place in Roman Litigation." *Journal of Roman Studies* 66:132–38.

Damon, C. 1997. *The Mask of the Parasite: A Pathology of Roman Patronage.* Ann Arbor.

Damon, C., and C. S. MacKay. 1995. "On the Prosecution of C. Antonius in 76 B.C." *Historia* 44:37–55.

Dickey, E. 2002. *Latin Forms of Address from Plautus to Apuleius.* New York-Oxford.

Drummond, A. 1999. "Tribunes and Tribunician Programmes in 63 B.C." *Athenaeum* 87:121–67.

———. 2000. "Rullus and the Sullan *possessores*." *Historia* 82:126–53.

Dudley, D. R. 1941. "Blossius of Cumae." *Journal of Roman Studies* 31:94–99.

Duplá, A. 2011. "Consulares populares." In *Consuls and res publica: Holding High Office in the Roman Republic*, edited by H. Beck, A. Duplá, M. Jehne, and F. Pina Polo, 279–98. Cambridge.

Dyck, A. R. 1996. *A Commentary on Cicero,* De officiis. Ann Arbor.

———. 2004. *A Commentary on Cicero,* De legibus. Ann Arbor.

———. 2008. "Rivals into Partners: Hortensius and Cicero." *Historia* 57:142–73.

———, ed., comm. 2010. *Cicero: Pro Sexto Roscio.* Cambridge.

———, ed., trans., comm. 2012. *Cicero: Speeches on Behalf of Marcus Fonteius and Marcus Aemilius Scaurus.* Oxford.

———. 2019. Three Textual Notes on Cicero, *De lege agraria* 2, *Classical Quarterly* 69:901–3.

———. Forthcoming. *Cicero: The Man and His Works.*

GENERAL BIBLIOGRAPHY

Eckert, A. 2016. "'There is No One Who Does not Hate Sulla': Emotion, Persuasion and Cultural Trauma." In *Emotion and Persuasion in Classical Antiquity*, edited by E. Sanders and M. Johncock, 133–45. Stuttgart.

———. 2018. "Good Fortune and the Public Good: Disputing Sulla's Claim to Be *felix*." In *Institutions and Ideology in Republican Rome: Speech, Audience and Decision*, edited by H. van der Blom, C. Gray, and C. Steel, 283–98. Cambridge.

Edmondson, J. 2016. "Investing in Death: Gladiators as Investment and Currency in the Late Republic." In *Money and Power in the Roman Republic*, edited by H. Beck, M. Jehne, and J. Serrati, 37–52. Brussels.

Egmond, F. 1995. "The Cock, the Dog, the Serpent, and the Monkey: Reception and Transmission of a Roman Punishment, or Historiography as History." *International Journal of the Classical Tradition* 2:159–92.

Eich, A. 2008. "Überlegungen zur juristischen und sozialen Bewertung der Fälschung öffentlicher Urkunden während der späten Republik und der Kaiserzeit." *Zeitschrift für Papyrologie und Epigraphik* 166:227–46.

Elster, M. 2014. "Die römischen *leges de civitate* von den Gracchen bis zu Sulla." In *Gesetzgebung und politische Kultur in der römischen Republik*, edited by U. Walter, 183–226. Heidelberg.

Espluga, X. 2016. "Cicero. Speeches. An Overview." In *From the Protohistory to the History of the Text*, edited by J. Velaza, 55–101. Bern.

Farney, G. D. 2007. *Ethnic Identity and Aristocratic Competition in Republican Rome*. Cambridge.

Ferrary, J.-L. 1988. "Rogatio Servilia agraria." *Athenaeum* 66:141–64.

GENERAL BIBLIOGRAPHY

Flower, H. I. 1996. *Ancestor Masks and Aristocratic Power in Roman Culture*. Oxford.

Freyburger, G. 1986. *Fides. Étude sémantique et religieuse depuis les origins jusqu'à l'époque augustéenne*. Paris.

Frier, B. 1983. "Urban Praetors and Rural Violence: The Legal Background of Cicero's *Pro Caecina*." *Transactions of the American Philological Association* 113:221–41.

———. 1985. *The Rise of the Roman Jurists*. Princeton.

Fuhrmann, M. 1990. "Mündlichkeit und fiktive Mündlichkeit in den von Cicero veröffentlichten Reden." In *Strukturen der Mündlichkeit in der römischen Literatur*, edited by G. Vogt-Spira, 53–62. Tübingen.

Gabba, E. 1973. *Esercito e società nella tarda repubblica romana*. Florence.

———. 1976. *Republican Rome, the Army and the Allies*. Translated by P. J. Cuff. Berkeley-Los Angeles.

García Morcillo, M. 2016. "Placing the *hasta* in the Forum: Cicero and the Topographical Symbolism of Patrimonial Sales." In *Ruin or Renewal? Places in the Transformation of Memory in the City of Rome*, edited by M. García Morcillo, J. H. Richardson, and F. Santangelo, 113–33. Rome.

Garofalo, P. 2019. "Sulla, i Caecilii Metelli e Lanuvium." *Hermes* 147:42–52.

Garuti, I., ed. 1965. *M. Tulli Ciceronis Pro M. Tullio oratio*. Milan.

Gnoli, F. 1979. *Ricerche sul crimen peculatus*. Milan.

Greenidge, A. H. J. 1901. *The Legal Procedure of Cicero's Time*. Oxford.

Guérin, C. 2015. *La voix de la vérité. Témoin et témoignage dans les tribunaux romains du Ier siècle avant J.-C.* Paris.

GENERAL BIBLIOGRAPHY

Hall, J. 2014. *Cicero's Use of Judicial Theater*. Ann Arbor.

Harries, J. 2011. "Violating the Principles of Partnership: Cicero on Quinctius and Naevius." In Smith and Covino, 127–43.

Hartung, H.-J. 1974. "Religio und sapientia iudicum: Einige grundsätzliche Bemerkungen zu einem Geschworenenspiegel in Ciceros Reden." *Hermes* 102:556–66.

Harvey, P. B. 1982. "Cicero, Consius, and Capua: II. Cicero and M. Brutus' Colony." *Athenaeum* 60:145–71.

Hermann, M. 2012. "Die Wahrscheinlichkeit als Argumentationsmittel in Ciceros Rede 'Pro Qunctio.'" *Gymnasium* 119:523–42.

Hinard, F. 1976. "Remarques sur les 'praecones' et le 'praeconium' dans la Rome de la fin de la République." *Latomus* 35:730–46.

———. 1985a. "Le 'Pro Quinctio,' un discours politique?" *Revue des Études Anciennes* 87:88–107.

———. 1985b. *Les proscriptions de la Rome républicaine*. Rome.

Hinard, F., and Y. Benferhat, eds., trans. 2006. *Cicéron: Discours*, 1.2: *Pour Sextus Roscius*. Paris.

Hopkins, K. 1980. "Taxes and Trade in the Roman Empire." *Journal of Roman Studies* 70:101–25.

Jonkers, E. J. 1963. *A Social and Economic Commentary on Cicero's* De lege agraria orationes tres. Leiden.

Kaser, M. 1956. "Infamia und ignominia in den römischen Rechtsquellen." *Zeitschrift der Savigny-Stiftung für Rechtsgeschichte, Romanistische Abteilung* 73:220–78.

Kaser, M., and K. Hackl. 1996. *Das römische Zivilprozessrecht*. 2nd ed. Munich.

Kasten, H., ed. 1968. *M. Tullius Cicero: Oratio Pro Sex. Roscio Amerino*. Leipzig.

GENERAL BIBLIOGRAPHY

Kaster, R. A., ed., trans., comm. 2006. *Cicero: Speech on Behalf of Publius Sestius*. Oxford.

Kay, P. 2014. *Rome's Economic Revolution*. Oxford.

Keaveney, A. 2005. *Sulla: The Last Republican*. 2nd ed. London-New York.

Kenty, J. 2016. "Congenital Virtue: *mos maiorum* in Cicero's Orations." *Classical Journal* 111:429–62.

Khrustalyov, W. K. 2018. "*Sic est (non) iusta causa belli?* Issues of Law and Justice in the Debate Concerning a Roman Annexation of Egypt in 65 B.C." *Hyperboreus* 24:244–64.

Kinsey, T. E., ed., comm. 1971. *M. Tulli Ciceronis Pro P. Quinctio oratio*. Sydney.

———. 1985. "The Case against Sextus Roscius of Ameria." *Antiquité classique* 49:188–96.

Kleve, K. 1996. "How to Read an Illegible Papyrus: Towards an Edition of *PHerc.* 78, Caecilius Statius, *Obolostates sive Faenerator*." *Cronache ercolanesi* 26:5–14.

Klingner, F. 1953. *Ciceros Rede für den Schauspieler Roscius. Eine Episode in der Entwicklung seiner Kunstprosa*. Sitzungsberichte der Bayerischen Akademie der Wissenschaften, Philosophisch-historische Klasse, 4. Munich.

Kragelund, P. 2001. "Dreams, Religion and Politics in Republican Rome." *Historia* 50:3–95.

Krostenko, B. A. 2023. *The Voices of the Consul: The Rhetorics of Cicero's* De lege agraria *I and II*. New York.

Kühnert, B. 1989. "*Populus Romanus* und *sentina urbis*: zur Terminologie der *plebs urbana* der späten Republik bei Cicero." *Klio* 71:43–62.

Kumaniecki, K. 1972. "L'orazione 'Pro Quinctio' di Marco Tullio Cicerone." In *Studi Classici in onore di Quintino Cataudella* 3:129–57. Catania.

GENERAL BIBLIOGRAPHY

Kunkel, W., and R. Wittmann. 1995. *Staatsordnung und Staatspraxis der römischen Republik*, 2: *Die Magistratur*. Munich.

La Bua, G. 2005. "*Obscuritas* e *dissimulatio* nella *pro Tullio* di Cicerone." *Rhetorica* 23:261–80.

———. 2019. *Cicero and Roman Education: The Reception of the Speeches and Ancient Scholarship*. Cambridge.

Lausberg, H. 1998. *Handbook of Literary Rhetoric: A Foundation for Literary Study*. Translated by M. T. Bliss, A. Jansen, and D. E. Orton. Edited by D. E. Orton and R. D. Anderson. Leiden = *Handbuch der literarischen Rhetorik*. 3rd ed. Stuttgart, 1990.

Lebek, W. D. 1996. "Moneymaking on the Roman Stage." In *Roman Theater and Society*, edited by W. J. Slater, 29–48. E. Togo Salmon Papers I. Ann Arbor.

Lenel, O. 1927. *Das Edictum perpetuum*. 3rd ed. Leipzig. Reprint, Aalen, 1956.

Lennon, J. J. 2022. *Dirt and Denigration: Stigma and Marginalisation in Ancient Rome*. Tübingen.

Leonhardt, J. 1998–1999. "Senat und Volk in Ciceros Reden *De lege agraria*." *Acta Classica Universitatis Scientiarum Debreceniensis* 34–35:279–92.

Leovant-Cirefice, V. 2000. "Le rôle de l'apostrophe aux *Quirites* dans les discours de Cicéron adressés au peuple." In Achard and Ledentu, 43–55.

Lintott, A. 1999. *The Constitution of the Roman Republic*. Oxford.

———. 2008. *Cicero as Evidence: A Historian's Companion*. Oxford.

Lo Cascio, E. 2006. "Realtà e rappresentazione: la caratterizzazione degli *homines ex municipiis rusticanis* nella

pro Roscio Amerino." In *Lo spettacolo della giustizia: le orazioni di Cicerone*, edited by G. Petrone. and A. Casamento, 49–62. Palermo.

Loutsch, C. M. 1979. "Remarques sur Cicéron, *Pro Sexto Roscio Amerino*." *Liverpool Classical Monthly* 4.6:107–12.

———. 1982. "Cicéron et l'affaire Rabirius (63 av. J.-C.)." *Museum Helveticum* 39:305–15.

———. 1994. *L'exorde dans les discours de Cicéron*. Brussels.

Macaulay, T. B. 2008. *The Journals of Thomas Babington Macaulay*. Edited by W. Thomas. 5 vols. London.

Mantovani, D. 2009. "Cicerone storico del diritto." *Ciceroniana* n.s. 13:297–367.

Manuwald, G. 2011. *Roman Republican Theatre*. Cambridge.

———, ed., trans., comm. 2018. *Cicero: Agrarian Speeches*. Oxford.

———. 2020. *Roman Comedy*. Leiden-Boston.

———, ed., trans., comm. 2021. *Cicero:* Post reditum *Speeches*. Oxford.

Marek, V., ed. 1983. *M. T. Cicero: Orationes de lege agraria, Pro C. Rabirio*. Leipzig.

Marinone, N., and E. Malaspina. 2004. *Cronologia ciceroniana*. 2nd ed. Rome-Bologna.

Marzano, A. 2007. *Roman Villas in Central Italy: A Social and Economic History*. Leiden-Boston.

Maslowski, T., ed. 1995. *M. Tullius Cicero: Orationes in P. Vatinium testem, Pro M. Caelio*. Stuttgart-Leipzig.

May, J. M. 1988. *Trials of Character: The Eloquence of Ciceronian Ethos*. Chapel Hill.

Meister, J. B. 2009. "Pisos Augenbrauen. Zur Lesbarkeit

aristokratischer Körper in der späten römischen Republik." *Historia* 58:71–95.

Mette, H. J. 1965. "Der junge Zivilanwalt Cicero." *Gymnasium* 72:10–27.

Mollea, S. 2022. "*Humanitas* dei giudici, colpevolezza dell'imputato in alcune orazioni ciceroniane?" *Ciceroniana On Line* 6:233–57.

Mommsen, T. 1887–1888. *Römisches Staatsrecht*. 3rd ed. 3 vols. in 5. Berlin.

———. 1899. *Römisches Strafrecht*. Leipzig.

Moreau, P. 2006. "*Quem honoris causa appello*. L'usage public des noms de personne et ses règles à Rome." In *"Aere perennius": en hommage à Hubert Zehnacker*, edited by J. Champeaux and M. Chassignet, 293–307. Paris.

Morstein-Marx, R. (as Kallet-Marx, R.) 1995. *Hegemony to Empire: The Development of the Roman Imperium in the East from 148 to 62 B.C.* Berkeley-Los Angeles-Oxford.

———. 2004. *Mass Oratory and Political Power in the Late Roman Republic*. Cambridge.

———. 2014. "Persuading the People in the Participatory Roman Context." In *A Companion to Greek Democracy and the Roman Republic*, edited by D. Hammer, 294–309. Chichester.

Mouritsen, H. 2011. *The Freedman in the Roman World*. Cambridge.

———. 2022. *The Roman Elite and the End of the Republic: The* Boni, *the Nobles, and Cicero*. Cambridge.

Narducci, E. 2004. *Cicerone e i suoi interprete: studi sull'opera e la fortuna*. Pisa.

GENERAL BIBLIOGRAPHY

Nicolet, C. 1970. "Les *finitores ex equestri loco* de la loi Servilia de 63 av. J.-C." *Latomus* 29:72–103.

———. 1974. *L'ordre équestre à l'époque républicaine (312–43 av. J.-C.)*. Vol. 2: *Prosopographie des chevaliers romains*. Paris.

Noble, F. M. 2014. "Sulla and the Gods: Religion, Politics and Propaganda in the *Autobiography* of L. Cornelius Sulla." PhD diss., Newcastle.

Oakley, S. P. 1997–2005. *A Commentary on Livy Books VI–X*. 4 vols. Oxford.

Ogilvie, R. M. 1965. *A Commentary on Livy Books 1–5*. Oxford.

Opelt, I. 1965. *Die lateinischen Schimpfwörter und verwandte sprachliche Erscheinungen. Eine Typologie.* Heidelberg.

Otto, A. 1890. *Die Sprichwörter und sprichwörtlichen Redensarten der Römer*. Leipzig.

Paterson, J. 2004. "Self-reference in Cicero's Forensic Speeches." In Powell and Paterson, 79–95.

Petrucci, A. 2022. "Due cause in materia commerciale a confronto: il caso di Tiziano Primo (Paul. 1 *Decr.* D. 14, 5, 8) e la *Pro Quinctio* di Cicerone." *Ciceroniana On Line* 6:197–217.

Peyron, A., ed. 1824. *M. Tulli Ciceronis Orationum Pro Scauro, Pro Tullio et In Clodium fragmenta inedita*. Stuttgart-Tübingen.

Pieper, C. 2020. "*Nox rei publicae*? Catiline's and Cicero's Nocturnal Activities in the *Catilinarians*." In *The Values of Nighttime in Classical Antiquity. Between Dusk and Dawn*, edited by J. Ker and A. Wessels, 210–33. Leiden.

Pina Polo, F. 2018. "How Much History Did the Romans Know? Historical References in Cicero's Speeches to

the People." In *Omnium Annalium Monumenta: Historical Writing and Historical Evidence in Republican Rome*, edited by K. Sandberg and C. Smith, 205–33. Leiden-Boston.

———. 2019. "Rhetoric of Fear in Republican Rome: The Ciceronian Case." In *Communicating Public Opinion in the Roman Republic*, edited by C. Rosillo-López, 191–209. Stuttgart.

Platschek, J. 2005. *Studien zu Ciceros Rede für P. Quinctius.* Munich.

———. 2011. "Zum Text von Cic. *Q.Rosc.* 4, 11–12." *Philologus* 155:369–74.

Pocock, L. G. 1926. *A Commentary on Cicero In Vatinium*. London.

Potůček, P. 1998. "The Argumentation *ab humanitate* in Cicero's Judicial Speeches." *Graecolatina Pragensia* 16–17:83–94.

Powell, J. G. F., and J. Paterson, eds. 2004. *Cicero the Advocate*. Oxford.

Ramsey, J. T. 2021. "Asconius on Cicero's Son-in-Law Lentulus, His Apprenticeship under Pupius Piso, and the *De Othone*." *Ciceroniana On Line* 5.1:7–28.

Rauh, N. K. 1989. "Auctioneers and the Roman Economy." *Historia* 38:451–71.

Reeve, M. D., ed. 1992. *M. Tullius Cicero: Oratio pro P. Quinctio*. Stuttgart.

Reinhardt, T. 2003. *Cicero's* Topica, *Edited with an Introduction, Translation and Commentary*. Oxford.

Reynolds, L. D., ed. 1983. *Texts and Transmission: A Survey of the Latin Classics*. Oxford.

Richardson, L. J., Jr. 1992. *A New Topographical Dictionary of Ancient Rome*. Baltimore-London.

GENERAL BIBLIOGRAPHY

Riesenweber, T. 2015. *C. Marius Victorinus, Commenta in Ciceronis Rhetorica*. 2 vols. Berlin-Boston.

Riggsby, A. M. 1999. *Crime and Community in Ciceronian Rome*. Austin.

———. 2010. "Form as Global Strategy in Cicero's Second Catilinarian." In *Form and Function in Roman Oratory*, edited by D. H. Berry and A. Erskine, 94–104. Cambridge.

Robinson, A. 1994. "Cicero's Use of the Gracchi in Two Speeches before the People." *Atene e Roma* n.s. 39:71–76.

Roby, H. J. 1902. *Roman Private Law in the Times of Cicero and of the Antonines*. Vol. 2. Cambridge.

Rosenberger, V. 1992. *Bella et expeditiones. Die antike Terminologie der Kriege Roms*. Stuttgart.

Rosenstein, N. 1995. "Sorting Out the Lot in Republican Rome." *American Journal of Philology* 116:43–75.

Rüfner, T. 2008. Review of Platschek 2005. *Zeitschrift der Savigny-Stiftung für Rechtsgeschichte, Romanistische Abteilung* 125:766–74.

Rüpke, J. 2008. *Fasti sacerdotum*. Translated by D. M. B. Richardson. Oxford.

Russo, F. 2014. "Rhetorical Strategy and Judicial Subterfuges in Cicero's *Pro Tullio*." *Acta Classica* 57:155–64.

Santalucia, B. 2009. "Le formalità introduttive del processo per quaestiones tardo-repubblicano." In *La repressione criminale nella Roma repubblicana fra norma e persuasione*, edited by B. Santalucia, 93–114. Pavia.

Santangelo, F. 2012. "*Sullanus* and *Sullani*." *Arctos* 46:187–91.

Scheuermann, E. S. 2015. *Cicero und das Geld*. Frankfurt am Main.

GENERAL BIBLIOGRAPHY

Schindel, U. 2000. Review of A. L. Castelli Montanari, *Iulius Severianus*. *Gnomon* 72:414–18.

Schmid, W. 1954. Review of Klingner 1953. *Gnomon* 26:317–22.

Schmitthenner, W. 1960. "Politik und Armee in der späten Römischen Republik." *Historische Zeitschrift* 190:1–17.

Schmitz, D. 1985. *Zeugen des Prozeßgegners in Gerichtsreden Ciceros*. Prismata 1. Frankfurt am Main.

Schultz, C. E. 2006. "Juno Sospita and Roman Insecurity in the Social War." In *Maxima debetur magistro reverentia: Essays on Rome and the Roman Tradition in Honor of Russell T. Scott*, edited by P. B. Harvey, Jr., and C. Conybeare, 193–206. Como.

Schulze, W. 1904. *Zur Geschichte lateinischer Eigennamen*. Berlin.

Scullard, H. H. 1970. *Scipio Africanus: Soldier and Politician*. Bristol.

Seager, R. 2007. "The Guilt or Innocence of Sex. Roscius." *Athenaeum* 95:895–910.

Shackleton Bailey, D. R., ed., comm. 1977. *Cicero: Epistulae ad famliares*. 2 vols. Cambridge.

———. 1979. "On Cicero's Speeches." *Harvard Studies in Classical Philology* 83:237–85.

———. 1992. *Onomasticon to Cicero's Speeches*. 2nd ed. Stuttgart-Leipzig.

Shatzman, I. 1972. "The Roman General's Authority over Booty." *Historia* 21:177–205.

———. 1975. *Senatorial Wealth and Roman Politics*. Brussels.

Smith, C., and R. Covino, eds. 2011. *Praise and Blame in Roman Republican Rhetoric*. Swansea.

GENERAL BIBLIOGRAPHY

Strasburger, H. 1956. *Concordia ordinum*. Amsterdam. Original, 1931.

Stroh, W. 1975. *Taxis und Taktik: Die advokatorische Dispositionskunst in Ciceros Gerichtsreden*. Stuttgart.

Tan, J. 2008. "*Contiones* in the Age of Cicero." *Classical Antiquity* 27:163–201.

Tansey, P. 2016. "A Selective Prosopographical Study of Marriage in the Roman Elite in the Second and First Centuries B.C.: Revisiting the Evidence." PhD diss., Macquarie University, Sydney, Australia.

Tarpin, M. 2009. "Les *manubiae* dans la procédure d'appropriation du boutin." In *Praeda. Butin de guerre et société dans la Rome républicaine*, edited by M. Coudry and M. Humm, 81–102. Stuttgart.

Thein, A. 2017. "*Percussores*: A Study in Sullan Violence." *Tyche* 32:235–50.

Thilo, R. M. 1980. *Der Codex accepti et expensi im Römischen Recht. Ein Beitrag zur Lehre von der Litteralobligation*. Göttingen.

Tracy, C. 2008–2009. "The People's Consul: The Significance of Cicero's Use of the Term 'Popularis.'" *Illinois Classical Studies* 33–34:181–99.

Treggiari, S. 1969. *Roman Freedmen during the Late Republic*. Oxford.

Urso, G. 2019. *Catilina, le faux populiste*. Bordeaux.

van der Blom, H. 2017. "Sulla in the 'contio': An Oratorical Episode in Pieces." In *Fragments, Holes, and Wholes: Reconstructing the Ancient World in Theory and Practice*, edited by T. Derda, J. Hilder, and J. Kwapisz, 181–95. Warsaw.

Vasaly, A. 1988. "*Ars dispositionis*: Cicero's Second Agrarian Speech." *Hermes* 116:409–27.

———. 1993. *Representations: Images of the World in Ciceronian Oratory*. Berkeley-Los Angeles-Oxford.

———. 2009. "Cicero, Domestic Politics, and the First Action of the Verrines." *Classical Antiquity* 28:101–137.

Verboven, K. 2002. *The Economy of Friends: Economic Aspects of* amicitia *and Patronage in the Late Republic*. Brussels.

Vervaet, F. J. 2018. "The Date, Modalities and Legacy of Sulla's Abdication of the Dictatorship: A Study in Sullan Statecraft." *Historia Antiqua* 36:31–82.

Ville, G. 1981. *La gladiature en occident des origines à la mort de Domitien*. Rome.

Walter, U. 2014. "*Lex incognita*. Vom 'Übersetzen' der feindlichen *rogatio* in Ciceros Rede *De lege agraria* II." In *Gesetzgebung und politische Kultur in der römischen Republik*, edited by U. Walter, 168–82. Heidelberg.

Webster, T. B. L. 1960. *Studies in Menander*. 2nd ed. Manchester.

Weische, A. 1972. *Ciceros Nachahmung der attischen Redner*. Heidelberg.

Wieacker, F. 1988. *Römische Rechtsgeschichte. Quellenkunde, Rechtsbildung, Jurisprudenz und Rechtsliteratur*. Vol. 1. Munich.

Wiseman, T. P. 1967. "T. Cloelius of Terracina." *Classical Review* 18:263–64.

Wissowa, G. 1912. *Religion und Kultus der Römer*. 2nd ed. Munich. Reprint, 1971.

Wolf, J. G. 2010. "La stigma dell'ignominia." In *Homo, caput, persona. La costruzione giuridica dell'identità nell'esperienza romana dell'epoca di Plauto a Ulpiano*, edited by A. Corbino, M. Humbert, and G. Negri, 491–549. Pavia.

GENERAL BIBLIOGRAPHY

Yakobson, A. 2010. "Traditional Political Culture and the People's Role in the Roman Republic." *Historia* 59:282–302.

Zetzel, J. E. G. 2013. "A Contract on Ameria: Law and Legality in Cicero's *Pro Roscio Amerino*." *American Journal of Philology* 134:425–44.

IN DEFENSE OF
PUBLIUS QUINCTIUS

INTRODUCTION

During the 80s BC the young Cicero enjoyed the finest education available at Rome in philosophy, rhetoric, and the law. He was slow, however, to enter the lists as an advocate in court, partly perhaps because of the unsettled political climate, partly because of his desire as a product of a nonpolitical family and of Arpinum, a town outside Rome, to make a self-confident debut and not learn the advocate's trade in the forum (*Brut.* 311). In any case, his earliest surviving defense is a version of his speech for the trial of P. Quinctius, which occurred in the late summer of 81.[1] By this date Cicero's mentors, such as L. Crassus, who had charge of his early education (*De or.* 2.2), and the Scaevolae, who allowed him to listen to their responses to clients (the way the law was learned at Rome), were already dead.[2] The impetus to tackle this defense came from Cicero's contacts in the theatrical world, in particular the actor Q. Roscius Gallus, who was the brother-in-law of

---

[1] The date follows both from Cicero's age (twenty-five) at the time of the trial (Gell. *NA* 15.28.3) and from the roughly two-year interval between Quinctius' appearance before the praetor on September 13 of 83 and the trial: §§40, 41, 67; cf. Platschek 2005, 2–3n9.

[2] Q. Mucius Scaevola (cos. 117) and his homonymous distant relative (cos. 95): *Leg.* 1.13; *Brut.* 306; *Amic.* 1; he comments on their teaching at *Leg.* 2.47–53.

INTRODUCTION

Quinctius and who pushed Cicero to take on the case at short notice after Quinctius' previous advocate, M. Iunius, had withdrawn (§§77–79).[3]

Quinctius' case was not straightforward. His brother Gaius had been a partner of Sextus Naevius, an auctioneer (*praeco*) by profession, in a business with property in Gaul. Upon Gaius' death, Publius inherited his brother's estates, including his share of the business and his debts (§§11–12, 14). Naevius claimed that Gaius had owed him money from their partnership and filed an action to collect it from Publius. Claiming that the latter had defaulted on an agreed court date secured by bail (*vadimonium*), Naevius applied to the praetor P. Burrenus for authorization to take possession (*missio in possessionem*) of Quinctius' property, which was granted while Quinctius was in Gaul. After ejecting Quinctius from their joint Gallic property, Naevius proceeded to post notices of a sale of Quinctius' seized property (§§25, 28). Thereupon, Quinctius' agent Sextus Alfenus intervened to hinder the sale and prevent Naevius' seizure of one of Quinctius' slaves (§27). Alfenus refused, however, to litigate if he were required to provide security and called on the assistance of a tribune; it was then agreed that the trial be postponed until Quinctius returned from Gaul (§§63–67). On September 13 of 83, Quinctius presented himself in court (§29).

The terms of the trial were then negotiated. Naevius wanted Quinctius to offer security on the ground that,

---

[3] Identification with any of the other known Iunii of the period is uncertain; cf. Platschek 2005, 6n25; Lintott 2008, 44n4. The withdrawal of Iunius is surely related to the complaints that Hortensius brought to the praetor the day before the current trial (§§33–34, cf. §3).

PRO QUINCTIO

since his property had been taken into possession under a praetor's edict for thirty days, which would make him *infamis*, that is, having lost some of his rights as a Roman citizen, his credit was suspect. Quinctius, however, denied that his property had been so taken into possession. To clear the way for litigation over Naevius' property claim, the praetor ordered an initial trial taking the form of a wager (*sponsio*) on Quinctius' assertion. Since Naevius presented prima facie evidence that Quinctius' property had been possessed for thirty days under the praetor's edict, the latter was assigned the role of plaintiff challenging that proposition.

Cicero did not take on the case because of any long-standing tie to Quinctius. Rather, he evidently saw this as an opportunity to make a name for himself, reckoning that the matter would attract attention since Rome's leading advocate, Q. Hortensius, was representing the other side.[4] The legal issue is the narrow one of whether Quinctius' property had been possessed for thirty days under the praetor's edict. One might, therefore, have expected the thirty-day deadline to be contested, but it is not. (It was presumably met.) Rather, Cicero employs an unusual strategy to counter Naevius and Hortensius. He adopts from the beginning a querulous tone, seeking pity for his own inexperience and his client's resourcelessness pitted against the formidable power and influence possessed by the other side (§§1–2).[5] The procedure itself, he claims, is unfair, forcing Quinctius into the position of plaintiff who

---

[4] So Kinsey 1971, 6. On Hortensius, his career, and his relations with Cicero, cf. Dyck 2008.

[5] On this "strategy of lament," see May 1988, 21.

INTRODUCTION

must speak first when he is really defending his rights of citizenship (*caput*), which would be compromised by a conviction (§8). Moreover, their opponents sought unfairly to exert pressure on the praetor to limit the amount of time available to the defense (§§33–34). The case is a civil one tried by a single judge, C. Aquilius, a coeval of Cicero's but already established as a leading jurist,[6] advised by a council of three other jurists (named at §54). Cicero repeatedly appeals to them as the sole hope of Quinctius in view of the powers arrayed against him.

The unorthodox approach continues in the argumentation, which begins with the claim that there was no reason for Naevius to seek an order for possession (*missio in possessionem*) of Quinctius' goods, a point irrelevant to the legal issue but one that can serve to blacken Naevius' character by suggesting that he acted, if not illegally, at least inappropriately (§§37–59). He repeatedly exploits prejudice against Naevius' profession as an auctioneer, not well regarded in upper-class circles, and his status as the son of a freedman (cf. on §§11 and 55). Cicero enlivens his argumentation with direct addresses to Naevius (§53) and bits of (imagined) speeches and dialogue, whereby he boldly puts words into his opponent's mouth (§§43, 45, 46–47, 55, 71–72) or projects the councilors' likely response to a query (§54). Cicero's second major topic is that Naevius did not take possession of Quinctius' goods "in accord with the edict" because he sent a messenger to expel Quinctius from their joint property before he had obtained the praetor's order for possession (§§60–85). But "in accord with

[6] On him, cf. Nicolet 1974, 783–84; Frier 1985, 148; Wieacker 1988, 601–2.

PRO QUINCTIO

the edict" was perhaps merely inserted to characterize the action, not truly part of the *sponsio*.[7] Here Cicero might at most have stirred prejudice against Naevius' greed, though he inflates his fault to an "unheard-of crime" (*inauditum facinus*, §79). The third argument, mostly lost in the lacuna at §85, was that Naevius had not taken possession of Quinctius' goods in the true sense, because he had not taken possession of all of them.

Now, a private case pleaded before a single judge would, according to Cicero's later doctrine, call for the Low Style (*Orat.* 72, *Opt. gen.* 8–10), that is, it should be down to earth, not elevated. But the young orator pulls out all the stops in a lengthy, emotional peroration (§§91–99). Here once again he homes in on the characterological contrast, hoping to make the case into a competition between Quinctius' austere lifestyle and the lavish and dissipated life of Naevius (§92), an association of lifestyle and mores anticipating Cicero's approach to the defense of Sextus Roscius. Perhaps he thought that this argument would appeal to Aquilius, whom he had known since his student days.

The speech is precocious, deftly handling the political background of the case by castigating Naevius' change of sides from Marian to Sullan, in contrast to Quinctius' refusal to betray his former friends (§§70, 93), displaying skill in complex argumentation,[8] and filling in gaps in his evidence with arguments from probability.[9] The speech is not perfect. There are some inconsistencies, for in-

[7] So Platschek 2005, 113.
[8] §§86–87, with Platschek 2005, 182–86.
[9] Cf. Hermann 2012.

stance, on the question of whether Quinctius owed Naevius money (denied at §37 but implicitly admitted at §21). The main divisions of the speech are marked with a heavy hand, as one might expect from a beginner. And the style falls short of Cicero's later polish.[10]

Nonetheless, it is, all in all, a creditable performance in a difficult case that the young orator took on at short notice. It is not attested whether Cicero won this case.[11]

NOTE ON MANUSCRIPTS AND EDITIONS

The oldest known copy of our speech consists of three leaves in rustic capitals from a fifth-century palimpsest discovered at Turin in 1820 by A. Peyron,[12] ten of Cicero's speeches, all from the same book, having been overwritten to make room for a text of Augustine.

The other evidence we have for the speech derives from a lost archetype written in Beneventan script. The first author to mention the speech in modern times was Antonio Loschi, secretary to the Duke of Milan, who between 1391 and 1405 wrote a work discussing eleven Ciceronian speeches, including *Pro Quinctio*. The same eleven speeches appear in the same order in a number of French and Italian manuscripts from the late four-

[10] Cf. Kinsey 1971, 6–9, esp. 7 ("the effect . . . is not so much of a florid as of an arid *redundantia*").

[11] Opinion is divided. I argue elsewhere that he might have won; see Dyck forthcoming.

[12] Edited in Peyron 1824, 214–16; the manuscript was destroyed in a fire in 1904.

teenth century onward. Moreover, Petrarch (1304–1374) is known to have acquired nine of the speeches, and he refers to the tenth, *Pro Flacco*, in a marginal note. It is therefore plausibly conjectured that this group reflects Petrarch's library.[13]

The text is based on the following witnesses:

P   Taurinensis a II 2*, s. V
C   Venetus Marcianus Lat. XI 122 (4117), s. XIV^2
D   Vaticanus Palatinus Lat. 1478, a. 1413 scriptus
E   Vaticanus Lat. 9305, s. XIV$^{3/3}$
F   Parisinus Lat. 7778, s. XIV$^{ex.}$
G   Parisinus Lat. 16226, s. XIV$^{ex.}$
H   Vaticanus Ottobonianus Lat. 1710, s. XIV$^{ex.}$ vel XV$^{in.}$
L   Vaticanus Lat. 2903, paulo ante a. 1415 scriptus
X   Laurentianus plut. 48.11, circa a. 1415 scriptus
Y   Scorialensis R I 12, circa a. 1420 scriptus
Ω   Archetype[14]

Their relations can be represented as follows (after Reeve 1992, xxx):

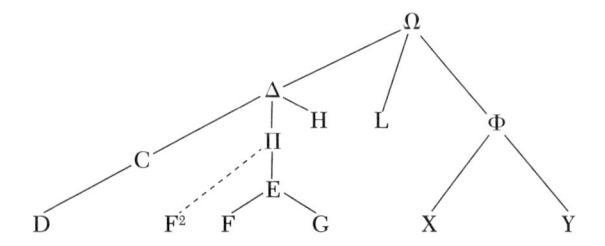

INTRODUCTION

The following are the major editions cited in the notes to the Latin text (for further references, see Reeve 1992, lxvii–lxx):

ed. Rom.	Rome, 1471
ed. Ven.	Venice, 1471
Angelius	Florence, 1515
Naugerius	Venice, 1519
Naugerius	Venice, 1534
Manutius	Venice, 1540
Stephanus	Paris, 1543
Hotoman	Paris, 1554 (commentary)
Lambinus	Paris, 1565
Lallemand	Paris, 1768
Ernesti	Halle, 1773
Garatoni	Naples, 1777
Halm	Zurich, 1854
Kayser	Leipzig, 1861
Reeve	Stuttgart-Leipzig, 1992

---

[13] Cf. Rouse and Reeve in Reynolds 1983, 87.

[14] This reconstruction is based on Reeve 1992, which is also the source of the manuscript readings reported here; see his edition for further detail.

PRO PUBLIO QUINCTIO

Quae res in civitate duae plurimum possunt, eae contra nos ambae faciunt in hoc tempore: summa gratia et eloquentia. Quarum alteram, C. Aquili, vereor, alteram metuo. Eloquentia Q. Hortensi ne me in dicendo impediat non nihil commoveor; gratia Sex. Naevi ne P. Quinctio 2 noceat, id vero non mediocriter pertimesco. Neque hoc tanto opere querendum videretur, haec summa in illis esse, si in nobis essent saltem mediocria; verum ita se res habet ut ego, qui neque usu satis et ingenio parum possum, cum patrono disertissimo comparer, P. Quinctius, cuius tenues opes, nullae facultates, exiguae amicorum 3 copiae sunt, cum adversario gratiosissimo contendat. Illud quoque nobis accedit incommodum, quod M. Iunius, qui hic, C. Aquili, totiens[1] apud te egit, homo et in aliis causis

---

[1] hic . . . totiens *Reeve*: hanc aliquotiens Ω

---

[1] The presiding judge, C. Aquilius Gallus, was a contemporary of Cicero; both would serve as praetors in the year 66 (*MRR* 2:152), but thereafter Aquilius devoted himself to the law. See further *OCD* s.v. Aquil(l)ius Gallus, Gaius; Nicolet 1974, 2:783–84; Frier 1985, 148; Wieacker 1988, 601–2.   [2] The leading orator at this period, later cos. 69 (*MRR* 2:131). For testimonies

IN DEFENSE OF PUBLIUS QUINCTIUS

The two things that have most power in the community—great influence and eloquence—are both working against us today. The one fills me with apprehension, Gaius Aquilius,[1] the other with dread. I feel some concern that the eloquence of Quintus Hortensius[2] may be a hindrance to my pleading, but I greatly fear that the influence of Sextus Naevius may damage Publius Quinctius' case.[3] Yet these supreme advantages of theirs would not seem so very deplorable if we had at least a moderate share of them. But the position is such that I, who have little natural ability and insufficient experience, am pitted against a most accomplished advocate, while Publius Quinctius, whose resources are small, who has no opportunities and only a few friends, is contending with a most influential adversary. An additional disadvantage for us is that Marcus Iunius,[4] who has pleaded here before you so many times, Gaius Aquilius, and who has great experience both in other cases

2

3

and fragments, cf. *FRLO* 92; on his career and relations with Cicero, see Dyck 2008.   [3] Rauh 1989, 464–65, suspects that Naevius "handled the auction sales of the ultrarich."   [4] Sometimes identified with the plebeian tribune of 83, M. Iunius Brutus; cf. on §65; Platschek 2005, 6n25, 262–63; Lintott 2008, 44n4.

11

exercitatus et in hac multum ac saepe versatus, hoc tempore abest nova legatione impeditus, et ad me ventum est,[2] qui ut summa haberem cetera, temporis quidem certe vix satis habui ut rem tantam, tot controversiis implicatam, possem cognoscere. Ita quod mihi consuevit in ceteris causis esse adiumento, id quoque in hac causa deficit; nam quod ingenio minus possum, subsidium mihi diligentia comparavi, quae quanta sit, nisi tempus et spatium datum sit, intelligi non potest.

Quae quo plura sunt, C. Aquili, eo te et eos qui tibi in consilio sunt meliori mente nostra verba audire oportebit, ut multis incommodis veritas debilitata tandem aequitate talium virorum recreetur. Quod si tu iudex nullo praesidio fuisse videbere contra vim et gratiam solitudini atque inopiae, si apud hoc consilium ex opibus, non ex veritate, causa pendetur, profecto nihil est iam sanctum atque sincerum in civitate, nihil est quod humilitatem cuiusquam gravitas et virtus iudicis consoletur. Certe aut apud te et eos qui tibi adsunt veritas valebit aut ex hoc loco repulsa vi et gratia locum ubi consistat reperire non poterit.

⟨Id⟩ non[3] eo dico, C. Aquili, quo mihi veniat in dubium tua fides et constantia aut quo non in eis quos tibi advocavisti, viris lectissimis civitatis, spem summam habere P. Quinctius debeat. Quid ergo est? Primum magnitudo periculi summo timore hominem adficit, quod uno iudicio

---

[2] ventum est $L^2\Phi$: venturus Ω: venitur *recentiores*   [3] id non *Ernesti*: non Δ*L*: non *post lac.* Φ: atque hoc non *Reeve in app.*

---

[5] The presiding judge appointed a panel of experts (*consilium*) to advise him; for this practice in civil jurisdiction, cf. Crook 1955, 6. The members are named at §54.

and in this one, is prevented by a new commission from being present today. So then I was approached—I who, even if I possessed all other qualifications in the highest degree, have scarcely had time enough to be able to acquaint myself with a matter of such importance and one involving so many disputed points. Thus what has generally been a help to me in other cases fails me in this one. For what I lacked in talent I supplemented by my industry, but how great it is cannot be perceived unless time and leisure are provided.

The more numerous these disadvantages are, Gaius Aquilius, the greater should be the goodwill with which you and the members of your council[5] listen to our words, so that truth, weakened by so many disadvantages, may at last be revived by the fairness of men such as you. But if you, as judge, show that you afford no protection to loneliness and distress against violence and influence; if, before this council, the case is weighed in the balance of resources and not in that of truth, then assuredly nothing sacred or pure any longer exists in the community, and there is no reason for the authority and integrity of any judge to console a humble citizen. No doubt either truth will prevail before you and your councilors, or, driven by violence and influence from this tribunal, will be unable to find a place in which to rest.

I say this, Gaius Aquilius, not because it occurs to me to doubt your firmness and integrity, or because Quinctius ought not to repose the best hope in these distinguished citizens whom you have summoned to be your councilors. What is the trouble, then? In the first place, his great peril instills the utmost fear in my client, since he is staking all

de fortunis omnibus decernit, idque cum cogitat non minus saepe ei venit in mentem potestatis quam aequitatis tuae, propterea quod omnes quorum in alterius manu vita posita est saepius illud cogitant, quid possit is cuius in dicione ac potestate sunt quam quid debeat facere. Deinde habet adversarium P. Quinctius verbo Sex. Naevium, re vera huiusce aetatis homines disertissimos, fortissimos, ornatissimos[4] nostrae civitatis, qui communi studio, summis opibus Sex. Naevium defendunt, si id est defendere, cupiditati alterius obtemperare quo is facilius quem velit iniquo iudicio opprimere possit. Nam quid hoc iniquius aut indignius, C. Aquili, dici aut commemorari potest quam me, qui caput alterius, famam fortunasque defendam, priore loco causam dicere, cum praesertim Q. Hortensius, qui hoc iudicio partes accusatoris obtinet, contra me sit dicturus, cui summam copiam facultatemque dicendi natura largita est? Ita fit ut ego, qui tela depellere et vulneribus mederi debeam, tum id facere cogar cum etiam telum adversarius nullum iecerit, illis autem id tempus impugnandi detur cum et vitandi illorum impetus potestas adempta nobis erit et si qua in re, id quod parati sunt facere, falsum crimen quasi venenatum aliquod telum iecerint, medicinae faciendae locus non erit. Id accidit praetoris iniquitate et iniuria, primum quod contra om-

[4] ornatissimos $L\Phi$: horrent- ΔL^{mg}: honestissimos *Flor. Bib. Nat. Conv. Sup. I IV 4*

[6] One's *caput*, so used in legal contexts, could be removed or diminished by a verdict entailing *infamia*; cf. *OLD* s.v. *caput* 1, 6a; Greenidge 1901, 195n1, 508, 510; Berger 1953 s.vv. Capitis deminutio, Caput.   [7] For the "recurrent imagery of weapons and bodily harm" in the speech, cf. Bannon 2000, 72, 86.

his fortunes on a single judgment; and when he reflects upon that, your power comes into his mind as often as your sense of justice; for all those whose life is in the hands of another think more often of what the man in whose absolute power they are is able to do than of what he ought to do. In the next place, Publius Quinctius has as his opponent nominally Sextus Naevius, but in reality the most eloquent men of our time, the most gallant and most distinguished members of our community, who with united efforts and vast resources are defending Naevius, if to subserve the greed of one of the parties in order that he can more easily overpower anyone he chooses by an unfair trial—if that can be called defending. For can anything more unfair or more outrageous be spoken of or mentioned, Gaius Aquilius, than the fact that I, who am defending the civil rights,[6] the good name and fortunes of one of the parties, am pleading my case first, above all, when Hortensius, who in this trial plays the role of the accuser, upon whom nature has lavishly bestowed a wealth of words and the greatest eloquence, is going to speak against me? Thus it comes about that I, who ought to repel darts and heal wounds, am compelled to do this, even before the adversary has launched a single dart, whereas time is granted them for making an attack when we shall have been deprived of the power of avoiding their assault, and when, if they launch some false charge like a poisoned dart, as they are ready to do, we shall have no opportunity of applying an antidote.[7] This has come to pass because of the praetor's unfairness and injustice:[8] in the first

7

8

9

---

[8] Cn. Cornelius Dolabella, named at §30; cf. *MRR* 2:76.

nium consuetudinem iudicium prius de probro quam de re maluit fieri, deinde quod ita constituit id ipsum iudicium ut reus ante quam verbum accusatoris audisset, causam dicere cogeretur. Quod eorum gratia et potentia factum est qui, quasi sua res aut honos agatur, ita diligenter Sex. Naevi studio et cupiditati morem gerunt et in eius modi rebus opes suas experiuntur in quibus quo plus propter virtutem nobilitatemque possunt, eo minus quantum possint debent ostendere.

10 Cum tot tantisque difficultatibus adfectus atque adflictus in tuam, C. Aquili, fidem, veritatem, misericordiam P. Quinctius confugerit, cum adhuc ei propter vim adversariorum non ius par, non agendi potestas eadem, non magistratus aequus reperiri potuerit, cum ei summam per iniuriam omnia inimica atque infesta fuerint, te, C. Aquili, vosque qui in consilio adestis orat atque obsecrat ut multis iniuriis iactatam atque agitatam aequitatem in hoc tandem loco consistere et confirmari patiamini. Id quo facilius facere possitis, dabo operam ut a principio res quem ad modum gesta et contracta sit cognoscatis.

11 C. Quinctius fuit P. Quincti huius frater, sane ceterarum rerum pater familias et prudens et attentus, una in re paulo minus consideratus, qui societatem cum Sex. Naevio fecerit, viro bono verum tamen non ita instituto ut iura

---

9 The praetor's decision (see §§30–31) may not have been so unfair: Naevius had a prima facie case that he was in possession of Quinctius' property and had been for at least thirty days; in challenging this claim, Quinctius placed himself in the plaintiff's role, with the present procedural consequences. Cf. Platschek 2005, 125–26.   10 Evidently alluding to Q. Hortensius and L. Marcius Philippus (see on §72).

place because, contrary to everyone's custom, he has preferred that the trial should deal with my client's dishonor before the fact at issue; in the second place, because he has so arranged the trial itself that the accused should be forced to plead his case before he has heard a single word from the accuser.[9] This is the result of the power and influence of those men who indulge the greedy desires of Sextus Naevius as zealously as if their own interests or honor were at stake, and test their resources in matters in which, the greater the power they possess owing to their merit and rank, the less they are required to show how great it is.[10]

Troubled and overwhelmed by so many and such great difficulties, Publius Quinctius has taken refuge in your protection, uprightness, and compassion, Gaius Aquilius. Since until now in view of the power of his opponents, he has been unable to find equal justice, the same opportunity for pleading, or an impartial magistrate; since, by the greatest injustice, he has had unfriendliness and hostility on every side, he begs and beseeches you, Gaius Aquilius, and you, the members of his council, to allow equity, buffeted and harassed by many acts of injustice, to find rest and support at last in this tribunal. To enable you to do this more easily, I will see to it that you become acquainted, from the beginning, with how the matter was handled and the relationship formed.

Publius Quinctius, my client, had a brother named Gaius, undoubtedly a careful and attentive head of household in all other respects but in one matter he was a bit less cautious—in that he joined into partnership with Sextus Naevius, a good man but one who had not been brought up in such a manner as to gain knowledge of the

CICERO

societatis et officia certi patris familias nosse posset. Non quo ei deesset ingenium; nam neque parum facetus scurra Sex. Naevius neque inhumanus praeco umquam est existimatus. Quid ergo est? Cum ei natura nihil melius quam vocem dedisset, pater nihil praeter libertatem reliquisset, vocem in quaestum contulit, libertate usus est quo impunius dicax esset. Quare quod[5] socium tibi eum velles adiungere nihil erat nisi ut in tua pecunia condisceret qui pecuniae fructus esset. Tamen inductus consuetudine ac familiaritate Quinctius fecit, ut dixi, societatem earum rerum quae in Gallia comparabantur. Erat ei pecuaria res ampla et rustica sane bene culta et fructuosa. Tollitur ab atriis Liciniis atque a praeconum consessu [in Galliam][6] Naevius et trans Alpes usque transfertur. Fit magna mutatio loci, non ingeni; nam qui ab adulescentulo quaestum sibi instituisset sine impendio, postea quam nescioquid impendit et in commune contulit, mediocri quaestu con-

12

---

[5] quod *ed. Rom.*: quidem *codd.*   [6] in Galliam *secl. Rinkes*

---

[11] Cicero will repeatedly undermine his initial characterization; by §19, "excellent man" is palpably ironic.

[12] Two character types on the comic stage; cf. May 1988, 175n8. On the *scurra* as a "social menace, a know-all and a dangerous gossip," cf. Corbett 1986, 58; Beard 2014, chs. 5–6, esp. 59–61; also §55. A *praeco* could perform a variety of services, auctioneering the most common. On Cicero's exploitation of Naevius' profession, cf. Hinard 1976, 744–45; May 1988, 15; Damon 1997, 197; for its unpopularity see Rauh 1989, 459–61; Bond 2016, ch. 1 and app. 1 (epigraphic evidence); a more sympathetic picture, ibid. 35.

[13] For this main qualification for a *praeco*, see Hinard 1976, 732, and cf. §95.

PRO QUINCTIO 11–12

rights of a partnership and the duties of a trustworthy head of household.[11] Not that he was without talent, for Naevius was never regarded as a buffoon who lacked wit or as an unmannerly auctioneer.[12] How, then, does the matter stand? Since nature had endowed him with nothing better than a voice,[13] and his father had left him nothing but his freedom,[14] he turned his voice to account and used his freedom to utter his witticisms with greater impunity. There was, therefore, no reason why you would want to take him into partnership except for him to thoroughly learn the use of property by handling your property.[15] Nonetheless, guided by their intimate friendship, Quinctius, as I have said, entered into a partnership in properties that were being purchased in Gaul.[16] He held a considerable grazing farm and well-cultivated and profitable rural estates. Naevius is removed from the Licinian auction halls[17] and the crowd of auctioneers and transported across the Alps. A great change of place ensues, but not of character. For the man who from early youth had resolved to make money for himself without any capital, after he had put a certain amount of capital into the partnership,

12

---

[14] Implying that Naevius' father was a freedman, exploiting prejudice against them; cf. Treggiari 1969, 230.

[15] Suggesting that Naevius contributed no property of his own but was brought in as a property manager. For *fructus* as "use," cf. *TLL* 6.1:1393.45.

[16] Explaining the origin of the partnership might have compromised Cicero's portrait of Naevius. "Were being purchased" suggests that it was not a fusion of all assets but formed for a specific purpose; cf. *OLD* s.v. *comparo* 3b; Platschek 2005, 13–15. Cf. §28.

[17] Located at the entrance to the market, cf. §25.

13 tentus esse non poterat. Nec mirum si is qui vocem venalem habuerat ea quae voce quaesiverat magno sibi quaestui fore putabat. Itaque hercule haud mediocriter de communi quodcumque poterat ad se in privatam domum sevocabat; qua in re ita diligens erat quasi ei qui magna fide societatem gererent [arbitrium][7] pro socio condemnari solerent. Verum his de rebus non necesse habeo dicere; ea quae me P. Quinctius cupit commemorare, tametsi causa postulat, tamen quia postulat, non flagitat, praeteribo.

14 Cum annos iam complures societas esset et cum saepe suspectus Quinctio Naevius fuisset neque ita commode posset rationem reddere earum rerum quas libidine, non ratione gesserat, moritur in Gallia Quinctius cum adesset Naevius, et moritur repentino. Heredem testamento reliquit hunc P. Quinctium, ut ad quem summus maeror morte sua veniebat, ad eundem summus honos quoque
15 perveniret. Quo mortuo, nec ita multo post, in Galliam proficiscitur Quinctius; ibi cum isto Naevio familiariter vivit. Annum fere una sunt, cum et de societate multa inter se communicarent et de tota illa ratione atque re

[7] *vulgo suspectum seclusi, Flac. 43 (pro socio damnatus est) collato: def. Garatoni, at cf. Platschek 2005, 25 adn. 102*

---

[18] Admitting that Naevius did invest capital in the partnership.

[19] Perhaps because of time constraints; cf. §§33–35.

[20] Hinting at embezzlement; evidence would be needed were this the point at issue; cf. Harries 2011, 133. Kinsey 1971, 71, suggests that "the fact that it was Naevius who eventually pressed for a settlement supports the view that he and not Quinctius" was

PRO QUINCTIO 12–15

could not be contented with a moderate profit.[18] Nor is it 13
surprising that he who had put up his voice for hire thought
that what he had acquired by it would be highly profitable
to him. Accordingly, he withdrew from the common stock
whatever he could, on a large scale, by Hercules, and put
it into his own pocket; and in this he displayed as much
care as if those who carried on a partnership with the
greatest honesty were regularly condemned for violation
of a partnership. But I need not discuss these matters;
though the case calls for me to speak of the points P.
Quinctius desires me to raise, still, since it calls for but
does not demand them, I will set them aside.[19]

When the partnership had already lasted for several 14
years and Naevius had more than once been suspected by
Quinctius and he was unable to render a satisfactory account of certain transactions that he had carried on as he
wished and not in accordance with the rules of business,[20]
Quinctius died in Gaul, while Naevius was there, and he
died suddenly.[21] By his will he left my client Publius
Quinctius as his heir so that he who felt the deepest grief
at his death might also receive the highest honor.[22] Upon 15
his death, not long afterward, Quinctius set out for Gaul;
there he lived on friendly terms with this Naevius. They
were together about a year, during which they discussed
the partnership at length and the entire relationship and

dissatisfied with his partner's conduct; that there were unpaid
debts of the partnership owing to Naevius at Gaius' death would
not necessarily show fraud.

[21] Planting the suspicion of foul play; cf. Damon 1997, 200.

[22] If P. Quinctius was his brother's closest relative, the legacy
was routine.

CICERO

Gallicana, neque interea verbum ullum interposuit Naevius aut societatem sibi quippiam debere aut privatim Quinctium debuisse.

Cum aeris alieni aliquantum esset relictum quibus nominibus pecuniam Romae curari oporteret, auctionem in Gallia P. hic Quinctius Narbone se facturum esse proscribit earum rerum quae ipsius erant privatae. Ibi tum vir optimus Sex. Naevius hominem multis verbis deterret ne auctionetur: eum non ita commode posse eo tempore quae[8] proscripsisset vendere; Romae sibi nummorum facultatem esse, quam, si saperet, communem existimaret pro fraterna illa necessitudine et pro ipsius adfinitate. (Nam P. Quincti consobrinam habet in matrimonio Naevius et ex ea liberos.) Quia quod virum bonum facere oportebat, id loquebatur Naevius, credidit Quinctius eum qui orationem bonorum imitaretur facta quoque imitaturum. Auctionem velle facere desistit, Romam proficiscitur, decedit ex Gallia Romam simul Naevius.

16

Cum pecuniam C. Quinctius P. Scapulae debuisset, per te, C. Aquili, decidit P. Quinctius quid[9] liberis eius dissol-

17

[8] quae $H^2L\Phi$: quo Δ
[9] *Baiter*: quod Ω

---

[23] A partnership was dissolved on the death of one of the partners (Gaius 3.152); this probably also applied in the late republic. Did Naevius and P. Quinctius agree to form a new partnership? Cf. the *societas* mentioned in §§48, 76 and Harries 2011, 130–32; they could be called "partners" (*socii*) if they held property in common (Platschek 2005, 23–24).

[24] That is, Gaius Quinctius.

the property in Gaul.[23] In the meantime, Naevius never put in a word to the effect that either the partnership owed him anything or that Quinctius had been personally indebted to him.[24]

Since a certain number of debts had been left unpaid for which money had to be paid at Rome, my client Publius Quinctius posted a notice in Gaul of an auction at Narbo of some of his private property.[25] At that time this excellent man Naevius argued at great length, dissuading him from holding the sale: the time was unfavorable for selling the goods he had announced; he himself had a supply of money at Rome, which, if he had any sense, he should consider as belonging to both, in view of his tie with his brother and his relationship by marriage to himself. (For Naevius was married to Publius Quinctius' cousin, by whom he had children.) Because Naevius spoke of what a good man ought to do, Quinctius believed that one who imitated the language of good men would also imitate their actions. Abandoning the desire to hold an auction, he set out for Rome; Naevius departed from Gaul for Rome at the same time.

Since Gaius Quinctius was indebted to Publius Scapula,[26] Publius Quinctius, with you as his agent, Gaius Aquilius, settled how much he had to pay to Scapula's

[25] Narbo Martius (mod. Narbonne), founded ca. 118 as the first Roman colony in Gaul.

[26] Possibly the P. Quinctius Scapula whom Plin. *HN* 7.183 mentions as having died while dining at the house of Aquilius Gallus; cf. Gundel, *RE* s.v. Quinctius 53. Accepting Gaius' inheritance also entailed taking on his debts, which were substantial (§73): Gaius 2.152–53.

CICERO

veret. Hoc eo per te agebatur[10] quod propter aerariam rationem non satis erat in tabulis inspexisse quantum deberetur nisi ad Castoris quaesisses[11] quantum solveretur. Decidis statuisque tu, propter necessitudinem quae tibi 18 cum Scapulis est, quid eis ad denarium solveretur. Haec omnia Quinctius agebat auctore et consuasore Naevio, nec mirum si eius utebatur consilio cuius auxilium sibi paratum putabat. Non modo enim pollicitus erat in Gallia sed Romae cotidie simul atque sibi hic adnuisset numeraturum se dicebat; Quinctius porro istum posse facere videbat, debere intelligebat, mentiri, quia causa cur mentiretur non erat, non putabat. Quasi domi nummos haberet, ita constituit Scapulis se daturum. Naevium certiorem 19 facit, rogat ut curet quod dixisset. Tum iste vir optimus (vereor ne se derideri putet quod iterum iam dico "optimus"), qui hunc in summas angustias adductum putaret, ut eum suis condicionibus in ipso articulo temporis ad-

---

[10] agebatur *L*Φ: cogebatur Δ: agi cogebatur *Platschek 2005, 35–36*

[11] nisi ad Castoris quaesisset Ω: nisi ad Catonis quaesisses *Arus. 32*: sine advocato nisi quaesisses *vel* advocato nisi quaesisset *Platschek 2005, 36–37*

---

[27] Presumably, Scapula himself had died in the meantime, and the money was now owed to his heirs.

[28] This translation assumes that the debt had been incurred either in kind or in foreign currency but was to be repaid in Roman currency; cf. *OLD* s.v. *aerarius* 2a; *ratio* 3a; Kinsey 1971, 73–74.

[29] The temple of Castor and Pollux in the southeast corner of the Forum was where the moneylenders had their tables; cf. I. Nielsen, *LTUR* s.v. Castor, aedes, templum.

PRO QUINCTIO 17–19

children.[27] The matter was handled by you, because, owing to the rate of exchange,[28] it was not enough to examine the account books for the amount of the debt, but you also had to make inquiries near the temple of Castor[29] as to how much he had to pay them. You settled the question, and, in consideration of your intimate friendship with the Scapulae, decided how much ought to be paid to them reckoning in denarii.[30] Quinctius was engaged in all these actions with the advice and encouragement of Naevius, nor was it surprising that Quinctius took the advice of a man of whose assistance he felt assured. For Naevius had not only made the promise in Gaul but kept asserting every day in Rome that he would pay down the money as soon as Quinctius had given him the nod. Moreover, Quinctius knew that he was able to pay and felt that he ought to; he did not think that he was telling him a lie, because there was no reason why he should do so. As if he had the money at home, he entered into a formal engagement to pay the Scapulae.[31] He informed Naevius, and asked him to attend to the payment, as he had promised. Then that excellent man (I fear he may think he is being mocked because I am now calling him "excellent" for the second time), who thought my client was reduced to dire straits so that he could tie him down at the critical moment

18

19

[30] It looks as though Aquilius (addressed as "you") was acting as an arbiter or judge in a dispute between Quinctius and the Scapulae; cf. Platschek 2005, 35.

[31] In Roman law, this was a *constitutum*, an agreement to pay a fixed amount by a fixed date; cf. Berger 1953 s.v. Constitutum; Platschek 2005, 38.

stringeret, assem sese negat daturum nisi prius de rebus rationibusque societatis omnibus decidissent[12] et scisset sibi cum Quinctio controversiae nihil futurum. "Posterius" inquit "ista videbimus" Quinctius; "nunc hoc velim cures, si tibi videtur, quod dixisti." Negat se alia ratione facturum; quod promisisset non plus sua referre quam si cum auctionem venderet domini iussu quippiam promisisset.

20 Destitutione illa perculsus Quinctius a Scapulis paucos dies aufert, in Galliam mittit ut ea quae proscripserat venirent, deteriore tempore absens auctionatur, Scapulis difficiliore condicione dissolvit. Tum appellat ultro Naevium ut quoniam suspicaretur aliqua de re fore controversiam, videret ut quam primum et quam minima cum
21 molestia tota res transigeretur. Dat iste amicum M. Trebellium, nos communem necessarium qui istius domi erat educatus et quo utebatur iste plurimum, propinquum nostrum Sex. Alfenum. Res convenire nullo modo poterat, propterea quod hic mediocrem iacturam facere cupiebat,

[12] *Reeve in app.*: -et Ω

---

[32] Harries 2011, 135, suggests rather that Naevius "belatedly realised there was no security" for the return of such a loan, and that his investigations may have raised "real doubts that even the first debt [owed by Quinctius] . . . would be repaid" and so was "unwilling to make a further commitment."

[33] That is, he does not feel bound by what he said; cf. §95 on Naevius' prostituting his voice, with Hinard 1976, 739, 743.

[34] He may have been obliged to pay a penalty because of his default on the previous agreement.

[35] Otherwise unknown: Münzer, *RE* s.v. Trebellius 7.

on his own terms,[32] refused to advance Quinctius a penny until they had reached a settlement in regard to all affairs and accounts of the partnership, and felt assured that he would have no cause of dispute with Quinctius. "We will see about that later," said Quinctius; "for the present, if you will be so kind, I should be glad if you would see about getting the money, as you promised." Naevius declared that he would not do so on any other terms, saying that his promise had no more to do with him than any other promise that he had made on the owner's orders when selling goods at auction.[33]

Shattered by this betrayal, Quinctius obtains a few days' grace from the Scapulae and sends word to Gaul that the goods that he had advertised should be sold; the auction takes place during his absence at a less favorable time, and he pays off the Scapulae on harder terms.[34] He then takes the initiative, calling upon Naevius, since he suspected there might be a dispute about something or other, to see about getting the whole affair settled as soon as possible and with the least trouble. Naevius appoints his friend Marcus Trebellius to represent him;[35] we appoint a man connected by common ties with both parties, a man who had been brought up in Naevius' house and was an intimate friend of his, a relative of ours, Sextus Alfenus.[36] No agreement was possible, because my client wished to suffer only a moderate loss, while Naevius was not content

20

21

---

[36] "Of ours," that is, Quinctius'. Alfenus is known only from our speech; he was proscribed by Sulla (§76): Klebs, *RE* s.v. Alfenus 1; Nicolet 1974, 769–70; Hinard 1985a, 96–97, and 1985b, 329–30.

CICERO

22 iste mediocri praeda contentus non erat. Itaque ex eo tempore res esse in vadimonium coepit. Cum vadimonia saepe dilata essent et cum aliquantum temporis in ea re esset consumptum neque quicquam profectum esset, venit ad vadimonium Naevius. Hoc quaeso,[13] C. Aquili vosque qui adestis in consilio, ut diligenter attendatis, ut singulare genus fraudis et novam rationem insidiarum cognoscere
23 possitis. Ait se auctionatum esse in Gallia; quod sibi videretur se vendidisse; curasse ne quid sibi societas deberet; se iam neque vadari amplius neque vadimonium promittere; si quid agere secum velit Quinctius, non recusare. Hic, cum rem Gallicanam cuperet revisere, hominem in praesentia non vadatur. Ita sine vadimonio disceditur.

Deinde Romae dies xxx fere Quinctius commoratur; cum ceteris quae habebat vadimonia differt, ut expeditus
24 in Galliam proficisci possit; proficiscitur. Roma egreditur ante diem iiii[14] kalend. Februarias Quinctius Scipione et Norbano coss. Quaeso ut eum diem memoriae mandetis. L. Albius Sex. filius Quirina, vir bonus et cum primis ho-

[13] hoc quaeso *Reeve*: hoc se quo Ω: obsecro $\eta H^2 L^2$
[14] *cf.* §57

---

[37] Literally, *res esse in vadimonium coepit* = "the matter began to be at the stage between the defendant's giving of a *vadimonium* [= bail, that is, a guarantee that the party will appear before a magistrate] and his appearance in court": *OLD* s.v. *vadimonium* 2e; Greenidge 1901, 142n3; Berger 1953 s.v. Vadimonium; Platschek 2005, 45–56.   [38] Cicero fails to explain why Quinctius wished to go to Gaul at this point (to collect evidence of debts owed him by Naevius?); cf. Kinsey 1971, 82.

[39] January 27 (four days before the Kalends of February) is

with moderate plunder. And so from that time the matter 22
began to be litigated.[37] After several appointments had
been made and adjourned, considerable time was wasted
on the matter and no progress was made, Naevius appeared in court. I beg you, Aquilius, and you, the members
of his council, to give me your earnest attention, so that
you can understand an unparalleled kind of fraud and a
new method of trickery. Naevius declared that he had 23
conducted an auction in Gaul; he had sold whatever he
thought fit; that he had taken care that the partnership
should not be indebted to him; that he no longer claimed
that Quinctius should produce bail, nor would he promise
bail to him; but if Quinctius wished to bring any action
against him, he had no objection. Since my client desired
to pay another visit to his property in Gaul, for the present
he did not bind Naevius over to appear.[38] They thus departed without any appointment for appearance in court.

Next, Quinctius remains in Rome for about thirty days;
he postponed any suits that he had with others, so that he
might be able to set out for Gaul free from anxiety. He set
out. Quinctius left Rome on January 27,[39] during the consulship of Scipio and Norbanus.[40] I beg you to commit this 24
date to memory. Lucius Albius, the son of Sextus, of the
tribe of Quirinus, a worthy and especially honorable man,

---

the date given here by the manuscripts, but this is at odds with
"the day before the Kalends of February," i.e., January 29, at §57.
A scribal error seems likelier than that Cicero was inconsistent in
citing this important date. The longer number is likelier to have
been truncated than the shorter one lengthened, and "the day
before" would be expressed by *pridie* (for a different view, cf.
Platschek 2005, 60–61).   [40] That is, the year 83: *MRR* 2:62.

nestus, una profectus est. Cum venissent ad Vada Volaterrana quae nominantur, vident perfamiliarem Naevi qui ex Gallia pueros venales isti adducebat, L. Publicium, qui, ut Romam venit, narrat Naevio quo in loco viderit Quinctium. Quod ubi ex Publicio audivit,[15] pueros circum amicos dimittit, ipse suos necessarios ab atriis Liciniis et a faucibus macelli corrogat ut ad tabulam Sextiam sibi adsint hora secunda postridie. Veniunt frequentes; testificatur[16] iste P. Quinctium non stetisse et se stetisse; tabulae maximae signis hominum nobilium consignantur; disceditur. Postulat a Burreno[17] praetore Naevius ut ex edicto bona possidere liceat; iussit[18] bona proscribi eius quicum familiaritas fuerat, societas erat, adfinitas liberis istius vivis divelli nullo modo poterat. Qua ex re intellegi facile potuit

[15] audivit *Rau*: *lac.* Ω
[16] η: -antur Ω
[17] a burreno *H²*: aburrieno *L, alii alia (cf.* §§30, 69)
[18] iussit: ius sit *Platschek 2005, 91*

---

[41] About 186 Roman miles from Rome along the Via Aemilia.

[42] Known only from this passage: Münzer, *RE* s.v. Publicius 10.

[43] Evidently, a picture of the exploits of L. Sextius Calvinus (cos. 124), who conquered the Ligurians, Salluvii, and Vocontii (*MRR* 1:511, 515, and 518), located near the praetor's office: so Pocock 1926, 180–81, followed by Shackleton Bailey 1977, 1:288, and Platschek 2005, 65–70.

[44] Ironic; cf. Platschek 2005, 72n276.

[45] Known only from our speech (cf. §§30 and 69). The manuscripts have *Burrenus* and *Burrienus*, but *Bur(r)enius* is epigraphically attested four times (cf. Schulze 1904, 110n1). *MRR*

PRO QUINCTIO 24–26

set out with him. After they had reached the Fords of Volaterrae, as they are called,[41] they saw an intimate friend of Naevius, Lucius Publicius,[42] who was bringing him some slaves from Gaul for sale, who, on his arrival at Rome, told Naevius where he had seen Quinctius. When he had heard this from Publicius, Naevius sent his slaves round to all his friends and personally invited his acquaintances from the Licinian halls and the entrance to the market to meet him at the picture of Sextius[43] at the second hour the following day. They attended in great numbers. Naevius called them to witness that Publius Quinctius had not answered to his bail, and that he [Naevius] had answered; a grand document[44] was attested to by the seals of the distinguished witnesses; the meeting broke up. Naevius then applied to the praetor Burrenus[45] for permission to take possession of the defaulter's property in accordance with the edict.[46] He ordered to be put up for sale the property of the man whose friend he had been, whose partner he still was, and whose kinship by marriage was indissoluble as long as Naevius' children still lived. From this fact it could be easily understood

2:62 gives the praenomen as P. with a query and the spelling as Burrienus; Klebs, *RE* s.v. Burrienus.

[46] The praetor could issue an "order for possession" (*missio in possessionem*) on the presumption that Quinctius had committed one of the offenses listed in the edict. Cf. Berger 1953 s.vv. Edictum praetoris, Missiones in possessionem. Cicero depicts the process leading to the issuance of the edict as "staged" by Naevius in response to word received from Publicius about Quinctius' travel to Gaul. But Cicero was not privy to communications between Publicius and Naevius.

CICERO

nullum esse officium tam sanctum atque sollemne quod non avaritia comminuere atque violare soleat; etenim si veritate amicitia, fide societas, pietate propinquitas colitur, necesse est iste qui amicum socium adfinem fama ac fortunis spoliare conatus est vanum se et perfidiosum et
27 impium esse fateatur. Libellos Sex. Alfenus, procurator P. Quincti, familiaris et propinquus Sex. Naevi, deicit, servulum unum quem iste prenderat abducit, denuntiat sese procuratorem esse, istum aequum esse famae fortunisque P. Quincti consulere et adventum eius expectare; quod si facere nolit atque imbiberit eius modi rationibus illum ad suas condiciones perducere, sese nihil precari et si quid agere velit, ‹paratum esse›[19] iudicio defendere.

28 Haec dum Romae geruntur, Quinctius interea contra ius consuetudinem edicta praetorum de saltu agroque communi a servis communibus vi detruditur. Existima, C. Aquili, †id†[20] modo et ratione omnia Romae Naevium fecisse si hoc quod per litteras istius in Gallia gestum est recte atque ordine factum videtur. Expulsus atque eiectus e praedio Quinctius, accepta insigni iniuria, confugit ad C. Flaccum imperatorem, qui tum erat in provincia (quem, ut ipsius dignitas poscit, honoris gratia nomino). Is eam

[19] *inser. Reeve, §66 coll.*
[20] id *del. Angelius*: ea *Kinsey*: ita *Reeve: fort.* illa

---

[47] These are two customary and symbolic acts demonstrating that Quinctius' interests are being protected; cf. Platschek 2005, 233–37.
[48] Perhaps Naevius was thereby merely "managing that part of the estate that [he] was claiming as his from the partnership"

PRO QUINCTIO 26–28

that there is no duty so sacred and solemn that it would not generally be compromised and violated by avarice. For if friendship is maintained by truth, partnership by good faith, and kinship by a sense of duty, the man who has attempted to rob his friend, his partner, his kinsman of his reputation and fortunes must admit that he is untrustworthy, treacherous, and undutiful. Sextus Alfenus, Publius Quinctius' agent, the friend and relative of Sextus Naevius, tore down the bills of sale, carried off one young slave whom Naevius had seized,[47] declared that he was Quinctius' agent, that it was right that Naevius should have regard for the reputation and fortunes of Publius Quinctius and await his arrival; if he refused to do this and was determined to use such methods to bring him to his terms, he asked no favor, and if Naevius chose to bring an action, he was ready to defend Quinctius in court.

While these events were occurring at Rome, in the meantime Quinctius, contrary to law, custom, and the edicts of praetors, was forcibly driven from the common pastures and land by slaves belonging to the partners.[48] Gaius Aquilius, you may think all actions Naevius took at Rome correct and regular if what was done by his letter in Gaul seems to have been done correctly and regularly. Quinctius, expelled and driven out of the estate, having been subjected to such flagrant injustice, took refuge with the governor Gaius Flaccus, who was at that time in the province (whom, as his rank demands, I mention with all

27

28

(Lintott 2008, 54); or Naevius feared that in Gaul Quinctius would sell off the partnership's property and present him with a fait accompli (Platschek 2005, 87).

rem quam vehementer vindicandam putarit ex decretis eius poteritis cognoscere.

29   Alfenus interea Romae cum isto gladiatore vetulo cotidie pugnabat. Utebatur populo sane suo propterea quod iste caput petere non desinebat. Iste postulat ut procurator iudicatum solvi satis daret. Negat Alfenus aequum esse procuratorem satis dare quod reus satis dare non deberet si ipse adesset. Appellantur tribuni, a quibus cum esset certum auxilium petitum, ita tum disceditur ut Idibus Septembribus P. Quinctium sisti Sex. Alfenus promitteret.

30   Venit Romam Quinctius, vadimonium sistit. Iste, homo acerrimus, bonorum possessor expulsor ereptor, annum et sex menses nihil petit; quiescit; condicionibus hunc quoad potest producit; a Cn. Dolabella denique praetore postulat ut sibi Quinctius iudicatum solvi satis det ex formula

---

[49] C. Valerius Flaccus (cos. 93) was proconsul in Transalpine Gaul perhaps as early as 85 and until 81; cf. *MRR* 2:58–59, 60n3, 61, 64, 70, 77–78. "Decrees" may be a rhetorical plural. Flaccus could have issued an *interdictum de vi* restoring Quinctius to the property from which he had been forcibly ejected (cf. Greenidge 1901, 214–15). However, at the time of the dispossession, Quinctius did not know about the *missio in possessionem*, so Flaccus will have acted without knowledge of it. He may subsequently have changed his assessment. Cicero's way of referring to him shows that he will not give evidence for Quinctius at trial. See Platschek 2005, 93–94.   [50] Not used literally but as a term of abuse; cf. *OLD* s.v. 1 vs. 2; Opelt 1965, 136, 209.

[51] Aiming at the opponent's vital organs was unpopular because it shortened the combat. There is a pun on *caput* in the literal and legal senses; cf. on §8.

[52] That is, if Quinctius lost his case.

PRO QUINCTIO 28–30

due respect). How severely he thought this action should be punished, you will be able to learn from his decrees.[49]

Meanwhile, at Rome Alfenus was fighting daily with this veteran gladiator.[50] He no doubt had the people on his side, because his opponent unremittingly aimed at the head.[51] The other demands that the agent give security that a judgment would be paid.[52] Alfenus says it is not fair that an agent should give a security that the defendant, if present in person, would not be required to give.[53] Appeal is made to the tribunes; after definite assistance had been asked from them, they departed upon Alfenus promising that Publius Quinctius would appear in court on September 13.[54]

Quinctius returns to Rome and appears to his bail. The other, a bitterly hostile man who had taken possession of his property, who had driven him out and robbed him of it, raised no claim for a year and six months, kept quiet, led my client on as long as he could by proposing terms, and finally demands from the praetor Gnaeus Dolabella[55] that Quinctius should give him security for his claim under

29

30

---

[53] The demand for surety from Quinctius' agent is legally justified (Gai. *Inst.* 4.101). Cicero merely reports the ground given by Alfenus for his refusal, but this is likely to have been a delaying tactic; see further Kinsey 1971, 92–93; Platschek 2005, 253–54.

[54] The date when business resumed after the Roman Games. On Alfenus' appeal to the tribunes, see further §§63–65 with notes. [55] Cn. Cornelius Dolabella, praetor 81, possibly praetor urbanus: so with a query *MRR* 2:76; *TLRR* 135. The delay in pressing the claim may have been due at least in part to political considerations, Naevius presuming he could make no progress as long as M. Brutus was tribune (cf. §65) but taking heart once Sulla was firmly in power.

quod ab eo petat quoniam eius[21] ex edicto praetoris bona dies xxx possessa sint. Non recusabat Quinctius quin ita satis dare iuberet si bona possessa essent ex edicto. Decernit quam aequum nihil dico; unum hoc dico: novum, et hoc ipsum tacuisse mallem, quoniam utrumque quivis intelligere potuisset. Iubet P. Quinctium sponsionem cum Sex. Naevio facere si bona sua ex edicto P. Burreni[22] praetoris dies xxx possessa non essent. Recusabant qui aderant tum Quinctio; demonstrabant de re iudicium fieri oportere, ut aut uterque inter se aut neuter satis daret; non 31 necesse esse famam alterius in iudicium venire. Clamabat porro ipse Quinctius sese idcirco nolle satis dare ne videretur iudicasse bona sua ex edicto possessa esse; sponsionem porro si istius modi faceret, se (id quod nunc evenit) de capite suo priore loco causam esse dicturum. Dolabella, quem ad modum solent homines nobiles seu recte seu perperam facere coeperunt (ita in utroque excellunt ut nemo nostro loco natus adsequi possit), iniuriam facere fortissime perseverat: aut satis dare aut sponsionem iubet facere, et interea recusantes nostros advocatos acerrime submoveri.

[21] quoniam eius Ω, *def. Platschek 2005, 104–13*: cuius *Manutius*: quoius *Augustinus*
[22] burreni *DH*: burceni *E*: burrieni *L*Φ *(cf. ad §25)*

[56] The point is that after thirty days the goods of the debtor are liable to be sold at auction and he becomes *infamis*; cf. Greenidge 1901, 285 and n. 3.
[57] Dolabella's decision was in Quinctius' favor, a fact that Cicero conceals; cf. Platschek 2005, 126.
[58] A *sponsio* is a wager used as a means to settle a dispute via litigation. Each party agrees to pay a nominal sum to the winner; see further Crook 1976.

PRO QUINCTIO 30–31

the formula, since according to the praetor's edict his goods have been possessed for thirty days.[56] Quinctius did not object to his ordering that he should give security, if his goods had been possessed in accordance with the edict. The praetor issued a decree—as to how fair it is, I say nothing; I only say this, that it was novel—and I should have preferred to remain silent even upon this point, since anyone could have understood either matter.[57] He ordered Publius Quinctius to enter into a wager[58] with Sextus Naevius on the question of whether his goods had not been possessed for thirty days according to the edict of the praetor Publius Burrenus. Those who were then present to support Quinctius demurred; they pointed out that the trial ought to deal with the real question, so that either both parties or neither of them should give security; that there was no need for the reputation of either party being put on trial.[59] Moreover, Quinctius himself cried out that his reason for being unwilling to give security was to avoid the appearance of himself passing judgment that his goods had been possessed in accordance with the editct. Furthermore, if he made such a wager, he would plead first in a matter affecting his civil rights, as has now come to pass. In the manner of noblemen who have set out on a course, whether right or wrong (they show such superiority in both kinds that is beyond the reach of one born in our station), Dolabella manfully persevered in acting wrongfully: he ordered [Quinctius] either to provide security or enter into a wager, and in the meantime ordered our supporters, who were protesting, to be ruthlessly removed from court.

31

[59] The "real question" (*res*), according to Cicero, was whether Quinctius owed Naevius money.

32 Conturbatus sane discedit Quinctius, neque mirum, cui haec optio tam misera tamque iniqua daretur, ut aut ipse se capitis damnaret si satis dedisset aut causam capitis si sponsionem fecisset priore loco diceret. Cum in altera re causae nihil esset quin secus iudicaret ipse de se, quod iudicium gravissimum est, in altera spes esset ad talem tamen virum iudicem veniendi unde eo plus opis auferret quo minus attulisset gratiae, sponsionem facere maluit; fecit; te iudicem, C. Aquili, sumpsit; ex sponso
33 egit. In hoc summa iudici causaque tota consistit. Iudicium esse, C. Aquili, non de re pecuniaria, sed de fama fortunisque P. Quincti vides. Cum maiores ita constituerint ut qui pro capite diceret, is posteriore loco diceret, nos inaudita criminatione accusatorum priore loco causam dicere intelligis; eos porro qui defendere consuerunt vides accusare, et ea ingenia converti ad perniciem quae antea versabantur in salute atque auxilio ferendo.

Illud etiam restiterat quod hesterno die fecerunt, ut te in ius adducerent ut nobis tempus quam diu diceremus praestitueres; quam rem facile a praetore impetrassent nisi tu quod esset tuum ius[23] officium potestasque do-
34 cuisses. Nec nobis adhuc praeter te quisquam fuit ubi

[23] ius *Reeve*: ius et Ω

[60] Only one certain prosecution by Hortensius is attested, that of L. Marcius Philippus for extortion as governor of a province in 95 (*TLRR* 90); another prosecution is possible, that of Q. Oppius in 74, but not certain (*TLRR* 157).

[61] Cf. Kinsey 1971, 104: "during the proceedings *in iure* the parties had agreed, with the approval of the praetor, on the case to be tried and the *iudex* to try it. Later interference by the prae-

Quinctius withdrew, shaken; and no wonder, since so 32
wretched and unfair a choice was offered him—either to
condemn himself to lose his civil rights if he gave security,
or, if he entered into a wager, to plead first in an action in
which they were at stake. Since in the one case there was
nothing to prevent him from passing adverse judgment on
himself, which is a judgment that is very weighty indeed,
while in the other there was the hope of coming before a
judge of such a character that the less influence he brought
to bear, the greater the assistance he might obtain, he
preferred to enter into the wager. He did so; he proposed
you as judge, Gaius Aquilius; and filed suit on the wager.
The essential point of the trial and the whole case is this: 33
you see, Gaius Aquilius, that at stake in the trial is not a
pecuniary matter, but the fame and fortunes of Publius
Quinctius. Although our ancestors established the rule
that a man pleading for his civil rights should speak in the
second place, you see that we are pleading our case first,
without having heard the prosecutors' charge. Moreover,
you see men prosecuting who have been in the habit of
speaking for the defense and talents being turned to the
work of destruction that formerly were engaged in bringing salvation and assistance.[60]

This point remained, and they accomplished it yesterday: to summon you to court, so that you might prescribe
to us how long we might speak. They would easily have
been granted this by the praetor, had you not taught him
your rights, your duties, and your power.[61] Up until now 34
there was no one except you from whom we might obtain

tor at the request of one party might be held to be a breach of
that agreement and to justify an appeal to the tribunes."

39

nostrum ius contra illos obtineremus, neque illis umquam satis fuit illud obtinere quod probari omnibus posset; ita sine iniuria potentiam levem atque inopem esse arbitrantur. Verum quoniam tibi instat Hortensius ut eas in consilium, a me postulat ne dicendo tempus absumam, queritur[24] priore patrono causam defendente numquam perorari potuisse, non patiar istam manere suspicionem, nos rem iudicari nolle. Neque illud mihi adrogabo, me posse causam commodius demonstrare quam antea demonstrata sit, neque tamen tam multa verba faciam, propterea quod et ab illo qui tum dixit iam informata causa est et a me, qui neque excogitare nec pronuntiare multa possum, brevitas postulatur, quae mihimet ipsi amicissima

35 est. Faciam quod te saepe animadverti facere, Hortensi: totam causae meae dictionem certas in partis dividam. Tu id semper facis, quia semper potes; ego in hac causa faciam, propterea quod in hac videor posse facere. Quod tibi natura dat ut semper possis, id mihi causa concedit ut hodie possim. Certos mihi fines terminosque constituam extra quos egredi non possim si maxime velim, ut et mihi sit propositum de quo dicam et Hortensius habeat exposita ad quae respondeat et tu, C. Aquili, iam ante animo prospicere possis quibus de rebus auditurus sis.

[24] *post* queritur *suppl. Kayser* enim

---

[62] Here and elsewhere, e.g., §45, *Ver.* 1.33, etc., Hortensius is addressed, by a kind of camaraderie of advocates, by a single name; cf. Kinsey 1971, 107; Adams 1978, 146–47.

[63] Indeed, Hortensius famously used his fingers to count out his points: *Div. Caec.* 45.

PRO QUINCTIO 34–35

our rights against them. Nor were they ever satisfied with obtaining what could be approved by everyone; so slight and inconsequential do they hold power to be unless it is used to inflict harm. But since Hortensius presses you to consult your councilors, demands that I not engage in a filibuster, and complains that, when the previous advocate was defending, the case could never be brought to a conclusion, I will not allow the suspicion to abide that we do not want a verdict to be reached. I shall not raise the arrogant claim that I can set out the case better than was previously done; yet I shall not speak at such great length, because the case has already been put into shape by the previous speaker, and also because brevity is required of me, which is most congenial to me, who am incapable of thinking up or delivering a long speech. I will do what I have often observed you doing, Hortensius:[62] I will divide my entire pleading into distinct sections.[63] You always do this, because you always can; I will do it in this case, because I think that I can do so here. What nature grants you to be able to do always, the case allows me to be able to do today.[64] I will set for myself fixed boundaries and limits beyond which I may not go, however much I may desire to do so. Hence I shall have the subject on which I am to speak and Hortensius will have the points expounded to which he is to reply and you, Gaius Aquilius, can already see in advance the matters about which you will hear.

35

[64] Cicero thus excuses his apparent imitation of Hortensius' procedure; for his selection of Hortensius as his model, cf. *Brut.* 317.

36   Negamus te bona P. Quincti, Sex. Naevi, possedisse ex edicto praetoris. In eo sponsio facta est. Ostendam primum causam non fuisse cur a praetore postulares ut bona P. Quincti possideres, deinde ex edicto te possidere non potuisse, postremo non possedisse. Quaeso, C. Aquili vosque qui estis in consilio, ut quid pollicitus sim diligenter memoriae mandetis; etenim rem facilius totam accipietis si haec memineritis et me facile vestra existimatione revocabitis si extra hos cancellos egredi conabor quos mihi ipse circumdedi. Nego fuisse causam cur postularet, nego ex edicto possidere potuisse, nego possedisse. Haec tria cum docuero, peroraro.

37   Non fuit causa cur postularet. Qui hoc intellegi potest? Quia Sex. Naevio neque ex societatis ratione neque privatim quicquam debuit Quinctius. Quis huic rei testis est? Idem qui acerrimus adversarius: in hanc rem te, te[25] inquam, testem, Naevi, citabo. Annum et eo diutius post mortem C. Quincti fuit in Gallia tecum simul Quinctius. Doce te petisse ab eo istam nescioquam innumerabilem pecuniam, doce aliquando mentionem fecisse, dixisse

38 deberi: debuisse concedam. Moritur C. Quinctius, qui tibi, ut ais, certis nominibus grandem pecuniam debuit. Heres eius P. Quinctius in Galliam ad te ipsum venit in agrum communem, eo denique ubi non modo res erat sed

[25] te te η: te Ω

---

[65] On the tripartite structure, cf. Craig 1985; Petrucci 2022, 211–12.

PRO QUINCTIO 36–38

We deny, Sextus Naevius, that you have taken possession of Publius Quinctius' goods in accordance with the praetor's edict. That is the matter about which the wager was made. I will first show that there was no reason to demand from the praetor that you should take possession of Quinctius' goods; next, that you could not have taken possession of them in accordance with the edict; finally, that you did not possess them. I beg you, Gaius Aquilius, and you, the members of his council, carefully to commit to memory the promise I have made. For you will more easily apprehend the entire case, if you remember these points, and by your judgment you will easily call me back if I endeavor to pass beyond the barriers with which I have surrounded myself. I deny that there was any reason to make the demand; I deny that he could have taken possession in accordance with the edict; I deny that he took possession. When I have proven these three claims, I will conclude.[65]

There was no reason for him to make the demand. How can this be shown? Because Quinctius owed Sextus Naevius nothing either from the partnership or privately. Who attests to this fact? The very man who is his bitterest opponent. I shall, I say, call you, you, Naevius, as a witness to this fact. Quinctius lived with you in Gaul for a year and more after the death of Gaius Quinctius. Show that you ever asked him to pay that enormous amount, whatever it was, show that you ever mentioned it or said that it was owed, and I will admit that he owed it. Gaius Quinctius died, who, as you assert, owed you a large sum of money on specific accounts. His heir Publius Quinctius came to Gaul, to yourself, to the joint estate—in fact, to the place where not only the property was, but also all the accounts

ratio quoque omnis et omnes litterae. Quis tam dissolutus in re familiari fuisset, quis tam neglegens, quis tam tui, Sexte, dissimilis qui, cum res ab eo quicum contraxisset recessisset et ad heredem pervenisset, non heredem, cum primum vidisset, certiorem faceret, appellaret, rationem adferret, si quid in controversiam veniret aut intra parietes aut summo iure experiretur? Itane est? Quod viri optimi faciunt si qui suos propinquos ac necessarios caros et honestos esse atque haberi volunt, id Sex. Naevius non faceret, qui usque eo fervit ferturque avaritia ut de suis commodis aliquam partem velit amittere ne quam partem huic
39 propinquo suo ullius ornamenti relinquat? Et is pecuniam, si qua deberetur, non peteret qui quia quod debitum numquam est, id datum non est, non pecuniam modo verum etiam hominis propinqui sanguinem vitamque eripere conatur? Huic tu molestus esse videlicet noluisti; quem nunc respirare libere non sinis, quem nunc interficere nefarie cupis, eum tum pudenter appellare nolebas. Ita credo: hominem propinquum, tui observantem, virum bonum, pudentem, maiorem natu, nolebas aut non audebas appellare. Saepe, ut fit, cum ipse te confirmasses, cum statuisses mentionem de pecunia facere, cum paratus meditatusque venisses, homo timidus virginali verecundia subito ipse te[26] retinebas; excidebat repente oratio; cum

[26] ipse te: te ipse *Reeve in app. (numeri causa, ut vid.)*

---

[66] Cicero addresses his opponent familiarly, showing contempt; cf. Adams 1978, 162; Dickey 2002, 64 and n. 48.
[67] That is, the two sides could agree to appoint an arbiter (*honorarius arbiter*) or take the dispute to the praetor.
[68] Namely, the stake he offered in the wager.

PRO QUINCTIO 38–39

and documents. Who would have been so careless in a matter of property, so heedless, so unlike you, Sextus,[66] that, after the property had left the hands of the man with whom he had made the contract and passed to his heir, he failed to notify the heir as soon as he saw him, claim the money, present the account, and if any dispute arose, seek a resolution either privately or with the full rigor of the law?[67] Is that so? Would Sextus Naevius have failed to do what good men do who wish their relations and friends to be and to be considered dear and honorable, Sextus Naevius, who was so seething and driven by greed that he would be willing to lose some portion of his assets[68] in order not to leave this relation of his a share in any ornament?[69] And if any money was owed, would the man fail to ask for it who, because that which was never owed was not paid, is endeavoring to snatch from his relation not only his money, but even his lifeblood? You evidently did not wish to annoy him: at that time you were unwilling to address a modest request for payment to a man whom you now do not allow to breathe freely, whom you criminally desire to murder. I suppose so: you were unwilling or did not dare to request payment from a man who was your relation, who respected you, a good, modest man, your elder. Many a time, as is common experience, when you had summoned courage, had decided to broach the topic of the money, when you had come prepared and practiced, timid man that you are of virginal modesty, you would immediately check yourself; words suddenly failed; though you were eager to ask for it, you did not dare to,

39

---

[69] That is, the full privileges of Roman citizenship that will be lost if Quinctius is convicted.

40 cuperes appellare, non audebas, ne invitus audiret. Id erit profecto, credamus hoc: Sex. Naevium, cuius caput oppugnet, eius auribus pepercisse. Si debuisset, Sexte, petisses, et petisses statim; si non statim, paulo quidem post; si non paulo, at aliquanto;[27] sex quidem illis mensibus profecto; anno vertente sine controversia. Anno et sex mensibus vero, cum tibi cotidie potestas hominis fuisset admonendi, verbum nullum facis: biennio iam confecto fere appellas. Quis tam perditus ac profusus nepos non adesa etiam pecunia sed abundanti[28] sic dissolutus fuisset ut fuit Sex. Naevius? Cum hominem nomino, satis mihi videor dicere. Debuit tibi C. Quinctius: numquam petisti.

41 Mortuus est ille, res ad heredem venit: cum eum cotidie videres, post biennium denique appellas. Dubitabitur utrum sit probabilius, Sex. Naevium statim si quid deberetur petiturum fuisse an ne appellaturum quidem biennio? "Appellandi tempus non erat." At tecum plus annum vixit in Gallia. "Agi non potuit." At et in provincia ius dicebatur et Romae iudicia fiebant. Restat ut aut summa neglegentia tibi obstiterit aut unica liberalitas. Si neglegentiam dices, mirabimur; si bonitatem, ridebimus; neque praeterea quid possis dicere invenio. Satis est argumenti nihil esse debitum Naevio quod tam diu nihil petivit.

[27] aliquanto *"vet." in ed. C. Stephani*: -ando Ω
[28] etiam pecunia sed abundanti *Reeve*: iam pecunia sed abundanti etiam pecunia Ω

---

70 As in §29, there is a play on *caput*.
71 An example of the use of dilemma "forcefully to conclude the discussion of a topic"; another will be found at §§64–65. Cf. Craig 1993, 173n8 (source of the quoted words).

PRO QUINCTIO 39–41

for fear he might be displeased at the words. No doubt 40
that will be the explanation. Let us believe then that Sextus Naevius spared the ears of the man whose head he would attack.[70] If he had owed you anything, Sextus, you would have asked for it, and done so at once; if not at once, a little later; if not a little later, at some time later; certainly within six months; without doubt before the end of the year. But for a year and six months, during which you daily had an opportunity of reminding him, you said not a word; now you make your request, when nearly two years have elapsed. What dissipated and extravagant spendthrift—not when money has been squandered but when it is still in abundant supply—would have been so careless as Naevius was? By the mere mention of the man's name I think I am saying enough. Gaius Quinctius owed you money; 41
you never asked for it. He died, and the estate passed to his heir. Although you saw him every day, you finally asked for payment after two years. Can there be any doubt which is the more probable: if anything was owed, that Sextus Naevius would have asked for it at once, or that he would not even have claimed it for two years? "I had no opportunity to claim it." But he lived with you in Gaul for more than a year. "One could not litigate." But justice was being administered in the province and the courts were convening in Rome. The remaining motives are extreme negligence or unparalleled generosity. If you plead negligence, we shall be astonished; if you plead generosity, we shall laugh; and I do not know what other excuse you can plead.[71] The fact that he failed to claim anything for so long is sufficient proof that he owed Naevius nothing.

42 Quid si hoc ipsum quod nunc facit ostendo testimonio esse nihil deberi? Quid enim nunc agit Sex. Naevius? Qua de re controversia est? Quod est hoc iudicium in quo iam biennium versamur? Quid negoti geritur in quo ille tot et tales viros defatigat? Pecuniam petit, nunc denique, ve-
43 rum tamen petat: audiamus. De rationibus et controversiis societatis vult diiudicari, sero, verum aliquando tamen: concedamus. "Non" inquit "id ago, C. Aquili, neque in eo nunc laboro. Pecunia mea tot annos utitur [C.][29] Quinctius: utatur sane, non peto." Quid igitur pugnas? An quod saepe multis in locis dixisti, ne in civitate sit, ne locum suum, quem adhuc honestissime defendit, obtineat, ne numeretur inter vivos, decernat de vita et ornamentis suis omnibus, apud iudicem causam priore loco dicat et eam cum orarit, tum denique vocem accusatoris audiat? Quid?
44 Hoc quo pertinet? Ut ocius ad tuum pervenias? At si id velles, iam pridem actum esse poterat. Ut honestiore iudicio conflictere? At sine summo scelere P. Quinctium propinquum tuum iugulare non potes. Ut facilius iudicium sit? At neque C. Aquilius de capite alterius libenter iudicat et Q. Hortensius contra caput non didicit dicere. Quid a

[29] *secl. Reeve in app.*: P. *Naugerius 1519*

---

[72] A regular way of referring to a person who is *infamis*; cf. *Rosc. Am.* 113.   [73] The current trial would not make Quinctius *infamis* but, if he lost, would entail that he was already *infamis*.

[74] A victory in this case would establish that Quinctius' property had been held under a praetor's edict for more than thirty days, which Naevius could then use as evidence that Quinctius had forfeited his bail (plea of *vadimonium desertum*), a prima facie proof that Quinctius owed him money.

But what if I show that the very thing that he [Naevius] 42
is now doing is evidence that nothing is owed to him?
What, in fact, is Naevius now doing? What is the matter
in dispute? What is this trial in which we have already
been engaged two years? What is this affair that is going
on now, with which he is wearing out so many eminent
men? He demands his money, at this late date, but nonetheless he demands it; let us hear what he has to say. He 43
wants the disputed accounts arising from the partnership
to be settled. It is rather late, but better late than never;
let us grant this. "This is not what I am aiming at, Gaius
Aquilius," he says; "I am not concerned about that at present. Quinctius has used my money for so many years. Let
him have it by all means; I do not ask for it." What, then,
are you fighting for? Is it, as you have said on many occasions, that he should not be in the body of citizens, that he
may not be able to keep his position, which until now he
has honorably maintained, that he may no longer be reckoned among the living,[72] that he may have to fight for his
life and all that makes it honorable, to plead his case first
before the judge, and only hear his accuser's words after
he has pleaded it? Well, what is the point of this? That you
may come into your own more speedily? But if this was 44
what you wanted, it could have been done long ago. That
you may contest the matter by a more honorable form of
procedure?[73] But you cannot, without committing an
abominable crime, murder your relation Publius Quinctius. That a trial may be facilitated?[74] But Aquilius takes
no pleasure in pronouncing sentence in a matter affecting
the civil rights of one of the parties, nor has Hortensius
learned the art of pleading against such rights. But what

CICERO

nobis autem, C. Aquili, refertur? Pecuniam petit: negamus deberi. Iudicium fiat statim; non recusamus. Quid[30] praeterea? Si veretur ut res iudicio facto parata sit, iudicatum solvi satis accipiat; quibus a me verbis satis acceperit,[31] eisdem ipse quod peto satis det. Actum iam potest esse, C. Aquili; iam tu potes discedere molestia prope
45 dicam non minore quam Quinctius liberatus.[32] Quid agimus, Hortensi? Quid de hac condicione dicimus? Possumus aliquando depositis armis sine periculo fortunarum de re pecuniaria disceptare? Possumus ita rem nostram persequi ut hominis propinqui caput incolume esse patiamur? Possumus petitoris personam capere, accusatoris deponere? "Immo" inquit "abs te satis accipiam; ego autem tibi satis non dabo." Quis tandem nobis ista iura tam aequa discribit? Quis hoc statuit, quod aequum sit in Quinctium, id iniquum esse in Naevium? "Quincti bona" inquit "ex edicto praetoris possessa sunt." Ergo id ut confitear postulas, ut quod numquam factum esse iudicio defendimus, id proinde quasi factum sit nostro iudicio
46 confirmemus. Inveniri ratio, C. Aquili, non potest ut ad suum quisque quam primum sine cuiusquam dedecore infamia pernicieque perveniat? Profecto si quid deberetur, peteret, non omnia iudicia fieri mallet quam unum illud unde haec omnia iudicia nascuntur. Qui inter tot

30 ut quid Ω: quid (ut *deleto*) *Angelius*
31 acceperit *Kayser*: acciperet Ω
32 liberatus *huc transposuit Reeve: ante* discedere Δ*L: om.* Φ

---

[75] Repeating the position taken by Quinctius' supporters before the praetor Dolabella that each side should provide securities (§30).   [76] Two senses of *iudicium* ("court" and "judgment") are contrasted.

PRO QUINCTIO 44–46

answer are we giving, Gaius Aquilius? He [Naevius] demands his money; we deny that any is owed. Let the trial begin at once; we make no objection. Is there anything further? If he is afraid that, after the decision has been given [*sc.* in his favor], the money will not be available, let him accept security and give security for what I claim in the same form as that in which he accepts security from me.[75] This can be settled now, Gaius Aquilius; you can now leave the tribunal, relieved of a matter, I might almost say, as troublesome to you as to Quinctius. What are we to do, Hortensius? What are we to say of this offer? Can we not at long last lay aside our arms and debate the question of money without imperiling anyone's fortunes? Can we not pursue our interests in such a way as to leave the civil rights of a relation unimpaired? Can we not assume the role of plaintiff and lay aside that of accuser? "No," says Naevius, "I will accept security from you, but I will give you none." Who is imposing such fair terms on us? Who has decided that what is fair for Quinctius is unfair for Naevius? "Quinctius' property," he says, "has been taken possession of in accordance with the praetor's edict." So then you demand that I should admit this, so that by our own judgment we confirm that something was done which in court we claim never occurred.[76] Can a way not be found, Gaius Aquilius, whereby each of the parties may come into his own[77] as soon as possible without bringing disgrace, infamy, and ruin upon the other? Surely if he [Naevius] were seeking what he was owed, he would not prefer that all kinds of trial should take place rather than that single one which is the source of all these trials. The

45

46

---

[77] Plays upon the traditional definition of justice, "to each his own" (*suum cuique*); cf. *Inv.* 2.160; *Off.* 1.21.

CICERO

annos ne appellarit quidem Quinctium, cum potestas esset agendi cotidie, qui quo tempore primum [male][33] agere coepit, in vadimoniis differendis tempus omne consumpserit, qui postea vadimonium quoque missum fecerit, hunc per insidias vi de agro communi deiecerit, qui, cum de re agendi nullo recusante potestas fuisset, sponsionem de probro facere maluerit, qui, cum revocetur ad id iudicium unde haec nata sunt omnia, condicionem aequissimam repudiet, fateatur se non pecuniam sed vitam et sanguinem petere, is non hoc palam dicit?: "Mihi si quid deberetur, peterem atque adeo iam pridem abstulissem.
47 Nihil hoc tanto negotio, nihil tam invidioso iudicio, nihil tam copiosa advocatione uterer si petendum esset. Extorquendum est invito atque ingratiis, quod non debet eripiendum atque exprimendum est, de fortunis omnibus P. Quinctius deturbandus est, potentes diserti nobiles omnes advocandi sunt, adhibenda vis est veritati, minae iactentur, pericula intendantur, formidines opponantur, ut his rebus aliquando victus et perterritus ipse se dedat."

33 *secl. Madvig (cf. §52 male agendi): frustra def. Platschek 2005, 50–57*

---

[78] This was, however, denied by Naevius; cf. §§38 and 68.

[79] The transmitted text has "act fraudulently" (*male agere*), but on Cicero's account, this was by no means the beginning of Naevius' "bad behavior"; that would have been when he tried to extort an agreement as a condition for providing Quinctius with money to repay the Scapulae (§19). Hence, Madvig's deletion of *male*, without which *agere* means "to litigate."

[80] *recusare* is a technical expression that recurs in §63 for rejecting the terms of litigation during the initial phase of a trial

man who for so many years never even asked Quinctius for payment when there was opportunity to go to court any day he chose;[78] who, when he first began to litigate,[79] wasted all the time in adjournments, who afterward gave up exacting bail, and treacherously drove my client by force from their common lands; who, when he had the opportunity of bringing an action on the main point without anyone objecting,[80] preferred to enter into a wager which might ruin his opponent's reputation;[81] who, when he is brought back to trying the question from which all these claims have arisen, rejects the fairest terms, would he not confess that it is not my client's money but his lifeblood that he is seeking? Does this man not openly declare, "If anything were owed to me, I would have claimed it and indeed recovered it long ago. I would by no means take so much trouble, engage in such invidious litigation, or employ such an abundance of advocates if collecting a debt were my goal. What he does not owe must be wrested from him against his will and under compulsion, it must be snatched and forced out. P. Quinctius must be driven headlong from all his fortunes; all powerful and eloquent nobles must be called upon to help; violence must be done to the truth, threats bandied, dangers brandished, intimidation applied, so that, frightened and defeated by these measures, he may finally surrender."

47

(*in iure*), when both litigants appeared before the magistrate; see Berger 1953 s.v. In iure; Platschek 2005, 51.

[81] But it was actually Quinctius who chose this procedure in view of the choices offered to him by the praetor (§32). Naevius would have "preferred" to litigate on the debt, but with Quinctius providing security, which the latter refused.

CICERO

Quae mehercule omnia, cum qui contra pugnent video et cum illum consessum considero, adesse atque impendere videntur neque vitari ullo modo posse; cum autem ad te, C. Aquili, oculos animumque rettuli, quo maiore conatu studioque aguntur, eo leviora infirmioraque existimo.

48 Nihil igitur debuit, ut tu ipse praedicas. Quid si debuisset, continuone causa fuisset cur a praetore postulares ut bona possideres? Non opinor id quidem nec ius esse nec cuiquam expedire. Quid igitur demonstrat? Vadimonium sibi ait esse desertum. Ante quam doceo id factum non esse, libet mihi, C. Aquili, ex[34] offici ratione atque ex omnium consuetudine rem ipsam et factum simul Sex. Naevi considerare.

Ad vadimonium non venerat, ut ais, is quicum tibi adfinitas, societas, omnes denique causae et necessitudines veteres intercedebant. Ilicone ad praetorem ire convenit? Continuone verum fuit postulare ut ex edicto bona possidere liceret? Ad haec extrema et inimicissima[35] iura tam cupide decurrebas ut tibi nihil in posterum quod gravius 49 aut crudelius facere posses reservares. Nam quid homini potest turpius, quid vero miserius aut acerbius usu venire? Quod tantum evenire dedecus, quae tanta calamitas inveniri potest? Pecuniam cuipiam si fortuna ademit aut si alicuius eripuit iniuria, tamen dum existimatio est integra,

---

[34] ex L^2: ea Ω (*om.* Φ)   [35] iniquissima Φ, *fort. recte*

---

[82] The ethical argument that it was improper for Naevius to go to law at once does not bear upon the legal issue but serves to blacken Naevius' character.

[83] That is, Naevius immediately resorted to the most extreme action possible.

PRO QUINCTIO 47–49

By Hercules, when I see his opponents and look at the people seated over there, all these actions seem to threaten, to be at hand, imminent and unavoidable. When, however, my eyes and thoughts return to you, Gaius Aquilius, the greater the zeal and effort that are exerted, the slighter and weaker I judge them to be.

So then, Quinctius owed you nothing, as you yourself declare. If he had owed you something, would there have been a reason for immediately demanding of the praetor that you should take possession of his goods?[82] I do not think that is either right or in anyone's interest. What, then, is he trying to prove? He claims that he [Quinctius] defaulted on his bail to his [Naevius'] disadvantage. Before I show that this did not occur, I should like, Gaius Aquilius, to consider the matter itself from the standpoint of the principle of duty and general custom and at the same time what Naevius has done.

As you assert, he had not appeared to his bail—this man between whom and yourself there existed a connection by marriage, a partnership—in short, all friendly relations and longstanding ties. Was it appropriate to go at once to the praetor? Was it right immediately to demand to be allowed to enter into possession of his property by virtue of the edict? You hastened so eagerly to exercise these extreme and most unfriendly rights that you held in reserve nothing more grievous or more cruel for future action.[83] For what can happen to a human being that is more disgraceful, what more wretched or more bitter? What disgrace or disaster of such magnitude can occur or be found? If fortune has deprived someone of money or if someone's wrongful act has snatched it away, nonetheless, as long as his standing is unimpaired, honorable

CICERO

facile consolatur honestas egestatem. At non nemo aut ignominia adfectus aut iudicio turpi convictus bonis quidem suis utitur, alterius opes, id quod miserrimum est, non expectat; hoc tamen in miseriis adiumento et solacio sublevatur. Cuius vero bona venierunt, cuius non modo illae amplissimae fortunae sed etiam victus vestitusque necessarius sub praeconem[36] cum dedecore subiectus est, is non modo ex numero vivorum exturbatur sed, si fieri potest, infra etiam mortuos amandatur; etenim mors honesta saepe vitam quoque inopem[37] exornat, vita turpis ne morti quidem honestae locum relinquit. Ergo hercule cuius bona ex edicto possidentur, huius omnis fama et existimatio cum bonis simul possidetur; de quo libelli in celeberrimis locis proponuntur, huic ne perire quidem tacite obscureque conceditur; cui magistri fiunt et domini constituuntur qui qua lege et qua condicione pereat pronuntient, de quo homine praeconis vox praedicat et pretium conficit, huic acerbissimum vivo videntique funus indicitur, si funus id habendum est[38] quo non amici conveniunt ad exsequias cohonestandas sed bonorum emptores ut carnifices ad reliquias vitae lacerandas et distrahendas.

[36] praeconem *Wesenberg*: -cone Ω
[37] inopem *Garatoni*: turpem Ω
[38] est *Halm*: sit Ω

[84] That is, if one suffers *infamia* either by a censorial mark (*nota*) against one's name on the census rolls or as a result of conviction for certain offenses; cf. Berger 1953 s.v. Actiones famosae.
[85] Namely, the retention of his property.

status affords ready consolation for poverty. But someone who suffers disgrace or is convicted by a judgment that entails disrepute,[84] though he continues to possess his property, does not expect anyone else's help, which is the most wretched fate of all; but amid his wretchedness he is nonetheless relieved by this assistance and comfort.[85] But one whose property has been sold, who has seen not only his rich possessions but even the necessities of food and clothing ignominiously subjected to the auctioneer's gavel—that person is not only driven from the company of the living, but is relegated, if possible, to a position lower than the dead.[86] In fact, an honorable death often confers luster even upon a life of poverty, whereas a disgraceful life leaves no room even for an honorable death. Well then, by Hercules, if a person's goods are possessed by virtue of an edict, his entire character and reputation are taken into possession together with the goods; if his name is posted up on notices in the most frequented places, he is not even allowed to die in silence and obscurity; if trustees are appointed and put in charge of his property, to set the terms and conditions of his ruin; if he hears the voice of an auctioneer crying out his name and fixing the price, then his own untimely funeral is announced to him while he is living and breathing,[87] if an event should be called a funeral for which there gather not his friends to lend honor to his obsequies but the purchasers of his goods, like butchers, to rend and scatter the remnants of his life.

50

[86] Evidently aiming to remind the judge of the victims of Sulla's proscriptions, though the latter were literally, not just metaphorically, dead; cf. Hinard 1985a, 102–4; 1985b, 148–49.

[87] Literally, "seeing."

CICERO

51   Itaque maiores nostri raro id accidere voluerunt; praetores ut considerate fieret comparaverunt; viri boni cum palam fraudantur, cum experiundi potestas non est, timide tamen et pedetemptim istuc descendunt, vi ac necessitate coacti, inviti, multis vadimoniis desertis, saepe inlusi ac destituti. Considerant enim quid et quantum sit alterius bona proscribere. Iugulare civem ne iure quidem quisquam bonus vult; mavult enim commemorare se cum posset perdere pepercisse quam cum parcere potuerit perdidisse. Haec in homines alienissimos, denique inimicissimos viri boni faciunt et hominum existimationis et communis humanitatis causa, ut cum ipsi nihil alteri scientes incommodarint, nihil in se[39] iure incommodi cadere

52   possit. Ad vadimonium non venit—quis? Propinquus. Si res ista gravissima sua sponte videretur, tamen eius atrocitas necessitudinis nomine levaretur. Ad vadimonium non venit—quis? Socius. Etiam gravius aliquid ei deberes concedere quicum te aut voluntas congregasset aut fortuna coniunxisset. Ad vadimonium non venit—quis? Is qui tibi praesto semper fuit. Ergo in eum qui semel hoc commisit ut tibi praesto non esset omnia tela coniecisti quae parata sunt in eos qui permulta male agendi causa fraudandique fecerunt?

53   Si dupundius tuus ageretur, Sex. Naevi, si in parvula re

[39] in se F^2 (cf. cum Reeve Sest. 30): ipse Ω

---

[88] The ancestors are typically invoked for establishing strict standards; cf., e.g., *Rosc. Am.* 69.   [89] Cf. fr. orat. 3 F 5 Cr.-D.

[90] The word *humanitas* (common feelings of humanity) appears here for the first time in extant Latin; it recurs at §97; cf. Mollea 2022.

PRO QUINCTIO 51–53

And so it was the will of our ancestors that this occur rarely;[88] and the praetors provided that it should occur only upon mature consideration. Even when they are openly defrauded, and when there is no opportunity of trying the case, good men resort to this measure with timidity and caution, driven by the force of necessity, unwillingly, after the defendant has failed to appear many times, and after they have often been flouted and left hanging. They take into account what it is—an enormous thing—to put another's property up for sale. No good man wants to put a citizen to death, even if he is within his rights; he would rather remember that he spared when he could have destroyed than that he destroyed when he could have spared.[89] This is how good men treat complete strangers, indeed, even their worst enemies, for the sake of public opinion and the common feelings of humanity.[90] Hence, having never themselves knowingly caused any unpleasantness for others, nothing disagreeable can justly befall them. He failed to appear to his bail—who? Your relation. Though that fact might seem grievous per se, its enormity should nonetheless have been palliated on account of the tie. He failed to appear to his bail—who? Your partner. You ought to have pardoned an even greater fault in a man with whom either your will had associated you or your fortune joined you. He failed to appear to his bail—who? The man who was always there for you. Have you on that account hurled all the missiles that are available against those who have committed a great many acts of chicanery and fraud, at the man who once failed to appear? 51 52

If a two-bit coin of your own were at stake, Sextus Naevius, if you feared being tricked in some trifling mat- 53

CICERO

captionis[40] aliquid vererere,[41] non statim ad C. Aquilium aut ad eorum aliquem qui consuluntur cucurrisses? Cum ius amicitiae societatis adfinitatis ageretur, cum offici rationem atque existimationis duci conveniret, eo tempore tu non modo non[42] ad C. Aquilium aut L. Lucilium[43] rettulisti sed ne ipse quidem te consuluisti, ne hoc quidem tecum locutus es?: "Horae duae fuerunt: Quinctius ad vadimonium non venit. Quid ago?" Si mehercule haec tecum duo verba fecisses, "Quid ago?," respirasset cupiditas atque avaritia, paulum aliquid loci rationi et consilio dedisses, tu te conlegisses, non in eam turpitudinem venisses ut hoc tibi esset apud tales viros confitendum, qua tibi vadimonium non sit obitum, eadem te hora consilium 54 cepisse hominis propinqui fortunas funditus evertere. Ego nunc pro te hos consulo post tempus et in aliena re, quoniam tu in tua re cum tempus erat consulere oblitus es. Quaero abs te, C. Aquili, L. Lucili,[44] P. Quintili, M. Marcelle—vadimonium mihi non obiit quidam socius et adfinis meus quicum mihi necessitudo vetus, controversia de re pecuniaria recens intercedit; postulone a praetore ut eius bona mihi possidere liceat, an, cum Romae domus

40 captionis *ed. Rom.*: captivis *vel* -tuus $\Delta L^1 \Phi$: captiptus L^2
41 vererere F^2 *Rufin.*: verere Ω
42 modo non P: modo Ω
43 lucilium P: lucullum Ω
44 lucili *Manutius*: -ille *Rufin.*: -ulli $\Delta\Phi$: -ulle L

___

91 L. Lucilius Balbus, one of Aquilius' three councilors for this case (§54). Cf. Münzer, *RE* s.v. Lucilius 19.
92 He names Aquilius and his three councilors. For Lucilius, see on §53. P. Quintilius is possibly the P. Quinctilius Varus who

PRO QUINCTIO 53–54

ter, would you not have hurried to consult Gaius Aquilius or some other legal advisor? But when the rights of friendship, partnership, and connection by marriage were at stake, when it was fitting to take account of duty and public standing, at that time did you not only not refer the matter to Gaius Aquilius or Lucius Lucilius[91] but not even consult yourself, not even engage in this dialogue? "It has been two hours. Quinctius failed to appear to his bail. What am I to do?" By Hercules, if you had uttered these words to yourself, "What am I to do?," greed and avarice would have paused, you would have given a little space to rational counsel, you would have come to your senses, you would not have plunged into the disgrace of having to confess before such men that at the very hour when he failed to meet his bail you decided to raze the fortunes of your relation to their foundations. I shall now consult 54 these men on your behalf, after the fact and on another's business, since you forgot to consult them on your own account when it was time. I ask you, Gaius Aquilius, Lucius Lucilius, Publius Quintilius, and Marcus Marcellus:[92] a certain man who is a partner of mine and connection by marriage failed to appear to his bail; I had a longstanding tie with him and a recent dispute about a pecuniary matter; shall I demand from the praetor that he permit me to take

was a witness in the case against Scamander in 74 (*Clu.* 53; *TLRR* 147); cf. Gundel, *RE* s.v. Quinctilius 2; *MRR* 3:177. M. (Claudius) Marcellus may have been C. Marius' legate at the victory at Aquae Sextiae and a legate of the consul Sextus Iulius Caesar in 90 during the Social War, when he led the defense of Aesernia, which was starved into submission; cf. Münzer, *RE* s.v. Claudius 226; *MRR* 1:569, 2:28.

eius, uxor, liberi sint, domum potius denuntiem? Quid est quod hac tandem de re vobis possit videri? Profecto si recte vestram bonitatem atque prudentiam cognovi, non multum me fallit, si consulamini, quid sitis responsuri: primum expectare, deinde, si latitare ac diutius ludificare videatur, amicos convenire, quaerere quis procurator sit, domum denuntiare—dici vix potest quam multa sint quae respondeatis ante fieri oportere quam ad hanc rationem extremam necessario[45] devenire.

55 Quid ad haec Naevius? Ridet scilicet nostram amentiam, qui in vita sua rationem summi offici desideremus et instituta virorum bonorum requiramus. "Quid mihi" inquit "cum ista summa sanctimonia ac diligentia? Viderint" inquit "ista officia viri boni. De me autem ita considerent: non quid habeam sed quibus rebus invenerim quaerant. Et quem ad modum natus et quo pacto educatus sim memini. Vetus est de scurra multo facilius divitem quam pa-
56 trem familias fieri posse." Haec ille, si verbis non audet, re quidem vera palam loquitur. Etenim si vult virorum bonorum instituto vivere, multa oportet discat ac dediscat, quorum illi aetati utrumque difficile est.

"Non dubitavi" inquit "cum vadimonium desertum esset, bona proscribere." Improbe, verum[46] quoniam tu id

[45] necessario *Gulielmius*: -iam Ω
[46] verum *Paris. Lat.* 7779: utrum Ω

[93] In Latin, *bonus* can be used in a moral sense ("a good man") but also to indicate "a man of property." Naevius, as represented here, is a *bonus* in the latter sense, but not the former.
[94] For the proverbial saying, cf. Otto 1890 s.v. *scurra*; the point was prepared at §11, where see note.

PRO QUINCTIO 54–56

possession of his property or since his house, his wife, and his children are at Rome, should I first give notice at his house? What may seem best to you as regards this matter? If I have rightly gauged your kindness and good sense, I have little doubt as to what reply you will give if you are consulted: first, wait; then, if he seems to hide and flout you for any length of time, meet with his friends, ask who his agent is, give notice at his house. It is almost past numbering the many steps that you would reply should be taken before being compelled to resort to this extreme measure.

What does Naevius say to this? No doubt he is laughing at our folly in seeking in his life a regard for strict duty or looking for the practices of good men. "What do I have to do with such severe morality and conscientiousness?" he says. "Let good men look to those duties," he says. "But as for me, let them consider as follows: let them ask not what I possess but by what means I have acquired it.[93] I remember in what circumstances I was born and the manner in which I was brought up. There is an old saying: 'it is much easier for a buffoon to become rich than a head of household.'"[94] This is what he openly declares in fact, even if he does not dare to say it in words. For if indeed he desires to live according to the practices of good men, he must learn and unlearn many things—both of which are difficult at his time of life.

"I did not hesitate," he says, "to put his goods up for sale, since he had forfeited his bail."[95] Shamelessly said,

55

56

---

[95] Cicero elides the step of obtaining the praetor's order so as to "make Naevius' action seem worse than it was": Kinsey 1971, 144.

63

CICERO

tibi adrogas et concedi postulas, concedamus. Quid? Si numquam deseruit, si ista causa abs te tota per summam fraudem et malitiam ficta[47] est, si vadimonium omnino tibi cum P. Quinctio nullum fuit, quo te nomine appellemus? Improbum? At etiam si desertum vadimonium esset, tamen in ista postulatione et proscriptione bonorum improbissimus reperiebare. Malitiosum? Non negas. Fraudulentum? Iam id quidem adrogas tibi et praeclarum putas. Audacem, cupidum, perfidiosum? Vulgaria et obsoleta sunt, res autem nova atque inaudita. Quid ergo est? Vereor mehercule ne aut gravioribus utar verbis quam natura[48] fert aut levioribus quam causa postulat. Ais esse vadimonium desertum. Quaesivit a te statim ut Romam rediit Quinctius quo die vadimonium istuc factum esse diceres. Respondisti statim Nonis Februariis. Discedens in memoriam redit Quinctius quo die Roma in Galliam profectus sit. Ad ephemeridem revertitur, invenitur dies profectionis pridie Kal. Februarias. Nonis Februariis si Romae fuit, causae nihil dicimus quin tibi vadimonium promiserit. Quid? Hoc inveniri qui potest? Profectus est una L. Albius, homo cum primis honestus; dicet[49] testimonium. Prosecuti sunt familiares et Albium et Quinctium: dicent hi quoque testimonium. Litterae P. Quincti, testes

[47] ficta *Paris. Lat.* 7779: facta Ω
[48] natura: natura mea *Reeve in app., Pis. fr. 9 coll.*
[49] dicet *Vat. Ottobonianus Lat. 1991²*: -it Ω

96 Perhaps exploiting a slip or misunderstanding on the part of Naevius: when Quinctius asked him about the date, he may have understood the date of the scheduled appearance rather

but since you claim this as your right, and demand that it should be allowed, let us allow it. Tell me this: if he never forfeited, if that entire claim was invented by you with utmost fraud and wickedness, if between you and Publius Quinctius there was no engagement to appear, by what name shall we call you? A criminal? But even if he had forfeited his bail, you nonetheless showed yourself to be an utter criminal in making that demand [of the praetor] and putting his goods up for sale. Full of malice? You do not deny it. Fraudulent? You even lay claim to it and think it a distinction. Bold, covetous, treacherous? They are commonplace qualities, but this is a novel and unheard of occurrence. What is it, then? By Hercules, I hesitate to use harsher words than my nature allows or milder ones than the case demands. You assert that the bail was forfeited. As soon as he returned to Rome, Quinctius asked you to tell him on what day he had given bail to appear. You immediately answered: on the 5th of February.[96] On leaving you, Quinctius tried to recall the day on which he set out from Rome for Gaul. He consulted his diary and found that the 29th of January was the day of his departure. If he was at Rome on the 5th of February, we admit there is no reason why he should not have entered into an engagement with you to appear. Well then, how can this be found out? Lucius Albius, an eminently honorable man, set out with him; he will give evidence. Some friends accompanied both Albius and Quinctius; they also will give evidence. The documents of Quinctius, those numer-

57

58

than the date of the agreement to appear. Cf. Mette 1965, 15, followed by Platschek 2005, 83–84; Lintott 2008, 35, 52–53.

tot quibus omnibus causa iustissima est cur scire potuerint, nulla cur mentiantur, cum astipulatore tuo comparabuntur—et in hac eius modi causa P. Quinctius laborabit et diutius in tanto metu miser periculoque versabitur, et vehementius eum gratia adversari perterrebit quam fides iudicis consolabitur? Vixit enim semper inculte atque horride, natura tristi ac recondita fuit: non ad solarium, non in campo, non in conviviis versatus est. Id egit ut amicos observantia, rem parsimonia retineret; antiquam offici rationem dilexit, cuius splendor omnis his moribus obsolevit. At si in causa pari discedere inferior videretur, tamen esset non mediocriter conquerendum. Nunc in causa superiore ne ut par quidem sit postulat: inferiorem esse se[50] patitur, dumtaxat usque eo ne cum bonis, fama fortunisque omnibus Sex. Naevi cupiditati crudelitatique dedatur.

60 Docui quod primum pollicitus sum, C. Aquili, causam omnino cur postularet non fuisse, quod neque pecunia debebatur et, si maxime deberetur, commissum nihil esse

---

[50] esse se *ed. Paris. 1527*: esse Ω

---

[97] An *adstipulator* is another creditor to whom the same promise was made and who can likewise sue in the event of non-payment; cf. Berger 1953 s.v. Adstipulatio (adstipulator), but here the word seems to have the more general meaning "supporter." Cf. Kinsey 1971, 148; Platschek 2005, 78. On the misleading contrast drawn here, see Kinsey 1971, 148.

[98] An item of plunder brought to Rome by M'. Valerius Messalla (cos. 263) and installed on a column in the Forum near the Rostra, where it became a natural meeting place; cf. Münzer, *RE* s.v. Valerius 247; E. Papi, *LTUR* s.v. Solarium.

ous witnesses, all of whom had the strongest reason why they would have been able to know the facts and none for lying, shall be confronted with your supporter[97]—and is it in a case of this kind that poor Quinctius will struggle, will live for a long time in such great fear and peril, will be more terrified by the influence of his opponent than reassured by the integrity of the judge? In fact, he has always led a rude and boorish life; he has always been gloomy and withdrawn; he never frequented the sundial,[98] the Campus Martius,[99] or dinner parties. It was his aim to keep his friends by treating them with respect, and his property by frugality;[100] he loved the old-fashioned principle of duty, all the glory of which has gone out of fashion amid our modern manners. But if in a case in which both sides were equal, he were to be seen coming off defeated, even then one would raise a loud complaint. But as things stand, though his case is superior, he does not even demand that it be on an equal footing; he accepts coming off defeated, but only so far as not to be handed over with all his goods, reputation, and fortunes to the greed and cruelty of Sextus Naevius.

I have demonstrated, Gaius Aquilius, the first point that I promised, that there was no reason at all for him [Naevius] to make his demand [of the praetor], because no money was owed and even if it were, no fault had been committed on account of which he should have resorted

---

[99] Used as a recreational area by Roman males; cf. *Off.* 1.104; Ov. *Ars am.* 3.383–85.

[100] Cf. the similar portrait at *Rosc. Am.* 39 and 75.

CICERO

quare ad istam rationem perveniretur. Attende nunc ex edicto praetoris bona P. Quincti possidere nullo modo potuisse. [Tractat edictum.][51] QUI FRAUDATIONIS CAUSA LATITABIT.[52] Non est is Quinctius, nisi si latitant qui ad negotium suum relicto procuratore proficiscuntur. CUI HERES NON EXTABIT. Ne is quidem. QUI EXILI CAUSA SOLUM VERTERIT. ⟨. . .⟩[53] Quo tempore existimas oportuisse, Naevi, absentem Quinctium defendi aut quo modo? Tum cum postulabas ut bona possideres? Nemo adfuit; neque enim quisquam divinare poterat te postulaturum, nec quemquam attinebat id recusare quod praetor 61 non fieri sed ex edicto suo fieri iubebat. Qui locus igitur absentis defendendi procuratori primus datus est? Cum proscribebas. Ergo adfuit, non passus est, libellos deiecit Sex. Alfenus; qui primus erat offici gradus servatus est a procuratore summa cum diligentia. Videamus quae deinde sint consecuta. Hominem P. Quincti deprehendis in publico, conaris abducere. Non patitur Alfenus, vi tibi adimit, curat ut domum reducatur ad Quinctium; hic quoque summe constat procuratoris diligentis officium. Debere tibi dicis Quinctium: procurator negat. Vadari vis:

[51] *seclusi duce Platschek 2005, 157 adn. 528*   [52] latitabit *Mommsen, Dig. 42.4.7.1 coll.*: -arit *Naugerius 1534: om.* Ω
[53] *lac. statuit Naugerius 1519: nulla in* Ω

---

[101] The second major division of Cicero's argumentation; see note on §30.
[102] But did Quinctius appoint Alfenus his agent at his departure? There are grounds for doubt; see Platschek 2005, 230–33.
[103] The denial that this clause of the edict applies to Quinctius is lost, possibly along with other arguments. Rüfner 2008, 773–74,

PRO QUINCTIO 60–61

to that measure. Now learn that he could by no means have possessed Publius Quinctius' property in accordance with the praetor's edict.[101] "Whoever shall keep himself hidden in order to defraud." This is not Quinctius unless persons who set out on their own business while leaving an agent behind are keeping themselves hidden.[102] "A man whose heir will not come forward." Not even this. "He who has changed his abode because of exile" . . .[103] When or how do you think, Naevius, that Quinctius should have been defended in his absence? At the time when you were demanding leave to take possession of his goods? No one was present,[104] nor could anyone have guessed that you would make the demand nor was it anyone's business to object to what the praetor ordered not to be done but to be done in accordance with his edict. What, then, was the first opportunity the agent had of defending the absent man? When you were posting up notices of the sale of the property. And so Sextus Alfenus was on hand, disallowed it, tore down the notices: the agent punctiliously observed the first stage of duty. Let us observe the sequel. You catch a slave of Publius Quinctius' in a public place and attempt to lead him away. Alfenus disallows it, forcibly wrests him from you and sees to it that he is returned to Quinctius.[105] In this case, too, a conscientious agent's duty is fulfilled to the letter. You assert that Quinctius owes you money; the agent denies it. You wish to set a court date guaranteed by security; he promises security. You summon him

61

argues that an edict against absenting oneself from court proceedings was cited here, but this is doubted by Platschek 2005, 157–230. [104] That is, in the praetor's court.
[105] That is, to his house, since Quinctius himself was in Gaul.

69

promittit. In ius vocas: sequitur. Iudicium postulas: non recusat. Quid aliud sit absentem defendi ego non intelligo.

62 At quis erat procurator? Credo aliquem electum hominem egentem, litigiosum, improbum, qui posset scurrae divitis cotidianum convicium sustinere. Nihil minus: eques Romanus locuples, sui negoti bene gerens, denique is quem quotiens Naevius in Galliam profectus est, procuratorem Romae reliquit—et audes, Sex. Naevi, negare absentem defensum esse Quinctium? Cum eum defenderit idem qui te solebat et cum is iudicium acceperit[54] pro Quinctio cui tu et rem et famam tuam commendare proficiscens et concredere solebas, conaris hoc dicere, neminem exstitisse qui Quinctium iudicio defenderet?

63 "Postulabam" inquit "ut satis daret." Iniuria postulabas (ita videbare);[55] recusabat Alfenus. "Ita, verum praetor decernebat." Tribuni igitur appellabantur. "Hic te" inquit "teneo: non est istud[56] pati neque iudicio defendere, cum auxilium a tribunis petas." Hoc ego, cum attendo qua prudentia sit Hortensius, dicturum esse eum non arbitror; cum autem antea dixisse audio et causam ipsam considero, quid aliud dicere possit non reperio. Fatetur enim libellos Alfenum deiecisse, vadimonium promisisse, iudicium quin acciperet in ea ipsa verba quae Naevius edebat non recusasse, ita tamen ‹. . .›[57] more et instituto, per eum

[54] acceperit *Bodl. Canon. Class. Lat. 226*: acciperet Ω (*perperam def. Platschek 2005, 106 adn. 376*)

[55] ita videbare: ita ut edebas recte *Platschek 2005, 241–42*: *fort.* ut videbare

[56] istud: istud iudicio *Kayser, at cf. Platschek 2005, 242 adn. 796, Ver. 2.2.31 (si patitur, ducas) coll.*

[57] *lac. statuit Kübler*

PRO QUINCTIO 61–63

to court; he follows. You demand a trial; he raises no objection. If this is not defending an absent man, I do not know what is.

But who was the agent? Presumably some poor man, a litigious scoundrel, selected to be able to endure a rich buffoon's daily abuse. Nothing of the kind: a well-to-do Roman knight, who managed his own affairs well, finally the man whom Naevius left as his agent at Rome whenever he set out for Gaul—and do you dare, Sextus Naevius, to deny that Quinctius was defended in his absence? When the same man defended him who was wont to defend you and when the man accepted the trial on Quinctius' behalf to whom you were wont to commit and entrust your property and reputation when you went on a journey, are you trying to claim that no one came forward to defend Quinctius in court?

"I was demanding," he [Naevius] says, "that he give security." You were demanding wrongly (so it appeared); Alfenus kept refusing. "Well, but the praetor issued a decree." Therefore appeal was made to the tribunes. "Here I have caught you," he says. "This is not submitting or putting up a defense in court when you seek assistance from the tribunes." When I consider Hortensius' good sense, I think he will not use this argument; but when I hear that he previously said it[106] and contemplate the case itself, I do not see what else he can say. For he admits that Alfenus tore down the notices, promised security, did not object to stand trial on the same terms that Naevius proposed but on the condition . . . by customary practice, by

---

[106] At previous hearings of the case, known to Cicero from hearsay, since M. Iunius had been Quinctius' advocate (§3).

64 magistratum qui auxili causa constitutus est. Aut haec facta non sint necesse est aut C. Aquilius, talis vir, iuratus hoc ius in civitate constituat, cuius procurator non omnia iudicia quae quisque in verba postularit ‹recusarit›,[58] cuius procurator a praetore tribunos appellare ausus sit, eum non defendi, eius bona recte possideri posse, ei misero, absenti, ignaro ‹periculi›[59] fortunarum suarum omnia vitae ornamenta per summum dedecus et ignominiam
65 deripi convenire. Quod si probari nemini potest, illud certe probari omnibus necesse est, defensum esse iudicio absentem Quinctium. Quod cum ita sit, ex edicto bona possessa non sunt. "At enim tribuni plebis ne audierunt quidem." Fateor, si ita est, procuratorem decreto praetoris oportuisse parere. Quid? Si M. Brutus intercessurum se dixit palam nisi quid inter ipsum Alfenum et Naevium conveniret, videturne intercessisse appellatio tribunorum non morae sed auxili causa?
66   Quid deinde fit? Alfenus, ut omnes intelligere possent

[58] *huc transp. Reeve*: ante omnia *Bodl. Canon. Class. Lat. 226 (aliter Platschek 2005, 243–45)*: om. Ω
[59] *add. Schuetz, coll. §45*

---

[107] The lacuna contained the stipulation—presumably that Naevius should give security on the same terms (cf. §44)—and that, upon his refusal, the plebeian tribunes were called upon to block the proceedings (see on §65); when the text resumes, their function is being described.
[108] That is, the tribunes' interference could not count as a judicial process.
[109] The tribune who intervened (*MRR* 2:63), the father of

PRO QUINCTIO 63–66

means of that magistrate who has been appointed for the sake of providing assistance.[107] It must be the case that either these actions did not occur or Gaius Aquilius, a man of such quality, should on oath lay down as the law in the state: the man whose agent has not objected to all judicial proceedings that each person has demanded under a set form of words, whose agent dared to appeal from the praetor to the tribunes, is not being defended, his goods can be rightly taken into possession, and it is fitting for that unhappy man, in his absence, in ignorance of the danger to his fortunes, to be stripped, in utmost disgrace and ignominy, of all that had makes life honorable. If that can be approved by no one, this at least must be approved by everyone: that in his absence Quinctius was being defended in court. That being so, his goods were not taken into possession in accordance with the edict. "But the plebeian tribunes did not even give him a hearing."[108] Granted, if it is the case that the agent should have obeyed the praetor's decree. Tell me: if Marcus Brutus[109] said openly that he would interpose a veto unless Alfenus himself and Naevius reached some agreement, does it seem that the tribunes were called upon to intervene, not to delay but to render assistance?[110]

What happened next? So that all could understand that 66

Caesar's assassin and a member of the popular party; cf. Münzer, *RE* s.v. Iunius 52.

[110] A recognized function of plebeian tribunes, with which even Sulla did not tamper; cf. Lintott 1999, 125–28. This is Cicero's only mention of the possibility that the tribune's intervention could have produced a delay, but he is vague; cf. Platshek 2005, 260–63.

iudicio defendi Quinctium, ne qua subesse posset aliena aut ipsius officio aut huius existimatione suspicio, viros bonos complures advocat. Testatur isto audiente se pro communi necessitudine id primum petere, ne quid atrocius in P. Quinctium absentem sine causa facere conetur; sin autem inimicissime atque infestissime contendere perseveret, se paratum esse omni recta atque honesta ratione defendere quod petat non deberi, se iudicium id quod 67 edat accipere. Eius rei condicionisque tabellas obsignaverunt viri boni complures. Res in dubium venire non potest. Fit rebus omnibus integris, neque proscriptis neque possessis bonis, ut Alfenus promittat Naevio sisti Quinctium. Venit ad vadimonium Quinctius. Iacet[60] res in controversiis isto calumniante biennium usque dum inveniretur qua ratione res ab usitata consuetudine recederet et in hoc singulare iudicium causa omnis concluderetur.

68 Quod officium, ⟨C.⟩[61] Aquili, commemorari procuratoris potest quod ab Alfeno praeteritum esse videatur? Quid adfertur quare P. Quinctius negetur absens esse defensus? An vero id quod Hortensium, quia nuper iniecit et quia Naevius semper id clamitat, dicturum arbitror, non fuisse Naevio parem certationem cum Alfeno illo tempore illis dominantibus? Quod si velim confiteri, illud, opinor, concedant, non procuratorem P. Quincti neminem fuisse sed gratiosum fuisse. Mihi autem ad vincendum satis est

[60] iacet *Angelius*: tacet Ω   [61] *add. Lambinus*

[111] Suggesting that Naevius has given up possession of Quinctius' goods, but in that case he would have entered into a wager he was bound to lose; cf. Platschek 2005, 259–60.
[112] The Marian faction, led at that time by Cinna.

PRO QUINCTIO 66–68

Quinctius was being legally defended and so that no latent suspicion might linger unfavorable to his own performance of duty or my client's reputation, he called together several honorable men. When he [Naevius] was listening, he called them to witness that he asked in the first place that in view of their shared ties, he not undertake, without justification, any extreme action against Publius Quinctius in his absence; but if he continued to exert himself in an unfriendly and hostile manner, he [Alfenus] was prepared to maintain by every right and honorable means that what he was claiming was not owed; and that he accepts any action he [Naevius] may propose. Several honorable gentlemen signed the tablets recording the statement and terms. The fact is not open to doubt. When all matters were open and the property had neither been taken into possession[111] nor offered for sale, it came to pass that Alfenus promised Naevius that Quinctius would appear in court. Quinctius did so. The matter languished amid disputes, with him [Naevius] disseminating slanders, for two years until a means could be discovered by which the matter would be removed from the usual procedure and the entire case enclosed in this unparalleled form of litigation.

67

What agent's duty can be named, Gaius Aquilius, that Alfenus appears to have omitted? What proof is adduced for denying that Publius Quinctius was defended in his absence? The point that I think Hortensius is going to raise, since he recently injected it and since Naevius has always been loudly proclaiming it, namely that at that time, with those people in power,[112] he was engaged in an unequal contest with Alfenus? If I were willing to admit this, I suppose that they would concede that far from having no agent, he had an influential one. For me to carry

68

CICERO

fuisse procuratorem quicum experiretur; qualis is fuerit, si modo absentem defendebat per ius et per magistratum, 69 nihil ad rem arbitror pertinere. "Erat" inquit "illarum partium." Quidni, qui apud te esset eductus, quem tu a puero sic instituisses ut nobili ne gladiatori quidem faveret? Si, quod tu semper summe cupisti, idem volebat Alfenus, ea re tibi cum eo par contentio non erat? "Bruti" inquit, "erat familiaris; itaque is intercedebat." Tu contra Burreni qui iniuriam[62] decernebat, omnium denique illorum qui tum et poterant per vim et scelus plurimum et quod poterant id audebant. An omnes tu istos vincere volebas qui nunc tu ut vincas tanto opere laborant? Aude id dicere non palam sed eis[63] ipsis quos advocasti—tametsi nolo eam rem commemorando renovare cuius omnino rei memoriam 70 omnem tolli funditus ac deleri arbitror oportere. Unum illud dico: si propter partium studium potens erat Alfenus, potentissimus Naevius; si fretus gratia postulabat aliquid iniquius Alfenus, multo iniquiora Naevius impetrabat. Neque enim inter studium vestrum quicquam, ut opinor, interfuit: ingenio, †vetustate,[64] artificio tu facile vicisti. Ut alia omittam, hoc satis est: Alfenus cum eis et propter eos periit quos diligebat, tu post quam qui tibi erant amici non poterant vincere ut amici tibi essent qui vincebant effe-

[62] iniuria *Manutius ex ant. libro*
[63] eis: his Ω: *om.* P   [64] vetustate: venustate *Turnebus et Muretus, teste Lallemand: fort.* varietate

---

[113] A pun on *nobilis* in two senses, "famous" and "a member of the nobility."
[114] That is, the defeat of the nobility, in the civil war between Sulla and the Marians.

PRO QUINCTIO 68–70

my point it is enough that there was an agent with whom the case could be litigated; I think that it is irrelevant how the agent is described as long as he was defending him in his absence legally and before a magistrate. "He [Alfenus] belonged to the other side," he says. Of course, since he was brought up in your house and from his boyhood you had trained him not even to root for a noble gladiator.[113] You could not compete on an equal footing with him because he wanted the same thing that you always intensely desired?[114] "Brutus was his friend," he says; "that is why he interposed his veto." You, on the other hand, were the friend of Burrenus, who issued the unjust decision and, in short, of all those who then held power by force and utmost wickedness and dared to do what they were able to. Or did you want all those men to prevail who are now working so hard for your victory? Dare to say this, not openly but to those very men whom you have called to support you—and yet I am unwilling to reopen, by mentioning it, the matter whose memory I think should be altogether eliminated and blotted out.[115] I say only this: if Alfenus was powerful because of party spirit, Naevius is very powerful indeed; if relying on his influence, Alfenus made an unfair request, Naevius gained concessions that were much more unfair. And in my opinion, there was no difference between you in partisanship, but in talent, experience, and artistry you easily won the victory. To leave the rest aside, it is enough to say that Alfenus perished along with and because of those of whom he loved, whereas when those who were your friends were unable to prevail, you saw to it that those who were winning were

69

70

---

[115] Namely, the recent civil war.

CICERO

71 cisti. Quod si tum par tibi ius cum Alfeno fuisse non putas, quia tamen aliquem contra te advocare poterat, quia magistratus aliqui reperiebatur apud quem Alfeni causa consisteret, quid hoc tempore Quinctio statuendum est, cui neque magistratus adhuc aequus inventus est neque iudicium redditum est usitatum, non condicio, non sponsio, non denique ulla umquam intercessit postulatio, mitto aequa, verum ante hoc tempus ne fando quidem audita? "De re pecuniaria cupio contendere." "Non licet." "At ea controversia est." "Nihil ad me attinet. Causam capitis dicas oportet." "Accusa ubi ita necesse est." "Non" inquit "nisi tu ante novo modo priore loco dixeris." "⟨Ita⟩[65] dicendum necessario est." "Praestituentur[66] ho-
72 rae ad arbitrium nostrum; iudex ipse coercebitur." "Quid tum?" "Tu aliquem patronum invenies, hominem antiqui offici, qui splendorem nostrum et gratiam negligat. Pro me pugnabit L. Philippus, eloquentia gravitate honore florentissimus civitatis; dicet Hortensius, excellens ingenio nobilitate existimatione; aderunt autem homines nobilissimi ac potentissimi: eorum frequentiam et consessum non modo P. Quinctius, qui de capite decernit, sed quivis
73 qui extra periculum sit perhorrescat." Haec est iniqua certatio, non illa qua tu contra Alfenum ⟨utebare. Aliquid

---

[65] ita (i.e. priore loco) addidi: diu add. Pluygers
[66] praestituentur Madvig: restituendum Ω

---

[116] That is, as the first speaker.   [117] Cf. §§33–35.
[118] Of a noble family and educated in Greek rhetoric, L. Marcius Philippus (cos. 91, cens. 86) was one of Rome's most influential politicians from the late 90s until well into the 70s; cf. Münzer, *RE* s.v. Marcius 75. On Hortensius, see on §1.

PRO QUINCTIO 70–73

your friends. But if you think that at that time you had no equal rights with Alfenus because he could, in spite of all, call someone in for support against you, because a magistrate was found before whom Alfenus' case held its ground, what should Quinctius decide to do at this time, when he has so far failed to find a fair magistrate, an ordinary trial has been denied to him, no terms, no wager, finally no demand has intervened—I do not say a fair one but, down to the present time, one that has even received a hearing. "I want to litigate on the question of money." "That is not permitted." "But that is the point at issue." "I do not care. You must plead the case for your civil rights." "Make the charge in the proper place."[116] "I will not prosecute," he says, "unless you speak first under the new rule." "I will have to speak that way." "The timetable will be prescribed at our whim: the judge himself will be placed under constraint."[117] "What then?" "You will find some advocate, a man with the old-fashioned sense of duty, a man to treat our glamour and influence with indifference. Lucius Philippus will fight for me, a man of the greatest eminence in the state for his eloquence, authority, and position; Hortensius will speak for me, a man distinguished for his talent, nobility, and reputation;[118] moreover, I shall have the support of men of the highest birth and the greatest power, so many of them sitting there as to cause not only Quinctius to tremble, who is fighting for his civil rights, but even a person who is not at risk." *This* is an unequal contest, not the one in which you engaged against Alfenus. And yet you

71

72

73

tamen Alfeno⟩ aequi dabas:[67] huic ne ubi consisteret quidem contra te locum reliquisti.

Quare aut doceas oportet Alfenum negasse se procuratorem esse, non deiecisse libellos, iudicium accipere noluisse, aut, cum haec ita facta sint, ex edicto te bona P. Quincti non possedisse concedas.

Etenim si ex edicto possedisti, quaero cur bona non venierint, cur ceteri sponsores et creditores non convenerint. Nemone fuit cui deberet Quinctius? Fuerunt, et complures fuerunt, propterea quod C. frater aliquantum aeris alieni reliquerat. Quid ergo est? Homines erant ab hoc omnes alienissimi et eis debebatur, neque tamen quisquam inventus est tam insignite improbus qui violare P. 74 Quincti existimationem absentis auderet. Unus fuit adfinis socius necessarius, Sex. Naevius, qui cum ipse ultro deberet ⟨. . .⟩,[68] qui quasi eximio praemio sceleris exposito cupidissime contenderet ut per se adflictum atque eversum propinquum suum non modo honeste partis bonis verum etiam communi luce privaret. Ubi erant ceteri creditores? Denique hoc tempore ubi sunt? Quis est qui fraudationis causa latuisse dicat, quis qui absentem defensum 75 neget esse Quinctium? Nemo invenitur. At contra omnes quibuscum ratio huic aut est aut fuit adsunt, defendunt,

[67] utebare . . . aequi dabas *Madvig*: equitabas Ω
[68] *lac. statuit A. Klotz*

---

[119] The claim is that Naevius owed money to Quinctius (§44); perhaps an explanation is lost in a following lacuna.
[120] Loss of civil rights (*caput*) is treated metaphorically as a loss of life (also expressed by *caput*).
[121] Quoting the language of the law (cf. §60).

PRO QUINCTIO 73–75

granted Alfenus some bit of justice; but to my client you have not even left a place where he could make a stand against you.

Therefore you must either prove that Alfenus denied that he was his agent, that he did not tear down the notices of sale, refused to accept the trial; or since these things did occur, you must admit that you did not take possession of Publius Quinctius' property in accordance with the edict.

For in fact, if you did take possession in accordance with the edict, I ask why the property was not sold, why other sureties and creditors failed to converge. Was there no one to whom Quinctius owed money? There were, a number of them, because his brother Gaius had left some amount of debt. What is the case, then? All were total strangers to my client and were owed money, but nonetheless no one was found who was so egregious a scoundrel as to dare to attack Publius Quinctius' reputation in his absence. Sextus Naevius, his connection by marriage, his partner, and friend was the only one, who, though himself owed him money . . .[119] who, as if an extraordinary prize had been offered for his crime, exerted himself with utmost greed to undermine and ruin his relation and deprive him not only of property honestly acquired but even of the light shared by all.[120] Where were the other creditors? Indeed, where are they now? Who is there to assert that Quinctius kept out of the way to perpetrate fraud[121] or to deny that he was defended in his absence? No one is found [to make the claim]. On the contrary, all persons with whom my client has or had dealings are on hand, are defending him, are exerting themselves to see that his

74

75

CICERO

fides huius multis locis cognita ne perfidia Sex. Naevi derogetur laborant. In huius modi sponsionem testes dare oportebat ex eo numero qui haec dicerent: "Vadimonium mihi deseruit, me fraudavit, a me nominis eius quod infitiatus esset diem petivit, ego experiri non potui, latitavit, procuratorem nullum reliquit." Horum nihil dicitur: parantur testes qui hoc dicant. Verum, opinor, viderimus cum dixerint. Unum tamen hoc cogitent, ita se graves esse ut si veritatem volent retinere, gravitatem possint obtinere; si eam negligent,[69] ut[70] omnes intellegant non ad obtinendum mendacium, sed ad verum probandum auctoritatem adiuvare. Ego haec duo quaero, primum qua ratione Naevius susceptum negotium non[71] transegerit, hoc est cur bona quae ex edicto possidebat non vendiderit, deinde cur ex tot creditoribus alius ad istam rationem nemo accesserit, ut necessario confiteare neque tam temerarium quemquam fuisse neque te ipsum id quod turpissime suscepisses perseverare et transigere potuisse.

Quid si tu ipse, Sex. Naevi, statuisti bona P. Quincti ex edicto possessa non esse? Opinor tuum testimonium, quod in aliena re leve esset, id in tua, quoniam contra te est, gravissimum debet esse. Emisti bona Sex. Alfeni L.

[69] negligent *Bodl. Canon. Class. Lat. 226*: -ligerunt Ω
[70] ut *Madvig*: ita leves sint ut Ω
[71] negotium non $L^2\Phi$: negotium ΔL^1

---

[122] This reflects the give-and-take in court: Cicero at first claims there are no such witnesses, but Hortensius puts in that there will be; cf. Platschek 2005, 229–30.
[123] Naevius could reply that he was prevented by Alfenus' intervention.

PRO QUINCTIO 75–76

credit, well known in many places, is not damaged by Sextus Naevius' treachery. In support of a wager like this, he [Naevius] would have to offer from their number witnesses to say this: "He defaulted on his bail to my disadvantage; he cheated me; he sought a trial date from me for a debt of his that he denied owing, but I could not litigate; he kept out of the way and left no agent behind." None of these things is claimed; witnesses are being prepared to say it.[122] We shall see the truth, I think, when they have spoken. And yet, let them consider this one point: they carry weight to the extent that they can maintain their weight if they are willing to adhere to the truth; but if they slight it [*sc.* the truth], that all may see that authority helps to establish the truth, not to maintain a lie. I pose these two questions: first, why did Naevius fail to complete the business he had undertaken, that is, why did he not sell the goods of which he was in possession in accordance with the edict;[123] second, why, among so many creditors, did no one else join in that plan? The upshot is that you must admit that no one else was so rash and that you yourself were unable to persist in and complete the disgraceful plan you had undertaken. 76

What if you yourself, Sextus Naevius, have declared that the property of Publius Quinctius was not taken into possession according to the edict? I think that your evidence, which would have little weight in another person's case, ought to weigh very heavily in your own, since it is against you. You bought the property of Sextus Alfenus when the dictator Lucius Sulla was offering it for sale.[124]

---

[124] This shows that Alfenus was killed in the proscriptions; cf. *Off.* 2.27 with van der Blom 2017; Hinard 1985b, 329–30.

Sulla dictatore vendente. Socium tibi in eis bonis edidisti Quinctium. Plura non dico. Cum eo tu voluntariam societatem coibas qui te in hereditaria societate fraudarat, et eum iudicio tuo comprobabas quem spoliatum[72] fama fortunisque omnibus arbitrabare?

77 Diffidebam mehercule, C. Aquili, satis animo certo et confirmato me posse in hac causa consistere. Sic cogitabam, cum contra dicturus esset Hortensius et cum me esset attente auditurus Philippus, fore uti permultis in rebus timore prolaberer. Dicebam huic Q. Roscio, cuius soror est cum P. Quinctio, cum a me peteret et summe contenderet ut propinquum suum defenderem, mihi perdifficile esse contra tales oratores non modo tantam causam perorare sed omnino verbum facere conari. Cum cupidius instaret, homini pro amicitia familiarius dixi mihi videri ore durissimo esse qui praesente eo gestum agere conarentur;[73] qui vero cum ipso contenderent, eos, etiam si quid antea recti aut venusti habere visi essent,[74] id amittere; ne quid mihi eiusdem modi accideret cum contra 78 talem artificem dicturus essem me vereri. Tum mihi Roscius et alia multa confirmandi mei causa dixit (et[75] mehercule si nihil diceret, tacito ipso officio et studio quod habebat erga propinquum suum quemvis commoveret; etenim

[72] *fort.* spoliandum   [73] conarentur *Halm*: -aretur Ω
[74] essent *Ernesti*: sunt Ω   [75] *Paris. Lat.* 7779: ut Ω

---

[125] Roscius was present presumably to offer support for his brother-in-law as an *advocatus*. On the famous actor and his career, cf. Lebek 1996, 36–39. Cicero parades Quinctius' connection with Roscius and his own friendship with the actor; cf. Kumaniecki 1972, 150–51.

PRO QUINCTIO 76–78

You declared that Quinctius was your partner in those goods. I say no more. Were you entering into a voluntary partnership with the man who had cheated you in a hereditary partnership, and by your judgment were you issuing approval of a man whom you thought had been stripped of his reputation and all his fortunes?

By Hercules, Gaius Aquilius, I mistrusted my ability to stand my ground with sufficient courage and resolution in this case. I thought that, since Hortensius was going to speak in opposition and Philippus was going to be hearing me attentively, I would take fright and fall into many a mistake. I was telling Quintus Roscius here,[125] whose sister is married to Publius Quinctius, when he was begging and earnestly imploring me to defend his relative, that it was very difficult for me not merely to plead so important a case to the end in opposition to orators of such quality but to try to utter a single word. When he pressed me keenly, I replied with a friend's familiarity that people seem to me brazen who would attempt to make a gesture in his presence;[126] that those who competed with him lost whatever aptness or grace they seemed previously to have had; and that I was afraid that something of the kind would happen to me if I were to speak in opposition to an artist of such quality [*sc.* as Hortensius]. Then Roscius told me a great many other things to steady me, and by Hercules, if he had said nothing, he would have deeply affected anyone, even without words, merely by his eagerness to do his duty by his relative; for he is such an artist that he

---

[126] Cicero closely studied Roscius' art of gesture; cf. *De orat.* 3.102.

cum artifex eius modi est[76] ut solus dignus videatur esse qui in scaena spectetur, tum vir eius modi est ut solus dignus esse videatur qui eo non accedat). Verum tamen "Quid si" inquit "habes eius modi causam ut hoc tibi planum sit faciendum, neminem esse qui possit biduo aut summum triduo septingenta milia passuum ambulare, tamenne vereris ut possis hoc contra Hortensium contendere?" "Minime" inquam "sed quid id ad rem?" "Nimirum" inquit "in eo causa consistit." "Quo modo?" Docet me eius modi rem et factum simul Sex. Naevi quod si solum proferretur, satis esse deberet. Quod abs te, C. Aquili, et a vobis qui estis in consilio quaeso ut diligenter attendatis. Profecto intelligetis illinc ab initio cupiditatem pugnasse et audaciam, hinc veritatem et pudorem quoad potuerit restitisse.

79

Bona postulas ut ex edicto possidere liceat: quo die? Te ipsum, Naevi, volo audire; volo inauditum facinus ipsius qui id commisit voce convinci. Dic, Naevi, diem. "A. d.[77] v Kalend. intercalares." Bene ais. Quam longe est hinc in saltum vestrum Gallicanum? Naevi, te rogo. "DCC milia passuum." Optime. De saltu deicitur Quinctius: quo die? Possumus hoc quoque ex te audire? Quid taces? Dic, inquam, diem. Pudet dicere; intelligo, verum et sero et nequicquam pudet. Deicitur de saltu, C. Aquili, pridie Kalend. intercalares. Biduo post aut, ut statim de iure aliquis

[76] *Quint.* 9.3.86: sit Ω
[77] diem ante diem *Manutius*: diem ante Ω

---

[127] Stroh 1975, 98n56, regards this and similar anecdotes in Cicero's speeches as fiction. The matter was not so simple as Cic-

PRO QUINCTIO 78–79

alone appears worthy to be seen on the stage but also such a man that he alone appears worthy not to mount it. But all the same, he said, "What if you have a case such that you must show that there is no one who could walk seven hundred miles in two or at most three days? Would you still fear being unable to maintain this against Hortensius?" "No," I said, "but what is the relevance?" "The case," he said, "rests, of course, on this point." "How so?" He advised me of a matter and deed of Sextus Naevius' of such a kind that if it alone were adduced, it ought to be sufficient.[127] Gaius Aquilius, and you, members of his council, please listen attentively to this; you will surely come to realize that on the other side the battle was waged from the beginning by greed and audacity but on our side truth and modesty, insofar as possible, put up resistance.

You demanded permission to take possession of his property in accordance with the edict—on what day? I want to hear from you yourself, Naevius; I want an unheard-of crime to be proven by the voice of the very man who committed it. Tell me the day, Naevius. "February 20." Right. How far is it from here to your pastureland in Gaul? I am asking you, Naevius. "Seven hundred miles." Excellent. Quinctius was expelled from the pasturage—on what day? Can we hear this from you as well? Why are you silent? Tell me the day, I say. He is ashamed to say; I know, but he is ashamed too late and to no purpose. He was expelled from the pasturage, Gaius Aquilius, on February 23. Seven hundred miles were covered in the space of two

ero claims; if it had been, M. Iunius would scarcely have failed to raise the point, rather than resorting to delaying tactics. Cf. Kinsey 1971, 183.

cucurrerit non toto triduo, DCC milia passuum conficiuntur. O rem incredibilem! O cupiditatem inconsideratam! O nuntium volucrem! Administri et satellites Sex. Naevi Roma trans Alpes in Sebaginnos[78] biduo veniunt. O hominem fortunatum, qui eius modi nuntios seu potius Pegasos habeat! Hic ego, si Crassi omnes cum Antoniis existant, si tu, L. Philippe, qui inter illos florebas, hanc causam voles cum Hortensio dicere, tamen superior sim necesse est. Non enim, quem ad modum putatis, omnia sunt in eloquentia: est quaedam tamen ita perspicua veritas ut eam infirmare nulla res possit. An, ante quam postulasti ut bona possideres, misisti qui curaret ut dominus de suo fundo a sua familia vi deiceretur? Utrumlibet elige: alterum incredibile est, alterum nefarium, et ante hoc tempus utrumque inauditum. Septingenta milia vis esse decursa biduo? Dic. Negas. Ante igitur misisti. Malo. Si enim illud diceres, improbe mentiri viderere; cum hoc confiteris, id te admisisse concedis quod ne mendacio quidem tegere possis. Hoc consilium Aquilio et talibus viris tam cupidum, tam audax, tam temerarium probabitur? Quid haec amentia, quid haec festinatio, quid haec immaturitas tanta significat? Non vim, non scelus, non latrocinium, non denique omnia potius quam ius, quam officium, quam pudorem? Mittis iniussu praetoris: quo consilio? Iussurum sciebas.

---

[78] in sebaginnos Δ*L*: in sebagranos Φ: inter agrarios *Platschek 2005, 13 adn. 41*

---

[128] The Sebaginni, or Sebagrani, are otherwise unknown. Platschek 2005, 13n41, suggests *inter agrarios* ("among the settlers"), but an ethnic or a geographic name seems to be required.

days or, supposing that he ran straight from court, not quite three days. Incredible feat! Reckless greed! A winged messenger! Sextus Naevius' agents and henchmen crossed the Alps to the territory of the Sebaginni[128] in two days! Lucky man, to have such messengers, or rather Pegasuses, at his disposal! On this point, even if all the Crassi and Antonii were to rise from the dead, if you, Lucius Philippus, who were distinguished among them, will be willing to join Hortensius in pleading this case, I must prevail nonetheless. For it is not the case that, as you suppose, everything depends upon eloquence: there is a truth so evident that nothing can weaken it. Can it really be that you sent an agent to see that the owner was forcibly expelled from his estate by his own slaves before you made a demand to take possession of his property? Choose whichever you please: the one is incredible, the other wicked, and both were previously unheard of. Do you claim that seven hundred miles were covered in two days? Tell me. You say no. Then you sent your agent first. I prefer that. For if you were to say the former, you would show yourself to be a bald-faced liar; when you admit the latter, you admit that you did something that you could not even cover up by a lie. Will Aquilius and men of such quality approve this plan, so greedy, so bold, so reckless? What is the meaning of this madness, this haste, this premature action?[129] Does it not point to force, wickedness, robbery, in short, anything other than law, duty, modesty? You sent your agent without a praetor's order—with what plan? You

---

[129] Naevius had sold some property of the partnership to compensate him for debts he claimed he was owed (§23); he may have feared that Quinctius would do the same. Cf. Kinsey 1971, 189.

Quid? Cum iussisset, tum mittere nonne poteras? Postulaturus eras. Quando? Post dies xxx. Nempe si te nihil impediret, si voluntas eadem maneret, si valeres, denique si viveres. Praetor scilicet iussisset. Opinor, si vellet, si valeret, si ius diceret, si nemo recusaret qui ex ipsius decreto et satis dare[79] et iudicium accipere vellet. Nam per deos immortales si Alfenus procurator P. Quincti tibi tum satis dare[80] et iudicium accipere,[81] denique omnia quae postulares facere voluisset, quid ageres? Revocares eum quem in Galliam miseras. At hic quidem iam de fundo expulsus, iam a suis dis penatibus praeceps eiectus, iam, quod indignissimum est, suorum servorum manibus nuntio atque imperio tuo violatus esset. Corrigeres haec scilicet postea. Tu[82] de cuiusquam vita dicere audes, qui hoc concedas necesse est, ita te caecum cupiditate et avaritia fuisse ut cum postea quid futurum esset ignorares, accidere autem multa possent, spem malefici praesentis in incerto relicui temporis eventu conlocares?

Atque haec perinde loquor quasi ipso illo tempore cum te praetor iussisset ex edicto possidere, si in possessionem misisses, debueris aut potueris P. Quinctium de possessione deturbare. Omnia sunt, C. Aquili, eius modi quivis ut perspicere possit in hac causa improbitatem et gratiam cum inopia et veritate contendere. Praetor te quem ad

[79] dare *Ernesti*: daret Ω
[80] dare *Lambinus*: daret Ω
[81] accipere *Gulielmius*: accipere vellet Ω
[82] postea tu *Reeve (Ver. 2.3.48, 4.112 coll.)*: tu postea Ω

---

[130] About the time it would take to reach Gaul.

knew he would give the order. Well then, could you not send him once he had given the order? You were going to make your demand. When? In thirty days.[130] Certainly, if nothing hindered you, if you continued to want to, if you remained healthy, finally, if you were alive. The praetor would certainly have ordered it. I suppose so, if he wanted to, if he were in good health, if he were in court, if no one objected who was willing, as provided for in his decree, both to provide security and to stand trial. For, by the immortal gods, if at that time Alfenus, Quinctius' agent, had been willing to provide security and stand trial, in short, to do everything that you demanded, what would you have done? You would have recalled the agent you had sent to Gaul. But my client had already been expelled from his estate, cast headlong out of his hearth and home, already—and this is the greatest outrage—been attacked by the hands of his own slaves at a command sent by you. You would, of course, have subsequently made this right. Do you dare to speak of anyone's life, you who must admit that you were so blinded by greed and avarice that, although you did not know what would happen afterward—and many things might have happened—you founded the hope of gain from a present crime on a doubtful future outcome?

And yet I am saying this as if at that very time when the praetor ordered you to take possession in accordance with his edict, if you had dispatched an agent for possession, you should or could have expelled Publius Quinctius from possession. All the facts are such, Gaius Aquilius, that anyone can see that in this case criminality and influence are competing with helplessness and the truth. How did the praetor order you to take possession? On the basis of his

83

84

modum possidere iussit? Opinor ex edicto. Sponsio quae in verba facta est? SI EX EDICTO PRAETORIS BONA P. QUINCTI POSSESSA NON SUNT. Redeamus ad edictum. Id quidem quem ad modum iubet possidere? Numquid est causae, C. Aquili, quin si longe aliter possedit quam praetor edixit, iste ex edicto non possederit, ego sponsionem[83] vicerim? Nihil opinor. Cognoscamus edictum. QUI EX EDICTO MEO IN POSSESSIONEM VENERINT (de te loquitur, Naevi, quem ad modum tu putas; ais enim te ex edicto venisse; tibi quid facias definit, te instituit, tibi praecepta dat), EOS ITA VIDETUR IN POSSESSIONE ESSE OPORTERE—quo modo? QUOD IBIDEM RECTE CUSTODIRE POTERUNT, ID IBIDEM CUSTODIANT; QUOD NON POTERUNT, ID AUFERRE ET ABDUCERE LICEBIT. Quid tum? DOMINUM inquit INVITUM DETRUDERE NON PLACET. Eum ipsum qui fraudandi causa latitet, eum ipsum quem iudicio nemo defendat, eum ipsum qui cum omnibus creditoribus suis male agat, invitum de praedio detrudi vetat.

85 Proficiscenti tibi in possessionem praetor ipse, Sex. Naevi, palam dicit: ita possideto ut tecum simul possideat Quinctius, ita possideto ut Quinctio vis ne adferatur. Quid? Tu id quem ad modum observas? Mitto illud dicere, eum qui non[84] latitarit, cui Romae domus, uxor, liberi, procurator esset, eum qui tibi vadimonium non deseruis-

---

[83] sponsionem *Neapol. Bibl. Nat. IV B 7*: -e Ω
[84] non *F²*: *om.* Ω

PRO QUINCTIO 84–85

edict, I presume. On what terms was the wager drawn up? "If Publius Quinctius' property was not possessed on the basis of the praetor's edict." Let us go back to the edict. How does it order one to take possession? Is there any reason, Gaius Aquilius, why I should not win the wager if he [Naevius] took possession in a far different manner than the praetor decreed, and did not take possession in accord with the edict? None, I believe.[131] Let us acquaint ourselves with the edict. "Those who have come into possession in accordance with my edict" (he is speaking of you, Naevius, as you suppose; for you claim to have come into possession on the basis of the edict; it lays down what you may do, instructs you, gives you directions) "it seems best that they should be in possession in this way" (how?) "what they could safely guard on the spot, let them guard there; what they could not, they may carry or drive away." What next? "It is not good," he says, "to expel the owner against his will." He forbids even the man who kept out of the way to perpetrate fraud, the man whom no one defends in court, the man who cheats all his creditors, to be expelled from his estate against his will. As you proceeded to take possession, the praetor himself plainly said to you, Sextus Naevius: take possession in such a way that Quinctius may be in possession jointly with you and that no violence is used.[132] Tell me then, how did you observe this rule? I forbear to mention that he was a man who did not keep out of the way, had a home, a wife, children, and an agent at Rome, did not default on bail—I leave all these facts

---

[131] Even so, it would not follow that Cicero had necessarily won his case; Aquilius might still decide that, in equity, Quinctius had lost. See further Kinsey 1971, 193.

[132] Inferred from the praetor's edict just cited.

93

CICERO

set—haec omnia mitto: illud dico, dominum expulsum esse de praedio, domino a familia sua manus adlatas esse ante suos lares familiaris. Hoc edicti

* * *[85]

Si qui unum aliquem fundum quavis ratione possideat, ipsum autem dominum patiatur cetera praedia tenere, is, ut opinor, praedium, non bona videatur alterius possidere.

* * *

Quid est possidere? Nimirum in possessione esse earum rerum quae possunt eo tempore possideri.

* * *

cum domus erat Romae, servi, in ipsa Gallia privata P. Quincti praedia, quae numquam ausus es possidere

* * *

Quod si bona P. Quincti possideres, possidere omnia[86] eo iure deberes.[87]

* * *

biennium[88] ne appellasset quidem Quinctium cum simul esset et experiri posset cotidie; deinde quod omnia iudicia difficillima cum summa sua invidia maximoque periculo P. Quincti fieri mallet quam illud pecuniarium iudicium quod uno die transigi posset, ex quo uno haec omnia nata

---

[85] *lac. statuit Naugerius 1519*
[86] omnia *Severiani cod.* V: omnes *cett.*
[87] si qui unum . . . deberes *ex Severiano 16 (101.8 Castelli Montanari) deprompta ("sic Cicero pro Quinctio")*
[88] *Reeve in adn.*: nuum ΔL^1: unum L^n: num Φ

---

[133] Perhaps confusing the standard of possession that applied in *usucapio* (acquisition of ownership through uninterrupted possession) with that of a praetor's *missio in possessionem*; cf. Platschek 2005, 275.

PRO QUINCTIO 85

aside. I say this: the owner was expelled from his estate, his own slaves laid violent hands upon the owner in the presence of his household gods. This . . . of the edict

* * *

If anyone takes possession of some single farm by any means but allows the owner to hold the other estates, he seems, I believe, to possess the other man's farm but not his property.

* * *

What is it to possess? To be in possession, obviously, of the things that can be possessed at that time.[133]

* * *

when he had a house and slaves at Rome, in Gaul itself private estates belonging to Publius Quinctius, which you never dared to take into possession.

* * *

But if you possessed the property of Publius Quinctius, you ought under that law to possess it all.[134]

* * *

[I have shown in the first place that][135] for two years he did not even apply to Quinctius, although he lived with him and could have gone to law with him any day; next, that he preferred for all the most troublesome legal proceedings to be convened, with great prejudice to himself and the greatest danger to Publius Quinctius, rather than a pecuniary action, the one source and origin of all these proceedings, as he admits, which could have been finished

---

[134] The preceding four excerpts are cited by the mid-fifth-century (cf. Schindel 2000, 416) rhetorician Iulius Severianus with attribution to this speech.

[135] Supplied *exempli gratia*.

et profecta esse concedit, quo in loco condicionem tuli, si vellet pecuniam petere, P. Quinctium iudicatum solvi satis daturum dum ipse, si quid peteret, pari condicione uteretur. Ostendi quam multa ante fieri convenerit quam hominis propinqui bona possideri postularentur, praesertim cum Romae domus eius, uxor, liberi essent et procurator aeque utriusque necessarius. Docui, cum desertum esse dicat vadimonium, omnino vadimonium nullum fuisse; quo die hunc sibi promisisse dicat, eo die ne Romae quidem eum fuisse; id testibus me pollicitus sum planum facturum qui et scire deberent et causam cur mentirentur non haberent.

Ex edicto autem non potuisse bona possideri demonstravi quod nec fraudandi causa latitasset[89] neque exili causa solum vertisse diceretur. Relicuum est ut eum nemo iudicio defenderit; quod contra copiosissime defensum esse contendi non ab homine alieno neque ab aliquo calumniatore atque improbo sed ab equite Romano, propinquo ac necessario suo, quem ipse Sex. Naevius procuratorem relinquere antea consuesset; neque eum, si tribunos appellarit, idcirco minus iudicio pati paratum fuisse, nec potentia procuratoris Naevio ius ereptum; contra istum potentia sua tum tantummodo superiorem fuisse, nunc nobis vix respirandi potestatem dare. Quaesivi quae causa fuisset cur bona non venissent cum ex edicto possideren-

---

[89] latitasset Ω, *def. Platschek 2005, 181 (cf. §§60, 85)*: -asse *Angelius*

---

[136] Naevius' rights were not abridged in that he could still litigate, but not on his terms, because Alfenus was prepared neither to offer security nor to allow Quinctius' property to be sold; cf. Kinsey 1971, 199.

in one day. On that occasion I proposed the terms that, if he intended to sue for the money, Quinctius should give security for the payment of the judgment, provided that he [Naevius] himself, in case Quinctius claimed any money, should give the same security to him. I have shown how many steps should have been taken before application was made for possession of the goods of a relative, especially as he had at Rome a house, a wife, children, and an agent, a friend of both parties. I have proved that though he [Naevius] claims bail was forfeited, there was no bail at all; that on the day he [Naevius] claims my client promised it to him, he was not even at Rome; I have undertaken to prove this by testimony of witnesses, who both ought to know and have no motive to lie.

I have shown, moreover, that the property could not have been taken into possession in accordance with the edict because he neither kept out of the way to perpetrate fraud nor was it asserted that he left the country to go into exile. There remains the claim that no one defended him in court; I have maintained that, on the contrary, he was lavishly defended, not by some stranger, by some unscrupulous pettifogger, but by a Roman knight, his friend and relative, whom Sextus Naevius himself had previously been wont to leave behind as his agent; and if he called upon the tribunes for assistance, he was not any less on that account prepared to submit to a trial, nor were Naevius' rights abridged by the agent's power;[136] on the contrary, he [Naevius] was then merely superior by virtue of his power, but he now scarcely gives us the power to breathe freely. I asked what had been the reason why the goods had not been sold if they were taken into possession

CICERO

tur. Deinde illud quoque requisivi, qua ratione ex tot creditoribus nemo nec tum idem fecerit neque nunc contra dicat omnesque pro P. Quinctio pugnent, praesertim cum in tali iudicio testimonia creditorum existimentur ad rem maxime pertinere. Postea sum usus adversari testimonio, qui sibi eum nuper edidit socium quem quo modo nunc intendit ne in vivorum quidem numero tum demonstrat fuisse. Tum illam incredibilem celeritatem seu potius audaciam protuli: confirmavi necesse esse aut biduo DCC milia passuum esse decursa aut Sex. Naevium diebus compluribus ante in possessionem misisse quam postularet ut ei[90] liceret bona possidere. Postea recitavi edictum quod aperte dominum de praedio detrudi vetaret, in quo constitit Naevium ex edicto non possedisse cum confiteretur ex praedio vi detrusum esse Quinctium.

Omnino[91] autem bona possessa non esse constitui quod bonorum possessio spectetur non in aliqua parte sed in universis quae teneri et possideri possint. Dixi domum Romae fuisse, quo iste ne aspirarit quidem, servos complures, ex quibus iste possederit neminem, ne attigerit quidem; unum fuisse quem attingere conatus sit, prohibitum[92] quievisse; in ipsa Gallia cognostis in praedia privata Quincti Sex. Naevium non venisse; denique ex hoc ipso

[90] ei Ω: eius *E, fort. recte (cf. §54)*
[91] omnino *Stephanus*: omnia Ω
[92] prohibitum *Madvig*: prohibitum fuisse Ω

[137] When Alfenus' goods, seized in the proscriptions, were sold; see on §76. "Not even among the living" refers to a person who is *infamis* (cf. on §43), which would describe Quinctius if his

PRO QUINCTIO 88–90

in accord with the edict. Then I also posed this question: why out of so many creditors none either did the same [as Naevius] or now is speaking in opposition but all are fighting on Publius Quinctius' behalf, especially since in a trial of this kind creditors' testimonies are considered particularly relevant. Next I used the testimony of our opponent, who recently declared that that man was his partner, who, according to his present claim, he is trying to show was not even among the living at that time.[137] Then I cited that incredible speed, or rather, audacity: I established that either seven hundred miles must have been covered in two days or Sextus Naevius had dispatched a messenger for possession several days before he demanded that he be permitted to take possession of the property. Afterward I read out the edict that explicitly forbade an owner from being ejected from his estate, whereby he[138] established that Naevius had not taken possession in accordance with the edict, since he [Naevius] admitted that Quinctius was ejected from the estate by force.

89

Moreover, I established that his property was not taken into possession at all, since the possession of property is not judged with regard to some part but all that can be held and possessed. I said that [Quinctius'] house was at Rome, which he [Naevius] did not even approach; he had a number of slaves, none of whom he [Naevius] took possession of or even touched; there was one whom he did try to approach, but he was prevented and ceased; you have learned that in Gaul itself Sextus Naevius did not enter Quinctius' private estates; finally, from the very pasturage

90

---

goods had been possessed for thirty days according to the praetor's edict, as claimed by Naevius.   [138] Namely, the praetor.

saltu quem per vim expulso socio possedit servos privatos Quincti omnes[93] eiectos esse.

Ex quo et ex ceteris dictis factis cogitatisque Sex. Naevi quivis potest intellegere istum nihil aliud egisse neque nunc agere nisi uti per vim, per iniuriam, per iniquitatem iudici totum agrum qui communis est suum facere possit.

91 Nunc causa perorata res ipsa et periculi magnitudo, C. Aquili, cogere videtur ut te atque eos qui tibi in consilio sunt obsecret obtesteturque P. Quinctius per[94] senectutem ac solitudinem suam nihil aliud nisi ut vestrae naturae bonitatique obsequamini, ut cum veritas hac[95] faciat, plus huius inopia possit ad misericordiam quam illius opes ad
92 crudelitatem. Quo die ad te iudicem venimus, eodem die illorum minas, quas ante horrebamus, negligere coepimus. Si causa cum causa contenderet, nos nostram perfacile cuivis probaturos statuebamus: quod vitae ratio cum ratione vitae decerneret, idcirco nobis etiam magis te iudice opus esse arbitrati sumus. Ea res enim nunc in discrimine versatur, utrum possitne se contra luxuriem ac licentiam rusticana illa atque inculta parsimonia defendere an deformata atque ornamentis omnibus spoliata
93 nuda cupiditati petulantiaeque addicatur. Non comparat se tecum gratia P. Quinctius, Sex. Naevi; non opibus, non

[93] omnes Ω, *def. Platschek 2005, 269–74*: non omnes *F¹*
[94] per *F² pro* ac *E*: per se ac *cett. (CHLΦ)*
[95] hac *Reeve, G. Luck, Mus. Rhenan. 105, 1962, 351 coll.*: haec Ω: cum hoc *Angelius*

---

[139] That is, Naevius did not take possession of the slaves, so that Naevius' possession of Quinctius' property also remains incomplete in this respect; cf. §89; Platschek 2005, 274–76.

PRO QUINCTIO 90–93

that he possessed once his partner had been expelled by force, all Quinctius' private slaves were ejected.[139]

From this and from Sextus Naevius' other words, deeds, and plans, anyone can recognize that he was and is now striving for nothing other than to be able to make the entire farm, which is common property, his own by force, by injustice, and by the unfairness of the court.

Now that the case has been pleaded to the end, the facts themselves and extremity of the danger seem to compel Publius Quinctius to beg and beseech you, Gaius Aquilius, and the members of your council, in the name of his advanced years and solitude, for nothing other than for you to follow your own good nature, so that, since truth is active on this side, his helplessness may have greater influence for pity than the other man's resources for cruelty.[140] On the very day we came before you as judge, we began to despise their threats, which we previously dreaded. If one case be pitted against the other, we judged that we would easily prove ours to anyone; since one lifestyle is competing with another, we thought that we needed you as judge all the more. This matter is now at issue: whether rustic and boorish frugality can defend itself against luxury and licentiousness or, disfigured and stripped of all adornments, is to be surrendered naked to greed and wantonness.[141] Publius Quinctius does not pit himself against you in popularity, Sextus Naevius, does not compete in

91

92

93

---

[140] Here begins the lengthy peroration, extending to §99; cf. Kinsey 1971, 213.

[141] Ethical qualities are associated with a certain type of lifestyle briefly here and more elaborately in the defense of Sextus Roscius; cf. Mouritsen 2022, 32.

facultate contendit. Omnes tuas artes quibus tu magnus es tibi concedit. Fatetur se non belle dicere, non ad voluntatem loqui posse, non ab adflicta amicitia transfugere atque ad florentem aliam devolare, non profusis sumptibus vivere, non ornare magnifice splendideque convivium, non habere domum clausam pudori et sanctimoniae, patentem atque adeo expositam cupiditati et voluptatibus; contra sibi officium, fidem, diligentiam, vitam omnino semper horridam atque aridam cordi fuisse. Ista superiora esse ac plurimum posse his moribus sentit. Quid ergo est?—non usque eo tamen ut in capite fortunisque hominum honestissimorum dominentur ei qui relicta virorum bonorum disciplina et quaestum et sumptum Galloni sequi maluerunt atque etiam, quod in illo non fuit, cum audacia perfidiaque vixerunt. Si licet vivere eum quem Sex. Naevius non vult, si est homini honesto locus in civitate invito Naevio, si fas est respirare P. Quinctium contra nutum dicionemque Naevi, si, quae pudore ornamenta sibi peperit, ea potest contra petulantiam me[96] defendente obtinere, spes est hunc[97] miserum atque infelicem aliquando tandem posse consistere. Sin et poterit Naevius id quod libet et ei libebit id quod non licet, quid agendum est? Qui deus appellandus est? Cuius hominis fides imploranda est? Qui denique questus, qui maeror dignus inveniri in calamitate tanta potest?

[96] me *Madvig*: te Ω   [97] hunc *Paris. Lat.* 7779: et hunc Ω

---

[142] Characteristic of the buffoon (*scurra*); cf. §11.
[143] Gallonius, who, like Naevius, was a *praeco* (cf. on §11), was a gormandizer satirized by Lucilius (frr. 198–212 W.); cf. *Fin.* 2.90; Hor. *Sat.* 2.2.47–48.

PRO QUINCTIO 93–94

resources or skill. He grants you all your arts by which you have become great. He admits that he cannot offer neat remarks,[142] make agreeable conversation, betray a troubled friendship and fly to one that is brilliant, live amid lavish expenditures, adorn a banquet in grand and splendid style, have a house closed to modesty and purity but open to, or rather set out for, greed and pleasure; on the contrary, he always cherished duty, loyalty, industry, in short, a life that is unkempt and austere. He knows that those other qualities are superior and have very great influence amid the manners of our time. What is the case, then? This influence has not, however, gone to the point that those who have abandoned the principles of good men and preferred to follow the moneymaking and expenditure of Gallonius[143] and have even lived audaciously and treacherously (which he did not do), may lord it over the civil rights and fortunes of most honorable men. If a man may live whom Sextus Naevius does not want to, if there is room in the community for an honorable man contrary to Naevius' wishes, if it is right for Publius Quinctius to recover his breath contrary to Naevius' nod and power, if he can, with me as his advocate, maintain the distinctions he has acquired by his modesty against impudent aggressiveness, there is hope that this wretched and unfortunate man can finally stand his ground. But what should be done if Naevius will be able to do as he pleases and will please to do what is impermissible? What god should we appeal to? What man's protection should we beseech? In short, what appropriate lamentation or grief can be found amid so great a disaster?

94

95 Miserum est exturbari fortunis omnibus, miserius[98] iniuria; acerbum est ab aliquo circumveniri, acerbius a propinquo; calamitosum est bonis everti, calamitosius cum dedecore; funestum est a forti atque honesto viro iugulari, funestius ab eo cuius vox in praeconio quaestu prostitit; indignum est a pari vinci aut superiore, indignius ab inferiore atque humiliore; luctuosum est tradi alteri cum bonis, luctuosius inimico; horribile est causam capitis dicere,
96 horribilius priore loco dicere. Omnia circumspexit Quinctius, omnia periclitatus est, C. Aquili. Non praetorem modo a quo ius impetraret invenire potuit, atque adeo ne unde arbitratu quidem suo postularet, sed ne amicos quidem Sex. Naevi,[99] quorum saepe et diu ad pedes iacuit stratus, obsecrans per deos immortales ut aut secum iure contenderent aut iniuriam sine ignominia sibi imponerent.
97 Denique ipsius inimici vultum superbissimum subiit, ipsius Sex. Naevi lacrimans manum prehendit in propinquorum bonis proscribendis exercitatam; obsecravit per fratris sui mortui cinerem, per nomen propinquitatis, per ipsius coniugem et liberos, quibus propior P. Quinctio nemo est, ut aliquando misericordiam caperet, aliquam si non propinquitatis at[100] aetatis suae, si non hominis at humanitatis rationem haberet, ut secum aliquid integra

[98] miserius *Paris. Lat. 7779*: miserius est Ω
[99] commovere potuit *vel sim. fort. hoc loco supplenda*
[100] at F^2HL^2: et Ω

144 See on §11.   145 "He could not even move" is supplied here to complete the sense; *commovere potuit* or the like may have dropped out of the Latin text. Cf. Kinsey 1971, 209.
146 Cf. §§25, 61.
147 See on §51; Potůček 1998, esp. 92–93.

PRO QUINCTIO 95–97

It is wretched to be expelled from all one's fortunes, more wretched to be expelled wrongfully; it is bitter to be cheated by anyone, more bitter by a relation; it is disastrous to be driven from one's property, more disastrous with disgrace attached; it is lamentable to be murdered by a brave and honorable man, more lamentable by one whose voice has been prostituted in the auctioneer's trade; it is outrageous to be defeated by an equal or superior, more outrageous by an inferior or humbler person;[144] it is grievous to be handed over together with one's possessions to another, more grievous to an enemy; it is horrible to plead a case for one's civil rights, more horrible to plead first. Quinctius has looked all around, Gaius Aquilius, has made trial of every possibility. He was not only unable to find a praetor by whom he might be granted his rights or even of whom he might demand a trial according to his wishes, but he could not even move Sextus Naevius' friends, at whose feet he often and for a long time lay prostrate, beseeching them by the immortal gods either to contest with him according to the law or to inflict a wrong upon him without disgrace.[145] Finally, he comes before the haughty face of his enemy himself; weeping, he grasps the hand of Sextus Naevius, a hand practiced in posting the property of his relations up for sale;[146] he beseeched him by the ashes of his deceased brother, by the name of their kinship, by his own wife and children, to whom Publius Quinctius is the nearest relative, that at long last he should feel pity, have some consideration, if not for his kinship, for his age, that he should have consideration if not for the man, for human feeling,[147] so that, with his reputation intact, he might arrive at a settlement with him

sua fama qualibet dum modo tolerabili condicione transigeret. Ab ipso repudiatus, ab amicis eius non sublevatus, ab omni magistratu agitatus atque perterritus, quem praeter te appellet habet neminem; tibi se, tibi suas omnes opes fortunasque commendat, tibi committit existimationem ac spem relicuae vitae; multis vexatus contumeliis, plurimis iactatus iniuriis, non turpis ad te sed miser confugit. E fundo ornatissimo deiectus, ignominiis omnibus appetitus, cum illum in suis paternis bonis dominari videret, ipse filiae nubili dotem conficere non posset, nihil tamen alienum vita superiore commisit. Itaque hoc te obsecrat, C. Aquili, ut quam existimationem, quam honestatem in iudicium tuum prope acta iam aetate decursaque attulit, eam liceat ei secum ex hoc loco efferre, ne is de cuius officio nemo umquam dubitavit sexagesimo denique anno dedecore macula turpissimaque ignominia notetur, ne ornamentis eius omnibus Sex. Naevius pro spoliis abutatur, ne per te †ferat[101] quo minus quae existimatio P. Quinctium usque ad senectutem perduxit, eadem usque ad rogum prosequatur.

[101] ferat Ω: *fort.* fer<ens praedam nefariam prohibe>at

PRO QUINCTIO 97–99

on any terms, provided they be tolerable. Spurned by the 98
man himself, not aided by his [Naevius'] friends, buffeted
and intimidated by every magistrate, he has no one to call
upon for assistance except you; to you he entrusts all his
resources and fortunes, to you he commits his reputation
and hope for the rest of his life; harassed by many insults,
buffeted by a great many wrongs, not disgraced[148] but
wretched, he flees to you for refuge. Though expelled
from a well-equipped estate, assailed by all manner of
indignity, when he saw the other man lording it over his
own patrimony, while he himself was unable to get together a dowry for his marriageable daughter, he did nothing at odds with his previous life. He therefore beseeches 99
you, Gaius Aquilius, that he be permitted to carry with
him from this place the honorable reputation that he
brought to your court, with his life now practically finished
and done, so that a man about whose sense of duty no one
was ever in doubt may not finally, in his sixtieth year, be
marked with the stain of dishonor and most foul disgrace,
that Sextus Naevius not use all his distinctions as spoils, so
that he may not . . .[149] through your decision prevent the
reputation that guided Publius Quinctius to old age from
following him all the way to the pyre.

[148] "Disgraced" (*turpis*) is nontechnical for *infamis*.
[149] The transmitted text appears to be impossible: *fero* occurs intransitively only in a couple of senses that do not fit this context (*OLD* s.v. 6 and 7), and it appears to be unparalleled with *quominus*.

IN DEFENSE OF
SEXTUS ROSCIUS
OF AMERIA

INTRODUCTION

After handling Quinctius' case, Cicero was invited by a Valerius Messalla to defend one Sextus Roscius of Ameria, a town (*municipium*) in Umbria with territory extending west to the Tiber. Messalla was a young nobleman whose invitation the young Cicero did not feel able to refuse (§§4, 149).[1] Cicero's description of the situation in the opening of his speech may reflect the arguments used to persuade him: the fact that he was young and had not yet held public office meant that he could take on the case with relatively little risk, as opposed to others whose words might carry greater weight (§§2–3). Cicero's agreement is a sign of his ambition: though he is twenty-six and too young to hold office—he speaks of "not yet" having done so (*nondum* at §3)—successful candidature will require the backing of such nobles as Messalla.

Sextus Roscius' case was not an easy one. It was a case of parricide, Sextus being accused of having organized his father's murder. The motive alleged by the prosecution was that his father, also named Sextus Roscius, planned to

[1] It is not quite clear whether this was M. Valerius Messalla Niger (cos. 61) or M. Valerius Messalla Rufus (cos. 53); see Dyck 2010 on §149.

INTRODUCTION

disinherit his son, who acted to forestall that outcome (§§40, 52–53). Moreover, the matter was complicated by property issues. The thirteen farms held by the elder Roscius had been sold at auction for a fraction of their value to L. Cornelius Chrysogonus (§6), a freedman of the dictator Sulla, who had seen to it that the father's name had been added to the list of those proscribed, on the ground that he had been slain behind enemy lines (§127, *apud adversarios occisum*). To oppose the prosecution and inquire more closely into the elder Roscius' death would thus seem to pose a challenge to Chrysogonus and, ultimately, Sulla himself. Finally, there was by now, after years in which the criminal courts had been held in abeyance, pent-up outrage over the unchecked bloodletting of the Sullan proscriptions (§11). The jurors might be expected to share that mood. The question was whether the prosecution or the defense could tap into it more effectively.

Cicero's defense took an unexpected tack, foregrounding the sale of the Roscian estates, a matter not within the scope of the tribunal handling trials for murder.[2] He thus boldly frames Chrysogonus as the real opponent from the beginning and the real underlying issue as that of Roscius' property. The implied subnarrative, to which the jurors and the general public could relate, is that the real driver of the proscriptions was greed for the property of others, and he makes Chrysogonus the figurehead of that greed and the current trial the final result: not content with having despoiled Roscius' property, Chrysogonus cannot rest

---

[2] Cf. the vivid depiction of surprise on the prosecution's side of the courtroom: §60.

PRO ROSCIO AMERINO

easy unless he has deprived him of his (civic) life (*caput*) as well.[3]

With that penetrating psychological analysis, Cicero has found a way to present his client to the jurors as a resourceless victim and his opponent as a man of great power, first introduced as "a young man, at the present time perhaps the most powerful in the state" (§6, *adulescens vel potentissimus hoc tempore nostrae civitatis*). But he also needs to place the other actors appropriately within this basic frame. He begins doing this with a narrative featuring two estranged relatives of the deceased, T. Roscius Magnus and T. Roscius Capito (§17). After making the important point that the elder Roscius was slain in Rome, not behind enemy lines (§18), Cicero dilates on the sequel at Ameria: suspicions are roused by the depiction of the speedy arrival of the news of the murder, with Mallius Glaucia, a freedman of Magnus, making an all-night journey to deliver it to Capito, then its report four days later to Chrysogonus in Sulla's camp; the haste with which young Roscius was dispossessed and the general reaction of the people of Ameria heighten sympathy for him, as does the narrative of the threat to his life that led him to seek refuge with his father's friends in Rome (§§19–27). A lament (*conquestio*) reinforces the sudden and total reversal of fortunes from the client's point of view (§§29–32). Cicero divides the case, somewhat artificially, into three

---

[3] §§7–8. If convicted by the jurors, Roscius would have had the option of going into exile, rather than face the death penalty. Nonetheless, Cicero describes the ghastly punishment visited upon a parricide who confessed to the crime (§71) as if it might apply to his client.

INTRODUCTION

parts, the charge, the criminality, and the power, that deal with (1) Erucius, the prosecuting attorney, (2) Magnus and Capito, and (3) Chrysogonus.

Erucius was a professional prosecutor whom Cicero would face in another early case (fr. orat. 1 F 10 Cr.-D.). Cicero undercuts him in various ways, suggesting that he came to trial ill prepared (§72), that he lifted parts of his speech from another case entirely (§82), that it was merely the recent slaughter of Marian prosecutors that made him seem up to the task (§89), and hinting, none too subtly, that he was a slave by birth (§46). He reminds him pointedly of the Remmian law, which provided severe penalties for knowingly launching an unfounded criminal prosecution (§55).[4] In fact, as Cicero complains, Erucius had not presented much of a case. He alleged bad feeling between father and son that led to the father's plan to disinherit him, but his only proof was the fact that the father had sent his son to the country to manage his estates, while the father lived in Rome (§§40–42, 52, 54). He rounded this off with a picture of the younger Roscius as boorish and antisocial, remaining on his estates and not cultivating friendships (§52). Cicero does not attempt to refute this portrait; rather, he embraces it and makes it the centerpiece of his own argument that the father's treatment of his son, entrusting him with the cultivation of the estates, was, on the contrary, a mark of approbation—an old custom still maintained in the rural *municipia* of Italy (§§50–51).[5] Cicero reinforces Erucius' failure to supply a credible motive for the murder with a famous digression on

[4] See further Centola 1999, 15–60.
[5] Cf. Lo Cascio 2006, 56–59.

113

parricide and its punishment, claiming that the perpetrator must virtually be caught with blood on his hands in order for the charge to be credible (§§61–73). He then deploys the dialectical tool of division (*diairesis*), acquired in his philosophical studies, in combination with the town/country dichotomy taken over from Erucius' analysis of father-son relations, to show the implausibility of the claim that his client had arranged the murder: he lacked the means or contacts that would have been required, and, in general, such criminality is characteristic of the city, not the countryside (§§73–78).[6]

In a modern court, this argument might have sufficed, but the evidence suggests that in the Roman murder court an alternative suspect was virtually *de rigueur*.[7] Hence, in the second division of his argument, Cicero fingers two alternative suspects, Magnus and Capito, though he really does not have much evidence. Thus he deploys the *cui bono*? ("to whose advantage?") argument, pointing to the fact that the murder was profitable to Capito and Magnus, but not to his client (§§84–88), whereby he seems to advance Magnus from Chrysogonus' agent (§§21, 23) to joint owner (§108). But at the moment of the elder Roscius' death, the son was in prospect of inheriting, other property interests having arisen only after the fact. He also seeks to stir suspicion again based on Mallius Glaucia's breakneck journey to bring word of the murder to Ameria and his connections as the freedman of Magnus and bearer

---

[6] For Cicero's use of this argument, see further Benferhat 2003–2004; Blandenet 2017.

[7] Cf. Riggsby 1999, 110.

INTRODUCTION

of the news to Capito. He now implies even more strongly that Glaucia wielded the murder weapon (§§97–98). For Capito, Cicero has insinuations of previous crimes that he threatens to divulge if he takes the witness stand—a barely concealed attempt at witness intimidation (§§99–100). He likewise warns Magnus, who is a junior prosecutor (*subscriptor*) at this trial, against testifying (§104). He narrates the embassy of ten leading citizens of Ameria, including Capito, to Sulla's camp at Volaterrae in Etruria to argue the injustice of the confiscation of the Roscian property. The incident shows that Capito betrayed his fellow ambassadors by reaching a separate agreement with Chrysogonus and thwarting the meeting with Sulla (§§109–15). But Capito thus secured his share later and was no party to a "partnership" (*societas*) formed in the immediate aftermath of the murder, as previously claimed (§20).[8] Cicero also wants to use the fact that Roscius' slaves, now in the possession of Chrysogonus, were not made available for questioning under torture as evidence that something is being concealed (§§119–23).

But the virtuoso performance in this speech is the section on Chrysogonus. With a devastating portrait of the Greek freedman and his extravagant lifestyle, including ostentatious enjoyment of the estates and goods of formerly leading Roman families, Cicero succeeds in gathering all the jurors' bitter, pent-up resentment against the proscriptions and their results and channeling it toward this one figure (§§124–35).

Though Cicero began the speech with the diffidence

[8] On the "partnership," see further Zetzel 2013.

expected of a very junior speaker (cf. *Off.* 2.46), by the end he is prepared to offer political commentary, which, however, he carefully prefaces by making the point that, once a peaceful settlement proved to be impossible, he favored the side that won (§§136–37).[9] He describes the outcome as a victory for the nobility but goes on to add some advice as to how this victory should be used and how nobles should behave, whereby Caecilia and Messalla, Roscius' protectors, are held up as models (§149).[10] Otherwise, he raises the specter of a second and still worse set of proscriptions (§§153–54).

The speech won acquittal for his client against what must have seemed formidable odds (*Brut.* 312; *Off.* 2.51). There was risk in taking this position, but he managed that risk carefully, separating Sulla from Chrysogonus, and Chrysogonus from the commission of the crime. There was, however, corruption at the heart of the matter in the addition of the elder Roscius' name to the proscription list, since he was slain in Rome, not behind enemy lines, and after the deadline of June 1 of 81 for the proscriptions (§128), though Cicero wants to claim that this was done by Chrysogonus behind Sulla's back (§§127, 131). The young Cicero shows himself astute in reading the public mood

---

[9] This was no doubt felt to be necessary because, as a fellow Arpinate, he could otherwise easily be taken for a partisan of Marius.

[10] Caecilia Metella was a well-connected woman, daughter of one consul (Metellus Balearicus, cos. 123) and wife of another, (Ap. Claudius, cos. 79), to whom she bore several children, including Clodia and P. Clodius; her dream led to the restoration of the cult of Juno Sospita; cf. Münzer, *RE* s.v. Caecilius 135; see on §27.

and winning over his audience with initial emotional appeals for pity in light of his client's devastating losses. That he held his audience in the palm of his hand is shown by the storm of applause that greeted the purple passage on the parricide's punishment, later noted by Cicero with slight embarrassment (*Orat.* 107). He is also adept at sizing up his courtroom adversary Erucius and ferreting out the weaknesses in his case and appropriating the elements useful for his own argument, such as the portrait of his client as a rustic, and the urban/rural dichotomy. He also adroitly aligns himself with traditional Roman values and uses his training in dialectic to dissect the prosecution's claim about the commission of the crime. Finally, his deft characterizations, especially the portrait of Chrysogonus, sealed the victory.

NOTE ON MANUSCRIPTS AND EDITIONS

Our speech is one of several that survived thanks to a single manuscript (C), which by AD 1158–1161 was located in the monastery at Cluny. A. C. Clark was the first to identify this witness and show its importance.[11] At the Council of Constance (AD 1414–1417), the French scholar Jean de Montreuil called the manuscript to the attention of Poggio Bracciolini, who brought it to Italy, where it was copied and lost. Before C left France, however, Nicolas de Clamanges copied it at Paris (V = Paris lat. 14749). Poggio's traveling companion Bartolomeo da

[11] Clark 1905.

Montepulciano also copied excerpts from C, which are preserved in Florence (Laurentianus 54.5 = B).[12]

Before it disappeared, C was copied numerous times. Whether these progeny of C derive directly from it or via one or more lost intermediaries remains to be clarified.[13] Editors divide them between two families: (1) Laurentianus 48.10 (A), Perusinus E71 (π), and Laurentianus 52.1 (ϕ); (2) Pistoriensis A.32 (σ), Laurentianus 48.25 (χ), and Laurentianus 90 sup. 69 (ψ). For §§1–5 we have access to an earlier stage of tradition thanks to a palimpsest fragment of the fifth century preserved in Vatican Pal. lat. 24 (P).

In addition, quotations in scholia, grammarians, and rhetoricians occasionally provide readings worthy of consideration.

The text is based on the following manuscripts:

P   Vaticanus Palatinus lat. 24, s. V, rescr. VII/VIII (§§1–5)
V   Parisinus lat. 14749, olim S. Victoris 91, s. XV$^{med.}$
B   Laurentianus 54.5, s. XV$^{in.}$ (excerpta Bartolomaei de Monte Politiano)
A   Laurentianus 48.10, a. 1416 scriptus
π Perusinus E71, a. 1417 scriptus
σ Pistoriensis A.32, s. XV$^{in.}$
ϕ Laurentianus 52.1, a. 1420–30 scriptus
χ Laurentianus 48.25, s. XV$^{in.}$
ψ Laurentianus 90 sup. 69, s. XV$^{in.}$
ω consensus of A$\pi\sigma\phi\chi\psi$
Ω all codices except P and B

[12] Cf. Rouse and Reeve, in Reynolds 1983, 88–91; Maslowski 1995, xliv–vi; Hinard and Benferhat 2006, lxxvii–lxxxviii.

[13] Rouse and Reeve, in Reynolds 1983, 89. Readings are reported according to Kasten 1968, supplemented by Hinard and Benferhat 2006.

INTRODUCTION

The following are the major editions cited in the notes to the Latin text:

ed. Rom.	Rome, 1471
ed. Ven.	Venice, 1471
Guarino	Brescia, 1473
ed. Mediol.	Milan, 1498
Beroaldo	Bologna, 1499
Angelius	Florence, 1515
Naugerius	Venice, 1519
Stephanus	Paris, 1539
Manutius	Venice, 1540
Hotoman	Paris, 1554 (commentary)
Lambinus	Paris, 1565
Puteanus	Paris, 1566
Ursinus	Venice, 1581
Gruter	Hamburg, 1618
Ernesti	Halle, 1773
Garatoni	Naples, 1777
Schuetz	Leipzig, 1814–1823
Buechner	Leipzig, 1835
Madvig	The Hague, 1841
Kayser	Leipzig, 1861
Eberhard	Leipzig, 1874
Richter	Leipzig, 1889^3
R. Klotz	Leipzig, 1894
Clark	Oxford, 1905
Landgraf	Leipzig, 1914
A. Klotz	Leipzig, 1949

PRO SEXTO ROSCIO AMERINO

Credo ego vos, iudices, mirari quid sit quod, cum tot summi oratores hominesque nobilissimi sedeant, ego potissimum surrexerim, is qui neque aetate neque ingenio neque auctoritate sim cum his qui sedeant comparandus. Omnes enim hi quos videtis adesse in hac causa iniuriam novo scelere conflatam putant oportere defendi, defendere ipsi propter iniquitatem temporum non audent. Ita fit ut adsint propterea quod officium sequuntur, taceant autem idcirco quia periculum vitant. Quid ergo? Audacissimus ego ex omnibus? Minime. An tanto officiosior quam ceteri? Ne istius quidem laudis ita sum cupidus ut aliis eam praereptam velim. Quae me igitur res praeter ceteros impulit ut causam Sex. Rosci reciperem? Quia, si qui istorum dixisset quos videtis adesse, in quibus summa auctoritas est atque amplitudo, si verbum de re publica fecisset, id quod in hac causa fieri necesse est, multo plura dixisse quam dixisset putaretur. Ego autem si omnia quae dicenda sunt libere dixero, nequaquam tamen similiter oratio mea

IN DEFENSE OF
SEXTUS ROSCIUS OF AMERIA

I suppose that you are wondering, gentlemen of the jury, when so many eminent orators and men of the nobility remain seated, why I, rather than any of them, have risen to speak, one who in neither age, nor ability, nor authority can be compared with those who remain seated. All those whom you see here supporting the accused are of the opinion that in this case an unjust charge, concocted by an unprecedented act of wickedness, should be repelled, but on account of the unfavorable times dare not repel it themselves. Hence it is that they are present in fulfillment of a duty, but remain silent because they are trying to avoid danger. Well then, am I the boldest of all? By no means. Or am I so much keener to render a service than the rest? I am not so eager even for that merit, as to wish others to be deprived of it. What then was the reason that impelled me, more than anyone else, to undertake the defense of Sextus Roscius? The reason is that if any of those whom you see here present, in whom the highest authority and dignity are vested, had uttered a word about public affairs—a thing that must be done in this case—it would be thought that he had said much more than he really did. But as for me, even if I were to say freely all that needs to be said, my words can by no means be spread abroad in

CICERO

exire atque in vulgus emanare poterit. Deinde quod ceterorum neque dictum obscurum potest esse propter nobilitatem et amplitudinem neque temere dicto concedi propter aetatem et prudentiam, ego si quid liberius dixero, vel occultum esse propterea quod nondum ad rem publicam accessi vel ignosci adulescentiae meae poterit; tametsi non modo ignoscendi ratio verum etiam cognoscendi consuetudo iam de civitate sublata est. Accedit illa quoque causa quod a ceteris forsitan ita petitum sit ut dicerent ut utrumvis salvo officio se facere posse arbitrarentur; a me autem ii contenderunt qui apud me et amicitia et beneficiis et dignitate plurimum possunt. Quorum ego nec benevolentiam erga me ignorare nec auctoritatem aspernari nec voluntatem neglegere debebam.[1] His de causis ego huic causae patronus exstiti, non electus unus qui maximo ingenio sed relictus ex omnibus qui minimo periculo possem[2] dicere, neque uti satis firmo praesidio defensus Sex. Roscius verum uti ne omnino desertus esset.

Forsitan quaeratis qui iste terror sit et quae tanta formido quae tot ac tales viros impediat quominus pro capite et fortunis alterius, quemadmodum consuerunt, causam velint dicere. Quod adhuc vos ignorare non mirum est, propterea quod consulto ab accusatoribus eius rei quae

[1] debeam: *corr. Ernesti*
[2] possum: *corr. edd.*

[1] As becomes a young man (cf. *Off.* 2.46), Cicero is concerned to show himself modest about his abilities and the significance of his opinions. He speaks a bit more confidently at §148. That the scions of the noble families who were backing Roscius (cf. on §15)

the same manner and leak to the general public. In the next place, no word of the others can pass unnoticed, owing to their rank and dignity, nor can any rashness of speech be allowed in their case owing to their age and wisdom; whereas, if I speak too freely, my words will either be inconspicuous, because I have not yet entered public life, or pardoned owing to my youth, although not only the practice of pardon, but even the custom of judicial inquiry has now been abolished from the state. A further reason is this: while others were perhaps asked to speak in such a way that they supposed they were at liberty either to consent or refuse without violating their obligations, I have been pressed to do so by men who have great influence with me by virtue of their friendship, acts of kindness, and rank, whose goodwill toward myself I was bound not to ignore, nor to disdain their authority, nor to slight their wishes. For these reasons I have come forward as the advocate in this case—not chosen as the one who could speak with the greatest ability, but of them all the one left who could speak with the least risk. I have been chosen not that Sextus Roscius might be adequately defended, but to prevent his being altogether abandoned.[1]

You may perhaps ask, what is that terror, that dread so dire as to prevent so many and such eminent men from consenting, in accordance with their constant practice, to plead the case of a party whose civil rights and property are at stake. It is not surprising that you are still unaware of this, since the accusers have purposely failed to mention

had much to fear may be doubted, however. Perhaps they thought the case too trivial to take on personally.

6 conflavit hoc iudicium mentio facta non est. Quae res ea est? Bona patris huiusce Sex. Rosci, quae sunt sexagiens, quae de viro fortissimo et clarissimo[3] L. Sulla, quem honoris causa nomino, duobus milibus nummum sese dicit emisse adulescens vel potentissimus hoc tempore nostrae civitatis, L. Cornelius Chrysogonus. Is a vobis, iudices, hoc postulat ut, quoniam in alienam pecuniam tam plenam atque praeclaram nullo iure invaserit quoniamque ei pecuniae vita Sex. Rosci obstare atque officere videatur, deleatis ex animo suo suspicionem omnem metumque tollatis: sese hoc incolumi non arbitratur huius innocentis patrimonium tam amplum et copiosum posse obtinere, damnato et eiecto sperat se posse quod adeptus est per scelus, id per luxuriam effundere atque consumere. Hunc sibi ex animo scrupulum, qui se dies noctesque stimulat ac pungit, ut evellatis postulat, ut ad hanc suam praedam tam nefariam adiutores vos profiteamini.

7 Si vobis aequa ⟨ea⟩[4] et honesta postulatio videtur, iudices, ego contra brevem postulationem adfero et, quomodo mihi persuadeo, aliquanto aequiorem. Primum a Chrysogono peto ut pecunia fortunisque nostris contentus sit, sanguinem et vitam ne petat; deinde a vobis, iudices,

[3] clarissimo et fortissimo ψ *Arus.*
[4] *add. Havet*

---

[2] Romans disliked having their names bandied in public discourse; therefore Cicero is careful to indicate his respect for Sulla, who was consul and probably still dictator this year (*MRR* 2:79; Vervaet 2018). He accords similar treatment to the nobles mentioned in §§15 and 27 but shows no such consideration for Chrysogonus; see further Moreau 2006. According to Cicero, the

the reason that has brought about this trial. What is this 6
reason? The property of the father of my client Sextus
Roscius is valued at 6,000,000 sesterces, and it is from
a most valiant and illustrious man, Lucius Sulla (whose
name I mention with respect), that a young man, at the
present time perhaps the most powerful in the state,
claims to have bought the same for 2,000 sesterces—Lucius Cornelius Chrysogonus.[2] What he demands from you,
gentlemen, is this, that because he has illegally seized this
rich and splendid property of another, and because the
existence of Sextus Roscius appears to be a hindrance and
an obstacle to that property, you should remove all uneasiness from his mind and put an end to his apprehension. As long as he [Sextus Roscius] is alive, he [Chrysogonus] thinks himself unable to retain possession of the large
and rich inheritance of an innocent man like my client; but
if he is condemned and driven out, he hopes to be able to
squander and use up in luxury what he has obtained by
crime. He calls upon you to pluck this pebble from his
mind, which torments and stings him night and day, and
to avow yourselves his supporters in securing his ill-gotten
plunder.[3]

If this demand seems to you fair and honorable, gentlemen, I put forward in opposition another demand, which 7
is brief, and, I feel convinced, a bit more equitable. In the
first place, I request Chrysogonus to be satisfied with our
wealth and property, and not to ask for our lifeblood. Sec-

naming of Chrysogonus here and in the sequel unleashed frenzied activity on the prosecution side (§60).

[3] Cicero audaciously frames the issue in the case from his opponent's point of view, just as he had attributed a cynical evaluation of the case to Naevius at *Quinct.* 55.

CICERO

ut audacium sceleri resistatis, innocentium calamitatem levetis et in causa Sex. Rosci periculum quod in omnes
8 intenditur propulsetis. Quodsi aut causa criminis aut facti suspicio aut quaelibet denique vel minima res reperietur quamobrem videantur illi nonnihil tamen in deferendo nomine secuti, postremo si praeter eam praedam quam dixi quicquam aliud causae inveneritis, non recusamus quin illorum libidini Sex. Rosci vita dedatur. Sin aliud agitur nihil nisi ut iis ne quid desit quibus satis nihil est, si hoc solum hoc tempore pugnatur ut ad illam opimam praeclaramque praedam damnatio Sex. Rosci velut cumulus accedat, nonne cum multa indigna tum hoc vel[5] indignissimum est, vos idoneos habitos per quorum sententias iusque iurandum id adsequantur quod antea ipsi scelere et ferro adsequi consuerunt? Qui ex civitate in senatum propter dignitatem, ex senatu in hoc consilium delecti estis propter severitatem, ab his hoc postulare homines sicarios atque gladiatores, non modo ut supplicia vitent quae a vobis pro maleficiis suis metuere atque horrere debent, verum etiam ut spoliis ex hoc iudicio ornati auctique discedant?

9 His de rebus tantis tamque atrocibus neque satis me commode dicere neque satis graviter conqueri neque satis libere vociferari posse intellego. Nam commoditati inge-

---

[5] hoc vel *Havet*: vel hoc Ω

---

[4] Though Cicero does not show a universal danger, at §§145 and 152–53 he widens the peril to the children of the proscribed generally.

[5] For Cicero's tendency to assume such an expansive burden of proof, cf. Riggsby 1999, 30, 56.

[6] The point is elaborated at §§26–29.

ondly, I ask you, gentlemen, to resist the wickedness of audacious men, to alleviate the misfortunes of the innocent, and in the case of Sextus Roscius to avert a danger that threatens everyone.[4] But if any ground for the accusation, any suspicion of guilt or even the slightest thing can be discovered on account of which they appear to have had some reason for bringing the charge, and lastly if you find any other explanation of it than the plunder of which I have spoken, we make no objection to the life of Roscius being abandoned to their desire.[5] But if the goal is for those who are never satisfied to lack nothing, if the only object of the present struggle is for the condemnation of Sextus Roscius to crown the seizure of that rich and splendid plunder, is it not the greatest of the many indignities for you to be thought the appropriate tools, through the instrument of your vote given under oath, for them to obtain what they themselves have formerly been accustomed to obtain by crime and the sword?[6] You were chosen for the senate from the rest of the citizens owing to your public standing and from the senate for this court owing to your strict sense of justice; is it from you that these assassins and gladiators demand not only that they may escape the punishment for their misdeeds, which they ought to fear and dread from you, but also that they may leave this court adorned and enriched with spoils?[7]

Of crimes so great and so appalling as these I feel that I can neither speak in sufficient language, nor make my complaint with sufficient impressiveness, nor raise my voice with sufficient freedom: my poor abilities hinder the use of appropriate language, my youth limits my impres-

[7] Cicero frames the issue as a binary choice between two sets of defendants, whereas in fact only his client is on trial.

CICERO

nium, gravitati aetas, libertati tempora sunt impedimento. Huc accedit summus timor quem mihi natura pudorque meus attribuit et vestra dignitas et vis adversariorum et Sex. Rosci pericula. Quapropter vos oro atque obsecro, iudices, ut attente bonaque cum venia verba mea audiatis.
10 Fide sapientiaque vestra fretus plus oneris sustuli quam ferre me posse intellego. Hoc onus si vos aliqua ex parte allevabitis, feram ut potero studio et industria, iudices; sin a vobis—id quod non spero—deserar, tamen animo non deficiam et id quod suscepi, quoad potero, perferam. Quod si perferre non potero, opprimi me onere offici malo quam id quod mihi cum fide semel impositum est aut propter perfidiam abicere aut propter infirmitatem animi
11 deponere. Te quoque magnopere, M. Fanni, quaeso ut qualem te iam antea populo Romano praebuisti, cum huic eidem quaestioni iudex praeesses, talem te et nobis et rei publicae hoc tempore impertias. Quanta multitudo hominum convenerit ad hoc iudicium vides; quae sit omnium mortalium exspectatio, quae cupiditas ut acria ac severa iudicia fiant intellegis. Longo intervallo iudicium inter sicarios hoc primum committitur, cum interea caedes indignissimae maximaeque factae sunt; omnes hanc quaestionem te praetore manifestis maleficiis cotidianoque sanguine dimiss‹o virtutis ostent›ui[6] sperant futuram.

[6] dimisso virtutis ostentui *Dyck*: dimissui *vel* dimissius Ω: dimisso ire *sch. Gronov.*

[8] An attempt to enlist the jurors' goodwill (*captatio benevolentiae*) by assuming the role of the underdog, as in Quinctius' trial (§§1–10).   [9] M. Fannius was a serving praetor (*MRR* 2:80). He had had charge of the homicide court as *iudex*

PRO ROSCIO AMERINO 9–11

siveness, and the times my freedom of speech. A further obstacle is the extreme nervousness imposed upon me by my natural modesty, by your dignity, the power of my opponents, and the peril of Sextus Roscius. For these reasons, gentlemen, I beg and beseech you to listen to my words with attention and kindly indulgence. Relying on your integrity and good sense, I feel that I have taken upon myself a burden heavier than I can bear. If you lighten this burden to some extent, I will bear it as well as I can, gentlemen, by dint of zeal and energy; but if I am abandoned by you—which I do not expect—I will nonetheless not lose courage, but will accomplish to the best of my ability the task which I have undertaken. But if I cannot accomplish it, I prefer to succumb to the burden of duty rather than to renounce through treachery or lay aside through lack of courage a task that has once been imposed upon me in reliance upon my good faith.[8] You also, Marcus Fannius, I earnestly request to show yourself to us and the republic today such a man as you did on a previous occasion to the Roman people, when you presided over this same court.[9] You see what a large crowd has assembled for this trial; you are aware of what everyone expects, what everyone desires—that strict and severe rulings be produced. After a long interval this is the first trial for murder that is being convened, although in the meantime outrageous and egregious murders have been committed; everyone hopes that this court, under your praetorship, will put an end to open crimes and daily bloodshed and be a model of virtue.[10]

quaestionis some time between 85 and 81; cf. Alexander 2002, 168–69, 307n44.   [10] The text has been supplemented conjecturally; see note on the Latin.

12 Qua vociferatione in ceteris iudiciis accusatores uti consuerunt, ea nos hoc tempore utimur qui causam dicimus. Petimus abs te, M. Fanni, a vobisque, iudices, ut quam acerrime maleficia vindicetis, ut quam fortissime hominibus audacissimis resistatis, ut hoc cogitetis, nisi in hac causa qui vester animus sit ostendetis, eo prorumpere hominum cupiditatem et scelus et audaciam ut non modo clam verum etiam hic in foro ante tribunal tuum, M. Fanni, ante pedes vestros, iudices, inter ipsa subsellia 13 caedes futurae sint. Etenim quid aliud hoc iudicio temptatur nisi ut id fieri liceat? Accusant ii qui in fortunas huius invaserunt, causam dicit is, cui praeter calamitatem nihil reliquerunt; accusant ii quibus occidi patrem Sex. Rosci bono fuit, causam dicit is cui non modo luctum mors patris attulit verum etiam egestatem; accusant ii qui hunc ipsum iugulare summe cupierunt, causam dicit is qui etiam ad hoc ipsum[7] iudicium cum praesidio venit ne hic ibidem ante oculos vestros trucidetur; denique accusant ii quos populus poscit, causam dicit is qui unus relictus ex illorum 14 nefaria caede restat. Atque ut facilius intellegere possitis, iudices, ea quae facta sunt indigniora esse quam haec sunt quae dicimus, ab initio res quemadmodum gesta sit vobis exponemus, quo facilius et huius hominis innocentissimi miserias et illorum audacias cognoscere possitis et rei publicae calamitatem.

15 Sex. Roscius, pater huiusce, municeps Amerinus fuit, cum genere et nobilitate et pecunia non modo sui municipi verum etiam eius vicinitatis facile primus, tum gratia

[7] [ipsum] *Havet*

---

[11] This is presumably said with a gesture to those seated on the prosecutor's side of the court.

12 The vehement appeal that accusers are accustomed to make in other trials, we, the accused, make today. We ask you, Marcus Fannius, and you, gentlemen, to punish crimes with the utmost severity, to resist the most audacious of men with all your courage, and to bear in mind that, unless in this case you show what your temper is, men's greed, wickedness, and audacity are likely to break bounds to such an extent that murders will be committed, not only in secret, but even here in the forum before your tribunal, Marcus Fannius, at your feet, gentlemen of the jury, and amid the very benches on which you sit. 13 For what is being tested by this trial, if not that this be permitted? They are the accusers, who have laid hands upon the property of my client, he is the defendant, to whom they have left nothing but ruin; they are the accusers, who profited by the murder of Sextus Roscius' father, he is the defendant, to whom his father's death brought not only sorrow, but also poverty; they are the accusers, who keenly desired to murder my client himself, he is the defendant who has come even to this trial with a guard, for fear he may be killed in this very spot before your eyes; lastly, they are the accusers, whom the people demands for trial, he is the defendant, who is the sole survivor of their wicked murder. 14 And that you may more readily understand, gentlemen, that the deeds are more outrageous than my words describe, we will put before you the course of events from the beginning, so that you can more easily understand the misfortunes of this completely innocent man, the audacity of those people,[11] and the disaster of the state.

15 Sextus Roscius, my client's father, was a townsman of Ameria; by birth, descent, and fortune he was easily the leading citizen not only of his own town, but also of its

atque hospitiis florens hominum nobilissimorum. Nam cum Metellis, Serviliis, Scipionibus erat ei non modo hospitium verum etiam domesticus usus et consuetudo, quas, ut aequum est, familias honestatis amplitudinisque gratia nomino. Itaque ex suis omnibus commodis hoc solum filio reliquit; nam patrimonium domestici praedones vi ereptum possident, fama et vita innocentis ab hospitibus amicisque paternis defenditur. Hic cum omni tempore nobilitatis fautor fuisset tum hoc tumultu proximo, cum omnium nobilium dignitas et salus in discrimen veniret, praeter ceteros in ea vicinitate eam partem causamque opera, studio, auctoritate defendit. Etenim rectum putabat pro eorum honestate se pugnare propter quos ipse honestissimus inter suos numerabatur. Posteaquam victoria constituta est ab armisque recessimus, cum proscriberentur homines atque ex omni regione caperentur ii qui adversarii fuisse putabantur, erat ille Romae frequens atque in foro et in ore omnium cotidie versabatur, magis ut exsultare victoria nobilitatis videretur quam timere ne quid ex ea calamitatis sibi accideret.

16

---

12 The Metelli receive pride of place, Q. Caecilius Metellus Pius being currently Sulla's colleague in the consulship (*MRR* 2:79). It was, in fact, Caecilia Metella who had given Roscius refuge after his expulsion from his ancestral estates (§27), and another Metellus had attempted to secure the testimony of slaves who had witnessed the murder, an effort that was assisted by a P. Scipio (see further on §77). It is not clear how the Servilii may have helped the defense, but the family certainly was influential, its leading member P. Servilius Vatia being a *triumphator* and destined to be consul in 79 (*MRR* 2:43 and 82).   13 The claim of "brigands belonging to his family" (*domestici praedones*), thrown out as a paradox, will be explained beginning at §17.

region; he was also distinguished by his influence and relations of hospitality with those of the highest rank. For he not only enjoyed relations of hospitality with the Metelli, Servilii, and Scipios,[12] but also private contacts and intimacy with those families, whose names I mention with the respect due to their high character and dignity. And so, of all his advantages, this was the only one that he bequeathed to his son, since his inheritance was snatched by force and is in the hands of brigands belonging to his family, while the reputation and life of the innocent son are being defended by the guests and friends of his father.[13] Since the latter had always supported the nobles, especially in the latest disturbance, when the standing and safety of all nobles were at risk, he, more than anyone else in the region, defended their party and cause by his efforts, zeal, and influence. In fact, he thought it right to fight for the honor of those thanks to whom he was reckoned the most honorable man among his fellow citizens. After their victory had been established and we were no longer at war, when people were being proscribed and those from every region who were supposed to have belonged to the opposite party were being seized, he was constantly in Rome, and went about every day in the forum before the eyes of all, so that he seemed to triumph in the victory of the nobles rather than fear that it might prove disastrous to him.[14]

16

[14] This (unexplained) activity of the elder Roscius in the forum has given rise to the suspicion that he was a *sector*, that is, one who bought up properties of the proscribed at auction and divided them up for resale (from *seco*, "cut"); cf. Loutsch 1979, 108; in general, Thein 2017, 241n38. If that was the case, he may have made himself a target of reprisals.

17 Erant ei veteres inimicitiae cum duobus Rosciis Amerinis, quorum alterum sedere in accusatorum subselliis video, alterum tria huiusce praedia possidere audio; quas inimicitias si tam cavere potuisset quam metuere solebat, viveret. Neque enim, iudices, iniuria metuebat. Nam duo isti sunt T. Roscii—quorum alteri Capitoni cognomen est, iste qui adest Magnus vocatur—homines eiusmodi: alter plurimarum palmarum vetus ac nobilis gladiator habetur, hic autem nuper se ad eum lanistam contulit, quique[8] ante hanc pugnam tiro esset, quod sciam, facile ipsum ma-
18 gistrum scelere audaciaque superavit. Nam cum hic Sex. Roscius esset Ameriae, T. autem iste Roscius Romae, cum hic filius assiduus in praediis esset cumque se voluntate patris rei familiari vitaeque rusticae dedisset, iste autem frequens Romae esset, occiditur ad balneas Pallacinas rediens a cena Sex. Roscius. Spero ex hoc ipso non esse obscurum ad quem suspicio malefici pertineat; verum id quod adhuc est suspiciosum, nisi perspicuum res ipsa fecerit, hunc adfinem culpae iudicatote.
19 Occiso Sex. Roscio primus Ameriam nuntiat Mallius Glaucia quidam, homo tenuis, libertinus, cliens et fami-

[8] qui: *corr. Havet*

---

[15] Cicero speaks metaphorically, "gladiator" being used of a cutthroat; *lanista* (trainer of gladiators) was a despised profession and term of reproach; cf. Opelt 1965, 136, and, on our passage, 209; Ville 1981, 272–76; Edmondson 2016, 40–43; Lennon 2022, 126–32.

[16] Known only from this passage; evidently in the "district of Pallacina" in the Campus Martius mentioned at §132; cf. Richardson 1992 s.v. Balneae Pallacinae; Lega, *LTUR* s.v. Pallacinae.

PRO ROSCIO AMERINO 17–19

Longstanding feuds had existed between him and two other Roscii of Ameria, one of whom I see sitting on the accusers' benches, while I hear that the other is in possession of three farms that belong to my client; and had he been able to be as much on his guard against these feuds as he was continually in fear of them, he would be alive today. For, in fact, gentlemen, his fears were not unfounded. For those two Titi Roscii—one of whom is surnamed Capito, while the other, who is present, is called Magnus—are men of the following character. The first is reputed to be a famous and experienced gladiator, who has won many victories, the second recently went to the other for training, and although, so far as I know, before this last fight he was only a novice, he has easily surpassed the master himself in wickedness and audacity.[15] Now, while my client was at Ameria, and that Titus Roscius [Magnus] at Rome; while the son was always engaged upon his farms, and, in accordance with his father's wish, devoted himself to the management of the estate and a country life, whereas Magnus was constantly at Rome, Sextus Roscius [the father], while returning from supper, was killed near the baths of Pallacina.[16] I hope that from this very circumstance it is clear on whom suspicion of having committed the crime falls; but unless the facts themselves change what is still only suspicion into certainty, you are welcome to decide that my client is implicated in the murder.

After Sextus Roscius had been killed, the news was first brought to Ameria by one Mallius Glaucia, a man of no means, a freedman, a client and friend of this Titus Ros-

17

18

19

liaris istius T. Rosci, et nuntiat domum non fili sed T. Capitonis inimici; et cum post horam primam noctis occisus esset, primo diluculo nuntius hic Ameriam venit; decem horis nocturnis sex et quinquaginta milia passuum cisiis pervolavit, non modo ut exoptatum inimico nuntium primus adferret sed etiam cruorem inimici quam recentissimum telumque paulo ante e corpore extractum ostenderet.

20 Quadriduo quo haec gesta sunt res ad Chrysogonum in castra L. Sullae Volaterras defertur; magnitudo pecuniae demonstratur; bonitas praediorum—nam fundos decem et tres reliquit qui Tiberim fere omnes tangunt—, huius inopia et solitudo commemoratur; demonstrant, cum pater huiusce Sex. Roscius, homo tam splendidus et gratiosus, nullo negotio sit occisus, perfacile hunc hominem incautum et rusticum[9] et Romae ignotum de medio tolli posse; ad eam rem operam suam pollicentur. Ne diutius

21 teneam, iudices, societas coitur. Cum nulla iam proscriptionis mentio fieret, cum etiam qui antea metuerant redirent ac iam defunctos sese periculis arbitrarentur, no-

---

[9] rus: *corr. ed. Guar.*

---

[17] That is, soon after nightfall, the Romans dividing both the day and the night into twelve equal segments; cf. *OLD* s.v. *hora*. The chronology is vague, however, the murder having occurred "some months" after June 1 according to §128, so it is impossible to fix the hour with any precision.

[18] A *cisium* was a light Gallic two-wheeled vehicle, the word borrowed along with the object (*OLD* s.v.). The use of the plural suggests that the plot was well organized, with new vehicles ready at intervals to relieve the exhausted horses.

[19] About fifty-two modern miles (eighty-four km).

cius, and it was brought to the house, not of the son, but of his [the father's] enemy, Titus Capito. Although the murder had been committed after the first hour of the night,[17] the messenger reached Ameria at daybreak. During the night, in ten hours, with relays of light vehicles,[18] he rapidly covered fifty-six miles,[19] not only to be the first to bring the longed-for message to the enemy, but even to show him the still reeking blood of his enemy and the dagger pulled shortly before out of his body.[20] Four days after these events, the news of the matter was brought to Sulla's camp at Volaterrae, to Chrysogonus. The fortune [of Roscius] was shown to be large, the excellence of his farms (for he left thirteen, nearly all bordering the Tiber) and my client's helplessness and isolation were recounted. It was represented that, since my client's father Sextus Roscius, a man of such distinction and popularity, had been killed without any difficulty, it would be very easy to get rid of my client, unsuspicious as he was, living in the country, and unknown in Rome. They [the Titi Roscii] promised their assistance for this purpose. In short, gentlemen, the partnership was formed. Although the proscriptions were no longer mentioned, and even those who had formerly been kept away by fear were returning, thinking that they were now out of danger, the name of

---

[20] During the proscriptions, presentation of the victim's decapitated head to Sulla was the "proof of performance" required in order to claim the reward; cf. *Tabula Heracleensis* 122; Suet. *Iul.* 11.2; Hinard 1985b, 40–41; Urso 2019, 101. The bloody dagger may have had a similar function in this case, or so Cicero seems to suggest; cf. §§97–98, where he again implies that Glaucia was the murderer.

men refertur in tabulas Sex. Rosci, hominis studiosissimi nobilitatis, ⟨cuius bonorum⟩[10] manceps fit Chrysogonus; tria praedia vel nobilissima Capitoni propria traduntur, quae hodie possidet; in reliquas omnes fortunas iste T. Roscius nomine Chrysogoni, quemadmodum ipse dicit, impetum facit. [Haec bona HS emuntur duobus milibus nummum.][11] Haec omnia, iudices, imprudente L. Sulla facta esse certo scio. Neque enim mirum, cum eodem tempore et ea quae praeterita sunt ⟨sanet⟩[12] et ea quae videntur instare praeparet, cum et pacis constituendae rationem et belli gerendi potestatem solus habeat, cum omnes in unum spectent, unus omnia gubernet, cum tot tantisque negotiis distentus sit ut respirare libere non possit, si aliquid non animadvertat, cum praesertim tam multi occupationem eius observent tempusque aucupentur ut, simul atque ille despexerit, aliquid huiusce modi moliantur. Huc accedit quod, quamvis ille felix sit, sicut est, tamen in[13] tanta felicitate nemo potest esse in magna familia qui neminem neque servum neque libertum improbum habeat.

23   Interea iste T. Roscius, vir optimus, procurator Chrysogoni, Ameriam venit, in praedia huius invadit, hunc mise-

[10] *add. Dyck,* bonorum *tantum H. J. Mueller*
[11] *ex §6 repet., del. Kayser*
[12] *add. Rinkes*   [13] *secl. Lambinus*

---

[21] Here, in painting his picture of the partnership (*societas*) between Chrysogonus and the T. Roscii, Cicero makes it appear that Capito came into immediate possession of his three farms, whereas at §110 it becomes clear that he did so only under the pressure of the embassy of the "ten leading citizens" of Ameria. On the partnership, see further Zetzel 2013.

PRO ROSCIO AMERINO 21–23

Sextus Roscius, a zealous supporter of the nobles, was entered on the proscription list; Chrysogonus became the purchaser of his goods. Three farms, the very finest, were handed over to Capito as his own property, and he is in possession of them this very day.[21] As for the rest of the property, this Titus Roscius, as he himself says, seized it in the name of Chrysogonus. I know for a fact, gentlemen, that all this took place without Sulla's knowledge. For when he is simultaneously repairing the past and preparing in advance for possible threats; when he alone possesses the means of establishing peace and the power of waging war; when all eyes are fixed upon him alone, and he alone exercises universal rule; when he is distracted by so many and such important affairs that he cannot breathe freely, it is no surprise if something escapes his notice, especially as so many are on the lookout for the time when he is busy and are watching for an opportunity, as soon as he is off guard, to start some such plan as this. Furthermore, however "fortunate" he may be, as he really is, no one can be so fortunate as not to have some dishonest slave or freedman in a large household.[22]

Meanwhile, Titus Roscius, an excellent man,[23] Chrysogonus' agent, comes to Ameria; he seizes my client's farms,

---

[22] The first of four passages separating Sulla from the abuses committed by his freedman; cf. §§91, 127, 131. Sulla adopted "Fortunate" (*Felix*) as a second cognomen and had it inscribed beside his name on his equestrian statue; cf. App. *B Civ.* 1.97.451; Keaveney 2005, 135; Noble 2014, esp. 224–26, 230n25 (on the statue); Eckert 2018, 293–94.

[23] Ironically applied, as to Naevius at *Quinct.* 19.

rum, luctu perditum, qui nondum etiam omnia paterno funeri iusta solvisset, nudum eicit[14] domo atque focis patriis disque penatibus praecipitem, iudices, exturbat, ipse amplissimae pecuniae fit dominus. Qui in sua re fuisset egentissimus, erat, ut fit, insolens in aliena: multa palam domum suam auferebat, plura clam de medio removebat, non pauca suis adiutoribus large effuseque donabat, reliqua constituta auctione vendebat.

24 Quod Amerinis usque eo visum est indignum ut urbe tota fletus gemitusque fieret. Etenim multa simul ante oculos versabantur: mors hominis florentissimi Sex. Rosci[15] crudelissima, fili autem eius egestas indignissima, cui de tanto patrimonio praedo iste nefarius ne iter quidem ad sepulcrum patrium reliquisset, bonorum emptio flagitiosa, possessio, furta, rapinae, donationes. Nemo erat qui non ardere omnia mallet quam videre in Sex. Rosci, viri optimi atque honestissimi, bonis iactantem se ac domi-
25 nantem T. Roscium. Itaque decurionum decretum statim fit ut decem primi proficiscantur ad L. Sullam doceantque eum qui vir Sex. Roscius fuerit, conquerantur de istorum scelere et iniuriis, orent ut et illius mortui famam et fili innocentis fortunas conservatas velit. Atque ipsum decretum, quaeso, cognoscite.

[14] eiecit: *corr. ed. Ven.*
[15] Sex. Rosci *secl. Bake*

and before the unhappy man, overwhelmed with grief, had completed all his father's funeral rites, strips and throws him out of his house, and drives him headlong from his parental hearth and home and his household gods, gentlemen, while he himself becomes the owner of an ample property. Having formerly lived in penury on his own means, once in possession of another's property, he was arrogant (as is generally the case). He was openly carrying much away to his own house, secretly removing more, distributing much with a liberal and lavish hand among his helpers, and organizing an auction and selling what was left.

This seemed so outrageous to the inhabitants of Ameria that the whole town was filled with tears and lamentations. Many sights passed before their eyes at the same time: the cruel murder of Sextus Roscius, a most distinguished man; the scandalous poverty of his son, to whom that wicked bandit had not even left, out of so rich an inheritance, the right of way to the paternal burial site; the infamous purchase of the property, its seizure, the thefts, plunderings, donations. There was no one who would not have preferred for the world to be consumed in a conflagration than to see Titus Roscius showing off and lording it over the property of Sextus Roscius, a most excellent and honorable man. Accordingly the decurions immediately issued a decree that their ten chief members were to approach Sulla and inform him what kind of man Sextus Roscius was, to lodge a complaint regarding the iniquitous crimes of these men, and to beg him to be willing to see that the reputation of the dead man and the fortune of his innocent son should be protected. I ask you to listen to the terms of the decree.

CICERO

DECRETUM DECURIONUM.

Legati in castra veniunt. Intellegitur, iudices, id[16] quod iam ante dixi, imprudente L. Sulla scelera haec et flagitia fieri. Nam statim Chrysogonus et ipse ad eos accedit et homines nobiles allegat[17] qui peterent ne ad Sullam adirent et omnia Chrysogonum quae vellent esse facturum pollicerentur. Usque adeo autem ille pertimuerat ut mori mallet quam de his rebus Sullam doceri. Homines antiqui qui ex sua natura ceteros fingerent, cum ille confirmaret sese nomen Sex. Rosci de tabulis exempturum, praedia vacua filio traditurum, cumque id ita futurum T. Roscius Capito, qui in decem legatis erat, adpromitteret, crediderunt; Ameriam re inorata reverterunt. Ac primo rem differre cotidie ac procrastinare isti coeperunt, deinde aliquanto lentius nihil agere atque deludere, postremo, id quod facile intellectum est, insidias vitae huiusce Sex. Rosci parare neque sese arbitrari posse diutius alienam pecuniam domino incolumi obtinere. Quod hic simul atque sensit, de amicorum cognatorumque sententia Romam confugit et sese ad Caeciliam, Nepotis ‹sororem, Balearici›[18] filiam, quam honoris causa nomino, contulit, qua pater usus erat plurimum. In qua muliere, iudices, etiamnunc, id quod omnes semper existimaverunt, quasi

[16] ut: *corr. Naugerius*   [17] allegat iis *vel* allegatus: *corr. Ernesti*   [18] sororem Balearici *add. Garatoni*

---

[24] In light of the foregoing, a surprising point, suggesting that no one in Ameria connected him with the murder.
[25] One of the touches of humor Cicero included in this speech; cf. *Orat.* 108.

THE DECREE OF THE DECURIONS.

The delegation reached the camp. It is clear, gentlemen, that, as I have said before, these infamous crimes were committed without the knowledge of L. Sulla. For Chrysogonus immediately went to meet the delegates in person and deputed certain men of rank to beg them not to approach Sulla and to promise them that Chrysogonus would do everything they wished. He was so alarmed that he would have preferred death to Sulla being informed about these matters. When Chrysogonus assured them that he himself would strike Sextus Roscius' name from the proscription list, hand over the farms unoccupied to the son, and when Titus Roscius Capito, who was one of the ten delegates,[24] added his promise that this would be done, the delegates, men of the good old stock, projecting the character of others from their own, believed these assurances, and returned to Ameria without having pleaded their case [before Sulla]. At first these men [the Titi Roscii] began to put off the matter day by day and defer it to tomorrow, then to be a bit more sluggish in their inactivity,[25] and dupe the delegates; finally, as it was quite easy to see, they began to hatch a plot against the life of my client Sextus Roscius, thinking that they could no longer retain possession of the property of another while the real owner was alive. As soon as he perceived this, on the advice of his friends and relatives my client took refuge in Rome, and went to Caecilia, the sister of Nepos, the daughter of Balearicus (whose name I mention with respect), formerly a good friend of his father. In this woman, gentlemen, even today, as has always been the general opinion, there still

CICERO

exempli causa vestigia antiqui offici remanent. Ea Sex.
Roscium inopem, eiectum domo atque expulsum ex suis
bonis, fugientem latronum tela et minas recepit domum
hospitique oppresso iam desperatoque ab omnibus opitulata est. Eius virtute, fide, diligentia factum est ut hic potius vivus in reos quam occisus in proscriptos referretur.

28 Nam postquam isti intellexerunt summa diligentia vitam Sex. Rosci custodiri neque sibi ullam caedis faciendae potestatem dari, consilium ceperunt plenum sceleris et audaciae ut nomen huius de parricidio deferrent, ut ad eam rem aliquem accusatorem veterem compararent qui de ea re posset[19] dicere aliquid in qua re nulla subesset suspicio, denique ut, quoniam crimine non poterant, tempore ipso pugnarent. Ita loqui homines: quod iudicia tam diu facta non essent, condemnari eum oportere qui primus in iudicium adductus esset; huic autem patronos propter Chrysogoni gratiam defuturos; de bonorum venditione et de ista societate verbum esse facturum neminem; ipso nomine parricidi et atrocitate criminis fore ut hic nullo negotio tolleretur, cum ab nullo defensus esset.[20]

29 Hoc consilio atque adeo hac amentia impulsi quem ipsi,

[19] possit: *corr. ed. Mediol.*
[20] cum . . . esset *secl. Fleckeisen, fort. recte*

---

[26] Caecilia Metella was the daughter of Q. Caecilius Metellus Balearicus (cos. 123) and sister of Q. Caecilius Metellus Nepos (cos. 98). In the year 90 a dream of hers, reported in the senate, led to the repair of the temple of Juno Sospita; cf. *Div.* 1.4, 1.99, 2.136a; Kragelund 2001; Schultz 2006; Garofalo 2019, 46–48. She was also the wife of Ap. Claudius Pulcher (cos. 79) and mother of

survive, as if to serve as a model, traces of the old sense of duty.[26] She took into her house Sextus Roscius, when he was destitute, driven out of his home, and expelled from his property, fleeing from the daggers and threats of bandits, and assisted her friend, by now overwhelmed and despaired of by all. Thanks to her courage, loyalty, and care, he lived to be entered in the list of the accused, instead of in the list of the proscribed after his death.

In fact, when these men perceived that Sextus Roscius' life was being guarded with the utmost diligence and that no opportunity was offered them for putting him to death, they formed the villainous and audacious plan of prosecuting him for parricide; of procuring some veteran accuser for the purpose, the kind who could say something about a matter in which there was no latent suspicion; and lastly, since they could not fight by means of a charge, they would employ the times themselves as a weapon. They said to themselves: since no trials have taken place for so long a time, the first person brought to trial has to be condemned; owing to the influence of Chrysogonus, my client would have no one to defend him; no one would say a word about the sale of the property and that partnership; by the mere name of parricide and the odiousness of the charge my client would be removed without difficulty, since no one would defend him. Driven by this plan, or rather by this 29

28

Cicero's later bête noire, P. Clodius Pulcher. Cf. Münzer, *RE* s.v. Caecilius 135. Her husband is not mentioned here, whether because they were divorced or because he declined to participate in order not to antagonize Sulla and/or his underlings; cf. Tansey 2016, 136–37.

cum cuperent, non potuerunt occidere, eum iugulandum vobis tradiderunt.

Quid primum querar aut unde potissimum, iudices, ordiar aut quod aut a quibus auxilium petam? Deorumne immortalium, populine Romani vestramne qui summam potestatem habetis hoc tempore fidem implorem? Pater occisus nefarie, domus obsessa ab inimicis, bona adempta, possessa, direpta, fili vita infesta, saepe ferro atque insidiis appetita. Quid ab his tot maleficiis sceleris abesse videtur? Tamen haec aliis nefariis cumulant atque adaugent, crimen incredibile confingunt, testes in hunc et accusatores huiusce pecunia comparant; hanc condicionem misero ferunt ut optet utrum[21] malit cervices ⟨T.⟩[22] Roscio dare an insutus in culleum [supplicium parricidarum][23] per summum dedecus vitam amittere. Patronos huic defuturos putaverunt; [desunt][24] qui libere dicat, qui cum fide defendat, id quod in hac causa satis ⟨est⟩,[25] [quoniam quidem suscepi][26] non deest profecto, iudices. Et forsitan in suscipienda causa temere impulsus adulescentia fecerim; quoniam quidem semel suscepi, licet hercules undique

[21] optet utrum *Beroaldus*: optetur utrum ω
[22] *add. Ernesti*   [23] *secl. Hotoman*
[24] *secl. Dyck*   [25] *add. ed. Mediol.*
[26] *secl. Heusinger*

---

[27] The orator's dilemma was a topos going back at least to C. Gracchus (*FRLO* 48 F 61; Bonnet 1906); cf. fr. orat. 5 F 3 Cr.-D.; *Lig.* 1 ("So I do not know where to turn"); Narducci 2004, 215–26.

[28] T. Roscius is presumably Magnus, again depicted as a gladiator (cf. §17). Offering the throat (so that it could be cut) was

madness, they have handed over to you to murder the man whom they could not kill, though they wanted to.

What should I complain of first? From what point, gentlemen, should I best begin? What assistance am I to ask for or from whom? Should I beg for the protection of the immortal gods, of the Roman people, or yours, gentlemen, who at this moment possess the supreme power?[27] The father wickedly murdered, his house besieged by enemies, his property removed, taken into possession, and pillaged, his son's life endangered, often assailed by treachery and the sword—from these misdeeds so numerous what crime seems to be missing? Yet they crown and aggravate them by other wicked acts. They invent an incredible charge, bribe with my client's own money witnesses and accusers to appear against him, and they offer the unhappy man these terms: to choose whether he prefers to offer his throat to Titus Roscius[28] or to be sewn up in a sack and lose his life in utter disgrace.[29] They thought that he would lack defenders. But the kind of man who would speak freely, who would loyally defend him—and this is enough in this case—is certainly not lacking, gentlemen. Perhaps, in undertaking this case, I may have acted rashly under the impulse of youth; but since I have once undertaken it, though threats, terrors, and dangers of ev-

---

what the defeated gladiator was expected to do; cf. Ville 1981, 424–25.

[29] This punishment, further elaborated at §70, was originally a ritual for removing a prodigy from the community. It appears to have applied, however, only if the defendant confessed to the charge (Suet. *Aug.* 33.1); cf. Egmond 1995 and other literature at Dyck 2010, 1–2.

CICERO

omnes minae, terrores periculaque impendeant, omnia succurram ac subibo. Certum est deliberatumque quae ad causam pertinere arbitror omnia non modo dicere verum etiam libenter, audacter libereque dicere; nulla res tanta exsistet, iudices, ut possit vim mihi maiorem adhibere metus quam fides. Etenim quis tam dissoluto animo est qui haec cum videat tacere ac neglegere possit? "Patrem meum, cum proscriptus non esset, iugulastis, occisum in proscriptorum numerum rettulistis, me domo mea per vim expulistis, patrimonium meum possidetis." Quid vultis amplius? Etiamne ad subsellia cum ferro atque telis venistis ut hic aut iuguletis aut condemnetis Sex. Roscium?

33   Hominem longe audacissimum nuper habuimus in civitate C. Fimbriam et, quod inter omnes constat, nisi inter eos qui ipsi quoque insaniunt, insanissimum. Is cum curasset in funere C. Mari ut Q. Scaevola vulneraretur, vir sanctissimus atque ornatissimus nostrae civitatis, de cuius laude neque hic locus est ut multa dicantur neque plura tamen dici possunt quam populus Romanus memoria reti-

---

[30] An invented speech put into another's mouth is called a *sermocinatio*; the device recurs at §145.

[31] This is the first of five digressions in the speech, a total surpassed only by *Ver.* 2.4, where there are eight (cf. Canter 1931, 352), perhaps a sign of a dearth of materials and a weak case. C. Flavius Fimbria (ca. 115/14–85) was the son of the homonymous *novus homo* consul of 104. The younger Fimbria was a partisan of C. Marius and participated in the worst excesses that followed the capture of Rome by Cinna and Marius in 87. Marius himself died on January 13 of 86; cf. *MRR* 2:46 and 53. Fimbria was later a legate in the war against Mithridates in Asia Minor, during which he betrayed his commanding officer, L. Valerius Flaccus, and took over his army. He committed suicide when Sulla closed in on him: *MRR* 2:53 and 59; Münzer, *RE* Flavius 88.

ery kind menace on every side, by Hercules, I will meet and undergo them all. It is my deliberate and fixed intention not only to say all that I consider relevant to the case, but also to say it willingly, boldly, and freely; no obstacle will arise that is so great, gentlemen, that fear would exert greater influence over me than loyalty. For is there anyone with such a weak will that when he sees these things he would be able to hold his tongue and ignore them? "My father you murdered, although he had not been proscribed; after he had been killed, you entered his name in the proscription list; as for me, you drove me out of my house by force; as for my patrimony, you are in possession of it."[30] What more do you want? Have you even come to these benches with weapons of steel so as either to murder or convict Sextus Roscius in this place?

By far the most audacious man that we have recently had in the community was Gaius Fimbria, and also the maddest, as is generally agreed by all except those who are mad themselves.[31] He contrived that, at the funeral of Gaius Marius, the most upright and illustrious man in our state, Quintus Scaevola, should be wounded; this is neither the place to speak at length in his praise, nor, if it were, could more be said than what is retained in the memory of the Roman people.[32] When he was informed

---

[32] One of Cicero's early teachers, Q. Mucius Scaevola (cos. 95) was pontifex maximus from ca. 89 (cf. Rüpke 2008, §2478) and an eminent jurist, to whom an eighteen-book treatise on the civil law is credited (*Dig.* 49.15.5), though only scattered opinions survive. Though the wound inflicted by Fimbria was not fatal, he was killed in 82 by order of the younger Marius in a liquidation of enemies as he abandoned Rome before Sulla's advance. Cf. Münzer, *RE* Mucius 22; on him as a jurist, Wieacker 1988, 596ff.

net, diem Scaevolae dixit posteaquam comperit eum posse vivere. Cum ab eo quaereretur quid tandem accusaturus esset eum quem pro dignitate ne laudare quidem quisquam satis commode posset, aiunt hominem, ut erat furiosus, respondisse: quod non totum telum corpore recepisset. Quo populus Romanus nihil vidit indignius nisi eiusdem viri mortem, qui[27] tantum potuit ut omnes occisus perdiderit et afflixerit, quos quia servare per compositionem[28] volebat, ipse ab eis interemptus est. Estne hoc illi dicto atque facto Fimbriano simillimum? Accusatis Sex. Roscium. Quid ita? Quia de manibus vestris effugit, quia se occidi passus non est. Illud, quia in Scaevola factum est, magis indignum videtur, hoc, quia fit a Chrysogono, non est ferendum. Nam per deos immortales! quid est in hac causa quod defensionis indigeat? Qui locus ingenium patroni requirit aut oratoris eloquentiam magnopere desiderat? Totam causam, iudices, explicemus atque ante oculos expositam consideremus; ita facillime quae res totum iudicium contineat et quibus ⟨de⟩[29] rebus nos dicere oporteat et quid vos sequi conveniat intellegetis.

35 Tres sunt res, quantum ego existimare possum, quae obstent hoc tempore Sex. Roscio, crimen adversariorum et audacia et potentia. Criminis confictionem [accusator][30] ⟨C.⟩[31] Erucius suscepit, audaciae partes Roscii sibi popo-

[27] quae: *corr. Dyck* [28] servare per compositionem *ed. Rom.*: servare per conservare posicionem $V\chi^1$, *alii alia*
[29] *add.* ψ^2 [30] *secl. Richter*
[31] *add. Dyck*

---

[33] Cf. *TLRR* 119 for Fimbria's possible status at the time of the prosecution; the case was evidently dropped.

PRO ROSCIO AMERINO 33–35

that he [Scaevola] might possibly recover, he [Fimbria] laid an accusation against Scaevola.[33] When he was asked whatever was the reason why he was going to accuse a man whom no one could even praise as he merited, he is said to have answered, like the madman that he was, "because he had not received the whole of the weapon in his body."[34] The Roman people never saw anything more outrageous than this, unless it was the death of this same man [Scaevola], who had such influence that in death he brought ruin and disaster on the whole body of citizens, since he himself was slain by the persons whom he desired to save by means of an amicable settlement. Is the present case not very similar to what Fimbria said and did? You are accusing Sextus Roscius. Why? Because he escaped from your hands, because he did not allow himself to be killed. The earlier crime, because it was committed in the case of Scaevola, seems more outrageous; but this crime, because it is committed by Chrysogonus, is intolerable. For, by the immortal gods, what is there in this case that needs defense? What point requires an advocate's talent or greatly needs the eloquence of an orator? Let us unfold the whole case, gentlemen, and examine it once it has been put before your eyes; in this way you will most readily understand on what the whole trial depends, on what matters I must speak, and what you should be guided by. 34

As far as I can judge, three factors currently stand in Sextus Roscius' way: the accusation brought by his adversaries, their audacity, and their power. Gaius Erucius undertook to concoct the charge; the Roscii claimed the role 35

---

[34] That is, as a good gladiator should.

151

scerunt, Chrysogonus autem, is qui plurimum potest, potentia pugnat. De hisce omnibus rebus me dicere oportere intellego. Quid igitur est? Non eodem modo de omnibus, ideo quod prima illa res ad meum officium pertinet, duas autem reliquas vobis populus Romanus imposuit: ego crimen oportet diluam, vos et audaciae resistere et hominum eiusmodi perniciosam atque intolerandam potentiam primo quoque tempore exstinguere atque opprimere debetis.

Occidisse patrem Sex. Roscius arguitur. Scelestum, di immortales! ac nefarium facinus atque eiusmodi quo uno maleficio[32] scelera omnia complexa esse videantur! Etenim si, id quod praeclare a sapientibus dicitur, vultu saepe laeditur pietas, quod supplicium satis acre reperietur in eum qui mortem obtulerit parenti, pro quo mori ipsum, si res postularet, iura divina atque humana cogebant? In hoc tanto, tam atroci, tam singulari maleficio, quod ita raro exstitit ut, si quando auditum sit, portenti ac prodigi simile numeretur, quibus tandem tu,[33] C. Eruci, argumentis accusatorem censes uti oportere? Nonne et audaciam eius qui in crimen vocetur singularem ostendere et mores feros immanemque naturam et vitam vitiis flagitiisque omnibus deditam, [et][34] denique omnia ad perniciem profligata atque perdita? Quorum tu nihil in Sex. Roscium ne obiciendi quidem causa contulisti.

[32] *secl. A. Eberhard*   [33] te: *corr. R. Klotz*
[34] *secl. Madvig*

---

[35] The formal division (*partitio*) of the speech; the argumentation/refutation breaks down as follows: (1) Erucius (§§37–82); (2) Magnus and Capito (§§83–123); (3) Chrysogonus (§§124–49).

of audacity; and Chrysogonus, who has the greatest influence, is fighting by means of his power.[35] I know I must discuss all these matters. How, then, am I to proceed? Not in the same way about all of them, because the first point relates to my duty, whereas the Roman people has assigned the two others to you [the jurors]. I have to refute the charge; but you ought to resist audacity and blot out and suppress the ruinous and intolerable power of men of this kind at the very first opportunity.

Sextus Roscius is accused of having killed his father— a criminal and wicked act, immortal gods, of such a nature that all crimes seem to be subsumed in this single evil deed! In fact, if, as is well said by philosophers, filial duty is often violated by a look,[36] what punishment sufficiently severe can be found for one who has caused his father's death, for whom laws divine and human would have bound him to die himself, if circumstances demanded? In the case of a crime so grave, so appalling, so unusual, and one which arises so rarely that, whenever it is heard of, it is regarded as akin to a portent and prodigy, what arguments, I ask you, do you, Gaius Erucius, think an accuser ought to employ? Should he not show the remarkable audacity of the man who is charged with it, his savage character and brutal nature, a life devoted to every kind of vice and infamy, in short, all elements depraved and reduced to ruin? You have imputed none of these qualities to Sextus Roscius, not even for the sake of throwing them in his teeth.[37]

---

[35] He will later appeal to this division in order to dissociate Chrysogonus from the commission of the crime (§122).
[36] Cf. *Off.* 1.146 on mental states disclosed by tiny details of behavior.   [37] That is, let alone proving them.

39   Patrem occidit Sex. Roscius. Qui homo? Adulescentulus corruptus et ab hominibus nequam inductus? Annos natus maior quadraginta. Vetus videlicet sicarius, homo audax et saepe in caede versatus? At hoc ab accusatore ne dici quidem audistis. Luxuries igitur hominem nimirum et aeris alieni magnitudo et indomitae animi cupiditates ad hoc scelus impulerunt? De luxuria purgavit Erucius cum dixit hunc ne in convivio quidem ullo fere interfuisse. Nihil autem umquam[35] debuit. Cupiditates porro quae possunt esse in eo qui, ut ipse accusator obiecit, ruri semper habitarit et in agro colendo vixerit? Quae vita maxime disiuncta ⟨a⟩[36] cupiditate et cum officio ⟨coniuncta est⟩.[37]

40   Quae res igitur tantum istum furorem Sex. Roscio obiecit? "Patri" inquit "non placebat." Patri non placebat? Quam ob causam? Necesse est enim eam quoque iustam et magnam et perspicuam fuisse. Nam ut illud incredibile est, mortem oblatam esse patri a filio sine plurimis et maximis causis, sic hoc veri simile non est, odio fuisse parenti

41 filium sine causis multis et magnis et necessariis. Rursus igitur eodem revertamur et quaeramus quae tanta vitia fuerint in unico filio quare is patri displiceret. At perspicuum est nullum fuisse. Pater igitur amens, qui odisset eum sine causa quem procrearat? At is quidem fuit omnium constantissimus. Ergo illud iam perspicuum profecto est, si neque amens pater neque perditus filius fuerit, neque odi causam patri neque sceleris filio fuisse.

42   "Nescio" inquit "quae causa odi fuerit; fuisse odium intellego quia antea, cum duos filios haberet, illum alte-

[35] umquam cuiquam *Bake*
[36] *add. ed. Guar.*
[37] coniuncta est *suppl* G^2s, coniuncta *tantum* $\sigma\chi^2\psi$

Sextus Roscius killed his father. What kind of man is 39 he? A corrupted young man led astray by worthless companions? He is more than forty years old. He is doubtless a veteran assassin, a man of audacity and often involved in murder? But you have not heard this even claimed by his accuser. No doubt, then, it was a life of indulgence, enormous debts, and his unbridled desires that drove him to commit this crime? As for a life of indulgence, Erucius has cleared him from that by saying that he hardly ever took part in any dinner party; he never had any debts; further, what desires could there be in one who, as his accuser himself has said reproachfully, always inhabited the country and lived by cultivating his land? This life is most removed from desires and inseparable from duty.

What, then, implanted such extreme madness in Sextus 40 Roscius? "His father disliked him," he says. His father disliked him? For what reason? It must be a valid, strong, and obvious one, for, just as it is incredible that a son should have inflicted death upon his father unless he had numerous and weighty motives, so it is improbable that a father loathed his son without many strong and cogent reasons. Let us return to the point and inquire what out- 41 size vices there were in an only son such as to make his father dislike him. But it is obvious that there were none. Was his father mad, then, to hate, without reason, the son whom he had begotten? On the contrary, he was the most steadfast of all men. Consequently, it is by now indeed obvious that, if the father was not out of his mind nor his son depraved, the father had no motive for hatred, nor the son for murder.

"I do not know," he says, "what the motive for the ha- 42 tred was; but I know that it existed, since previously, when

CICERO

rum qui mortuus est secum omni tempore volebat esse, hunc in praedia rustica relegavit." Quod Erucio accidebat in mala nugatoriaque accusatione, idem mihi usu venit in causa optima: ille quomodo crimen commenticium confirmaret non inveniebat, ego res tam leves qua ratione infirmem ac diluam reperire non possum. Quid ais, Eruci? Tot praedia, tam pulchra, tam fructuosa Sex. Roscius filio suo relegationis ac supplici gratia colenda ac tuenda tradiderat? Quid? Hoc patres familiae qui liberos habent, praesertim homines illius ordinis ex municipiis rusticanis, nonne optatissimum sibi putant esse filios suos rei familiari maxime servire et in praediis colendis operae plurimum studique consumere? An amandarat hunc sic ut esset in agro ac tantummodo aleretur ad villam, ut commodis omnibus careret? Quid? Si constat hunc non modo colendis praediis praefuisse sed certis fundis patre vivo frui solitum esse, tamenne haec a te vita eius[38] rusticana relegatio atque amandatio appellabitur? Vides, Eruci, quantum distet argumentatio tua ab re ipsa atque ⟨a⟩[39] veritate: quod consuetudine patres faciunt, id quasi novum reprehendis; quod benevolentia fit, id odio factum criminaris; quod honoris causa pater filio suo concessit, id eum supplici causa fecisse dicis. Neque haec tu non intellegis, sed usque eo quid arguas non habes, ut non modo

[38] a te vita eius *Vahlen*: attente vita et Ω   [39] *add.* ψ

---

[38] For use of a single name in addressing the opposing counsel, cf. on *Quinct.* 35.   [39] For Cicero's argument here and at §§50–51 that the old Roman custom by which fathers entrusted management of their estates to their sons persisted in rural Italy, cf. Lo Cascio 2006, 56–59.

he had two sons alive, he wanted the one who is now dead to be always with him, but relegated this son to his farms in the country." The same point that occurred to Erucius in bringing a malicious and frivolous accusation proves useful to me in arguing an excellent case. He failed to find a means of proving his made-up charge, whereas I cannot discover a means of disproving and refuting such trifling allegations. What are you claiming, Erucius?[38] Did Sextus Roscius hand over so many fine and productive farms to his son to cultivate and look after merely for the sake of relegating and punishing him? Tell me: do not the heads of households who have children, especially those of Roscius' class from the country towns, think it most desirable for themselves that their sons should devote themselves most of all to their property and spend the greatest part of their labor and pains on cultivating their farms?[39] Or did he send him away on such terms that he might remain on the estate and merely have his food given him at the country house but be deprived of all benefits? Tell me: if it is agreed that my client not only was in charge of the cultivation of the farms, but during his father's lifetime, generally had the usufruct of certain estates, will you still call his life a relegation and banishment to the country? You see, Erucius, how far your argument differs from the facts and reality. You criticize as a novelty what fathers customarily do; what is done out of kindness you denounce as done out of hatred; what a father has granted his son as a mark of esteem, you assert he did as a punishment. It is not that you do not understand this, but you are so lacking in argu-

tibi contra nos dicendum putes verum etiam contra rerum naturam contraque consuetudinem hominum contraque opiniones omnium.

"At enim, cum duos filios haberet, alterum a se non dimittebat, alterum ruri esse patiebatur." Quaeso, Eruci, ut hoc in bonam partem accipias; non enim exprobrandi causa sed commonendi gratia dicam. Si tibi fortuna non dedit ut patre certo nascerere ex quo intellegere posses qui animus patrius in liberos esset, at natura certe dedit ut humanitatis non parum haberes; eo accessit studium doctrinae, ut ne a litteris quidem alienus esses. ‹Ec›quid[40] tandem tibi videtur, ut ad fabulas veniamus, senex ille Caecilianus minoris facere Eutychum filium rusticum quam illum alterum, Chaerestratum—nam, ut opinor, hoc nomine est—alterum in urbe secum honoris causa habere, alterum rus supplici causa relegasse? "Quid ad istas ineptias abis?" inquies. Quasi vero mihi difficile sit quamvis multos nominatim proferre, ne longius abeam, vel tribules vel vicinos meos qui suos liberos, quos plurimi faciunt, agricolas assiduos esse cupiunt! Verum homines notos sumere odiosum est, cum et illud incertum sit velintne ii sese nominari, et nemo vobis magis notus futurus sit quam

[40] *suppl. Stephanus*

---

[40] Cicero implies that Erucius was born a slave.

[41] Cicero shows a bit of hesitancy in order not to appear too learned; cf. §125 on the Valerian Law, and *Ver.* 2.4.5, where he pretends to be unsure about the name of the artist Polyclitus.

[42] Caecilius Statius was an Insubrian Gaul who came to Rome, probably as a prisoner of war ca. 200, and went on to a brilliant career as a comic poet; see Manuwald 2011, 234–42; 2020, 43–44.

ments, that you think you must speak not only against us, but even against nature, the custom of mankind, and everyone's opinion.

"But when he had two sons, he never sent the one away from him, but allowed the other to live in the country." I beg you, Erucius, to take what I am going to say in good part, for I speak not to reproach you, but to remind you. If fortune did not grant you to be born of a determinate father,[40] from whom you could have learned what a father's feeling is toward his children, at least nature has given you no small share of human feeling, combined with the pursuit of learning, so that you are not even a stranger to literature. To take an example from the stage, is it the case that you think the old man in the play of Caecilius thinks less of Eutychus, the son who lives in the country, than of the other, Chaerestratus (I think that was his name),[41] and that he keeps the one with him in the city as a token of esteem, while he has sent the other into the country as a punishment?[42] "Why go off into such irrelevancies?" you will say. As if it would be difficult for me—so as not to "go off" very far—to name as many as you please of my fellow tribesmen or neighbors who desire that their sons, whom they value highly, should be painstaking farmers! But it is not in good taste to take as examples men who are well known, since it is uncertain whether they would like their names to be given;[43] besides, none of them is

Some four hundred to five hundred verses of his discovered in a papyrus roll in Herculaneum await publication; cf. Kleve 1996. Cicero alludes to the *Hypobolimaeus*, based on a comedy of Menander; for reconstruction of the plot, see Webster 1960, 100–101. [43] See on §6.

est hic Eutychus, et certe ad rem nihil intersit utrum hunc ego comicum adulescentem an aliquem ex agro Veiente nominem. Etenim haec conficta arbitror esse a poetis ut effictos nostros mores in alienis personis expressamque imaginem nostrae[41] vitae cotidianae videremus. Age nunc, refer animum sis ad veritatem et considera non modo in Umbria atque in ea vicinitate sed in his veteribus municipiis quae studia a patribus familias[42] maxime laudentur; iam profecto te intelleges inopia criminum summam laudem Sex. Roscio vitio et culpae dedisse. Ac non modo hoc patrum voluntate liberi faciunt sed permultos et ego novi et, nisi me fallit animus, unus quisque vestrum, qui et ipsi incensi sunt studio quod ad[43] agrum colendum attinet, vitamque hanc rusticam, quam tu probro et crimini putas esse oportere, et honestissimam et suavissimam esse arbitrantur. Quid censes hunc ipsum Sex. Roscium quo studio et qua intellegentia esse in rusticis rebus? Ut ex his propinquis eius, hominibus honestissimis, audio, non tu in isto artificio accusatorio callidior es quam hic in suo. Verum, ut opinor, quoniam ita Chrysogono videtur, qui huic nullum praedium reliquit, et artificium obliviscatur et studium deponat licebit. Quod tametsi miserum et indignum est, feret tamen aequo animo, iudices, si per vos vi-

[41] nostram: *corr. Hotoman, secl. Madvig*
[42] familiis: *corr. ed. Guar.*
[43] quod ad *Angelius*: quod *vel* quo ad ω

[44] The introduction of an example from comedy and the transition to and from it are handled somewhat clumsily here; in this respect *QRosc.* and *Cael.* are more deft.

likely to be better known to you than this Eutychus, and certainly it makes no difference whether I name this young man in the comedy or someone from the territory of Veii. I think, in fact, that these fictions have been created by the poets so we may see our manners represented in other persons and a vivid picture of our daily life. Come now, bring your mind back, if you please, to reality[44] and consider what pursuits are most praised by heads of households, not only in Umbria and that region, but in our old municipal towns; you will surely realize that, for lack of charges, you have claimed Sextus Roscius' greatest merit to be a vice and a fault. And sons do not do this only in obedience to their fathers' wishes, but I myself, and, unless I am mistaken, each of you also knows very many men who, on their own, are fired with enthusiasm for agriculture, and consider this country life, which you think should be subject to shame and accusation, to be most honorable and most agreeable. What do you think of my client Roscius himself, what enthusiasm and understanding he has shown in agriculture? As I learn from his relatives here, most honorable men, you are not shrewder in your own trade of accuser than he is in his.[45] But I suppose that, since it so pleases Chrysogonus, who has not left him a single farm, he will be allowed to forget his trade and lay aside his interest in it. Although it is wretched and an indignity, he will nonetheless bear it with equanimity, gentlemen, if your verdict enables him to retain his life and

48

49

---

[45] Cicero alludes in passing to Roscius' relatives; the demonstrative *his* suggests that they are present in court to support him. Here Cicero refers neutrally to Erucius' "trade"; it will become a target for criticism at §§54–57.

tam et famam potest obtinere; hoc vero est quod ferri non potest, si et in hanc calamitatem venit propter praediorum bonitatem et multitudinem et quod ea studiose coluit, id erit ei maxime fraudi, ut parum miseriae sit quod aliis coluit, non sibi, nisi etiam quod omnino coluit crimini fuerit.

50   Ne tu, Eruci, accusator esses ridiculus, si illis temporibus natus esses cum ab aratro arcessebantur qui consules fierent. Etenim qui praeesse agro colendo flagitium putes, profecto illum Atilium quem sua manu spargentem semen qui missi erant convenerunt hominem turpissimum atque inhonestissimum iudicares. At hercule maiores nostri longe aliter et de illo et de ceteris talibus viris existimabant itaque ex minima tenuissimaque re publica maximam et florentissimam nobis reliquerunt. Suos enim agros studiose colebant, non alienos cupide appetebant; quibus rebus et agris et urbibus et nationibus rem publicam atque
51   hoc imperium et populi Romani nomen auxerunt. Neque ego haec eo profero quo conferenda sint cum hisce de quibus nunc quaerimus, sed ut illud intellegatur, cum apud maiores nostros summi viri clarissimique homines, qui omni tempore ad gubernacula rei publicae sedere debebant, tamen in agris quoque colendis aliquantum operae temporisque consumpserint, ignosci oportere ei

---

46 This sentence underlines the irony that precisely Roscius' zealous devotion to agriculture has been his undoing, in two respects: the resulting quality of the farms caught the eye of others, who were greedy to own them; and Erucius used his devotion to agriculture as proof of his father's dislike (and therefore a motive for murder).

reputation. But what is intolerable is that he has arrived at this misfortune owing to the quality and number of his farms, and the fact that he zealously cultivated them will in particular be prejudicial to him and that the misfortune that he cultivated them for others, not himself, would be insufficient unless he was charged because he cultivated them at all.[46]

In truth, Erucius, you would be an absurd accuser if you had been born in the times when men used to be summoned from the plow to be made consuls. For, seeing that you think it a disgrace to be in charge of cultivating the land, you would surely have considered the illustrious Atilius, whom the delegation found sowing seed with his own hand, a most disgraceful and dishonorable man. And yet, by Hercules, our ancestors had a very different opinion of Atilius and others like him.[47] And by such practices they have left us, instead of a very small and poor republic, one that is very great and prosperous. For they used to cultivate their own lands zealously, they did not greedily seek to obtain those of others; and by such conduct, with lands and cities and nations they enlarged the republic, this empire, and the renown of the Roman people. I do not cite these facts so that they should be compared with these we are now investigating, but so that it may be understood that, as among our ancestors men of the highest rank and distinction, who at any time had to sit at the helm of the republic, nevertheless also spent a good deal of time and effort on the cultivation of their lands, so a man ought

[50]

[51]

---

[47] It is not clear which of the consular Atilii is meant; cf. *MRR* 1:208n1. Val. Max. 4.4.5, otherwise dependent on our passage, makes him a *triumphator*.

homini qui se fateatur esse rusticum, cum ruri assiduus semper vixerit, cum praesertim nihil esset quod aut patri gratius aut sibi iucundius aut re vera honestius facere posset.

52 Odium igitur acerrimum patris in filium ex hoc, opinor, ostenditur, Eruci, quod hunc ruri esse patiebatur. Numquid est aliud? "Immo vero" inquit "est; nam istum exheredare in animo habebat." Audio; nunc dicis aliquid quod ad rem pertineat; nam illa, opinor, tu quoque concedis levia esse atque inepta: "Convivia cum patre non inibat." Quippe qui ne in oppidum quidem nisi perraro veniret. "Domum suam istum non fere quisquam vocabat." Nec mirum, qui neque in urbe viveret neque revocaturus es-
53 set. Verum haec tu quoque intellegis esse nugatoria; illud quod coepimus videamus, quo certius argumentum odi reperiri nullo modo potest. "Exheredare pater filium cogitabat." Mitto quaerere qua de causa; quaero qui scias; tametsi te dicere atque enumerare causas omnes oportebat, et id erat certi accusatoris officium qui tanti sceleris argueret explicare omnia vitia ac peccata fili quibus incensus parens potuerit animum inducere ut naturam ipsam vinceret, ut amorem illum penitus insitum eiceret ex animo, ut denique patrem esse sese obliviceretur; quae sine magnis huiusce peccatis accidere potuisse non arbitror.
54 Verum concedo tibi ut ea praetereas quae, cum taces, nulla esse concedis; illud[44] quidem, voluisse exheredare,

[44] illum: *corr. Gulielmius*

to be excused if he confesses himself a rustic, since he has always lived in the country, especially since there was nothing he could do that would be more agreeable to his father, more pleasant to himself, or in fact more honorable.

So then, I suppose, Erucius, the father's bitter hatred against the son is shown by his allowing him to remain in the country! Is there anything else? "Certainly there is," he says; "for he intended to disinherit him." I see; now you are saying something that may pertain to the case, for even you admit, I believe, that these arguments are trifling and absurd: "He would not attend dinner parties with his father"; of course not, since he rarely came into town. "Almost no one invited him to his house"; no surprise, seeing that he did not live in the city, and could not return the invitation. But you are also aware that these arguments are worthless. Now let us consider what we began to speak of, which is the surest proof of hatred that can possibly be found. "The father intended to disinherit the son." I forbear to ask for what reason; I ask how you know it. Certainly you ought to have stated and enumerated all the reasons, and it would have been the duty of a true accuser, who was arguing for conviction on so monstrous a crime, to set forth all the vices and transgressions of the son, by which the father was so enraged as to be able to bring himself to overcome his natural feelings, to drive out of his mind that deeply rooted love, in short, to forget that he was a father. I think that this could not have happened unless there were grave transgressions on the part of my client. However, I give you permission to pass over matters which, by your silence, you admit are nonexistent; this, however, the claim that he intended to disinherit him, you

CICERO

certe tu planum facere debes. Quid ergo adfers quare id factum putemus? Vere nihil potes dicere; finge aliquid saltem commode ut ne plane videaris id facere quod aperte facis, huius miseri fortunis et horum virorum talium dignitati illudere. "Exheredare filium voluit." Quam ob causam? "Nescio." Exheredavitne? "Non." Quis prohibuit? "Cogitabat." Cogitabat? Cui dixit? "Nemini." Quid est aliud iudicio ac legibus ac maiestate vestra abuti ad quaestum atque ad libidinem nisi hoc modo accusare atque id obicere quod planum facere non modo non possis 55 verum ne coneris quidem? Nemo nostrum est, Eruci, quin sciat tibi inimicitias cum Sex. Roscio nullas esse; vident omnes qua de causa huic[45] inimicus venias; sciunt huiusce pecunia te adductum esse. Quid ergo est? Ita tamen quaestus te cupidum esse oportebat ut horum existimationem et legem Remmiam putares aliquid valere oportere.

Accusatores multos esse in civitate utile est, ut metu contineatur audacia; verumtamen hoc ita est utile ut ne plane illudamur ab accusatoribus. Innocens est quispiam, verumtamen, quamquam abest a culpa, suspicione tamen non caret; tametsi miserum est, tamen ei qui hunc accuset possim aliquo modo ignoscere. Cum enim aliquid habeat

---

[45] huc: *corr. Beroaldus*

---

[48] The claim was raised in a more general form at §30.

[49] The Remmian Law defined *calumnia* (false accusation) as a criminal offense to be tried before the same court that heard the original case. Conviction entailed being branded on the forehead with the letter *k* (for *kalumniator*) and *infamia*; cf. *LPPR*

certainly ought to prove. What, then, can you bring forward to cause us to believe that this occurred? You can say nothing that agrees with the truth, but at least invent something plausible that you may not be clearly seen to be doing what you are openly doing—mocking the misfortunes of my wretched client and the dignity of judges so eminent as these. "The father intended to disinherit the son." For what reason? "I do not know." Did he disinherit him? "No." Who prevented him? "He was thinking of it." Thinking of it? To whom did he say that? "To nobody." What is it to abuse the court and the laws and your [the jurors'] majesty arbitrarily and for gain other than to conduct an accusation in this form and throw out a claim that you not only cannot prove but do not even try to? There is not one of us, Erucius, who does not know that you have no personal enmity with Sextus Roscius; everybody is aware why you appear in court as his enemy; everybody knows that you have been brought in by my client's money.[48] What is the case, then? Though eager for gain, you should have been eager in such a way as to consider that the opinion these men hold of you and the Remmian law must carry some weight.[49]

It is useful for there to be a number of accusers in the community, so that criminality may be held in check by fear, but it is useful only on condition that they do not openly mock us. So-and-so is innocent; but although he is free from guilt, he is not free from suspicion. Although it is a misfortune for him, still, I could to a certain extent pardon the man who accuses him. For since he has some-

363–64; Mommsen 1899, 491–98; Greenidge 1901, 468–70; Berger 1953 s.v. calumnia; Centola 1999, 15–60.

quod possit[46] criminose ac suspiciose dicere, aperte ludificari et calumniari sciens non videatur. Quare facile omnes patimur esse quam plurimos accusatores, quod innocens, si accusatus sit, absolvi potest, nocens, nisi accusatus fuerit, condemnari non potest; utilius est autem absolvi innocentem quam nocentem causam non dicere. Anseribus cibaria publice locantur et canes aluntur in Capitolio ut significent si fures venerint. At fures internoscere non possunt, significant tamen si qui noctu in Capitolium venerint quia id est suspiciosum, et[47] tametsi bestiae sunt, tamen in eam partem potius peccant quae est cautior. Quodsi luce quoque canes latrent cum deos salutatum aliqui venerint, opinor, eis crura suffringantur, quod acres sint etiam tum cum suspicio nulla sit. Simillima est accusatorum ratio. Alii vestrum anseres sunt, qui tantummodo clamant, nocere non possunt, alii canes, qui et latrare et mordere possunt. Cibaria vobis praeberi videmus; vos autem maxime debetis in eos impetum facere qui merentur; hoc populo gratissimum est. Deinde, si voletis, etiam tum cum verisimile erit aliquem[48] commisisse, in suspicione latratote; id quoque concedi potest. Sin autem sic agetis ut arguatis aliquem patrem occidisse neque dicere possitis aut quare aut quomodo, ac tantummodo sine suspicione latrabitis, crura quidem vobis nemo suffringet, sed, si ego

[46] possim: *corr. Angelius*
[47] et *post* venerint *hab.* Ω: *huc transp. Krueger (verbis* tametsi . . . tamen *deletis*)
[48] aliquem aliquid *Hotoman*

[50] On rewards for successful prosecution in the criminal courts, cf. Alexander 1985.

PRO ROSCIO AMERINO 55–57

thing that he can say to incriminate and create suspicion, he may not appear to be openly fooling us or knowingly engaging in slander. We all tolerate that there are as many accusers as possible because an innocent man, if he is accused, can be acquitted, but a guilty person cannot be convicted unless he has been accused; and it is more advantageous for an innocent man to be acquitted than for a guilty man not to be brought to trial. On the Capitol food is provided for the geese at public expense, and dogs are fed there, to give the alarm in case thieves should break in. Though they cannot distinguish thieves from others, yet they give the alarm if any persons have entered the Capitol by night, because it is suspicious, and although they are animals, they err on the side of caution. But if the dogs should bark by daylight as well, when people come to worship the gods, they would have their legs broken, I believe, for being fierce even when there is no ground for suspicion. The case of the accusers is just the same. Some of you are geese, who only cackle but cannot do any harm, others are dogs, who can both bark and bite. We see that food is provided for you,[50] but you ought especially to attack those who deserve it; this is most agreeable to the people. Then, if you like, bark if you have any suspicions, even when there is [merely] a probability that someone has committed a crime; that also is permissible. But if you act in such a manner as to argue that someone has murdered his father, but cannot say why or how,[51] if you only bark when there is no cause for suspicion, no one will break your legs, but, if I know these gentlemen well, they

[51] Cicero anticipates: he will turn to the modality of the crime at §73b.

hos bene novi, litteram illam cui vos usque eo inimici estis ut etiam kalendas omnes[49] oderitis ita vehementer ad caput affigent ut postea neminem alium nisi fortunas vestras accusare possitis.

58   Quid mihi ad defendendum dedisti, bone accusator? Quid hisce autem ad suspicandum? "Ne exheredaretur veritus est." Audio, sed qua de causa vereri debuerit nemo dicit. "Habebat pater in animo." Planum fac. Nihil est; non quicum deliberarit,[50] quem certiorem fecerit, unde istud vobis suspicari in mentem venerit. Cum hoc modo accusas, Eruci, nonne hoc palam dicis: "Ego quid acceperim scio, quid dicam nescio; unum illud spectavi quod Chrysogonus aiebat neminem isti patronum futurum; de bonorum emptione deque ea societate neminem esse qui verbum facere auderet hoc tempore"? Haec te opinio falsa in istam fraudem impulit; non mehercules verbum fecisses, si tibi quemquam responsurum putasses.

59   Operae pretium erat, si animadvertistis, iudices, neglegentiam eius in accusando considerare. Credo, cum vidisset qui homines in hisce subselliis sederent, quaesisse[51] num ille aut ille defensurus esset; de me ne suspicatum quidem esse, quod antea causam publicam nullam dixerim. Posteaquam invenit neminem eorum qui possunt et solent, ita neglegens esse coepit ut, cum in mentem veniret ei, resideret, deinde spatiaretur, nonnumquam etiam

[49] kalendas omnes *Pighius*: calo(m)ni(i)s Ω
[50] deliberavit: *corr. ed. Ven.*
[51] quaesisset: *corr. ed. Rom.*

will so deeply brand your head with that letter, which is so odious to you that you even hate all the kalends, that in future you will have no one to accuse but your own ill luck.[52]

What then have you given me to refute, my worthy accuser? What grounds for suspicion have you given these gentlemen? "He was afraid of being disinherited." I hear you say so, but no one says why he should have been afraid of this. "His father intended to." Prove it. There is no proof—not with whom he consulted, whom he informed, why it occurred to you to form this suspicion. When you bring an accusation in this manner, Erucius, are you not openly declaring: "I know what I have received, I do not know what I am to say; the one thing I considered was that Chrysogonus was asserting that no one would represent this man, there was no one in times like these who would dare to utter a word about the purchase of the goods or that partnership"? This mistaken opinion pushed you into that deceit; by Hercules, you would not have said a word if you had thought that anyone would reply to you.

It would have been worth your while, gentlemen, if you noticed it, to consider his carelessness in making his accusation. When he saw who were the men sitting on these benches, I think he asked whether this one or that one was likely to undertake the defense; he did not even form a suspicion about me, because I had not previously pleaded a criminal case. When he found none of those who can and generally do defend, he began to be so indifferent that, when it occurred to him, he sat down, then he walked

---

[52] See on §55. The kalends were the first day of the month, abbreviated with the letter *k*.

puerum vocaret, credo, cui cenam imperaret, prorsus ut vestro consessu et hoc conventu pro summa solitudine abuteretur. Peroravit aliquando, adsedit; surrexi ego. Respirare visus est quod non alius potius diceret. Coepi dicere. Usque eo animadverti, iudices, eum iocari atque alias res agere antequam Chrysogonum nominavi; quem simul atque attigi, statim homo se erexit, mirari visus est. Intellexi quid eum pepugisset. Iterum ac tertio nominavi. Postea homines cursare ultro et citro non destiterunt, credo qui Chrysogono nuntiarent esse aliquem in civitate qui contra voluntatem eius dicere auderet; aliter causam agi atque ille existimaret, aperiri bonorum emptionem, vexari pessime societatem, gratiam potentiamque eius neglegi, iudices diligenter attendere, populo rem indignam videri. Quae quoniam te fefellerunt,[52] Eruci, quoniamque vides versa esse omnia, causam pro Sex. Roscio, si non commode at libere dici, quem dedi putabas defendi intellegis, quos tradituros sperabas vides iudicare, restitue nobis aliquando veterem tuam illam calliditatem atque prudentiam, ⟨aut⟩ confitere ⟨te⟩[53] huc ea spe venisse quod putares hic latrocinium, non iudicium futurum.

De parricidio causa dicitur; ratio ab accusatore reddita non est quam ob causam patrem filius occiderit. Quod in minimis noxiis et in his levioribus peccatis quae magis

[52] fefellerint: *corr. ed. Ven.*
[53] ⟨aut⟩ confitere ⟨te⟩: *suppl. Hotoman*

---

[53] A rare tableau of the pragmatics of the Roman court, either improvised at trial or added to the published version of the speech; cf. Fuhrmann 1990, 57.

about, sometimes called for his slave (I suppose to order supper); so that, all in all, he treated you who sit in judgment and the public in attendance as if he had been absolutely alone. At last he concluded and sat down; I got up. 60 He seemed to breathe a sigh of relief, because no one other than myself was speaking. I began to speak. I observed, gentlemen, that he was joking and paid no attention, until I mentioned the name of Chrysogonus; as soon as I touched upon him, the man immediately sat bolt upright; he seemed to be astonished. I understood what had stung him. I mentioned Chrysogonus a second and a third time. After that, men continually ran to and fro, I suppose to inform Chrysogonus that there was someone in the community who was bold enough to speak contrary to his will, that the case was being pleaded differently than he thought, that the purchase of the goods was revealed, that the partnership was being severely criticized, that his influence and power were disregarded, that the jury was listening attentively, that the people thought the matter outrageous.[53] Since you were mistaken in these matters, 61 Erucius, and since you see that everything is changed, that Sextus Roscius' case is being pleaded, if not adequately, at least with freedom; since you see that he whom you thought abandoned is being defended, that those who you hoped would give him up are acting as judges, show us again, at last, your old shrewdness and sagacity, or confess that you came here with this hope: you thought that here would be not a tribunal but a robbery.

A case of parricide is being argued; the accuser has provided no motive for the son to kill his father. In the case 62 of the most trifling offenses and trivial misdemeanors, which we know are more frequent and now of almost daily

crebra et iam prope cotidiana sunt et[54] maxime et primum quaeritur, quae causa malefici fuerit, id Erucius in parricidio quaeri non putat oportere. In quo scelere, iudices, etiam cum multae causae convenisse unum in locum atque inter se congruere videntur, tamen non temere creditur, neque levi coniectura res penditur, neque testis incertus auditur, neque accusatoris ingenio res iudicatur. Cum multa antea commissa maleficia, cum vita hominis perditissima, tum singularis audacia ostendatur necesse est, neque audacia solum sed summus furor atque amentia. Haec cum sint omnia, tamen exstent oportet expressa sceleris vestigia, ubi, qua ratione, per quos, quo tempore maleficium sit admissum. Quae nisi multa et manifesta sunt, profecto res tam scelesta, tam atrox, tam nefaria credi non potest. Magna est enim vis humanitatis; multum valet communio sanguinis; reclamitat istius modi suspicionibus ipsa natura; portentum atque monstrum certissimum est esse aliquem humana specie et figura qui tantum immanitate bestias vicerit ut, propter quos hanc suavissimam lucem aspexerit, eos indignissime luce privarit, cum etiam feras inter sese partus atque educatio et natura ipsa conciliet.

63

Non ita multis ante annis aiunt T. Cloelium[55] quendam Tarracinensem, hominem non obscurum, cum cenatus cubitum in idem conclave cum duobus adulescentibus filiis isset, inventum esse mane iugulatum. Cum neque ser-

64

---

[54] id: *corr. R. Klotz*   [55] Caelium *V. Max.*

---

[54] Nothing more is known of this man than is stated here; cf. Münzer, *RE* s.v. Caelius 15. For the transmitted Cloelius as the correct form of the name, cf. Wiseman 1967; Shackleton Bailey 1992, 14.

occurrence, the point that is investigated first and most fully, what was the motive of the offense, this, in a case of parricide, Erucius does not think needs to be investigated. As regards this crime, gentlemen, even when many motives appear to converge in one place and to be consistent with each other, it is nonetheless not believed without due consideration, the matter is not decided by mere conjecture, no unreliable witness is listened to, nor is the case judged by the accuser's ability. It must be shown not only that many crimes were previously committed and the defendant's life was utterly depraved, but also his unparalleled criminality, and not that alone but also the height of frenzy and madness. But even if all this is proven, unmistakable traces of the crime must be found: where, how, by what agents, and at what time the evil deed was committed. And unless these proofs are many and evident, an act so criminal, so appalling, and so wicked surely cannot be believed. For the power of human feeling is great; the ties of blood are strong; nature itself cries out against such suspicions; it is undoubtedly an unnatural and monstrous phenomenon, that a being of human form and figure should exist who so far surpasses the beasts in savagery as to have most outrageously deprived of the light of day those thanks to whom he has seen this sweet light, whereas even the beasts are united among themselves by the ties of birth and rearing and by nature itself.

Not many years ago, it is said, a certain Titus Cloelius of Tarracina, a well-known man, went to bed after supper in the same room as his two adolescent sons, and was found in the morning with his throat cut.[54] As no slave or

CICERO

vus quisquam reperiretur[56] neque liber ad quem ea suspicio pertineret, id aetatis autem duo filii propter cubantes ne sensisse quidem se dicerent, nomina filiorum de parricidio delata sunt. Quid poterat tam esse[57] suspiciosum aut tam inauditum?[58] Neutrumne sensisse? Ausum autem esse quemquam se in id conclave committere eo potissimum tempore cum ibidem essent duo adulescentes filii qui et sentire et defendere facile possent? Erat porro
65 nemo in quem ea suspicio conveniret. Tamen, cum planum iudicibus esset factum aperto ostio dormientes eos repertos esse, iudicio absoluti adulescentes et suspicione omni liberati sunt. Nemo enim putabat quemquam esse qui, cum omnia divina atque humana iura scelere nefario polluisset, somnum statim capere potuisset,[59] propterea quod qui tantum facinus commiserunt non modo sine cura quiescere sed ne spirare quidem sine metu possunt.
66 Videtisne quos nobis poetae tradiderunt patris ulciscendi causa supplicium de matre sumpsisse, cum praesertim deorum immortalium iussis atque oraculis id fecisse dicantur, tamen ut eos agitent Furiae neque consistere umquam patiantur, quod ne pii quidem sine scelere esse potuerunt? Sic se res habet, iudices: magnam vim, magnam necessitatem, magnam possidet religionem paternus maternusque sanguis; ex quo si qua macula concepta est, non modo elui[60] non potest verum usque eo permanat ad animum ut summus furor atque amentia consequatur.
67 Nolite enim putare, quemadmodum in fabulis saepenu-

---

[56] reperiebatur: *corr. Angelius* est V: sane $A\pi\phi$: satis est $\sigma\chi\psi$ [57] tam esse *Gruter*: sā   [58] aut tam inauditum *Busche*: autem Ω [59] potuisse: *corr. edd. Ven. et Rom.*
[60] elui *Victorius*: levi *vel* leni Ω

free man was found on whom suspicion might have fallen, but at that time the two sons who slept nearby declared that they had not even noticed anything, the sons were indicted for parricide. What could be so suspicious or unheard of? For neither of them to have noticed anything? For someone to have dared to venture into that room at the very time when the two adolescent sons were there, who could easily have seen the crime and offered resistance? Moreover, there was no one who might have been reasonably suspected. However, when it was proven to the judges that they had been found asleep when the door was opened, the young men were acquitted and cleared of all suspicion. In fact, no one thought there was any man who could have gone to sleep immediately after he had violated all laws divine and human by an impious crime, because those who have committed so great a crime are not only unable to rest peacefully, but cannot even breathe without fear.

Do you not know that those sons who, as the poets have handed down to us, exacted punishment on their mother to avenge their father, even though they are said to have done this in obedience to the commands and oracles of the immortal gods, were nonetheless hounded by the Furies and never allowed to rest, because they could not even fulfill their duty without committing a crime? For this is the case, gentlemen: the blood of a father and mother has great power, restraining force, and sanctity; from this if a stain has been produced, it not only cannot be washed out, but it penetrates even to the heart, to be succeeded by the height of frenzy and madness. For do not suppose, as you often see in plays, that those who have committed any

mero videtis, eos qui aliquid impie scelerateque commiserunt agitari et perterreri Furiarum taedis ardentibus. Sua quemque fraus et suus terror maxime vexat, suum quemque scelus agitat amentiaque adficit, suae malae cogitationes conscientiaeque animi terrent; hae sunt impiis assiduae domesticaeque Furiae quae dies noctesque parentium poenas a consceleratissimis filiis repetant.

68 Haec magnitudo malefici facit ut, nisi paene manifestum parricidium proferatur, credibile non sit: nisi turpis adulescentia, nisi omnibus flagitiis vita inquinata, nisi sumptus effusi cum probro atque dedecore, nisi prorupta audacia, nisi tanta temeritas ut non procul abhorreat ab insania. Accedat huc oportet odium parentis, animadversionis paternae metus, amici improbi, servi conscii, tempus idoneum, locus opportune captus ad eam rem; paene dicam, respersas manus sanguine paterno iudices videant oportet, si tantum facinus, tam immane, tam acerbum credituri sunt.

69 Quare hoc quo minus est credibile, nisi ostenditur, eo magis est, si convincitur, vindicandum. Itaque cum multis ex rebus intellegi potest maiores nostros non modo armis plus quam ceteras nationes verum etiam consilio sapientiaque potuisse, tum ex hac re vel maxime quod in impios singulare supplicium invenerunt. Qua in re quantum pru-

---

55 A sophisticated argument, assuming (again) some knowledge of the theater on the part of the jurors. They may have known plays depicting Alcmaeon driven mad in the aftermath of his matricide, a subject of plays by Ennius and Accius (vv. 16–31 J. = *FRL* 12–14 and pp. 228–30 Dangel, respectively). (Orestes' madness, depicted in Aeschylus' *Eumenides*, is not known to have been dramatized at Rome by this date.) Cicero's psychological

impious and wicked act are harassed and terrified by the blazing torches of the Furies. It is their own evil deed, their own terror that most torments them; each of them is harassed and driven to madness by his own crime; his own evil thoughts and the stings of conscience terrify him. These are the unremitting personal Furies which, day and night, claim the parents' expiation from their wicked children.[55] It is owing to the enormity of the crime that, unless an act of parricide is produced [in court] that is beyond a doubt, it is incredible. Unless the suspect's youth has been disgraceful, his life stained with shameful acts of every kind, his expenditures lavish and accompanied by shame and disgrace, his audacity unrestrained, his rashness so extreme as to be not far removed from madness; to this should be added hatred on his father's part, the fear of paternal punishment, reprobates as friends, slaves as accomplices, a favorable opportunity, a place suitably chosen for the purpose—I would almost say that the jury must see his hands sprinkled with his father's blood, if they are to believe a crime so great, so monstrous, and so cruel. 68

This is the reason why, the less credible parricide is, unless it is demonstrated, the more severely it should be punished, if it is proven. And so, while from many other things we can understand that our ancestors have surpassed other nations, not only in arms, but also in counsel and wisdom, this is especially shown by the fact that they devised a unique punishment for the violators of the parental bond. In this matter, consider how far they excelled 69

---

reinterpretation of the parricide's madness is indebted to Aeschines, *Against Timarchus* 190–91; cf. Weische 1972, 24–25. He returns to the theme at *Pis.* 46 and *Leg.* 1.40.

dentia praestiterint iis qui apud ceteros sapientissimi fuisse dicuntur considerate. Prudentissima civitas Atheniensium, dum ea rerum potita est, fuisse traditur; eius porro civitatis sapientissimum Solonem dicunt fuisse, eum qui leges quibus hodie quoque utuntur scripserit. Is cum interrogaretur cur nullum supplicium constituisset in eum qui parentem necasset, respondit se id neminem facturum putasse. Sapienter fecisse dicitur, cum de eo nihil sanxerit quod antea commissum non erat, ne non tam prohibere quam admonere videretur. Quanto nostri maiores sapientius! Qui cum intellegerent nihil esse tam sanctum quod non aliquando violaret audacia, supplicium in parricidas singulare excogitaverunt ut, quos natura ipsa retinere in officio non potuisset, ii[61] magnitudine poenae a maleficio summoverentur.

Insui voluerunt in culleum vivos atque ita in flumen deici. O singularem sapientiam, iudices! Nonne videntur hunc hominem ex rerum natura sustulisse et eripuisse cui repente caelum, solem, aquam terramque ademerint ut, qui eum necasset unde ipse natus esset, careret iis rebus omnibus ex quibus omnia nata esse dicuntur? Noluerunt feris corpus obicere ne bestiis quoque quae tantum scelus attigissent immanioribus uteremur; non sic nudos in flumen deicere ne, cum delati essent in mare, ‹mare›[62] ipsum polluerent quo cetera quae violata sunt expiari putan-

---

[61] ii *Naugerius*: in *V*: *om. cett.*
[62] *add. Richter*

---

[56] This is overstated; most of Solon's laws had by now been replaced or amended.
[57] Cf. §63.

in sagacity those who are said to have been the wisest men of other nations. According to tradition, while it possessed the hegemony, Athens was the most sagacious of states; moreover, the wisest of its citizens is said to have been Solon, the man who drafted the laws which are still in force among them at the present day.[56] When he was asked why he had not fixed a punishment for a man who had killed his father, he answered that he thought no one would do this. He is said to have acted wisely in not appointing any penalty for a crime which had not previously been committed, for fear he might appear to suggest rather than prevent it. How much wiser were our ancestors! Since they understood that nothing was so sacred that it might not some day be violated by an act of audacity, they thought up a unique punishment for parricides, in order, by the severity of the punishment, to deter from crime those whom nature alone had been unable to keep within the bounds of duty.

It was their [the ancestors'] will that they [parricides] should be sewn alive into a sack, and then thrown into a river. A unique piece of wisdom, gentlemen! Do they not seem to have removed and torn this man out of the natural world, when they suddenly deprived him of the sky, the sun, water, and earth, so that one who had killed him to whom he owed his birth might be without all those elements from which all things are said to have been born? They did not want to throw the body to wild beasts, lest we find the beasts, too, more savage for having come in contact with such an offense;[57] they did not want to throw such men, simply naked, into a river, for fear that, carried down into the sea, they might pollute the very sea by which all other polluted things are thought to be cleansed;

tur; denique nihil tam vile neque tam vulgare est cuius partem ullam reliquerint. Etenim quid tam est commune quam spiritus vivis, terra mortuis, mare fluctuantibus, litus eiectis? Ita vivunt, dum possunt, ut ducere animam de caelo non queant, ita moriuntur ut eorum ossa terra non tangat, ita iactantur fluctibus ut numquam alluantur,[63] ita postremo eiciuntur ut ne ad saxa quidem mortui conquiescant. Tanti malefici crimen, cui maleficio tam insigne supplicium est constitutum, probare te, Eruci, censes posse talibus viris, si ne causam quidem malefici protuleris? Si hunc apud bonorum emptores ipsos accusares eique iudicio Chrysogonus praeesset, tamen diligentius paratiusque venisses. Utrum quid agatur non vides, an apud quos agatur? Agitur de parricidio, quod sine multis causis suscipi non potest; apud homines autem prudentissimos agitur, qui intellegunt neminem ne minimum quidem maleficium sine causa admittere.

Esto, causam proferre non potes. tametsi statim vicisse debeo, tamen de meo iure decedam et tibi quod in alia causa non concederem in hac concedam fretus huius innocentia. Non quaero abs te quare patrem Sex. Roscius occiderit, quaero quomodo occiderit. Ita quaero abs te, C. Eruci, quomodo, et sic tecum agam ut meo[64] loco vel

[63] *Cic. Orat. 107*: abluantur Ω
[64] in eo: *corr. Madvig*

---

[58] The famous passage about the parricide's punishment, relating it to the four elements (the sun being a proxy for fire). Cicero later cites it, with slight embarrassment over the storm of applause that it roused (*Orat.* 107).

in a word, there is nothing so cheap or common that they left them any share in it. For what is so common as breath to the living, earth to the dead, the sea to those tossed by the waves, the shore to those cast up by the sea? They live, while they can, without being able to draw breath from heaven; they die without earth coming in contact with their bones; they are tossed by the waves without ever being cleansed by washing; lastly, they are finally cast ashore without being able, after death, to find rest even on the rocks.[58] Do you think, Erucius, that you can prove a charge of such a crime, for which so unique a punishment has been imposed, to men such as these, if you have not even cited a motive for the crime? If you were accusing my client before the very purchasers of his property, and Chrysogonus were presiding at the trial, you should nevertheless have come more carefully prepared.[59] Do you not see what issue is being tried, or before what men? It is a trial for parricide, which no one attempts to commit without many motives; it is pleaded before men of the greatest shrewdness, who understand that no one commits even the most trifling misdemeanor without a motive.

Very well; you cannot adduce a motive. Although I ought already to have won my case, I will step back from my right, and will make a concession to you in this case, which I would not make in any other, so convinced am I of my client's innocence. I do not ask you to say why Sextus Roscius killed his father, I ask you how he killed him. I ask you how, Gaius Erucius, and will deal with you on the terms that, though it is my turn to speak, I give you permis-

---

[59] Cf. §82, where Cicero accuses Erucius of lifting part of his speech from another case (for lack of material).

respondendi vel interpellandi tibi potestatem faciam vel etiam, si quid voles, interrogandi. Quomodo occidit? Ipse percussit an aliis occidendum dedit? Si ipsum arguis, Romae non fuit; si per alios fecisse dicis, quaero: quos?[65] Servosne an liberos? ⟨Si liberos⟩,[66] quos homines? Indidemne Ameria an hosce ex urbe sicarios? Si Ameria, qui sunt ii? Cur non nominantur? Si Roma,[67] unde eos noverat Roscius, qui Romam multis annis non venit neque umquam plus triduo fuit? Ubi eos convenit? Qui collocutus[68] est? Quomodo persuasit? "Pretium dedit": cui dedit? Per quem dedit? Unde aut quantum dedit? Nonne his vestigiis ad caput malefici perveniri solet? Et simul tibi in mentem veniat facito quemadmodum vitam huiusce depinxeris: hunc hominem ferum atque agrestem fuisse, numquam cum homine quoquam collocutum esse, numquam in oppido constitisse. Qua in re praetereo illud quod mihi maximo argumento ad huius innocentiam poterat esse, in rusticis moribus, in victu arido, in hac horrida incultaque vita istius modi maleficia gigni non solere. Ut non omnem frugem neque arborem in omni agro reperire possis, sic non omne facinus in omni vita nascitur. In urbe luxuries creatur, ex luxuria exsistat avaritia necesse est, ex avaritia

[65] quos V: *om. cett.*
[66] si liberos *add. Madvig*
[67] Romae: *corr. Stephanus*
[68] qui collocutus *Krueger*: quicum locutus Ω

[60] Here Cicero capitalizes on his study of dialectic: he divides the category into slaves and free men and examines and rejects both possibilities.

[61] Cicero now turns Erucius' complaints about Roscius' anti-

sion to reply or interrupt or even ask questions, if you wish. How did he kill him? Did he strike the blow himself, or entrust the task to others? If you maintain that he did it himself, he was not in Rome; if you say that he acted through others, I ask: who were they? Slaves or free men?[60] If free men, who are they? From the same place, Ameria, or some of these assassins from the city? If from Ameria, who are they? Why are their names not given? If from Rome, how did Roscius, who for many years did not come to Rome and never stayed there more than three days, make their acquaintance?[61] Where did he meet them? How did he get an interview with them? How did he persuade them? "He gave them a bribe." To whom, and through whom, did he give it? Where did the money come from, and how much was it? Is it not by following such tracks that the origin of the crime is usually reached? And at the same time call to mind how you described my client's life: you said that he was a savage and a boor, that he never talked to anyone, that he had never stayed in town [i.e., Ameria]. In this connection, I pass over what might have been a very strong argument for me in favor of his innocence—that such rustic manners, frugal living, a rough and uncivilized life do not generally give birth to such misdeeds.[62] As you could not find every kind of crop or tree on every soil, so every kind of life does not produce every crime. The city creates luxury, from which avarice inevitably springs, while from avarice audacity breaks

---

social nature (§52) into an argument against his client's involvement with the murder, a move prepared at §39.

[62] Not really passed over, the point was raised at §39 and will be immediately elaborated here.

erumpat audacia, inde omnia scelera ac maleficia gignuntur. Vita autem haec rustica, quam tu agrestem vocas, parsimoniae, diligentiae, iustitiae magistra est.

76 Verum haec missa facio; illud quaero: is homo ⟨qui⟩,[69] ut tute dicis, numquam inter homines fuerit, per quos homines hoc tantum facinus, tam occultum, absens praesertim, conficere potuerit? Multa sunt falsa, iudices, quae tamen argui suspiciose possunt; in his rebus si suspicio reperta erit, culpam inesse concedam. Romae Sex. Roscius occiditur cum in agro Amerino esset filius. Litteras, credo, misit alicui sicario qui Romae noverat neminem. "Arcessivit aliquem." Quem aut[70] quando? "Nuntium misit." Quem aut ad quem? "Pretio, gratia, spe, promissis induxit aliquem." Nihil horum ne confingi quidem potest; et tamen causa de parricidio dicitur.

77 Reliquum est ut per servos id admiserit. O di immortales, rem miseram et calamitosam! Quod in tali crimine quod innocenti saluti solet esse, ut servos in quaestionem polliceatur,[71] id Sex. Roscio facere non licet? Vos qui hunc accusatis omnes eius servos habetis; unus puer victus cotidiani administer ex tanta familia Sex. Roscio relictus non est. Te nunc appello, P. Scipio, te, ⟨M.⟩[72] Metelle: vobis

[69] *add.* ψ^2
[70] quem aut *Prisc. GL 2:534.25*: aut V: at *cett.*
[71] -antur ω: *corr. Sylvius*
[72] *add. Krause*

forth, the source of all crimes and misdeeds. On the other hand, this country life, which you call boorish, teaches thrift, carefulness, and justice.[63]

But I leave these reflections aside. I put this question: this man, who, as you yourself say, never mixed among men, by whose help was he able to perpetrate so great a crime, one so well concealed, especially in his absence? An accusation is often false, gentlemen, but yet can be argued in such a way as to give rise to suspicion; in our circumstances, if anything suspicious is found, I will admit that there is guilt. Sextus Roscius was killed at Rome when his son was in the territory of Ameria. I suppose he, who knew nobody in Rome, sent a letter to some assassin. "He sent for someone." Whom or when? "He sent a messenger." Whom or to whom? "He persuaded someone by a bribe, by his influence, by raising hopes, and by promises." None of these can even be fabricated, and yet a case of parricide is being pleaded.

There remains the possibility that he committed the crime by the agency of slaves. O immortal gods, what a misfortune! What a calamity! Is Sextus Roscius not permitted to do what is generally the salvation of an innocent man in an accusation of this kind—to offer his slaves for questioning?[64] You who are accusing my client have possession of all his slaves; out of so numerous a household, not a single boy has been left to him to attend to his daily meals. I now call upon you, Publius Scipio, and you, Mar-

[63] For Cicero's exploitation of town/country stereotypes in the speech, cf. Benferhat 2003–2004; Blandenet 2017.

[64] Slaves were required to give evidence under torture; cf. Mommsen 1899, 416–18; Greenidge 1901, 479–80.

advocatis, vobis agentibus aliquotiens duos servos paternos in quaestionem ab adversariis Sex. Roscius postulavit; meministisne T. Roscium[73] recusare? Quid? Ii servi ubi sunt? Chrysogonum, iudices, sectantur; apud eum sunt in honore et in pretio. Etiamnunc ut ex iis quaeratur ego postulo, hic orat atque obsecrat. Quid facitis? Cur recusatis? Dubitate etiamnunc, iudices, si potestis, a quo sit Sex. Roscius occisus, ab eone qui propter illius mortem in egestate et insidiis versatur, cui ne quaerendi quidem de morte patris potestas permittitur, an ab iis qui quaestionem fugitant, bona possident, in caede atque ex caede vivunt. Omnia, iudices, in hac causa sunt misera atque indigna; tamen hoc nihil neque acerbius neque iniquius proferri potest: mortis paternae de servis paternis quaestionem habere filio non licet! Ne tam diu quidem dominus erit in suos dum ex iis de patris morte quaeratur? Veniam, neque ita multo post, ad hunc locum; nam hoc totum ad Roscios pertinet, de quorum audacia tum me dicturum pollicitus sum cum Eruci crimina diluissem.

79   Nunc, Eruci, ad te venio. Conveniat mihi tecum necesse est, si ad hunc maleficium istud pertinet, aut ipsum sua manu fecisse, id quod negas, aut per aliquos liberos

---

[73] meministisne t. roscium *Stephanus*: meministine t. rosci Ω

[65] This P. Scipio may be P. Cornelius Scipio Nasica (pr. 93), one of whose sons was adopted by the Caecilii Metelli, a sign of strong ties. If the praenomen is correctly restored, our Metellus may be the son of C. Metellus Caprarius and thus cousin of Roscius' protector, Caecilia Metella; he later served as praetor in 69. Cf. *MRR* 2:14 and 131–32; Münzer, *RE* s.v. Cornelius 351, Caecilius 78.

cus Metellus:[65] when you were supporting him and acting on his behalf, Sextus Roscius several times demanded two of his father's slaves from his adversaries for questioning. Do you not remember that Titus Roscius refused?[66] Well? Where are those slaves? Gentlemen, they attend upon Chrysogonus; at his house they are highly esteemed and valued. Even now, I demand that they be put to questioning, my client begs and entreats you. What will you do? Why do you refuse? Hesitate still, gentlemen, if you can, to decide by whom Sextus Roscius was killed; whether it was by him who, owing to his death, finds himself in poverty and in the midst of plots, who is not even allowed the opportunity of making an inquiry into his father's death, or whether it was those who repeatedly shirk any inquiry, are in possession of his property, who live in murder and by murder. Everything in this case, gentlemen, is pitiable and outrageous, but nothing can be cited that is harsher or more unfair than this—that a son should not be allowed to submit his father's slaves to questioning in regard to his father's death. Is he not even to remain master of his own slaves long enough for them to be questioned about his father's death? I will shortly deal with this topic; for this entire matter has to do with the [Titi] Roscii, and I promised to speak of their audacity as soon as I had refuted Erucius' charges.

78

Now, Erucius, I come to you. You and I must agree that, if my client is connected with this crime, he either committed it with his own hand, which you deny, or by the agency of some free men or slaves. Free men? You are

79

[66] That is, T. Roscius Magnus refused in his capacity as Chrysogonus' administrator; cf. §23.

189

aut servos. Liberosne? Quos neque ut convenire[74] potuerit neque qua ratione inducere neque ubi neque per quos neque qua spe aut quo pretio potes ostendere. Ego contra ostendo non modo nihil eorum fecisse Sex. Roscium sed ne potuisse quidem facere, quod neque Romae multis annis fuerit neque de praediis umquam temere discesserit. Restare tibi videbatur servorum nomen, quo quasi in portum reiectus a ceteris suspicionibus confugere posses; ubi scopulum offendis eiusmodi ut non modo ab hoc crimen resilire videas verum omnem suspicionem in vosmet ipsos recidere intellegas. Quid ergo est quo tandem[75] accusator inopia argumentorum confugerit? "Eiusmodi tempus erat" inquit "ut homines vulgo impune occiderentur; quare hoc tu propter multitudinem sicariorum nullo negotio facere potuisti." Interim mihi videris, Eruci, una mercede duas res assequi velle, nos iudicio perfundere, accusare autem eos ipsos a quibus mercedem accepisti. Quid ais? Vulgo occidebantur? Per quos et a quibus? Nonne cogitas te a sectoribus huc adductum esse? Quid postea? Nescimus[76] per ista tempora eosdem fere sectores fuisse collorum et bonorum? Ii denique qui tum armati dies noctesque concursabant, qui Romae erant assidui, qui omni tempore in praeda et sanguine versabantur, Sex. Roscio temporis illius acerbitatem iniquitatemque obicient et illam sicariorum multitudinem, in qua ipsi duces

[74] -veniret: *corr. ed. Guar.*   [75] tamen V
[76] an nescimus *Vinkelsteyn*

[67] A pun on *sector*, variously translated as "brokers" or "purchasers of property" (of the proscribed) but here "cutpurses"; for the term see on §16.

unable to show how he was able to meet them, by what means he persuaded them, where, by what agents, what expectations he raised, what bribe he offered. I, on the contrary, show that Sextus Roscius not only did not do, but could not have done, any of these things, seeing that for many years he had neither been in Rome nor had ever left his farm without good reason. It seemed to you that the only thing left was the category of slaves, to which, when driven from your other suspicions, you could take refuge as if to a harbor; but there you have struck upon such a rock that you not only see the charge rebound from my client, but also understand that every suspicion recoils upon yourselves. Well then, where has the accuser finally taken refuge for lack of arguments? "The times were such," he says, "that men were being killed with impunity as an ordinary occurrence; therefore, since there were so many assassins, you could have committed this crime without difficulty." Sometimes, Erucius, you seem to me to want to kill two birds with one stone, to flood us with litigation and to accuse those very persons from whom you received payment. What do you say? Men were being killed as an ordinary occurrence? Through whom and by whom? Do you not reflect that you were brought here by the purchasers of confiscated goods? What next? Do we not know that, during the times you mention, the same men were generally cutthroats and cutpurses?[67] Finally, shall these men, who were then running about armed night and day, who never left Rome, who were always engaged in plundering and murdering—shall they reproach Sextus Roscius with the cruelty and injustice of those times, and imagine that the crowd of assassins, of

ac principes erant, huic crimini putabunt fore, qui non modo Romae non fuit sed omnino quid Romae ageretur nescivit,[77] propterea quod ruri assiduus, quemadmodum tute confiteris, fuit?

82 Vereor ne aut molestus sim vobis, iudices, aut ne ingeniis vestris videar diffidere, si de tam perspicuis rebus diutius disseram. Eruci criminatio tota, ut arbitror, dissoluta est; nisi forte expectatis ut illa diluam quae de peculatu ac de eiusmodi rebus commenticiis inaudita nobis ante hoc tempus ac nova obiecit. Quae mihi iste visus est ex alia oratione declamare quam in alium reum commentaretur; ita neque ad crimen parricidi neque ad eum qui causam dicit pertinebant.[78] De quibus quoniam verbo arguit, verbo satis est negare. Si quid est quod ad testes reservet, ibi quoque nos, ut in ipsa causa, paratiores reperiet quam putabat.

83 Venio nunc eo quo me non cupiditas ducit sed fides. Nam si mihi liberet accusare, accusarem alios potius ex quibus possem crescere; quod certum est non facere dum utrumvis licebit. Is enim mihi videtur amplissimus qui sua virtute in altiorem locum pervenit, non qui ascendit per alterius incommodum et calamitatem. Desinamus[79] ali-

[77] nesciret: *corr. Madvig*   [78] -bat: *corr. Naugerius*
[79] ⟨sed⟩ desinamus *Lehmann*

---

[68] Embezzlement (*peculatus*) was self-enrichment with public funds and ordinarily applied to magistrates; cf. Gnoli 1979. Possibly it was claimed that Roscius had held back some of his patrimony, which had become state property as a result of the proscription.

[69] The prosecutor might hold some testimony or other evi-

which they themselves were the leaders and chiefs, will be a ground for accusing my client, who was not only not at Rome, but was entirely ignorant of what was going on at Rome, because, as you yourself admit, he always remained in the country?

I am afraid, gentlemen, of either boring you or appearing to distrust your intelligence, if I continue to discuss matters that are so obvious. Erucius' entire accusation, I think, has been refuted, unless perhaps you are waiting to hear me answer the charge of embezzlement[68] and such made-up accusations that he has brought, charges which are new and which we never heard of before today. He seemed to me to be rehearsing them from another speech, which he was preparing against another defendant, so little did they apply to the charge of parricide or to him who is on trial. But since he has argued them merely with his word, it is enough to deny them with a word. If he is keeping back anything for the witnesses, there, too, as in the case itself, he will find us better prepared than he expected.[69]

I now come to a matter to which I am led, not by my eagerness, but by loyalty [to my client]. For if prosecution were to my taste, I would rather accuse other persons, at whose expense I could increase my reputation; but I am resolved not to do this, as long as the choice of accusing or not is open to me. For that man seems to me most important who attains a higher position by his own merit, not the man who finds a means of rising in another's misfortune and disaster. Let us at last cease to examine idle

dence in reserve to take the defense by surprise; cf. Quint. *Inst.* 7.10.13; Guérin 2015, 203.

quando ea scrutari quae sunt inania; quaeramus ibi[80] maleficium ubi et est et inveniri potest; iam intelleges, Eruci, certum crimen quam multis suspicionibus coarguatur, tametsi neque omnia dicam et leviter unumquidque[81] tangam. Neque enim id facerem, nisi necesse esset, et id erit signi me invitum facere quod non persequar[82] longius quam salus huius et mea fides postulabit.

84   Causam tu nullam reperiebas in Sex. Roscio; at ego in T. Roscio reperio. Tecum enim mihi res est, T. Rosci, quoniam istic sedes ac te palam adversarium esse profiteris.[83] De Capitone post viderimus si, quemadmodum paratum esse audio, testis prodierit: tum alias quoque suas palmas cognoscet, de quibus me ne audisse quidem suspicatur. L. Cassius ille, quem populus Romanus verissimum et sapientissimum iudicem putabat, identidem in causis quaerere solebat "cui bono" fuisset. Sic vita hominum est ut ad maleficium nemo conetur sine spe atque emolumento 85 accedere. Hunc quaesitorem ac iudicem fugiebant atque horrebant ii quibus periculum creabatur ideo quod, tametsi veritatis erat amicus, tamen natura non tam propensus ad misericordiam quam applicatus[84] ad severitatem videbatur. Ego, quamquam praeest huic quaestioni vir et

---

[80] ubi: *corr.* σ²   [81] unumquodque: *corr. Wesenberg*
[82] prosequar: *corr. Lambinus*
[83] -tearis: *corr. ed. Rom. et Ven.*
[84] implicatus: *corr. Novák*

---

[70] That is, Magnus, whose presence in court was already signaled at §17. He was evidently acting as a junior prosecutor (*subscriptor*) in the case; cf. Guérin 2015, 100.

[71] A barely concealed attempt at witness intimidation; cf.

charges; let us seek the crime where it is and can be discovered. You will soon understand, Erucius, how many suspicious circumstances it takes to prove a genuine accusation, although I shall not mention all of them and shall touch upon each point lightly. And I would not even do that, unless it were necessary, and the proof that I am acting unwillingly will be the fact that I shall not go further than the safety of my client and my loyalty demand.

You could find no motive in Sextus Roscius, but I find one in Titus Roscius. It is you, Titus Roscius, with whom I have to deal, since you are sitting over there [on the accusers' bench], and openly avow yourself our opponent.[70] We will deal with Capito afterward, if, as I understand he is ready to do, he comes forward as a witness; he will then learn of other laurels of his, which he does not suspect that I have even heard of.[71] The illustrious Lucius Cassius, whom the Roman people used to regard as the most upright and wisest judge, was in the habit of asking repeatedly in trials, "who had profited by it?"[72] Human nature is such that no one attempts to commit a crime without the hope of profit. He was avoided and dreaded as a presiding judge and juror by those who were threatened by a criminal charge, because, although he was a friend of the truth, he appeared by nature not so much disposed to mercy as devoted to severity. Although a man is in charge of this

Schmitz 1985, 36. Cicero takes up the characterization of Capito as a "famous and experienced gladiator" who has many palms to his credit (§17).

[72] Lucius Cassius Longinus Ravilla (cos. 127, cens. 125), a severe judge, notably in the second trial of the Vestal Virgins for unchastity in the year 113 after their initial acquittal: *TLRR* 43.

contra audaciam fortissimus et ab innocentia clementissimus, tamen facile me pateretur vel illo ipso acerrimo iudice quaerente vel apud Cassianos iudices, quorum etiamnunc ii quibus causa dicenda est nomen ipsum reformidant, pro Sex. Roscio dicere. In hac enim causa cum viderent illos amplissimam pecuniam possidere, hunc in summa mendicitate esse, illud quidem non quaererent, cui bono fuisset, sed eo perspicuo[85] crimen et suspicionem potius ad praedam adiungerent quam ad egestatem. Quid si accedit eodem ut tenuis antea fueris? Quid si ut avarus? Quid si ut audax? Quid si ut illius qui occisus est inimicissimus? Num quaerenda ⟨causa⟩[86] quae te ad tantum facinus adduxerit? Quid ergo horum negari potest? Tenuitas hominis eiusmodi est ut dissimulari non queat atque eo magis eluceat quo magis occultatur. Avaritiam praefers qui societatem coieris de municipis cognatique fortunis cum alienissimo. Quam sis audax, ut alia obliviscar, hinc omnes intellegere potuerunt quod ex tota societate, hoc est ex tot sicariis, solus tu inventus es qui cum accusatoribus sederes atque os tuum non modo ostenderes sed etiam offerres. Inimicitias tibi fuisse cum Sex. Roscio et magnas rei familiaris controversias concedas necesse est. Restat, iudices, ut hoc dubitemus, uter potius Sex. Roscium occiderit, is ad quem morte eius divitiae venerint, an is ad quem mendicitas, is qui antea tenuis fuerit, an is qui postea factus sit

[85] perspicuum: *corr. Puteanus*
[86] *add. cod. Helmstad.*

[73] On M. Fannius, cf. on §11.
[74] "Cassian judges" were proverbially severe; cf. Otto 1890, 77 s.v. Cassius.

inquiry who is both courageous in the face of criminality and mild in regard to innocence,[73] I would nonetheless willingly consent to plead on behalf of Sextus Roscius even with that very keen judge himself presiding or before Cassian jurors, whose very name even now strikes defendants with terror.[74] For in this case, when they saw the accusers in possession of vast property and my client reduced to utter beggary, they would not inquire "who had profited by it," but, since that was obvious, they would connect the charge and the suspicion rather with the plunder than the poverty. What if, in addition, you were formerly poor? What if you were avaricious? What if you were audacious? What if you were the bitterest enemy of the man who was murdered? Need any other motive be sought, which drove you to this abominable crime? Can any of these facts be denied? A man's poverty is such that it cannot be concealed, and, the greater the efforts that are made to hide it, the more conspicuous it appears. You put your avarice on display, seeing that you have entered into a partnership with a perfect stranger concerning the fortune of a kinsman and fellow townsman. Not to mention other things, everyone could understand how audacious you are from the fact that, out of all the members of the partnership, in other words, out of all those assassins, you alone were recruited to sit among the accusers, and not only let us see your shameless face but even make a show of it. You must admit that enmity and serious property disputes existed between you and Sextus Roscius. The only thing that remains, gentlemen, is for us to consider which of the two is more likely to be the murderer of Sextus Roscius, he to whom this murder has brought wealth, or he to whom it has brought beggary; he who previously was poor, or he

egentissimus, is qui ardens avaritia feratur infestus in suos, an is qui semper ita vixerit ut quaestum nosset nullum, fructum autem eum solum quem labore peperisset, is qui omnium sectorum audacissimus sit, an is qui propter fori iudiciorumque insolentiam non modo subsellia verum etiam urbem ipsam reformidet, postremo, iudices, id quod ad rem mea sententia maxime pertinet, utrum inimicus potius an filius.

89 Haec tu, Eruci, tot et tanta si nanctus esses in reo, quam diu diceres! Quo te modo iactares! Tempus hercule te citius quam oratio deficeret. Etenim in singulis rebus eiusmodi materies est ut dies singulos possis consumere. Neque ego non possum; non enim tantum mihi derogo, tametsi nihil adrogo, ut te copiosius quam me putem posse dicere. Verum ego forsitan propter multitudinem patronorum in grege adnumerer, te pugna Cannensis accusatorem sat bonum fecit. Multos caesos non ad Trasimennum lacum sed ad Servilium vidimus. "Quis ibi non est
90 vulneratus ferro Phrygio?" Non necesse est omnes commemorare Curtios, Marios, denique Memmios[87] quos iam aetas a proeliis avocabat, postremo Priamum ipsum [se-

---

[87] memmios *Ursinus*: mammeos Ω: omnes eos *Martin*

---

[75] The battle of Cannae, fought in June 216, was the proverbial slaughter of Roman history; cf. Otto 1890, 72–73. An earlier defeat in the Hannibalic War at Lake Trasimennus (June 21 of 217) provides an analogue to the Servilian Cistern in Rome, where the heads of the proscribed were displayed (presumably after they became too numerous to be contained in Sulla's house); cf. Richardson 1992 s.v. Lacus Servilius; La Regina, *LTUR* s.v. Lacus Servilius.

who afterward was reduced to poverty; he who, inflamed by avarice, rushes to attack his own relatives, or he who has always lived such a life that he knew nothing about gain but only about the fruit that his own work produced; he who is the most audacious of all the brokers, or he who, owing to his inexperience of the forum and the courts, dreads not only the sight of the benches, but even the city itself; lastly, gentlemen—and this, in my opinion, is of the greatest relevance to the matter—one who was his enemy or his son.

If you, Erucius, had these arguments, so many and so weighty, as regards a defendant, at what length would you speak! How you would throw yourself about! You would run short of time, by Hercules, sooner than words. In fact, the material is so abundant that you might spend a whole day on each point. Not that I could not do the same; for, without making arrogant claims, I have not so poor an opinion of myself as to think you capable of speaking at greater length than I can. But perhaps, considering the large number of defending counsel, I may only be reckoned as one of a crowd, while the battle of Cannae has made you an adequate accuser. We have seen many slain, not near Lake Trasimennus, but at the Servilian Cistern.[75] "Who was not wounded there by Phrygian steel?"[76] There is no need to enumerate them all, the Curtii, the Marii, and lastly the Memmii, already withdrawn by age from the battles; last of all, Priam himself, Antistius, prohibited

---

[76] A verse from an unknown Ennian tragedy (312 J. = *FRL* 144), the words attributed by the Gronovian Scholiast to Ulysses when asked by Ajax why he has run from battle.

nem],[88] Antistium, quem non modo aetas sed etiam leges pugnare prohibebant. Iam quos nemo propter ignobilitatem nominat, sescenti sunt qui inter sicarios et de veneficiis accusabant; qui omnes, quod ad me attinet, vellem viverent. Nihil enim mali est canes ibi quam plurimos esse ubi permulti observandi multaque servanda sunt. Verum, ut fit, multa saepe imprudentibus imperatoribus vis belli ac turba molitur. Dum is in aliis rebus erat occupatus qui summam rerum administrabat, erant interea qui suis vulneribus mederentur; qui, tamquam si offusa rei publicae[89] sempiterna nox esset, ita ruebant in tenebris omniaque miscebant; a quibus miror ne quod iudiciorum esset vestigium, non subsellia quoque esse combusta; nam et accusatores et iudices sustulerunt. Hoc commodi est quod ita vixerunt ut testes omnes, si cuperent, interficere non possent; nam, dum hominum genus erit, qui accuset eos non deerit, dum civitas erit, iudicia fient. Verum, ut coepi dicere, et Erucius, haec si haberet in causa quae commemoravi, posset ea quamvis diu dicere, et ego, iudices, possum; sed in animo est, quemadmodum ante dixi, leviter transire ac tantummodo perstringere unam quamque rem ut omnes intellegant me non studio accusare sed officio defendere.

91

[88] *del. Madvig*
[89] rei publicae *Arusianus*: re p. Ω

[77] The Marian prosecutors mentioned here are not identifiable with any certainty; cf. Dyck 2010, ad loc. For P. Antistius, a rare example of an orator who improved his speaking style, cf. *Brut.* 226–27, with Charrier 2003, 83–84; in general *FRLO* 78

PRO ROSCIO AMERINO 90–91

from fighting, not only by his age, but also by the laws.[77] Further, there are hundreds whose name is never mentioned owing to their obscurity, who used to prosecute in cases of murder and poisoning. As far as I am concerned, I could wish that they were all living. For there is no harm in there being as many dogs as possible where a great many people have to be watched and many things guarded.[78] But, as happens, the violence and turmoil of war often set many events in motion that generals are unaware of. While he who was managing the whole state was occupied with other matters, there were some who in the meantime were attending to their own wounds; these people, as if eternal night had enveloped the republic, were rushing about in the darkness and throwing everything into confusion. I am surprised that they did not also burn the benches, so that there would be no trace left of the courts; for they eliminated both accusers and jurors. But fortunately they led such a life that they could not slay all the witnesses, even if they so desired; for as long as the human race exists, there will be no lack of men to accuse them; as long as the state lasts, trials will take place. But, as I was saying, if in his case Erucius had the facts I have mentioned, he would be able to speak on them as long as he pleased, and, gentlemen of the jury, I can do the same. But, as I said before, it is my intention to pass lightly over and only touch upon each matter, that everyone may understand that I am not making an accusation from inclination, but offering a defense out of duty.

91

(which our passage supplements). Cicero alludes again to the Remmian Law; cf. on §55.   [78] The analogy of prosecutors to guard dogs is taken up from §§56–57.

CICERO

92 Video igitur causas esse permultas quae istum impellerent; videamus nunc ecquae[90] facultas suscipiendi malefici fuerit. Ubi occisus est Sex. Roscius?—"Romae."—Quid? Tu, T. Rosci, ubi tunc eras?—"Romae. Verum quid ad rem? Et alii multi."—Quasi nunc id agatur quis ex tanta multitudine occiderit, ac non hoc quaeratur, eum qui Romae sit occisus utrum verisimilius sit ab eo esse occisum qui assiduus eo tempore Romae fuerit, an ab eo qui multis
93 annis Romam omnino non accesserit. Age nunc ceteras quoque facultates[91] consideremus. Erat tum multitudo sicariorum, id quod commemoravit Erucius, et homines impune occidebantur. Quid? Ea multitudo quae erat? Opinor aut eorum qui in bonis erant occupati aut eorum qui ab iis conducebantur ut aliquem occiderent. Si eos putas qui alienum appetebant, tu es in eo numero qui nostra pecunia dives es; sin eos quos qui leviore nomine appellant percussores vocant, quaere in cuius fide sint et clientela; mihi crede, aliquem de societate tua reperies; et, quicquid tu contra dixeris, id cum defensione nostra contendito; ita facillime causa Sex. Rosci cum tua conferetur.
94 Dices: "Quid postea, si Romae assiduus fui?" Respondebo: "At ego omnino non fui."—"Fateor me sectorem esse, verum et alii multi."—"At ego, ut tute arguis,

[90] et quae: *corr. Ursinus*
[91] quoque facultates *edd. Rom. et Ven.*: facultates quoque Ω

---

[79] Cicero takes up Erucius' claim quoted at §80 and subjects it to division (*diairesis*), as he had the modality of the murder; see on §74. This leads to the posing of a dilemma, on which see Craig 1993, 37–38.   [80] "Hit man" (*percussor*) was used as a euphemism for "assassin" (*sicarius*) and largely supplanted the lat-

I see, then, that there were many motives that might 92
have driven him. Let us now see whether he had any opportunity of committing the crime. Where was Sextus Roscius killed? "At Rome." Well, Titus Roscius, where were you at that time? "At Rome. But what has that to do with it? Many others were as well." As if the present question were to find out who, out of so great a number, committed the murder, and not rather whether it is more likely that one who was killed at Rome was killed by one who at the time was constantly in Rome, or by one who for many years had not gone to Rome at all. Come now, let us also 93
consider the other means. As Erucius mentioned, at that time there was a crowd of assassins, and men were being killed with impunity. Well, of whom was this crowd composed?[79] I imagine either of those who were occupied in buying properties or of those who were hired by them to murder somebody. If you think the criminals were those who coveted others' property, you are one of that number, you who are enriched by our wealth; but if you think they were those who are called by the milder name of hit men,[80] inquire under whose protection, whose clients they are, and trust me, you will find someone from your partnership. Whatever you may say to the contrary, compare it with my defense; in this way, it will be very easy to contrast the case of Sextus Roscius with your own. You will 94
say, "If I was constantly in Rome, what follows from that?" I shall reply, "But I was not there at all." "I confess that I am a broker, but so are many others." "But I, as you your-

ter, except in technical legal language, during the empire; cf. Adams 1973, 290n69; Thein 2017, 237n13, 239–43. On *sicarius* in our speech, cf. Cloud 1969, 271–76.

agricola et rusticus."—"Non continuo, si me in gregem sicariorum contuli, sum sicarius."—"At ego profecto, qui ne novi quidem quemquam sicarium, longe absum ab eiusmodi crimine." Permulta sunt quae dici possunt quare intellegatur summam tibi facultatem fuisse malefici suscipiendi; quae non modo idcirco praetereo quod te ipsum non libenter accuso verum eo magis etiam quod, si de illis caedibus velim commemorare quae tum factae sunt ista eadem ratione qua Sex. Roscius occisus est, vereor ne ad plures oratio mea pertinere videatur.

95 Videamus nunc strictim, sicut cetera, quae post mortem Sex. Rosci abs te, T. Rosci, facta sunt; quae ita aperta et manifesta sunt ut medius fidius, iudices, invitus ea dicam. Vereor enim, cuicuimodi[92] es, T.[93] Rosci, ne ita hunc videar voluisse servare ut tibi omnino non pepercerim. Cum hoc vereor et cupio tibi aliqua ex parte quod salva fide possim parcere, rursus immuto voluntatem meam; venit enim mihi in mentem oris tui. Tene, cum ceteri socii tui fugerent ac se occultarent, ut hoc iudicium non de illorum praeda sed de huius maleficio fieri videretur, potissimum tibi partes istas depoposcisse ut in iudicio versarere et sederes cum accusatore! Qua in re nihil aliud assequeris nisi ut ab omnibus mortalibus audacia tua cognoscatur
96 et impudentia. Occiso Sex. Roscio quis primus Ameriam

[92] *Priscian*: quidquidmodi Ω
[93] es t. *edd.*: est Ω

---

[81] There is a similar move, turning away from a topic that might seem to implicate others, at fr. orat. 5 F 36 Cr.-D.

[82] Cicero tendentiously creates a motive for the absence of

self argue, am a farmer and a rustic." "If I have mixed with a crowd of assassins, it does not follow at once that I am an assassin." "But surely I, who do not even know any assassin, am far beyond the reach of such an accusation." There are a great many things that can be said to make it clear that you had the greatest means of committing this crime; but I pass over them, not only because I take no pleasure in accusing you, but more so because, if I wished to speak of the murders that were committed then the same way as Sextus Roscius was killed, I fear that my words would seem to be aimed at a number of people.[81]

Let us now examine—cursorily, like the other points— your deeds, Titus Roscius, after Sextus Roscius' death; they are so obvious and palpable, that, by divine faith, gentlemen, I speak of them unwillingly. For I am afraid that, whatever kind of man you are, Titus Roscius, I may be thought to have desired to save my client without sparing you at all. But when I have this fear and desire to spare you to some extent as far as I can without compromising my pledge [to my client], I again change my mind, for I remember your brazenness. To think that you, when the rest of your partners took flight and kept themselves hidden, so that this trial might not seem to be about their plunder, but my client's crime[82]—to think that you should have claimed this role in particular for yourself, that you should appear in court and take a seat by the accuser! By this you accomplish nothing else than to make your audacity and impudence recognized by everyone. After Sextus Roscius was killed, who first brought the news to Ameria?

Chrysogonus and Capito from the courtroom and simultaneously reframes the question at issue in the trial.

nuntiat? Mallius Glaucia, quem iam antea nominavi, tuus cliens et familiaris. Quid attinuit eum potissimum nuntiare quod, si nullum iam ante consilium de morte ac de bonis eius inieras nullamque societatem neque sceleris neque praemi cum homine ullo coieras, ad te minime omnium pertinebat?—"Sua sponte Mallius nuntiat."— Quid, quaeso,[94] eius intererat? An, cum Ameriam non huiusce rei causa venisset, casu accidit ut id quod Romae audierat primus nuntiaret? Cuius rei causa venerat Ameriam? "Non possum" inquit "divinare." Eo rem iam adducam ut nihil divinatione opus sit. Qua ratione ⟨T.⟩[95] Roscio Capitoni primo[96] nuntiavit? Cum Ameriae Sex. Rosci domus uxor liberique essent, cum tot propinqui cognatique optime convenientes, qua ratione factum est ut iste tuus cliens, sceleris tui nuntius, T. Roscio Capitoni potissimum nuntiaret? Occisus est a cena rediens; nondum lucebat 97 cum Ameriae scitum est. Quid hic incredibilis cursus, quid haec tanta celeritas festinatioque significat? Non quaero quis percusserit; nihil est, Glaucia, quod metuas; non excutio te, si quid forte ferri habuisti, non scrutor; nihil ad me arbitror pertinere; quoniam cuius consilio occisus sit invenio, cuius manu sit percussus non laboro. Unum hoc sumo quod mihi apertum tuum scelus resque manifesta dat: ubi aut unde audivit Glaucia? Qui tam cito scivit? Fac

---

[94] quasi: *corr. Angelius*   [95] *suppl. Richter*
[96] primum: *corr. Richter*

---

[83] Cf. §19, where he was mentioned with the same characterization.   [84] But if he really planned a prosecution, establishing and prosecuting the agent could be a step toward securing the conviction of the mastermind, as when in the year 74, A. Cluen-

Mallius Glaucia, whom I have mentioned before, your client and friend.[83] What was the point for him in particular to announce a fact that, had you not previously hatched a plot concerning his death and goods and formed a partnership with anyone in the crime and its reward, had less to do with you than anyone else? "Mallius brought the news of his own accord." What, I ask, had it to do with him? Or, if he had not come to Ameria for this purpose, was it by accident that he was the first to announce what he had heard in Rome? For what reason did he come to Ameria? "I cannot guess," he says. I will soon bring the matter to such a point that there will be no need of guessing. For what reason did he first announce it to Titus Roscius Capito? Though Sextus Roscius had a house, a wife, and children at Ameria, though he had so many relatives and kinsmen with whom he was on the best of terms, for what reason did it come about that this man, your client, who brought the news of your crime, announced it to Titus Roscius Capito in particular? He was killed when returning from supper; before daybreak it was known at Ameria. What is the meaning of this incredibly rapid journey, this great speed and haste? I do not ask who struck the blow; you have nothing to fear, Glaucia; I am not investigating you; I do not search you to see if you had any weapon; I do not think it has anything to do with me; since I am seeking to discover who planned the murder, I do not care whose hand struck the blow.[84] I bring forward this one point, which your obvious crime and the clear facts supply me: where and from whom did Glaucia hear of it? How

tius Habitus prosecuted three men in succession for attempting to murder him (*TLRR* 147–49).

audisse statim; quae res eum nocte una tantum itineris contendere coegit? Quae necessitas eum tanta premebat ut, si sua sponte iter Ameriam faceret, id temporis Roma proficisceretur, nullam partem noctis requiesceret?

98 Etiamne in tam perspicuis rebus argumentatio quaerenda aut coniectura capienda est?[97] Nonne vobis haec quae audistis cernere oculis videmini, iudices? Non illum miserum, ignarum casus sui redeuntem a cena videtis, non positas insidias, non impetum repentinum? Non versatur ante oculos vobis in caede Glaucia? Non adest iste T. Roscius? Non suis manibus in curru collocat Automedontem illum, sui sceleris acerbissimi nefariaeque victoriae nuntium? Non orat ut eam noctem pervigilet, ut honoris sui 99 causa laboret, ut Capitoni quam primum nuntiet? Quid erat quod Capitonem primum scire vellet? Nescio, nisi hoc video, Capitonem in his bonis esse socium; de tribus et decem fundis tres nobilissimos fundos eum video pos100 sidere. Audio praeterea non hanc suspicionem nunc primum in Capitonem conferri; multas esse infames eius[98] palmas, hanc primam esse tamen lemniscatam quae Roma ei[99] deferatur; nullum modum esse hominis occidendi quo ille non aliquot occiderit, multos ferro, multos veneno. Habeo etiam dicere quem contra morem maiorum mino-

[97] sit: *corr. Madvig*   [98] infames eius *Gruter*: infamius Ω
[99] Roma ei *Ernesti*: Romae Ω

---

[85] Automedon, Achilles' charioteer, was a byword for speed; cf. Juv. 1.60–61.
[86] With "victory" Cicero conjures the picture of Magnus as a gladiator painted at §17; this is then taken up with the reference to Capito's "palms," including one "adorned with ribbons" (*lemniscatam*) as a mark of special distinction at §100.

did he come to know it so quickly? Suppose that he heard of it at once; what forced him to make so long a journey in a hurry in a single night? What great necessity was pressing him, if he was going to Ameria of his own accord, to set out from Rome at that hour, and rest for no part of the night?

When the facts are so evident, is there need to seek for arguments or grasp at conjectures? Does it not seem to you, gentlemen, that you can see with your eyes what you have heard? Do you not see that unfortunate man returning from supper, unsuspecting of his fate? Do you not see the ambush laid, the sudden attack? Is not Glaucia before your eyes stalking amid the gore? Is not this Titus Roscius present? Does he not with his own hands place that Automedon in the chariot,[85] the messenger of his most heinous crime and impious victory?[86] Does he not beg him to spend a sleepless night, to exert himself out of personal regard for him, to carry the news to Capito without delay? What was his reason for wishing that Capito should be the first to know it? I do not know, but I notice this point, that Capito is a partner in the property of Roscius; I know that out of thirteen farms he is in possession of three of the finest. Further, I have heard that this is not the first time that Capito has been suspected of such actions, that he possesses a number of palms for infamous victories, but this is the first one adorned with ribbons to be brought to him from Rome; there is no method of murder which he has not employed for killing a certain number of men, many by the dagger, many by poison.[87] I can even tell of

---

[87] He thus names the two most widespread methods that gave their name to Sulla's law dealing with murder; cf. Cloud 1968.

rem annis LX de ponte in Tiberim deiecerit. Quae,[100] si prodierit atque adeo cum prodierit—scio enim proditurum esse—audiet. Veniat modo, explicet suum volumen illud quod ei planum facere possum Erucium conscripsisse; quod aiunt illum Sex. Roscio intentasse et minitatum[101] esse se omnia illa pro testimonio esse dicturum. O praeclarum testem, iudices! O gravitatem dignam exspectatione! O vitam honestam atque eiusmodi ut libentibus animis ad eius testimonium vestrum ius iurandum accommodetis! Profecto non tam perspicue nos istorum[102] maleficia videremus, nisi ipsos caecos redderet cupiditas et avaritia et audacia. Alter ex ipsa caede volucrem nuntium Ameriam ad socium atque magistrum suum misit ut, si dissimulare omnes cuperent se scire ad quem maleficium pertineret, tamen ipse apertum suum scelus ante omnium oculos poneret. Alter, si dis immortalibus placet, testimonium etiam in Sex. Roscium dicturus est; quasi vero id nunc agatur utrum is quod dixerit credendum ac non[103] quod fecerit vindicandum sit! Itaque more maiorum comparatum est ut[104] in minimis rebus homines amplissimi testimonium de sua re non dicerent. Africanus, qui suo

---

[100] qui: *corr. Naugerius*   [101] meditatum: *corr. Hotoman*
[102] nos istorum ψ^2: istorum *vel* nonistorum Ω
[103] ac non *Jeep*: an Ω   [104] ut *vel Havet*

---

[88] A grim joke. Cicero alludes to an obscure proverb "sixty-year-olds from the bridge" (*sexagenarios de ponte*); cf. Otto 1890, 320–21, and other references at Dyck 2010, 163.

[89] A scarcely veiled attempt to intimidate a prospective witness; cf. on §84.

one man, whom, though less than sixty, he threw from a bridge into the Tiber, contrary to the custom of our ancestors.[88] He will hear these exploits of his, if, or rather when, he comes forward as a witness—for I know that he will do so.[89] Only let him come, let him open his roll, which I can prove was written for him by Erucius—the roll that he is said to have brandished in the face of Sextus Roscius, with the threat that he would state all the facts contained in it as evidence.[90] What a brilliant witness, gentlemen! A mighty authority worth waiting for! An honorable character, to whose evidence you should willingly adapt your sworn verdict! We would not, of course, see these men's crimes so clearly, unless they themselves were blinded by greed and avarice and audacity. One of them, immediately after the murder, sent a speedy messenger to his partner and master at Ameria,[91] so that, even if all desired to conceal that they knew who was implicated in the murder, he himself would nonetheless put his crime on display before everyone's eyes. The other—would you believe it?—is even going to give evidence against Sextus Roscius, as if it were now a question whether his words should be believed, and not rather whether his actions should be punished! And so it was established by the custom of our ancestors, that, even in the least important matters, men of the greatest distinction should not give evidence in a case concerning their interests. Africanus, who shows by his

[90] This was probably not Capito's testimony written out for him by Erucius, as Cicero claims, but a document that he planned to read out in the course of his testimony; cf. Guérin 2015, 200.

[91] Cicero takes up the (alleged) student–teacher relationship of Magnus and Capito from §17.

cognomine declarat tertiam partem orbis terrarum se subegisse, tamen, si sua res ageretur, testimonium non diceret; nam illud in talem virum non audeo dicere: si diceret, non crederetur. Videte nunc quam versa et mutata in peiorem partem sint omnia. Cum de bonis et de caede agatur, testimonium dicturus est is qui et sector est et sicarius, hoc est qui et illorum ipsorum bonorum de quibus agitur emptor atque possessor est et eum hominem occidendum curavit de cuius morte quaeritur.

104 Quid? Tu, vir optime, ecquid habes quod dicas? Mihi ausculta: vide ne tibi desis; tua quoque res permagna agitur. Multa scelerate, multa audaciter,[105] multa improbe fecisti, unum stultissime, profecto tua sponte non de Eruci sententia: nihil opus fuit te istic sedere;[106] neque enim accusatore muto neque teste quisquam utitur eo qui de accusatoris subsellio surgit. Huc accedit quod paulo tamen occultior atque tectior vestra ista cupiditas esset. Nunc quid est quod quisquam ex vobis audire desideret, cum quae facitis eiusmodi sint ut ea dedita opera a nobis contra vosmet ipsos facere videamini?

105 Age nunc illa videamus, iudices, quae statim consecuta sunt. Ad Volaterras in castra L. Sullae mors Sex. Rosci quadriduo quo is occisus est Chrysogono nuntiatur. Quaeritur etiamnunc quis eum nuntium miserit? Nonne perspicuum est eundem qui Ameriam? Curat Chrysogonus ut

[105] *Priscian*: audacter Ω
[106] istic sedere *Hotoman*: isti credere Ω

[92] This assumes the threefold division of the world (Europe, Asia, Africa) established by Hecataeus of Miletus (ca. 500 BC).
[93] Cicero now turns from Capito to Magnus; for his having

surname that he conquered a third of the world,[92] would nevertheless not give evidence if his interests were at stake: for I do not venture to say in regard to such a man that, if he were to speak, he would not be believed. Consider now how everything has changed and altered for the worse. When property and murder are at issue, a man is going to give evidence who is both a broker and an assassin, that is, who is the purchaser and possessor of the very properties which are at stake, and contrived the murder of the man whose death is the subject of investigation.

Well then, most honorable sir, what do you have to say?[93] Listen to me. Take care that you do not desert yourself. Your own considerable interest is also at stake. You have committed many wicked, audacious, and shameless acts; but you have also done one very foolish thing, undoubtedly of your own accord, not on the advice of Erucius. There was no need for you to sit there; for no one employs an accuser who is dumb or a witness who gets up from the accuser's bench. In addition, that greed of yours would be a bit more secret and concealed. But as it is, what is there that anyone would desire to hear from you, since what you are doing is such that you seem intentionally to be acting on our behalf against yourselves?

Come now, gentlemen, let us see what events immediately followed. Four days after he had been killed, the death of Sextus Roscius was reported to Chrysogonus in the camp of Lucius Sulla at Volaterrae. Does anyone still ask who sent the messenger? Is it not clear that it was the same man who sent him to Ameria? Chrysogonus saw to

taken a seat on the prosecutor's side of the court, cf. §87. He is clearly trying to forestall any plan for him to testify.

eius bona veneant statim, qui non norat hominem aut rem. At qui ei venit in mentem praedia concupiscere hominis ignoti quem omnino numquam viderat? Soletis, cum aliquid huiusce modi audistis, iudices, continuo dicere: "Necesse est aliquem dixisse municipem aut vicinum; ii plerumque indicant, per eos plerique produntur." Hic nihil est quod suspicione ⟨me ponere⟩[107] hoc putetis. Non enim ego ita disputabo: "Verisimile est Roscios istam rem ad Chrysogonum detulisse, erat enim eis cum Chrysogono iam antea amicitia; nam cum multos veteres a maioribus Roscii patronos hospitesque haberent, omnes eos colere atque observare destiterunt ac se in Chrysogoni fidem et clientelam contulerunt." Haec possum omnia [vere][108] dicere, sed in hac causa coniectura nihil opus est; ipsos certo scio non negare ad haec bona Chrysogonum accessisse impulsu suo. Si eum qui indicivae partem acceperit oculis cernetis, poteritisne dubitare, iudices, qui indicarit? Qui sunt igitur in istis bonis quibus partem Chrysogonus dederit? Duo Roscii. Numquisnam praeterea? Nemo est, iudices. Num ergo dubium est quin ii obtulerint hanc praedam Chrysogono qui ab eo partem praedae tulerunt?

Age nunc ex ipsius Chrysogoni iudicio Rosciorum factum consideremus. Si nihil in ista pugna Roscii quod operae pretium esset fecerant, quam ob causam ⟨a⟩[109] Chrysogono tantis praemiis donabantur? Si nihil aliud

---

[107] *Sydow*: suspicionem Ω [108] *secl. Dyck*
[109] *add. Ascensius*

---

[94] Cf. the politically convenient change of friends attributed to Naevius at *Quinct.* 70.

it that Roscius' property was sold at once, although he knew neither who Roscius was nor the facts of the case. But how did it come into his head to covet the farms of an unknown man whom he had never seen? Gentlemen, on hearing anything of this kind, you are accustomed to say at once: "Some fellow townsman or neighbor must have told him; it is generally they who give information, it is by them that most people are betrayed." In this case there is no reason for you to think that I claim this on mere suspicion. For I shall not argue as follows: "It is likely that the Roscii informed Chrysogonus about the matter, for they had previously been on friendly terms with Chrysogonus; in fact, although the Roscii had many longstanding hereditary patrons and guest-friends, they ceased to treat all of them with attention and respect, and put themselves under the protection and patronage of Chrysogonus."[94] I can say all these things, but in this case there is no need of conjecture. I am convinced that they themselves do not deny that Chrysogonus turned to this property at their instigation. If you see with your own eyes the man who has received a share as the finder's fee, can you doubt, gentlemen, who gave the information? Who then are the people to whom Chrysogonus has given a share in this property? The two Roscii. Is there anyone else? Nobody, gentlemen. Can there be any doubt, then, that this plunder was offered to Chrysogonus by those who obtained a share of the plunder from him?

Come now, let us consider the deed of the Roscii from the standpoint of the judgment of Chrysogonus himself. If they had rendered no valuable service in that fight, why were they endowed by Chrysogonus with such splendid prizes? If they did nothing else but report the fact [of the

fecerunt nisi rem detulerunt, nonne satis fuit iis gratias agi, denique, ut perliberaliter ageretur, honoris aliquid haberi? Cur tria praedia tantae pecuniae statim Capitoni dantur? Cur quae reliqua sunt iste ⟨T.⟩[110] Roscius omnia cum Chrysogono communiter possidet? Nonne perspicuum est, iudices, has manubias Rosciis Chrysogonum re cognita concessisse?

109 Venit in decem primis legatus in castra Capito. Totam vitam, naturam moresque hominis ex ipsa legatione cognoscite. Nisi intellexeritis, iudices, nullum esse officium, nullum ius tam sanctum atque integrum quod non eius scelus[111] atque perfidia violarit et imminuerit, virum optimum esse eum iudicatote. 110 Impedimento est quominus de his rebus Sulla doceatur, ceterorum legatorum consilia et voluntatem Chrysogono enuntiat, monet ut provideat ne palam res agatur, ostendit, si sublata sit venditio bonorum, illum pecuniam grandem amissurum, sese capitis periculum aditurum; illum acuere, hos qui simul erant missi fallere, illum identidem monere ut caveret, hisce insidiose spem falsam ostendere, cum illo contra hos inire consilia, horum consilia illi enuntiare, cum illo partem suam depecisci, hisce aliqua fretus mora[112] semper omnes aditus ad

[110] *add. Richter*   [111] eius scelus *Stephanus*: eiusce vis Ω
[112] fretus mora *cod. Guelferb.*: fretum ora Ω

---

[95] This is doubly misleading: the three farms were not given "immediately" (*statim*) to Capito, as Cicero himself shows in the sequel (§115); and Magnus, formerly said to have been Chrysogonus' administrator (§21), is now advanced to joint ownership.

[96] See §§25–26.

[97] For a similarly expansive burden of proof, cf. §18.

elder Roscius' death], would it not have been enough to thank them, or, to act with utmost generosity, to give them some gratuity? Why are three such valuable farms immediately given to Capito? Why is Titus Roscius in joint possession with Chrysogonus of all the rest?[95] Is it not clear, gentlemen, that Chrysogonus, upon investigation, gave up these spoils to the Roscii?

Capito came to the camp as a delegate among the ten leading decurions.[96] Learn the man's entire manner of life, nature, and character from the legation alone. If you have not realized, gentlemen, that there is no duty, no right so sacred and inviolable that his wickedness and treachery have not violated and compromised it, you may judge him to be an excellent man.[97] He prevented Sulla from being informed about these matters; he divulged the plans and intentions of the other delegates to Chrysogonus; he warned him to take measures to prevent the affair being dealt with openly; he pointed out that, if the sale of the property were canceled, he [Chrysogonus] would lose a large sum of money and he himself would be in capital danger;[98] he incited him [Chrysogonus] and deceived his fellow delegates; he repeatedly warned the former to be on his guard and treacherously held out false hopes to the latter; he formed plans against them with him, and divulged their plans to him; he bargained with him for a share in the plunder, while to them he always barred all

109

110

---

[98] Cicero can have had no information about this conversation, if indeed it ever occurred. Chrysogonus hardly needed to have his own property interests pointed out to him, and Capito is unlikely to have revealed his own vulnerability. The narrative has been framed to shield Chrysogonus.

Sullam intercludere. Postremo isto hortatore, auctore, intercessore ad Sullam legati non adierunt; istius fide ac potius perfidia decepti, id quod ex ipsis cognoscere poteritis, si accusator voluerit testimonium eis denuntiare, pro re certa spem falsam domum rettulerunt. In privatis rebus si qui rem mandatam non modo malitiosius gessisset sui quaestus aut commodi causa verum etiam neglegentius, eum maiores summum admisisse dedecus existimabant. Itaque mandati constitutum est iudicium non minus turpe quam furti, credo propterea quod quibus in rebus ipsi interesse non possumus, in eis operae nostrae vicaria fides amicorum supponitur; quam qui laedit, oppugnat omnium commune praesidium et, quantum in ipso est, disturbat vitae societatem. Non enim possumus omnia per nos agere; alius in alia est re magis utilis. Idcirco amicitiae comparantur ut commune commodum mutuis officiis gubernetur. Quid recipis mandatum si aut neglecturus aut ad tuum commodum conversurus es? Cur mihi te offers

111

112

---

99 In spite of the leading role given to Capito here, it was only Chrysogonus who was in a position to block access to Sulla.

100 Though only the prosecutor could compel witness testimony (Mommsen 1899, 403–5; Greenidge 1901, 485–86; Guérin 2015, 112), witnesses could come forward voluntarily, which these men did not do, whether because they had been bribed or were embarrassed to admit that they had been duped.

101 A mandate (*mandatum*) is "a consensual contract by which a person assumed the duty to conclude a legal transaction or to perform a service gratuitously in the interest of the mandator or of a third party": Berger 195 s.v. Mandatum. This was one of various kinds of transactions in which good faith (*bona fides*) was required, with *infamia* as a consequence of conviction for a viola-

access to Sulla, alleging some reason for delay. Finally, with him [Capito] urging, suggesting, and mediating, the ambassadors did not meet with Sulla.[99] Deceived by his word, or rather, by his broken word—as you will be able to learn from themselves, if the accuser is willing to summon them as witnesses[100]—instead of an assured result they took home with them nothing but false hopes. In private affairs, one who had carried out a mandate, not only maliciously for his own profit or advantage, but even somewhat carelessly was thought by our ancestors to have committed a most disreputable act. Accordingly, an action for violation of a mandate was established that involved as much disgrace as an action for theft.[101] I suppose the reason for this was that, in matters in which we cannot take a personal part, the promise of our friends is a proxy for our own efforts; and one who violates this promise attacks what is the common safeguard of all, and, as far as it is in his power, disrupts social life. For we cannot do everything by ourselves; one party is more proficient in one area, another in another. That is why friendships are formed—that the common interest may be guided by mutual services.[102] Why do you accept a mandate if you intend either to neglect it or turn it to your own advantage?

111

112

tion; see also Greenidge 1901, 203–4. Here Cicero turns to account his knowledge of civil law, which he learned at the feet of Q. Mucius Scaevola ("the Augur") and later the homonymous pontifex; see *Amic.* 1.

[102] Lacking a developed service economy, the Romans evolved this form of friendship—what we might call "business friendships." See the detailed study by Verboven 2002.

ac meis commodis officio simulato officis et obstas? Recede de medio; per alium transigam. Suscipis onus offici quod te putas sustinere ⟨non⟩[113] posse; quod minime videtur leve[114] iis qui minime ipsi leves sunt. Ergo idcirco turpis haec culpa est quod duas res sanctissimas violat, amicitiam et fidem. Nam neque mandat quisquam fere nisi amico neque credit nisi ei quem fidelem putat. Perditissimi est igitur hominis simul et amicitiam dissolvere et fallere eum qui laesus non esset, nisi credidisset. Itane est? In minimis rebus qui mandatum neglexerit, turpissimo iudicio condemnetur necesse est, in re tanta cum is cui fama mortui, fortunae vivi commendatae sunt atque concreditae, ignominia mortuum, ⟨inopia vivum⟩[115] affecerit, is inter honestos homines atque adeo inter vivos numerabitur? In minimis privatisque rebus etiam neglegentia in crimen mandati iudiciumque infamiae[116] vocatur,[117] propterea quod, si recte fiat, illum neglegere oporteat qui mandarit, non illum qui mandatum receperit; in re tanta, quae publice gesta atque commissa sit, qui non neglegentia privatum aliquod commodum laeserit sed

113 *add. Kayser*
114 leve *H. J. Mueller*: grave Ω
115 inopia vivum *add. Havet*
116 infamia: *corr. Puteanus*
117 revocatur: *corr. Lambinus*

103 The text is uncertain. The restoration adopted here assumes that Cicero is describing the circumstances in which a withdrawal from a mandate is appropriate. The point is reinforced by repetition of *levis* (translated here as "trivial" and "shallow").

Why do you offer to help me, and by pretended service stand in the way of and thwart my interests? Get out of the way; I will get someone else to transact my business. You undertake a burdensome service that you think you cannot sustain—a burden which seems by no means trivial to those who are themselves by no means shallow.[103] That, then, is why this fault [i.e., failure to carry out a mandate] is disgraceful, because it violates two things that are most sacred—friendship and good faith. For as a rule no one entrusts a mandate except to a friend, and no one trusts anyone except one whom he believes to be faithful. It is therefore the act of an utterly abandoned man simultaneously to destroy friendship and to deceive one who would not have suffered injury unless he had trusted him. Is it not so? If in a matter of very little importance a man who has neglected a mandate must be condemned by a most disgraceful sentence, in a case so important, when the man to whom the reputation of the dead and the fortunes of the living have been committed and entrusted has tainted the dead with ignominy and the living with poverty, shall he be reckoned among honorable men, or rather, among the living? In private affairs of the least importance, even negligence is summoned to trial on a charge of [betrayal of] mandate with a sentence of infamy,[104] because, if all is in order, negligence should be on the part of the one who has given the mandate, not the one who has accepted it. In a matter of such importance, which was publicly entrusted and carried out, if someone has not merely damaged some private interest by his care-

---

[104] *Infamia* was a status involving loss of various civil rights; see further Greenidge 1901, 508; Kaser 1956; Wolf 2010.

CICERO

perfidia legationis ipsius caerimoniam polluerit maculaque affecerit, qua is tandem poena afficietur aut quo
114 iudicio damnabitur? Si hanc ei rem privatim Sex. Roscius mandavisset ut cum Chrysogono transigeret atque decideret inque eam rem fidem suam, si quid opus esse putaret, interponeret illeque[118] sese facturum recepisset, nonne, si ex eo negotio tantulum in rem suam convertisset, damnatus per arbitrum et rem restitueret et honestatem omnem
115 amitteret? Nunc non hanc ei rem Sex. Roscius mandavit sed, id quod multo gravius est, ipse Sex. Roscius cum fama, vita bonisque omnibus a decurionibus publice ⟨T.⟩[119] Roscio mandatus est; et ex eo T. Roscius non paululum nescioquid in rem suam convertit sed hunc funditus evertit bonis, ipse tria praedia sibi depectus est, voluntatem decurionum ac municipum omnium tantidem quanti fidem suam fecit.

116 Videte iam porro cetera, iudices, ut intellegatis fingi maleficium nullum posse quo iste sese non contaminarit. In rebus minoribus socium fallere turpissimum est aequeque turpe atque illud de quo ante dixi; neque iniuria, propterea quod auxilium sibi se putat adiunxisse qui cum altero rem communicavit. Ad cuius igitur fidem confugiet, cum per eius fidem laeditur cui se commiserit? Atque ea sunt animadvertenda peccata maxime quae difficillime praecaventur. Tecti esse ad alienos possumus, intimi multa apertiora videant necesse est; socium cavere qui possu-

[118] ille qui: *corr. Madvig*
[119] *add. Schuetz*

---

[105] The Latin involves a play on the word *fides*, first rendered as "protection," then as "faith."

222

lessness, but by his treachery has violated and defiled the sacred character of the legation itself, what punishment, I ask, shall be inflicted or to what sentence shall he be condemned? If as a private person Sextus Roscius had entrusted this matter to him to settle and reach an agreement with Chrysogonus, and, if he thought it necessary, give his word for that purpose; and if he [Capito] had undertaken to do so, and if out of the transaction he had made ever so little profit, would he not be condemned by an arbitrator, make restitution, and entirely lose his good name? As it is, Sextus Roscius did not entrust this matter to him but—what is far more serious—Sextus Roscius himself, together with his reputation, life, and all his property was publicly entrusted to Titus Roscius by the decurions, and from that affair Titus Roscius has turned no small trifle to his own advantage, but has totally overthrown my client in respect to his property and bargained for three farms for himself, and has shown as little regard for the wishes of the decurions and all his fellow townsmen as for his own word.

Moreover, gentlemen, consider now the rest of his actions, that you may understand that no misdeed can be imagined with which he has not defiled himself. It is most disgraceful to deceive a partner in trifling matters, as disgraceful as the conduct I have mentioned before. And rightly so, because a man who has entered into partnership with another thinks that he has brought in assistance for himself. To whose protection shall he take refuge, when injured by his faith in the man to whom he has entrusted himself?[105] Besides, those offenses against which it is most difficult to take precautions must be punished most severely. We can be reserved toward strangers, but our intimate friends must see many matters more clearly; but how

mus, quem etiam si metuimus, ius offici laedimus? Recte igitur maiores eum qui socium fefellisset in virorum bonorum numero non putarunt haberi oportere. At vero T. Roscius non unum rei pecuniariae socium fefellit—quod tametsi grave est, tamen aliquo modo posse ferri videtur—verum novem homines honestissimos eiusdem muneris,[120] offici mandatorumque socios, induxit, decepit, destituit, adversariis tradidit, omni fraude et perfidia fefellit; qui de eius scelere suspicari nihil potuerunt, socium offici metuere non debuerunt, eius malitiam non viderunt, orationi vanae crediderunt. Itaque nunc illi homines honestissimi propter istius insidias parum putantur cauti providique fuisse; iste qui initio proditor fuit, deinde perfuga, qui primo sociorum consilia adversariis enuntiavit, deinde societatem cum ipsis adversariis coiit, terret etiam nos ac minatur tribus praediis, hoc est praemiis sceleris, ornatus.

In eiusmodi vita, iudices, in his tot tantisque flagitiis hoc quoque maleficium de quo iudicium est reperietis. Etenim quaerere ita debetis: ubi multa avare, multa audacter, multa improbe, multa perfidiose facta videbitis, ibi scelus quoque latere inter illa tot flagitia putatote. Tametsi hoc quidem minime latet quod ita promptum et propositum est ut non ex illis maleficiis quae in illo constat esse hoc intellegatur verum ex hoc etiam, si quo[121] de illorum forte dubitabitur, convincatur. Quid tandem, quaeso,

[120] *post* muneris *hab.* ω legationis, *del. Fleckeisen*
[121] quod: *corr. Gulielmius*

---

106 That is, an action "on behalf of a partner" (*pro socio*), no less than one for betraying a mandate, involved a violation of good faith (*bona fides*), and resulted in *infamia*; cf. Greenidge 1901, 204, 542; Berger 1953 s.v. Societas.

can we take precautions against a partner, since even to feel uneasy about his conduct is a violation of the law of duty? Rightly, therefore, our ancestors thought that one who had deceived his partner ought not to be reckoned among honorable men.[106] But in truth Titus Roscius did not deceive merely a single partner in a matter of money, which, although a grave offense, seems to a certain extent tolerable, but he led on, deceived, deserted, handed over to their adversaries, and cheated by every kind of fraud and perfidy nine most honorable men, associated with him in the same function, duty, and mandate. These men could not have the least suspicion of his wickedness, they were bound not to feel any anxiety about the man who was their partner in duty, they did not see his wickedness, they believed his delusive words. This is why those most honorable men, owing to his snares, are now considered to have been wanting in caution and foresight; he who was in the beginning a traitor, then a deserter, who first divulged the plans of his associates to their adversaries, and then formed a partnership with those adversaries themselves, even intimidates and threatens us, and is decorated with three farms, the reward of his crime.

117

In a life of this kind, gentlemen, among shameful acts so many and so monstrous, you will also find the crime that is the subject of this trial. For you ought to conduct your inquiry as follows: wherever you find many acts performed with greed, audacity, depravity, and treachery, assume that there the crime also lies concealed among so many shameful acts. And yet this is by no means hidden—a matter that is so plainly visible and exposed that it is understood not only from the crimes that are securely attributed to him [Capito], but if there is doubt about any of them, it is even

118

iudices? Num aut ille lanista omnino iam a gladio recessisse[122] videtur aut hic[123] discipulus magistro tantulum de arte concedere? Par est avaritia, similis improbitas, eadem impudentia, gemina audacia.

119   Etenim, quoniam fidem magistri cognostis, cognoscite[124] nunc discipuli aequitatem. Dixi iam antea saepenumero postulatos esse ab istis duos servos in quaestionem. Tu semper, T. Rosci, recusasti. Quaero abs te, iine qui postulabant indigni erant qui impetrarent, an is te non commovebat pro quo postulabant, an res ipsa tibi iniqua videbatur? Postulabant homines nobilissimi atque integerrimi nostrae civitatis quos iam antea nominavi; qui ita vixerunt talesque a populo Romano putantur ut quicquid dicerent nemo esset qui non aequum putaret. Postulabant autem pro homine miserrimo atque infelicissimo, qui vel ipse sese in cruciatum dari cuperet dum de patris morte
120 quaereretur. Res porro abs te eiusmodi postulabatur ut nihil interesset, utrum eam rem recusares an de maleficio confiterere. Quae cum ita sint, quaero abs te quam ob causam recusaris. Cum occiditur Sex. Roscius ibidem fuerunt. Servos ipsos, quod ad me attinet, neque arguo neque purgo; quod a vobis oppugnari video ne in quaestionem dentur, suspiciosum est. Quod vero apud vos ipsos in ho-

[122] gladio recessisse *Madvig*: gladiatore cessisse Ω
[123] hic *schol.*: (h)is Ω
[124] cognoscite *Vχψ*: cognoscitis *Aπσφ*

[107] Transition to the topic of the testimony of Sextus Roscius' slaves. The real obstacle was not Magnus, but Chrysogonus; Magnus merely acted as his agent.

[108] He refers back to Scipio and Metellus, mentioned at §77.

proven by this crime. Well then, I ask you, gentlemen: that trainer of gladiators [Capito] surely does not seem to have retired altogether from the fray or this pupil [Magnus] to yield to him even a little bit as regards the art, does he? Their greed is equal, their criminality similar, their brazenness identical, their audacity twin.

And indeed, since you have learned the master's good faith, now learn the pupil's fairness.[107] I said previously that two slaves were often demanded from our opponents for questioning. You, Titus Roscius, always refused. I ask you: were those who were making the request unworthy of obtaining what they requested? Or did the man on whose behalf they requested fail to arouse your sympathy? Or did the request appear to you unjust? Those who made the request were the noblest and most upright men in our community, whose names I have already mentioned; they have lived such a life and are regarded by the Roman people with such esteem that, whatever they might say, no one would think it unfair.[108] Moreover, they made the request on behalf of a most miserable and unfortunate man, who would even be ready to give himself to the torture, provided there were an inquiry into his father's death. Further, the request made of you was of such a kind that it made no difference whether you refused it or confessed the crime. This being so, I ask you why you refused. When Sextus Roscius was killed, they were on the spot. The slaves themselves, for my part, I neither accuse nor exculpate. But I see you resisting their being submitted to questioning; this is suspicious. Further, since they are held in

119

120

The esteem of the Roman people is inferred from Scipio's election to office; see ad loc.

CICERO

nore tanto sunt, profecto necesse est sciant aliquid quod, si dixerint, perniciosum vobis futurum sit.—"In dominos quaeri de servis iniquum est."—At non[125] quaeritur: Sex. enim Roscius reus est neque [enim],[126] cum de hoc quaeritur, ⟨in dominos quaeritur⟩;[127] vos enim dominos esse dicitis.—"Cum Chrysogono sunt."—Ita credo; litteris eorum et urbanitate Chrysogonus ducitur ut inter suos omnium deliciarum atque omnium artium puerulos ex tot elegantissimis familiis lectos velit hos versari, homines paene operarios, ex Amerina disciplina patris familiae rusticani.

121 Non ita est profecto, iudices; non est verisimile ut Chrysogonus horum litteras adamarit aut humanitatem, non ut rei familiaris negotio diligentiam cognorit eorum et fidem. Est quiddam quod occultatur; quod quo studiosius ab istis[128] opprimitur et absconditur, eo magis eminet

122 et apparet. Quid igitur? Chrysogonus suine[129] malefici occultandi causa quaestionem de iis haberi non vult? Minime, iudices; non in omnes arbitror omnia convenire. Ego in Chrysogono, quod ad me attinet, nihil eiusmodi suspicor; neque hoc mihi nunc primum in mentem venit dicere. Meministis me ita distribuisse initio causam: in crimen cuius tota argumentatio permissa Erucio est et in audaciam cuius partes Rosciis impositae sunt. Quicquid

[125] ne: *corr. Buechner*   [126] *del. Plasberg*
[127] in dominos quaeritur *add. Havet*
[128] ipsis: *corr. Havet*
[129] suine *cod. Paris. 6369*: tuine $V\psi^2$: tui *cett.*

109 Cicero stirs prejudice at Chrysogonus' household as newly collected (thanks to the proscriptions) from many fine families, and he again exploits the town/country dichotomy. In fact, the

such great honor among you, they must surely know something that, if they were to say it, would be ruinous to you. "It is unjust for slaves to be interrogated about their masters." But there is no such interrogation, for Sextus Roscius is the defendant, and when an interrogation is conducted about him, it is not against their masters, for you say that you are their masters. "They are with Chrysogonus." I suppose so; Chrysogonus is drawn to them by their culture and refinement so that he wants them—men who are practically laborers, bumpkins with a country householder's training from Ameria—to have their place among his own boys schooled in all pleasures and all arts whom he has chosen from so many refined families.[109] No, gentlemen, this is certainly not the case; it is unlikely that Chrysogonus took a fancy to their culture and refinement or that he discerned their diligence and fidelity in handling his property. Something is being concealed; the more zealously they suppress it and hide it away, the more evident and conspicuous it becomes. Well then, does Chrysogonus refuse an inquiry concerning them in order to conceal his own crime? No, gentlemen; I do not think that all charges fit all parties. As far as I am concerned, I harbor no such suspicion concerning Chrysogonus; and it does not only now occur to me to say this. You recall that I divided up my case in the beginning into the charge, the entire presentation of which was entrusted to Erucius; into audacity, a role which was assigned to the Roscii.

slaves who were with the elder Roscius on the night of his murder were evidently part of his household in Rome and are unlikely to have fallen below general standards of urban refinement; cf. Alexander 2002, 305–6n33.

malefici, sceleris, caedis erit, proprium id Rosciorum esse debebit. Nimiam gratiam potentiamque Chrysogoni dicimus et nobis obstare et perferri nullo modo posse et a vobis, quoniam potestas data est, non modo infirmari verum etiam vindicari oportere. Ego sic existimo, qui quaeri velit ex eis quos constat, cum caedes facta sit, adfuisse, eum cupere verum inveniri;[130] qui recuset, eum profecto, tametsi verbo non audeat, tamen re ipsa de maleficio suo confiteri.

Dixi initio, iudices, nolle me plura de istorum scelere dicere quam causa postularet ac necessitas ipsa cogeret. Nam et multae res afferri possunt et una quaeque earum multis cum argumentis dici potest. Verum ego quod invitus ac necessario facio neque diu neque diligenter facere possum. Quae praeteriri nullo modo poterant, ea leviter, iudices, attigi; quae posita sunt in suspicionibus, de quibus, si coepero dicere, pluribus verbis sit disserendum, ea vestris ingeniis coniecturaeque committo.

Venio nunc ad illud nomen aureum [Chrysogoni][131] sub quo nomine tota societas latuit;[132] de quo, iudices, neque quomodo dicam neque quomodo taceam reperire possum. Si enim taceo, vel maximam partem relinquo; sin

[130] invenire: *corr. Pluygers*
[131] *secl. Weidner*
[132] statuit: *corr. Madvig*

[110] Cicero argues that Chrysogonus should be separated from the murder plot, but feebly, merely citing his own previous division of his case (§35). The distinction between parts (2) criminality and (3) power is not hard and fast. Even if the Roscii were the agents immediately responsible for the murder, Chrysogonus

PRO ROSCIO AMERINO 122–124

Whatever misdeed, crime, or murder there will be, it will have to be owned by the Roscii. We assert that Chrysogonus' excessive influence and power are both an obstacle to us and are by no means tolerable, and since you have the power, they ought not only to be weakened but even to be punished by you.[110] I am of this opinion: he is eager for the truth who wants an inquiry made from those who, it is agreed, were present when the murder occurred; he who refuses surely makes a confession about his commission of the crime by the fact itself, even if he does not dare do so in words.

I said, at the beginning, gentlemen, that I did not wish to say more about these men's crime than the case required and necessity compelled me.[111] For many allegations can be made, and each of them could be asserted with many arguments. But I cannot do at length or in detail what I am doing unwillingly and under compulsion. I have touched lightly, gentlemen, on the points that could by no means be passed over; I entrust to your intelligence and powers of conjecture points that rest on suspicion, about which, if I were to broach them, I would have to speak at length.

I come now to that golden name under which the entire partnership has been hidden; about this, gentlemen, I can discover neither how I should speak nor how I should keep silent.[112] If I keep silent, I abandon the greatest part

---

could have been the mastermind behind it. He was certainly the main beneficiary. Hence Stroh 1975, 74–75, suspects "figured speech" here, that is, that Cicero is saying one thing but means something else; cf. also Seager 2007, 908.

111 Cf. §83. 112 Another orator's dilemma; cf. on §29.

CICERO

autem dico, vereor ne non ille solus, id quod ad me nihil attinet, sed alii quoque plures laesos sese[133] putent. Tametsi ita se res habet ut mihi in communem causam sectorum dicendum nihil magnopere videatur; haec enim causa nova profecto et singularis est. Bonorum Sex. Rosci emptor est Chrysogonus.[134] Primum hoc videamus: eius hominis bona qua ratione venierunt aut quomodo venire potuerunt? Atque hoc non ita quaeram, iudices, ut id dicam esse indignum, hominis innocentis bona venisse—si enim haec audientur ac libere dicentur, non fuit tantus homo Sex. Roscius in civitate ut de eo potissimum conqueramur—verum ego hoc quaero: qui potuerunt ista ipsa lege quae de proscriptione est, sive Valeria est sive Cornelia—non enim novi nec scio—verum ista ipsa lege bona Sex. Rosci venire qui potuerunt? Scriptum enim ita dicunt esse: ut aut eorum bona veneant[135] "qui proscripti sunt"—quo in numero Sex. Roscius non est—aut eorum "qui in adversariorum praesidiis occisi sunt." Dum praesidia ulla fuerunt, in Sullae praesidiis fuit; posteaquam ab armis ⟨omnes⟩[136] recesserunt, in summo otio rediens a cena Ro-

---

[133] sese *Stephanus clausulae causa*: se esse ω

[134] emptor est Chrysogonus *cod. Helmstad.*: emptorē Chrysogonus V: emptorem Chrysogonum ω

[135] veneant σ: veniant *cett.*   [136] add. *Clark*

---

[113] A discreet allusion to Sulla.

[114] Cicero alludes to the Valerian Law of 82 by which Sulla was appointed dictator and a Lex Cornelia (quoted below), regulating the scope and legal consequences of the proscriptions; cf. *LPPR* 348–49; *RS* §49. There might have been ambiguity if the proscriptions began before the dictatorship and the former in-

[of my case]; but if I speak, I fear that not he alone—which does not matter to me—but also several others may think they have been insulted.[113] The matter is, however, such that it seems to me that I need say nothing against the brokers' common cause; for this case is surely novel and unparalleled. Chrysogonus purchased Sextus Roscius' property. In the first place, let us examine this point: on what ground were this man's goods sold or how could they have been sold? And I am not asking this, gentlemen, so as to claim that it is outrageous for an innocent man's goods to have been sold—if this argument is to be freely made and heard, Sextus Roscius was not so important a figure in the community that we should complain about him in particular—my question is this: under that very law about the proscription, whether it is the Valerian or the Cornelian [Law]—I am not familiar with it and do not know—but by that very law how could Sextus Roscius' goods have been sold?[114] For it is said that it reads as follows: that the property, either of those "who have been proscribed"—of whom Sextus Roscius is not one—or of those "who have been slain within the enemy's fortifications" should be sold.[115] As long as there were any fortifications, he was within those of Sulla. After all had laid down their arms, during a time of perfect peace, he was slain at Rome, when returning from supper. If he was slain

125

126

cluded a clause confirming Sulla's previous acts; cf. App. *B Civ.* 1.97; Mommsen 1887–1888, 2:736.   [115] Cicero is deliberately vague in his reference to this law, professing not to know its precise name and merely citing what people say (*dicunt*) it said. Inquiring too closely into the law about the proscriptions might have raised suspicions from Sulla's point of view.

CICERO

mae occisus est. ⟨Si⟩[137] lege, bona quoque lege venisse fateor. Sin autem constat contra omnes non modo veteres leges verum etiam novas occisum esse, bona quo iure aut quo more[138] aut qua lege venierint quaero.

127 In quem hoc dicam quaeris, Eruci. Non in eum quem vis et putas; nam Sullam et oratio mea ab initio et ipsius eximia virtus omni tempore purgavit. Ego haec omnia Chrysogonum fecisse dico, ut ementiretur, ut malum civem Roscium fuisse fingeret, ut eum apud adversarios occisum esse diceret, ut hisce ⟨de⟩[139] rebus a legatis Amerinorum doceri L. Sullam passus non sit. Denique etiam illud suspicor, omnino haec bona non venisse; id quod
128 postea, si per vos, iudices, licitum erit, aperietur. Opinor enim esse in lege quam ad diem proscriptiones venditionesque fiant, nimirum Kalendas Iunias. Aliquot post menses et homo occisus est et bona venisse dicuntur. Profecto aut haec bona in tabulas publicas nulla redierunt nosque ab isto nebulone facetius eludimur quam putamus, aut, si redierunt, tabulae publicae corruptae aliqua ratione sunt; nam lege quidem bona venire non potuisse constat. Intellego me ante tempus, iudices, haec scrutari et propemodum errare qui, cum capiti Sex. Rosci mederi debeam, reduviam curem. Non enim laborat de pecunia, non ullius rationem sui commodi ducit; facile egestatem suam se laturum putat, si hac indigna suspicione et ficto crimine

---

[137] *add.* ψ²   [138] modo: *corr. Ernesti*
[139] *add. Ascensius*

---

[116] He raises some grounds for suspicion at §128, but if there was a more detailed argument, it may have been lost in the lacuna at §132.   [117] A proverbial expression; cf. Otto 1890, 295.

by virtue of the law, I admit that his property also was sold by virtue of the law. But if it is established that he was slain contrary to all laws, not only the old ones but also the new ones, I ask by what right or by what custom or by virtue of what law his goods were sold.

You ask, Erucius, against whom my words are directed. Not against him whom you claim and think them to be, for my speech from its beginning and his own eminent character at all times have exonerated Sulla. I assert that all this is the work of Chrysogonus—that he lied, that he misrepresented Roscius as a bad citizen, that he said that he had been slain among Sulla's enemies, that he prevented Sulla being informed about these matters by the Amerians' delegates. Lastly, I even suspect that this property has not been sold at all, as I will afterward show, gentlemen, if you allow me to do so.[116] Now I believe that the deadline up to which proscriptions and sales may take place is stated in the law—namely, the 1st of June. Some months afterward the man was slain and his property is said to have been sold. Either these goods were not entered on the public registers, and we are being cheated by this rascal more cleverly than we think, or, if they were, the public registers have been tampered with in some way, for it is evident that the property could not have been sold by virtue of the law. I am aware, gentlemen, that I am examining this question prematurely and that I am almost on the wrong road, in that while I ought to be trying to save my client's life, I am treating a hangnail.[117] For he is not concerned about money; he takes no account of his own interest; he thinks that he will easily endure his poverty, provided he is freed from this unworthy suspicion

129 liberatus sit. Verum quaeso a vobis, iudices, ut haec pauca quae restant ita audiatis ut partim me dicere pro me ipso putetis, partim ⟨pro⟩[140] Sex. Roscio. Quae enim mihi ipsi indigna et intolerabilia videntur quaeque ad omnes, nisi providemus, arbitror pertinere, ea pro me ipso ex[141] animi mei sensu ac dolore pronuntio; quae ad huius vitam [casum][142] causamque pertineant et quid hic pro se dici velit et qua condicione contentus sit, iam in extrema oratione nostra, iudices, audietis.

130 Ego haec a Chrysogono mea sponte remoto Sex. Roscio quaero: primum quare civis optimi bona venierint, deinde quare hominis eius qui ⟨neque proscriptus⟩[143] neque apud adversarios occisus est bona venierint,[144] cum in eos solos lex scripta sit, deinde quare aliquanto post eam diem venierint quae dies in lege praefinita est, deinde cur tantulo venierint. Quae omnia si, quemadmodum solent liberti nequam et improbi facere, in patronum suum voluerit conferre, nihil egerit; nemo est enim qui nesciat propter magnitudinem rerum multa multos ⟨partim improbante⟩,[145] partim imprudente L. Sulla commisisse.

131 Placet igitur in his rebus aliquid imprudentia praeteriri? Non placet, iudices, sed necesse est. Etenim si Iuppiter Optimus Maximus, cuius nutu et arbitrio caelum, terra mariaque reguntur, saepe ventis vehementioribus aut im-

---

[140] add. edd. Rom. et Ven.   [141] et: corr. Naugerius
[142] vitae casum: corr. Richter
[143] neque proscriptus add. Hotoman
[144] venierunt VA   [145] partim improbante add. Clark

---

[118] The strategy of dissociating his client from a certain line of argument is also used at *Clu.* 143–60. This tactic enables Cicero to advance an argument that may influence the jurors but

and false accusation. But I beg you, gentlemen, to listen 129
to the few things that remain with the understanding that
I am speaking partly for myself, and partly for Sextus Roscius. Things which seem to me outrageous and intolerable,
and which, in my opinion, may affect us all, unless we take
precautions, these I declare on my own account sincerely
and with indignation; things which concern my client's life
and his case and what he wishes to be said on his behalf,
what conditions will satisfy him, you will hear presently,
gentlemen, at the end of my speech.

I put the following questions to Chrysogonus on my 130
own account, leaving Sextus Roscius out of the matter:[118]
first, why has the property of an excellent citizen been
sold; next, why has the property of a man been sold who
was neither proscribed nor slain among the enemy, although they are the only persons against whom the law
has been drafted; next, why has it been sold some time
after the deadline prescribed by the law; next, why was it
sold at so low a price? If, after the usual manner of a
worthless and wicked freedman, he should wish to make
his patron responsible for all this, he will gain nothing, for
everybody knows that many men have committed many
crimes of which Sulla partly disapproved and partly was
ignorant, owing to the magnitude of his undertakings.
Does it seem right, then, that in matters of this kind any- 131
thing should be overlooked through inattention? It does
not seem right, gentlemen, but it is inevitable. In fact, if
Jupiter, Greatest and Best, whose nod and will governs
heaven, earth, and seas, has often done grievous harm to

without compromising the portrait he paints of his client's character.

CICERO

moderatis tempestatibus aut nimio calore aut intolerabili frigore hominibus nocuit, urbes delevit, fruges perdidit, quorum nihil pernicii[146] causa divino consilio sed vi ipsa et magnitudine rerum factum putamus, at contra commoda[147] quibus utimur lucemque qua fruimur spiritumque quem ducimus ab eo nobis dari atque impertiri videmus, quid miramur, iudices,[148] L. Sullam, cum solus rem publicam regeret orbemque terrarum gubernaret imperique maiestatem quam armis receperat, tum[149] legibus confirmaret, aliqua animadvertere non potuisse? Nisi hoc mirum est quod vis divina assequi non possit, si id mens humana adepta non sit. Verum ut haec missa faciam quae iam facta sunt, ex iis quae nunc cum maxime fiunt nonne quivis potest intellegere omnium architectum et machinatorem unum esse Chrysogonum? Qui Sex. Rosci nomen deferendum curavit [hoc iudicium],[150] cuius honoris causa accusare se dixit Erucius . . .[151]

In vico Pallacinae
Maxime metuit

[146] pernicii *Caesell. apud Gell. 9.14.19 et Non. 486.25*: pernicie Ω   [147] commoda *cod. Mon. 15734*: commodis a *V*: commodis ω   [148] iudices *schol.*: om. Ω
[149] tum *V*: cum σχψ: ut Aπφ   [150] secl. *Madvig*
[151] *lac. indic. Aπ, fragmenta ex scholiis sumpta*

---

[119] Here, in spite of his division of the case (§§35, 122), he comes close to admitting that Chrysogonus was the mastermind.
[120] At this point there is a lacuna in the transmitted text; the following are fragments recovered from the scholia.

PRO ROSCIO AMERINO 131–132

men by furious winds, violent storms, excessive heat, or unbearable cold, destroyed their cities and ruined their crops, we do not attribute any of these disasters to a divine plan and a desire for causing destruction, but to the mere force and the mighty agency of nature. But, on the other hand, the advantages of which we avail ourselves, the light which we enjoy, the air we breathe, we see as favors given and bestowed upon us by him [Jupiter]. Why then, gentlemen, are we surprised that Lucius Sulla, when he alone guided the republic and governed the world, when he was strengthening by laws the majesty of the supreme power that he had regained by force of arms, should have been unable to notice a few things? Unless we ought to be surprised that human intelligence has not achieved that of which divine power is incapable. But, leaving aside these matters that are already past, can anyone fail to understand, from what is going on just now, that Chrysogonus alone is the architect and contriver of them all?[119] The man who caused Sextus Roscius to be accused and out of regard for whom Erucius declared he brought the accusation . . .[120]

132

In the Pallacine quarter[121]
He most feared[122]

---

[121] The scholiast says that this identifies the location where the elder Roscius dined on the fatal night (as one might expect from his murder "near the baths of Pallacina," §18).

[122] Sulla is to be supplied as the object, according to the scholiast; Chrysogonus will be the subject.

239

CICERO

Derivat tamen et ait se
Manupretia[152] praediis
Hic ego audire istos cupio

... aptam et ratione dispositam se habere existimant qui in Sallentinis aut in Bruttiis habent unde vix ter in anno audire nuntium possunt. Alter tibi descendit de Palatio et aedibus suis; habet animi causa rus amoenum et suburbanum, plura praeterea praedia neque tamen ullum nisi praeclarum et propinquum. Domus referta vasis Corinthiis et Deliacis, in quibus est authepsa illa quam tanto pretio nuper mercatus est ut cum[153] praetereuntes id[154] praeconem[155] nuntiare[156] audiebant fundum venire arbitrarentur. Quid praeterea caelati argenti, quid stragulae vestis, quid pictarum tabularum, quid signorum, quid marmoris apud illum putatis esse? Tantum scilicet quantum e multis splendidisque familiis in turba et rapinis coa-

[152] manu praedia: *corr. Orelli*
[153] cum *Dyck (i.e., quom)*: qui Ω
[154] id (*sc. pretium*) *Dyck*: quid Ω, *del. A. Klotz*
[155] praeconem *A. Klotz*: preconum (*sup.* e *litt.* a *s.l.*) V: praeco σχ: praetium *vel* precium Aϕψπ: pecuniam B
[156] nuntiare π: enuntiare χ: numerare VABϕψ: enumerare σ

---

[123] According to the scholiast, the subject is Chrysogonus, who goes on to claim that he removed Roscius' goods so quickly (cf. the reference to "plunderings" [*rapinae*] at §24) not for fear that Sulla would take them, but because he was building a house in the region of Veii.

[124] Perhaps a reference to the three farms Chrysogonus ceded to Capito (§99).

[125] When continuous text resumes, Cicero seems to be con-

PRO ROSCIO AMERINO 132–133

He, however, distracts attention and says that he[123]
Rewards by means of farms[124]
In this connection, I am keen to hear them

... People who have estates in the territory of the Sallentini or Bruttii, whence they can get news scarcely three times a year, think that they possess a country house, convenient and suitably arranged.[125] Here you have the other[126] coming down from his house on the Palatine: he has for his relaxation a pleasant country estate and a suburban villa, besides a number of farms all of them excellent and near the city; a house crammed with Corinthian and Delian vases, among them that self-cooker,[127] which he recently bought at so high a price that when passersby heard the auctioneer announce the price, they thought that an estate was being sold. What quantities besides of embossed silver, of coverlets, pictures, statues, marble do you imagine are in his home? As much, of course, as could be heaped up in a single house, taken from many illustrious families amid the confusion and plundering. But what

133

trasting properties owned by Sulla's favorites, some preferring to have estates as far from Rome as possible, as opposed to Chrysogonus, whose properties and pleasures are described at §133. The Sallentini, a people of Illyrian origin, lived in southern Calabria, whereas the Bruttii lived in the mountainous southwest of Italy, where some of Sulla's followers established large estates; cf. Seager, *CAH* 9:204.

[126] "The other" (of two) implies a comparison with a person identified in the foregoing, perhaps the defendant (Cicero had compared him with Magnus at §§86 and 88).

[127] That is, a cooker containing its own heating element. The word *authepsa* occurs only here.

cervari una in domo potuit. Familiam vero quantam et quam variis cum artificiis habeat quid ego dicam? Mitto hasce artes vulgares, coquos, pistores,[157] lecticarios; animi et aurium causa tot homines habet ut cotidiano cantu vocum et nervorum et tibiarum nocturnisque conviviis tota vicinitas personet. In hac vita, iudices, quos sumptus cotidianos, quas effusiones fieri putatis, quae vero convivia? Honesta, credo, in eiusmodi domo, si domus haec habenda est potius quam[158] officina nequitiae ac deversorium flagitiorum omnium. Ipse vero quemadmodum composito et diliburo capillo passim per forum volitet cum magna caterva togatorum videtis, iudices; videtis[159] ut omnes despiciat, ut hominem prae se neminem putet, ut se solum beatum, solum potentem putet.

Quae vero efficiat et quae conetur si velim commemorare, vereor, iudices, ne quis imperitior existimet me causam nobilitatis victoriamque voluisse laedere. Tametsi meo iure possum, si quid in hac parte mihi non placeat, vituperare; non enim vereor ne quis alienum me animum habuisse a causa nobilitatis existimet. Sciunt ii qui me norunt me pro mea[160] tenui infirmaque parte, posteaquam

[157] pictores: *corr. Naugerius*
[158] quam *Bσχψ: om. VAπφ*
[159] videtis iudices videtis *Reid*: videtis iudices et invidetis iudices et unum videtis *V*: videtis iudices etiam videtis iudices *ω*
[160] illa: *corr. Madvig*

[128] The villain's appearance in the central square is a rhetorical topos going back to Demosthenes' picture of Aeschines at 19.314 (cf. Weische 1972, 28–29); cf. also *Rhet. Her.* 4.62. Chrysogonus carefully coiffed and perfumed is reminiscent of Gabinius

am I to say about his vast household of slaves and the variety of their technical skills? I say nothing about these common skills, the cooks, bakers, litter bearers: he has so many people to charm his mind and ears that the whole neighborhood resounds daily with the strains of vocal music, stringed instruments, and flutes, and with the noise of nighttime banquets. When a man leads this life, gentlemen, can you imagine what daily expenses, what lavish displays, what banquets occur? Quite respectable, I suppose, in such a house, if this can be considered a house rather than a manufactory of wickedness and a lodging for every sort of outrageous conduct. You see how the man himself, gentlemen, with hair carefully arranged and perfumed, gads about through the forum accompanied by a large crowd of toga-clad men;[128] you see how he despises everyone, how he considers no one a human being compared with himself, and believes that he alone is wealthy and powerful.[129]

If I wished to mention what he is achieving and attempting to do, I am afraid, gentlemen, that some uninformed person may think that I wanted to attack the cause and victory of the nobility. And yet I can rightfully censure it if anything displeases me in that party; for I have no fear of anyone thinking that I harbored feelings unfriendly to the cause of the nobility. Those who know me are aware that, to the best of my poor and feeble abilities, after a

as portrayed at *Red. sen.* 12–13 and 16; for such traits being viewed as marks of effeminacy, cf. Herter, *RAC* s.v. Effeminatus.

[129] This takes up previous references to Chrysogonus' (informal) power (*potentia*) at §§6, 35, 60, and 122, now with the suggestion of overreach; cf. Buchheit 1975, 200–201.

id quod maxime volui fieri non potuit, ut componeretur, id maxime defendisse ut ii vincerent qui vicerunt. Quis enim erat qui non videret humilitatem cum dignitate de amplitudine contendere? Quo in certamine perditi civis erat non se ad eos iungere quibus incolumibus et domi dignitas et foris auctoritas retineretur. Quae perfecta esse et suum cuique honorem et gradum redditum gaudeo, iudices, vehementerque laetor eaque omnia deorum voluntate, studio populi Romani, consilio et imperio et felicitate L. Sullae gesta esse intellego. Quod animadversum est in eos qui contra omni ratione pugnarunt, non debeo reprehendere; quod viris fortibus quorum opera eximia in rebus gerendis exstitit honos habitus est, laudo. Quae ut fierent idcirco pugnatum esse arbitror meque in eo studio partium fuisse confiteor. Sin autem id actum est et idcirco arma sumpta sunt ut homines postremi pecuniis alienis locupletarentur et in fortunas uniuscuiusque impetum facerent, et id non modo re prohibere non licet sed ne verbis quidem vituperare, tum vero [in][161] isto bello non recreatus neque restitutus sed subactus oppressusque populus Romanus est.

137

Verum longe aliter est: nil horum est, iudices. Non

138

[161] *secl. Garatoni*

---

[130] In this he followed his mentor Scaevola; see §33.
[131] Paterson 2004, 85–87, sketches the background. Cf. also *Ver.* 2.1.37, where Cicero says that Verres did not become a Sullan "in order for honor and rank to be restored to the nobility," which would presumably, in his view, have been an acceptable reason.
[132] Cf. *Rep.* 1.43, where Scipio criticizes democracy for confusing social distinctions (*gradus dignitatis*).

peaceful settlement, which I desired above all,[130] became impossible, I earnestly supported the victory of those who have won it. For was there anyone who failed to see that men of low birth were contending with men of rank for the highest honors?[131] In this contest it would have been the act of a desperate citizen not to join those who, by their safety, assured that proper rank would be maintained at home and authority abroad. I am glad, gentlemen, and highly delighted that this has been accomplished, that each has had his status and rank restored;[132] and I am aware that all these actions have been carried out by the will of the gods, the zeal of the Roman people, and the counsel, supreme power, and good fortune of Lucius Sulla.[133] I ought not to find fault that punishment has been inflicted on those who fought against us in every way they could; I commend that honor has been bestowed on the brave men who displayed outstanding service in the conduct of affairs. I am of the opinion that the object of the struggle was that these results should be attained, and I confess that I was associated with that party. But if this was done and arms were taken up so that the lowest of people might be enriched with others' wealth and might attack everyone's property; if it is not only unlawful to prevent this by action, but even to censure it with words, then indeed, instead of being refreshed and restored, the Roman people has been subdued and crushed by this war.

But it is quite otherwise; none of these things is the

[133] "Good fortune" (*felicitas*), glancing at Felix ("fortunate"), Sulla' second cognomen (see on §22), chimes in with the dictator's propaganda.

modo non laedetur[162] causa nobilitatis, si istis hominibus resistetis, verum etiam ornabitur. Etenim qui haec vituperare volunt[163] Chrysogonum tantum posse queruntur; qui laudare volunt concessum ei non esse commemorant. Ac iam nihil est quod quisquam aut tam stultus aut tam improbus sit qui dicat: "Vellem quidem liceret; hoc dixissem." Dicas licet. "Hoc fecissem." Facias licet; nemo prohibet. "Hoc decrevissem." Decerne, modo recte; omnes approbabunt. "Hoc iudicassem." Laudabunt omnes, si recte et ordine iudicaris. Dum necesse erat resque ipsa cogebat, unus omnia poterat; qui posteaquam magistratus creavit legesque constituit, sua cuique procuratio auctoritasque est restituta. Quam si retinere volunt ii qui reciperarunt in perpetuum poterunt obtinere; sin has caedes et rapinas et hos tantos tamque profusos sumptus aut facient aut approbabunt—nolo in eos gravius quicquam ne ominis[164] quidem causa dicere, unum hoc dico: nostri isti nobiles nisi vigilantes et boni et fortes et misericordes erunt, iis hominibus in quibus haec erunt ornamenta sua concedant necesse est. Quapropter desinant aliquando dicere male aliquem locutum esse, si qui vere ac libere locutus sit, desinant suam causam cum Chrysogono com-

[162] laeditur: *corr. Angelius*
[163] volunt *Aσχψ*: volent *Vπφ*
[164] hominis: *corr. Manutius*

---

[134] Though it has been claimed that this passage shows that Sulla yielded power in stages with abdication of the dictatorship in 81, Vervaet 2018 argues convincingly that the evidence is compatible with abdication at the beginning of 79.

PRO ROSCIO AMERINO 138–140

case, gentlemen. Not only will no harm be done to the cause of the nobles by your resisting these people, but it will even be enhanced. In fact, those who wish to censure the present state of affairs complain that Chrysogonus has so much power; those who wish to praise it declare that it has not been granted to him. There is now no reason why anyone should be so foolish or dishonest as to say: "I wish it were allowed; I would have said this." You may say it. "I would have done this." You may do it; no one prevents you. "I would have made this determination." Make it, provided you determine rightly; everyone will approve. "I should have judged thus." Everyone will praise you, if you judge rightly and properly. While it was necessary and the state of affairs demanded, one man alone possessed all power; but after he appointed magistrates and established laws, everyone's sphere of responsibility and authority was restored to him.[134] If they desire to retain it, those who have recovered it will be able to hold it in perpetuity; but if they commit or approve of these acts of murder and plundering, of such great and lavish expenses—I do not wish to say anything harsh against them, if only for the omen's sake.[135] I say only this: this nobility of ours, unless they are watchful, good, brave, and merciful, must yield their distinctions to those who possess these qualities. Therefore let them at last cease to say that someone has spoken treasonably if he has spoken with truth and frankness; let them cease to make common cause with Chry-

139

140

---

[135] Cf. *Fam.* 4.3[203].3: *Caesar . . . dixit se senatui roganti de Marcello ne ominis quidem causa negaturum* ("Caesar . . . declared that, if only for the omen's sake, he would not say no to the Senate's petition": trans. Shackleton Bailey).

municare, desinant, si ille laesus sit, de se aliquid detractum arbitrari, videant ne turpe miserumque sit eos qui equestrem splendorem pati non potuerunt servi nequissimi dominationem ferre posse. Quae quidem dominatio, iudices, in aliis rebus antea versabatur, nunc vero quam viam munitet et quod iter affectet videtis: ad fidem, ad ius iurandum, ad iudicia vestra, ad id quod solum prope in civitate sincerum sanctumque restat. Hicne etiam sese putat aliquid posse Chrysogonus? Hicne etiam potens esse vult? O rem miseram atque acerbam! Neque mehercules hoc indigne fero, quod verear ne quid possit, verum quod ausus est, quod speravit sese apud tales viros aliquid posse[165] ad perniciem innocentis, id ipsum queror. Idcircone spectata[166] nobilitas armis atque ferro rem publicam reciperavit ut ad libidinem suam liberti servulique nobilium bona fortunas vitasque nostras[167] vexare possent? Si id actum est, fateor me errasse qui hoc maluerim, fateor insanisse qui cum illis senserim; tametsi inermis, iudices, sensi. Sin autem victoria nobilium ornamento atque emolumento rei publicae populoque Romano debet esse, tum vero optimo et nobilissimo cuique meam orationem gratissimam esse oportet. Quod si quis est qui et se et causam laedi putet cum Chrysogonus vituperetur, is causam igno-

141

142

---

[165] *add.* χψ
[166] exspectata: *corr. Landgraf*
[167] vitasque nostras *Luterbacher*: vestrasque nostras V: vestras atque nostras Aπϕψ: vestras nostrasque σχ

---

136 Before a senatorial audience, Cicero does not draw nice distinctions between slaves and freedmen; cf. Achard 1981, 215–16.

sogonus; let them cease to think that if he is injured, they themselves have suffered a loss; let them consider whether it is not disgraceful and miserable that they, who could not suffer the splendor of the equestrian order, should be able to endure the domination of the basest of slaves.[136] This domination, gentlemen, was formerly exercised on other matters, but now you see "what road it is constructing, what course it is entering upon":[137] one that leads to your good faith, your oath, your verdicts, to almost the only thing that is left in the community uncorrupted and inviolable. Does Chrysogonus think that even in this he possesses some influence? Does he wish to be powerful even in this? How miserable! How bitter! And, by Hercules, I am not indignant at this because I am afraid of his having any power, but because he has dared, because he has hoped with men such as these to have some influence to cause the ruin of an innocent man, *that* is what I complain of. Did the respected nobles recover the republic by arms and the sword only in order that freedmen and worthless slaves of the nobles might be able to harass our property, fortunes, and lives at will? If this has been achieved, I confess that I made a mistake in preferring this course; I confess that I lost my mind in agreeing with their opinions, although I did so, gentlemen, without taking part in the fight. But if the victory of the nobles is to be a glory and an advantage to the republic and the Roman people, then indeed my words ought to be most welcome to all who are best and noblest. But if there is anyone who thinks that both he himself and the cause suffer injury when Chryso-

141

142

---

[137] Cicero cites a verse from an unknown drama; cf. Dyck 2010, 195; Krostenko 2023, 271 and n. 59.

rat, se ipsum probe[168] novit; causa enim splendidior fiet, si nequissimo cuique resistetur, ille improbissimus Chrysogoni fautor qui sibi cum illo rationem communicatam putat laeditur, cum ab hoc splendore causae separatur.

143   Verum haec omnis oratio, ut iam ante dixi, mea est, qua me uti res publica et dolor meus et istorum iniuria coegit. Sed Roscius horum nihil indignum putat, neminem accusat, nihil de suo patrimonio queritur. Putat homo imperitus morum, agricola et rusticus, ista omnia quae vos per Sullam gesta esse dicitis more, lege, iure gentium facta; culpa liberatus et crimine nefario solutus cupit a vobis
144 discedere; si hac indigna suspicione careat, animo aequo se carere suis omnibus commodis dicit. Rogat oratque te, Chrysogone, si nihil de patris fortunis amplissimis in suam rem convertit, si nulla in re te fraudavit, si tibi optima fide sua omnia concessit, adnumeravit, appendit, si vestitum quo ipse tectus erat anulumque de digito[169] suum tibi tradidit, si ex omnibus rebus se ipsum nudum neque praeterea quicquam excepit, ut sibi per te liceat innocenti
145 amicorum opibus vitam in egestate degere. "Praedia mea tu possides, ego aliena misericordia vivo; concedo, et quod animus aequus est et[170] quia necesse est. Mea domus tibi patet, mihi clausa est; fero. Familia mea maxima tu[171] uteris, ego servum habeo nullum; patior et ferendum puto.

[168] probe *Madvig*: prope non Ω
[169] de digito *Boemoraeus*: dedit os Ω
[170] est et *Angelius*: esset Ω
[171] maxima tu *cod. Helstad.*: maximat V: maxima *cett.*

[138] Cf. §130.

gonus is attacked, he does not understand the cause, but forms a good estimate of himself: for the cause will become more glorious if it shall offer resistance to every scoundrel, but the shameless supporter of Chrysogonus, who thinks that he and Chrysogonus have a common interest, does suffer injury, for he is cut off from the glory of the cause.

But, as I have already stated,[138] all that I have just said is my own; the republic, my indignation, and the injustice of those men compelled me to use this language. But Roscius thinks none of these acts outrageous, he accuses no one, he makes no complaint about his inheritance. Inexperienced in the ways of the world, this farmer and rustic believes that all the actions that you assert were taken by Sulla were done in accordance with custom, law, and the law of nations. He desires to depart from you free from blame and acquitted of a nefarious accusation; if he is free of this unworthy suspicion, he declares that he is resigned to the loss of all his property. If out of his father's ample fortune he has turned nothing to his own advantage, if he has defrauded you in no respect, if he has yielded all his property to you with the utmost good faith, has counted and weighed each item separately, if he has delivered to you the very clothes that covered him and the ring from his finger, if, of all his belongings he has only reserved his naked body and nothing else, he begs and beseeches you, Chrysogonus, to allow him, an innocent man, to pass his life in poverty, with the resources of his friends. "You possess my farms; I am living on the charity of others; I allow it, because I am resigned and because I must. My house is open to you, but shut to me; I bear it. You have at your disposal my numerous household; I have not a single slave;

CICERO

Quid vis amplius? Quid insequeris? Quid oppugnas? Qua in re tuam voluntatem laedi a me putas? Ubi tuis commodis officio? Quid tibi obsto?" Si spoliorum causa vis hominem occidere, spoliasti; quid quaeris amplius? Si inimicitiarum, quae sunt tibi inimicitiae cum eo cuius ante praedia possedisti quam ipsum cognosti? Sin metus,[172] ab eone aliquid metuis quem vides ipsum ab se tam atrocem iniuriam propulsare non posse? Sin, ⟨quod⟩[173] bona quae Rosci fuerunt tua facta sunt, idcirco hunc illius filium studes perdere, nonne ostendis id te vereri quod praeter ceteros tu metuere non debeas, nequando liberis proscrip-
146 torum bona patria reddantur? Facis iniuriam, Chrysogone, si maiorem spem emptionis tuae in huius exitio ponis quam in iis rebus quas L. Sulla gessit. Quodsi tibi causa nulla est cur hunc miserum tanta calamitate affici velis, si tibi omnia sua praeter[174] animam tradidit nec sibi quicquam paternum ne monumenti quidem causa clam reservavit,[175] per deos immortales! quae ista tanta crudelitas est, quae tam fera immanisque natura? Quis umquam praedo fuit tam nefarius, quis pirata tam barbarus ut, cum integram praedam sine sanguine habere posset, cruenta
147 spolia detrahere mallet? Scis hunc nihil habere, nihil audere, nihil posse, nihil umquam contra rem tuam cogitasse, et tamen oppugnas eum quem neque metuere potes neque odisse debes nec quicquam iam habere reliqui

[172] metuis: *corr. Madvig*
[173] *add. Naugerius*
[174] praeter σχψ: propter VAπφ
[175] clam reservavit *recentiores*: clare servavit Ω

I suffer it and think that it must be endured. What more do you want? Why pursue me? Why attack me? In what respect do you think I have thwarted your wishes? Where have I opposed your interests? In what do I stand in your way?" If you wish to murder a man for the sake of the spoils, you have despoiled him; what more do you ask for? If it is from enmity, what enmity can exist between you and one whose farms you took possession of before you knew the man himself? If it is from fear, do you fear anything from one whom you see to be incapable of warding off from himself so appalling an injustice? But if it is because the property that belonged to Sextus Roscius has become yours that you are eager to destroy his son, do you not show that you are afraid of that of which you of all men should not fear—lest their patrimony ever be restored to the children of the proscribed? You do wrong, Chrysogonus, if you place greater hope of preserving your purchase in the destruction of my client than the actions carried out by Sulla. But if you have no reason for wishing this unhappy man to be afflicted by so great a calamity, if he has handed over to you everything except the breath in his body, if he has not secretly kept back even as a keepsake anything that belonged to his father, by the immortal gods, what is the meaning of this monstrous cruelty, this savage inhumanity? Was ever a robber so wicked, was ever a pirate so barbarous, as to prefer to strip off spoils dripping with gore when he could have the whole prize without bloodshed? You know that my client possesses nothing, that he dares do nothing, can do nothing, that he has never contemplated any action against your interests; and do you nonetheless attack him whom you cannot fear and ought not to hate, who you see has nothing left of which you can

CICERO

vides quod ei detrahere possis? Nisi hoc indignum putas, quod vestitum sedere in iudicio vides quem tu e patrimonio tamquam e naufragio nudum expulisti. Quasi vero nescias hunc et ali et vestiri a Caecilia Baliarici[176] filia, Nepotis sorore, spectatissima femina, quae cum patrem clarissimum, amplissimos patruos, ornatissimum fratrem haberet, tamen, cum esset mulier, virtute perfecit ut, quanto honore ipsa ex illorum dignitate afficeretur, non minora illis ornamenta ex sua laude redderet.

148 An, quod diligenter defenditur, id tibi indignum facinus videtur? Mihi crede, si pro patris huius hospitiis[177] et gratia vellent omnes huic[178] hospites adesse et auderent libere defendere, satis copiose defenderetur; sin autem pro magnitudine iniuriae proque eo quod summa res publica in huius periculo temptatur haec omnes vindicarent, consistere mehercule vobis isto in loco non liceret. Nunc ita defenditur, non sane ut moleste ferre adversarii de-
149 beant neque ut se potentia superari putent. Quae domi gerenda sunt, ea per Caeciliam transiguntur, fori iudicique rationem ⟨M.⟩[179] Messalla, ut videtis, iudices, suscepit; qui, si iam satis aetatis ac roboris haberet, ipse pro Sex. Roscio diceret. Quoniam ad dicendum impedimento

[176] baliaris: *corr. Manutius*
[177] hospitis: *corr. ed. Ven.*
[178] huius: *corr. A. Eberhard*
[179] *add. Garatoni*

---

139 Cf. fr. orat. 14 F 6 Cr.-D. (of Clodius after the Bona Dea trial): "he emerged from that trial naked as if from a shipwreck."

140 For Caecilia's father and brother, cf. on §27. Her three paternal uncles were L. Caecilius Metellus Diadematus (cos.

rob him? Unless you think it scandalous to see him wearing his clothes and sitting in court—the man whom you have driven out of his patrimony naked as if he had suffered shipwreck.[139] As if you do not know that my client is fed and clothed by Caecilia, the daughter of Balearicus, the sister of Nepos, a woman highly esteemed, who, although she had a most illustrious father, most distinguished uncles, and a most eminent brother, has yet, woman though she is, by her character brought it about that, great as is the honor which she herself derives from their eminence, she gives back to them no lesser distinction through her own merits.[140]

Or does it seem to you scandalous that he is being scrupulously defended? Believe me, if, in consideration of his father's hospitality and popularity, all his guest-friends would be willing to be present and dare to defend him openly, he would have plenty of defenders; but if, in consideration of the greatness of the injustice, and of the fact that the highest interests of the state are being attacked in my client's danger, all men were to punish these acts, by Hercules, you would not be allowed to stand where you are. As it is, he is not being defended in such a way as ought to annoy our opponents, or make them think that they are being defeated by superior power. As for his domestic affairs, they are looked after by Caecilia; the conduct of his affairs in the forum and in court, as you see, gentlemen, has been undertaken by Marcus Messalla. If he were old and strong enough, he would himself plead for Sextus Roscius; but since his youth and his modesty, which is an

117), M. Caecilius Metellus (cos. 115), and C. Caecilius Metellus Caprarius (cos. 113).

est aetas et pudor, qui ornat aetatem, causam mihi tradidit, quem sua causa cupere ac debere intellegebat, ipse assiduitate, consilio, auctoritate, diligentia perfecit ut Sex. Rosci vita erepta de manibus sectorum sententiis iudicum permitteretur. Nimirum, iudices, pro hac nobilitate pars maxima civitatis in armis fuit; haec acta res est ut ii[180] nobiles restituerentur in civitatem qui hoc facerent quod facere Messallam videtis, qui caput innocentis defenderent, qui iniuriae resisterent, qui quantum possent in salute alterius quam in exitio mallent ostendere; quod si omnes qui eodem loco nati sunt[181] facerent, et res publica ex illis et ipsi ex invidia minus laborarent.

150 Verum si a Chrysogono, iudices, non impetramus ut pecunia nostra contentus sit, vitam ne petat, si ille adduci non potest ut, cum ademerit nobis omnia quae nostra erant propria, ne lucem quoque hanc quae communis est eripere cupiat, si non satis habet avaritiam suam pecunia explere, nisi etiam crudelitati sanguis praebitus[182] sit, unum perfugium, iudices, una spes reliqua est Sex. Roscio eadem quae rei publicae, vestra pristina bonitas et misericordia. Quae si manet, salvi etiam nunc esse possumus; sin ea crudelitas quae hoc tempore in re publica[183] versata est vestros quoque animos—id quod fieri profecto non potest—duriores acerbioresque reddit, actum est, iudices;

[180] ut ii *Madvig*: uti Ω [181] sunt σχψ: sint VAπφ
[182] crudelitati sanguis praebitus *Madvig*: crudelitate (-i) sanguinis praeditus Ω [183] in re p. *ed. Mediol.*: in rem p. Ω

---

[141] Probably M. Valerius Messalla Niger (cos. 61). He will have been two to four years younger than Cicero, so, in spite of Cicero's excuses, taking on the prosecution would not have been

ornament to it, prevent him from speaking, he has entrusted the case to me, who he knew desired it for his sake and was under an obligation to undertake it.[141] By his unwearied attention, his advice, influence, and diligence, he succeeded in rescuing the life of Sextus Roscius from the hands of the brokers and entrusting it to the verdict of his judges. There is no doubt, gentlemen, that a majority of the citizens took up arms for such nobles; their object was that these nobles should be restored to the community who would do what you see Messalla doing—defend the civil existence of an innocent man, resist injustice, and prefer to show the extent of their power in saving rather than ruining another man. If all those who have been born in the same rank were to do this, the republic would suffer less from them, and they themselves would suffer less from jealousy.

But if Chrysogonus does not grant our request to be content with our money and not to aim at our life; if, after having taken away everything that belonged to us, he cannot be induced to abstain from desiring to rob us even of this light of day which is common to all; if he is not content to glut his avarice with money unless blood is provided to assuage his cruelty, then, gentlemen, the only refuge, the only hope left for Sextus Roscius is the same as that for the republic—the kindliness and compassion that you showed in earlier times. If these feelings abide, we can even now be saved. But if that cruelty, which in these times is rife in the republic, also hardens and embitters your hearts— which surely cannot come to pass—then, gentlemen, it is 150

out of the question. The alternative candidate is Niger's cousin M. Valerius Messalla Rufus (cos. 53), who was two years younger.

inter feras satius est aetatem degere quam in hac tanta
151 immanitate versari. Ad eamne rem vos reservati estis, ad eamne rem delecti ut eos condemnaretis quos sectores ac sicarii iugulare non potuissent? Solent hoc boni imperatores facere cum proelium committunt, ut in eo loco quo fugam hostium fore arbitrentur milites collocent, in quos si qui ex acie fugerint de improviso incidant. Nimirum similiter arbitrantur isti bonorum emptores vos hic, tales viros, sedere qui excipiatis eos qui de suis manibus effugerint. Di prohibeant, iudices, ut hoc quod maiores consilium publicum vocari voluerunt praesidium sectorum
152 existimetur! An vero, iudices, vos non intellegitis[184] nihil aliud agi nisi ut proscriptorum liberi quavis ratione tollantur et eius rei initium in vestro iure iurando atque in Sex. Rosci periculo quaeri? Dubium est ad quem maleficium pertineat, cum videatis ex altera parte sectorem, inimicum, sicarium eundemque accusatorem hoc tempore, ex altera parte egentem, probatum suis filium, in quo non modo culpa nulla sed ne suspicio quidem potuit consistere? Numquid hic aliud videtis obstare Roscio nisi quod patris bona venierunt?
153 Quodsi id vos suscipitis et eam ad rem[185] operam vestram profitemini, si idcirco sedetis ut ad vos adducantur eorum liberi quorum bona venierunt, cavete, per deos immortales! iudices, ne nova et multo crudelior per vos

[184] intellegitis: intellegetis *VA*
[185] eam ad rem *Gulielmius*: ea(n)dem rem Ω

---

[142] The claim that the prosecution is instrumentalizing the jurors to commit the murder they previously failed to carry out is reprised from §8.

all over; it would be better to spend one's life among wild beasts than in the midst of such frightful barbarism. Is it for this that you have been preserved, is it for this that you have been chosen, that you might condemn those whom the brokers and cutthroats have been unable to murder?[142] When they join battle, good generals usually post soldiers at the spot to which they think the enemy will retreat, so that they may make an unexpected attack upon any who have fled the line of battle. No doubt these purchasers of confiscated goods think that in the same manner men like you are sitting here to catch those who have escaped from their hands. Heaven forbid, gentlemen, that this which our ancestors wanted to be called a public council, should be thought to be a bodyguard for the brokers! Do you not understand, gentlemen, that the only aim is that the children of the proscribed should be removed at all costs, and that the first step in this process is being sought in your verdict and the peril of Sextus Roscius? Is there any doubt who is implicated in the crime, when you see on the one side a broker, an enemy, an assassin, and likewise the current accuser; on the other, a man reduced to poverty, a son approved by his relatives, to whom not only no culpability, but not even a suspicion could be attached? Surely you do not see that anything else is opposed to Roscius except that his father's property has been sold, do you?

But if you support that cause and offer your efforts for that purpose; if you are sitting in order that the children of those whose goods have been sold may be brought before you, by the immortal gods, gentlemen, take care lest you be seen to have inaugurated a new and far more cruel

proscriptio instaurata esse videatur. Illam priorem, quae facta est in eos qui arma capere potuerunt, tamen senatus suscipere noluit, ne quid acrius quam more maiorum comparatum <est>[186] publico consilio factum videretur, hanc vero quae ad eorum liberos atque ad infantium puerorum incunabula pertinet nisi hoc iudicio a vobis reicitis et aspernamini, videte per deos immortales! quem in locum rem publicam perventuram putetis! Homines sapientes et ista auctoritate et potestate praeditos qua vos estis ex quibus rebus maxime res publica laborat, iis maxime mederi convenit. Vestrum nemo est quin intellegat populum Romanum, qui quondam in hostes lenissimus existimabatur, hoc tempore domestica crudelitate laborare. Hanc tollite ex civitate, iudices, hanc pati nolite diutius in hac re publica versari. Quae non modo id habet in se mali, quod tot cives atrocissime sustulit verum etiam hominibus lenissimis ademit misericordiam consuetudine incommodorum. Nam cum omnibus horis aliquid atrociter fieri videmus aut audimus, etiam qui natura mitissimi sumus assiduitate molestiarum sensum omnem humanitatis ex animis amittimus.

[186] *add. ed. Rom.*

proscription. The first one, which was directed against those who were able to take up arms, the senate nonetheless refused to support, for fear that an act more severe than what was ordained by ancestral custom might appear to have been performed by a public council. The second, which concerns their children and infants in the cradle, unless you reject it with contempt in this trial, by the immortal gods, consider to what a state you think the republic will be brought. It behooves wise men, furnished with the authority and power which you possess, to apply remedies especially to those evils from which the republic most suffers. There is no one among you who does not know that the Roman people, who were once considered to be most lenient toward their enemies, is currently suffering from domestic cruelty. Banish this cruelty from the community, gentlemen; do not allow it to roam at large any longer in this republic. It does not only involve this evil, that it has eliminated so many citizens by a most appalling death, but by inuring them to evils it has also removed pity from even the mildest men. For when, every hour, we see or hear of an act of cruelty, even those of us who are by nature most merciful, by the constant presence of trouble, lose from our hearts all feeling of humanity.

IN DEFENSE OF
QUINTUS ROSCIUS
THE COMIC ACTOR

INTRODUCTION

Quintus Roscius Gallus was the leading actor of Cicero's day and an old friend of the orator going back to the 80s, when he had referred Cicero to his first known client, P. Quinctius, the actor's brother-in-law. His acting was much admired.[1] This trial, which probably occurred in 72 or 71,[2] involved a claim for a specific sum (*condictio certae pecuniae*), namely 50,000 sesterces filed against Roscius by C. Fannius Chaerea, who was represented by P. Saturius, an experienced advocate (cf. §22; *FRLO* 106). The case was tried before a single judge, C. Calpurnius Piso (cos. 67), assisted by a council (§12).[3]

Interpretation of the speech is made difficult by the fact that it has survived in mutilated form, with both the beginning and the end lost. The formal narrative, if there was one,[4] has not survived, so the background must be gathered from various passages of the extant part, the argumentation/refutation.[5] Roscius and Fannius had entered into partnership as joint owners of the slave Panur-

---

[1] Cf. §§29–30. For instance, at *De or.* 1.130 "Crassus" declares that "Roscius" is used as a byword for excellence in any art. Lebek 1996, 36–39, discusses Roscius' life and career.

[2] For detailed arguments, see Dyck forthcoming, Appendix 2.

[3] Cf. *TLRR* 166.

[4] Doubted by Mette 1965, 17–18, and Stroh 1975, 137.

[5] I follow in essentials the reconstruction of Stroh 1975, ch. 5.

gus, purchased by Fannius and trained in acting by Roscius (§§27–29). Panurgus had, however, been killed by one Q. Flavius of Tarquinii (§32). Fannius filed suit against Flavius for damages under the Aquilian Law (§32), both in his own name and as legal representative (*cognitor*) of Roscius (§32).[6] Flavius agreed to an out-of-court settlement with Roscius, whereby he presented the actor with a farm valued by Fannius at 100,000 sesterces; this occurred fifteen years before the current trial (§§32, 37). Three years before our trial, Fannius had found out about Roscius' settlement with Flavius and, in the belief that Roscius was withholding property that rightfully belonged to the partnership, filed suit for theft (§§26, 32). A conviction on this charge, or even a settlement, would have been very damaging to Roscius, since it would have resulted in *infamia*, with entailed loss of various civil rights.[7] Fannius and Roscius evidently came to an out-of-court agreement (*pactio*), though this is denied by Cicero (§26). This agreement led to an arbitration between the two, whereby the current judge, C. Piso, served as arbitrator (ibid.). The result of the arbitration was that Piso "asked" (*rogasti*) Roscius to pay Fannius a sum of money (the figure is corrupted in our manuscripts) for representing him in the suit with Flavius and that Fannius made a counterstipulation (*restipulatio*) that he would pay Roscius half of any settlement received from Flavius (§38). It would thus appear that the suit with Flavius over Panurgus' death was to be taken up again at this stage.[8] Cicero

[6] *TLRR* 125.

[7] Cf. Mommsen 1899, 754 and 997.

[8] Contrast Stroh 1975, 131, who suggests that Flavius was acquitted when the matter first came to trial.

cites these facts as part of his argument that Roscius made a settlement for himself alone and that the claims of the partnership remained open. The amount of 50,000 sesterces that Fannius is claiming in the current trial is the balance remaining on the 100,000 sesterces that Roscius promised as part of the *pactio* that led Fannius to drop his charges (§§4, 51).[9] Cicero, however, claims that the suit was dropped because Roscius was innocent (§26), and he probably argued in the lost end of the speech that the 50,000 sesterces already paid were a generous gift made by Roscius.[10]

A theory of the case that would explain the attitudes of the two principals would be this: in accepting the farm from Flavius, Roscius took the (legally naive) view that he was the chief contributor to Panurgus' value and was entitled to receive the lion's share of the compensation without reference to Fannius, who could make his own arrangements; he also thought that Fannius overvalued the farm, which was not worth so much when first acquired (this attitude peeks out in the argument at §§27–33). Fannius, meanwhile, was apparently unable to make any prog-

[9] Not from the arbitration; cf. Stroh 1975, 112. Though Fannius would have a claim to half the value of the farm, which he estimated at 100,000, a double penalty applied in cases of theft (so Stroh 1975, 118); alternatively, the difference may have been compensation for the income derived from the farm over the twelve years when it had been in Roscius' possession (so Lintott 2008, 66).

[10] So Stroh 1975, 145–46; this was the second option offered at §16 and would comport both with Cicero's claim of his client's innocence and with his general portrait of his client's character (§§18, 21, 27).

INTRODUCTION

ress in his lawsuit against Flavius and learned of his partner's settlement only twelve years later. (The settlement was probably made on a confidential basis.) If Fannius had learned of the settlement at the time and cited it in court, it would have significantly damaged Flavius' case. Fannius was understandably peeved at Roscius for having betrayed his interests in this way[11] and filed suit for theft. Under this pressure, Roscius agreed to the *pactio*, whereby Fannius agreed to drop the suit in exchange for payment of 100,000 HS, including an initial installment of 50,000. Roscius, however, came to regret this agreement, believing that Fannius' contribution to the partnership (6,000 HS, the initial purchase price of Panurgus, §29) was hardly worth so much. He may also have heard the rumor that Fannius had received 100,000 HS from Flavius (§42) and concluded that Fannius had been amply compensated.[12] For three years he showed no inclination to pay the balance of 50,000 owed to Fannius. The latter's patience finally broke, and he filed suit for the fixed sum of 50,000 HS.

Cicero, then, was presented with a case that was legally weak (the law of partnership was clear that income from joint property must be divided between the partners).[13] But he compensated for this weakness in two ways: by a careful arrangement of his arguments so as to highlight his opponent's weakness and conceal his own; and by a skillful appeal to the audience gathered to observe the case in the

[11] Stroh 1975, 134–35.

[12] Stroh 1975, 136.

[13] Cf. Berger 1953 s.v. Societas. The counterstipulation quoted at §37 shows that this was established as a partnership of two equals.

PRO ROSCIO COMOEDO

forum (the *corona*), perhaps consisting mostly of theater people and fans of Roscius, in the hope that their enthusiasm, once roused, would spill over to the judge.[14]

The argument can be outlined as follows, with the lost parts indicated by square brackets:

[I. Proem (probably including an attack on Fannius' character)]
II. Nontechnical proofs (ἄτεχνοι πίστεις) (§§1–13)
III. *Divisio* (§§14–15)
IV. Technical proofs (ἔντεχνοι πίστεις) (§§16–56)
    A. Roscius was innocent of the charge of theft (§§16–26)
    B. Legal position with respect to the charge of theft (§§27–56)
        1. Digression: Roscius' contribution to the partnership was the more important (§§27–31)
        2. The claim that Roscius had settled for the partnership (§§32–51)
        3. The claim that a settlement by a partner belongs to the partnership (§§52–56)
[C. A claim that Roscius paid Fannius 50,000 HS out of generosity (?)
V. Peroration][15]

Cicero probably launched early on, as in the defense of Quinctius, an attack on the character of the rival litigant as a treacherous partner who should not have resorted to law (hinted at by the reference to "this hand, full of treachery," §1). What are labeled above, from the standpoint of

[14] Cf. Axer 1980, 28; 1989, 305.
[15] Cf. Stroh 1975, 147.

INTRODUCTION

rhetorical theory, nontechnical and technical proofs are differently described by Cicero: he claims that II. is the central question at issue and that his arguments here are sufficient to ensure victory in the trial and that the subject of the rest of the speech is beyond the scope of the legal case and is pursued merely to save his client's reputation (§14). But this analysis is misleading and merely emphasizes one type of evidence (documentary proofs), where the prosecutor's case is weak (Fannius supported his claim by an entry in his daybook [*adversaria*], not his ledger [*tabulae*]), at the expense of arguments from probability, where the prosecutor's case was strong (Saturius could claim that Roscius was strongly motivated to reach an out-of-court settlement on the charge of theft and persuaded Fannius to omit the corresponding entry from his ledger to spare his reputation).

What is remarkable about Cicero's claim of Roscius' innocence on the charge of theft (IV.A.) is that he argues solely on the basis of character, not on the facts or the legal position. Moreover, he frames this as a comparison, arguing from probability that Fannius would be likelier to have cheated Roscius than vice-versa (though Fannius was not on trial for cheating his partner). Not only that, but he offers as proof not anything that Fannius did, but merely his appearance. If at *Rosc. Am.* 46–47 Cicero introduced an example from the comic stage with an elaborate apologia, here, in a case dealing with a comic actor, he slips naturally into the comparison, citing the similarity of Fannius' face, with eyebrows shaved, to the mask of the stock figure of the pimp (*leno*) Ballio in Plautus' *Pseudolus*, often played by Roscius on the stage (§20). The audience will remember the famous scene of competitive insults in

which Ballio is reproached as a "cheater of partners" (*sociofraude*, *Pseud.* 362) and apply it to Fannius.[16] Allusion and suggestion do the work of logical argument.

Cicero continues the theatrical mood in the sequel as he stages various imagined dialogues between the persons involved in the case. These include his own dialogues with Fannius (§§24, 25, 43), between Roscius and Fannius (§§26, 32), and himself and Saturius (§§22, 27, 40). To heighten the drama, he sometimes even invents "stage directions": "he blushes, he does not know what to answer" (§8); "shuffling back and forth" (§37). These scenes culminate in a sarcastically cynical dialogue between Roscius and Cluvius about the possibility of the latter telling a lie to further the actor's interests, similar to several conversations between crooks in Plautus' plays (§49).[17] There is also the reconciliation between Fannius and Roscius imagined as a scene in which a jilted lover seeks restoration to the favor of the beloved (§26). In style, too, the speech borrows heavily from the racy, colloquial diction of comedy, as Axer shows in detail.[18]

Besides playing to the crowd, Cicero also offers some facts and figures to engage the attention of Piso. Axer's study of the numerical notation in the manuscript yields the first convincing account of Cicero's financial argument, which is essentially that Fannius has already obtained half of the value he attributes to the farm received

[16] Cf. Lennon 2022, 35–38.

[17] Cf. Axer 1980, 29–30.

[18] Axer 1980, 34–37; 1989, 305–6. The attempt of Klingner 1953 to analyze the diction as Asianist is unconvincing; cf. Schmid 1954; Axer 1980, 10–13, 37–39.

INTRODUCTION

by Roscius, and he should be content with that, even if it is less than he wanted: it would be unfair for Roscius, who contributed so much value to the partnership, to have to bear an additional burden.[19]

Cicero has postponed to near the end his rather weak arguments countering the prosecution's legal claims (IV.B.). He points out that when Roscius settled with Flavius he did not provide security to guarantee that no subsequent suit would be filed against him, implying that Fannius' right of action was still open (§§35–36). However, if Flavius insisted that Roscius hold their agreement in confidence, he may have felt sufficiently protected against a successful suit by Fannius. In addition, Cicero points out that under the arbitration agreement Fannius made a counterstipulation to pay Roscius half of any settlement received from Flavius (§§37–38), with the implication that the claims of the partnership were still open. Cicero also claims that Fannius received 100,000 HS from Flavius without reference to Roscius. This would at most show that Fannius made the same kind of side-agreement with Flavius as Roscius, but his proof is weak, relying on hearsay (§§39–51).[20] Finally, he seeks to undermine the point that proceeds of the partnership must be returned

[19] Axer 1980, 82.

[20] C. Cluvius, the source of the information, had been judge in the trial of Fannius vs. Flavius. If the matter was settled out of court, however, he would not necessarily have known the details. Cicero does not say that he had died in the meantime (as he surely would have done, had that been the case). Perhaps, as Stroh 1975, 145n130, suspects, Roscius was unable to persuade him to testify at trial.

to the partnership with the analogy of the partners to the heirs under a will (§§39–51). But the analogy misleads: the heirs owe no duties to each other, whereas partners are bound by duties to one another under a good faith contract.

Cicero seems to have made the best he could of a difficult case, emphasizing Fannius' weak documentation of his agreement with Roscius, downplaying the underlying legal issues, offering a confusing and desultory presentation of the facts, and leaning heavily on the popular actor's good reputation. He wants to suggest, while not saying so explicitly, that Fannius is too greedy (cf. §21) and that, in equity, he should be content with what he has already received. If Cicero won a victory in this case, it will have been, as in the defense of Cluentius, by enveloping the judge in darkness.[21]

NOTE ON MANUSCRIPT AND EDITIONS

The text of the defense of Q. Roscius survived the Middle Ages in a single mutilated manuscript that Poggio discovered, perhaps at Cologne.[22] He made a copy, which he brought back to Italy. Poggio's copy was rediscovered in 1948 by A. Colonna and was used by Axer as the basis for his 1976 edition, on which this edition is based:

V   Vaticanus latinus 11458, a. 1471 scriptus

[21] Quint. *Inst.* 2.17.21.
[22] Cf. Axer 1976, v–viii; Rouse and Reeve, in Reynolds 1983, 83 and 91.

INTRODUCTION

The following are the major editions cited in the notes:

Ascensius	Paris, 1511
Angelius	Florence, 1515
Aldus	Venice, 1519 (edited by Naugerius)
Dubois	Paris, 1532
Naugerius	Venice, 1534
Manutius	Venice, 1540
Lambinus	Paris, 1566
Ernesti	Halle, 1773
Garatoni	Naples, 1777–1778
R. Kotz	Leipzig, 1837
Baiter, Halm	Zurich, 1845–1863
Müller	Leipzig, 1894
Clark	Oxford, 1909
A. Klotz	Leipzig, 1922

PRO ⟨QUINTO⟩
ROSCIO COMOEDO

... malitiam naturae crederetur. Is scilicet vir optimus et singulari fide praeditus in suo iudicio suis tabulis testibus uti conatur. Solent fere dicere qui per tabulas hominis ⟨prob⟩ati[1] pecuniam expensam tulerunt: "Egone talem virum corrumpere potui, ut mea causa falsum in codicem referret?" Expecto quam mox Chaerea hac oratione utatur: "Egone hanc manum plenam perfidiae[2] et hos digitos meos impellere potui ut falsum perscriberem[3] nomen?" Quod si ille suas proferet tabulas, proferet suas quoque Roscius. Erit in illius tabulis hoc nomen, at ⟨in⟩[4] huius 2 non erit. Cur potius illius quam huius crederetur?—Scripsisset[5] ille, si non iussu huius expensum tulisset?—Non scripsisset hic quod sibi expensum ferre iussisset? Nam quem ad modum turpe est scribere quod non debeatur,

---

[1] *Axer*: citi *(post spat. vac. 3–4 litt.)* V: honesti *Manutius*
[2] plenam perfidiae *suspicatus est Ernesti*
[3] -erent *Manutius*
[4] *add. Dubois*   [5] scripsisse V: *corr. Aldus*

---

[1] Ironic reference to the plaintiff, C. Fannius Chaerea, who must prove that Roscius had contracted a debt of 100,000 HS. "Account books" renders *tabulae*; a synonym is the *codex accepti*

IN DEFENSE OF QUINTUS ROSCIUS THE COMIC ACTOR

... would be thought ... a vice of character. He, of course, as a fine gentleman and endowed with singular integrity, is attempting to use his own account books as evidence in his own trial.[1] Those who have cited the payment of money by the account books of a man of proven character generally say: "Could I have bribed a man of such quality to make a false entry in his books for my sake?" I am waiting to see how long it will be before Chaerea uses the following argument: "Could I have induced this hand, full of treachery, and these fingers of mine to make a false entry of a debt?" But if he produces his account books, Roscius, too, will produce his. This entry will be found in the former's books, but not in my client's. Why should credence be given to the former rather than the latter?—Would he (Chaerea) have made the entry unless he had made the expenditure on his (Roscius') instructions?—Would my client not have made an entry of money he had bidden (Chaerea) to disburse to himself? For just as it is disgraceful to enter an amount that is not owed, so it is dishonest

2

et expensi (book of receipts and expenditures) mentioned in §4; see further Thilo 1980, 162–70.

sic improbum est non referre quod debeas. Aeque enim tabulae condemnantur eius qui verum non rettulit et eius qui falsum perscripsit. Sed ego copia et facultate causae confisus vide quo progrediar. Si tabulas C. Fannius accepti et expensi profert suas in suam rem suo arbitratu scriptas, 3 quominus secundum illum iudicetis non recuso. Quis hoc frater fratri, quis parens filio tribuit ut quodcumque rettulisset, id ratum haberet? Ratum habebit Roscius; profer; quod tibi fuerit persuasum, huic erit persuasum, quod tibi fuerit probatum, huic erit probatum. Paulo ante M. Perpennae, P. Saturi tabulas poscebamus, nunc tuas, C. Fanni Chaerea, solius flagitamus et quominus secundum eas lis 4 detur non recusamus; quid ita non profers? Non confecit tabulas? Immo diligentissime. Non refert parva nomina in codices? Immo omnis summas. Leve et tenue hoc nomen est? HS CCCIƆƆ sunt. Quomodo tibi tanta pecunia extraordinaria iacet? Quomodo HS CCCIƆƆ in codice accepti et expensi non sunt? Pro di immortales! essene quemquam tanta audacia praeditum qui quod nomen referre in tabulas timeat, id petere audeat, quod in codicem ⟨in⟩iuratus[6] referre noluerit, id iurare in litem non dubitet, quod sibi probare non possit, id persuadere alteri conetur!

[6] iniuratus *recentiores*: iuratus V

---

[2] Cf. *Rosc. Am.* 73 for a similar self-confident concession.
[3] M. Perpenna (better, Perperna), cos. 92, cens. 86 (*MRR* 2:17, 54; Münzer, *RE* s.v. Perperna 5), evidently a witness at this trial (*TLRR* 166), probably a friend and supporter of Saturius; cf. the reference to his supporter(s) (*advocatio*) at §15; Stroh 1975, 138n113.

not to enter what you do owe. For the account books of one who failed to enter what is true are as blameworthy as those of one who has written down what is false. But see how far I am prepared to go, relying upon the abundant resources of my case.[2] If Gaius Fannius produces his accounts of receipts and disbursements taken down in his own interest and at his own discretion, I make no objection to your passing judgment in his favor. What brother has granted to his brother or what father to his son the concession of regarding as confirmed whatever he has entered in his books? Roscius will regard it as confirmed; produce your books; what you may have been convinced of, he will be convinced of; what you may have approved, he will approve. A little while ago we asked for the account books of Marcus Perpenna[3] and Publius Saturius;[4] we now urgently call for yours alone, Gaius Fannius Chaerea, and have no objection to judgment being rendered according to them; why in this case do you not produce them? Did he not keep books? On the contrary, most carefully. Does he not enter small debts in his ledgers? On the contrary, every sum. Is this debt unimportant and trivial? It is 100,000 sesterces. How is it you allow such an extraordinarily large sum of money to lie neglected? How is it that 100,000 sesterces fail to appear in the ledger? Immortal gods, to think that there can be a man so audacious as to dare to claim a debt that he is afraid to enter in his account books; as not to hesitate to swear to a debt for a lawsuit which, when not under oath, he refused to enter in his ledger; as to endeavor to persuade another of something that he cannot prove to himself!

[4] Counsel for the plaintiff; cf. *FRLO* 106; Münzer, *RE* s.v. Saturius 1.

CICERO

5 Nimium cito ait me indignari de tabulis; non habere se hoc nomen in codicem accepti et expensi relatum confitetur, sed in adversariis patere contendit. Usque eone te diligis et magnifice circumspicis ut pecuniam non ex tuis tabulis sed adversariis petas? Suum codicem testis loco recitare arrogantiae est; suarum perscriptionum et litura‑
6 rum adversaria proferre non amentia est? Quod si eandem vim, diligentiam auctoritatemque habent adversaria quam tabulae, quid attinet codicem instituere, conscribere, ordinem conservare, memoriae tradere litterarum vetustatem? Sed si, quod adversariis nihil credimus, idcirco codicem scribere instituimus, quod etiam apud omnes leve et infirmum est, id apud iudicem grave et sanctum esse duceretur?
7 Quid est quod neglegenter scribamus adversaria? Quid est quod diligenter conficiamus tabulas? Qua de causa? Quia haec sunt menstrua, illae sunt aeternae; haec delentur statim, illae servantur sancte; haec parvi temporis memoriam, illae perpetuae existimationis fidem et religionem amplectuntur; haec sunt disiecta,[7] illae sunt in ordinem confectae. Itaque adversaria in iudicium protulit nemo; codicem protulit, tabulas recitavit. Tu, C. Piso, tali fide, virtute, gravitate, auctoritate ornatus, ex adversariis
8 pecuniam petere non auderes. Ego quae clara sunt consuetudine diutius dicere non debeo. Illud vero quod ad rem vehementer pertinet quaero: quam pridem hoc nomen, Fanni, in adversaria rettulisti? Erubescit, quid re‑

---

[7] disiecta *Hotoman*: deiectae V

---

[5] *adversaria* = "rough book for preliminary recording of accounts, daybook": *OLD* s.v. *adversaria,*[2] ordinarily entered in regular account books at the end of each month (§§7–8).

PRO ROSCIO COMOEDO 5–8

He says that I am too hasty in expressing my indignation about the account books; he admits that he does not have this item entered in his ledger, but maintains that it appears in his daybook.[5] Are you so in love with yourself, do you have such a high regard for yourself, as to ask for money not on the basis of your account books, but of your daybooks? It is presumptuous to read out one's own ledger as a witness; but is it not sheer madness to produce rough notes of one's entries and erasures? But if daybooks have the same value, the same exactness, and the same authority as account books, what is the use of establishing a ledger, of writing down, keeping an ordered list, and entrusting past events to a written record? But if we begin to keep a ledger because we have no faith in daybooks, would something that everyone views as trivial and weak be held to be weighty and exalted in the eyes of a judge? Why do we write our daybooks carelessly but keep our ledgers carefully? It is because daybooks are for a month, ledgers are permanent; daybooks are immediately destroyed, ledgers are religiously preserved; daybooks embrace the record of a moment, ledgers encompass the good faith and honesty of one's reputation for all time; daybooks are scattered, ledgers are put together in order. This is why no one has produced daybooks in court; it is ledgers that have been produced and account books that have been read out. You, Gaius Piso, a man distinguished by such integrity, character, dignity, and authority, would not venture to claim money on the basis of daybooks. I myself ought not to speak any longer on matters that are clear by custom. I ask this question, which is highly relevant to the subject at hand: how long ago, Fannius, did you enter this debt in your daybooks? He blushes, he does not know what to

CICERO

spondeat nescit, quid fingat extemplo non habet. "Sunt duo menses" dices. Iam[8] tum in codicem accepti et expensi[9] ⟨referri⟩[10] debuit. Amplius? Sunt sex menses? Cur tam diu iacet hoc nomen in adversariis? Quid si tandem amplius triennium est? Quomodo, cum omnes qui tabulas conficiant menstruas paene rationes in tabulas transferant, tu hoc nomen triennium amplius in adversariis iacere

9 pateris? Utrum cetera nomina in codicem accepti et expensi digesta[11] habes an non? Si non, quomodo tabulas conficis? Si etiam, quam ob rem, cum cetera nomina in ordinem referebas, hoc nomen triennio amplius, quod erat in primis magnum, in adversariis relinquebas? Nolebas sciri debere tibi Roscium; cur scribebas? Rogatus eras ne referres; cur in adversariis scriptum habes?[12]

Sed haec quamquam firma esse video, tamen ipse mihi satis facere non possum nisi a C. Fannio ipso testimonium sumo hanc pecuniam ei non deberi. Magnum est quod conor, difficile est quod polliceor: nisi eundem et adversa-

10 rium et testem habuerit Roscius, nolo vincat. Pecunia tibi debebatur[13] certa, quae nunc petitur per iudicem, in qua

---

[8] dices. iam *Axer*: iam dices V

[9] acceptum et expensum V: *corr. Turnebus et item infra*

[10] referri *recentiores*: *om.* V: referre *Axer clausulae causa*

[11] digesta *recentiores*: et diggesta V

[12] habebas: *corr. Lambinus*

[13] debeatur V: *corr. Naugerius*

---

[6] Though Fannius had a reasonable explanation (he left the item out of his account book at Roscius' request, but kept it in his daybook for his own records), by use of the dilemma form, Cicero seeks to make this seem implausible; cf. Craig 1993, 75–76.

answer, he cannot invent anything on the spur of the moment. "It is two months ago," you will say. Already at that time it ought to have been entered in the ledger of receipts and disbursements. Still longer? Six months? Why did this item remain so long forgotten in the daybook? What then if it is more than three years ago? How is it that, when all other people who keep account books transfer their accounts nearly every month into their books, you allow this debt to lie neglected in your daybook for more than three years? Have you organized all the other debts in the ledger of receipts and disbursements or not? If not, how do you keep your books? If you have, why is it that, when you were entering all the other debts in order, you left this debt, which was extremely large, for more than three years in your daybook? You did not want it to be known that Roscius was indebted to you. Why then did you write it down? You had been asked not to enter it. Why do you have it written in your daybook?[6]

But although I think that this is secure, nonetheless I cannot feel satisfied unless I obtain evidence from Fannius himself that this money is not owed to him. What I am attempting is a great task; what I am promising is difficult: unless Roscius shall have the same man both as his opponent and his witness, I do not want him to win his case. A specific sum of money was owed to you, which you now claim before a judge; concerning this a wager[7] was

---

[7] For the *sponsio* (wager), see on *Quinct.* 30.

legitimae partis sponsio facta est. Hic tu si amplius HS[14] nummo petisti quam tibi debitum est, causam perdidisti propterea quod aliud est iudicium, aliud est arbitrium. Iudicium est pecuniae certae, arbitrium incertae; ad iudicium hoc modo venimus ut totam litem aut obtineamus aut amittamus; ad arbitrium hoc animo adimus ut neque nihil neque tantum quantum postulavimus consequamur.

11 Ei rei ipsa verba formulae testimonio sunt. Quid est in iudicio? Derectum, asperum, simplex: SI PARRET[15] HS IƆƆƆ[16] DARI. Hic nisi planum facit HS IƆƆƆ ad libellam sibi deberi, causam perdit. Quid est in arbitrio? Mite, moderatum: QUANTUM[17] AEQUIUS ET MELIUS ID DARI. Ille iam[18] confitetur plus se petere quam debeatur, sed satis superque habere dicit quod sibi ab arbitro tribuatur. Itaque

12 alter causae confidit, alter diffidit. Quae cum ita sint, quaero abs te quid ita de hac pecunia, de his ipsis HS IƆƆƆ, de tuarum tabularum fide compromissum feceris, arbitrum sumpseris, quantum[19] aequius et melius sit dari re-

[14] HS *recentiores*: SS V   [15] parret V, *def. Platschek 2011, 370 adn. 6, TLL 10.1:371 coll.*: peteret V$^{mg.}$
[16] IƆƆƆ *Naugerius*: LIII V *(ita semper)*
[17] quantum *Manutius*: quanto V
[18] *Axer*: tamen *ex* tam V: tamen *recentiores*
[19] *Manutius*: quanto V

---

8 Fannius has filed suit for a fixed sum of money (*actio certae creditae pecuniae*); cf. Greenidge 1901, 198–200; Berger 1953 s.v. Mutuum. The sum in question is 50,000 sesterces, the balance remaining from the 100,000 Roscius agreed to pay Fannius in the agreement that led Fannius to drop the charge of theft.

9 The events narrated in §12 and the dénouement described

agreed to pay the part required by law.[8] In this case, if you claimed a sesterce more than is owed to you, you have lost your case, because a trial is one thing, arbitration is another. A trial deals with a fixed sum, arbitration with an indefinite sum. We come to trial on the understanding that we either gain or lose the suit entirely; we come before an arbitrator with the expectation of gaining something but not as much as we asked. The terms of the formula are themselves evidence of this. What is the formula in a trial? It is straightforward, severe, and simple: "if it is shown that 50,000 sesterces ought to be paid." Unless he (the claimant) proves that 50,000 sesterces to a penny are owed to him, he loses his case. What is the formula in arbitration?[9] It is mild and moderate: "as much as it seems fair and just should be given." He (the claimant) already admits that he is asking for more than is due to him, but he says that he will be satisfied and more than satisfied with what is awarded him by the arbitrator. Thus the one has confidence in his case, the other does not. This being so, I ask you why, in regard to this money, to these very 50,000 sesterces on the basis of your account books you entered into a joint agreement,[10] you accepted an arbitrator as to how much it seems "fair and just" should be given or

at §§37–38 show that this is an *arbitrium ex compromisso* (arbitration based on an agreement [sc. of the parties]) and not an *arbitrium pro socio* (arbitration initiated by one partner against another); cf. Platschek 2011, 371.

[10] That is, "a joint promise or undertaking made by two or more persons, and guaranteed by a deposit of money, to abide by the decision of an arbiter": *OLD* s.v. *compromissum*.

promittique si prior es.[20] Quis in hanc rem fuit arbiter? Utinam is quidem Romae esset! Romae est. Utinam[21] adesset in iudicio! Adest. Utinam sederet in consilio C. Pisonis! Ipse C. Piso est. Eundemne tu arbitrum et iudicem sumebas? Eidem[22] et infinitam largitionem remittebas et eundem in angustissimam formulam sponsionis concludebas? Quis umquam ad arbitrum, quantum petiit, tantum abstulit? Nemo; quantum enim aequius esset sibi dari,[23] petiit. De quo nomine ad arbitrum adisti, de eo ad iudicem venisti! Ceteri cum ad iudicem causam labefactari animadvertunt, ad arbitrum confugiunt, hic ab arbitro ad iudicem venire est ausus! Qui cum de hac pecunia ⟨de⟩[24] tabularum fide arbitrum sumpsit, iudicavit sibi pecuniam non deberi.

13

Iam duae partes causae sunt confectae; adnumerasse[25] sese negat, expensum tulisse non dicit, cum tabulas non recitat. Reliquum est ut stipulatum se esse dicat; praeterea enim quem ad modum certam pecuniam petere possit non reperio. Stipulatus es—ubi, quo die, quo tempore, quo praesente? Quis spopondisse me dicit? Nemo. Hic ego si finem faciam dicendi, satis fidei et diligentiae meae, satis

14

[20] si prior es *Platschek 2011, 374*: si peieres V
[21] nam utinam *codd.*: nam *del. codd. nonnulli*
[22] eidem *Angelius*: idem V
[23] dari *recentiores*: pari V
[24] de *inser. Ascensius (cf. §12)*
[25] *Camerarius*: adulterasse V

[11] Namely, the one who "has confidence in his case," as described at the end of §11.

[12] C. Calpurnius Piso (cos. 67), later defended by Cicero on a

promised if you are the former.[11] Who was the arbitrator for this matter? If only he were in Rome! He is in Rome. If only he were present in court! He is. If only he were sitting as Piso's assessor! It is Piso himself.[12] Did you accept the same man as arbitrator and judge? Did you allow the same man unlimited freedom of action and also confine him within the very narrow formula of the wager? Who ever obtained all that he claimed before an arbitrator? Nobody; for he only claimed for as much as seemed fair and right to be given him. You have come before a judge with a claim for the same amount as that for which you approached an arbitrator! When others perceive that their case is likely to be undermined before a judge, they have recourse to an arbitrator, but this man (Fannius) has ventured to go from an arbitrator to a judge! When he accepted an arbitrator on the evidence of his account books as regards this sum of money, he passed judgment that the money was not owed to him.

Two parts of the case are now finished. Fannius admits that he did not pay the money, he does not say that he entered it as paid, since he does not quote his account books. His only remaining alternative is to say that he made a stipulation.[13] For I cannot think of any other way for him to be able to claim a fixed sum of money. You made a stipulation. When? On what day? At what time? In whose presence? Who says that I made a promise? Nobody. If I were to finish my pleading at this point, I should

charge of extortion: *MRR* 2:142; *TLRR* 225; Münzer, *RE* s.v. Calpurnius 63.

[13] That is, a solemn agreement entered into before witnesses; cf. §14; Berger 1953 s.v. Stipulatio.

causae et controversiae, satis formulae et sponsioni, satis etiam iudici fecisse videar cur secundum Roscium iudicari debeat. Pecunia petita est certa; cum tertia parte sponsio facta est. Haec pecunia necesse est aut data aut expensa lata aut stipulata sit. Datam non esse Fannius confitetur, expensam latam non esse codices Fanni confirmant, stipulatam non esse taciturnitas testium concedit. Quid ergo est? Quod et reus is[26] est cui et pecunia levissima et existimatio sanctissima fuit semper, et iudex est is quem nos non minus bene de nobis existimare quam secundum nos iudicare velimus, et advocatio ea est quam propter eximium splendorem ut iudicem unum[27] vereri debeamus, perinde ac si in hanc formulam omnia iudicia legitima, omnia arbitria honoraria, omnia officia domestica conclusa et comprensa sint, perinde dicemus. Illa superior fuit oratio necessaria, haec erit voluntaria, illa ad iudicem, haec ad C. Pisonem, illa pro reo, haec pro Roscio, illa victoriae, haec bonae existimationis causa comparata.

16   Pecuniam petis, Fanni, a Roscio. Quam? Dic audacter et aperte. Utrum ⟨quae⟩[28] tibi ex societate debeatur an

[26] reus is *Manutius*: res eius V
[27] ut iudicem unum: *secl. Beck*: alii alia
[28] *inser. recentiores*

---

[14] For similar (premature) claims of completion, cf. *Arch.* 8, *Balb.* 15; Casamento 2013, 5–7.

[15] For initiation of litigation by wager, see on *Quinct.* 30.

[16] Literally, "entered as paid out": *OLD* s.v. *fero* 24b.

[17] Cf. §11.

[18] Pretending that the private agreement between Roscius and Flavius, the heart of the case, is legally irrelevant and pursued

think that I had done enough to prove my good faith and carefulness, enough for the case and the question at issue, enough for the formula and the wager, enough even to convince the judge why a decision ought to be given in favor of Roscius.[14] A fixed sum of money has been claimed; a wager has been made for a third of it.[15] This money must either have been a loan or debited[16] or promised by stipulation. Fannius admits that it was not lent; his ledgers prove that it was not debited; the silence of witnesses proves that it was not a stipulation. What, then, is the case? Since the defendant is a man who has always thought very little of money, but has considered his reputation to be most sacred; since the judge is a man whom we wish to think well of us as much as we wish him to decide in our favor; and since the distinguished assembly of counsel is of such quality that we ought to stand in awe of them for their outstanding brilliance as we would a single judge, I shall speak just as if all civil and equity actions and all private duties were included and comprised in this formula.[17] What I said before was necessary; what I am about to say will be voluntary. That was addressed to a judge, this to Gaius Piso; that was a plea for a defendant, this one is for Roscius; my former speech was prepared in order to win a case, the latter for the sake of good reputation.[18]

Fannius, you are claiming money from Roscius. What money? Speak boldly and frankly. Was it money that was owed to you from the partnership, or money that had been

merely for the sake of Roscius' reputation; cf. Stroh 1975, 140; Craig 1993, 77–78.

quae ex liberalitate huius promissa sit et ostentata? Quorum alterum est gravius et odiosius, alterum levius et facilius. Quae ex societate debeatur? Quid ais? Hoc iam neque leviter ferendum est neque neglegenter defendendum. Si qua enim sunt privata iudicia summae existimationis et paene dicam capitis, tria haec sunt, fiduciae, tutelae, societatis. Aeque enim perfidiosum et nefarium est fidem frangere quae continet vitam, et pupillum fraudare qui in tutelam pervenit, et socium fallere cui[29] se in negotio coniunxit. Quae cum ita sint, quis sit qui socium fraudarit et fefellerit consideremus; dabit enim nobis iam tacite vita acta in alterutram partem firmum et grave testimonium. Q. Roscius? Quid ais? Nonne, ut ignis in aquam coniectus continuo restinguitur et refrigeratur, sic refervens falsum crimen in purissimam et castissimam vitam conlatum statim considit[30] et exstinguitur? Roscius socium fraudavit! Potest hoc homini huic haerere peccatum? Qui medius fidius—audacter dico—plus fidei quam artis, plus veritatis quam disciplinae possidet in se, quem populus Romanus meliorem virum quam histrionem esse arbitratur, qui ita dignissimus est scaena propter artificium, ut dignissimus sit curia propter abstinentiam. Sed quid ego ineptus de

[29] cui *R. Klotz*: qui *codd.*
[30] *Axer (coll. Brut. 93)*: concidit V

[19] Another deceptive dilemma: the money Fannius is seeking ultimately had its origin in the partnership (i.e., in Roscius' acceptance of a farm from Flavius in compensation for the murder of the slave Panurgus) but more immediately in the agreement by which Fannius agreed to drop his suit for theft in exchange for which Roscius would pay 100,000 HS. In the following paragraphs (§§17–24), however, Cicero takes the line that the money

promised and offered to you by my client's generosity?[19] The one is a serious and hateful charge, the other less important and easier to deal with. Is it money owed on the basis of the partnership? What do you say? This is a charge that should not be lightly borne or carelessly repelled. For if there are any private actions that affect one's overall reputation—I might almost say one's life—they are these three: actions covering trust, guardianship, and partnership. For it is as treacherous and criminal to break good faith, on which life depends, as to defraud a ward who has come under our guardianship or to cheat the partner with whom one has joined in business. This being so, let us consider who it is that has cheated and deceived his partner; for his past life will now tacitly afford us secure and weighty evidence for one or the other. Quintus Roscius? What do you say to this: is it not the case that, just as fire, when thrown into water, is immediately chilled and extinguished, so fiery slander, when directed at a life of the greatest innocence and purity, immediately dies down and is blotted out? Roscius cheated his partner! Can this offense be attached to this man? A man who, by divine faith—I say it boldly—has in him more good faith than art, more truth than method; a man whom the Roman people values more highly as a man than as an actor, who, while worthy of the stage because of his artistry, is worthy of the senate because of his self-restraint. But why am I so fool-

is owed from the partnership so that he can argue from Roscius' character that he would never cheat a partner; cf. Stroh 1975, 118–19, 121, 141. Cicero may be preparing a claim, to be elaborated in the lost conclusion of the speech, that the 50,000 HS paid to Fannius was a generous gift (ibid., 145–56).

Roscio apud Pisonem dico? Ignotum hominem scilicet pluribus verbis commendo. Estne quisquam omnium mortalium de quo melius existimes tu? Estne quisquam qui tibi purior, pudentior, humanior, officiosior liberaliorque videatur? Quid? Tu, Saturi, qui contra hunc venis, existimas aliter? Nonne, quotienscumque in causa in nomen huius incidisti, totiens hunc et virum bonum esse dixisti et honoris causa appellasti? Quod nemo nisi aut honestissimo aut amicissimo facere consuevit. Qua in re mihi ridicule es visus esse inconstans, qui eundem et laederes et laudares, et virum optimum et hominem improbissimum esse diceres. Eundem tu et honoris causa appellabas et virum primarium esse dicebas et socium fraudasse arguebas? Sed, ut opinor, laudem veritati tribuebas, crimen gratiae concedebas; de hoc ut existimabas praedicabas, Chaereae arbitratu causam agebas.

Fraudavit Roscius! Est hoc quidem auribus animisque hominum absurdum. Quid si tandem aliquem timidum dementem divitem inertem[31] nactus esset qui experiri non posset? Tamen incredibile esset. Verum tamen quem fraudarit videamus. C. Fannium Chaeream Roscius fraudavit! Oro atque obsecro vos qui nostis, vitam inter se utriusque conferte, qui non nostis, faciem utriusque considerate.

[31] *fort. delendum*

[20] Playing on the words *laudare* (praise) and *laedere* (attack); cf. *Font.* 35 with Dyck 2012, 69.

[21] At *Phil.* 2.30 Cicero similarly capitalizes on Antony's polite reference to M. Brutus on September 19 of 44. For Roman naming conventions, see in general Moreau 2006.

ish as to speak of Roscius before Piso? I am evidently praising a stranger at some length. Is there anyone in the world whom you would esteem more highly? Is there anyone whom you think more virtuous, more modest, more refined, more dutiful, or more generous? Tell me: do you, Saturius, who appear against him, think otherwise? Is it not the case that, whenever you had occasion in your pleading to mention his name, you declared each time that my client was both an honorable man and that you spoke of him with respect—which is generally done only to a most honorable person or a close friend? In this matter you seemed to me to be absurdly inconsistent, in praising and attacking the same man,[20] in calling him both a most excellent man and a crook. Did you mention the man out of respect and call him a leading citizen, and at the same time try to prove that he cheated his partner?[21] But, I suppose, you granted your praise to the truth, but yielded your accusation as a concession to influence. You made mention of my client as you truly thought; but you were pleading the case at Chaerea's discretion.

Roscius cheated. *This* strikes our ears and feelings as preposterous. What if he had come upon some wealthy man, nervous, crazed, or idle, who was incapable of going to law with him? Even then it would be incredible. All the same, let us see whom he cheated. Roscius cheated Gaius Fannius Chaerea! I beg and beseech you who know them: compare both their lives against each other; you who do not know them, look at both their faces.[22] Do not his very

---

[22] Cf. *Ver.* 2.3.22, drawing inferences from the face of the tithe-collector Apronius.

Nonne ipsum caput et supercilia illa penitus adrasa[32] olere malitiam et clamitare calliditatem videntur? Non ab imis unguibus usque ad verticem summum, si quam coniecturam affert hominibus tacita corporis figura, ex fraude, fallaciis, mendaciis constare totus videtur? Qui idcirco capite et superciliis semper est rasis, ne ullum pilum viri boni habere dicatur; cuius personam praeclare Roscius in scaena tractare consuevit, neque tamen pro beneficio ei par gratia refertur. Nam Ballionem illum improbissimum et periurissimum lenonem cum agit, agit Chaeream; persona illa lutulenta, impura, invisa in huius[33] moribus, natura vitaque est expressa. Qui quam ob rem Roscium similem sui in fraude et malitia existimarit, mihi causa non videtur, nisi forte quod praeclare hunc imitari se in persona lenonis animadvertit. Quam ob rem etiam atque etiam considera, C. Piso, quis quem fraudasse dicatur. Roscius Fannium? Quid est hoc? Probus improbum, pudens impudentem, periurum castus, callidum imperitus, liberalis avidum? Incredibile est. Quem ad modum, si Fannius Roscium fraudasse diceretur, utrumque ex utriusque persona veri simile videretur, et Fannium per malitiam fecisse, et Roscium per imprudentiam deceptum esse, sic, cum Roscius Fannium fraudasse arguatur, utrumque incredibile est, et Roscium quicquam per avaritiam appetisse et Fannium quicquam per bonitatem amisisse.

21

22   Principia sunt huiusmodi; spectemus reliqua. HS

---

[32] abrasa *recentiores*   [33] huius: istius *Halm*

---

[23] Considered a mark of effeminacy; cf. Meister 2009, 78–79.
[24] Allusion to a proverbial saying; cf. Otto 1890 s.v. *pilus* 1.
[25] Cf. Pl. *Pseud.* 967, with Lennon 2022, 35–38.

head and those clean-shaven eyebrows seem to reek of malice and proclaim craftiness? If the silent form of his body allows one to conjecture, does he (Fannius) not seem to be composed entirely of fraud, trickery, and lies from his toenails to the top of his head? He always has his head and eyebrows shaved,[23] so that he may not be said to have a single hair of an honorable man on him;[24] Roscius has constantly portrayed his character brilliantly on the stage—and yet he is not rewarded with gratitude equal to his kindness. For when he plays Ballio, that most crooked and perjured pimp,[25] he is playing Chaerea; that filthy, impure, and detested character has been reproduced in his manners, disposition, and life. It seems to me there is no reason why he should have thought Roscius was like himself in fraud and wickedness, unless perhaps he noticed that my client imitated him outstandingly in the character of the pimp. Therefore, consider again and again, Gaius Piso, who is said to have cheated whom. Roscius cheated Fannius? What does this mean? Did a good man cheat a crook, a modest man a shameless one, a blameless man a perjurer, an inexperienced man a crafty one, a generous man a greedy one? It is incredible. Just as, if Fannius were said to have cheated Roscius, each point would appear probable, judging from the character of both men—that Fannius had acted wickedly and that Roscius had been deceived by his lack of caution—so when Roscius is accused of having cheated Fannius, each point is incredible—that Roscius sought to obtain anything out of greed and that Fannius lost anything because of his good nature.

Such is the starting point; let us examine the sequel. 22

ɪↃↃↃ[34] Q. Roscius fraudavit Fannium. Qua de causa? Subridet Saturius, veterator, ut sibi videtur; ait propter ipsa HS ɪↃↃↃ. Video; sed tamen cur ipsa HS ɪↃↃↃ tam vehementer concupierit quaero; nam tibi, M. Perpenna, ⟨tibi⟩[35] C. Piso, certe tanti non fuisset ut socium fraudaretis. Roscio cur tanti fuerit[36] causam requiro. Egebat? Immo locuples erat. Debebat? Immo in suis nummis versabatur. Avarus erat? Immo etiam ante quam locuples, semper liberalissimus munificentissimusque fuit. Pro deum hominumque fidem, qui HS CCCIↃↃↃ CCCIↃↃↃ CCCIↃↃↃ quaestus facere noluit—nam certe HS CCCIↃↃↃ CCCIↃↃↃ CCCIↃↃↃ[37] merere et potuit et debuit, si potest Dionysia HS CCCIↃↃↃ CCCIↃↃↃ[38] merere—is per summam fraudem et malitiam et perfidiam HS ɪↃↃↃ appetiit? Et illa fuit pecunia immanis, haec parvula, illa honesta, haec sordida, illa iucunda, haec acerba, illa propria, haec in causa et in iudicio collocata. Decem his annis proximis hic[39] sexagiens honestissime consequi potuit; noluit. Laborem quaestus recepit, quaestum[40] laboris reiecit; populo Romano adhuc servire non destitit, sibi servire iam pridem destitit. Hoc tu umquam, Fanni, faceres? Sed[41] si hos quaestus recipere pos-

[34] ɪↃↃↃ: *hic et infra cf. ad §11*   [35] *add. Clark*
[36] fuisset . . . fuerit: fuissent . . . fuerint *Turnebus, at cf. K–S 1:62*   [37] CCCIↃↃↃ CCCIↃↃↃ CCCIↃↃↃ *hic et supra Naugerius*: CCCLIII CCCLIII CCCLIII *V*
[38] CCCIↃↃↃ CCCIↃↃↃ *Naugerius*: CCCLIII CCCLIII *V*
[39] *Dyck*: hoc *Axer*: HS *V*   [40] quaestum *Beroaldus*: -us *V*
[41] sed: et *Lambinus, at cf. Axer 1977a, 234*

---

[26] A famous dancer at this period; cf. *FRLO* 146 F 2 = 92 F 39 = Gell. *NA* 1.5.3.

PRO ROSCIO COMOEDO 22–24

Quintus Roscius cheated Fannius of 50,000 sesterces. For what reason? Saturius smiles, the cunning old fellow, as he thinks himself to be; he says, on account of the same 50,000 sesterces. I see; but nonetheless I ask why he so keenly desired those 50,000 sesterces; for certainly they would not have been so valuable to you, Marcus Perpenna, or to you, Gaius Piso, that you would cheat a partner. I ask why it was worth so much to Roscius. Was he in need? No, he was wealthy. Was he in debt? No, he had plenty of money. Was he a miser? No, even before he became rich, he was always most liberal and generous. Good heavens, a man who refused to make a profit of 300,000 sesterces— for certainly he could and ought to have earned 300,000 sesterces if Dionysia can earn 200,000 sesterces[26]—did he seek to obtain 50,000 sesterces by means of utmost fraud, wickedness, and treachery? The former sum was enormous, the latter trivial; the former honorably gained, the latter sordid; the former agreeable, the latter bitter; the former his own, the latter dependent on litigation and a trial. In the last ten years my client could have honorably earned sixty times as much;[27] he chose not to.[28] He undertook the work that would bring the profit; but he rejected the profit the work brought. He has never yet ceased to serve the Roman people; but he has long since ceased to serve his own interests. Would you ever do this, Fannius? But if you could make such profits, would you not gesticu-

---

[27] That is, an annual income of 300,000 could have earned 3,000,000, sixty times 50,000; cf. Axer 1980, 61–64.

[28] By acting for pay he would forfeit the status of knight (*eques*) granted by Sulla; cf. Macrob. *Sat.* 3.14.13.

ses, non eodem tempore et gestum et animam ageres? Dic nunc te ab Roscio HS IƆƆƆ circumscriptum esse, qui tantas et tam infinitas pecunias non propter inertiam laboris sed propter magnificentiam liberalitatis repudiarit. Quid ego nunc illa dicam quae vobis in mentem venire certo scio? Fraudabat te in societate Roscius. Sunt iura, sunt formulae de omnibus rebus constitutae, ne quis aut in genere iniuriae aut ratione actionis errare possit. Expressae sunt enim ex uniuscuiusque damno, dolore, incommodo, calamitate, iniuria publicae[42] a praetore formulae, ad quas
25 privata lis accommodatur. Quae cum ita sint, cur non arbitrum[43] pro socio adegeris Q. Roscium quaero. Formulam non noras? Notissima erat. Iudicio gravi experiri nolebas? Quid ita? Propter familiaritatem veterem? Cur ergo laedis? Propter integritatem hominis? Cur igitur insimulas? Propter magnitudinem[44] criminis? Itane vero? Quem per arbitrum circumvenire non posses, cuius de ea re proprium non erat iudicium, nunc[45] per iudicem condemnabis, cuius de ⟨ea⟩[46] re nullum est arbitrium? Quin tu hoc crimen aut obice ubi licet agere, aut iacere[47] noli ubi non oportet. Tametsi iam hoc tuo testimonio crimen sublatum est. Nam tu, quo tu tempore illa formula uti noluisti, nihil

[42] publicae *Naugerius*: publica hae (h *s.l. add.*) V: in publico hae *Axer 1977b, 233–34*
[43] arbitrum: ad arbitrum *Ascensius, at cf. OLD s.v. adigo 8*
[44] magnitudinem *Manutius*: aegritudinem V
[45] nunc: hunc *Manutius, at cf. Axer 1977a, 235*
[46] *add. Manutius*   [47] iacere *Manutius*: tacere V

[29] For *animam agere*, cf. *Tusc.* 1.19; *OLD* s.v. *ago* 9.
[30] The arbitrator had no jurisdiction, because his appointment

late until you drew your last breath?[29] Say now that you have been cheated of 50,000 sesterces by Roscius, who refused such vast, such enormous sums, not because of the laziness of his work habits, but because of the magnificence of his generosity. Why should I now say, gentlemen, what I feel certain you are thinking? Roscius cheated you in a partnership. There are laws, there are formulae established for all matters, so that no one could be mistaken about the kind of harm or the means of taking action. In fact, from each person's loss, suffering, harm, misfortune, or injury, formulae have been extracted for public use by the praetor, to which a private lawsuit is adapted. This being so, I ask why you did not compel Quintus Roscius to appear before an arbitrator in a case of partnership. Did you not know the formula? But it was well known. Were you unwilling to bring an action entailing a severe penalty? Why so? On account of your longstanding friendship? Why then do you attack him? On account of the man's integrity? Why then do you accuse him? On account of the gravity of the charge? Is that really so? Will you now secure conviction by a judge, who has no discretion concerning the matter, of a man whom you could not get the better of before an arbitrator, who had no proper jurisdiction concerning the matter?[30] Either bring this charge where it is permitted to litigate it or do not launch it where it may not be brought. This charge has, however, already been refuted by your own evidence. For at the time when you refused to employ that formula, you passed judgment

was extralegal, by consent of the parties, whereas the judge had no discretion, being bound to rule according to the formula; cf. §11.

hunc in societate fraudis fecisse iudi‹casti. Con›dicionis⁴⁸
tabulas habet an non? Si non habet, quem ad modum
26 pactio est? Si habet, cur non nomina?⁴⁹ Dic nunc Roscium
abs te petisse ut familiarem suum sumeres arbitrum. Non
petiit. Dic pactionem fecisse ut absolveretur. Non pepigit.
Quaere quare sit absolutus. Quod erat summa innocentia
et integritate. Quid enim factum est? Venisti domum ultro
Rosci, satis fecisti quod ‹te›⁵⁰ temere commisisti in iudicium; ut denuntiaret rogasti, ut ignosceret; te affuturum
negasti, debere tibi ex societate nihil clamitasti. Iudici hic
denuntiavit; absolutus est. Tamen fraudis ac furti mentionem facere audes? Perstat in impudentia. "Pactionem
enim" inquit "mecum fecerat, idcirco videlicet ne condem-
naretur." Quid erat causae cur metueret ne condemnare-
tur? "Res erat manifesta, furtum erat apertum."

27   Cuius rei furtum factum erat? Exorditur magna cum
expectatione Saturius⁵¹ histrionis exponere societatem.
"Panurgus" inquit "fuit Fanni; is fit⁵² ei cum Roscio com-

---

⁴⁸ iudicasti condicionis *Axer 1977b, 235–36 (Quinct. 67 coll.)*: iudid *(del.)* iudiditionem V: iudicasti *(ut vid.)* V¹ *in mg.*, iudicio *(ut vid.)* V¹, *fort. alia manu*   ⁴⁹ nomina *Stroh 1975, 114*: nominas V   ⁵⁰ *add. Axer 1977b, 237*   ⁵¹ *Dyck*: veterem *Axer 1977b, 238–39*: veteris V   ⁵² fit *Passow*: fuit V

---

[31] In fact, Fannius had dropped his suit for theft following his agreement with Roscius. That Fannius is now suing under a different law does not acquit Roscius of violating the laws of partnership.   [32] Reading *nomina* for *nominas*, that is, the entries in his account book that would confirm the agreement.

[33] Saturius evidently claimed that Roscius asked Fannius to abort the trial and instead appoint his friend C. Piso as extrajudi-

that my client had committed no fraud in the partnership.[31] Does he have the records of the terms or not? If not, how can there be an agreement? If he has them, why does he not have the entries?[32] Say now that Roscius asked you to accept his own friend as arbitrator. He did not do so.[33] Say that he made an agreement in order to be acquitted. He made no agreement. Ask why he was acquitted. Because he was perfectly innocent and a man of the highest integrity. What, in fact, took place? You went to Roscius' house of your own accord; you apologized for having rashly gone to court; you begged him to announce this[34] and that he pardon you; you said that you would not appear, and loudly declared that nothing was owing to you from the partnership. Roscius informed the judge and was acquitted. Do you still venture to mention fraud and theft?[35] He (Fannius) persists in his impudence. "Yes," he says, "because he had made an agreement with me, obviously, in order to avoid being convicted." What reason was there why he should be afraid of being convicted? "The fact was clear, the theft was obvious."

What was stolen? With everyone in a state of heightened suspense, Saturius begins to expound the partnership in the actor. "Panurgus," he says, "was the slave of Fannius, and became the common property of him and

cial arbitrator, and Fannius agreed to this after Roscius had promised payment of 100,000 HS. Cicero denies both claims. Cf. Stroh 1975, 117.   [34] That is, their arrangement, as Roscius did, according to the next sentence.   [35] Fannius' documentation being inadequate, Saturius had to mention fraud and theft to support his claim that Roscius owed the money at issue to Fannius on the basis of an agreement to drop his suit for theft.

munis." Hic primum questus est non leviter Saturius communem factum esse gratis cum Roscio, qui pretio proprius fuisset Fanni. Largitus est scilicet homo liberalis et dissolutus et bonitate adfluens Fannius Roscio. Sic puto. Quoniam ille hic constitit paulisper, mihi quoque[53] necesse est paulum commorari. Panurgum tu, Saturi, proprium Fanni dicis fuisse. At ego totum Rosci fuisse contendo. Quid erat enim Fanni? Corpus. Quid Rosci? Disciplina. Facies non erat, ars erat pretiosa. Ex qua parte erat Fanni, non erat HS IƆƆ∞,[54] ex qua parte erat Rosci, amplius erat HS IƆƆƆƆ CCCIƆƆƆ;[55] nemo enim illum ex trunco corporis spectabat, sed ex artificio comico aestimabat;[56] nam illa membra merere per se non amplius poterant duodecim aeris, disciplina, quae erat ab hoc tradita, locabat se non minus HS CCCIƆƆƆ.[57] O societatem captiosam et iniquam,[58] ubi alter HS D,[59] alter IƆƆƆ[60] quod sit in societatem adfert! Nisi idcirco moleste pateris quod HS IƆƆ∞[61] tu ex arca proferebas, ⟨hic⟩[62] HS IƆƆƆƆ CCCIƆƆƆ[63] ex disciplina et artificio promebat. Quam enim spem[64] et expectationem, quod studium et quem favorem secum in scaenam attulit Panurgus quod Rosci fuit discipulus! Qui diligebant hunc, illi

[53] mihi quoque *recentiores*: quoque mihi V
[54] *Mommsen*: LIII∞ V   [55] *Axer*: CCCLIII CCCL V
[56] *recentiores*: extimabat V   [57] *Naugerius*: CCCLIII V
[58] indignam: *corr. Lambinus*   [59] *Axer*: LII∞ V
[60] *Axer*: LIII V   [61] *Mommsen*: LIII∞ V
[62] *add. A. Klotz*   [63] *Axer*: CCCLIII LIII V
[64] *Boemoraeus*: rem V

---

[36] Though Cicero pretends that he is merely following Saturius' procedure, the following section establishes a moral case

PRO ROSCIO COMOEDO 27–29

Roscius." At this point Saturius first complained bitterly that he had become joint possession with Roscius for nothing, since he had been bought by Fannius as his private property. Of course Fannius, that generous man, careless, and overflowing with kindness, made a present of him to Roscius. I suppose so! Since he (Saturius) dwelt for some time on this point, I also must linger a bit.[36] You assert, Saturius, that Panurgus was the private property of Fannius. But I contend that he belonged entirely to Roscius. For what part of him belonged to Fannius? His body. What part belonged to Roscius? His training. Not his personal appearance, but his art was of value. What belonged to Fannius was not worth more than 6,000 sesterces; what belonged to Roscius was worth more than 600,000 sesterces, for no one judged him by his body, but valued him by his skill as a comic actor; his limbs, by themselves, could not earn more than twelve *asses*,[37] but the training, which he had received from my client, yielded no less than 100,000 sesterces. What a deceptive and unequal partnership, to which one of the partners contributes 500 sesterces, the other something worth 50,000! Unless you are annoyed that you drew 6,000 sesterces from your strong box, whereas my client drew 600,000 from his training and skill.[38] What hopes, what expectations, what enthusiasm, what favor did Panurgus bring to the stage, because he was the pupil of Roscius! Those who

---

for Roscius as the partner who contributed by far the greater value to Panurgus.   [37] The lowest denomination of Roman currency, twelve *asses* (= three sesterces), apparently the daily wage of an unskilled worker; cf. Axer 1980, 71.   [38] For the reconstruction of the numbers, cf. Axer 1980, 67–75.

favebant, qui admirabantur hunc, illum probabant, qui denique huius nomen audierant, illum eruditum et perfectum existimabant. Sic est volgus: ex veritate pauca, ex opinione multa aestimat.[65] Quid sciret ille perpauci animadvertebant, ubi didicisset omnes quaerebant; nihil ab hoc pravum et pervorsum produci posse arbitrabantur. Si veniret ab Statilio, tametsi artificio Roscium superaret, adspicere nemo posset; nemo enim, sicut ex improbo patre probum filium nasci, sic ex pessimo histrione bonum comoedum fieri posse existimaret. Quia veniebat a Roscio, plus etiam scire quam sciebat videbatur. Quod item nuper in Erote comoedo usu venit. Qui posteaquam e scaena non modo sibilis sed etiam convicio explodebatur, sicut in aram confugit in huius domum, disciplinam, patrocinium, nomen; itaque perbrevi tempore, qui ne in novissimis quidem erat histrionibus, ad primos pervenit comoedos. Quae res extulit eum? Una commendatio huius; qui tamen Panurgum illum, non solum ut Rosci discipulus fuisse diceretur, domum recepit, sed etiam summo cum labore, stomacho miseriaque erudiit. Nam[66] quo quisque est sollertior et ingeniosior, hoc docet iracundius et laboriosius; quod enim ipse celeriter arripuit, id cum tarde percipi videt discruciatur. Paulo longius oratio mea provecta est hac de causa, ut condicionem societatis diligenter cognosceretis.

[65] *recentiores*: extimat V
[66] *Dubois*: iam V (*def. Axer 1977a, 236*)

[39] Known only from this passage: Münzer, *RE* s.v. Statilius 1.
[40] Known only from this passage: Münzer, *RE* s.v. Eros 4.

were devoted to my client favored him (Panurgus); those who admired my client approved of him; in short, all who had heard my client's name thought him (Panurgus) accomplished and perfect. This is the way of the crowd: few of its judgments are founded on truth, most on opinion. Very few noticed what he knew, everybody kept asking where he had learned it. They thought that nothing wrong or misguided could come from my client. If he had come from Statilius,[39] although he might have surpassed Roscius in skill, no one would be able to notice; for no one would think that a good comic actor could be made out of a very bad actor any more than an honest son could be born from a crooked father. Because he (Panurgus) came from Roscius he seemed to know even more than he did. The same thing also happened recently in the case of the comic actor Eros.[40] After he was driven off the stage not only by hisses but even abuse, he fled for refuge, as if to an altar, to my client's house, his training, his patronage, and his reputation; and so, in a very short time, he who had not even been among actors of the lowest class advanced to comic actors of the first rank. What was it that raised him so high? My client's recommendation alone; in the case of Panurgus, however, he did not only take him into his house so that he could be said to have been Roscius' pupil, but even taught him with the greatest pains, irritability, and discomfort. In fact, the cleverer and more talented a person is, the more ill-tempered and distressed he is as a teacher; for when he sees that a pupil is slow at grasping what he himself rapidly mastered, he is tormented. I have been led to speak at somewhat greater length, in order that you might have an accurate knowledge of the terms on which the partnership was formed.

32   Quae deinde sunt consecuta? "Panurgum" inquit "hunc servum communem Q. Flavius Tarquiniensis quidam interfecit. In hanc rem" inquit "me cognitorem dedisti. Lite contestata, iudicio damni iniuria constituto tu sine me cum Flavio decidisti." Utrum pro dimidia parte an pro tota ⟨re⟩?[67] Planius dicam: utrum pro me an et pro me et pro te? Pro me? Potui exemplo multorum, licitum est iure, fecerunt multi, nihil in ea re tibi iniuriae feci. Pete tu tuum, exige et aufer quod debetur; suam quisque partem iuris possideat et persequatur.—"At enim tu tuum negotium gessisti bene."—Gere et tu tuum bene.—"Magno tuam dimidiam partem decidisti."—Magno et tu tuam partem decide.—"HS Q CCCIↃↃ[68] tu abstulisti." Si
33 fuit hoc vere,[69] HS Q ⟨CCCIↃↃ⟩ tu quoque[70] aufer. Sed hanc decisionem Rosci oratione et opinione augere licet, re et veritate mediocrem et tenuem esse invenietis. Accepit enim agrum temporibus iis cum iacerent pretia praediorum; qui ager neque villam habuit neque ex ulla parte fuit cultus; qui nunc multo pluris est quam tunc fuit. Neque id est mirum. Tum enim propter rei publicae calamitates omnium possessiones erant incertae, nunc deum immortalium benignitate omnium fortunae sunt certae;

[67] tota re *R. Klotz (cf. §34; Mur. 48)*: re tota *Clark*
[68] Q CCCIↃↃ *Mommsen*: que CCCLIII *V*
[69] si fuit hoc vere *Axer*: si fit hoc vero *V*
[70] Q CCCIↃↃ tu quoque *Axer*: quoque tu *V*

---

[41] That is, the formalities of litigation had been settled before a magistrate (*in iure*) prior to submission of the case to a judge (*iudex*); cf. Berger 1953 s.v. Litis contestatio. The Lex Aquilia provided *inter alia* twofold restitution for damage caused by the

PRO ROSCIO COMOEDO 32–33

What followed next? "Panurgus, this joint slave," he 32
(Fannius) says, "was killed by a certain Quintus Flavius of
Tarquinii. You appointed me as your agent for this affair.
After suit had been entered upon, and an action for damages had been established,[41] you came to an agreement
with Flavius without consulting me." Was it for a half share
or for the whole amount? To put it more plainly: was it for
me or for both me and you? For me? I could do so, following many precedents; it is allowed by law; many have
done it; I have done you no injury in this respect. Ask for
your share; get paid and take what is due to you; let each
seek and possess the share to which he is entitled. "Well,
you managed your business very cleverly." Manage your
business cleverly also. "You got a very high price for your
half." Get a high price for yours as well. "You got 100,000
sesterces." If this was really the case, get 100,000 sesterces
also.[42] But although this settlement of Roscius' is exaggerated by talk and public opinion, in fact and truth you will 33
find it to be moderate and inconsiderable. He received a
farm at a time when the prices of country properties were
low; it contained no villa and was entirely uncultivated;
today it is worth far more than it was then. This is not
surprising. For at that time, owing to the disasters by
which the republic was afflicted, no one's property was
secure; now, thanks to the kindness of the immortal gods,
everyone's possessions are assured. Then the farm was

---

killing of a slave or domestic quadruped by a wrongful act (*damnum iniuria datum*), not self-defense or accident; see *LPPR*
241–42; *MRR* 1:186n2; Berger 1953 s.v. Lex Aquilia.

[42] Though in this imagined dialogue Roscius accepts the valuation of the farm conditionally, Cicero disputes this in the sequel.

tum erat ager incultus sine tecto, nunc est cultissimus cum optima villa. Verum tamen quoniam natura tam malivolus es, numquam ista te molestia et cura liberabis. Praeclare suum negotium gessit Roscius, fundum fructuosissimum abstulit; quid ad te? Tuam partem dimidiam quem ad modum vis decide. Vertit hic rationem et id quod adprobare non potest fingere conatur. "De tota re" inquit "decidisti."

Ergo huc universa causa deducitur, utrum Roscius cum Flavio de sua parte an de tota societate fecerit pactionem. Nam ego Roscium, si quid communi nomine pepigit,[71] confiteor praestare debere societati.—Societatis, non suas litis redemit, cum fundum a Flavio accepit.—Quid ita satis non dedit amplius [a se][72] neminem petiturum? Qui de sua parte decidit, reliquis integram relinquit actionem, qui pro sociis transigit, satis dat neminem eorum postea petiturum. Quid ita Flavio sibi cavere non venit in mentem? Nesciebat videlicet Panurgum fuisse in societate. Sciebat. Nesciebat Fannium Roscio esse socium.—Praeclare ‹sciebat›;[73] nam iste cum eo litem contestatam habebat. Cur igitur decidit et non restipulatur neminem amplius ‹a se›[74] petiturum? Cur de fundo decedit et iudi-

[71] pepigit *Lambinus*: tetigit *codd.*

[72] *om. recentiores, del. Garatoni (cf. §36)*: assem *Clark (§49 coll.)*: ab eo *Lambinus*

[73] *inser. Kayser*

[74] *huc transp. Dyck (nam haec supra perperam post* amplius *posita sunt), post* neminem *Baiter*

uncultivated, without a building upon it; now it is highly cultivated and there is an excellent villa. However, since you are so spiteful by nature, you will never free yourself from that worry and anxiety. Roscius managed his business brilliantly and got a most productive farm; what does that have to do with you? Make any settlement you like as to your half share. Now he changes his tactics and tries to invent what he is unable to prove. "It was about the whole business," he says, "that you made a settlement."[43]

The whole case, then, comes down to this: did Roscius make an agreement with Flavius only for his own share or for the partnership as a whole? For if Roscius made any agreement on account of the partnership, I admit that he ought to hand it over to the partnership. "When he accepted the farm from Flavius, he made a settlement on behalf of the partnership, not for himself alone." Why then did he not give security that no one would make a further demand? Anyone who makes an agreement for himself alone leaves to the others their right of action unimpaired; one who makes an agreement for his partners gives security that none of them shall make any further claim. Why then did it not occur to Flavius to look after his own interests? I suppose he did not know that Panurgus belonged to the partnership. He did know it. He did not know that Fannius was Roscius' partner. He knew it perfectly well, for he was in litigation with him. Why then does he make a settlement without requiring a counter-stipulation that no one should make any further claim

---

[43] Pretending that Saturius has changed his tactics when, in fact, he has been insinuating that the settlement was too large to have been merely for a half share; cf. Stroh 1975, 144.

cio non absolvitur? Cur tam imperite facit ut nec[75] Roscium stipulatione alliget neque a Fannio iudicio se absolvat? Est hoc primum et ex condicione iuris et ex consuetudine cautionis firmissimum et gravissimum argumentum, quod ego pluribus verbis amplecterer, si non alia certiora et clariora testimonia in causa haberem.

37

Et ne forte me hoc frustra pollicitum esse praedices, te, te inquam, Fanni, ab tuis subselliis contra te testem suscitabo. Criminatio tua quae est? Roscium cum Flavio pro societate decidisse. Quo tempore? Abhinc annis xv. Defensio mea quae est? Roscium pro sua parte cum Flavio transegisse. Repromittis tu abhinc triennium Roscio. Quid? Recita istam restipulationem clarius. Attende, quaeso, Piso; Fannium invitum et huc atque illuc tergiversantem testimonium contra se dicere cogo. Quid enim restipulatio clamat? QUOD A FLAVIO ABSTULERO, PARTEM DIMIDIAM INDE ROSCIO ME SOLUTURUM SPONDEO. Tua vox est, Fanni. Quid tu auferre potes a Flavio, si Flavius nihil debet? Quid hic porro nunc restipulatur quod iam pridem ipse exegit? Quid vero Flavius tibi daturus est, qui Roscio omne quod debuit dissolvit?[76] Cur in re tam vetere,[77] in negotio iam[78] confecto, in societate dissoluta nova haec restipulatio interponitur? Quis est huius restipulationis scriptor, testis arbiterque? Tu, Piso; tu enim Q. Roscium pro opera ⟨et⟩[79] labore, quod cognitor fuisset, quod vadimonia obisset, rogasti ut Fannio daret HS

38

[75] nec *ed. Rom.*: ne V
[76] *fort.* dissolverit
[77] *ed. Rom.*: veteri V
[78] iam *Gulielmius*: tam V
[79] *dubitanter Baiter, coll. Att. 16.16.8, De orat. 1.234*

against him? Why does he give up the farm without getting himself released from his suit? Why does he act so ignorantly as to neither bind Roscius by a stipulation nor free himself in court from Fannius? This is the first argument and the strongest and weightiest one, derived from both the state of the law and the customary stipulation; I would develop it at greater length, if I did not have other surer and clearer evidence in the case.

But so that you may not perhaps say that I have made this promise in vain, it is you, you, I say, Fannius, whom I will rouse from your benches as a witness against yourself. What is your accusation? That Roscius made a settlement with Flavius on behalf of the partnership. When? Fifteen years ago. What is my defense? That Roscius made an agreement with Flavius for his own share. Three years ago you gave Roscius a guarantee. What? Read out that counterstipulation. Listen please, Piso. Against his will, shuffling back and forth, Fannius is compelled by me to give evidence against himself. What does the counterstipulation proclaim? "I promise to pay Roscius half of what I receive from Flavius." These are your own words, Fannius. What can you get from Flavius, if he owes nothing? Why does my client now make a counterstipulation regarding a sum that he obtained long ago? What is Flavius going to give you, since his payment to Roscius covered all his debts? Why, in a matter of so long ago, in a matter that is already settled, in the case of a partnership that is dissolved, is this new counterstipulation introduced? Who drew it up, who witnessed it, and who was the arbitrator? You, Piso; for it was you who requested that Roscius give

CICERO

†CCCLIII† hac condicione ut, si quid ille exegisset a Flavio, partem eius dimidiam Roscio dissolveret. Satisne ipsa restipulatio[80] dicere tibi videtur aperte Roscium pro se
39 decidisse? At[81] enim forsitan hoc tibi veniat in mentem, repromisisse Fannium Roscio,[82] si quid a Flavio exegisset, eius partem dimidiam, sed omnino exegisse nihil. Quid tum?[83] Non exitum exactionis, sed initium repromissionis spectare debes. Neque si ille iure consequi ⟨non potuit⟩,[84] non, quod in se fuit, iudicavit Roscium suas, non societatis lites redemisse. Quid si tandem planum facio post decisionem veterem Rosci, post repromissionem recentem hanc Fanni HS CCCIƆƆ Fannium a Q. Flavio[85] Panurgi nomine abstulisse? Tamen diutius inludere viri optimi existimationi Q. Rosci audebit?

40 Paulo ante quaerebam, id quod vehementer ad rem pertinebat, qua de causa Flavius, cum de tota lite faceret pactionem, neque satis acciperet a Roscio neque iudicio absolveretur a Fannio. Nunc vero id quod mirum et incredibile est requiro: quam ob rem, cum de tota re decidisset cum Roscio, HS CCCIƆƆ[86] separatim Fannio dissolvit? Hoc loco, Saturi, quid pares respondere scire cupio:

---

[80] restipulatio *Manutius*: stipulatio *V (def. Stroh 1975, 125 adn. 75, Axer 1977a, 237)*   [81] *Manutius*: et *V*

[82] Fannium Roscio *recentiores*: Fannium Roscium *V*: Fannio Roscium *V¹*   [83] tum *Lambinus*: tu *V*   [84] iure consequi non potuit *Axer 1977a, 238, Ver. 2.5.51 coll.*: in ecsequendum *V*: id exsequendum non iudicavit *Clark*   [85] CCCIƆƆ Fannium a Q. Flavio *Naugerius*; CCCLIII Fannium a Flavio *V*

[86] CCCIƆƆ *hic et identidem §§40–43 Naugerius*: CCCLIII *V*

---

[44] The transmitted figure is too low, and is corrupted else-

Fannius 353 sesterces[44] to compensate him for his trouble and labor, because he had been his agent, because he had given security and appeared in court, on condition that Fannius would pay Roscius half of what he recovered from Flavius. Does the counterstipulation itself seem to you to argue with sufficient clarity that Roscius made an agreement for himself? But perhaps the possibility may occur to you that Fannius made a guarantee to pay Roscius half of what he might get from Flavius, but that he got nothing at all. What then? You ought to consider, not the result of the claim, but the origin of the guarantee. Even if he had not been able to achieve this in court,[45] he did not thereby, as far as it depended on him, judge that Roscius had settled his own claim, not that of the partnership. But what if I prove that, after the old agreement of Roscius and after this recent guarantee of Fannius, Fannius recovered 100,000 sesterces from Quintus Flavius on account of Panurgus? Will he still dare to scoff at the reputation of that most excellent man, Quintus Roscius?

A little before I asked a question highly relevant to the matter: why did Flavius, when he was making an agreement about the whole action, neither get security from Roscius nor obtain release from the suit from Fannius? But now I am asking about something that is strange and incredible: why, after he had come to a settlement with Roscius about the whole affair, did he make a separate payment of 100,000 sesterces to Fannius? On this point, Saturius, I should like to know what answer you propose

where from 100,000, but that seems too high. Lambin suggested 15,000; cf. Stroh 1975, 123–24.

[45] On the text, cf. Axer 1977a, 238.

utrum omnino Fannium ⟨a⟩[87] Flavio[88] HS CCCIƆƆ non
41 abstulisse an alio nomine et alia de causa abstulisse?[89] Si alia de causa, quae ratio tibi cum eo intercesserat? Nulla. Addictus erat tibi? Non. Frustra tempus contero. "Omnino" inquit "HS CCCIƆƆ a Flavio non abstulit neque Panurgi nomine neque cuiusquam." Si planum facio post hanc recentem stipulationem Rosci HS CCCIƆƆ a Flavio te abstulisse, numquid causae erit[90] quin ab iudicio abeas turpissime victus? Quo teste igitur hoc planum faciam?
42 Venerat, ut opinor, haec res in iudicium. Certe. Quis erat petitor? Fannius. Quis reus? Flavius. Quis iudex? Cluvius. Ex his unus mihi testis est producendus qui pecuniam datam dicat. [Quis est ex his gravissimus? Sine controversia qui omnium iudicio comprobatus est iudex.][91] Quem igitur ex his tribus a me testem ⟨ex⟩spectabis?[92] Petitorem? Fannius est; ⟨is⟩[93] contra se numquam testimonium dicet. Reum? Flavius est. Is[94] iam pridem est mortuus; si viveret, verba eius audiretis. Iudicem? Cluvius est. Quid is dicit? HS CCCIƆƆ Panurgi nomine Flavium Fannio dissolvisse. ⟨Quis est ex his gravissimus? Sine controversia qui omnium iudicio comprobatus est iudex.⟩[95] Quem tu si ex censu spectas, eques Romanus est, si ex vita,

[87] *recentiores*
[88] *Laur. plut. 48.26 in mg.*: fabio V
[89] abstulisse . . . abstulisse *recentiores*: -isset . . . -isset V
[90] causae erit *ex* causare *corr.* V
[91] *cf. quae sequuntur*
[92] *recentiores*: spectabis V
[93] *add. Axer 1977a, 240*
[94] est. is *ed. Rom.*: testis V
[95] *huc transponenda censuit Axer 1977a, 239–40*

to make: that Fannius never got 100,000 sesterces at all from Flavius or that he got them on some other claim or for some other reason? If for some other reason, what dealings did you have with him previously? None. Had he been handed over to you as a debtor? No. I am wasting time uselessly. "Fannius," he says, "did not get 100,000 sesterces from Flavius, either on account of Panurgus or anything else." If I prove that, after this recent stipulation of Roscius,[46] you got 100,000 sesterces from Flavius, surely there will be no reason why you should not leave the court defeated and disgraced, will there? By whose evidence then shall I prove this? This affair, I believe, came into court. Certainly. Who was the plaintiff? Fannius. Who was the defendant? Flavius. Who was the judge? Cluvius.[47] I must produce one of these men as a witness to say that the money was paid. Which of these three men, then, will you expect me to produce as a witness? The plaintiff? It is Fannius; he will never give evidence against himself. The defendant? It is Flavius; he has been dead a long time; if he were alive, you would hear him speak. The judge? It is Cluvius. What does he say? That Flavius paid Fannius 100,000 sesterces on account of Panurgus. Who carries the greatest weight? Indisputably, the judge, who has been approved of by the judgment of all. If you consider his income, he is a Roman knight;[48] if his life, he is a man of the greatest distinction; if his

[46] That is, Roscius' demand that Fannius give a guarantee (*repromissio*); cf. Stroh 1975, 111n33.   [47] C. Cluvius, a Roman *eques* known only from this speech: Münzer, *RE* s.v. Cluvius 3.

[48] Knights were required to have an annual income of 400,000 sesterces; cf. *OLD* s.v. equites.

CICERO

homo clarissimus est, si ex fide,[96] iudicem sumpsisti, si ex veritate, id quod scire potuit et debuit dixit. Nega, nega nunc equiti Romano, homini honesto, iudici tuo credi oportere! Circumspicit, aestuat, negat nos Cluvi testimonium recitaturos. [Recitabimus.][97] Erras; inani et tenui spe te consolaris. Recita testimonium T. Manili et C. Lusci Ocreae, duorum senatorum, hominum ornatissimorum, qui ex Cluvio audierunt. ⟨TESTIMONIUM T. MANILI ET C. LUSCI OCREAE.⟩[98] Utrum dicis Luscio et Manilio[99] an etiam[100] Cluvio non esse credendum? Planius atque apertius dicam: utrum Luscius et Manilius nihil de HS CCCIƆƆ ex Cluvio audierunt, an Cluvius falsum Luscio et Manilio dixit? Hoc ego loco soluto et quieto sum animo, et quorsum recidat responsum tuum non magno opere laboro; firmissimis enim et sanctissimis testimoniis virorum optimorum causa Rosci communita est. Si iam tibi deliberatum est quibus abroges fidem iuris iurandi, responde. Manilio et Luscio negas esse credendum? Dic, aude; est tuae contumaciae, arrogantiae vitaeque universae vox. Quid? Exspectas quam mox ego Luscium et Manilium dicam ordine esse senatores, aetate grandes natu, natura sanctos et religiosos, copiis rei familiaris locupletes et pecuniosos? Non faciam; nihil mihi detraham, cum illis exactae aetatis severissime fructum, quem meruerunt, retribuam. Magis mea adulescentia indiget illorum bona

---

[96] fide *Kayser (cf. §45)*: te *V*: re *Axer 1977a, 240*
[97] *seclusi*
[98] *suppl. Hotoman*
[99] Manilio *recentiores*: Manl- *V (et identidem in sequentibus)*
[100] etiam *Clark*: et *codd.*

reliability, you accepted him as judge; if his truthfulness, he said what he could and ought to have known. Say now, say that a Roman knight, an honorable man, your judge, ought not to be believed! He is looking around, he is agitated, he says that we are not going to read the evidence of Cluvius. You are mistaken; you are comforting yourself with a vain and feeble hope. Read the evidence of Titus Manilius and Gaius Luscius Ocrea, two senators, most distinguished men, who heard it from Cluvius.[49] "Evidence of Titus Manilius and Gaius Luscius Ocrea." Do you say that we ought not to believe Luscius and Manilius or even Cluvius? I will speak more clearly and more frankly. Did Luscius and Manilius hear nothing from Cluvius about the 100,000 sesterces, or did Cluvius tell a lie to Luscius and Manilius? On this point I am calm and free from anxiety. I do not care greatly what you may fall back upon in reply, for the case of Roscius is fortified by the strongest and most sacred evidence of most excellent men. If you have already made up your mind which of them you would refuse to believe on oath, answer. Do you assert that Manilius and Luscius ought not to be believed? Say so, if you dare; such words are on a par with your obstinacy, your arrogance, and your whole life. Well then? Are you waiting to see how long it will be before I tell you that Luscius and Manilius are senators in rank, in years old men, in character, upright and scrupulous, in private resources, rich and wealthy? I shall not do this: I will not do prejudice to myself by rendering to them the well-deserved credit for a life passed with the greatest austerity. The need of my own youth for their good opin-

---

[49] Roman senators known only from this speech; cf. Münzer, *RE* s.vv. Manilius 16, Luscius 2.

existimatione[101] quam illorum severissima senectus desiderat meam laudem. Tibi vero, Piso, diu deliberandum et concoquendum est utrum potius Chaereae iniurato in sua lite an Manilio et Luscio iuratis in alieno iudicio credas. Reliquum est ut Cluvium falsum dixisse Luscio et Manilio contendat. Quod si facit, qua impudentia est! Eumne testem improbabit quem iudicem probarit? Ei negabit credi oportere cui ipse crediderit? Eius testis ad iudicem fidem infirmabit cuius propter fidem et religionem iudicis testes compararit?[102] Quem ego si ferrem iudicem, refugere non deberet, cum testem producam, reprehendere audebit?

"Dicit enim" inquit "iniuratus Luscio et Manilio." Si diceret iuratus,[103] crederes? At quid interest inter periurum et mendacem? Qui mentiri solet, peierare consuevit. Quem ego ut mentiatur inducere possum, ut peieret exorare facile potero. Nam qui semel a veritate deflexit, hic non maiore[104] religione ad periurium quam ad mendacium perduci consuevit. Quis enim deprecatione deorum, non conscientiae fide commovetur? Propterea, quae poena ab dis[105] immortalibus periuro, haec eadem mendaci constituta est; non enim ex pactione verborum quibus ius iurandum comprehenditur, sed ex perfidia et malitia per quam insidiae tenduntur alicui, di immortales hominibus irasci et suscensere[106] consuerunt. At ego hoc ex

[101] bona existimatione *recentiores*: bona extimatione *ex* extimatione bona *corr.* V
[102] compararit *Halm*: comparabat V
[103] iuratus *recentiores*: iniuratus V
[104] maiore *recentiores*: minore V
[105] dis: diis V
[106] suscensere *Lambinus*: succ- V

ion is greater than any desire on the part of their austere old age for any praise of mine. It is for you, Piso, to deliberate and ponder well whether you would rather believe Chaerea, not under oath, in a case in which he is personally interested, rather than Manilius and Luscius under oath in one with which they are not concerned. There remains the alternative, for him to maintain that Cluvius lied to Luscius and Manilius. If he does this, what an impudent man he is! Will he disapprove of the man as a witness of whom he approved as a judge? Will he claim that the man should not be trusted whom he himself trusted? Will he undermine before a judge the reliability of a witness on account of whose reliability and scrupulousness as a judge he brought witnesses before him? If I should propose him as a judge, he would be bound not to reject him, and shall he dare to find fault with him when I bring him forward as a witness?

"Well, but," he says, "Cluvius spoke to Luscius and Manilius when he was not under oath." If he told them under oath, would you believe him? But what is the difference between a perjurer and a liar? A man who is in the habit of lying has grown used to committing perjury. If I can persuade a person to tell a lie, I shall easily be able to induce him to commit perjury. For one who has once deviated from the truth generally has no greater scruples about being persuaded to commit perjury than to tell a lie. For who is there that is moved by a curse of the gods though not by the honesty of his own conscience? Because the same punishment has been set by the gods for the perjurer and the liar; for it is not the form of the words, in which an oath is embodied, but the perfidy and wickedness whereby a snare is set for someone, that generally incites the wrath and indignation of the immortal gods. But I on

contrario contendo: levior esset auctoritas Cluvi, si diceret iuratus, quam nunc est, cum dicit iniuratus. Tum enim forsitan improbis[107] nimis cupidus videretur, qui qua de re iudex fuisset testis esset; nunc omnibus inimicis necesse est castissimus et constantissimus esse videatur, qui id quod scit familiaribus suis dicit.

48 Dic nunc, si potes, si res, si causa patitur, Cluvium esse mentitum! Mentitus est Cluvius? Ipsa mihi veritas manum iniecit et paulisper consistere et commorari cogit. Unde hoc totum ductum et conflatum mendacium est? Roscius est videlicet homo callidus et versutus. Hoc initio cogitare coepit: "quoniam Fannius a me petit HS IƆƆ,[108] petam a C. Cluvio, equite ⟨Romano⟩,[109] ornatissimo homine, ut mea causa mentiatur, dicat decisionem factam esse quae facta non est, HS CCCIƆƆ[110] a Flavio data esse Fannio quae data non sunt." Est hoc principium improbi animi,

49 miseri ingeni, nulli[111] consili. Quid deinde? Posteaquam se praeclare confirmavit, venit ad Cluvium. Quem hominem? Levem? Immo gravissimum. Mobilem? Immo constantissimum. Familiarem? Immo alienissimum. Hunc postea quam salutavit, rogare coepit blande et concinne scilicet: "mentire mea causa; viris optimis tuis familiaribus praesentibus dic Flavium cum Fannio de Panurgo decidisse qui nihil transegit; dic HS CCCIƆƆ[112] dedisse qui assem nullum dedit." Quid ille respondit? "Ego vero cupide et libenter mentiar tua causa, et si quando me peie-

---

[107] *imperitis Axer 1977a, 241–42*
[108] *Naugerius*: LIII V
[109] *add. recentiores*
[110] *Naugerius*: CCCLIII V
[111] nullius *recentiores: tradita def. A. Klotz, Ter. Andr. 608 coll.*
[112] *et hic et §51 Naugerius*: CCCLIII V

the contrary maintain that Cluvius' authority would have less weight if he had spoken under oath than it now has, when he is not under oath. For then malicious people might perhaps think him all too eager if he were acting as a witness in a case in which he had been judge; but as things stand, even all his enemies must consider him to be a man of the highest integrity and the greatest steadfastness, who tells his friends what he knows.

Say now, if you can, if the fact, if the case allows you, that Cluvius lied! Cluvius lied? Truth itself has laid hands on me and compels me to stop and dwell upon this point for a few moments. What was the source from which this entire lie was derived and concocted? Roscius of course is a cunning and crafty fellow. At the outset, he began to reason thus: "since Fannius is claiming 50,000 sesterces from me, I will ask Gaius Cluvius, a Roman knight, a man of the highest distinction, to tell a lie for my sake, to say that an agreement was made which was not made, that 100,000 sesterces were given by Flavius to Fannius, which were not given." This is the starting point of a dishonest mind, of a pitiable nature, of a lack of sense. What next? After he successfully plucked up his courage, he approached Cluvius. What kind of man is he? Shallow? No, most serious. Pliable? No, most firm. A friend (of Roscius)? No, a perfect stranger. After he greeted him, he began to ask him (Cluvius) in flattering and smooth language, namely: "tell a lie for my sake; in the presence of some fine gentlemen who are friends of yours say that Flavius settled with Fannius about Panurgus, although he did nothing of the kind; say that he gave him 100,000 sesterces, although he did not give him a penny." What answer did he give? "Certainly, I will tell a lie for your sake gladly and with alacrity; and, if at any time you want me

CICERO

rare ⟨vis⟩,[113] ut paululum tu compendi facias, paratum fore scito; non fuit causa cur tantum laborem caperes et ad me venires; per nuntium hoc quod erat tam leve trans-
50 igere potuisti." Pro deum hominumque fidem! hoc aut Roscius umquam a Cluvio petisset, si HS miliens in iudicium haberet, aut Cluvius Roscio petenti concessisset, si universae praedae particeps esset? Vix medius fidius tu, Fanni, a Ballione aut aliquo eius simili hoc et postulare[114] auderes et impetrare posses. Quod cum est veritate falsum, tum ratione quoque est incredibile; obliviscor enim Roscium et Cluvium viros esse primarios; improbos tem-
51 poris causa esse fingo. Falsum subornavit testem Roscius Cluvium! Cur tam sero? Cur cum altera pensio solvenda esset, non tum cum prima? Nam iam antea HS IↃↃↃ[115] dissolverat. Deinde si iam persuasum erat Cluvio ut mentiretur, cur potius HS CCCIↃↃↃ quam CCCIↃↃↃ CCCIↃↃↃ CCCIↃↃↃ[116] data dixit Fannio a Flavio, cum ex restipulatione pars eius dimidia Rosci esset? Iam intellegis, C. Piso, sibi soli, societati nihil Roscium petisse. Hoc cum sentiat[117] Saturius esse apertum, resistere et repugnare contra veritatem non audet, aliud fraudis et insidiarum in eodem vestigio deverticulum repperit.
52 "Petisse" inquit[118] "suam partem Roscium a Flavio confiteor, vacuam et integram reliquisse Fanni concedo;

[113] peierare vis *Clark*: vis peierare *ed. Rom.*
[114] et postulare *Garatoni*: expostulare V
[115] *Naugerius*: LIII V
[116] CCCIↃↃↃ CCCIↃↃↃ CCCIↃↃↃ *Naugerius*: CCCLIII CCCLIII CCCLIII V
[117] sentiat *Müller*: sentit V
[118] inquit *Angelius*: inquam V

PRO ROSCIO COMOEDO 49–52

to commit perjury, so that you may make a little profit, you may feel sure that I shall be ready. There was no reason for you to take all this trouble to come to me; you could have arranged so trivial a matter through a messenger." Great heavens! Would Roscius ever have asked this of Cluvius, even if he had had millions at stake in the trial, or would Cluvius have agreed to Roscius' request, even if his share were to be the whole prize? By divine faith, Fannius, you would hardly dare to demand and be able to obtain this from Ballio or someone like him. Not only is this false as regards the truth; it is also incredible as a matter of common sense; for I am forgetting that Roscius and Cluvius are leading men in the community; I am pretending that they are crooks to suit the occasion. Roscius suborned Cluvius as a false witness. Why was this done so late? Why when the second installment was to be paid, rather than the first? For Roscius had already paid 50,000 sesterces. Then, if Cluvius had been persuaded to make a false statement, why did he say that 100,000 had been given by Flavius to Fannius rather than 300,000 sesterces, since, according to the counterstipulation, half of the sum belonged to Roscius? By now you understand, Gaius Piso, that Roscius claimed for himself alone, but nothing for the partnership. Since Saturius realizes that this is clear, he does not dare to resist and fight against the truth, but has instantly discovered another loophole for fraud and treachery.

"I admit," he says, "that Roscius claimed his own share from Flavius; I grant that he left Fannius' share free and untouched; but I maintain that what he obtained for him-

sed quod sibi exegit, id commune societatis factum esse contendo." Quo nihil captiosius neque indignius potest dici. Quaero enim potueritne Roscius ex societate suam partem petere necne. Si non potuit, quem ad modum abstulit? Si potuit, quem ad modum non sibi exegit? Nam

53 quod sibi petitur, certe alteri non exigitur. An ita est: si quod[119] universae societatis fuisset petisset, quod cum redactum esset aequaliter omnes partirentur, numquid petierit quod suae partis esset? Numquid cum abstulit, soli sibi exegit? Quid interest inter eum qui per se litigat et qui cognitor est datus?[120] Qui per se litem contestatur, sibi soli petit; alteri nemo potest nisi qui cognitor est factus. Itane vero? Cognitor si fuisset tuus, quod vicisset iudicio, ferres tuum; suo nomine petit, quod abstulit, sibi non

54 tibi exegit. Quod si quisquam petere potest alteri qui cognitor non est factus, quaero quid ita, cum Panurgus esset interfectus et lis contestata cum Flavio damni iniuria esset, tu in eam litem cognitor Rosci sis factus, cum praesertim ex tua oratione quodcumque tibi peteres huic peteres, quodcumque tibi exigeres, id in societatem recideret. Quodsi ad Roscium nihil perveniret quod tu a Flavio abstulisses, nisi te in suam litem dedisset cognitorem, ad te pervenire nihil debet quod Roscius pro sua parte exegit,

55 quoniam tuus cognitor non est factus. Quid enim huic rei respondere poteris, Fanni? Cum de sua parte Roscius transegit cum Flavio, actionem tibi tuam reliquit an non?

[119] quod *Angelius*: quid V
[120] cognitor est datus *Manutius*: cognitorem dat V

---

[50] Saturius probably made only the last assertion. It is unlikely that he made the first two concessions, which contradict his position; cf. Stroh 1975, 128.

self became the common property of the partnership."[50] No statement can be more treacherous or outrageous than this. I ask: could Roscius have claimed his share on the basis of the partnership or not? If he could not, how did he get the money? If he could, how was it that he did not demand it for himself? For what is claimed for oneself is certainly not demanded for another. Or is this the case: if he had claimed what belonged to the partnership as a whole and which, when it had been recovered, would have been shared equally by all, would he not have claimed his share? What he took he surely did not demand for himself alone, did he? What is the difference between a man who carries on a suit by himself and one who is appointed as agent? He who begins an action by himself claims for himself only; no one, unless he has been appointed agent, can claim for another. Is that so? If he (Roscius) had been your agent, you would have got as your own what he received after winning his case; but since he claimed what he got in his own name, he demanded it for himself and not for you. But if anyone can claim for another, but has not been appointed his agent, I ask why, after Panurgus had been killed, and an action for damages had been begun against Flavius, you were appointed Roscius' agent for that action, especially since, as you argued, whatever you claimed for yourself, you claimed for him, and whatever you got for yourself fell to the partnership. But if nothing that you would have obtained from Flavius would have come to Roscius, unless he had appointed you as agent for his suit, nothing of what Roscius demanded as his share ought to come to you, since he was not appointed your agent. What answer will you be able to make to this, Fannius? When Roscius made an arrangement with Flavius for his own share, did he leave you your right of action or

CICERO

Si non reliquit, quem ad modum HS CCCIƆƆ[121] ab eo postea exegisti? Si reliquit, quid ab hoc petis quod per te persequi et petere debes? Simillima enim et maxime gemina societas hereditatis est; quem ad modum socius in societate habet partem, sic heres in hereditate habet partem. Ut heres sibi soli non coheredibus petit, sic socius sibi soli, non sociis petit; et quem ad modum uterque pro sua parte petit, sic pro sua parte dissolvit, heres ex ea[122] parte qua hereditatem adiit, socius ex ea qua societatem 56 coiit. Quem ad modum suam partem Roscius suo nomine condonare potuit Flavio, ut eam tu non peteres, sic cum exegit suam partem et tibi integram petitionem reliquit, tecum partiri non debet, nisi forte tu perverso more quod huius est ‹si›[123] ab alio extorquere non potes, huic eripere potes. Perstat in sententia Saturius, quodcumque sibi petat socius, id societatis fieri. Quod si ita est, qua[124]—malum—stultitia fuit Roscius, qui ex iuris peritorum consilio et auctoritate restipularetur a Fannio diligenter, ut quod is[125] exegisset a Flavio dimidiam partem sibi dissolveret,[126] si quidem sine cautione et repromissione nihilo minus id Fannius societati, hoc est Roscio, debebat! * * *

---

[121] *Naugerius*: CCCLIII V [122] ea *Madvig*: sua V
[123] *inseruit Kayser* [124] qua *Manutius*: quae V
[125] is V *s.l.*: eius V*ac*
[126] dissolveret *ed. Rom.*: dissolvere˜ V

---

[51] Misleading: heirs (*heredes*) to an inheritance have no obligations to one another, whereas partners (*socii*) in a partnership (*societas*) are bound by mutual obligations under a *bonae fidei* (good faith) contract to share relevant income with their partners.

PRO ROSCIO COMOEDO 55–56

not? If not, how did you afterward demand 100,000 sesterces from him (Flavius)? If he did, why do you claim from my client what you ought to claim and try to obtain yourself? In fact, a partnership is very like and in general a twin of an inheritance; just as a partner has a share in a partnership, so an heir has a share in an inheritance. As an heir claims for himself alone, not for his coheirs, so a partner claims for himself alone, not for his partners; and as each claims for his own share, so he pays for his own share, the heir in proportion to the share for which he entered on the inheritance, the partner in proportion to the share for which he joined the partnership.[51] Just as Roscius could have given up his share in his own name to Flavius, so that you might not claim it, so, when he got his share and left you the right of claiming unimpaired, he ought not to share with you, unless perhaps, by a perversion of custom, if you cannot extort from another what belongs to my client, you can rob him of it. Saturius stubbornly maintains that whatever a partner claims for himself becomes the property of the partnership. But if this is so—confound it!—what a fool Roscius was, who on the advice and authority of men learned in the law, made a precise counterstipulation with Fannius that he should pay him half of what he got from Flavius, since, without any security or guarantee, Fannius nonetheless owed it to the partnership, that is, to Roscius![52] . . .

[52] This argument would apply if the partnership still existed at the time of the counterstipulation, but by then the partnership had been dissolved, as Cicero acknowledges at §38. Therefore, Roscius could protect his interests only by a counterstipulation, not under the law of partnership.

IN DEFENSE OF
MARCUS TULLIUS

INTRODUCTION

This speech casts light on social conditions in the Italian countryside in the aftermath of Spartacus' revolt. The case was a private one, probably tried in 71.[1] The litigants were the owners of neighboring properties near the south Italian city of Thurii, which had been occupied by Spartacus' band (App. *B Civ.* 1.117.547). Cicero's client, M. Tullius, apparently no relation,[2] was suing P. Fabius for damages inflicted when Fabius' slaves attacked some of Tullius' slaves, who occupied a hut on a disputed territory, the *centuria Populiana*, located between the two estates; they not only killed the slaves but also damaged the hut. Though Tacitus criticized the prolixity of this defense

[1] So dated with a query at *TLRR* 173. The date would follow from the mention of a Metellus as praetor at §39, which could refer to L. Caecilius Metellus, cos. 68: so with a query *MRR* 2:122. This chronology assumes that L. Quinctius, the counsel for the defendant, though attested as legate or cavalry commander under M. Crassus for his six-month campaign against Spartacus (latter part of 72–beginning of 71), was by now discharged from service (for Quinctius' role in the war, cf. Frontin. *Str.* 2.5.34; Plut. *Vit. Crass.* 11.4 [giving the name as Quintus]; for the duration, cf. App. *B Civ.* 1.121.560). Cf. also Frier 1983, 225 and n. 18; 1985, 52 and n. 39.

[2] Cicero claims mere homonymity, not a blood tie, with his client (§4). He is known only from this speech; cf. Münzer, *RE* s.v. Tullius 12.

INTRODUCTION

(*Dial.* 20.1),[3] it now survives only in fragments preserved in two palimpsests, comprising perhaps half of the full speech.

The case was governed by an *intentio* (statement of charge) based on a *formula* drawn up by M. Lucullus as peregrine praetor of 76[4] and incorporated by subsequent praetors, including the current one, Metellus, in their edicts. It can be reconstructed as "loss of how much money was inflicted on M. Tullius by force by men armed or assembled with malice aforethought (*dolo malo*) of the slaves (*familia*) of P. Fabius, a quadruple of so much money let the commissioners condemn P. Fabius (to pay) M. Tullius; if it does not appear (to be the case), let them acquit him."[5] The matter was now in its second hearing (*actio*) before a board of commissioners (*recuperatores*);[6] Cicero complains that the opposing counsel, L. Quinctius, used up all the previous day with his pleading and did not finish before nightfall, so the trial had to be adjourned and recommenced the next day (§6).[7]

In preliminary remarks, Cicero touches on the change

---

[3] Tacitus complains about the lengthy exposition of the praetor's edict, perhaps because by his day it was long settled; cf. Frier 1983, 239; 1985, 52–56.

[4] So Frier 1983, 232, followed by Broughton, *MRR* 3:204; but he may have held both the peregrine and the urban praetorships; cf. Balzarini 1968, 328n14; Damon and Mackay 1995, 52.

[5] §7, supplemented by Lenel 1927, 395, omitting *aut noxae dedere* as alien to the republican version.

[6] A board, usually of three, that provided for somewhat expedited proceedings; cf. §§10–11; Frier 1985, 197–212.

[7] On Quinctius (tr. pl. 74, pr. 68), a *popularis* politician not esteemed by Cicero (cf. *Brut.* 223), see Gundel, *RE* s.v. Quinctius 12; *FRLO* 107.

329

in the opponent's tactics: Quinctius is now apparently prepared to accept the facts of the case as narrated by Cicero in view of the strength of the witnesses' testimony (cf. §24).[8] He also issues an apology in advance for personal attacks on P. Fabius[9] and a request to Quinctius not to engage in a mere filibuster but allow the trial to come to a conclusion (§§1–6). Then Cicero turns to examine M. Lucullus' *formula*. He explains that the purpose was to check the lawlessness of bands of slaves (*familiae*) that were roaming the countryside under arms and endangering not only private property but also the state interest (§8). He contrasts this with the earlier Aquilian Law that punished "loss wrongfully inflicted" (*damnum iniuria datum*) with a penalty double the value of the affected property.[10] Cicero claims that Lucullus deliberately stiffened the penalty to fourfold and eliminated the potential defense of justifiable action by omitting "wrongfully" (*iniuria*) from the *formula*, since abuses had in the meantime become much worse (§§9–12; cf. §41).[11]

In the following narrative, Cicero draws a characterological contrast of his client, who inherited his estate from his father (the generally approved method of property transfer, also used to his client's advantage in *Rosc.*

[8] This would be a shift from a conjectural case (*causa coniecturalis*), about the facts of the case, to a *causa qualitatis*, claiming that the attack was justified. Cf. Lausberg 1998, §§79–138, in particular §§99–107, 123–30. For a different view, cf. Stroh 1975, 163, 165n27.

[9] Cf. *Rosc. Am.* 83.

[10] See on *QRosc.* 32.

[11] For the historical background to Lucullus' *formula*, cf. Balzarini 1968, 355–58; Frier 1983, 233–34, and 1985, 52, citing Lepidus' rebellion of 78/77; Mantovani 2009, 351–54.

INTRODUCTION

Am.[12]), and his adversary P. Fabius, a former officer in Sulla's campaigns in Macedonia and Asia Minor.[13] Though details are obscure due to damage to the text, he suggests that Fabius enriched himself by underhanded means (§15). Cicero later uses the connection to stir prejudice, when he calls Fabius "that wealthy Asiatic head of household" (§19).[14] Fabius chose to invest some of his newly acquired wealth in the estate neighboring to Tullius', and he bought it for a dear price in partnership with one Cn. Acerronius (§§14, 16).[15] The farm was, however, in poor shape, uncultivated and with all its buildings burned down, a fact that can be plausibly attributed to Spartacus' rampaging band (§14).[16] Unhappy with its condition, Fabius decided to put the property up for sale and was engaged in discussions about selling his share to Acerronius (§§16–17). Fabius[17] also brought in bands of armed men, who caused damage and destruction, including the murder of two slaves (§§18–19). When Fabius noticed one of Tullius' slaves in the *centuria Populiana*, he went to Tullius' villa to complain. Tullius and Fabius agreed to go through a ceremonial ejection from property (*deductio*) as a preliminary to litigation over ownership.[18] Fabius gave Tullius his choice of roles, and he chose to play the part

---

[12] Cf. Benferhat 2003–2004, 267.

[13] Known only from this speech; cf. Münzer, *RE* s.v. Fabius 28.

[14] The tactic also appears in other speeches; cf. Vasaly 1993, 98–205; Arweiler 2008.

[15] Also known only from this speech; cf. Klebs, *RE* s.v. Acerronius 1.

[16] Cf. Münzer, *RE* 6.2:1748.5–11.

[17] Not Tullius; see on §18.

[18] On the procedure, cf. Frier 1985, 79–92.

of owner, so that Fabius would set foot on the property, and Tullius and his men would escort him out (§20). But the following night Fabius' slaves entered the property, forced their way into the building where the slaves were living, and slew all of them except one, who, though gravely wounded, escaped and reported the events to Tullius. Thereupon Tullius summoned his friends from the district to witness the scene where the attack had occurred and filed suit (§§21–23).

The unexplained point in Cicero's narrative is the fact that Fabius brought a band of armed thugs to the area (§§18–19). Only toward the end of the extant text does the motive come to light, when Cicero quotes Fabius' claim that his house had been burned down by Tullius' men and that he feared for his personal safety (§§54–55). Quinctius apparently wanted to frame the incident as a justified act of revenge and hence sought to have the word "wrongfully" (*iniuria*) added to the *formula*, a request denied by the praetor Metellus (§§38–39). As in other forensic speeches, Cicero softens the impact of his adversary's case by an arrangement that severs causal connections.[19] Stroh poses a fundamental challenge to Cicero's narrative by claiming that Tullius' men were the aggressors, and he points out that they are not described as unarmed.[20] Though Cicero does not say explicitly that Tullius' men were unarmed, he does say that Fabius' men *were* armed and that Tullius' slaves offered no resistance (as might have been expected had they been armed) and that all Tullius' slaves were killed or wounded and none of Flavius' slaves were (§§21–22, 55). Stroh's hypothesis that Fabius'

[19] Cf. in general Stroh 1975.
[20] Stroh 1975, 162, followed by La Bua 2005, 273n38.

INTRODUCTION

slaves acted in self-defense ("Notwehr") is not supported by the text, nor is his idea that one of Fabius' slaves was killed or that Tullius' slaves burned a building on disputed land.[21] In view of the facts of Cicero's narrative (§21), which the defense evidently did not dispute (§1), this was a clandestine attack by Fabius' slaves. Quinctius may have claimed that there was provocation on the other side—Stroh points to the phrase "even under provocation" (*etiam lacessiti*, §8)—but it is not clear what the provocation might have been. The occupation of the Populian tract? Or did Fabius blame Tullius' men for the burning of his buildings (when it might have been due to Spartacus' band)? In view of its timing on the night following the agreement between Tullius and Fabius regarding the formal removal of the latter from the property (*deductio*), it seems likely that Fabius came to regret having allowed Tullius to choose the role of ejector and so intervened to clear the *centuria Populiana* of Tullius' men so that he could turn the land over unoccupied to Acerronius and thus complete the sale (cf. §17). He perhaps thought that he would be better placed to win a suit over ownership if he was in possession of the property and did not consider the possibility that he might face a suit "on grounds of force and men armed or assembled."[22]

Toward the end of the extant speech, Cicero responds

---

[21] Stroh 1975, 162.

[22] Cf. Roby 1902, 508: "It would appear as if Fabius repented of his offer of the option to Tullius, and thought it would be wise to get possession himself." For a similar evasion of an agreed *deductio*, cf. *Caec.* 20–22. Frier 1985, 84–89, remarks that such moves suggest that the procedure was by now poorly understood; it fell into desuetude under the empire.

PRO TULLIO

to points raised by Quinctius, beginning with the words "by malice aforethought" (*dolo malo*) included in the *formula*. Quinctius tried to argue that this requirement made the *formula* inapplicable to the facts of the current case, since a body of slaves could not act "by malice aforethought," as if possessing a single mind (§35).[23] Cicero argues that, to the contrary, "by malice aforethought" was added for the benefit of the prosecutor, not the defendant, since the lawgiver thereby widened the scope for prosecution to include not only the agents who carried out the act but also the mastermind who planned it (§§26–33). This explanation of the phrase is, however, one-sided and ad hoc, as his subsequent arguments show:[24] the individual actions comprising the events of the fatal night all required malice aforethought, and violence itself implied it,[25] so the whole incident inevitably did also (§34). Quinctius also appears to have argued that Cicero's case rested on an exaggerated regard for human life and cited a provision of the Twelve Tables (8.12) and of the laws bound by oath (*leges sacratae*) that licensed killing (§47). Cicero replies that the permission is narrowly circumscribed and does not apply to the circumstances of this case and that in general ancestral law establishes a high bar for homicide (§§48–52). Even the damage caused by Fabius' slaves to the house on the disputed property would have to be compensated for under the law (§53). And if Fabius feared

[23] Stroh 1975, 163, argues that Cicero has twisted Quinctius' point, but it is unclear how, on the facts apparently admitted by both sides, Quinctius could have claimed self-defense; see above.

[24] Cf. Stroh 1975, 168 and n. 39.

[25] Accepted by later jurists; cf. Ulp. *Dig.* 47.8.2.8.

INTRODUCTION

for his life, as Quinctius claimed, that would hardly justify preemptive murder (§§55–56).

Even though Cicero may exaggerate the incompatibility of violence with Roman law (§42 *fin.*),[26] he and his client appear to have selected their legal ground carefully and to have a solid case. Success in this trial would have strongly prejudiced subsequent litigation over the ownership of the *centuria Populiana*.

NOTE ON MANUSCRIPTS AND EDITIONS

The text is based on the following witnesses:

A   Ambrosius S. P. 11.66, olim R. 57 sup., s. V, rescr. VII
T   Taurinensis A.II.2*, olim D.IV.22, s. V, rescr. VII[27]

The following are the major editions cited in the notes:

Mai	Milan-Rome, 1814
Peyron	Stuttgart-Tübingen, 1824
Leclerc	Paris, 1825
Beier	Leipzig, 1825
P. E. Huschke	Leipzig, 1826 (in *Analecta Litteraria*, ed. I. G. Hushke)

[26] Cf. Costa 1927, 1:151.
[27] Readings are cited according to Garuti 1965. Uncredited interventions are those of Peyron.

PRO MARCO TULLIO

A⟨ntea sic hanc causam⟩[1] a⟨gere⟩ s⟨tatue⟩ra⟨m,[2] recupe⟩ratores,[3] ut ⟨infitias i⟩turos[4] adversarios arbitrarer tantam caedem et tam atrocem ad familiam suam pertinere. Itaque animo soluto a cura et a cogitatione veneram, quod intellegebam facile id me testibus planum facere posse. Nunc vero postea quam non modo confessus est vir primarius, L. Quin⟨ctius⟩[5] . . . ⟨la⟩borabam[6] ut, quod arguebam, id factum esse ostenderem; nunc in eo consumenda est oratio, ut ne adversarii, quod infitiari nullo modo potuerunt, cum maxime cuperent, id cum confessi sunt, meliore

2 loco esse videantur. Itaque tum vestrum difficilius iudicium,[7] mea facilis defensio fore videbatur. Ego enim omnia in testib⟨us⟩ . . .[8] Quid est facilius quam de eo qui confitetur iudicare? Mihi autem difficile est satis copiose de eo dicere quod nec atrocius verbis demonstrari potest

---

[1] *suppl. Peyron*   [2] *suppl. Beier*   [3] *suppl. Peyron*
[4] *Schöll (propter spatium)*: infitiaturos *Orelli*
[5] *suppl. Peyron*   [6] *suppl. Peyron in lac.* VI *versuum octonarum denarum fere litterarum*
[7] difficilius iudicium *Peyron*: diudicium *T*
[8] *suppl. Peyron in lac.* VII *versuum*

IN DEFENSE OF
MARCUS TULLIUS

Before I had decided to plead the case assuming, commissioners,[1] that our opponents would deny that a slaughter so horrendous and on such a scale had anything to do with their slaves. Accordingly, I came with a mind free of anxiety, since I knew that I could easily substantiate this with witnesses. Now, however, since the eminent man, Lucius Quinctius,[2] has not only confessed this . . . I was at pains to show that what I was arguing did occur. Now I must use my pleading to show that our opponents are not better placed when they have confessed what they could by no means deny, although they very much wanted to do so. And so it seemed then that your verdict would be more difficult but my defense would be easy. For I (rested?) my entire case on witnesses . . . What is easier than to pass judgment on a man who confesses? It is hard for me to speak with sufficient eloquence about a thing that cannot be more hideously depicted in words than it

[1] On this body, see above, 329n6.
[2] Plebeian tribune in 74 (*MRR* 2:103), negatively characterized at *Clu.* 77, 79, 108–12, and *Brut.* 223. Cf. Gundel, *RE* s.v. Quinctius 12; *FRLO* 107.

quam re ipsa est, neque apertius oratione mea fieri quam ipsorum confessione factum est.

3   Cum in hac re quam commemoravi mihi mutanda ratio defensionis . . .[9] minus diligenter illius existimationem quam rem M. Tulli viderer defendere. Nunc quoniam Quinctius ad causam pertinere putavit res ita multas, falsas praesertim et inique confictas, proferre de vita et moribus et existimatione M. Tulli, multis de causis mihi Fabius debebit ignoscere, si minus eius famae parcere
4   videbor quam antea consului. Pri . . .[10] ore[11] putavit ad officium suum pertinere adversario nulla in re parcere, quid me oportet Tullium pro Tullio facere, homine coniuncto mecum non minus animo quam nomine? Ac mihi ⟨non⟩[12] magis illud laborandum videtur, recuperatores, ut quod antea nihil in istum dixi probar⟨e possi⟩m quam[13] ⟨ne⟩[14] in eo reprehendar quod hoc tempore respondeo.
5   Verum et tum id feci quod oportuit, et nunc faciam quod necesse est. Nam cum esset de re pecuniaria controversia, quod damnum datum M. Tullio diceremus, alienum[15] mea natura videbatur quicquam de existimatione P. Fabi dicere, non quia[16] res postulare non videretur. Quid ergo est? Tametsi postulat causa, tamen, nisi plane cogit ingratiis, ad male dicendum non soleo descendere. Nunc cum coactus dicam, si quid forte dicam, tamen id ipsum vere-

[9] *desiderantur* VII *versus*   [10] VI *versus desiderantur*
[11] *incipit cod. A; fort.* ⟨suo m⟩ore   [12] *supplevi*
[13] probare possim quam *Cramer*: probar . . . sumquam *A*
[14] *post Leclerc suppl. Mommsen*
[15] alienum ⟨a⟩ *Mai, quod ipse postea reiecit (cf. OLD s.v.* alienus *8a)*
[16] quin *A: corr. Mai*

PRO TULLIO 2–5

in fact is and cannot be made more blatant by my speaking than it has been by the confession of the perpetrators.

Since I had to change my defense strategy in the respect that I have mentioned ... (I was afraid?) that I would seem to be defending the reputation of Marcus Tullius with less care than his property. But now since Quinctius has thought it relevant to the case to adduce so many matters, in particular mendacious and malignant inventions, concerning Marcus Tullius' life, character, and reputation, Fabius will for many reasons have to pardon me if I am found to be less sparing of his reputation than I previously planned to be. In the first place (?) ... Since, in his usual fashion, my opponent (?) thought that it was his duty to spare his adversary in no respect, what should I, a Tullius, do on behalf of a Tullius, a man allied with me in feelings no less than in name?[3] I think, commissioners, that I must not exert myself more to be able to justify the fact that I said nothing against him previously than lest I be reproached for the reply I currently offer. Then I did what I should have done, and now I am doing what I must. When the dispute was about a financial matter, the fact that we claimed that a loss had been inflicted on Marcus Tullius, it seemed out of character for me to say anything about Publius Fabius' reputation, not that the case did not seem to call for it. Why so? Even if the case calls for it, unless it clearly compels me against my will, it is not my practice to indulge in attacks on character. But now, since I am speaking under constraint, whatever I say will be said

3

4

5

---

[3] For a similar bond with his client based on a shared characteristic, cf. *Mur.* 3.

CICERO

cunde modiceque[17] faciam, tantum ut, quoniam sibi me non esse inimicum potuit priore actione Fabius iudicare, nunc M. Tullio fidelem certumque amicum esse cognoscat.

6 Unum hoc abs te, L. Quincti, pervelim impetrare—quod tametsi eo volo quia mihi utile est, tamen abs te idcirco quia aequum est postulo—ut ita tibi multum temporis ad dicendum sumas ut his aliquid ad iudicandum relinquas. Namque antea non defensionis tuae modus, sed nox tibi fine⟨m⟩ dicendi fecit; nunc, si tibi placere potest, ne idem facias, id abs te postulo. Neque hoc idcirco postulo quod te aliquid censeam praeterire oportere aut non quam ornatissime et copiosissime dicere, verum ut semel una quaque de re dicas; quod si facies, non vereor ne dicendo dies eximatur.

7 Iudicium vestrum est, recuperatores, QUANTAE PECUNIAE PARET DOLO MALO FAMILIAE P. FABI VI HOMINIBUS ARMATIS COACTISVE DAMNUM DATUM[18] ESSE M. TULLIO. Eius rei taxationem nos fecimus; aestimatio vestra est; iudicium datum est in qudruplum.

8 Cum omnes leges omniaque iudicia quae paulo graviora atque asperiora videntur esse ex improborum iniquitate et iniuria nata sunt, tum hoc iudicium paucis hisce annis propter hominum malam consuetudinem nimiamque licentiam constitutum est. Nam cum multae familiae

---

[17] modique *A*: *corr. Heinrich*   [18] datum *T*: factum *A*

---

[4] For several hearings being required, cf. *Caec.* 6.
[5] *familia* is literally "the slaves of a household": *OLD* s.v. 2. The master bears legal responsibility; cf. Greenidge 1901, 554.

PRO TULLIO 5–8

with such modesty and moderation that, while in the prior hearing Fabius could have judged me to be no enemy of his,[4] in the current one he may come to know me as a loyal and reliable friend of Marcus Tullius.

I should like very much for you to grant this one request, Lucius Quinctius—although I crave this because it is to my benefit, I ask it of you because it is fair—namely that you take for yourself so much time for speaking as to leave the commissioners some time for judging the case. In fact, previously it was not the termination of your defense but the onset of night that put an end to your speech; I ask you, please do not do the same now. I am not making this request because I think you ought to omit anything or not speak as elegantly and copiously as possible, but so that you will speak about each matter once only; if you do this, I have no fear that the daylight will be exhausted by your speaking.

The matter for you to decide, commissioners, is, "Loss of how much money appears to have been inflicted on Marcus Tullius by malice aforethought of the slaves[5] of Publius Fabius by force by means of men armed or assembled." We have offered an estimate of this; your task is to fix the assessment; a quadruple penalty applies.[6]

All laws and all tribunals that are thought to be a bit stern and harsh have arisen from the wrongful and injurious acts of wicked persons. This tribunal in particular was established in these past few years because of people's bad practices and excessive permissiveness. In fact, since

[6] That is, the plaintiff proposed a maximum penalty (*taxatio*), while the commissioners fixed the final amount; cf. Greenidge 1901, 210, 553.

dicerentur in agris longinquis et pascuis armatae esse caedisque facere, cumque ea consuetudo non solum ad res privatorum sed ad summam rem publicam pertinere videretur, M. Lucullus, qui summa aequitate et sapientia ius dixit, primus hoc iudicium composuit et id spectavit ut omnes ita familias suas continerent ut non modo armati damnum nemini darent verum etiam lacessiti iure se pot-

9 ius quam armis defenderent; et cum sciret de damno legem esse Aquiliam, tamen hoc ita existimavit, apud maiores nostros cum et res et cupiditates minores essent et familiae non magnae magno metu continerentur ut perraro fieret ut homo occideretur, idque nefarium ac singulare facinus putaretur, nihil opus fuisse iudicio de vi coactis armatisque hominibus; quod enim usu non veniebat, de eo si quis legem aut iudicium constitueret, non tam pro-

10 hibere videretur quam admonere. His temporibus cum ex bello diuturno atque domestico res in eam consuetudinem venisset ut homines minore religione armis uterentur, necesse putavit esse et in universam familiam iudicium dare, quod a familia factum diceretur, et recuperatores

11 dare, ut quam primum res iudicaretur, et poenam graviorem constituere, ut metu comprimeretur audacia, et illam latebram tollere: "damnum iniuria." Quod in aliis causis debet valere et valet lege Aquilia, id ex huius modi

---

7 M. Terentius Varro Lucullus, praetor peregrinus for 76, issued the edict on armed bands of slaves; cf. *MRR* 2:93 and 625; Münzer, *RE* s.v. Licinius 109. For his office, see above, 329n4.

8 See on *QRosc.* 32.

9 Cf. *Rosc. Am.* 70.

10 The civil war between Sulla and the faction of Cinna, culminating in Sulla's election as dictator in 82 (*MRR* 2:66–67).

many bands of slaves were said to be under arms in distant fields and pastures and to be perpetrating murders, and since this practice seemed to have a bearing not only on the property of private individuals but also on the state interest, Marcus Lucullus, whose jurisprudence was marked by supreme fairness and wisdom, was the first to set up this tribunal and intended that all persons restrain their own slaves so that not only would they not inflict damage on anyone with armed force but that even under provocation they would defend themselves by law rather than by arms.[7] Although he knew that there was an Aquilian law on loss (of property),[8] he took the view that in our ancestors' time when property and cupidity were on a smaller scale and slaves were not numerous and were held in check by intense fear so that it was quite rare for a person to be killed, and this was considered a wicked and unique crime, there had been no need for a tribunal about violence and people assembled and armed: if someone were to establish a law or tribunal about a matter that was not occurring, he would seem not so much to prohibit as to advise it.[9] In our time, since as a result of a prolonged war at home,[10] the practice had developed for people to use arms with less inhibition, he thought it needful both to provide a tribunal for an entire household's slaves for a crime said to have been committed by the household's slaves and to provide commissioners, so that the matter could be adjudicated as soon as possible, and to set a stiffer penalty, so that criminality could be held in check by fear, and to eliminate the loophole "loss by wrongful action." What ought to apply in other cases and does apply by the Aquilian law, this, on the basis of a loss of such a kind that

9

10

11

CICERO

12 damno quod vi per servos armatos datum esset...[19] ⟨ne⟩[20] ipsi statuerent quo tempore possent suo iure arma capere, manum cogere, homines occidere. Cum iudicium ita daret[21] ut hoc solum in iudicium veniret,[22] videreturne vi hominibus coactis armatisve damnum dolo malo familiae datum, neque illud adderet "iniuria," putavit se audaciam improborum sustulisse, cum spem defensionis nullam reliquisset.

13 Quoniam quod iudicium et quo consilio constitutum sit cognostis, nunc rem ipsam, ut gesta sit, dum breviter vobis
14 demonstro, attendite. Fundum habet in agro Thurino[23] M. Tullius paternum, recuperatores, quem se habere usque eo non moleste tulit, donec vicinum eius modi nactus est qui agri finis armis proferre mallet quam iure defendere. Nam P. Fabius nuper emit agrum de C. Claudio senatore, cui fundo erat adfinis M. Tullius, sane magno, dimidio fere pluris incultum exustis villis omnibus quam quanti integrum atque ornatissimum carissimis pretiis
15 ipse Claudius ⟨emerat⟩...[24] clam circumscripsisse isti a

19 VII *versiculi ternarum denarum fere litterarum desiderati sunt*   20 *exempli gratia suppl.*
21 daretur A: *corr. Heinrich*
22 venire A: *corr. Beier*
23 Thurino *Quint. 4.2.131:* Thyrino A
24 emerat *suppl. Heinrich;* XI *versus desunt*

---

11 Probably, "ought not to apply in current conditions" or the like should be supplied; that is, Lucullus closed the "loophole" of the Aquilian law by disallowing "rightful action" as a defense.

12 The subject is probably "slaves," and Cicero is describing circumstances to be averted by Lucullus' edict.

PRO TULLIO 11–15

it was inflicted by force by armed slaves . . .[11] lest (?) they themselves decide at what time they could rightfully take up arms, assemble a band, commit murder.[12] Since he provided a tribunal of such a kind that this was the sole offense that was adjudicated, namely whether it seemed that loss was inflicted by force by men assembled or armed by the malice aforethought of the household's slaves, and did not add "wrongfully," he thought he had put an end to the criminality of wicked persons, since he had left them no hope of a defense.

Seeing that you have learned what tribunal has been established and with what purpose, now give ear while I briefly narrate for you how the facts of the case occurred.[13] Marcus Tullius has a farm inherited from his father in the Thurine country,[14] commissioners. He was content with this possession until he encountered the kind of neighbor who preferred to expand his boundaries by arms rather than defend them at law. In fact, Publius Fabius recently bought a farm from the senator Gaius Claudius,[15] a farm of which Marcus Tullius was a neighbor, for a substantial price, half again more, though all its outbuildings were burned down, than the dear price at which Claudius himself had bought it when it was pristine and well-equipped . . . secretly defrauded from the consular provinces Mace-

---

[13] Beginning of the narrative; cf. *Mil.* 23, with Keeline 2021, 153.

[14] That is, the district around Thurii, a city on the Bay of Tarentum where a Roman colony (Copia) was established in 193.

[15] Not identifiable with any known Claudius; cf. Münzer, *RE* Suppl. 3 s.v. Claudius 20a.

consulari Macedonia et Asia. Etiam illud addam quod ad rem pertinet: imperatore mortuo pecuniam nescio quo modo quaesitam dum vult in praedio ponere, non posuit sed abiecit. Nihil adhuc m . . .[25] ⟨imprudentiam su⟩am[26] calamitate[27] vicinorum corrigit, et quod stomachum suum

16 damno Tulli ⟨ex⟩plere[28] conatus est. Est in eo agro centuria quae Populiana nominatur, recuperatores, quae semper M. Tulli fuit, quam etiam pater pos⟨sederat⟩ . . .[29] posita esse et ad fundum eius convenire. Ac primum, quod eum negoti totius et emptionis suae paenitebat, fundum proscripsit; eum autem emptum habebat cum socio Cn.

17 Acerronio, viro op⟨timo⟩ . . .[30] modum proscripsisse. Hominem appellat. Iste sane arroganter quod commodum fuit respondit. Nequedum finis auctor demonstraverat. Mittit ad procuratorem litteras et ad vilicum Tullius . . .[31] facturum negavit; illis absentibus finis Acerronio demonstravit neque tamen hanc centuriam Populianam vacuam tradidit. Acerronius, quo modo potuit, se de tota[32] re ex⟨imit⟩ . . . um . . .[33] ⟨ex discri⟩mine[34] eius modi semustilatus effugit.

[25] *versus* X *desunt*   [26] imprudentiam suam *e.g. supplevi*: stultitiam *Mai*   [27] calamitatem *A: corr. Mai*
[28] *suppl. Mai: vel possis* complere   [29] possederat *suppl. Mai, versus* XI *desunt*   [30] optimo *suppl. Mai, versus* XI *desunt*   [31] *desunt* X *versus*   [32] tora *A:* tota *Niebuhr*
[33] eximit *e.g. supplevi, versus* X *desunt*
[34] ex discrimine *suppl. Heinrich*

16 This appears to be the last part of the abuse of Fabius' character (cf. §§3, 5), alleging some sort of financial irregularity during the war with Mithridates; cf. Münzer, *RE* s.v. Fabius 28.

PRO TULLIO 15–17

donia and Asia.[16] I will also add this relevant point: when, upon his commander's death, he wanted to invest the money he had somehow acquired in a farm, he did not invest it, but threw it away. Nothing as yet ... he corrected his imprudence (?) by inflicting disaster on his neighbors and tried to appease his displeasure at Tullius' expense. In that district there is a unit of land called the Populian, commissioners, which has always belonged to Marcus Tullius, which his father had also possessed ... was located and fit with his farm.[17] At first, since he regretted his purchase and the entire business, he advertised the farm for sale. He had, however, purchased it in partnership with Gnaeus Acerronius, an excellent man[18] ... had advertised for sale. He hailed the man. The other, arrogantly enough, made a reply as he pleased. The sponsor had not yet pointed out the boundaries.[19] Tullius sent a letter to his administrator and his steward ... He refused to do it; in their absence he pointed out the boundaries to Acerronius and yet did not hand over this Populian property unoccupied.[20] As far as he could, Acerronius removed himself (?) from the entire matter ... He escaped such a danger, albeit singed.[21]

---

[17] Probably an explanation of Fabius' desire for the Populian property.   [18] Known only from our speech: Klebs, *RE* s.v. Acerronius 1.   [19] "The sponsor" (*sc.* of the sale), that is, Fabius, who evidently wanted to sell his share to Acerronius; cf. Greenidge 1901, 552.   [20] The subject is evidently Fabius; that he turn over the Populian property unoccupied would have been a condition of sale but could not be fulfilled as long as it was occupied by Tullius' slaves.   [21] Evidently a metaphorical reference to Acerronius, who distanced himself just in time to avoid being implicated in Fabius' crime.

CICERO

18   Adducit iste interea in saltum homines electos maximis animis et viribus et eis arma quae cuique habilia[35] atque apta essent comparat, prorsus ut quivis intellegeret non eos ad rem rusticam, verum ad caedem ac pugnam com-
19   parari. Brevi illo tempore Q. Cati Aemiliani, hominis honesti, quem vos nostis, duo homines occiderunt; multa alia fecerunt; passim vagabantur armati, non obscure, sed ut plane intellegeretur[36] ad quam rem parati essent; agros, vias denique infestas habebant. Venit in Thurinum interea Tullius. Deinde iste pater familias Asiaticus beatus, novus arator et idem pecuarius, cum ambularet in agro, animadvertit in hac ipsa centuria Populiana aedificium non ita
20   magnum servumque M. Tulli Philinum.[37] "Quid vobis," inquit, "istic negoti in meo est?" Servus respondit pudenter, at non stulte, dominum esse ad villam; posse eum cum eo disceptare si quid vellet. Rogat Fabius Acerronium—nam ibi tum erat—ut secum simul veniat ad Tullium. Venitur. Ad villam erat Tullius. Appellat Fabius ut aut ipse Tullium deduceret aut ab eo deduceretur. Dicit deducturum se Tullius, vadimonium Fabio Romam promissurum. Manet in ea condicione Fabius. Mature disceditur.

35 habilia *Heinrich*: abitalia *A*
36 intellegeretur *scripsi*: intellegere viderentur *A*
37 Philinum *Mai*: filium *A*

---

22 That is, Fabius; cf. §55. Contrast Frier 1985, 82, who cites §§16–17 as evidence that "Tullius . . . directed his procurator and bailiff to seize it [i.e., the Populian property]." But surely this is a move by Fabius in preparation for the assault described at §21.
23 Otherwise unknown; not in the *RE*.
24 Fabius is clearly identified both by his "newness" and by the

PRO TULLIO 18–20

Meanwhile the other[22] brought into the estate men selected for courage and strength and provided them arms that were easily wielded and suitable for each so that anyone could understand that they were being prepared not for field work but for battle and slaughter. In that brief period they murdered two slaves belonging to Quintus Catius Aemilianus, an honorable man whom you know;[23] they perpetrated many other crimes; they wandered here and there under arms and did so openly so that it was clearly understood what they were ready for; in short, they kept the fields and roads insecure. Meanwhile Tullius came to the Thurine district. Then that wealthy Asiatic head of household, a new plowman and cattle breeder,[24] while walking in the field noticed on this very Populian property a building of modest size and Philinus, a slave of Marcus Tullius'. "What business do you have here on my property?" he asked. The slave replied modestly, but not stupidly, that his master was at the villa; if he wanted, he could dispute the matter with him. Fabius asks Acerronius—for he was there at that time—to go with him to Tullius. They go. Tullius was at the villa. Fabius demands that either he escort Tullius off the property or be escorted off by him. Tullius replies that he will escort Fabius off and will promise Fabius security for a court appearance at Rome. Fabius adheres to these terms.[25] They part without further ado.

18

19

20

source of his wealth; cf. §§14 and 15. Asiatic connections can be used to stir prejudice; see above, 331n14.

[25] A formal ceremony is thus agreed to identify the property in question preliminary to litigation over ownership, Tullius playing the role of the possessor and Fabius that of the plaintiff; cf. Greenidge 1901, 186; Frier 1985, 81–84.

21 Proxima nocte, iam fere cum lux adpropinquaret, ad illud aedificium de quo antea dixi, quod erat in centuria Populiana, servi P. Fabi frequentes armatique veniunt; introitum ipsi sibi ⟨vi⟩[38] manuque patefaciunt; homines magni preti servos M. Tulli nec opinantis adoriuntur; quod⟨que⟩[39] facile factu fuit, neque tam multos neque repugnantis multi armati paratique occidunt tantumque odi crudelitatisque ⟨hab⟩uerunt[40] ut eos omnis gurgulionibus insectis relinquerent, ne, si quem semivivum ac spirantem etiam reliquissent, minor eis honor haberetur; praeterea tectum
22 villamque disturbant. Hanc rem tam atrocem, tam indignam, tam repentinam nuntiat M. Tullio Philinus, quem antea nominavi, qui graviter saucius e caede effugerat. Tullius statim dimittit ad amicos, quorum ex[41] vicinitate
23 Thurina[42] bona atque honesta copia praesto fuit. Omnibus acerba res et misera videbatur. Cum amici in comm . . .[43] turbarunt.[44]

24 Audite, quaeso, in eas res quas commemoro hominum honestorum testimonium. Haec quae mei testes dicunt, fatetur adversarius eos vere dicere; quae mei testes non dicunt, quia non viderunt nec sciunt, ea dicit ipse adversarius. Nostri testes dicunt occisos homines; cruorem in locis pluribus, deiectum aedificium se vidisse dicunt; nihil amplius. Quid Fabius? Horum nihil negat. Quid ergo ad-
25 dit amplius? Suam familiam fecisse dicit. Quo modo? Vi hominibus armatis. Quo animo? Ut id fieret quod factum est. Quid est id? Ut homines M. Tulli occiderentur. Quod

[38] *suppl. Heinrich*   [39] *suppl. Huschke*
[40] *suppl. in lac. Mai*   [41] ex *Beier*: ea *A*
[42] Thurina *Pluygers*: tum illa *A*   [43] *deficit cod.* A; *multa desunt*   [44] *incipit cod.* T

The next night, when dawn was approaching, Publius Fabius' slaves arrive in force and under arms at the building on the Populian property that I previously mentioned. They force an entry. They attack valuable slaves of Marcus Tullius caught unawares. Armed men, numerous and prepared, slew others who were less numerous and did not resist—an easy job. Their hatred and cruelty were such that they left them all with their throats cut, for fear of losing face if they had left anyone breathing and half-dead. They demolished the roof and the house besides. The aforementioned Philinus, who had fled the slaughter seriously wounded, announced this sudden, outrageous atrocity to Marcus Tullius. Tullius immediately sent to his friends, honorable men, of whom the neighboring Thurine district had a good supply available. All of them found the matter bitter and wretched. When his friends . . . they threw into confusion.

Please attend to the testimony of honorable men on the matters I am discussing. My opponent admits that my witnesses are telling the truth in their testimony; my opponent, for his part, is asserting things that my witnesses do not, since they did not see them and do not know about them. Our witnesses say that men were killed; bloodshed occurred in a number of places; they assert that they saw the building demolished; that is all. What does Fabius say? He denies none of these points. What does he say in addition? He says that his slaves perpetrated it. How? By force, by means of armed men. With what intent? To achieve what was done. What is that? That Marcus Tullius' people be slain. If something was done with the intent that

ergo eo animo factum est ut homines unum in locum convenirent, ut arma caperent, ut certo consilio certum in locum proficiscerentur, ut idoneum tempus eligerent, ut caedem facerent, id si voluerunt et cogitarunt et perfecerunt, potestis eam voluntatem, id consilium, id factum a
26 dolo malo seiungere? At istuc totum "dolo malo" additur in hoc iudicio eius causa qui agit, non illius quicum agitur. Id ut intellegatis, recuperatores, quaeso ut diligenter attendatis; profecto quin ita sit non dubitabitis.

27 Si ita iudicium daretur ut id concluderetur quod a familia factum esset, si quae familia ipsa in caede interesse noluisset et homines aut servos aut liberos coegisset aut conduxisset, totum hoc iudicium et praetoris severitas dissolveretur. Nemo enim potest hoc[45] iudicare, qua in re familia non interfuisset, in ea re eam ipsam familiam vi armatis hominibus damnum dedisse. Ergo, id quia poterat fieri et facile poterat, idcirco non satis habitum est quaeri quid familia ipsa fecisset, verum etiam illud, quid familiae
28 dolo malo factum esset. Nam cum facit ipsa familia vim[46] armatis coactisve hominibus et damnum cuipiam dat, id dolo malo fieri necesse est; cum autem rationem init ut id[47] fiat, familia ipsa non facit, fit tamen[48] dolo malo eius. Ergo addito "dolo malo" actoris et petitoris fit causa copiosior. Utrum enim ostendere potest, sive eam ipsam familiam sibi damnum dedisse, sive consilio et opera eius familiae factum esse, vincat necesse est.

[45] hoc *Leclerc*: haec *T*
[46] vim *Halm*: vi *T*
[47] id *Leclerc*: ea *T*   [48] tamen *scripsi*: autem *T*

---

[26] That is, without the requirement of "malice aforethought."
[27] A rather far-fetched hypothesis; cf. Stroh 1975, 164n23.

men gather in a single place, seize arms, by a concerted plan set out to a specific place, choose a suitable time, perpetrate murder, if they wanted this, plotted it, and carried it out, can you separate that intent, that plot, that deed from malice aforethought? But this entire concept of "malice aforethought" was added in this tribunal for the sake of the plaintiff, not the defendant. In order to understand this point, commissioners, please listen carefully; you will surely not be in doubt that this is the case.

If the tribunal was granted on the terms that the point at issue would be what was done by the household's slaves,[26] if the household's slaves had refused to take part in the slaughter personally and compelled or hired slaves or free men (as their agents),[27] this entire tribunal and the praetor's severity would be annulled. For in a matter in which the household slaves did not participate, no one can judge that the household's slaves themselves inflicted loss by means of force and armed men. Therefore, since this could be done and done easily, an inquiry into what the household slaves themselves had done was held to be insufficient, but what was done by the malice aforethought of the household's slaves also had to be investigated. For when the household's slaves themselves engage in violence by means of men armed or assembled and inflict loss on anyone, this is necessarily done by malice aforethought; when, however, the household's slaves form a plan that this occur but do not perform it themselves, it occurs nonetheless by their malice aforethought. Therefore by the addition of "by malice aforethought" the case of the plaintiff and prosecutor becomes enhanced. For whichever he can show, whether that the household's slaves themselves caused his loss or that it was done by the planning and effort of that household's slaves, he must prevail.

29   Videtis praetores per hos annos interdicere[49] hoc modo, v⟨elut inter⟩[50] me et M. Claudium: UNDE [DE][51] DOLO MALO TUO, M. TULLI, M. CLAUDIUS AUT FAMILIA AUT PROCURATOR EIUS VI DETRUSUS EST, cetera ex formula. Si, ubi[52] ita interdictum est et sponsio facta, ego me ad iudicem sic[53] defendam, ⟨ut⟩[54] vi me deiecisse confitear, dolo malo negem, ecquis[55] me audiat? Non opinor equidem,[56] quia, si vi deieci M. Claudium, dolo malo deieci; in vi enim dolus malus inest, et Claudio utrumvis satis est planum facere, vel se a me ipso vi deiectum esse
30 vel me consilium inisse ut vi deiceretur. Plus igitur ⟨datur⟩ Claudio, cum ⟨ita⟩[57] interdicitur, unde dolo malo meo vi deiectus sit, quam si daretur, unde a me vi deiectus esset. Nam in hoc posteriore, nisi ipse egomet deiecissem, vincerem sponsionem; in illo priore, ubi dolus malus additur,[58] sive consilium inissem [ut vi deieceretur],[59] sive ipse deiecissem, necesse erat eum[60] dolo malo meo vi deiec-
31 tum iudicari. Hoc persimile atque adeo plane idem est in hoc iudicio, recuperatores. Quaero enim abs te, si ita iudi-

[49] interdicere *Madvig*: intercedere *T*
[50] *suppl. Huschke*
[51] *del. Baiter*
[52] si ubi *Kayser*: sicut *T*
[53] sic *Kayser*: si *T*
[54] *suppl. Peyron*
[55] etquis *T*: *corr. Leclerc*
[56] quidem *T*: *corr. Halm*
[57] igitur . . . Claudio cum . . . *T*: *suppl. Beier*
[58] auditur *T*: *corr. Beier*
[59] *del. Keller*
[60] eum *scripsi*: te *T*

PRO TULLIO 29–31

You notice that in recent years the praetors draft their interdicts in this form, for instance between me and Marcus Claudius:[28] "whence, Marcus Tullius, Marcus Claudius or his household slaves or his manager was thrust out by violence by your malice aforethought," and the rest of the words from the formula.[29] If, when the interdict has been thus formulated and the wager has been made,[30] I should defend myself to the judge in that I confess that I thrust him out by violence but deny that it was done by malice aforethought, is there anyone who would give me a hearing? I think not, since if I thrust Marcus Claudius out by violence, I did so by malice aforethought; malice aforethought is inherent in violence, and it suffices for Claudius to prove either of the two, either that he was violently thrust out by me or that I formed the plan for him to be thrust out by violence. Therefore, Claudius is given more when the interdict is so formulated, "whence he was thrust by violence by my malice aforethought," than if he were granted, "whence he was violently thrust by me." For in this latter formulation, unless I myself had thrust him out, I would win the wager; in the former one, in which malice aforethought is added, whether I formed the plot or thrust him out myself, he must be judged to have been thrust out by violence by my malice aforethought. This is very similar and in fact quite the same in the current trial, commissioners. I ask you, if the trial were granted on these terms, "A

29

30

31

---

[28] A fictive name, as we would say "John Doe."

[29] *Sc.* "thereto shall you restore him" (*eo restituas*). This interdict had in the meantime been superseded; see §46 with note.

[30] For the wager (*sponsio*) initiating litigation, see on *Quinct.* 30.

cium datum esset: QUANTAE PECUNIAE PARET A FAMILIA P. FABI ⟨VI⟩[61] HOMINIBUS ARMATIS DAMNUM M. TULLIO DATUM,[62] quid haberes quod diceres? Nihil, opinor. Fateris enim omnia et familiam P. Fabi fecisse et vi hominibus armatis fecisse. Quod additum est "dolo malo," id te aduvare putas, in quo opprimitur et excluditur omnis tua defensio? Nam si additum id non esset ac tibi libitum esset ita defendere,[63] tuam familiam non fecisse, vinceres, si id probare potuisses. Nunc, sive illa defensione uti voluisses sive hac qua uteris, condemneris necesse est; nisi putamus eu⟨m in iudi⟩cium[64] venire qui consilium inierit, illum qui fecerit non venire, cum consilium sine facto intellegi possit, factum sine consilio non possit. An, quod factum eius modi est ut sine occulto consilio, sine nocte, sine vi, sine damno alterius, sine armis, sine caede, sine maleficio fieri non potuerit, id sine dolo malo factum iudicabitur? An, qua in re praetor[65] illi improbam defensionem tolli voluit, in ea re mihi difficiliorem actionem factam putabitis? Hic mihi isti singulari ingenio videntur esse qui et id quod mihi contra illos datum est ipsi arripiunt et scopulo atque saxis pro portu stationeque utuntur. Nam in dolo malo volunt delitescere, in quo, non modo cum omnia ipsi fecerunt quae fatentur, verum etiam si per alios id fecissent, hae-

32

33

[61] *suppl. Huschke*   [62] *litteras* DA *legit Keller, teste Baiter*
[63] defenderem *T: corr. Peyron*   [64] *suppl. Peyron*
[65] praetor *Peyron:* p.r. *T*

[31] That is, proof of malice aforethought (*dolus malus*) and of the criminal act are alternative paths to conviction; cf. Greenidge 1901, 554.

loss of how much money appears to have been inflicted on Marcus Tullius by the slaves of the household of Publius Fabius by force by armed men," what would you have to say? Nothing, I presume. In fact, you confess that the slaves of the household of Publius Fabius did everything and did it by force and armed men. Do you suppose that the fact that "by malice aforethought" has been added helps your case, the point by which your entire defense is overwhelmed and excluded? For if this point had not been added and you were free to offer the defense that the slaves of your household did not perpetrate (the crime), you would prevail, if you had been able to prove it. But as things stand, whether you had wished to use that defense or the one you are using, you must be convicted; unless we suppose that the person who formed the plan is on trial and not the perpetrator, since a plan without a deed is comprehensible, but not a deed without a plan.[31] Or if something is done in such a way that it could not be done without a hidden plan, night, violence, loss to another party, arms, bloodshed, crime, is it going to be judged to have been done without malice aforethought? Or are you going to suppose that my case is made more difficult in the respect in which the praetor wanted a shameless defense to be excluded? In this context, those persons seem to me to have a unique talent who snatch for themselves what has been granted to me against them and use a rocky reef as a harbor and anchorage. For they want to take refuge in "malice aforethought," by which they are caught and held fast not only if they themselves did everything they admit but even if they had done it using others as their

34 rerent ac tenerentur. Ego non in una re sola, quod mihi satis est, [neque in universa re solum quod mihi satis est][66] sed singillatim in omnibus dolum malum exstare dico. Consilium capiunt ut ad servos M. Tulli veniant; dolo malo faciunt. Arma capiunt; dolo malo faciunt. Tempus ad insidiandum atque celandum idoneum eligunt; dolo malo faciunt. Vi in tectum inruunt; in ipsa vi dolus est. Occidunt homines, tectum diruunt; nec homo occidi nec consulto alteri damnum dari sine dolo malo potest. Ergo si omnes partes sunt eius modi ut in singulis dolus malus haereat, universam rem et totum facinus sine dolo malo factum iudicabitis?

35 Quid ad haec Quinctius? Sane nihil certum neque unum, in quo non modo possit verum putet se posse consistere. Primum enim illud iniecit,[67] nihil posse dolo malo familiae fieri. Hoc loco non solum fecit ut defenderet Fabium, sed ut omnino huisce modi iudicia dissolveret. Nam si venit id in iudicium de familia quod omnino familia nulla potest committere, nullum est iudicium, absolvantur omnes de simili causa necesse est, [hoc solum][68]
36 bona, me hercule, ‹fide›![69] Si hoc solum esset, tamen vos, tales viri, nolle deberetis maximam rem coniunctam cum summa re publica fortunisque privatorum, severissimum

[66] *delevi, praeeunte Francken, qui* re solum . . . satis est *del.*
[67] in c t *T: suppl. Peyron*
[68] *del. Madvig (cf. quae sequuntur)*   [69] *add. Huschke*

[32] That is, the addition of "malice aforethought" (*dolus malus*) to the edict expands the options of the prosecution so that not merely the agent but also the planner and instigator is liable.

[33] That is, the impossibility of a household's slaves acting "with

PRO TULLIO 33–36

tools.[32] I assert that malice aforethought exists not in a single matter alone, which is sufficient for my case, but in all the components individually. They form the plan to go to Marcus Tullius' slaves; they act with malice aforethought. They take up arms; they act with malice aforethought. They select a time suitable for concealment and ambush; they act with malice aforethought. They force entry into the building; malice is inherent in the force itself. They slay the men and destroy the building; a man cannot be killed nor can loss be deliberately inflicted on another without malice aforethought. So then, if all the parts are of such a kind that malice aforethought is inherent in them individually, are you going to judge that the entire matter and the whole crime was done without malice aforethought?

What rebuttal does Quinctius offer to this? No stable, unified point such that he could take a stand on it or even think that he can do so. In the first place, he inserted the claim that nothing can be done by malice aforethought of a household's slaves. By this argument he not only achieved a defense of Fabius but a dissolution of such trials altogether. For if concerning a household's slaves a crime is brought to trial that no household's slaves can commit, there is no trial, all persons must be acquitted for a similar reason, by Hercules![33] If this were the sole consideration, even so, as men of such quality,[34] you should refuse for an important matter bound up with the state interest and the fortunes of private individuals, a severe

34

35

36

---

malice aforethought" (*dolo malo*), as claimed by the defense, would annul that *formula* altogether.

[34] For the flattery, cf. §§43, 53; Hartung 1974.

iudicium maximaque ratione compositum per vos videri esse dissolutum. Sed non id solum agitur ...

* * *

Hoc iudicium sic exspectatur ut non unae rei statui, sed omnibus constitui putetur.[70]

* * *

37 ego[71] intellego, et tamen dicendum est ad ea quae dixit Quinctius, non quo ad rem pertineat, sed ne quid, quia a me praetermissum sit,[72] pro concesso putetur.

38   Dicis oportere quaeri homines M. Tulli iniuria occisi sint[73] necne. De quo hoc primum quaero, venerit ea res in hoc iudicium necne. Si non venit, quid attinet aut nos dicere aut hos quaerere? Si autem venit, quid attinuit te tam multis verbis a praetore postulare ut adderet in iudicium "iniuria," et, quia non impetrasses, tribunos pl. appellare et hic in iudicio queri praetoris iniquitatem, quod
39 de iniuria non addidisset?[74] Haec cum praetorem postulabas, cum tribunos appellabas, nempe ita[75] dicebas, potestatem tibi fieri oportere ut, si posses, recuperatoribus[76] persuaderes non esse iniuria M. Tullio damnum datum.

[70] hoc ... putetur *ex Prisc. 6.1.5*
[71] *post lac. incipit* T
[72] sit *Baiter*: est *vel* sit T   [73] sint *Madvig*: essent T
[74] addidisset *Huschke*: addiderit (*vel* addidebet) T
[75] nempe ita *Peyron*: .. m. ... a T
[76] recuperatores T: *corr. Beier*

---

[35] That is, because of the recent origin of the *formula*, the decision of this court will establish a precedent; cf. Balzarini 1968, 326.   [36] Perhaps in reply to an imaginary objector quoted in the lacuna.   [37] Quinctius had evidently planned to argue

PRO TULLIO 36–39

tribunal and one put in place for a very good reason, to be seen to be dissolved by your action. But this is not the only thing at stake ...

* * *

This verdict is so highly anticipated that it is thought to be put in place not for a single matter but for all.[35]

* * *

I understand,[36] and yet I must speak in opposition to Quinctius' assertions, not because it is relevant but so that a point not be thought to have been conceded because it was omitted by me.

You claim that we must investigate whether Marcus Tullius' men were slain wrongfully or not.[37] As to this, I first ask whether this matter comes within the scope of this tribunal or not. If it does not, what is the point of our saying that they were or of these men conducting an inquiry? If it does fall within the scope, what was the point of your demanding at length from the praetor that he add "wrongfully" to the scope of the tribunal and, since you failed to obtain this, your calling upon the plebeian tribunes and in this connection complaining of the praetor's unfairness in the trial, since he made no addition about wrongful action? When you made these demands of the praetor, when you called upon the tribunes, you were, of course, asserting that you should be given leave to persuade the commissioners, if you could, that the loss was not wrongfully inflicted on Marcus Tullius. So then, although the point

that Fabius' slaves acted justifiably under provocation by Tullius' slaves and that the crimes of the latter included burning down a building on Quinctius' property and kidnapping one of Quinctius' slaves (§54).

361

Quod ergo ideo in iudicium addi voluisti, ut de eo tibi apud recuperatores dicere[77] liceret, eo non addito nihilo minus tamen ita dicis, quasi id ipsum a quo depulsus es impetraris? At quibus verbis in decernendo Metellus usus est ceterique quos appellasti? Nonne haec omnium fuit oratio, quod vi hominibus armatis coactisve familia fecisse diceretur, id tametsi nullo iure fieri potuerit, tamen se
40 nihil addituros? Et recte, recuperatores. Nam cum perfugio nullo constituto tamen haec scelera servi audacissime faciant, domini impudentissime confiteantur, quid censetis fore, si praetor iudicet eius modi caedis fieri iure posse? An quicquam interest utrum magistratus peccato defensionem consituant an peccandi potestatem licentiamque
41 permittant? Etenim, recuperatores, non damno commoventur magistratus ut in haec verba iudicium dent. Nam id ⟨si⟩[78] esset, nec recuperatores potius darent quam iudicem nec in universam familiam, sed in eum ⟨qui⟩cum[79] nominatim ageretur, nec in quadruplum, sed in duplum, et ⟨ad⟩[80] "damnum" adderetur "iniuria." Neque enim is qui hoc iudicium dedit de ceteris damnis ab lege Aquilia recedit, in[81] quibus nihil agitur nisi damnum, qua de re
42 praetor animum debet advertere. In hoc iudicio videtis agi de vi, videtis agi de hominibus armatis, videtis aedificiorum expugnationes, agri vastationes, hominum trucida-

[77] diceret *T: corr. Peyron*
[78] si *hoc loco suppl. Huschke, post* nam *Beier*
[79] *suppl. Peyron*
[80] *suppl. Beier*   [81] id *T (litt.* d *expuncta): corr. Peyron*

---

[38] Namely, his decision about the wording of the formula that would govern the trial; cf. Damon and MacKay 1995, 50.

was not added that you wanted added to the scope of the tribunal so that you might have leave to speak about it before the commissioners, are you nevertheless speaking as though the very point denied to you had been granted? But what was the language used by Metellus in formulating his decision[38] and by the others whom you called upon?[39] Did they not all say that although what a household's slaves were said to have done by force, by men armed or gathered, could not be done rightfully at all, nonetheless they would make no addition? Rightly so, commissioners. For when, although no refuge was put in place, slaves nonetheless boldly perpetrate these crimes and their masters brazenly admit them, what do you think will be the case if the praetor judges that such slaughter can rightfully occur? Or is there any difference whether magistrates set up a defense for wrongdoing or issue a license and permission for wrongdoing? The fact is, commissioners, that magistrates are not moved by a loss to provide a trial under these words. If that were the case, they would not provide commissioners rather than a judge and not against the whole of the household's slaves, but against the one who is the named defendant and not for a quadruple penalty but a double one, and "wrongfully" would be added to "loss." For the man who provided this tribunal did not deviate from the Aquilian law in regard to other losses, in which nothing is at issue except the loss, concerning which the praetor must exact punishment. You see that in this tribunal violence is at issue, armed men are at issue, the forcible seizure of buildings, the devastation of land, the slaying of men, arson, plunderings, bloodshed

---

[39] That is, the tribunes.

tiones, incendia, rapinas, sanguinem in iudicium venire, et miramini satis habuisse eos qui hoc iudicium dederunt id quaeri, utrum haec tam acerba, tam indigna, tam atrocia facta essent necne, non utrum iure facta an iniuria? Non ergo praetores a lege Aquilia recesserunt, quae de damno est,[82] sed de vi et armis[83] severum iudicium constituerunt, nec ius et iniuriam quaeri nusquam putarunt oportere, sed eos qui armis quam iure agere maluissent de iure et iniuria disputare noluerunt. Neque ideo de iniuria non addiderunt quod in aliis rebus non adderent, sed ne ipsi iudicarent posse homines servos iure arma capere et manum cogere, neque quod putarent, si additum esset, posse hoc talibus viris persuaderi[84] non iniuria factum, sed ne quod tamen[85] scutum dare in iudicio viderentur eis quos propter haec arma in iudicium vocavissent. Fuit illud interdictum apud maiores nostros de vi quod hodie quoque est: UNDE TU AUT FAMILIA AUT PROCURATOR TUUS ILLUM AUT FAMILIAM AUT PROCURATOREM ILLIUS IN HOC ANNO VI DEIECISTI. Deinde additur illius iam hoc causa quicum agitur: CUM ILLE POSSIDERET, et hoc amplius: QUOD NEC VI NEC CLAM NEC PRECARIO POSSIDERET. Multa dantur ei qui vi alterum detrusisse dicitur, quorum

[82] est T^{pc}: esset T^{ac} [83] armis T^{pc}: armatis T^{ac}
[84] persuaderi *(Beier) vel* persuadere T [85] *fort.* tamquam

---

[40] Cf. Greenidge 1901, 556, who suggests that Quinctius' position may have been that "this action was only an extension of that given by the *lex Aquilia*."

[41] The earliest known interdict "on violence" (*de vi*), dating probably from the early second century; the "exception on the ground of faulty possession" (*exceptio vitiosae possessionis*) al-

PRO TULLIO 42–45

are within the scope of the tribunal. Are we surprised that those who provided this tribunal considered it sufficient for the subject of inquiry to be whether these acts, so bitter, so outrageous, so monstrous occurred or not, not whether they occurred rightly or wrongfully? The praetors, then, did not deviate from the Aquilian law, which deals with loss, but they set up a severe tribunal that deals with violence and arms; nor was it their view that there should be no venue for inquiring into right and wrong, but they refused to allow those who had preferred to act under arms rather than under law to dispute over right and wrong.[40] Nor did they fail to add something about wrongful action because they did not add it in other matters, but lest they themselves judge that slaves could rightfully seize arms and gather a band, nor did they do so because they thought that if it had been added, men of such quality could be persuaded that it was not wrongfully done, but to avoid the impression that in their tribunal they were nonetheless handing a shield to those whom they had summoned to judgment because of these arms. Among our ancestors there was the following interdict about violence that still applies today: "whence you or the slaves of your household or your manager has thrust him or the slaves of his household or his manager by force this year."[41] Then the following is added for the sake of the defendant: "when he was in possession," and further this point: "a thing which he possessed neither by force nor by stealth nor at the pleasure of another." Many concessions are made to the party who is said to have displaced another by force;

43

44

45

luded to at Ter. *Eun.* 319–20, dated to 161, perhaps had its origin in this edict; cf. Frier 1983, 235 and n. 60; 1985, 53 and n. 41.

si unum quodlibet probare iudici potuerit, etiam si confessus erit se vi deiecisse, vincat necesse est: vel non possedisse eum qui deiectus sit, vel vi [ab se][86] possedisse, vel clam, vel precario. Ei qui de vi confessus esset tot defensiones tamen ad causam obtinendam maiores reliquerunt.

46 Age illud alterum interdictum consideremus, quod item nunc est constitutum propter eandem iniquitatem temporum nimiamque hominum ⟨licentiam⟩ . . .[87]

47 boni debent dicere. Atque ille legem mihi de XII tabulis recitavit, quae permittit ut furem noctu liceat occidere et luce,[88] si se telo defendat, et legem antiquam de legibus sacratis, quae iubeat impune occidi eum qui tribunum pl.
48 pulsaverit. Nihil, ut opinor, praeterea de legibus. Qua in re hoc primum quaero, quid ad hoc iudicium recitari istas leges pertinuerit. Num quem tribunum pl. servi M. Tulli pulsaverunt? Non opinor. Num furatum domum P. Fabi noctu venerunt?[89] Ne id quidem. Num[90] luce furatum venerunt et se telo defenderunt? Dici non potest. Ergo istis legibus quas recitasti certe non potuit istius familia
49 servos M. Tulli occidere. "Non" inquit "ad eam rem recitavi, sed ut hoc intellegeres, non visum esse maioribus

[86] *seclusi*
[87] licentiam *suppl. Peyron, deinde magna lacuna in* T
[88] luce *Peyron*: luci T
[89] venerint T: *corr. Peyron*   [90] nunc T: *corr. Peyron*

[42] That is, the same as mentioned at §8. Under this recently introduced interdict, Caecina's case was tried in 69. On the two interdicts, cf. Frier 1983, 236–37; 1985, 55–56.

[43] *Lex XII* 8.12, also cited at *Mil.* 9 to show that homicide is not a crime per se.   [44] By *leges sacratae* the plebeians banded

if he should be able to prove any one of these to the judge, even if he has admitted that he displaced him by force, he must prevail: either that the displaced person had not been in possession or that he was in possession by force or clandestinely or at the pleasure of another. Our ancestors left even the party who admitted the use of force so many defenses for prevailing in court. Come now, let us consider this other interdict that has likewise now been put in place on account of the same unfavorable times and people's excessive license . . .[42]

good men ought to say. And moreover, he read out to me a law from the Twelve Tables that allows that a thief may be slain by night and by day if he defends himself with a weapon,[43] and an ancient law from the laws bound by oath[44] that commands that whoever has beaten a plebeian tribune is slain with impunity. He said nothing further, I believe, about laws. In this connection, my first question is, what did the recital of those laws have to do with this tribunal? Surely Marcus Tullius' slaves did not beat any plebeian tribune, did they? I think not. Surely they did not go to Publius Fabius' house by night in order to commit theft, did they? Not even that. Surely they did not come to commit theft by day and defend themselves with a weapon? It cannot be claimed. Therefore the defendant's slaves certainly could not have slain the slaves of Marcus Tullius under the laws that you have read out. "I did not read them out," he replies, "for that purpose, but so that you would understand that homicide did not seem to our

together and dedicated themselves to self-help in opposition to the patricians; cf. Livy 2.33.3, with Ogilvie 1965, ad loc. The oath was originally sworn by Ceres.

nostris tam indignum istuc nescio quid quam tu putas, hominem occidi." At primum istae ipsae leges quas recitas, ut mittam cetera, significant quam noluerint maiores nostri, nisi cum pernecesse esset, hominem occidi. [Primum][91] Ista lex sacrata est, quam rogarunt armati, ut inermes sine periculo possent esse. Qua re non iniuria, quo magistratu munitae leges sunt, eius magistratus corpus legibus vallatum esse voluerunt. Furem, hoc est praedonem et latronem, luce occidi vetant XII tabulae; cum intra parietes tuos hostem certissimum teneas, nisi se telo defendit,[92] inquit, etiam si cum telo venerit, nisi utetur telo eo ac repugnabit, non occides. Quid[93] si repugnat? "Endoplorato," hoc est conclamato, ut aliqui audiant et conveniant. Quid ad hanc clementiam addi potest, qui ne hoc quidem permiserint, ut domi suae caput suum sine testibus et arbitris[94] ferro defendere liceret?

51   Quis est cui magis ignosci conveniat, quoniam me ad XII tabulas revocas, quam si quis quem imprudens occiderit? Nemo, opinor. Haec enim tacita lex est humanitatis, ut ab homine consili, non fortunae poena repetatur. Tamen huiusce rei veniam maiores non dederunt. Nam lex

[91] primum *ut repetitum del. Keller*
[92] defendit: defendet *Baiter*
[93] quid *Madvig*: quos *T*: quod *Peyron*
[94] arbitriis *T*: *corr. Peyron*

[45] A rare debate over what counts as ancestral custom; cf. Kenty 2016, 441.
[46] The "law hallowed by oath" (*lex sacrata*) was enacted, according to tradition, in 493 during the secession of the plebs, who were thus under arms; for sources, cf. *MRR* 1:15.

ancestors such an outrageous thing as you suppose." But in the first place, those very laws you read out (to set the rest aside) show how unwilling our ancestors were for homicide to occur unless it was utterly necessary.[45] That law that the men passed under arms was hallowed by oath so that unarmed persons could be free of danger.[46] Rightly, therefore, they wanted the body of that magistrate[47] hedged about by laws by whom the laws were fortified. The Twelve Tables forbid a thief, that is, a brigand and highwayman, from being killed by daylight; although you have caught the enemy red-handed within your house walls, unless he defends himself with a weapon, it says, even if he came with a weapon, unless he uses that weapon and fights back, you shall not kill him. What if he fights back? "Ask for help," that is, raise a cry so that some people may hear it and gather. What greater clemency can there be than that of those who did not even allow that a man has license in his own house to defend his life with a sword except with witnesses and spectators present?

Since you refer me to the Twelve Tables, whom is it more fitting to pardon than the one who has killed someone unintentionally? No one, I suppose. This is, in fact, an unspoken law of the human race that a penalty is sought for a person's plan, not their luck.[48] Nevertheless our ancestors issued no pardon for this case. For in the Twelve

[47] Namely, the plebeian tribune.
[48] The first hint in Cicero's corpus of natural law standing above individual enactments; cf. Classen 1985, 280.

est in XII tabulis: SI TELUM MANU FUGIT MA⟨GIS QUAM IECIT⟩[95] . . .

* * *

52 Si qui furem occiderit, iniuria occiderit. Quam ob rem? Quia ius constitutum nullum est. Quid, si se telo defenderit? Non iniuria. Quid ita? Quia constitutum est.[96]

* * *

53 tamen per vim[97] factum esset [non modo servos],[98] tamen in eo ipso loco qui tuus esset, non modo servos M. Tulli occidere iure non potuisti verum etiam, si tectum hoc insciente aut per vim demolitus esses, quod hic in tuo aedificasset et suum esse defenderet, id vi[99] aut clam factum iudicaretur. Tu ipse iam statue quam verum sit, cum paucas tegulas deicere impune familia tua non potuerit, maximam caedem sine fraude facere potuisse.[100] Ego ipse tecto illo disturbato si hodie postulem, quod vi aut clam factum sit, tu aut per arbitrum restituas aut sponsione condemneris necesse est; nunc hoc probabis viris talibus, cum aedificium tuo iure disturbare non potueris quod esset, quem ad modum tu vis, in tuo, homines qui in eo aedificio fuerint te tuo iure potuisse occidere? "At servus meus non
54 comparet, qui visus est cum tuis; at[101] casa mea est incensa a tuis." Quid ad haec respondeam? Ostendi falsa esse; ve-

[95] *cod. T expl.; suppl. Peyron*
[96] *ex Iul. Rufiniano (RLM, p. 40.21)*
[97] per vim *Beier*: verum *T*
[98] *del. Beier*
[99] vim *T: corr. Baiter*
[100] potuisset *T: corr. Beier*
[101] ad . . . ad *T: corr. Peyron*

Tables there is a law: "If a missile escapes from one's hand, rather than being thrown . . ."[49]

* * *

If anyone killed a thief, he did so wrongfully. Why? Because no right (to do so) has been established. What if he defended himself with a weapon? Rightly. Why so? Because (the right to do so) has been established. 52

* * *

although it was done by force and on the very ground that belonged to you, not only could you not rightly have killed Marcus Tullius' slaves but even if you had demolished without his knowledge or by force the building which he had built on your property and claimed as his own, this would be judged to have been done by force or clandestinely. You yourself decide how true it is, when your slaves could not with impunity have dislodged a few roof tiles, that they could be free of crime in perpetrating an enormous slaughter. If I myself were to raise an accusation today on the basis of that demolished building on the ground it was done by force or clandestinely, you would necessarily either make restitution by finding of an arbitrator or be convicted under a wager. But as things stand, are you going to prove to men of such quality that, though you could not rightfully destroy a building on the ground that it was, as you claim, on your property, you could rightfully kill the people who were in that building? "But my slave failed to appear, who was seen with your slaves; but my house was burned down by your slaves." What reply am I to make to these claims? I have shown that they are 53 54

---

[49] *Tab. XII* 8.24, also cited at *Top.* 64; cf. *Dig.* 48.8.1.3; Reinhardt 2003, 331–33.

rum tamen confitebor. Quid postea? Hoc sequitur, ut familiam[102] M. Tulli concidi oportuerit? Vix me hercule ut corium peti, vix ut gravius expostulari; verum ut esses durissimus, agi quidem usitato iure et cotidiana actione potuit. Quid opus fuit vi, quid armatis hominbus, quid 55 caede, quid sanguine? "At enim oppugnatum me fortasse venissent." Haec est illorum in causa perdita extrema non oratio neque defensio, sed coniectura et quasi divinatio. Illi oppugnatum venturi erant? Quem? Fabium. Quo consilio? Ut occiderent. Quam ob causam? Quid ut proficerent? Qui comperisti? Et ut rem perspicuam quam paucissimis verbis agam, dubitari hoc potest, recuperatores, utri oppugnasse videantur, qui ad villam venerunt, an qui in villa[103] manserunt? Qui occisi sunt, an ei ex quorum numero saucius factus est nemo? Quibus[104] cur facerent, 56 causa non fuit, an ei qui fecisse se confitentur? Verum ut hoc tibi credam, metuisse te ne oppugnarere, quis hoc statuit[105] umquam, aut cui concedi sine summo omnium periculo potest, ut eum iure potuerit occidere a quo metuisse se dicat ne ipse posterius occideretur?[106]

102 familia *T*: *corr. G. Müller*
103 villam *T*: *corr. Peyron*
104 quibus *Leclerc*: qui *T*
105 statuit *Quint. 5.13.21*: statut *T*
106 iure ... occideretur *Quint. 5.13.21*: *desiderantur in lac. in T*

false; but I will admit them nonetheless [sc. for the sake of argument]. What then? Does it follow that Marcus Tullius' slaves had to be cut down? Good heavens! Scarcely that they ought to be flogged or severely reprimanded; but to take the harshest line, it would have been possible to litigate under usual law and everyday complaint. What need was there for violence, armed men, slaughter, bloodshed? "But they would perhaps have come to attack me." In a lost cause, this is their final—I will not say speech or defense—but guesswork and, as it were, divination. They were going to come to attack? Whom? Fabius. With what intent? To kill him. For what reason? To accomplish what? How did you find out? To argue an obvious point as briefly as possible, is it open to doubt, commissioners, which of the two appears to have attacked, those who came to the building or those who remained in the building? Those who were slain or those of whose number none was wounded? Those who had no motive for doing so or those who admit to having done it? But, to lend credence to your claim that you feared being attacked, who ever decided or to whom can it be conceded without the utmost danger to the community that someone could rightly slay a person by whom he says he feared that he himself might later be slain?

CICERO

FRAGMENTA

1a Mar. Vict. 1.30 (p. 78.19–24 Riesenweber; cf. Riesenweber 2015, 2:130)

Illa superior species [sc. partitionis] cum proposuerit quid conveniat, id ipsum ad se inclinat, ut pro se faciat id quod adversarius confitetur, postea vero subiungit id quod sit[107] in controversia. Fecit hoc Cicero pro Tullio: "Dicam" inquit "vim factam a P. Fabii familia, adversarii non negant." Hic id[108] proposuit quod adversarii fateantur. Deinde ⟨id⟩[109] ipsum pro se fecit dicendo: "Damnum datum esse M. Tullio concedis: vici unam rem;[110] vi hominibus armatis non negas: vici alterum; dolo malo familiae P. Fabii, id non totum negas: a familia P. Fabii[111] factum esse concedis, dolo malo[112] negas: de hoc iudicium est."

1b Iul. Vict. *Ars rhet.* 65.4–9 Giomini-Celentano

Sic et Marcus Tullius fecit pro Tullio: damnum datum Tullio et vi hominibus armatis et a familia P. Fabi constare dicit, in controversia autem esse an dolo malo damnum datum sit, quod est τὸ κρινόμενον quodque adiuvatur plurimum ex his de quibus convenire constitit, id est: dolum malum esse cum familia armata sit, cum ad vim venerit, cum damnum intulerit.

[107] sit μ: fit FQ [108] *om.* μ
[109] *add. Riesenweber* [110] *quae sequuntur om.* μ
[111] id non ... Fabii Q: *om.* O
[112] dolo malo factum *Mar. Vict. 78.28 Riesenweber*

PRO TULLIO F 1a–1b

FRAGMENTS

1a Victorinus

The former type [of partition of the case] is when [the orator] has set out what is appropriate, he bends this very thing in his direction so that he turns his opponent's admission into a point in his favor, but afterward adds the matter that is in dispute. Cicero did this in *In Defense of Tullius*: "I will assert," he says, "that violence was perpetrated by the slaves of Publius Fabius; our opponents do not deny this." Here he has set out the point that his opponents admit. Then he turned that very point in his favor by saying: "You admit that loss was inflicted on Marcus Tullius; I have won one point. You do not deny that this was done by force by armed men; I have won the second point. You do not wholly deny that this was done by the malice aforethought of Publius Fabius' slaves; you admit that this was done by Publius Fabius' slaves; you deny that this was done by malice aforethought; this is the subject matter of the trial."

1b Iulius Victor, *Handbook of Rhetoric*

Marcus Tullius also did this [i.e., turned his opponent's admission into a point in his favor] in *In Defense of Tullius*: he says that it is agreed that loss was inflicted on Tullius both by force by armed men and by Publius Fabius' slaves, but that the matter in dispute is whether the loss was inflicted by malice aforethought, which is the what is being determined and which is greatly assisted by the points on which agreement is established, namely that malice aforethought is when a household's slaves are armed, have ventured upon violence, and have inflicted loss.

1c Mart. Cap. 5.556 (p. 196.7–11 Willis; cf. Stroh 1975, 167n35)

Et ea quae conveniunt tunc enumeranda, si nobis prosunt, ut Cicero pro M. Tullio ait: "Damnum passum esse M. Tullium convenit mihi cum adversario; vi hominibus armatis rem gestam esse non infitiantur, a familia P. Fabii commissam negare non audent; an[113] dolo malo factum sit ambigitur."

1d Grill. *Comm. in Cic. rhet.* 93.94–96 Jakobi

In obscuro genere ‹causae›[114] quid facere debes? Ut docilem facias auditorem, quod facit in Tulliana: "De hac re," inquit, "iudicabitis."[115]

2a Diom. *GL* 1.372.21

"Explicavi" legimus, ut est apud Ciceronem pro Tullio.

2b Macrob. *De diff. GL* 5.607.4

Cicero pro Tullio explicavi[116] ait.

---

[113] an *Vulcanius (ed. Basiliens. 1577)*: etiam *V*: iam *cett.*
[114] *add. Jakobi*
[115] *Fr. 1 fort. in lac. §23 ponendum; cf. Stroh 1975, 167 adn. 35*
[116] explicavit: *correxi*

1c Martianus Capella, *On the Marriage of Philology and Mercury*

And the points of agreement should then be enumerated if they are in our favor, as Cicero says in *In Defense of Marcus Tullius*: "My opponent and I agree that Marcus Tullius suffered a loss; they do not deny that the matter was carried out by force by armed men; they dare not deny that it was perpetrated by Publius Fabius' slaves; the point at issue is whether it was done by malice aforethought."

1d Grillius, *Commentary on Cicero's* Rhetorica

What should you do in an obscure type of case? Make the listener inclined to learn, which is what he [Cicero] did in the Tulliana: "This is the matter," he says, "about which you will pass judgment."

2a Diomedes

We read "I explained," as is in Cicero *In Defense of Tullius*.

2b Macrobius, *On Differences and Similarities of the Greek and Latin Verb*

In *In Defense of Tullius* Cicero says "I explained."

3 Fortun. 116.11, 19–22 Calboli Montefusco

Voluntas legis quot modis consideratur? Tribus . . . Quid tertio? Cum exemplo multarum legum probamus praesentem quoque legem ita sentire ut nos defendimus, sicut M. Tullius fecit pro M. Tullio et pro A. Caecina.

4 Iul. Vict. *Ars rhet.* 42.6–8 Giomini-Celentano

Ab eventu in fine [sc. argumenta ducuntur], ut M. Tullius Cicero:[117] "Si iudicaveritis sine dolo malo posse familiam congregari, hominem occidi, omnibus facinorosis eandem licentiam permiseritis."

[117] *fort.* pro Marco Tullio Cicero

PRO TULLIO F 3–4

3 Fortunatianus, *Handbook of Rhetoric*

How many ways is the intention of the law considered [sc. in a pleading]? Three . . . What is the third? When we argue with the examples of many laws that the present law also has the sense that we are claiming, as Marcus Tullius did in *In Defense of Marcus Tullius* and *In Defense of Aulus Caecina*.

4 Iulius Victor, *Handbook of Rhetoric*

(Arguments are derived) from the outcome by way of a conclusion, as Marcus Tullius Cicero (did): "If you judge that a household's slaves can gather and a man be killed without malice aforethought, you will grant the same license to all criminals."

ON THE AGRARIAN LAW

INTRODUCTION

On January 1 of 63, Cicero entered office as consul, presided over his first meeting of the senate, and there delivered a speech. He later included a version of this speech as the first in the corpus of consular orations that he prepared and published in the year 60 in order to promote an image of high statesmanship (*Att.* 2.1[21].3). The speech is mutilated at the beginning, but enough survives (perhaps two-thirds of its original length) to show that it was dominated by an issue that had arisen in the final weeks of 64, namely a proposal by the plebeian tribune P. Servilius Rullus to raise funds by allocating spoils of war collected by Rome's generals and by selling public land in the Roman provinces and Italy, and to use the proceeds to purchase farmland in Italy to be colonized by the urban plebs. Given this focus, the oration is conventionally named Cicero's first speech *On the Agrarian Law*.[1]

The theme running through this speech, as we have it, from beginning to end is the need to preserve the "standing" (*dignitas*) of the Roman people or of the republic

---

[1] The goals of Rullus' bill have been variously assessed by scholars; for a survey of opinions, see Manuwald 2018, xxiv–xxv; Krostenko 2023, 3–4, argues that the bill was both intelligent and politically astute.

INTRODUCTION

(1.2, 17, 22, 23, 27). The lost beginning of the speech probably offered remarks on Cicero's election to office, just as his second speech *On the Agrarian Law* does (2.1–10), with appropriate adjustments for the different audience, then a transition to the subject of Rullus' bill, followed perhaps, as in the second speech, by criticism of the method of election and powers of the board of ten (the Decemvirs) charged with administering the program.[2] When extant text begins, Cicero is discussing the collection of funds by appropriation of war booty and sale of taxable and other lands (1.1–13). The second half of the extant argumentation deals with the settlement of colonies, with particular emphasis on the plan to establish a colony at Capua, a bogey for the Romans since its defection to Hannibal during the Second Punic War (1.16–22). In the peroration, Cicero issues the surprising pledge that, circumstances permitting, he will not go to govern a province the year after his consulship, so as not to be beholden to the tribunes' goodwill. (They could use their veto to block appropriation of the funding.) He also assesses the current danger to the state as internal, and expresses his resolve to restore the standing of the senate (1.23–27).[3]

---

[2] Krostenko 2023, 93n97, suggests that the exordium also touched on the theme of the brave vs. ineffective consul raised at 1.3; possibly also the concept of the *popularis* consul (1.23) was introduced. He also suspects that "missing passages . . . would have argued that the bill's various legal 'permissions' enabled and reflected moral 'license'" (ibid., 265, with following argument).

[3] He later claimed that the foundations for the primacy of the senate were laid in this speech (*Fam.* 1.9[20].12).

This speech, even if preserved in full, would have been briefer than the second one,[4] delivered before the people, and although the basic topics are the same, they are argued along different lines. In general, the senators are given a view of events "from above," the people "from below."[5] Moreover, the senators were, for the most part, owners of large estates and had no interest in receiving small parcels of land. They were, therefore, accessible to arguments framed from the standpoint of state, not personal interest.[6] In view of these shared premises, Cicero can use the same invective techniques before the senate, but more briefly, without the need for lengthy illustrations in the form of quotations from the text of the bill (though he does cite one section of the bill at 1.2) or narratives of Cicero's own experiences (as at 2.13 or 92–94)[7] or of historical material (such as the previous attempt to annex Egypt, 2.41–44). Politically significant names are differently deployed. When he narrates the territories to be sold in Asia, in the senate he emphasizes the names of the generals who conquered them, since they will have reso-

[4] Cf. *De or.* 2.333 on speaking less elaborately (*minore apparatu*) in the senate and avoiding showing off one's skills (*vitanda . . . ingenii ostentationis suspicio*).

[5] Cf. Krostenko 2023, 46.

[6] Cf. *Part. or.* 92 with Leonhardt 1998–1999, 281, who rightly identifies the two types of audience (educated vs. uneducated) with the senate and the people, the former open to arguments about what is honorable (*honestas*), the latter to arguments from interests.

[7] Cf. Manuwald 2021, xxviii, on deployment of a more personal tone before the people than the senate in the speeches on his return from exile.

INTRODUCTION

nance before that body, but the names of the places before the people, possibly with the intent of dazzling them.[8] Sulla is named only twice before the senate, once merely as a chronological marker, the other a passing reference to his absolutism (1.10 and 21), and his son Faustus is mentioned sympathetically (1.12). Before the people, however, besides chronological references and a general allusion to his absolutism, Sulla is specifically criticized (2.56 and 81), as are the lands bestowed by Sulla and those who received them (2.68–70 and 98). The Gracchi are mentioned approvingly before the people (2.10, 31, 81), but before the senate as dispensers of largesse (1.21).[9]

In the peroration to the first speech, Cicero challenges Rullus to debate him in a public meeting (1.23), a challenge he did not immediately take up. So Cicero brought his case to the people himself some days later, with a version of that speech being the second in the agrarian law series.[10] Here Cicero finds himself in the rhetorically tricky position of arguing before the people in opposition to the people's own apparent interests. Rullus and his supporters had spread word that the urban plebs were to be settled as farmers on some of the choicest agricultural lands of Italy. Cicero will disappoint these ex-

---

[8] For the basic dichotomy, cf. Krostenko 2023, 250.

[9] For detailed comparison of the rhetoric deployed in the first and the second speeches, cf. Krostenko 2023.

[10] This speech and the following one were delivered at the first two *contiones* known to have been summoned by a consul in the post-Sullan period; cf. Tan 2008, 190 nos. 21–22. In referring to the senate speech here, he does not say that it was delivered "today" or "yesterday," as he might have done if that were the case; cf. Manuwald 2018, xxxiv and 183.

pectations, but not immediately. As in some of his more challenging forensic cases, he will back into the subject gradually and put off the most difficult part until he has established his own credibility and a certain rapport with the audience, an approach rhetoricians called *insinuatio*.[11] Cicero's speech is surprising, however, in the frequency of his appeals to the ancestors (*maiores*) both as a standard for behavior and as a foil for Rullus' actions, such appeals being expected, rather, before a senatorial audience.[12]

Cicero begins in the traditional manner, by thanking the people for his election but underscoring his unique position as a "new" man (*novus homo*) elected at the time of his earliest eligibility (*suo anno*).[13] He claims that with himself as their leader the people have "broken into" the consulship, the closely guarded stronghold of the nobility, so that it will in future be open to men of character (*virtus*, 2.3). He paints a picture of the current state of the republic, under threat, with new concentrations of power (*dominationes*) and indeed kingdoms (*regna*) being prepared (2.8). On the other side, Cicero quotes the pledge from his senate speech that he will be a consul "in the people's interest" (*popularis*, 2.9; cf. 1.23) and details what his program will be: domestic peace (*otium*) combined with rule (*imperium*) and worthy standing (*dignitas*, 2.9).[14] He goes

[11] Cf. Loutsch 1982, 311n35; 1994, 222–26.

[12] Cf. note 6 above with *De or.* 2.334–35; see further on 2.9.

[13] The claim of uniqueness may apply, however, only to recent cases; cf. Manuwald 2018, 194–95.

[14] This will later be simplified to the slogan "tranquility combined with worthy standing" (*cum dignitate otium*); see further Kaster 2006, 31–37, 322; Mouritsen 2022, 134–41.

INTRODUCTION

on to distinguish these values from other actions, such as the invalidation of judicial verdicts, restoration of those who have been condemned, and promises of agricultural land to the Roman people—all tribunician proposals floated at this time.[15] Cicero hastens to add that he does not oppose agrarian legislation per se and praises the Gracchi for their reforms (2.10). Cicero shows his own concern for the people's interests and casts doubt upon that of Rullus by narrating his overtures to the tribune, which were rebuffed, and highlighting Rullus' clandestine meetings by night, his change of demeanor upon election to the tribunate, and his incoherence at the *contio* he called to explain his bill (2.12–13). Having appointed clerks to transcribe the proposal when it was promulgated, Cicero read it, he claims, with an open mind, but discovered that it was nothing but a plot to seize wealth and power on a vast scale (2.14–15). He has a crier beside him who, on command, reads out portions of the text, on which he then comments. He thus presents himself as an authority on the bill who is examining it with the foresight necessary to protect the people's interests (2.25), in this respect like the Roman ancestors (2.90). He offers, however, bits of the law detached from context in such a way that they fail to yield a single complete clause.[16]

The body of the speech consists of sections on (1) the Decemvirs' mode of election and powers (2.16–35);

---

[15] The first two items refer to a proposal by another plebeian tribune L. Caecilius Rufus, which Cicero mischaracterizes; cf. on 2.9 and 10.

[16] Cf. Ferrary 1988, 160, 164; Drummond 2000, 133; Morstein-Marx 2004, 196; Manuwald 2018, xxii–xxiii.

(2) their collection of money to fund their project (2.35–62); (3) their purchases of land (2.63–72); and (4) the settlement of colonies (2.73–97). In introducing the first topic, Cicero immediately sounds what will be a major theme, namely that the bill would reduce the freedom of Roman citizens, in this case, by having the Decemvirs elected by only seventeen of the thirty-five tribes to which citizens were assigned (2.16).[17] He complains that Rullus, though the author of the bill, is allowed to canvass for the Decemvirate created by it (2.20–22). Pompey is excluded, however, since the candidates must present themselves in person, whereas he is still occupied with settling affairs in Asia. Cicero spins dark suspicions that the tribunes are deliberately excluding him from "the guardianship of your liberty" so that they can be free to pursue nefarious designs (2.23–25). Rullus may, however, have feared a loss of momentum that might result if all the Decemvirs were not present in Rome to oversee the project from the start.[18] Cicero concludes this section by emphasizing that Rullus assigns his Decemvirs more than regal powers (2.35) that will extend over a five-year period and include judicial authority not subject to appeal.[19]

Collection of funds (2) was a necessary step for Rullus, because, in order to launch his program successfully, he

[17] Cf. Krostenko 2023, 142–45. For Cicero's criticisms of abridgment of the people's freedom in this speech generally, cf. Arena 2012, 229–43; Krostenko 2023, ch. 4.

[18] Rullus had scheduled the first auctions under his bill for the current month (January): 1.4.

[19] Krostenko 2023, 225–26, argues that Cicero wants his audience to think of the Decemvirs of 450, who abused their absolute powers.

INTRODUCTION

needed a large amount of start-up capital to finance land purchases. Cicero ignores this fact, however, and represents the bill's revenue-generating provisions as resulting from greed (2.24, 25, 37, 63) and Rullus' own spendthrift character (2.48; cf. 1.2). Cicero's first specific complaint under this heading is that the properties to be sold in Italy are not specified, the bill merely indicating those authorized for sale by decree of the senate in or after the year 81 (2.35). He darkly suspects that the reason may be that Rullus is planning to expand the list of eligible properties by forging decrees (2.37). In addition, the Decemvirs are to sell public land outside Italy acquired by Rome in or after the year 88. This provision gives rise to the first "catalog passage," in which Cicero lists six prominent cities of Asia as likely to be claimed eligible by the Decemvirs, the aim being perhaps to bedazzle the contional audience and create the impression of power to be exercised on an enormous scale; he then expands the scope to "all Asia" (2.39). He adds Bithynia and Mytilene as places recently reconquered from Mithridates (2.40) and goes on to suspect that Rullus has his eye on "all Egypt," which had been bequeathed to the Roman people by the will of Ptolemy X Alexander I (ca. 140–88), a proposal to accept the legacy having been discussed in the senate in 65. While not committing himself on the substance of the issue, Cicero assumes that the same people are behind Rullus' bill and wonders why they are now trying to obtain by stealth what they had previously sought openly (2.41–44).

Lands subject to taxation (*vectigalia*) are also targeted for sale under Rullus' bill (2.47–55). Here Cicero uses a two-pronged attack. On the one hand, such lands are conceived as a kind of patrimony bequeathed to the Roman

people by their ancestors and won at great cost in successful military campaigns. By describing such property as "our own" (*proprium*), Cicero seeks to instill pride of ownership and reluctance to alienate property so acquired (2.48). On the other hand, Cicero singles out Pompey as the commander whose interests would be prejudiced. In fact, it is likely that Rullus and his collaborators had either concerted their plans with Pompey or designed their bill so as to appeal to him, because, with his campaign in Asia now winding down, he would need to take thought, as Roman commanders since Marius had done, for settling his time-served veterans on plots of land.[20] Cicero, however, resolutely ignores this aspect and insists that the bill his been framed "against Gnaeus Pompey" (3.16). Cicero adds point and vividness to his claim by offering a specimen of the arrogant letter he expects Rullus to send to Pompey, commanding him to be present at the sale of his own conquests (2.53).

Cicero appends criticisms of several administrative aspects of the property sales. First, the venue of sales is not specified, a fact that he contrasts with Sulla's sales of the property of the proscribed, which at least took place in Rome, before the eyes of the Roman people (2.55–56). Second, he notes that, though the Decemvirs are to conduct a general investigation of the status of land to de-

---

[20] For Marius' policy, cf. Sall. *Iug.* 86.2–3; Weynand, *RE* Suppl. 6:1401.7–1403.41 (s.v. Marius); Gabba 1976, 14–19, with attached notes. Pompey would later support the land bills of the tribune L. Flavius, in 60 (*Att.* 1.19[19].4), and of Julius Caesar, in 59. For a possible example of Rullus' consideration for Pompey in drafting his bill, cf. Krostenko 2023, 114 and n. 54.

INTRODUCTION

termine whether it is private or public, certain lands are excepted, with Cicero suggesting, of course, that skullduggery is at play (2.56–59). Finally, spoils of war are to be administered by the Decemvirs, not, as in the past, by the victorious generals, except for Pompey, but Cicero claims that the commander does not want this invidious exception (2.61).

Turning to the purchase of lands (3), Cicero first complains that this is nontraditional, Roman settlements having previously been placed on public lands from which private individuals were expelled (2.65). Another point of criticism is that the lands to be purchased have been inadequately defined, Rullus merely having specified Italy (2.66). He also finds fault with the provision that lands are to be purchased that "can be," rather than "have been plowed or cultivated" and foresees that money will be wasted on barren and rocky soil (2.67). His major point here, however, is that the bill has been framed so as to enable those like Rullus' father-in-law Valg(i)us,[21] who own lands assigned by Sulla, to sell their odious possessions for as high a price as they wish (2.68–70). In addition, there is no provision for returning excess funds to the treasury (2.72).

When Cicero finally addresses the settlement of colonies (4), he quickly focuses on the rich farmland of Campania and in particular the city of Capua and makes this into a competition between Capua and Rome (2.76, "If perchance there is anyone for whom Capua has a greater

[21] He is mentioned by name only in 3.3 in the genitive case; the nominative form is therefore ambiguous; for a possible identification, see on 1.14.

391

charm than Rome"). He activates the stereotype of Campanians as arrogant (2.91, 93, 95–97; cf. on 1.20), illustrated by personal reminiscences of his visit to the colony founded at Capua by M. Brutus in 83 (2.92–93). Capua's envy of Rome's primacy is shown by its defection during the Second Punic War (2.95). At the same time, Cicero pictures Rullus' intended colonists not as peaceloving citizens, like the urban plebs, but as unscrupulous and violent men (2.77, 82), who will establish garrisons throughout Italy and ultimately, with their capital in Capua, be positioned to threaten Rome itself (2.86).[22] His subsidiary arguments are that Rullus does not plan to benefit the urban plebs since he said that he would begin his land distributions with a rural tribe, the Romilian (2.79); and Campanian land is already occupied by rural plebeians, who should not be displaced (2.84).

The peroration begins with a summary of Cicero's criticisms of the bill. Moreover, since he had noticed the effectiveness of the charge that Rullus was plotting against Pompey (2.49), he escalates to the claim he had made before the senate (F 4), that the Decemvirs would enter Pompey's camp and put it up for sale if they thought it in their interest (2.98–99). Cicero concludes by taking up from the exordium his special position as a "new" man and its implications: because he has risen by his own merits, he pledges that he will conduct his office with alertness and care (2.100). He also resumes the topic of "consul in the people's interest" (*consul popularis*, 2.7, 102) and

[22] Memories of the behavior of Sullan colonists may have lent plausibility to this claim; cf. Krostenko 2023, 294 and n. 11.

INTRODUCTION

the "peace, tranquility, and quiet" (*pacem tranquillitatem otium*) that form his program (2.102), adding a brief allusion to his reconciliation with his colleague Antonius (2.103).

Cicero suggests at certain points that his assembly speech had a certain impact (2.49, 101, 103).[23] The charge that Rullus' bill favored the interests of the owners of Sullan allotments must particularly have stung, for Rullus called his own assembly and flung back the charge, claiming that Cicero was the one acting in the interests of the Sullan possessors (3.1, 3). Rullus' speech, too, was not without effect: when Cicero responded by calling another assembly, he noticed hostile murmurings and a very different facial expression than previously (3.2). The speech that Cicero delivered on that occasion—or part of it—is designated in the tradition as the third speech *On the Agrarian Law*. Much shorter than the other two, it is likely to be one of the two "excerpts" (ἀποσπάσματα) on the agrarian law within the consular corpus mentioned at *Att.* 2.1[21].3.

The debate seems now to have narrowed to the question of who should bear the invidious epithet "Sullan," Rullus or Cicero.[24] Cicero frames his argument with a comparison of a provision from the fortieth section of Rullus' bill with L. Valerius Flaccus' law of 82 naming Sulla dictator and retroactively legitimizing his acts, which Cic-

---

[23] Possibly, as Morstein-Marx 2004, 192, suggests, this success may be owing to the fact that Cicero's first *contio* was well attended by his supporters.

[24] On this as a factor in the debate, see Eckert 2016, 139–40.

ero describes as "most unjust and least like a law" (3.4–5; *LPPR* 348–49). Cicero argues that Rullus' bill is even worse, because he aims not merely to confirm the Sullan possessors in their holdings but to upgrade their status so that they are now held with "the best title" (*optimo iure*) and thus freed of any easements or other encumbrances to full possessory rights (3.7). It is doubtful, however, that this was the intent of the clause that Cicero cites. It was probably merely meant to reassure those in possession by full public authority, or who had acquired property from such persons, that their holdings were secure. The position he takes here is also different from the one he espoused in his previous speeches, which identified the benefit to the Sullan possessors as being able to sell their odious holdings at a price of their choosing (1.14, 2.68).[25] Rullus' father-in-law Valg(i)us features again, as in the previous speech, and is described as a Sullan; he and others like him will be the beneficiaries of Rullus' legislation (3.3, 13).

The third speech concludes with another challenge to Rullus to debate him in a *contio*, a challenge the plebeian tribune this time took up, summoning Cicero to a *contio* called by himself. Calling upon the senators to join him,[26] Cicero duly appeared and delivered the remarks he later published as the fourth speech *On the Agrarian Law* (the other "excerpt" mentioned to Atticus), but which do not survive.[27] After this debate, Rullus seems to have withdrawn his bill in the face of Cicero's determined opposi-

[25] Cf. Manuwald 2018, 419
[26] Plut. *Vit. Cic.* 12.5; Krostenko 2023, 286.
[27] Cf. Crawford 1984, 79–81; Krostenko 2023, 3n8.

tion and the threat of a veto by his fellow tribune L. Caecilius (*Sul.* 65).[28]

The fate of Rullus' proposal for distribution of agricultural land to the urban plebs played out mostly in public assemblies (*contiones*) since it was a proposal by a plebeian tribune to be enacted by plebiscite. Cicero opposed it aggressively and did not shrink from calling his own *contio* to face the plebeian tribune on his own turf. He constructs the problem as a contest between himself and Rullus as to who is the true "friend of the people" (*popularis*), who is acting in Pompey's interests, and who is acting in the interests of the possessors of property assigned by Sulla. He represents himself as a different kind of consul, a new man vigilant to guard the people's interests against a pseudo-*popularis* such as Rullus who, he claims, is actually tending his own interests and those of his relations. Rullus opened himself up to this charge by allowing his own eligibility for election to the Decemvirate, with the Decemvirs to be endowed with praetorian authority for five years.[29] Rullus also provided assistance to Sullan possessors, such as his father-in-law Valg(i)us. Cicero exploits the urban plebs' unfamiliarity with administrative procedures and terminology by claiming that the method of election by only seventeen of thirty-five tribes was a restriction of

---

[28] Pliny alone suggests that the bill came up for a vote (*HN* 7.117); the reference to the people's repudiation of the bill at *Rab. perd.* 32 and *Fam.* 13.4[318].1 may refer to sentiment rather than balloting.

[29] Both the five-year term and the praetorian power appear to be innovations in an agrarian reform bill; cf. Krostenko 2023, 223–24.

DE LEGE AGRARIA

freedom (though it was used to elect the pontifex maximus, 2.18–19), or that the vote of a curiate law for the Decemvirs was overreaching.[30] He claimed that the bill was prejudicial to Pompey (because it required candidates for the Decemvirate to present themselves in person, which he could not do, 2.24) even though it exempted Pompey from the seizure of generals' war booty (2.59–60).

Though Rullus' bill may have been an attempt to solve the problem of urban crowding, it was in some respects poorly drafted and open to abuse. Cicero seized upon weak elements in the bill and magnified them. Cicero's worry about the strain on the treasury (1.15; 2.10, 32, 36, 47, 98) chimes with concerns he expresses elsewhere (*Off.* 2.72) and thus appears to be sincere. He may, however, also have had other interests in view than the ones he names in his speeches. The equites in general and in particular their most prominent subgroup, the tax-farmers, had supported his political rise; Cicero had a strong tendency to back their interests.[31] They would be harmed by loss of taxable lands, especially in Asia. In addition, Volaterrae and Arretium, communities to which he had longstanding ties, had territories that were to be confiscated by a Sullan decree that had not been implemented (*Att.* 1.19[19].4); these might have been subject to sale if Rullus' proposal were enacted (cf. 3.12). Cicero later claimed credit for protecting their rights during his consulship, an apparent reference to the opposition to Rullus' bill (*Fam.* 13.4[318].1–2).

[30] 2.26–30, with Manuwald 2018, 247.
[31] Cf. Bleicken 1995.

INTRODUCTION

In the speeches *On the Agrarian Law*, then, Cicero achieves his goals by playing on fears of loss of liberty, excessive concentrations of power, Rome's potential rival, Capua, and self-dealing by the plebeian tribunes. At the same time, he positions himself as both an outsider (vis-à-vis the nobles) and an insider (as a supporter of the senate's authority) and as a more perceptive and articulate spokesman for the people's (true) interests than a tribune such as Rullus.[32]

NOTE ON MANUSCRIPTS AND EDITIONS

The text of the speeches *On the Agrarian Law* is based on the following manuscripts:

E	Erfurtensis, nunc Berolinensis lat. fol. 252, s. XII
e	Palatinus 1525, a. 1467 scriptus
ϵ	Erlangensis 618, a. 1466 scriptus
α	codd. Eeϵ
π	codicis Pithoeani lectiones margini exemplaris Heidelbergensis 262[a] N. 18 adscriptae
V	Vaticanus latinus 11458, a. 1417, a Poggio exaratus
M	Laurentianus Conv. Soppr. 13, olim Abbatiae Florentinae CL II 39
n	codd. familiae Cusanae, post a. 1426 scripti, a Lagomarsinio sub n. 1, 7, 8, 13, 24 collati

[32] On Cicero's self-presentation as both outsider and insider, cf. Vasaly 2009, 134 (with reference to *Ver.* 1); on his dispute with Rullus as to which is the true *popularis*, cf. Krostenko 2023, 191–93, 198–99.

DE LEGE AGRARIA

χ	S. Marci 254 (Lag.3)
Lag.9	cod. unus a Lagomarsinio adhibitus, s. XV
ψ	codices reliqui s. XV plerique consentientes
ς	codicum reliquorum s. XV unus vel nonnulli dissentientes, nonnumquam etiam hi codices suo nomine indicantur:
c	Oxoniensis Canonici 226
k	Parisinus 7779, a. 1459 scriptus
s	Monacensis Clm 15734
r	Monacensis 527, fin. s. XV
ω vel cett.	consensus codicum omnium (vel ceterorum omnium)

The relations of the major witnesses can be represented as follows:

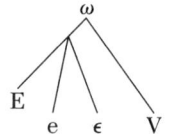

```
        ω
       /|\
      / | \
     E  |  \
       / \  \
      e   ε  V
```

E (12th century) is the oldest extant manuscript and heads the "German family," also represented by e and ε. V is the copy made by Poggio when he discovered a manuscript, probably at Cologne, in 1417. Poggio's copy was identified by A. Campana in 1948 and first used for the speeches *On the Agrarian Law* by Marek 1983; it is the source of the Italian branch of the tradition.[33]

---

[33] See further Rouse and Reeve, in Reynolds 1983, 83–85; Marek 1983, Praefatio; Manuwald 2018, li–liv.

INTRODUCTION

The following are the major editions cited in the notes to the Latin text:

ed. Rom.	Rome, 1471
ed. Ven.	Venice, 1471
Beroaldus	Bonn, 1499
Angelius	Venice, 1515
Naugerius	Venice, 1519
Camerarius	Basel, 1540
Manutius	Venice, 1540
Ramus	Paris, 1552/53
Turnebus	1553 (a review of Ramus 1552/53)
Lauredanus	Venice, 1558 (perhaps, rather, by C. Sigonius)
Lambinus	Paris, 1566
Gruterus	Hamburg, 1617–1619
Graevius	Amsterdam, 1695–1699
Ernesti	Halle, 1773
Ferratius	Padua, 1773
Garatoni	Naples, 1777–1778
Orelli	Zurich, 1826–1831
Baiter, Halm	Zurich, 1856 (new ed. of Orelli)
Kayser	Leipzig, 1862
Müller	Leipzig, 1885
Clark	Oxford, 1909
Boulanger	Paris, 1932
Marek	Leipzig, 1983
Manuwald	Oxford, 2018

The readings given here are as reported in Manuwald 2018.

DE LEGE AGRARIA
ORATIO PRIMA CONTRA
P. SERVILIUM RULLUM
TR. PLEB. IN SENATU

F 1 Char. *GL* 1.95.18 (p. 122.13 Barw)

imberba iuventute

F 2 Aq. Rom. 61.14 Elice (*RLM* 36.5)

Capuam colonis deductis occupabunt, Atellam[1] praesidio communient, Nuceriam, Cumas multitudine suorum obtinebunt, cetera oppida praesidiis devincient.

[1] Atellam *Aldus ex Mart. Cap.*: ac etiam *codd. plerique, alii alia*

ON THE AGRARIAN LAW I AGAINST THE PLEBEIAN TRIBUNE PUBLIUS SERVILIUS RULLUS IN THE SENATE

F 1 Charisius

Beardless youth.[1]

F 2 Aquila of Rome, *On Figures*

They will occupy Capua with settled colonists, they will fortify Atella with a garrison, they will hold Nuceria and Cumae with a throng of their own people, they will bind the other towns to obedience with garrisons.[2]

---

[1] Best taken as a reference to the surveyors mentioned at 2.45 as "selected young men." (Nicolet 1970 argues that Rullus wanted the sons of equites in this role so that they could exercise jurisdiction delegated by the Decemviri.) It is unlikely to refer to Rullus prior to taking office as plebeian tribune: his change of style for that role involved growing a fuller beard (*barba . . . maiore*), not a first beard (2.13).

[2] A list of places in Campania that will allegedly be taken over by Rullan colonists; cf. 2.86.

CICERO

F 3 Aq. Rom. 61.17 Elice (*RLM* 36.8)

Venibit[2] igitur sub praecone tota Propontis atque Hellespontus, addicetur omnis ora Lyciorum atque Cilicum, Mysia et Phrygia eidem condicioni legique parebunt.

F 4 Gell. *NA* 13.25.6 (Non. 697 L)

Praedam, manubias, sectionem,[3] castra denique Cn. Pompei sedente imperatore decemviri[4] vendent.

1   * * * quae res aperte petebatur, ea nunc occulte cuniculis oppugnatur. Dicent enim decemviri id quod et dicitur a multis et saepe dictum est, post eosdem consules regis Alexandrini[5] testamento regnum illud populi Romani esse factum. Dabitis igitur Alexandriam clam petentibus eis quibus apertissime pugnantibus restitistis? Haec, per deos immortales, utrum esse vobis consilia siccorum an vinu-

---

[2] venient *LN*: veniet *cett.*: *corr. Orelli*
[3] sectionem: sectiles *Non.*
[4] decemviri: censores *Non.*
[5] alexandrini χ¹: alexandri ωπ

---

[3] Places in Asia Minor Cicero imagines will be sold to fund Rullus' program; but Cicero's claims that all these areas are under Roman control, let alone eligible for sale as public land, are overstated; cf. Morstein-Marx 1995, 295n13. See also on 2.40.

[4] Similarly at 2.99; cf. also §5 below.

[5] Continuous text opens amid the Decemvirs' proposals for raising revenue for their plan, including an alleged scheme to annex Egypt. "The same men," evidently mentioned in the lost

402

DE LEGE AGRARIA 1 F 3–1

F 3 Aquila of Rome, *On Figures*

The whole of the Propontis and the Hellespont will be sold under the auctioneer's gavel, the entire Lycian and Cilician coast will be assigned, and Mysia and Phrygia will be subjected to the same legal terms.[3]

F 4 Aulus Gellius, *Attic Nights*

The Decemvirs will sell off the spoils, the plunder, the auction proceeds, finally the camp of Gnaeus Pompey while the commander is still in place.[4]

... the matter that was aimed at openly is now being secretly undermined. For the Decemvirs will say what is said by many and has often been said, that, after the consulship of the same men, that kingdom became the Roman people's by the will of the Alexandrian king.[5] Will you therefore give Alexandria to them when they ask for it secretly, although when they fought for it quite openly you resisted them?[6] By the immortal gods, do such ideas appear to you

1

beginning, will be L. Cornelius Sulla and Q. Pompeius, the consuls of 88: *MRR* 2:39; cf. 2.38. "The Alexandrian king" is Ptolemy X Alexander I (ca. 140–86), who received a loan from Roman equites to rebuild his fleet as a step toward recovering his kingdom and therefore bequeathed Egypt to Rome; cf. Badian 1967.

[6] Thus implying that the same people, that is, M. Crassus, stand behind Rullus' proposals as had promoted the seizure of Egypt in 65; for Cicero's speech on the question, cf. fr. orat. no. 7 Cr.-D. At 2.41–44 Cicero discusses the matter in greater detail, since the general public would not have been aware of the previous discussion in the senate; cf. Classen 1985, 318.

lentorum somnia, et utrum cogitata sapientium an optata furiosorum videntur?

2   Videte nunc proximo capite ut impurus helluo turbet rem publicam, ut a maioribus nostris possessiones relictas disperdat ac dissipet, ut sit non minus in populi Romani patrimonio nepos quam in suo. Perscribit in sua lege vectigalia quae decemviri vendant, hoc est, proscribit[6] auctionem publicorum bonorum. Agros emi vult qui dividantur; quaerit pecuniam. Videlicet excogitabit aliquid atque adferet. Nam superioribus capitibus dignitas populi Romani violabatur, nomen imperi in commune odium orbis terrae vocabatur, urbes pacatae, agri sociorum, regum status decemviris donabantur; nunc praesens pecunia,
3   certa,[7] numerata quaeritur. Exspecto quid tribunus plebis vigilans et acutus excogitet. "Veneat," inquit, "silva Scantia." Utrum tandem hanc silvam in relictis possessionibus an in censorum pascuis invenisti? Si quid est quod indagaris, inveneris, ex tenebris erueris, quamquam iniquum est, tamen consume sane quod[8] commodum est, quoniam quidem tu attulisti; silvam vero tu Scantiam vendas nobis consulibus atque hoc senatu? Tu ullum vectigal attingas, tu populo Romano subsidia belli, tu ornamenta pacis eripias? Tum vero hoc me inertiorem consulem iudicabo

---

[6] perscribit: *corr. e, ed. Ven. Clark*: praesens certa pecunia ω   [7] praesens pecunia certa   [8] quoniam: *corr. Orelli*

---

[7] Cicero pretends to go through the text of the law systematically, but is, in fact, highly selective.

[8] For this charge, cf. 2.48, also in the argument on taxable lands; Krostenko 2023, 79–81.

[9] The precise location is unknown.

DE LEGE AGRARIA 1.1–3

to be sober men's plans or the dreams of men drunk with wine, the thoughts of wise men or the hopes of raving madmen?

See now, in the next section,[7] how the vile wastrel throws the republic into turmoil, how he is ruining and squandering the possessions bequeathed by our ancestors, how he is as big a spendthrift of the patrimony of the Roman people as of his own.[8] In his law he lists in full the revenues that the Decemvirs may sell, that is, he is posting a notice of an auction of public property. He wishes lands to be bought for distribution; he is seeking money. I suppose he will think out some plan and bring it forward. For in the previous sections the dignity of the Roman people was violated, the name of our empire was made the object of the common hatred of all the world, cities that had been pacified, the lands of our allies, the status of kings were presented as gifts to the Decemvirs; now he wants ready money, a fixed sum, paid down in cash. I am waiting to see what our watchful and sagacious tribune of the plebs will think up. "Let the Scantian forest be sold,"[9] he says. Did you find this forest in the list of neglected possessions or in the pasturelands the censors lease? If there is anything that you have hunted out, discovered, dug out of the darkness, although it is unfair, yet by all means use up what is convenient, since you have brought it forward. But are you then to sell the Scantian forest with us as consuls and with this senate? Are you then to lay hands on any of the revenues? Are you then to rob the Roman people of their support in war, of their ornaments during peace? Then indeed I shall judge myself to be a less energetic consul

quam illos fortissimos viros qui apud maiores nostros fuerunt, quod quae vectigalia illis consulibus populo Romano parta sunt, ea me consule ne retineri quidem potuisse iudicabuntur. Vendit Italiae possessiones ex ordine omnes. Sane est in eo diligens; nullam enim praetermittit. Persequitur in tabulis censoriis totam Siciliam; nullum aedificium, nullos agros relinquit. Audistis auctionem populi Romani proscriptam a tribuno plebis, constitutam in mensem Ianuarium, et, credo, non dubitatis quin idcirco haec aerari causa non vendiderint ei qui armis et virtute pepererunt, ut esset quod nos largitionis causa venderemus.

5 Videte nunc quo adfectent[9] iter apertius quam antea. Nam superiore parte legis quem ad modum Pompeium oppugnarent, a me indicati sunt; nunc iam se ipsi indicabunt. Iubent venire agros Attalensium atque Olympenorum, quos[10] populo Romano ⟨P.⟩[11] Servili, fortissimi viri, victoria adiunxit, deinde agros in Macedonia regios, qui partim T. Flaminini,[12] partim L. Pauli, qui Persen vicit, virtute parti sunt, deinde agrum optimum et fructuosissimum Corinthium, qui L. Mummi imperio ac felicitate ad

---

[9] quo adfectent *R. Klotz*: quo affecerit ϵ: quoad (*vel* quod ad) fecerit ω   [10] hos: *corr. Lambinus*
[11] *add. Lauredanus*   [12] flam(m)inii: *corr. Manutius*

---

[10] Cf. also *Cat.* 1.4.   [11] For the poetic allusion, see on *Rosc. Am.* 140.   [12] F 4 will be from that part of the speech.

[13] Attalia, a town on the coast of Pamphylia, and Olympus, a seaport in Lycia, were among the territories conquered by P. Servilius Vatia Isauricus as proconsul in Cilicia in a campaign lasting from 77 to 75; cf. *MRR* 2:88n5; Morstein-Marx 1995, 294–96.

DE LEGE AGRARIA 1.3–5

than those gallant men who lived in the times of our ancestors,[10] because people will judge that the revenues which were obtained for the Roman people during their consulships cannot even be retained when I am consul. He is selling all the public possessions of Italy in order. No doubt he is attentive about that, for he does not let a single item pass. He searches through the whole of Sicily in the censors' registers; he leaves behind no building and no lands. You have heard the sale of (what belongs to) the Roman people publicly advertised by a plebeian tribune, scheduled for the month of January, and you have no doubt, I imagine, that the reason those who won it by the valor of their arms did not sell it for the sake of the treasury, was that there might be something that we could sell for the sake of largesse.

Now mark "the path they set out on"[11] more openly than before. For I have revealed how, in the previous part of the law, they attacked Pompey;[12] now they shall reveal it themselves. They order the lands of the inhabitants of Attalia and Olympus to be sold, which the victory of Publius Servilius, a gallant man, added to the territory of the Roman people;[13] next, the royal estates in Macedonia, acquired by the valor partly of Titus Flamininus, partly of Lucius Paullus, who conquered Perses;[14] next, the excellent and fruitful land of Corinth, which by the successful generalship of Lucius Mummius was added to the reve-

4

5

---

[14] T. Quinctius Flamininus, as proconsul in 197, defeated Philip V of Macedonia at Cynoscephalae; cf. *MRR* 1:334. L. Aemilius Paullus, as consul in 168, defeated Perses, or Perseus, king of Macedonia, at Pydna and later captured him; cf. *MRR* 1:427.

vectigalia populi Romani adiunctus est, post autem agros in Hispania apud Carthaginem novam duorum Scipionum eximia virtute possessos; tum vero ipsam veterem Carthaginem vendunt, quam P. Africanus nudatam tectis ac moenibus sive ad notandam Carthaginiensium calamitatem sive ad testificandam nostram victoriam sive oblata aliqua religione[13] ad aeternam hominum memoriam consecravit.
6 His insignibus atque infulis imperi venditis, quibus ornatam nobis maiores nostri rem publicam tradiderunt, iubent eos agros venire quos rex Mithridates in Paphlagonia, Ponto Cappadociaque possederit. Num obscure videntur prope hasta praeconis insectari Cn. Pompei exercitum, qui venire iubeant eos ipsos agros in quibus ille etiam nunc bellum gerat atque versetur?
7 Hoc vero cuius modi est, quod eius auctionis quam constituunt locum sibi nullum definiunt? Nam decemviris quibus in locis ipsis videatur vendendi potestas lege permittitur. Censoribus vectigalia locare nisi in conspectu

[13] oblata aliqua religione *Halm*: ad oblatam aliquam religionem ω

---

[15] As consul in 146, L. Mummius defeated the Achaeans at the Isthmus and captured and destroyed Corinth: *MRR* 1:465–66.

[16] In 211 the brothers P. Cornelius Scipio (cos. 218) and Cn. Cornelius Scipio Calvus (cos. 222) died fighting the Carthaginians in southern Spain; cf. *MRR* 1:274; Scullard 1970, 32–38.

[17] P. Cornelius Scipio Africanus Aemilianus (cos. 147, 134) captured and destroyed Carthage as a proconsul in 146.

[18] An *infula* is "a woollen headband knotted at intervals with ribbons," worn, for example, by priests as a mark of distinction: *OLD* s.v.; cf. Krostenko 2023, 252 and n. 12.

DE LEGE AGRARIA 1.5–7

nues of the Roman people;[15] and afterward the lands in Spain near New Carthage, which we possessed by the distinguished valor of the two Scipios;[16] then they sell old Carthage itself, which Publius Africanus consecrated as an eternal site of remembrance, stripped of its buildings and walls, either to mark the Carthaginians' disaster or as evidence of our victory or when some sort of religious impediment was presented.[17] After the sale of these distinctions and the crown[18] of our empire, which adorned the republic that our ancestors have handed down to us, they order those lands to be sold, that King Mithridates possessed in Paphlagonia, Pontus, and Cappadocia.[19] Are they not clearly seen to be practically pursuing the army of Gnaeus Pompey with the crier's spear,[20] when they bid you put up for sale those very lands in which he is even now waging war and actively engaged?

But what of the fact that they fail to define a location for the auction that they are scheduling? For the Decemvirs are given by the law the power to hold their sales in whatever places they please. The censors may not allow

[19] The chronologically latest items in the series, referring to the recently completed war against Mithridates VI of Pontus, though Cappadocia was not a Roman possession but an independent kingdom, albeit a Roman protectorate; and part of Pontus was assigned by Pompey to dynasts; cf. *OCD* s.vv. Paphlagonia, Pontus, Cappadocia.

[20] Blurring the military and administrative uses, a *hasta* stuck in the ground being a symbol of a public auction of war booty; cf. 2.53; *OLD* s.v. *hasta* 2a; García Morcillo 2016; Krostenko 2023, 154 and n. 22.

populi Romani non licet; his vendere vel in ultimis terris licebit? At hoc etiam nequissimi homines consumptis patrimoniis faciunt, ut in atriis auctionariis potius quam in triviis aut in compitis auctionentur; hic permittit sua lege decemviris ut in quibus commodum sit tenebris, ut in qua velint solitudine bona populi Romani possint divendere.

8 Iam illa omnibus in provinciis, regnis, liberis populis quam acerba, quam formidolosa, quam quaestuosa concursatio decemviralis futura sit, non videtis? Hereditatum obeundarum causa quibus vos legationes dedistis, qui et privati et privatum ad negotium exierunt, non maximis opibus neque summa auctoritate praediti, tamen auditis profecto quam graves eorum adventus sociis nostris esse soleant.

9 Quam ob rem quid putatis impendere hac lege omnibus gentibus terroris et mali, cum immittantur[14] in orbem terrarum decemviri summo cum imperio, summa cum avaritia infinitaque omnium rerum cupiditate? Quorum cum adventus graves, cum fasces formidolosi, tum vero iudicium ac potestas erit non ferenda. Licebit enim quod videbitur publicum iudicare, quod iudicarint vendere. Etiam illud quod homines sancti non facient, ut pecuniam accipiant ne vendant, tamen id eis ipsum per legem licebit. Hinc vos quas spoliationes, quas pactiones, quam denique

---

[14] immittantur *a*: mutantur *VM*: mittantur *cett.*

---

[21] Perhaps intended to enable locals to participate in the bidding; cf. Jonkers 1963, 98; Krostenko 2023, 17n57, 76.

[22] Showing that from the outset of his consulship Cicero was concerned about the senate's creation of "free embassies" (*legationes liberae*), enabling members to leave Rome on private business and claim support of the local communities they passed

DE LEGE AGRARIA 1.7–9

the farming of revenues except in the sight of the Roman people; shall these men be allowed to sell them even at the ends of the earth?[21] But even the most depraved of men, after their patrimony has been wasted, have their property auctioned in the auctioneers' halls rather than in the highways or crossroads, whereas by his law this man allows the Decemvirs to sell piecemeal the property of the Roman people in whatever obscurity it suits them or in whatever lonely place they choose. Do you not by now see 8 how harsh, how terrifying, how profitable the Decemvirs' journeying to and fro is bound to be throughout all provinces, kingdoms, and free peoples? You have doubtless heard how burdensome to our allies the arrivals generally are of those to whom you have given an embassy for the sake of entering upon an inheritance, though they have left the city as private individuals on private business, with no large resources and not vested with supreme authority.[22] Therefore what terror and calamity do you think 9 threaten all nations under this law, when the Decemvirs are let loose on the world with supreme power, utmost greed, and a boundless desire for all things? Their arrival will be burdensome, their fasces terrifying, their judicial power will be unbearable; for they will be allowed to judge whatever they please to be public property, and to sell what they have so judged. Even the thing that men of integrity will not do—take money for not selling—that very thing they will be allowed by law to do. Consequently, what plunderings, what bargainings, finally, what traffick-

through. He proposed legislation on the subject that was finally enacted in a compromise version; see further Dyck 2004, 490–91.

in omnibus locis nundinationem iuris ac fortunarum fore putatis? Etenim quod superiore parte legis praefinitum fuit, "Sulla et Pompeio consulibus," id rursus liberum infinitumque fecerunt. Iubet enim[15] eosdem decemviros omnibus agris publicis pergrande vectigal imponere, ut idem possint et liberare agros quos commodum sit et quos ipsis libeat publicare. Quo in iudicio perspici non potest utrum severitas acerbior an benignitas quaestuosior sit futura.

Sunt tamen in tota lege exceptiones duae non tam iniquae quam suspiciosae. Excipit enim in vectigali imponendo agrum Recentoricum Siciliensem, in vendendis agris eos agros de quibus cautum sit foedere. Hi sunt in Africa, qui ab Hiempsale possidentur. Hic quaero, si Hiempsali satis est cautum foedere et Recentoricus ager privatus est, quid attinuerit excipi; sin et foedus illud habet aliquam dubitationem et ager Recentoricus dicitur non numquam esse publicus, quem putet existimaturum duas causas in orbe terrarum repertas quibus gratis parceret? Num quisnam tam abstrusus usquam nummus videtur quem non architecti huiusce legis olfecerint? Provincias, civitates liberas, socios, amicos, reges denique exhauriunt, admovent manus vectigalibus populi Romani. Non est satis. Audite, audite[16] vos, qui amplissimo populi senatusque iudicio exercitus habuistis et bella gessistis: quod ad

---

[15] enim *a: om. cett.*   [16] audite *bis a: semel cett.*

---

[23] That is, the year 88; see on §1.   [24] Precise location unknown; the topic reappears at 2.57.   [25] Hiempsal II of Numidia was ousted by Marius' supporters in 87 but restored after Sulla's victory in 83; see further Manuwald 2018, 142–43.

DE LEGE AGRARIA 1.9–12

ing in the law and people's fortunes do you think there will be everywhere? For what was prescribed in the earlier part of the law, "when Sulla and Pompeius were consuls,"[23] they have again made unrestricted and unlimited. For he orders the same Decemvirs to impose a very high tax on all public lands, so that they may be able to free from it any lands that they find convenient, and to declare any that they please to be public property. In making this decision one cannot see whether their severity is likely to be harsher or their generosity more profitable.

Two exceptions in the entire law are, however, not so much unfair as suspicious. For in imposing the tax he makes an exception of the Recentoric territory in Sicily,[24] and in selling the lands, of those as to which a stipulation has been made by treaty. The latter are in Africa, lands that are possessed by Hiempsal.[25] In this connection I ask, if Hiempsal is sufficiently safeguarded by the treaty and the Recentoric territory is private property, what was the use of an exception being made? But if there is any uncertainty in the treaty, and the Recentoric land is sometimes said to be public property, who does he suppose will think that in the whole world two cases have been found that he spared free of charge? Does any coin ever seem so carefully hidden that the authors of this law have not sniffed it out? They are draining the provinces, the free states, our allies and friends, and finally, the kings: they are laying hands upon the revenues of the Roman people. That is not enough. Listen, listen, you who have commanded armies and waged wars by the distinguished judgment of the

quemque pervenerit ex praeda, ex manubiis, ex auro coronario, quod neque consumptum in monumento neque in aerarium relatum sit, id ad decemviros referri iubet. Hoc capite multa sperant: in omnes imperatores heredesque eorum quaestionem suo iudicio comparant, sed maximam pecuniam se a Fausto ablaturos arbitrantur. Quam causam suscipere iurati iudices noluerunt, hanc isti decemviri susceperunt:[17] idcirco a iudicibus fortasse praetermissam 13 esse arbitrantur quod sit ipsis reservata. Deinde etiam in reliquum tempus diligentissime sancit ut, quod quisque imperator habeat pecuniae, protinus ad decemviros deferat. Hic tamen excipit Pompeium simillime, ut mihi videtur, atque ut illa lege qua peregrini Roma eiciuntur Glaucippus excipitur. Non enim hac exceptione unus adficitur beneficio, sed unus privatur iniuria. Sed cui manubias remittit, in huius vectigalia invadit: iubet enim pecunia,[18] si qua post nos consules ex novis vectigalibus recipiatur, hac uti decemviros, quasi vero non intellegamus haec eos vectigalia quae Cn. Pompeius adiunxerit vendere cogitare.

14   Videtis iam, patres conscripti, omnibus rebus et modis constructam et coacervatam pecuniam decemviralem.

[17] suscepere *vel* suscipere: *corr. R. Klotz*
[18] pecuniam: *corr. Richter*

---

[26] The provision thus removes the Roman commander's traditional control of plunder seized in war, on which cf. Shatzman 1972; Churchill 1999; Tarpin 2009, esp. (on our passage) 89–90.

[27] Referring to an incident in 66 when an unknown plebeian tribune attempted to prosecute Sulla's son Faustus for self-enrichment with public funds (*peculatus*). But Cicero as praetor summoned a public meeting to influence opinion ahead of the

DE LEGE AGRARIA 1.12–14

people and senate: whatever shall come to anyone from the plunder, the spoils, the crown gold, and whatever has neither been spent on a monument nor paid into the treasury, is ordered to be paid to the Decemvirs.[26] With this section they entertain high hopes; they are preparing an investigation by their own tribunal into all the generals and their heirs, but they think that they will obtain the largest sum of money from Faustus. These Decemvirs have taken up a case that sworn jurors refused to accept; perhaps they think that it was passed over by the jurors since it was reserved for themselves.[27] Next, he most carefully ordains for the future that each general shall immediately pay to the Decemvirs whatever money he has. Yet here he excepts Pompey, in much the same way, as it seems to me, as Glaucippus is excepted by that law by which foreigners are expelled from Rome.[28] For by this exception one man is not done a kindness, but one man is freed from an injustice. But he attacks the revenues of the man whose spoils he waives. For he orders the Decemvirs to make use of any money received from fresh revenues after our consulship, as if we do not understand that these are the revenues acquired by Gnaeus Pompey that they are planning to sell.

By now you see, gentlemen of the senate, the Decemvirs' money, amassed and piled up by all sorts of ways and

13

14

trial, and the jury declined to hear the case; cf. *TLRR* 196; Mommsen 1899, 372 and n. 2; Santalucia 2009, 98–102.

[28] Referring to the Papian Law of 65, under which Cicero pleaded the cases of both Archias and Balbus; cf. *LPPR* 376; Elster 2014, 204–5. Glaucippus is otherwise unknown: *RE* s.v. Glaukippos 1.

415

Minuetur huius pecuniae invidia; consumetur enim in agrorum emptionibus. Optime. Quis ergo emet agros istos? Idem decemviri; tu, Rulle (missos enim facio ceteros), emes quod voles, vendes quod voles; utrumque horum facies quanti voles. Cavet enim vir optimus ne emat ab invito; quasi vero non intellegamus ab invito emere iniuriosum esse, ab non invito quaestuosum. Quantum tibi agri vendet, ut alios omittam, socer tuus? Et, si ego eius aequitatem animi probe novi, vendet non invitus. Facient idem ceteri libenter, ut possessionis invidiam pecunia commutent, accipiant quod cupiunt, dent quod retinere vix possunt.

15   Nunc perspicite[19] omnium rerum infinitam atque intolerandam licentiam. Pecunia coacta est ad agros emendos; ei porro ab invitis non ementur. Si consenserint possessores non vendere, quid futurum est? Referetur pecunia? Non licet. Exigetur? Vetat. Verum esto; nihil est quod non emi possit, si tantum des quantum velit venditor. Spoliemus orbem terrarum, vendamus vectigalia, effundamus aerarium, ut locupletatis aut invidiae aut pestilentiae possessoribus agri tamen emantur.

[19] perspicite *aς*: prospicite *cett.*

---

[29] Valgus, or Valgius, mentioned by name only at 3.3, is singled out to represent the group of Sullan possessors (on the several possible meanings of this phrase, see Manuwald 2018, 419). He has been identified with the C. Quinctius C.f. Valgus attested in Pompeian inscriptions and elsewhere; see further H. Gundel, *RE* s.v. Quinctius 56 and 57; Manuwald 2018, 427.

[30] Some of the Sullan colonies were on poor land, difficult to cultivate profitably; but the recipients were forbidden to alienate

DE LEGE AGRARIA 1.14–15

means. The unpopularity of this wealth will be lessened, for it will be used up in purchasing lands. Excellent! Who then is going to buy those lands? The same Decemvirs; you, Rullus—I say nothing about the rest—will buy what you like and you will sell what you like; you will do both of these at any price you like. For that excellent man takes care not to buy from an unwilling seller; as if we do not understand that it is wrong to buy from one who is unwilling, but profitable to buy from one who is willing. How much land will be sold to you—to leave the others aside—by your father-in-law?[29] And if I rightly understand his fair-mindedness, he will not be unwilling to sell. The rest will gladly do the same, to exchange the odium of their possession for money, to receive what they desire, to give away what they can scarcely retain.[30]

Now look closely at the unlimited and intolerable license of all these provisions. Money has been collected for buying lands; moreover, they will not be bought from those who are unwilling to sell. But if the owners have agreed not to sell, what will happen? Will the money be returned? It is not allowed. Will it be demanded (from the Decemvirs)? He forbids it. Let that pass; there is nothing that cannot be bought if you give as much as the seller wants. Let us despoil the world, let us sell the revenues, let us squander the treasury, in order that the lands may nonetheless be bought, with the owners of odium or pestilence enriched![31]

15

---

the land. Some of the land was also held under insecure title; see further Krostenko 2023, 25–26.

[31] Stirring hatred of those who possessed land granted by Sulla; see further Eckert 2016, 139–40.

CICERO

16   Quid tum? quae erit in istos agros deductio, quae totius rei ratio atque descriptio? "Deducentur," inquit, "coloniae." Quo<t>?[20] Quorum hominum? In quae loca? Quis enim non videt in coloniis esse haec omnia consideranda? Tibi nos, Rulle, et istis tuis harum omnium rerum machinatoribus totam Italiam inermem tradituros existimasti, quam praesidiis confirmaretis, coloniis occuparetis, omnibus vinclis devinctam et constrictam teneretis? Ubi enim cavetur ne in Ianiculo coloniam constituatis, ne urbem hanc urbe alia premere atque urgere possitis? "Non faciemus," inquit. Primum nescio, deinde timeo, postremo non committam ut vestro beneficio potius quam nostro consi-
17   lio salvi esse possimus. Quod vero totam Italiam vestris colonis[21] complere voluistis, id cuius modi esset neminemne nostrum intellecturum existimavistis?[22] Scriptum est enim: "Quae in municipia quasque in colonias decemviri velint, deducant colonos quos velint et eis agros adsignent quibus in locis velint," ut, cum totam Italiam militibus suis occuparint, nobis non modo dignitatis retinendae, verum[23] ne libertatis quidem recuperandae spes relinquatur. Atque haec a me suspicionibus et coniectura coarguuntur.
18   Iam omnis omnium tolletur error, iam aperte ostendent sibi nomen huius rei publicae, sedem urbis atque imperi,

---

[20] *corr. Lauredanus*   [21] coloniis: *corr. Manutius*
[22] existimavistis *a*: existimastis *Mψ*   [23] verum *E*: sed *cett.*

---

[32] First broached here, the potential military threat of the Rullan colonists is painted in detail at 2.73ff.

[33] The first hint, developed in the sequel, that Capua is being prepared as a "second Rome"; cf. also 2.86. For a different view,

Well then, what kind of settlement will be brought into those lands? What will be the method and plan of the whole affair? "Colonies will be brought in," he says. How many? Of what kind of men? To what places? For who fails to see that all these things have to be taken into consideration concerning colonies? Did you think, Rullus, that we would hand over to you and your engineers of all these schemes the whole of Italy unarmed, that you might strengthen it with garrisons, occupy it with colonies, and hold it bound and fettered by every kind of chain?[32] For where is there any guarantee against your establishing a colony on the Janiculum, against your being able to press and hem in this city by means of another one?[33] "We shall not do that," he says. First, I am not so sure; secondly, I am afraid; lastly, I will never cause our security[34] to depend upon your kindness rather than upon our wisdom. As to your wish to fill the whole of Italy with your colonists, did you suppose that none of us would understand the character of the plan? For it is written: "The Decemvirs shall settle any colonists they like in whatever towns and colonies they choose, and assign them lands in whatever places they please," so that, after they have occupied the whole of Italy with their soldiers, we may have little hope left not only of retaining our dignity, but even of recovering our liberty. And these points are proven by me on suspicion and conjecture.

Soon everyone's mistake will be eliminated; soon they will openly show that they dislike the name of this republic, the seat of our city and empire, finally, this temple of

that "the colony [is being] elevated to a 'city,'" see Krostenko 2023, 311.   [34] Literally, "for us to be able to be safe."

denique hoc templum Iovis Optimi Maximi atque hanc arcem omnium gentium displicere. Capuam deduci colonos volunt, illam urbem huic urbi rursus opponere, illuc opes suas deferre et imperi nomen transferre cogitant. Qui locus propter ubertatem agrorum abundantiamque rerum omnium superbiam et crudelitatem genuisse dicitur, ibi nostri coloni, delecti ad omne facinus, a decemviris collocabuntur, et, credo, qua in urbe homines in vetere[24] dignitate fortunaque nati copiam rerum moderate ferre non potuerunt, in ea isti vestri satellites modeste insolentiam suam continebunt. Maiores nostri Capua magistratus, senatum, consilium commune, omnia denique insignia rei publicae sustulerunt, neque aliud quicquam in urbe[25] nisi inane nomen Capuae reliquerunt, non crudelitate (quid enim illis fuit clementius qui etiam externis hostibus victis sua saepissime reddiderunt?), sed consilio, quod viderent, si quod rei publicae vestigium illis moenibus contineretur, urbem ipsam imperio domicilium praebere posse; vos haec, nisi evertere rem publicam cuperetis ac vobis novam dominationem comparare, credo, quam perniciosa essent non videretis. Quid enim cavendum est in coloniis de-

19

20

---

[24] veteri: *corr. Baiter*   [25] in urbe *a: om. cett.*

---

[35] The center of Jupiter's official cult on the Capitoline and the site of the senate's current meeting; cf. Bonnefond-Coudry 1989, 40. The cult title perhaps identifies him as the "greatest and best" of all Jupiters: so Wissowa 1912, 126.   [36] Rullus' bill probably included no specific reference to Capua: cf. 2.66. Cicero plays upon Romans' (irrational) fears of Capua, dating back to the city's defection to Hannibal in the aftermath of Cannae in 216. Cf. Vasaly 1988, 419–21, 426; Farney 2007, 187–90.

DE LEGE AGRARIA 1.18–20

Jupiter Best and Greatest and this citadel of all nations.[35] They want to settle colonists at Capua,[36] to set that city once again in opposition to this one; they are planning to transfer to that place their resources and the name of empire. In a place that, owing to the fertility of its lands[37] and abundance of all goods, is said to have given birth to arrogance and cruelty—there our colonists, chosen for every kind of crime, will be settled by the Decemvirs; and, I suppose, in a city in which men born to longstanding rank and fortune were unable to bear their abundance of goods moderately, in that city those henchmen of yours will curb their insolence with restraint. In Capua our ancestors abolished the magistrates, the senate, the popular assembly, and finally all the marks of a republic, leaving nothing else in the city except the empty name Capua,[38] not out of cruelty (for what was more merciful than they were, who frequently returned their property even to foreign enemies who had been conquered?), but by policy, for they saw that if any trace of a republic should be contained within those walls, the city itself could provide a home for empire: unless you desired to overthrow the republic and provide yourselves with a new despotism, you would not, I suppose, see how disastrous this was.[39] For what should

---

[37] Agreed to be the most fertile in Italy, according to Livy 26.16.7; cf. Plin. *HN* 18.111.

[38] Measures taken after the reconquest of Capua in 211; cf. Livy 26.16.9–10.

[39] Ironic. Expressed straightforwardly, Cicero says that Rullus and his followers would see the disastrous consequences of their plans were they not blinded by lust for power.

ducendis? Si luxuries, Hannibalem ipsum Capua corrupit; si superbia, nata inibi esse haec ex Campanorum fastidio videtur; si periculum,[26] non praeponitur huic urbi ista colonia, sed opponitur. At quem ad modum armatur, di immortales! Nam bello Punico quicquid potuit Capua, potuit ipsa per sese; nunc omnes urbes quae circum Capuam sunt a colonis per eosdem decemviros occupabuntur. Hanc enim ob causam permittit ipsa lex, in omnia quae velint oppida colonos ut decemviri deducant quos velint. Atque his colonis agrum Campanum et[27] Stellatem campum dividi iubet. Non queror deminutionem[28] vectigalium, non flagitium huius iacturae atque damni, praetermitto illa quae nemo est quin gravissime et verissime[29] conqueri possit, nos caput patrimoni publici, pulcherrimam populi Romani possessionem, subsidium annonae, horreum belli, sub signo claustrisque rei publicae positum vectigal servare non potuisse, eum denique nos agrum P. Rullo concessisse, qui ager ipse per sese et Sullanae dominationi et Gracchorum largitioni restitisset; non dico solum hoc in re publica vectigal esse quod amissis aliis remaneat, intermissis non conquiescat, in pace niteat, in bello non obsolescat, militem sustentet, hostem non pertimescat; praetermitto omnem hanc orationem et contioni re-

[26] periculum *Dyck*: praesidium ω
[27] et *an*: ac Mψ
[28] diminutionem: *corr. Manutius*
[29] gravissima et verissima: *corr. ed. Ven.*

[40] Cf. Livy 23.18.10–16; Strab. 5.4.13; Val. Max. 9.1ext.1.
[41] A proverbial characteristic; cf. Otto 1890 s.v. Campanus 2.

DE LEGE AGRARIA 1.20–21

be guarded against in establishing colonies? If it is luxury, Capua corrupted Hannibal himself;[40] if it is pride, this seems to have arisen there from the Campanians' haughtiness;[41] if danger, that colony is not set in front of this city, but is set against it. But, immortal gods, how it is armed! For in the Punic war, whatever power Capua had, it had by itself; but now all the cities that surround Capua will be occupied by settlers sent by the same Decemvirs. For this is the reason why the law itself allows the Decemvirs to settle such colonists as they wish in any towns they wish. And it orders the territory of Campania and the plain of Stellas to be divided among these colonists.[42] I do not complain of the decrease of the revenues, nor of the scandal of this loss and damage; I pass over those things which no one can help but lament most truly and most impressively—that we have been unable to preserve the chief part of the public heritage, the fairest possession of the Roman people, the support of the yearly grain supply, the war granary, the republic's revenue kept under seal and bar; finally, that we have yielded that land to Publius Rullus which by itself resisted both the absolutism of Sulla and the largesse of the Gracchi. I do not say that this is the only revenue in the state which is left after others have been lost; which does not remain idle, while others are interrupted; which flourishes in peace, and does not lose its value in time of war; which supports the soldiers and is not afraid of the enemy—I pass over this entire argument and reserve it for a public assembly. I am speaking of the dan-

[42] The *ager Campanus* is the area around Capua; the plain of Stellas (or Stellatis), also in Campania, is further north, south of Cales and near the river Volturnus; see Manuwald 2018, 164–65.

22 servo; de periculo salutis ac libertatis loquor. Quid enim existimatis integrum vobis[30] in re publica fore aut in vestra libertate ac dignitate retinenda,[31] cum Rullus atque ei quos multo magis quam Rullum timetis cum omni egentium atque improborum manu, cum omnibus copiis, cum omni argento et auro Capuam et urbis circa Capuam occuparint?

His ego rebus, patres conscripti, resistam vehementer atque acriter neque patiar homines ea me consule expro-
23 mere quae contra rem publicam iam diu cogitarint. Errastis, Rulle, vehementer et tu et non nulli collegae tui, qui sperastis vos contra consulem veritate, non ostentatione popularem posse in evertenda re publica populares existimari. Lacesso vos, in contionem voco, populo Romano disceptatore uti volo. Etenim, ut circumspiciamus omnia quae populo grata atque iucunda sunt,[32] nihil tam populare quam pacem, quam concordiam, quam otium reperiemus. Sollicitam mihi civitatem suspicione, suspensam metu, perturbatam vestris legibus et contionibus et de-

[30] vobis *anχ*: nobis *cett.*
[31] retinenda *E*: retinendā *ϵe*: retinendum *VM cett.*
[32] sint *a*

---

[43] On Cicero's claim that Rullus' proposal threatens Romans' freedom (*libertas*), cf. Arena 2012, 240–41; Krostenko 2023, ch. 4.

[44] Manuwald 2018, 169, suspects that these are "the people behind the bill"; cf. §26 below and the machinations described at fr. orat. 9 F 28 Cr.-D. Krostenko 2023, 274, thinks that they are "in part the *populares*."

DE LEGE AGRARIA 1.21–23

ger to our safety and freedom.[43] For what do you think will be left to you unimpaired in the republic or in the maintenance of your freedom and dignity, after Rullus and those whom you fear much more than Rullus,[44] with all his band of beggars and criminals, with all his forces, with all his silver and gold, have occupied Capua and the cities round about Capua?

I will, gentlemen of the senate, passionately and vigorously resist these measures; nor will I, while I am consul, allow men to bring forward plots that they have hatched against the state for a long time.[45] You and some of your colleagues, Rullus, have made a great mistake in hoping that, in opposition to a consul who was popular in reality and not for show, you could be considered popular in overthrowing the republic.[46] I challenge you, I summon you to a public meeting, I desire to employ the Roman people as our judge. For if we survey all the things that are pleasing and agreeable to the people, we shall find nothing so popular as peace, harmony, and quietness. You have handed over to me a state troubled by suspicion, on edge through fear, upset by your laws, your public meetings, and your

22

23

---

[45] Compare *Sul.* 67, quoting Cicero's claim in a letter to Pompey apropos of Catiline's conspiracy that "an incredible madness contracted two years ago burst forth in my consulate."

[46] "Popular" (*popularis*), labeling a political posture favoring the interests of the people and often claimed by plebeian tribunes, is here deftly appropriated by Cicero, implying that Rullus and likeminded tribunes were merely *popularis* "for show"; cf. 2.13 and the similar contest over the label with T. Labienus at *Rab. perd.* 11–15. Cf. Strasburger 1956, 67; Krostenko 2023, 191–93, 198–99.

ductionibus[33] tradidistis; spem improbis ostendistis, timorem bonis iniecistis, fidem de foro, dignitatem de re publica sustulistis. Hoc motu[34] atque hac perturbatione animorum atque rerum cum populo Romano vox et auctoritas consulis repente in tantis tenebris illuxerit, cum ostenderit nihil esse metuendum, nullum exercitum, nullam manum, nullas colonias, nullam venditionem vectigalium, nullum imperium novum, nullum regnum decemvirale, nullam alteram Romam neque aliam sedem imperi nobis consulibus futuram summamque tranquillitatem pacis atque oti, verendum, credo, nobis erit ne vestra ista praeclara lex agraria magis popularis esse videatur. Cum vero scelera consiliorum vestrorum fraudemque legis et insidias quae ipsi populo Romano a popularibus tribunis plebis fiant ostendero,[35] pertimescam, credo, ne mihi non liceat contra vos in contione consistere, praesertim cum mihi deliberatum et constitutum sit ita gerere consulatum quo uno modo geri graviter et libere potest, ut neque provinciam neque honorem neque ornamentum aliquod aut commodum neque rem ullam quae a tribuno plebis

[33] deductionibus *Kayser*: deditionibus ωπ: seditionibus ς
[34] motu: metu ψ*Lag.*9: modo ϵ   [35] *om.* Vψ

---

[47] The plebeian tribunes took office on December 10, thus enabling them to "set the tone" by initiating legislation before the inauguration of the new consuls on January 1.

[48] Here *fides* is probably "trust"; it has also been taken in the sense "credit," since financial markets were currently troubled by a crisis of liquidity (cf. Hopkins 1980, 111–12) and the war in Asia; hence there were calls for cancellation of debts (cf. *Off.* 2.84). Cf. Kay 2014, 257–59; Krostenko 2023, 196. But in this speech Cicero

DE LEGE AGRARIA 1.23–25

settling of colonists;[47] you have given hope to the wicked and inspired fear in the good; you have banished trust[48] from the forum, and dignity from the republic. In this confusion and disturbance of people's minds and affairs, when the authoritative voice of a consul has suddenly brought light for the Roman people amid utter darkness;[49] when it has shown that nothing need be feared; that as long as we are consuls there will be no army, no band, no colonies, no sale of revenues, no new command,[50] no autocratic rule of Decemvirs, no second Rome or other seat of empire; and that there will be the supreme tranquility of peace and quiet; then, I suppose, we shall have to fear that this excellent agrarian law of yours may appear more popular. But when I have revealed the wickedness of your designs, the cunning fraud of your law, and the snares that are being set for the Roman people itself by the "popular" tribunes of the plebs, then, I suppose, I shall be afraid that I shall not be permitted to stand against you in a public meeting,[51] especially as I have decided and made up my mind to carry on my consulship in the only manner in which it can be carried on with seriousness and freedom, namely that I will not seek to obtain a province, an honor, any distinction or advantage, or anything that a tribune of

---

says nothing about that; the nature of his current concern appears at 2.8 and 10; cf. Manuwald 2018, 174.

[49] For the metaphor, cf. Pieper 2020, 211–12 and n. 8; Krostenko 2023, 187.

[50] Rullus proposed to endow his Decemvirs with praetorian *imperium*; cf. 2.32.

[51] Compare *Cat.* 4.11, where Cicero likewise says he is undaunted about facing a public assembly (*contio*).

26 impediri possit appetiturus sim. Dicit frequentissimo senatu consul Kalendis Ianuariis sese, si status hic rei publicae maneat neque aliquod[36] negotium exstiterit quod honeste subterfugere non possit, in provinciam non iturum. Sic me in hoc magistratu geram, patres conscripti,[37] ut possim tribunum plebis rei publicae iratum coercere, mihi iratum contemnere.

Quam ob rem, per deos immortalis, colligite vos, tribuni plebis, deserite eos a quibus, nisi prospicitis, brevi tempore deseremini, conspirate nobiscum, consentite cum bonis, communem rem publicam communi studio atque amore defendite. Multa sunt occulta rei publicae vulnera, multa nefariorum civium perniciosa consilia; nullum externum periculum est, non rex, non gens ulla, non natio pertimescenda est; inclusum malum, intestinum ac domesticum est. Huic pro se quisque nostrum mederi atque hoc omnes sanare velle debemus. Erratis, si senatum probare ea quae a me dicuntur[38] putatis, populum autem esse in alia voluntate. Omnes qui se incolumis volent sequentur auctoritatem consulis soluti a cupiditatibus, liberi a delictis, cauti in periculis, non timidi in contentionibus. Quodsi qui vestrum spe ducitur se posse tur-

27

[36] aliquod *ack*: aliquid *EVMψ*: aliud *nχςLag.*9
[37] patres conscripti *ck*: p.r. *cett.*
[38] a me dicuntur *E*: dicuntur a me *VM*

---

[52] That is, as proconsul. A surprising move, without any known parallel in the previous history of the republic; it is conditioned, however, upon future developments. In the event, Cicero would lay down the province of Cisalpine Gaul (which he had received in an exchange with his colleague C. Antonius) at a

the plebs can block. On this 1st of January, in a fully attended senate, your consul declares that, if the republic continues in its present state, and unless some trouble arises that he cannot honorably avoid meeting, he will not go to a province.[52] I will so conduct myself in this office, gentlemen of the senate, that I can check a tribune of the plebs who is angry at the republic and can despise one who is angry at me.

Therefore, by the immortal gods, tribunes of the plebs, recover yourselves, abandon those by whom, unless you exercise foresight, you will soon be abandoned. Join with us, agree with the sound citizens, take up with a common zeal and affection the defense of our common country. Many are the republic's hidden wounds, many the pernicious designs of wicked citizens. There is no danger from without: no king, no people, no nation, is to be feared;[53] the evil is internal, inside, and domestic. Each and every one of us should for his own sake be willing to apply the remedy and cure it. You are mistaken if you think that the senate approves of my words, but that the people is of another opinion. All who wish to be safe will follow the authority of a consul released from desires, free from faults, wary in the midst of dangers, bold in controversy. But if any one of you is inspired by the hope of being able

public meeting, with the justification that he needed to devote himself exclusively to countering Catiline's conspiracy; cf. Marinone and Malaspina 2004, 85; Manuwald 2018, 178.

[53] Reflecting Roman self-confidence as the war against Mithridates VI in Asia winds down; similarly *Rab. perd.* 33 and *Cat.* 2.11.

bulenta ratione honori velificari suo, primum me consule id sperare desistat, deinde habeat me ipsum sibi documento, quem equestri ortum loco consulem videt, quae vitae via facillime viros bonos ad honorem dignitatemque perducat. Quodsi vos vestrum mihi studium, patres conscripti, ad communem dignitatem defendendam profitemini, perficiam profecto, id quod maxime res publica desiderat, ut huius ordinis auctoritas, quae apud maiores nostros fuit, eadem nunc longo intervallo rei publicae restituta esse videatur.

to set his sails for office by a disorderly policy, in the first place, let him abandon that hope as long as I am consul; and, secondly, let him take myself, whom he sees as consul, born of equestrian rank, as an example of what path of life most readily leads good men to office and dignity.[54] But if, gentlemen of the senate, you promise me your zeal in upholding the common dignity, I will certainly fulfill the most ardent wish of the republic, that the authority of this order, which existed in the time of our ancestors, may now, after a long interval, be seen to be restored to the state.[55]

[54] These remarks about his status as a "new" man (*novus homo*) were probably prepared in the lost beginning of the speech (cf. 2.3–4).

[55] Cicero would later claim that the foundations for strengthening the role of the senate were laid on the first day of his consulship: *Fam.* 1.9[20].12. This was also a goal of the legislation in *Leg.* 3; cf. Dyck 2004, 428–29. In this he follows the policy of the man who organized his education, L. Crassus; cf. *Brut.* 164 and (on Crassus' role in Cicero's education) *De or.* 2.1–2.

DE LEGE AGRARIA
ORATIO SECUNDA CONTRA
P. SERVILIUM RULLUM
TR. PLEB. AD POPULUM

Est hoc in more positum, Quirites, institutoque maiorum, ut ei qui beneficio vestro imagines familiae suae consecuti sunt eam primam habeant contionem,[1] qua gratiam benefici vestri cum suorum laude coniungant. Qua in oratione non nulli aliquando digni maiorum loco reperiuntur, plerique autem hoc perficiunt ut tantum maioribus eorum debitum esse videatur, unde etiam quod posteris solveretur redundaret. Mihi quidem[2] apud vos de meis maioribus dicendi facultas non datur, non quo non tales fuerint quales nos illorum sanguine creatos disciplinisque institutos videtis, sed quod laude populari atque honoris vestri luce caruerunt. De me autem ipso vereor ne arrogantis sit

2

[1] $an\chi^2$: orationem $VM\psi$
[2] mihi quidem $VM\psi$: mihique $a\pi n$: mihi quirites *Pithoeus*

---

[1] In assembly speeches (*contiones*), Cicero addresses the crowd as *Quirites*, an archaic designation of Roman citizens that reinforces their sense of tribal identity; cf. Leovant-Cirefice 2000, 55.

ON THE AGRARIAN LAW II AGAINST THE PLEBEIAN TRIBUNE PUBLIUS SERVILIUS RULLUS BEFORE THE PEOPLE

It is a custom, Romans,[1] established by our ancestors, that those who by your favor have obtained the right to have images in their family should, when delivering their first oration before the people, combine praise of their ancestors with an expression of gratitude for your favor.[2] And in such speeches some men are sometimes found to be worthy of the rank which their ancestors obtained, but the majority only make it seem that the debt due to their ancestors is so great that something is still left over to be paid to their posterity. As for myself, I have no opportunity of speaking of my ancestors before you; not that they were not such men as you see us to be, sprung from their blood and brought up in their principles, but because they never enjoyed the people's commendation or were rendered illustrious by the honor you bestowed. But to speak about myself before you I am afraid would show arrogance, to

[2] Noble Romans kept images of ancestors who had held public office in the atrium of the house and paraded them as masks worn by family members during festivals and funerals; see further Flower 1996.

apud vos dicere, ingrati tacere. Nam et quibus studiis hanc dignitatem consecutus sim memet ipsum commemorare perquam grave est, et silere de tantis vestris beneficiis nullo modo possum. Quare adhibebitur a me certa ratio moderatioque dicendi, ut quid a vobis acceperim commemorem, quare dignus vestro summo honore singularique iudicio sim, ipse modice dicam, si necesse erit, vos eosdem existimaturos putem qui iudicavistis.

3 Me perlongo intervallo prope memoriae temporumque nostrorum primum hominem novum consulem fecistis et eum locum quem nobilitas praesidiis firmatum atque omni ratione obvallatum tenebat me duce rescidistis virtutique in posterum patere voluistis. Neque me tantum modo consulem, quod est ipsum per sese amplissimum, sed ita fecistis quo modo pauci nobiles in hac civitate consules facti sunt, novus ante me nemo. Nam profecto si recordari volueritis de novis hominibus, reperietis eos qui sine repulsa consules facti sunt diuturno labore atque aliqua occasione esse factos, cum multis annis post petissent quam praetores fuissent, aliquanto serius quam per aetatem ac per leges liceret; qui autem anno suo petierint, sine repulsa non esse factos; me esse unum ex omnibus novis hominibus de quibus meminisse possimus,[3] qui consulatum petierim cum primum licitum sit, consul factus sim cum primum petierim, ut vester honos ad mei temporis diem petitus, non ad alienae petitionis occasionem inter-

[3] possimus *E*ϵ: possumus *cett.*

[3] A "new" man is defined as one with no officeholder in his ancestry; see further Manuwald 2018, 191–92; Krostenko 2023, 1n1.   [4] That is, the year of their first eligibility.

DE LEGE AGRARIA 2.2–3

remain silent ingratitude. For it is a very difficult matter for me to mention by what efforts I have obtained this dignity, and yet I can by no means keep silence about the great favors you have bestowed upon me. I shall therefore adopt a definite policy of moderate language such that I mention the honor I have received from you, but I will, if I must, speak moderately of the reason why I was worthy of your supreme honor and unparalleled judgment and suppose that you, who have passed the judgment, will abide by your opinion.

After a very long interval, you have made me consul as almost the first "new" man of our memory and lifetimes;[3] a position that the nobility was holding secured by guards and fortified in every way, with me as your leader, you have broken open with the intent that in future it should be open to merit. And you not only elected me consul, which in itself is a very high honor, but you did so in a way in which few nobles in this community have been made consuls, and no "new" man before me. For certainly, should you wish to call to mind the "new" men, you will find that those who were elected undefeated only obtained office after long labors and by seizing some opportunity, when they had canvassed many years after they had been praetors and somewhat later than their age and the laws allowed; but that those who became candidates in their own year[4] were not elected undefeated; that I am the only one of all the "new" men we can remember who canvassed for the consulship as soon as the law allowed and was elected in his first canvass, so that this honor bestowed by you, which I stood for at the date of my eligibility, appears not to have been seized when opportunity offered an inferior

3

ceptus, nec diuturnis precibus efflagitatus, sed dignitate
impetratus esse videatur. Est illud amplissimum, quod
paulo ante commemoravi, Quirites, quod hoc honore ex
novis hominibus primum me multis post annis adfecistis,
quod prima petitione, quod anno meo; sed tamen magnificentius atque ornatius esse illo nihil potest, quod meis
comitiis non tabellam vindicem tacitae libertatis, sed vocem unam[4] prae vobis indicem vestrarum erga me voluntatum ac studiorum tulistis. Itaque me non ⟨enumeratio⟩
extremae tribus[5] suffragiorum, sed primi illi vestri concursus, neque singulae voces praeconum, sed una vox[6] universi populi Romani[7] consulem declaravit.

Hoc ego tam insigne, tam singulare vestrum beneficium, Quirites, cum ad animi mei fructum atque laetitiam
duco esse permagnum, tum ad curam sollicitudinemque
multo maius.[8] Versantur enim, Quirites, in animo meo
multae et graves cogitationes, quae mihi nullam partem
neque diurnae neque nocturnae quietis impertiunt, primum tuendi consulatus, quae cum omnibus est difficilis et
magna ratio, tum vero mihi praeter ceteros, cuius errato
nulla venia, recte facto exigua laus et ab invitis expressa
proponitur; non dubitanti fidele consilium, non laboranti

[4] unam: vivam *ck*: *del. Mueller*

[5] enumeratio extremae tribus *Dyck 2019*: extrema tribus ω: extremae tribus *Ferratius*

[6] una vox *Kayser*: una voce ω

[7] universi p.r. *aπ*: universus p.r. *cett.*

[8] maius *a*: magis *cett.*

---

[5] The secret ballot replaced oral voting in electoral assemblies (*comitia*) by a Gabinian Law of 139 and was hailed in *popularis*

DE LEGE AGRARIA 2.3–5

rival, nor to have been urgently demanded with long canvassing, but to have been obtained by merit. And it is indeed an eminent distinction, as I have just mentioned, Romans, that I was the first of the "new" men upon whom after so many years you have bestowed this honor; that it was at the first canvass, that it was in my regular year; and yet nothing can be more glorious and more illustrious than the fact that at my election you bore before you not a voting tablet, a champion of silent liberty, but uttered a single voice as proof of your goodwill and enthusiasm for me.[5] Thus it was not the counting out of votes of the last tribe, but your first convergence [for voting[6]], not the individual voices of the criers,[7] but the single voice of the entire Roman people that proclaimed me consul.

This remarkable, extraordinary favor on your part, Romans, I consider both a great source of enjoyment and delight, and a cause of much more concern and anxiety. For my mind is occupied with many serious thoughts, which leave me no share of rest day or night—first, as regards maintaining the dignity of the consulate, a great and difficult task for anyone, but above all for myself, since no mistake of mine will meet with indulgence; but for any success scant praise is in prospect and that forced from unwilling people; if I am in doubt, the nobles offer no

---

rhetoric as the "champion of liberty." See further Dyck 2004, 529–30. There is an untranslatable pun on *vindex* (champion) and *index* (proof).

[6] This took place in the *Saepta*, the voting enclosures in the Campus Martius; cf. Richardson 1992 s.v. Ovile, Saepta Iulia.

[7] Announcing the tallies of the individual centuries, the voting units used for consular elections.

6 certum subsidium nobilitatis ostenditur. Quod si solus in discrimen aliquod adducerer, ferrem, Quirites, animo aequiore; sed mihi videntur certi homines, si qua in re me non modo consilio verum etiam casu lapsum esse arbitrabuntur, vos universos, qui me antetuleritis nobilitati, vituperaturi. Mihi autem, Quirites, omnia potius perpetienda esse duco quam non ita gerendum consulatum ut in omnibus meis factis atque consiliis vestrum de me factum consiliumque laudetur. Accedit etiam ille mihi summus labor ac difficillima ratio consulatus gerendi, quod non eadem mihi qua superioribus consulibus lege et condicione utendum esse decrevi, qui aditum huius loci conspectumque vestrum partim magnopere fugerunt, partim non vehementer secuti sunt. Ego autem non solum hoc in loco dicam, ubi est id dictu facillimum, sed in ipso senatu, in quo esse locus huic voci non videbatur, popularem me futurum esse consulem prima illa mea oratione Kalendis Ianuariis
7 dixi. Neque enim ullo modo facere possum ut, cum me intellegam non hominum potentium studio, non excellentibus gratiis paucorum, sed universi populi Romani iudicio consulem ita factum ut nobilissimis hominibus longe praeponerer, non et in hoc magistratu et in omni vita essem popularis. Sed mihi ad huius ⟨verbi⟩[9] vim et interpretationem vehementer opus est vestra sapientia. Versatur enim

[9] verbi *k Angelius*: om. cett.

[8] That is, the Rostra, the speaker's platform in the Comitium (between the forum and the senate house); see further Richardson 1992 s.v. Rostra, Suggestus, Tribunal.
[9] See on 1.23. This kind of rhetoric may have had some effect in view of Cicero's previous positions; cf. Yakobson 2010, 298–99.

trustworthy counsel, if I am struggling, no reliable support. But if I alone were brought into some danger, I would endure it, Romans, with greater calm; but there appear to me to be certain men who, if they think I have made a mistake in any matter not only intentionally but even by accident, will be ready to censure all of you for having preferred me to my noble competitors. But it is my opinion, Romans, that to suffer anything is better than failing to conduct my consulship in such a manner that in all my acts and policies, what you have done and advised concerning me may be commended. In addition, my method of conducting the consulship is most toilsome and difficult because I have made up my mind that I ought to follow a different system and principle from previous consuls, some of whom have especially avoided approaching this place[8] and meeting your gaze, while others have presented themselves halfheartedly. But not only in this place will I say it, where it is very easy to do, but in the senate itself, where there did not seem to be room for such language, I declared in that first speech of mine on the 1st of January that I would be the people's consul.[9] Since I am aware that I have been elected consul, not by the enthusiasm of men of influence, not by the distinguished favors of a few, but by the judgment of all the Roman people, in such a way that I was by a large majority preferred to men of the highest rank, I could not by any means fail to be the people's friend both in this magistracy and throughout my entire life. But I have urgent need of your wisdom in understanding the force and interpretation of this word. For

magnus error propter insidiosas non nullorum simulationes, qui, cum populi non solum commoda verum etiam salutem oppugnant et impediunt, oratione adsequi volunt ut populares esse videantur.

8 Ego qualem Kalendis Ianuariis acceperim rem publicam, Quirites, intellego: plenam sollicitudinis, plenam timoris; in qua nihil erat mali, nihil adversi quod non boni metuerent, improbi exspectarent; omnia turbulenta consilia contra hunc rei publicae statum et contra vestrum otium partim iniri, partim nobis consulibus designatis inita esse dicebantur; sublata erat de foro fides non ictu aliquo novae calamitatis, sed suspicione ac perturbatione iudici-
9 orum, infirmatione rerum iudicatarum; novae dominationes, extraordinaria non imperia, sed regna quaeri putabantur. Quae cum ego non solum suspicarer, sed plane cernerem—neque enim obscure gerebantur—dixi in senatu in hoc magistratu me popularem consulem futurum. Quid enim est tam populare quam pax? Qua non modo ei quibus natura sensum dedit sed etiam tecta atque agri mihi laetari videntur. Quid tam populare quam libertas? Quam non solum ab hominibus verum etiam a bestiis ex-

---

[10] At *Cat.* 1.15 Cicero alleges that Catiline plotted against his life when he was consul designate.

[11] Referring to two bills (evidently unrelated: Drummond 1999, 124 and 126) promulgated by the tribunes who took office on December 10 of 64: (1) by L. Caecilius Rufus, a stepbrother of P. Sulla, mitigating the penalty of lifelong exclusion from office applied to Sulla and P. Autronius, convicted in 66 under the Calpurnian Law on Electoral Malfeasance (*TLRR* 200; for a different view, cf. Krostenko 2023, 196); (2) Rullus' agrarian reform bill.

DE LEGE AGRARIA 2.7–9

a great error is being spread abroad through the malicious pretenses of certain individuals, who, while attacking and hindering not only the interests but even the safety of the people, are striving by their words to appear to be supporters of the people.

I am aware, Romans, what the condition of the republic was when it was handed over to me on the 1st of January; it was full of anxiety, full of fear; in it there was no evil, no calamity which good citizens did not dread, which the wicked were not hoping for. All kinds of seditious plots against the present form of government and against your quiet were reported—some as being formed, others as having been when we were named as consuls.[10] Trust had been banished from the forum, not by the stroke of some fresh calamity, but owing to suspicion and the disturbances of the law courts, the invalidation of decisions already made; new tyrannies, not merely extraordinary commands, but regal powers, were, it was supposed, being aimed at.[11] Since I not only suspected this, but saw it plainly (for it was done quite openly) I declared in the senate that, as long as I held this office, I would be the people's consul. For what is so welcome to the people as peace, which not only those animals which nature has endowed with sense, but even the houses and fields appear to me to enjoy? What is so welcome to the people as liberty, which you see is sought and preferred to everything else not only by men but also by beasts? What is so wel-

---

Caecilius soon withdrew his bill and later threatened to veto Rullus' bill (*Sull.* 65). For Rullus aiming at regal power, see §§15, 24, 75, etc.

peti atque omnibus rebus anteponi videtis. Quid tam populare quam otium? Quod ita iucundum est ut et vos et maiores vestri et fortissimus quisque vir maximos labores suscipiendos putet, ut aliquando in otio possit esse, praesertim in imperio ac dignitate. Quin idcirco etiam maioribus nostris praecipuam laudem gratiamque debemus, quod eorum labore est factum uti impune in otio esse possemus. Quare qui possum non esse popularis, cum videam haec omnia, Quirites, pacem externam, libertatem propriam generis ac nominis vestri, otium domesticum, denique omnia quae vobis cara atque ampla sunt in fidem et quodam modo in patrocinium mei consulatus esse collata? Neque enim, Quirites, illud vobis iucundum aut populare debet videri, largitio aliqua promulgata, quae verbis ostentari potest, re vera fieri nisi exhausto aerario nullo pacto potest; neque vero illa popularia sunt existimanda, iudiciorum perturbationes, rerum iudicatarum infirmationes, restitutio damnatorum, qui civitatum adflictarum perditis iam rebus extremi exitiorum solent esse exitus; nec, si qui agros populo Romano pollicentur, si[10] aliud quiddam[11] obscure moliuntur, aliud spe ac specie simulationis ostentant, populares existimandi sunt.

[10] si *k Angelius*: sed si $aV\psi c^2$: sed c^1 *Garatoni*
[11] quiddam *k Naugerius*: quidem $an\chi^2 c$: quid est *VMψLag*.9

---

[12] "Peace combined with worthy standing" (*cum dignitate otium*) would become a political ideal of Cicero's; see Kaster 2006, 31–37; Mouritsen 2022, 134–41.

[13] Appeal to the ancestors is usually associated with "standing" (*dignitas*) and hence with oratory in the senate; cf. *De or.*

DE LEGE AGRARIA 2.9–10

come to the people as tranquility, which is so pleasant that both you and your ancestors and the bravest of men think that the greatest labors ought to be undertaken in order to enjoy peace some day, especially when accompanied by authority and worthy standing?[12] In fact, the very reason we owe special praise and gratitude to our ancestors is because it is thanks to their labors that we are able to enjoy tranquility free from danger.[13] How then can I help being on the side of the people, Romans, when I see that all these things—peace abroad, the liberty characteristic of your nation and race, tranquility at home, in short, everything that you find important and dear, were entrusted to my keeping and, in a way, to the protection of my consulship? For neither, Romans, ought this to seem to you pleasant or in the interest of the people: for some largesse to proposed that can be promised in words but can in reality by no means be given without draining the treasury; nor are the disturbances of the courts, the invalidation of verdicts already rendered, the reinstating of the condemned, which are usually the final acts of the destruction of troubled states when their affairs are already hopeless, to be regarded as acts for the benefit of the people.[14] Nor, supposing some people promise lands to the Roman people, and supposing that, while they put this on display with hopes and specious pretenses, they are darkly engineering something different, do they deserve to be considered friends of the people.

10

2.334–35, but our speech contains more such references than any except *Phil.* 9; cf. Kenty 2016, 460–62.

[14] Tendentiously characterizing Caecilius' proposal; cf. *Sull.* 64.

CICERO

Nam vere dicam, Quirites, genus ipsum legis agrariae vituperare non possum. Venit enim mihi in mentem duos clarissimos, ingeniosissimos, amantissimos plebei[12] Romanae viros, Ti. et C. Gracchos, plebem in agris publicis constituisse, qui agri a privatis antea possidebantur. Non sum autem ego is consul qui, ut plerique, nefas esse arbitrer Gracchos laudare, quorum consiliis, sapientia, legibus
11 multas esse video rei publicae partis constitutas. Itaque, ut initio mihi designato consuli nuntiabatur legem agrariam tribunos plebis designatos conscribere, cupiebam quid cogitarent cognoscere; etenim arbitrabar, quoniam eodem anno gerendi nobis essent magistratus, esse aliquam oportere inter nos rei publicae bene administrandae
12 societatem. Cum familiariter me in eorum sermonem insinuarem ac darem, celabar, excludebar; et cum ostenderem, si lex utilis plebi Romanae mihi videretur, auctorem me atque adiutorem futurum, tamen aspernabantur hanc liberalitatem meam; negabant me adduci posse ut ullam[13] largitionem probarem. Finem feci offerendi mei ne forte mea sedulitas aut insidiosa aut impudens videretur. Interea non desistebant clam inter se convenire, privatos quosdam adhibere, ad suos coetus occultos noctem adiun-

[12] plebei *cod. Torr., ed. Rom.*: plebi ωπ
[13] illam πχn

---

[15] Cicero's attitude toward the Gracchi varies by audience and rhetorical goals; here before the people they serve as a foil for Rullus; cf. Robinson 1994; Bücher 2009, 102–4; Manuwald 2018, 168; Pina Polo 2018, 211–12.
[16] Suggesting that the tribunician elections preceded the consular elections in 64; see also §13.

DE LEGE AGRARIA 2.10–12

For, to speak frankly, Romans, I do not criticize the category of agrarian law itself. For I remember that two most illustrious men, most talented and the most devoted friends of the Roman plebs, Tiberius and Gaius Gracchus, settled the plebs on public lands that were formerly occupied by private persons. I am not a consul of such a kind that, like the majority, I think it a crime to praise the Gracchi, by whose advice, wisdom, and laws I see that many departments of the republic were set in order.[15] Accordingly, when I was informed at the outset, when I was consul elect, that the tribunes elect were drawing up an agrarian law, I felt a desire to learn what they were planning;[16] for I thought that, since we should have to carry out our magistracies in the same year, there ought to be some partnership between us, for governing the state well. But when I tried to take a friendly part in their conversations, I was kept in the dark, I was being shut out; and when I gave them to understand that, if the law seemed to me to be advantageous to the Roman plebs, I would support it and help to pass it, they nonetheless scorned my generous offer, and declared that I could never be brought to approve of any kind of largesse.[17] I terminated my offers of assistance, for fear that my persistence might perhaps appear either treacherous or insolent. In the meantime, they continued to meet secretly, to invite certain private individuals to join them, to employ darkness and solitude for

---

[17] For Cicero's fundamental opposition, see *Off.* 2.78–79. He did, however, offer partial support to a bill proposed in 60 by the plebeian tribune L. Flavius: *Att.* 1.19[19].4.

gere et solitudinem. Quibus rebus[14] quanto in metu fuerimus, ex vestra sollicitudine in qua illis temporibus fuistis facile adsequi coniectura poteritis. Ineunt tandem magistratus tribuni plebis; contio [tandem][15] exspectatur[16] P. Rulli, quod et princeps erat agrariae legis et truculentius se gerebat quam ceteri. Iam designatus alio vultu, alio vocis sono, alio incessu esse meditabatur, vestitu obsoletiore, corpore inculto et horrido, capillatior quam ante barbaque maiore, ut oculis et aspectu denuntiare omnibus vim tribuniciam et minitari rei publicae videretur. Legem hominis contionemque exspectabam; lex initio nulla proponitur, contionem in praesentia[17] advocari iubet. Summa cum exspectatione concurritur. Explicat orationem sane longam et verbis valde bonis. Unum erat quod mihi vitiosum videbatur, quod tanta ex frequentia inveniri nemo potuit qui intellegere posset quid diceret. Hoc ille utrum insidiarum causa fecerit an hoc genere eloquentiae delectetur nescio. Tametsi, [si] qui[18] acutiores in contione steterant, de lege agraria nescio quid voluisse eum dicere suspicabantur. Aliquando tandem me designato lex in publicum proponitur. Concurrunt iussu meo plures uno tempore librarii, descriptam legem ad me[19] adferunt.

[14] rebus ς *Naugerius*: in rebus ωπ
[15] *om. k, del. Lambinus*   [16] exspectatur *k*: exspectata ω
[17] in praesentia *Dyck 2019*: in pridie idus *Madvig*: in primis ω
[18] tametsi qui *Lambinus*: tametsi π: tamen si qui ω
[19] legem a me επ *(corr. edd.)*: a me legem *E*

---

[18] Creating the impression of something sinister afoot, as in highlighting the nocturnal meetings of Catiline; cf. Pieper 2020.
[19] December 10 of 64.

DE LEGE AGRARIA 2.12–13

their secret gatherings.[18] How great was my apprehension over these developments you can easily imagine from your own anxiety during those times. At last the plebeian tribunes enter office;[19] a speech of P. Rullus is awaited, because he was both the chief promoter of the agrarian law and was behaving more gruffly than any of his colleagues. As soon as he was elected, he practiced putting on a different expression, a different tone of voice, and a different gait; his clothes were more disheveled, his person was neglected and bristling, more hair about him than before and more beard, so that eyes and look seemed to put the world on notice of his tribunician power and to threaten the republic. I was waiting for the man's law and his speech. At first no law is proposed. He orders an assembly to be summoned for the present. A crowd gathers round with heightened anticipation. He unrolls a very long speech in very fine language. The only fault that appeared to me was that, among all the vast throng, no one could be found who was able to understand what he said. Whether he did this with some insidious purpose or takes pleasure in this type of eloquence, I cannot say.[20] Still, the more intelligent persons standing in the assembly suspected that he meant to say something or other about an agrarian law. At last, however, when I was consul elect, the law was publicly proposed. On my instructions several copyists converge simultaneously, transcribe it, and bring me the text.

13

[20] This speech supplements the collection in *FRLO*. This is the earliest example of stylistic criticism of an opponent in one of Cicero's speeches; cf. Achard 2000, 83; Walter 2014, 172.

CICERO

14   Omni hoc ratione vobis[20] confirmare possum, Quirites, hoc animo me ad legendam legem cognoscendamque venisse ut, si eam vobis accommodatam atque utilem esse intellegerem, auctor eius atque adiutor essem. Non enim natura neque discidio neque odio penitus insito bellum nescio quod habet susceptum consulatus cum tribunatu, quia persaepe seditiosis atque improbis tribunis plebis boni et fortes consules obstiterunt et quia vis tribunicia non numquam libidini restitit consulari. Non potestatum dissimilitudo, sed animorum disiunctio dissensionem fa-
15   cit. Itaque hoc animo legem sumpsi in manus ut eam cuperem esse aptam vestris commodis et eius modi quam consul re, non oratione popularis et honeste et libenter posset defendere. Atque ego a primo capite legis usque ad extremum reperio, Quirites, nihil aliud cogitatum, nihil aliud susceptum, nihil aliud actum nisi uti x reges aerari, vectigalium, provinciarum omnium, totius rei publicae, regnorum, liberorum populorum, orbis denique terrarum domini constituerentur legis agrariae simulatione atque nomine.

Sic confirmo, Quirites, hac lege agraria pulchra atque populari dari vobis nihil, condonari certis hominibus omnia, ostentari populo Romano[21] agros, eripi etiam libertatem, privatorum pecunias augeri, publicas exhauriri, denique—quod est indignissimum—per tribunum plebis, quem maiores praesidem libertatis custodemque esse

---

[20] ratione vobis $a\pi\chi^2 n$: vobis ratione *cett.*
[21] populi Romani $n\chi\varsigma$

---

[21] On Cicero's undermining of the usual dichotomy, cf. Morstein-Marx 2004, 224–25.

DE LEGE AGRARIA 2.14–15

I can earnestly assure you, Romans, that I applied to the reading and understanding of this law the attitude that if I found that it was suitable for you and in your interests, I would advocate and promote it. For it is neither owing to natural tendency nor disagreement nor deep-seated hatred that the consulship is engaged in a kind of war with the tribunate, because good and gallant consuls have very often withstood factious and crooked tribunes and the power of the tribunes has sometimes resisted the inordinate desires of the consuls. It is not the incompatibility of their powers, but the disunity of their minds that causes dissension.[21] Accordingly, I took this law into my hands with the attitude that I wanted it to be suited to your interests and such that a consul, who was a friend of the people in reality, not in words,[22] might honorably and gladly support. And from the first section to the last, Romans, I find that the only idea, the only scheme, the only aim is that ten kings should be set up as masters of the treasury, the revenues, all the provinces, the entire republic, of kingdoms, of free nations, finally, of the whole world, under the pretext of an agrarian law.

14

15

Thus I affirm, Romans, that this fine and popular agrarian law gives you nothing, but makes a present of everything to certain individuals; it holds lands before the eyes of the Roman people but robs them even of liberty; it increases the wealth of private persons and exhausts that of the state; lastly—the most outrageous thing of all—a tribune of the plebs, whom our ancestors intended to be the

---

[22] Similar distinction, with a similar implication that Rullus is a pseudo-*popularis*, at 1.23.

16 voluerunt, reges in civitate constitui. Quae cum, Quirites,[22] exposuero, si falsa vobis videbuntur esse, sequar auctoritatem vestram, mutabo meam sententiam; sin insidias fieri libertati vestrae simulatione largitionis intellegetis, nolitote dubitare plurimo sudore et sanguine maiorum vestrorum partam vobisque traditam libertatem nullo vestro labore consule adiutore defendere.

Primum caput est legis agrariae quo, ut illi putant, temptamini leviter quo animo libertatis vestrae deminutionem ferre possitis. Iubet enim tribunum plebis qui eam legem tulerit creare decemviros per tribus septemdecim,
17 ut, quem novem tribus fecerint, is decemvir sit. Hic quaero quam ob causam initium rerum ac legum suarum hinc duxerit ut populus Romanus suffragio privaretur. Totiens legibus agrariis curatores constituti sunt triumviri, quinqueviri, decemviri; quaero a populari tribuno plebis ecquando[23] nisi per xxxv tribus creati sint. Etenim cum omnes potestates, imperia, curationes ab universo populo Romano proficisci convenit, tum eas profecto maxime quae constituuntur ad populi fructum aliquem et commodum, in quo et universi deligant quem populo Romano maxime consulturum putent, et unus quisque studio et suffragio suo viam sibi ad beneficium impetrandum mu-

[22] quirites *Pithoeus*: q(ue) *Vaπ*: *om. cett.*
[23] ecquando *ed. Rom.*: haec quando *ω*: quando *nχ²*

---

[23] For liberty as the theme of the speech, cf. Krostenko 2023, ch. 4. [24] Cf. Krostenko 2023, 142: "Cicero has here transposed onto constitutional theory the people's own political practice . . . [of being] more keenly attentive when their own material interests . . . seemed to be directly at stake."

protector and guardian of liberty, is setting up kings in the state. After I have put all these facts before you, Romans, if they appear to you to be untrue, I will follow your authority and change my opinion. But if you recognize that, under the pretense of largesse, a plot is being laid against your liberty, do not hesitate, with a consul to help you, to defend that liberty which was won and passed down to you by your ancestors with so much sweat and blood but without any effort on your part.[23]

The first section of the agrarian law is one in which you are gently tested, as they think, as to the attitude with which you might be able to put up with a reduction of your liberty. For it orders the plebeian tribune, who has enacted that law, to elect Decemvirs by the votes of seventeen tribes, so that everyone who shall have been elected by nine tribes shall be Decemvir. Here I ask for what reason he has made depriving the Roman people of their vote the beginning of his proposals and laws. On all the occasions when triumvirs, quinquevirs, and decemvirs have been installed as administrators by agrarian laws, I ask this plebeian tribune, the friend of the people, when have they ever been elected except by the thirty-five tribes? For, as it is fitting that all powers, commands, and commissions should originate with the whole Roman people, this is especially the case in regard to those which are established for any benefit and interest of the people.[24] For it is then that the whole body of citizens elect the one who they think will best take thought for the Roman people, while each individual by his zeal and vote is able to pave the way for acquiring some benefit for himself. It

nire possit. Hoc tribuno plebis potissimum venit in mentem, populum Romanum universum privare suffragiis, paucas tribus non certa condicione iuris, sed sortis beneficio fortuito ad usurpandam libertatem vocare.

18 "Item," inquit, "eodemque modo," capite altero, "ut comitiis pontificis maximi." Ne hoc quidem vidit, maiores nostros tam fuisse populares ut, quod per populum creari fas non erat propter religionem sacrorum, in eo tamen propter amplitudinem sacerdoti voluerint populo supplicari? Atque hoc idem de ceteris sacerdotiis Cn. Domitius, tribunus plebis, vir clarissimus, tulit, quod populus per religionem sacerdotia mandare non poterat, ut minor pars populi vocaretur; ab ea parte qui esset factus, is a collegio 19 cooptaretur. Videte quid intersit inter Cn. Domitium, tribunum plebis, hominem nobilissimum, et P. Rullum, qui temptavit, ut opinor, patientiam vestram, cum se nobilem esse diceret: Domitius, quod per caerimonias populi fieri non poterat, ratione adsecutus est ut id, quoad posset, quoad fas esset, quoad liceret, populi ad partis daret; hic, quod populi semper proprium fuit, quod nemo imminuit, nemo mutavit, quin ei qui populo agros essent adsignaturi ante acciperent a populo beneficium quam darent, id totum eripere vobis atque e manibus extorquere conatus est.

---

[25] "This same measure," that is, popular election by a specified number of tribes: *LPPR* 329. According to Asc. 80.18–19C, Cicero refers to Cn. Domitius Ahenobarbus, plebeian tribune in 104; on Domitius and problems of dating the law and his tribunate, see further on fr. orat. 6 F 4–5 Cr.-D.   [26] P. Servilius Rullus' father was a moneyer, but no officeholder is known in his ancestry; cf. Stein *RE* s.v. Servilius 80. Hence the scorn for his claim to nobility, perhaps made in the speech reported at §13.

DE LEGE AGRARIA 2.17–19

occurred to this plebeian tribune before anyone else to deprive the entire Roman people of their votes, and to invite only a few tribes, not according to established legal rules but by accidental favor of the lot, to usurp their liberty.

"Likewise," he says, "and in the same manner," in the second section, "as at the election of the pontifex maximus." Did he not even see that our ancestors were so friendly to the people that, in a manner in which, on religious grounds, an election by the people was forbidden, they nonetheless, in view of the importance of the priesthood, wanted the people to be canvassed? Gnaeus Domitius, tribune of the plebs, a man of high distinction, enacted this same measure concerning the other priesthoods, since the people could not delegate priesthoods under religious law, namely that a minority of the people was summoned (to the election); he who has been elected by that part (of the citizen body) is co-opted by the college (of priests).[25] See the difference between Gnaeus Domitius, tribune of the plebs, a man of high nobility, and Publius Rullus, who in my opinion tested your patience by calling himself noble:[26] insofar as he could, insofar as it was religiously allowed, insofar as it was licit, Domitius, by a method, contrived to assign to a part of the people that which could not, because of religious obstacles, belong to the people; this man [Rullus], on the other hand, has endeavored to snatch from you entirely and wrest from your hands what has always belonged to the people, what no one has violated, what no one has altered—namely, that those who were to assign lands to the people should receive a benefit from the Roman people before bestowing one upon it. The one has given in a

18

19

Ille, quod dari populo nullo modo poterat, tamen quodam modo dedit; hic, quod adimi nullo pacto potest, tamen[24] quadam ratione eripere conatur.

20   Quaeret quispiam in tanta iniuria tantaque impudentia quid spectarit.[25] Non defuit consilium; fides erga plebem Romanam, Quirites,[26] aequitas in vos libertatemque vestram vehementer defuit. Iubet enim comitia decemviris habere creandis eum qui legem tulerit. Hoc dicam planius: iubet Rullus, homo non cupidus neque appetens, habere comitia Rullum. Nondum reprehendo; video fecisse alios. Illud quod nemo fecit, de minore parte populi, quo pertineat videte. Habebit comitia, volet eos renuntiare[27] quibus regia potestas hac lege quaeritur; universo populo neque ipse committit neque illi horum consiliorum
21   auctores committi recte putant posse. Sortietur[28] tribus idem Rullus. Homo felix educet[29] quas volet tribus. Quos novem tribus decemviros fecerint ab eodem Rullo eductae, hos omnium rerum, ut iam ostendam, dominos habebimus. Atque hi, ut grati ac memores benefici esse videantur, aliquid se novem tribuum notis hominibus debere

---

[24] potest tamen *Kahnt*: poterat potestate ω, *alii alia*
[25] spectant: *corr. Naugerius*   [26] quirites *Baiter*: -q. π: que *ee*: *om. cett.*   [27] denuntiare: *corr. Manutius*
[28] sortietur *k Naugerius*: sortitur ω   [29] educet α: educit *cett.*

---

[27] "Lucky" (*felix*) may hint at an identification of Rullus with Sulla; cf. on *Rosc. Am.* 22; Krostenko 2023, 205. In spite of Cicero's insinuation, tampering with lottery procedures was generally rare at Rome; cf. Rosenstein 1995.
[28] *notis hominibus*, "their friends" (i.e., "men known to" them; "leurs amis": Boulanger), is sometimes taken in a pejorative sense ("notorious men": Freese and Manuwald), but that usage seems

DE LEGE AGRARIA 2.19–21

certain way what could by no means be given to the people; the other is endeavoring to snatch away by a certain means what can by no means be removed.

Someone will ask what his object was in behaving with such injustice and impudence. He was not without a plan; but he was absolutely without good faith toward the Roman plebs, Romans, without fairness toward you and your liberty. For he orders that the elections for choosing the Decemvirs shall be held by the man who proposed the law. To put it more plainly: Rullus, a man who is neither avaricious nor grasping, orders that the elections should be held—by Rullus! I do not blame him as yet; I see that others have done the same. But consider what his object is in holding the election from a minority of the people, a thing that no one has done. He will hold the elections, he will want to declare those elected for whom royal authority is sought by this law. He himself neither entrusts it to the whole people, nor do those who were the instigators of these plans think that it can be rightly entrusted to it. Lots will be drawn for the tribes—by the same Rullus. The lucky man will draw the tribes he wishes.[27] As I will presently show, we shall have the Decemvirs chosen by the nine tribes drawn by the same Rullus as the masters of all our affairs. And they, to show themselves grateful and not forgetful of the favor, will acknowledge that they owe something to their friends in the nine tribes,[28] but as for

20

21

rather rare and generally signaled by the context; cf. *OLD* s.v. *notus* 7. The alleged improper behavior is that of the elected Decemviri, not those who voted for them. For a different view, that these are bribery agents (*divisores*), cf. Krostenko 2023, 146 and n. 14.

confitebuntur, reliquis vero sex et xx tribubus nihil erit quod non putent posse suo iure se[30] denegare. Quos tandem igitur decemviros fieri vult? Se primum. Qui licet? Leges enim sunt veteres neque eae consulares (si quid interesse hoc arbitramini) sed tribuniciae, vobis maioribusque vestris vehementer gratae atque iucundae: Licinia est lex et altera Aebutia, quae non modo eum qui tulerit de aliqua curatione ac potestate sed etiam collegas eius, cognatos, adfines excipit, ne eis ea potestas curativeve mandetur. Etenim si populo consulis, remove te a suspicione alicuius tui commodi, fac fidem te nihil nisi populi utilitatem et fructum quaerere, sine ad alios[31] potestatem, ad te gratiam benefici tui pervenire. Nam hoc quidem vix est liberi populi, vix vestrorum animorum ac magnificentiae. Quis legem tulit? Rullus. Quis maiorem partem populi suffragiis prohibuit?[32] Rullus. Quis comitiis praefuit, quis tribus quas voluit vocavit nullo custode sortitus, quis decemviros quos voluit creavit?[33] Idem Rullus. Quem principem renuntiavit? Rullum. Vix mehercule servis hoc eum suis, nedum[34] vobis omnium gentium dominis probaturum arbitror. Optimae leges igitur hac lege sine ulla su-

22

[30] se *hoc loco* eϵπ: *ante* putent *k*ς: *om. cett.*
[31] alios *Angelius*: illos ωπ
[32] perhibuit ϵ: privavit *n*χς
[33] creavit *Aquila*: renuntiavit ω   [34] nedum *Dyck*: non ω

[29] Little is known of the Licinian and Aebutian laws (*LPPR* 290); Cicero also cites the former at *Dom.* 51. Mommsen, 1887–1888, 1:501n2, suspected that they represent a reaction to Gracchan legislation, Tiberius Gracchus having accepted the post of triumvir under his agrarian law; cf. also Krostenko 2023, 201n58.

the remaining twenty-six there will be nothing that they do not hold themselves justified in refusing them. Whom then does he wish to be elected Decemvirs? Himself first. But how is that lawful? For old laws are in existence, not consular laws (if you think this of any importance), but tribunician ones, which were very acceptable and agreeable to you and your ancestors. There are a Licinian law and a second one, the Aebutian, which not only prohibit anyone who has enacted a law concerning any commission or power from being appointed to any such commission or power, but even excludes his colleagues, kinsfolk, and relatives by marriage.[29] Indeed, if you are taking thought for the people, avoid the suspicion of any personal benefit; prove that you seek nothing but the people's interest and advantage; let the power go to others and the gratitude for the favor to you. For this proposal is hardly worthy of a free people, of your spirit and grandeur. Who proposed the law? Rullus. Who kept the majority of the people from their votes? Rullus. Who presided over the elections? Who summoned the tribes he wanted, who drew lots for them, without any custodian being present?[30] Who declared the election of the Decemvirs whom he wanted? The same Rullus. Whom did he declare chief of the Decemvirs? Rullus. By Hercules, I hardly think that he would be able to persuade his own slaves to approve of this, still less you, the masters of the world. Therefore the best laws will be

22

[30] The *custodes* had charge of the ballot urn so as to ensure an accurate count, which they duly reported; no corresponding safeguard is known to have been used for sortition, however; cf. Krostenko 2023, 35n130.

spicione tollentur; idem lege sibi sua[35] curationem petet, idem maiore parte populi suffragiis spoliata comitia habebit, quos volet atque in eis se ipsum renuntiabit, et videlicet conlegas suos, ascriptores legis agrariae, non repudiabit, a quibus ei locus primus in indice et[36] in praescriptione legis concessus est; ceteri fructus omnium rerum qui in spe legis huius positi sunt communi cautione atque aequa ex[37] parte retinentur.

23 At videte hominis diligentiam, si aut Rullum ⟨haec⟩[38] cogitasse aut si Rullo potuisse in mentem venire arbitramini. Viderunt ei qui haec machinabantur, si vobis ex omni populo deligendi potestas esset data, quaecumque res esset in qua fides, integritas, virtus, auctoritas quaereretur, vos eam sine dubitatione ad Cn. Pompeium principem delaturos. Etenim quem unum ex cunctis delegissetis ut eum omnibus omnium gentium bellis terra et mari praeponeretis, certe in decemviris faciendis sive fides haberetur sive honos, et committi huic optime et ornari hunc 24 iustissime posse intellegebant. Itaque excipitur hac lege non adulescentia, non legitimum aliquod impedimentum, non potestas, non magistratus ullus aliis negotiis ac legibus impeditus, reus denique quo minus decemvir fieri possit non excipitur; Cn. Pompeius excipitur, ne cum P. Rullo—

[35] lege sibi sua *E*: legis sibi sua lege ω
[36] in indice et α: invidiae et *cett.*
[37] ex *cod. Torr.*: ei αVMψ: sibi *n*χ
[38] *add. C. F. W. Müller in app.*: illud *add. Clark*

[31] The co-sponsors (*ascriptores*) showed their support by adding their names to the text of the law (*adscribere*). He implies that the ten tribunes of the year will fill the ten seats on commission.

458

abolished by this law without leaving a trace. By virtue of his own law, he will seek a commission for himself; he will hold the elections, after the majority of the people has been stripped of their votes; he will declare those whom he pleases elected, including himself; and of course he will not reject his colleagues, the co-sponsors of the agrarian law,[31] who have granted him the first place in the title and heading of the law; the other profits from all the advantages that have rested upon the hope of this law are reserved by a mutual guarantee and in equal shares for themselves.[32]

But consider the care he took, if you think either that Rullus thought this up or that the idea could ever have occurred to Rullus.[33] Those who engineered this plot foresaw that, if you had the power of choosing from among all the citizens in any matter in which loyalty, integrity, courage, and authority were required, you would without hesitation entrust it to Pompey in the first place. For after you had chosen that one man out of all the citizens, placing him in charge of all your wars with all nations on land and sea, they certainly understood that, in electing Decemvirs, whether it was to be considered a position of trust or an honor, the matter could best be entrusted to him and that he could most justly be so honored. Accordingly, being under age, no legal impediment, no authority, no magistracy encumbered with other affairs and the laws, not even any legal accusation, is a bar to a man being elected a Decemvir; but Pompey is barred from being elected De-

23

24

---

[32] Suggesting the formation of a partnership to share profits equally; cf. Krostenko 2023, 207.

[33] For the insinuation, see 1.1 and note.

CICERO

taceo de ceteris—decemvir fieri possit. Praesentem enim profiteri iubet, quod nulla alia in lege umquam fuit, ne in eis quidem magistratibus quorum certus ordo est, ne, si[39] accepta lex esset, illum sibi collegam ascriberetis custodem ac vindicem cupiditatum.

Hic, quoniam video vos hominis dignitate et contumelia legis esse commotos, renovabo illud quod initio dixi, regnum comparari, libertatem vestram hac lege funditus 25 tolli. An vos aliter existimabatis? Cum ad omnia vestra pauci homines cupiditatis[40] oculos adiecissent, non eos in primis id acturos ut ex omni custodia vestrae libertatis, ex omni potestate, curatione, patrocinio vestrorum commodorum Cn. Pompeius depelleretur? Viderunt et vident, si per imprudentiam vestram, neglegentiam meam legem incognitam acceperitis, fore uti postea cognitis insidiis, cum decemviros creetis,[41] tum vitiis omnibus et sceleribus legis Cn. Pompei praesidium opponendum putetis. Et hoc parvum argumentum vobis erit, a certis hominibus dominationem potestatemque omnium rerum quaeri, cum videatis eum, quem custodem vestrae libertatis fore videant, expertem fieri dignitatis?

[39] ne si *Angelius*: sine *E*: sive ω
[40] *del. Baiter*   [41] creetis *Beroaldus*: crearetis ωπ

---

[34] That is, the regular cycle of magistracies with order and intervals specified by law (the *lex Villia annalis* of 180: *LPPR* 278–79). Cicero perhaps ridicules "an unnecessarily precise formulation," since declaration of candidacy in person was the norm and was therefore not ordinarily specified in legislation (so Manuwald 2018, 243), or exploits the people's ignorance of procedure.

[35] That this was Rullus' motive is doubtful. He may have

cemvir together with Publius Rullus (I say nothing of the rest). For he orders that one must declare one's candidacy in person, a thing which no other law has ever required, not even for the magistracies that have a fixed order,[34] for fear that, if his law were adopted, you might attach him to himself as a colleague to watch over and punish his desires.[35]

Here, since I see that you are moved by the dignity of the man and the insult offered by the law, I will repeat what I said at the outset, that a monarchy is being set up, that your liberty is entirely abolished by this law.[36] Or did you think otherwise? Did you not think that, when a few men had cast greedy eyes upon all your possessions, the first thing they would do would be to drive out Pompey from all guardianship of your liberty, from all authority and office, and from the protection of your interests? They have seen and still see that, if through lack of foresight on your part or inattention on my own you adopt a law about which you know nothing, the result will be that afterward, as soon as you perceive the snare, when electing the Decemvirs, you will think it your duty to oppose the protecting influence of Gnaeus Pompey to all the defects and criminal provisions of the law. And will you not find it a sufficient proof that certain persons are seeking absolute power and authority over everything, when you see the man whom they understand would be the guardian of your liberty excluded from this magistracy?

25

---

thought that he needed the full ten-man body on hand to make decisions as soon as they were elected, whereas Pompey was still settling affairs in Asia Minor.

[36] Referring back to §15.

26   Cognoscite nunc quae potestas decemviris et quanta detur. Primum lege curiata decemviros ornat. Iam hoc inauditum et plane novum, uti curiata lege magistratus detur qui nullis comitiis ante sit datus. Eam legem ab eo praetore populi Romani qui sit primus factus ferri[42] iubet. At quo modo? "Ut ei decemviratum habeant quos plebs designaverit." Oblitus est nullos a plebe designari. Et is orbem terrarum constringit novis legibus qui, quod[43] in secundo capite scriptum est, non meminit in tertio? Atque hic perspicuum est quid iuris a maioribus acceperitis, quid ab hoc tribuno plebis vobis relinquatur. Maiores de singulis magistratibus bis vos sententiam ferre voluerunt. Nam cum centuriata lex censoribus ferebatur, cum curiata ceteris patriciis magistratibus, tum iterum de eisdem iudicabatur, ut esset reprehendendi potestas, si populum benefici sui paeniteret. Nunc, Quirites,[44] prima illa comitia

27 tenetis, centuriata et tributa, curiata tantum auspiciorum causa remanserunt. Hic autem tribunus plebis, quia videbat potestatem neminem iniussu populi aut plebis posse habere, curiatis eam comitiis, quae vos non initis, confirmavit, tributa, quae vestra erant, sustulit. Ita cum maiores binis comitiis voluerint[45] vos de singulis magistratibus iu-

[42] fieri: *corr. Beroaldus*   [43] qui quod *Lambinus*: quicquod *V in mg.*: quicquid ω   [44] quirites *Lag.9 Baiter*: *om. e*ϵ: quia *cett.*   [45] voluerunt: *corr. Naugerius*

[37] That is, a law passed by the Roman people organized in *curiae*, the division of the citizen body established by Romulus and used to legitimize a magistrate's authority, but by the late republic obscure; hence Cicero can claim that Rullus is making unprecedented use of it. See further Manuwald 2018, 246–47.

DE LEGE AGRARIA 2.26–27

Learn now what power is conferred upon the Decemvirs, and how far it extends. In the first place he bestows upon the Decemvirs the honor of a curiate law.[37] Moreover, this is unheard of and entirely unprecedented, that a magistracy should be conferred by a curiate law without having been previously conferred at some elections. He orders the law to be enacted by that praetor of the Roman people who was first elected. But in what manner? "In order that those men may hold the Decemvirate who have been elected by the plebs." He has forgotten that none of them has been elected by the plebs. And is such a man to fetter the world with new laws, a man who in the third section forgets what has been laid down in the second? And here we clearly see what rights you have received from your ancestors, and what is left you by this tribune of the plebs. Our ancestors willed that you should give your votes twice for the election of each magistrate. For when a law of the centuries was proposed for the censors, and a curiate law for the other patrician magistrates, a second decision was arrived at regarding the same men, so that, if the people regretted the favor they had bestowed, they might have the power to take it back. Now, Romans, while you have kept those electoral assemblies as the chief, those of the centuries and of the tribes, the curiate assembly has been retained only for the sake of taking the auspices. But this tribune of the people, seeing that no one can exercise power except at the bidding of the people or the plebs, has confirmed that power by the curiate assembly, which you do not enter, and suppressed the tribal assembly, which was yours. Thus, while your ancestors desired that you should give a decision at two assemblies in the election of each magistrate, this "friend

dicare, hic homo popularis ne unam quidem populo comitiorum potestatem reliquit. Sed videte hominis religionem et diligentiam! Vidit et perspexit sine curiata lege decemviros potestatem habere non posse, quoniam per viiii tribus essent constituti; iubet ferre de his legem curiatam;[46] praetori imperat. Quam id ipsum absurde, nihil ad me attinet. Iubet enim, qui primus sit praetor factus, eum legem curiatam ferre; sin is ferre non possit,[47] qui postremus sit, ut aut lusisse in tantis rebus aut profecto nescio quid spectasse videatur. Verum hoc quod est aut ita perversum ut ridiculum, aut ita malitiosum ut obscurum sit, relinquamus; ad religionem hominis revertamur. Videt sine lege curiata nihil agi per decemviros posse. Quid postea, si ea lata non erit? Attendite ingenium. "Tum ei decemviri," inquit, "eodem iure sint quo qui optima lege." Si hoc fieri potest, ut in hac civitate, quae longe iure libertatis ceteris civitatibus antecellit, quisquam nullis comitiis imperium aut potestatem adsequi possit, quid attinet tertio capite legem curiatam ferre iubere, cum[48] quarto permittas ut sine lege curiata idem iuris habeant quod haberent si optima lege a populo essent creati? Reges constituuntur, non decemviri, Quirites, itaque ab his initiis

---

[46] curiatam *Lag.7, ed. Hervagiana*: centuriatam ωπ
[47] posset: *corr. Manutius*   [48] cum *Lambinus*: qm̄ (i.e. quom *vel* quoniam) *Ee*: quoniam V: quo ϵ

---

[38] The curiate assembly was under the presidency of the pontifex maximus; cf. Mommsen 1887–1888, 3:318.

[39] Afzelius 1940, 227, suspects that the tribunes had in mind appointing as a sympathetic presiding officer either the later Catilinarian conspirator P. Cornelius Lentulus Sura or C. Cosconius,

DE LEGE AGRARIA 2.27–29

of the people" has not left the power of even one of the assemblies to the people. But notice the scrupulous punctiliousness of the man! He saw and perceived that the Decemvirs could not have power without a curiate law, since they had been appointed by nine tribes. He therefore orders that a curiate law should be passed about them: he issues the command to the praetor. The absurdity of this arrangement is no concern of mine.[38] For he orders that the praetor who has been elected first shall enact the curiate law; but if he is unable to do so, then the last, so that it appears that he was either joking in matters of such importance or that he had some object or other in view.[39] But let us leave this arrangement, which is either as absurd as it is misguided or as difficult to understand as it is malicious; let us return to the man's punctiliousness. He sees that nothing can be done by the Decemvirs without a curiate law. What then, if the law is not passed? Notice his ingenuity. "In this case these Decemvirs shall have the same rights as magistrates elected in accordance with the most valid law." If it is possible that in this state, which far excels all other states in the right of freedom, anyone should be able to obtain civil or military power without the approval of any electoral assembly, what is the point of ordering, in the third section, a curiate law to be enacted, when in the fourth you allow that, without a curiate law, they should have the same rights as they would have if they had been elected by the people in accordance with the most valid law? It is kings that are being set up, Romans, not Decemvirs, and from these beginnings and

later a member of the board for implementing Caesar's agrarian legislation.

fundamentisque nascuntur, ut non modo cum ‹magistratum›[49] gerere coeperint, sed etiam cum constituentur, omne vestrum ius, potestas libertasque tollatur. At videte quam diligenter retineat ius tribuniciae potestatis. Consulibus legem curiatam ferentibus a tribunis plebis saepe est intercessum (neque tamen nos id querimur, esse hanc tribunorum plebis potestatem; tantum modo, si quis ea potestate temere est usus, ‹id querendum›[50] existimamus); hic tribunus plebis legi curiatae[51] quam praetor ferat adimit intercedendi potestatem. Atque hoc cum in eo reprehendendum est quod per tribunum plebis tribunicia potestas minuitur, tum in eo deridendum quod consuli, si legem curiatam non habet, attingere rem militarem non licet, hic, cui vetat intercedi,[52] ei potestatem, etiam si intercessum sit, tamen eandem constituit quam si lata esset lex, ut non intellegam quare aut hic vetet intercedere aut quemquam intercessurum putet, cum intercessio stultitiam intercessoris significatura sit, non rem impeditura.

31 Sint igitur decemviri neque veris comitiis, hoc est, populi suffragiis, neque illis ad speciem atque ad usurpationem vetustatis per xxx lictores auspiciorum causa adumbratis constituti. Videte nunc eos qui a vobis nihil potestatis acceperint quanto maioribus ornamentis adficiat quam omnes nos adfecti sumus quibus vos amplis-

---

[49] *add. Clark*
[50] id querendum *add. Dyck*, querendum *Marek*
[51] lege curiata: *corr. Manutius*
[52] huic cui vetat intercedendi: *corr. Clark*

---

[40] No example before 63 is recorded.

DE LEGE AGRARIA 2.29–31

foundations they are born in such a way that not only when they begin to exercise their office, but from the moment of their appointment, all your rights, all your powers, and all your liberty are swept away. But observe how carefully 30 he maintains the rights of the tribunate. The consuls, when enacting a curiate law, have often been obstructed by the veto of the plebeian tribunes;[40] we do not complain that the tribunes of the plebs have this power; but if anyone abuses that power, we think we ought to complain. But this plebeian tribune takes away the power of intercession for a curiate law that a praetor is enacting. And while it is blameworthy that the tribunician power is lessened by a tribune of the plebs, one cannot help laughing at the fact that, while a consul is not allowed to take a hand in military matters unless he is authorized to do so by a curiate law, to the man against whom he forbids intercession, he nonetheless gives the same power, even though there has been intercession, as if the law had been passed. Hence I fail to understand why he either forbids intercession or thinks that anyone will intercede, since intercession will not hinder the matter but will only show the folly of the interceder.

So then let there be Decemvirs appointed neither by 31 genuine elections, that is, by the votes of the people, nor the ones sketched out for show and to keep up the ancient practice by thirty lictors for the purpose of taking the auspices.[41] See now how much greater honors have been bestowed upon those who have received no power from you than upon all of us whom you have invested with the full-

---

[41] The *curiae* no longer voted themselves but were instead represented by thirty lictors; see on §26.

simas potestates dedistis. Iubet auspicato[53] coloniarum deducendarum causa decemviros habere pullarios "eodem iure," inquit, "quo habuerunt tresviri lege Sempronia." Audes etiam, Rulle, mentionem facere legis Semproniae, nec te ea lex ipsa commonet tresviros[54] illos xxxv tribuum suffragio creatos esse? Et cum tu a Ti. Gracchi aequitate ac pudore longissime remotus sis, id quod dissimillima ratione factum sit eodem iure putas esse oportere? Dat praeterea potestatem verbo praetoriam, re vera regiam; definit in quinquennium, facit sempiternam; tantis enim confirmat opibus et copiis ut invitis eripi nullo modo possit. Deinde ornat apparitoribus, scribis, librariis, praeconibus, architectis, praeterea mulis, tabernaculis, †centuriis,[55] supellectili; sumptum haurit ex aerario, suppeditat a sociis; finitores[56] ex equestri loco ducentos, vicenos[57] singulorum[58] stipatores corporis constituit, eosdem ministros et satellites potestatis.

Formam adhuc habetis, Quirites, et speciem [ipsam][59] tyrannorum; insignia videtis potestatis, nondum ipsam potestatem. Dixerit enim fortasse quispiam: "quid me ista laedunt, scriba, lictor, praeco, pullarius?" Omnia sunt haec

[53] auspicia: *corr. Orelli*
[54] iiiviros *Naugerius*: iiiviri *V*: treviri *E*: tales viros *cett.*
[55] centuriis: *locus conclamatus; alii alia*
[56] ianitores: *corr. Ant. Augustinus*
[57] in annos: *corr. Mommsen*
[58] singulorum *E*: singulos ω
[59] *del. Koch*

[42] Agrarian law enacted by plebiscite in 133 by Ti. Gracchus; cf. *LPPR* 298–300; *MRR* 1:493–94.

DE LEGE AGRARIA 2.31–32

est power. He orders the Decemvirs to have keepers of sacred chickens for the settlement of colonies upon taking of auspices, "enjoying the same rights," he says, "as the triumvirs by the Sempronian law."[42] Do you even dare to mention the Sempronian law, Rullus? Does not that law itself remind you that those triumvirs were elected by the votes of the thirty-five tribes? And though you fall far short of Tiberius Gracchus' justice and modesty, do you think what is done by a far different policy should have the same authority? Besides this, he gives the Decemvirs power that is nominally that of the praetors but is in reality that of a king. He limits it to five years, but makes it perpetual, for it is strengthened with such resources and forces that they cannot possibly be deprived of it against their will.[43] Then he equips them with attendants, clerks, secretaries, criers, and architects and in addition with mules, tents . . . furniture; he draws money for their expenses from the treasury and supplies them with more from the allies; two hundred surveyors from the equestrian order,[44] and twenty bodyguards for each are appointed as the servants and henchmen of their power.

Up to now, Romans, you have only the form and appearance of tyrants; you see the insignia of power, but not yet the power itself. Perhaps someone may say: "What harm do I get from a clerk, lictor, crier, or chicken keeper?" All these things are of such a kind, Romans, that one who

32

---

[43] Praetorian power was provided so that the Decemvirs had jurisdiction to settle property disputes; cf. §§33–34. Krostenko 2023, 225–26, thinks that Cicero means to conjure the arrogance of the Second Decemvirate of the year 450.

[44] See *Leg. agr.* 1 F 1 and §45 below.

huius modi, Quirites, ut ea qui habeat sine vestris suffragiis aut rex non ferendus aut privatus furiosus esse videatur. Perspicite quanta potestas permittatur: non privatorum insaniam, sed intolerantiam regum esse dicetis. Primum permittitur infinita potestas innumerabilis pecuniae conficiendae [de][60] vestris vectigalibus non fruendis, sed alienandis; deinde orbis terrarum gentiumque omnium datur cognitio sine consilio, poena sine provocatione, animadversio sine auxilio. Iudicare per quinquennium vel de consulibus vel de ipsis tribunis plebis poterunt; de illis interea nemo iudicabit; magistratus eis petere licebit, causam dicere non licebit; emere agros a quibus volent et quos volent, quam volent magno poterunt; colonias deducere novas, renovare veteres, totam Italiam suis colonis[61] ut complere liceat permittitur; omnis provincias obeundi, liberos populos agris multandi, regnorum vendendorum[62] summa potestas datur; cum velint, Romae esse, cum commodum sit, quacumque velint summo cum imperio iudicioque rerum omnium vagari ut liceat conceditur; interea dissolvant iudicia publica, e consiliis abducant quos velint, singuli de maximis rebus iudicent, quaesitori[63] permittant, finitorem mittant, ratum sit quod finitor uni illi a quo missus erit renuntiaverit. Verbum mihi deest, Quirites, cum ego hanc potestatem re-

---

[60] *del. Madvig*   [61] colonis *k*: coloniis ω
[62] vel dandorum ω: *corr. Camerarius*
[63] quaesitori *cod. Torr.*: quaestori ω

---

[45] Appeal ordinarily applies to criminal penalties, however; cf. Krostenko 2023, 222n17, 225n36.   [46] That is, those who assist magistrates making judicial decisions.

possesses them without your votes seems to be either a king and intolerable or a private individual and insane. Just observe what immense power is conferred upon them: you will say that it is not the madness of private individuals, but the intolerable insolence of kings. In the first place, they are allowed unlimited power of procuring enormous sums of money, not by profiting from your revenues, but by alienating them; in the second place, they are granted the jurisdiction without a council over the whole world and every people, penalty without appeal,[45] punishment without intervention of a tribune. For a period of five years they will be able to pass judgment on the consuls and even the plebeian tribunes themselves, while they will be judged by none; they will be allowed to canvass for magistracies, but they cannot be brought to trial; they will be able to buy any lands they choose from whomever they like, at whatever price they like. They are allowed to establish fresh colonies, to replenish old ones, to fill all Italy with their colonists; they have absolute authority to visit all the provinces, to confiscate the lands of free peoples, to sell kingdoms; when they like, they are allowed to remain at Rome, when it is convenient, to wander about wherever they please with absolute authority, military and judicial, in everything. Meanwhile, they can set aside sentences in criminal trials, remove from the councils of advisors[46] anyone they choose, decide individually upon most important affairs, delegate their power to a judge, send a surveyor, and ratify whatever the surveyor has reported to the one man by whom he has been sent. I fail to find the proper word, Romans, when I call such power kingly; it is

giam appello, sed profecto maior est quaedam. Nullum enim regnum fuit umquam quod non se, si[64] minus iure aliquo, at regionibus tamen certis contineret.[65] Hoc vero infinitum est, quo et regna omnia et vestrum imperium, quod latissime patet, et ea quae partim libera a vobis, partim etiam ignorata vobis sunt, permissu legis continentur.

Datur igitur eis primum ut liceat ea vendere omnia "de quibus vendendis senatus consulta facta sunt M. Tullio Cn. Cornelio consulibus post‹ve› ea."[66] Cur hoc tam est obscurum atque caecum? Quid? Ista omnia de quibus senatus censuit nominatim in lege perscribi nonne potuerunt? Duae sunt huius obscuritatis causae, Quirites, una pudoris (si quis pudor esse potest in tam insigni impudentia), altera sceleris. Nam neque ea quae senatus nominatim vendenda censuit audet appellare; sunt enim loca publica urbis, sunt sacella quae post restitutam tribuniciam potestatem nemo attigit, quae maiores in urbe ‹partim ornamenta urbis›,[67] partim periculi perfugia esse voluerunt. Haec lege tribunicia decemviri vendent. Accedet[68] eo mons Gaurus, accedent salicta ad Minturnas, adiungetur et[69] illa via vendibilis Herculanea multarum delicia-

36

[64] se si *Baiter*: si $V^c\chi^2k$: se *cett.*
[65] contineret $\alpha\pi$: continetur M^1: contineretur *cett.*
[66] postve ea *Richter*: postea: ω
[67] partim ornamenta urbis *add. Clark, praeeunte Lambino, qui* partim urbis ornamenta *post* perfugia *addiderat*
[68] accedit: *corr. Angelius*
[69] et $an\chi^2$: etiam V^c *cett.*

[47] M. Tullius Decula and Cn. Cornelius Dolabella, consuls in 81: *MRR* 2:74.

DE LEGE AGRARIA 2.35–36

surely something greater. For there has never been an instance of royal power which was not restrained, if not by some law, at least by fixed boundaries. But this one is without bounds: all the kingdoms, all your empire in its widest extent, all the lands, some of which are free from your rule and others with which you are not even acquainted, are included by permission of the law.

In the first place, they are permitted to sell everything "the sale of which was authorized by resolutions of the senate during the consulship of Marcus Tullius and Gnaeus Cornelius or afterward."[47] Why is this expressed so obscurely and opaquely? What is the reason? Could not all those objects in regard to which the senate expressly passed resolutions not have been set down in the law? There are two reasons for this obscurity, Romans: the one shame (if there can be any shame in such blatant shamelessness), the other criminality. For he does not dare to name those objects which the senate expressly resolved should be sold, for they are the public places of the city, sanctuaries upon which no one has laid hands since the restoration of the tribunician power, some of which our ancestors desired to be adornments for the city, others refuges from danger. These things will be sold by the Decemvirs by a tribunician law. Besides these there will be Mount Gaurus,[48] the willow groves near Minturnae,[49] that marketable Herculean road, of great value with its many

36

---

[48] A mountain in Campania noted for production of fine wines.

[49] A town near the Appian Way between Latium and Campania, near commercially valuable willow groves.

rum et magnae pecuniae, permulta alia quae senatus
propter angustias aerari vendenda censuit, consules prop-
37 ter invidiam non vendiderunt. Verum haec fortasse
propter pudorem in lege reticentur. Sed illud magis est
credendum et pertimescendum quod audaciae decemvirali corrumpendarum tabularum publicarum fingendo-
rumque senatus consultorum, quae facta numquam sint,[70]
cum ex eo numero qui per eos annos consules fuerunt
multi mortui sint, magna potestas permittitur. Nisi forte
nihil est aequum nos de eorum audacia suspicari quorum
cupiditati nimium angustus orbis terrarum esse videatur.
38 Habetis unum venditionis genus, quod magnum videri
vobis intellego. Sed attendite animos ad ea quae conse-
cuntur; hunc quasi gradum quendam atque aditum ad
cetera factum[71] intellegetis. "Qui agri, quae loca, aedificia." Quid est praeterea? Multa in mancipiis, in pecore,
auro, argento, ebore, veste, supellectili, ceteris rebus.
Quid dicam? Invidiosum putasse[72] hoc fore, si omnia nominasset? Non metuit invidiam. Quid ergo? Longum putavit et timuit ne quid praeteriret; ascripsit "aliudve quid,"
qua brevitate rem nullam esse exceptam videtis. Quicquid
igitur sit extra Italiam quod publicum populi Romani
factum sit L. Sulla Q. Pompeio consulibus aut postea, id
39 decemviros iubet vendere. Hoc capite, Quirites, omnis

[70] sunt: *corr. Ussing*
[71] iactum: *corr. Lauredanus*
[72] putasset: *corr. Puteanus*

---

[50] A raised road in Campania reputedly built by Hercules between the Lucrine Lake and the Mediterranean.

delightful surroundings,[50] and a number of other places that the senate decreed should be sold owing to the poverty of the treasury, but which the consuls did not sell for fear of unpopularity. However, it is perhaps owing to shame that these lands are not named in the law. But what is more credible and more to be feared is that great scope is allowed for the audacity of the Decemvirs for tampering with the public registers and forging resolutions of the senate that have never been passed, since many of those who were consuls during those years are dead.[51] Unless perhaps it is wrong for us to suspect the audacity of men for whose cupidity the world seems insufficient.

There you have one kind of sale, which I am aware seems important to you, but listen to those that follow: you will understand that this is only a sort of step and first approach to other goals. "Whatever lands, places, buildings." What else can there be? There is much property in slaves, cattle, gold, silver, ivory, clothing, furniture, and other things. What am I to say? That he thought it would cause unpopularity, if he had named everything? No, he had no fear of unpopularity. What then was the reason? He thought it was a lengthy list and was afraid of passing over anything; and so he added, "or anything else"; you see that, in spite of this brevity, nothing is excepted. He orders the Decemvirs to sell everything outside Italy that became the public property of the Roman people during the consulship of Lucius Sulla and Quintus Pompeius or afterward.[52] By this section, Romans, I assert that all peoples, nations,

---

[51] Hinting at a weakness in Roman administration: forged decrees were difficult to detect and root out; see Eich 2008.

[52] Namely, the year 88: *MRR* 2:39–40.

CICERO

gentis, nationes, provincias, regna decemvirum dicioni, iudicio potestatique permissa et condonata esse dico. Primum hoc quaero, ecqui[73] tandem locus usquam sit quem non possint decemviri dicere publicum populi Romani esse factum. Nam cum idem possit iudicare qui dixerit, quid est quod non liceat ei dicere cui [non][74] liceat eidem[75] iudicare? Commodum erit Pergamum, Smyrnam, Trallis, Ephesum, Miletum, Cyzicum, totam denique Asiam, quae post L. Sullam Q. Pompeium consules recuperata sit, populi Romani factam esse dicere: utrum oratio ad eius rei disputationem deerit, an, cum idem et disseret et iudicabit, impelli non poterit ut falsum iudicet? An, si condemnare Asiam nolet, terrorem damnationis et minas non quanti volet aestimabit?[76] Quid? Quod disputari contra nullo pacto potest, quoniam statutum a nobis est et iudicatum, quam hereditatem iam crevimus, regnum Bithyniae, quod certe publicum est populi Romani factum, num quid causae est quin omnes agros, urbis, stagna,[77]

40

---

[73] ecqui *Gebhardt*: enim qui ωπ
[74] *del. ed. Hervagiana*
[75] idem: *corr. Manutius*
[76] aestimabit *k, ed. Rom.*: existimabit ω
[77] stagna *a*: stativa *cett.*

---

[53] That is, Asia Minor was essentially lost but then reconquered by the Romans in the First Mithridatic War (89–85); cf. *OCD* s.v. Mithradates. Gabba 1973, 458, supposes that Pergamum, Tralles, Ephesus, and Miletus, which had joined Mithridates in the recent war, would have been mentioned in Rullus'

provinces, and kingdoms are handed over and made a free gift of to the dominion, jurisdiction, and power of the Decemvirs. In the first place, I ask, is there a place on earth of which the Decemvirs cannot say that it has become the public property of the Roman people? For when he who has said this is likewise able to decide, what is there that the same person may not be allowed to say, since he is also allowed to decide the matter? It will be to their interest to say that Pergamum, Smyrna, Tralles, Ephesus, Miletus, Cyzicus, in fact all Asia, which was recovered after the consulship of Lucius Sulla and Quintus Pompeius, has become the property of the Roman people.[53] Will he lack words to argue the matter, or since the same man will both argue and decide, will it be impossible for him to be induced to give a wrong decision? Or if he is unwilling to condemn Asia, will he not set as high a price as he wishes on the fear of the threatened condemnation?[54] What about a matter that cannot possibly be disputed, because it has been decided and judged by ourselves—the legacy upon which we have already entered, the kingdom of Bithynia, which certainly has become the public property of the Roman people? Is there anything to prevent them from selling all the lands, cities, still wa-

40

---

bill, but Cicero does not raise that claim, only that it would be "convenient" (*commodum*) to declare that they were eligible for sale; contrast the lands subject to taxation, said to have been listed "by name" (*nominatim*, §47). Cf. Vasaly 1988, 410–11.

[54] That is, in return for eliminating the fear.

CICERO

portus, totam denique Bithyniam decemviri vendituri sint? Quid? Mytilenae, quae certe vestrae, Quirites, belli lege ac victoriae iure factae sunt, urbs et natura ac situ et descriptione aedificiorum et pulchritudine in primis nobilis, agri iucundi et fertiles, nempe eodem capite inclusi

41 continentur. Quid? Alexandria cunctaque Aegyptus ut occulte latet, ut recondita est,[78] ut furtim tota decemviris traditur! Quis enim vestrum hoc ignorat, dici illud regnum testamento regis Alexae[79] populi Romani esse factum? Hic ego consul populi Romani non modo nihil iudico sed ne quid sentiam quidem profero; magna enim mihi res non modo ad statuendum sed etiam ad dicendum videtur esse. Video qui testamentum factum esse confirmet; auctoritatem senatus exstare hereditatis aditae sentio tum cum[80] Alexa mortuo legatos Tyrum misimus, qui ab illo pecu-

42 niam depositam nostris recuperarent. Haec L. Philippum

[78] est *ed. Mediol.*: sunt ω
[79] Alexae *edd.*: Alexa V *in marg.*: Alexandri ς
[80] cum *R. Klotz*: quando ω

[55] Bequeathed to Rome on the death of its king, Nicomedes IV, in 76 or 75; the senate "judged" the matter by accepting the legacy. However, Mithridates reacted by invading Bithynia in spring 73, thus starting the Third Mithridatic War; cf. *OCD* s.v. Mithradates. In the year 66 Cicero lamented its loss (*Leg. Man.* 5). The territory was recaptured by Pompey and joined with the former Pontic kingdom as a single province in 66–65; cf. *MRR* 2:155, 159–60.

[56] The principal city of the island of Lesbos joined Mithridates' side but was captured in 80 by M. Minucius Thermus

ters, harbors, in fact the whole of Bithynia?[55] What then? Mytilene, which certainly became yours, Romans, by the law of war and the right of victory, a city, especially famous by nature and position, and the plan and beauty of its buildings, with its pleasant and fertile lands, is surely included in the same section of the law.[56] What about Alexandria and the whole of Egypt? How secretly it is concealed! How it is kept hidden away! How stealthily it is handed over whole to the Decemvirs![57] Which of you is ignorant that it is decreed by the will of King Alexa that that kingdom has become the property of the Roman people?[58] On this point I, the consul of the Roman people, not only pass no judgment, but do not even put my opinion forward; for it seems to me a major matter not only to decide, but even to discuss. I see someone who asserts that the will was made; I am aware that an opinion of the senate exists stating that the inheritance was entered upon at the time when, upon the death of Alexa, we sent ambassadors to Tyre to recover for our people a sum of money deposited by him.[59] I remember that Lucius Philippus

41

42

(*MRR* 2:81) and later regained its freedom thanks to Pompey (Vell. Pat. 2.18.3; Plut. *Vit. Pomp.* 42.4). For a comparison of the places named in §§39–40 with *Leg. agr.* 1 F 3, see Krostenko 2023, 127n83.

[57] That is, it is not mentioned in the bill; Cicero merely infers that this is the intent.

[58] Referring to Ptolemy X Alexander I (ca. 140–88); see on 1.1.

[59] It was, in fact returned to Rome, according to the Bobbio Scholia (p. 92.19–20St).

CICERO

saepe in senatu confirmasse memoria teneo; eum qui regnum illud teneat hoc tempore neque genere neque animo regio esse inter omnis fere video convenire. Dicitur contra nullum esse testamentum, non oportere populum Romanum omnium regnorum ⟨ap⟩petentem[81] videri, demigraturos in illa loca nostros homines propter agrorum bonitatem et omnium rerum copiam. Hac tanta de re P. Rullus cum ceteris decemviris collegis suis iudicabit; et utrum[82] iudicabit? Nam utrumque ita magnum est ut nullo modo neque concedendum neque ferendum sit. Volet esse popularis; populo Romano adiudicabit. Ergo idem ex sua lege vendet Alexandriam, vendet Aegyptum, urbis copiosissimae pulcherrimorumque agrorum iudex, arbiter, dominus, rex denique opulentissimi regni reperietur.[83] Non sumet sibi tantum, non appetet; iudicabit Alexandriam regis esse, a populo Romano abiudicabit. Primum cur[84] ⟨de⟩ populi Romani hereditate[85] decemviri iudicent, cum vos volueritis de privatis hereditatibus cviros iudicare? Deinde quis aget causam populi Romani?

43

44

---

[81] *corr. Angelius*   [82] utrum *Puteanus*: verum ω
[83] reperietur χ^2ck: reperitur ω   [84] cur *Pluygers*: tum ωπ
[85] de p.r. hereditate *C. F. W. Müller*: p.r. hereditatem (de *omisso*) ω

---

[60] An "opinion" (*auctoritas*) of the senate was a decree thwarted by a veto. It was not written down; hence Cicero must rely for his knowledge of it on remarks made in the senate by L. Marcius Philippus (cos. 91), who, apart from the unimportant M. Perperna (or Perpenna; cos. 92), was the last survivor of the pre-Sullan senate when Cicero joined that body in 75; cf. Badian 1967, 180–81, 192.

DE LEGE AGRARIA 2.42–44

frequently affirmed these facts in the senate;[60] I see that nearly everyone agrees that he who occupies the throne today has neither the pedigree nor the mindset of a king.[61] On the other hand, it is said that there is no will, that the Roman people ought not to show itself eager to seize all kingdoms;[62] that our citizens are likely to emigrate to that country, attracted by the fertility of the land and its abundant supplies of everything. Rullus with his colleagues the Decemvirs will decide this important matter; and which way will he decide? For each alternative is of such importance that you must by no means either give way to him or put up with his decision. If Rullus desires to be the friend of the people, he will award the kingdom to the Roman people. And so too, by virtue of his law, he will sell Alexandria, he will sell Egypt, and we shall discover that he is the judge, the arbiter, the owner of a most wealthy city and of the most beautiful lands—in fine, the king of a most flourishing kingdom. Oh but he will not take so much for himself, he will not be greedy: he will decide that Alexandria is the king's, he will decide that it is not the Roman people's. In the first place, why are Decemvirs to decide about an inheritance of the Roman people, when you have wanted a hundred men to decide disputes about the inheritances of private persons?[63] Next, who will plead

[61] Alluding to the illegitimate birth of Ptolemy XII Auletes; cf. Khrustalyov 2018, 255.   [62] In the senate speech *On King Ptolemy* of 65, Cicero had argued against Crassus' plan to annex Egypt as showing greed; cf. fr. orat. 7 F 2 Cr.-D.

[63] The Centumviral court heard cases involving inheritance and property claims (*vindicationes*) of substantial value; see further Berger 1953 s.v. Centumviri.

Ubi res ista agetur? Qui sunt isti decemviri, quos prospiciamus[86] regnum Alexandriae Ptolomaeo gratis adiudicaturos? Quod si Alexandria petebatur, cur non eosdem cursus hoc tempore quos L. Cotta L. Torquato consulibus cucurrerunt? Cur non aperte, ut antea, cur non item, ut tum, derecto[87] et palam regionem illam petierunt? An qui etesiis,[88] qui per cursum rectum regnum tenere non potuerunt, nunc taetris[89] tenebris et caligine se Alexandriam perventuros arbitrati sunt?

45 Atque illud circumspicite vestris mentibus una, Quirites.[90] Legatos nostros,[91] homines auctoritate tenui, qui rerum privatarum causa legationes liberas obeunt, tamen exterae nationes ferre vix possunt. Grave est enim nomen imperi atque id etiam in levi persona pertimescitur, propterea quod vestro, non suo nomine, cum hinc egressi sunt, abutuntur. Quid censetis, cum isti decemviri cum imperio, cum fascibus, cum illa delecta finitorum iuventute per totum orbem terrarum vagabuntur, quo tandem animo, 46 quo metu, quo periculo miseras nationes futuras? Est in imperio terror; patientur. Est in adventu sumptus; ferent. Imperabitur aliquid muneris; non recusabunt. Illud vero quantum est, Quirites, cum is decemvir qui aliquam in

---

[86] prospiciamus *R. Klotz*: per- ω
[87] derecto *C. F. W. Müller*: decreto ω
[88] qui etesiis *Gulielmius*: quietis iis ωπ
[89] taetris *E*: tetris ω
[90] una quirites *Turnebus*: unaque ω
[91] nostros *an*: vestros *cett.*

---

[64] L. Aurelius Cotta and L. Manlius Torquatus, consuls of 65; for the earlier debate, cf. on §42.

DE LEGE AGRARIA 2.44–46

the case of the Roman people? Where will it be adjudicated? Who are the Decemvirs who we foresee are likely to award the kingdom of Alexandria to Ptolemy for nothing? But if Alexandria was aimed at, why not now follow the same course as that taken under the consulship of Lucius Cotta and Lucius Torquatus?[64] Why not now make for that location openly as before, why not straightforwardly and publicly, as they did then? Or did those men, who were unable to reach the kingdom by the trade winds, by a straight course, now imagine that they could arrive at Alexandria by foul mists and darkness?

Moreover, take a comprehensive view, Romans: our legates, men invested with little authority, who go on "free embassies" for the sake of their own private affairs, can nonetheless scarcely be endured by foreign nations.[65] For the mere name of empire is burdensome and greatly feared even in an insignificant representative, because, when they have left the city, it is not their own name, but yours, that they abuse. When these Decemvirs will be roaming about the entire world with supreme power, with the rods of office, with that picked band of young surveyors,[66] what feelings, apprehension, and danger do you think will come upon the unhappy nations? Supreme power[67] inspires terror; they will put up with it. Their arrival entails expense; they will bear it. If a gift is commanded, they will not refuse it. But what a shock would it be, Romans, if a Decemvir who has arrived in some city

45

46

---

[65] For the "free embassies," cf. on 1.8.

[66] See on *Leg. agr.* 1 F 1.

[67] *Imperium* was the power vested in the Decemvirs by Rullus' bill.

urbem aut exspectatus ut hospes aut repente ut dominus venerit illum ipsum locum quo venerit, illam ipsam sedem hospitalem in qua‹m›[92] erit deductus publicam populi Romani esse dicet![93] At quanta calamitas populi, si dixerit, quantus ipsi quaestus, si negarit! Atque idem qui haec appetunt queri non numquam solent omnis terras Cn. Pompeio atque omnia maria esse permissa. Simile vero est multa committi et condonari omnia, labori et negotio praeponi an praedae et quaestui, mitti ad socios liberandos an ad opprimendos! Denique, si qui est honos singularis, nihilne interest utrum populus Romanus eum cui velit deferat an is impudenter populo Romano per legis fraudem surripiatur?

47 Intellexistis quot res et quantas decemviri legis permissu venditori sint. Non est satis. Cum se sociorum, cum exterarum nationum, cum regum sanguine impleverint, incidant nervos populi Romani, adhibeant manus vectigalibus vestris, inrumpant in aerarium! Sequitur enim caput quo capite ne permittit quidem, si forte desit pecunia (quae tanta ex superioribus recipi potest ut deesse non debeat), sed, plane quasi ea res vobis[94] saluti futura sit, ita cogit[95] atque imperat ut decemviri vestra vectigalia vendant no-

[92] quam *ed. Hervagiana, Naugerius*: qua ω
[93] *post* dicet *hab. cett.* at: *om.* an
[94] vobis α: nobis *cett.*   [95] cogitat: *corr. Angelius*

---

[68] That is, after extorting a bribe.   [69] The first insinuation that Rullus' backers also opposed Pompey's extraordinary command in Asia; cf. 3.16. But the known opponents, Q. Lutatius Catulus and Q. Hortensius (*Leg. Man.* 51, 59–61, 63, 66), are very unlikely to have supported such a proposal.

DE LEGE AGRARIA 2.46–47

either expected as a guest or suddenly as a master should declare that the very place where he has arrived, the hospitable dwelling to which he has been escorted, is the public property of the Roman people! What a calamity for the people, if he says so! What a great gain for him, if he does not say so![68] And yet the very same people who are greedy for these things are sometimes in the habit of complaining that all lands and all seas are at the disposal of Pompey![69] It is, of course, the same thing to entrust large commissions and to make a comprehensive gift; to be put at the head of a laborious task or to be appointed to look after plunder and gain; to be sent to liberate our allies or to crush them! Lastly, if it is a case of some extraordinary honor, does it make no difference whether the Roman people bestows it upon the man it chooses or whether it is impudently stolen from the Roman people by a fraudulent law?

You now understand how many and what important 47 things the Decemvirs will sell by permission of this law. That is not enough. When they have gorged themselves with the blood of the allies, of foreign nations, and of kings, let them cut the sinews of the Roman people, let them lay hands on your revenues, let them break into the treasury! For next comes a section that does not simply give permission, if there should happen to be a want of money (which can be received in such quantities from the previous sections that there ought to be no lack of it), but, just as if it were a question of your salvation, absolutely compels and orders the Decemvirs to sell your revenue-producing lands, mentioning them by

48 minatim. Quam[96] tu mihi ex ordine recita de legis scripto populi Romani auctionem; quam mehercule ego praeconi huic ipsi[97] luctuosam et acerbam praedicationem futuram puto. ⟨Versatur⟩[98] ut in suis rebus, ita in re publica luxuriosus[99] nepos, qui prius silvas vendat quam vineas! Italiam percensuisti; perge in Siciliam: nihil est in hac provincia quod aut in oppidis aut in agris maiores nostri
49 proprium nobis reliquerint quin id venire iubeat. Quod partum recenti victoria maiores vobis in sociorum urbibus ac finibus et vinculum pacis et monumentum belli reliquerunt, id vos ab illis acceptum hoc auctore vendetis?

Hic mihi parumper mentes vestras, Quirites, commovere videor, dum patefacio vobis quas isti penitus abstrusas insidias se posuisse arbitrantur contra Cn. Pompei dignitatem. Et mihi, quaeso, ignoscite, si appello talem virum saepius. Vos mihi praetori biennio ante, Quirites, hoc eodem in loco personam hanc imposuistis ut, quibuscumque rebus possem, illius absentis dignitatem vobiscum una tuerer. Feci adhuc quae potui, neque familiaritate illius adductus nec spe honoris atque amplissimae dignitatis, quam ego, etsi libente illo, tamen absente, [illo][100] per vos

---

[96] quam ω *(cf. e.g. Att. 2.14.1, quantam tu mihi moves expectationem)*: quirites. eam *Clark*: quirites *tantum Shackleton Bailey 1979, 255–56*: iam *Manuwald*   [97] ipsam: *corr. Angelius*
[98] *add. Dyck*: auctio *add. Manutius*   [99] luxuriosos V^1M^1: luxuriosus ⟨est⟩ *Lambinus*   [100] *om. Lag.9, del. Manutius*

---

[70] Applying to Rullus a quasi-proverbial description of a wastrel; cf. Krostenko 2023, 79 and n. 40.

[71] "In this same place," that is, on the Rostra, referring to the first speech he delivered there as praetor in 66, *On the Manilian*

DE LEGE AGRARIA 2.47–49

name. Read out to me this auction list [of the property] 48
of the Roman people in order according to the text of
the law; by Hercules, I think that this announcement will
bring grief and bitterness even to this crier! Just as with
his own property, so in the case of the republic he is acting
as a spendthrift addicted to luxury, the kind who sells his
forests before his vineyards.[70] You have gone through the
property in Italy; go on into Sicily. There is nothing in this
province that our ancestors have left us as our own either
in the towns or countryside that he does not order to be
sold. As for the property acquired by a recent victory, 49
which your ancestors left to you, in the cities and in the
territories of our allies, both as a guarantee of peace and
a memorial of war, will you sell it at the bidding of this man
after you have received it from them?

Here, Romans, I believe I am briefly making an impression on your feelings, by revealing to you the deeply
hidden snares that they think they have laid against Pompey's standing. And pardon me, please, if I mention this
great man's name too often. Two years ago, in this same
place, when I was praetor, you imposed upon me, Romans,
the role of joining with you in defending his dignity during
his absence by whatever means I could.[71] Up to the present I have done what I could, although induced to do so
neither by friendship with him nor by hope of office and
high standing, which—with his goodwill,[72] albeit in his

Law, advocating Pompey's command in Asia (§§1 and 70); it is
unlikely that he refers here to Manilius' trial. See further Manuwald 2018, 299. [72] At *Att.* 1.1[10].2 Cicero is unsure
whether he has Pompey's support, but Q. Cic. (?) *Comment. pet.*
51 asserts that he does have it.

50 consecutus sum. Quam ob rem cum intellegam totam hanc fere legem ad illius opes evertendas tamquam machinam comparari, et resistam consiliis hominum et perficiam profecto, quod ego video, ut id vos universi non solum videre verum etiam tenere possitis.

Iubet venire quae Attalensium, quae Phaselitum,[101] quae Olympenorum[102] fuerint, agrumque Aperensem[103] et Oroandicum[104] et Gedusanum.[105] Haec P. Servili imperio et victoria, clarissimi viri,[106] vestra facta sunt. Adiungit agros Bithyniae regios, quibus nunc publicani fruuntur; deinde Attalicos agros in Cherroneso, in Macedonia qui regis Philippi sive Persae fuerunt, qui item a censoribus
51 locati sunt et certissimum vectigal ⟨adferunt⟩.[107] Ascribit eidem[108] auctioni Corinthios agros opimos et fertilis, et Cyrenenses, qui Apionis fuerunt, et agros in Hispania propter Carthaginem novam et in Africa ipsam veterem Carthaginem vendit, quam videlicet P. Africanus non propter religionem sedum illarum ac vetustatis de consili sententia consecravit, nec ut ipse locus eorum qui cum

[101] phasiletum: *corr. Naugerius*
[102] olimpinorum: *corr. Naugerius*
[103] agerensem: *corr. Zumpt*
[104] orindicum: *corr. Garatoni*
[105] gedusavum α   [106] clarissimi viri k: clarissimi l. viri ω
[107] *add. Clark*   [108] idem: *corr. Lambinus*

---

[73] Attalia was in Pamphylia, Phaselis and Olympus in Lycia; Apera (if that is the correct reading) was on the southern coast of Lycia; Oroanda was in southern Asia Minor between Pisidia and Isauria; Gedusa is otherwise unknown. See further Manuwald 2018, 130–31, 301–2. All these places were conquered, as he ex-

DE LEGE AGRARIA 2.49–51

absence—I have attained by your favor. Therefore, since 50
I understand that this law is almost entirely being set up
as a siege engine to overthrow that man's power, I will both
resist the men's designs and I will assuredly enable all of
you not only to see, but also to get a firm hold upon what
I see.

He orders the territories to be sold that belonged to
the inhabitants of Attalia, Phaselis, Olympus, and the land
of Apera, Oroanda, and Gedusa. These territories became
yours by the victorious command of the illustrious Publius
Servilius.[73] He adds the royal domains of Bithynia, from
which the tax farmers now reap profit; next the lands of
Attalus in the Chersonese;[74] those in Macedonia, which
belonged to Philip or Perses,[75] and were also farmed out
by the censors, and bring a sure source of revenue. He also 51
includes in the sale the rich and fertile lands of Corinth
and those of Cyrene, which belonged to Apion;[76] and sells
the territories in Spain near New Carthage and in Africa
old Carthage itself, which Publius Africanus I suppose
consecrated, by the advice of his council, not out of any
religious respect for its dwellings and its antiquity, nor that
the place itself might show traces of the disaster that over-

---

plains, by P. Servilius Isauricus; see on 1.5. Cicero's presentation seems to be deceptive, for Rullus probably listed no places outside Italy and Sicily; cf. Vasaly 1988, 411.

[74] The Thracian Chersonese (the modern peninsula Gallipoli) was among the territories that devolved upon the Roman people in 133 by the will of Attalus III of Pergamum: Liv. *per.* 58.

[75] See on 1.5.   [76] At his death in 75, Ptolemaeus Apion, king of Cyrenaica, left his domain to the Roman people; cf. Sall. *Hist.* 2.39 R. and note.

hac urbe de imperio decertarunt[109] vestigia calamitatis ostenderet, sed non fuit tam diligens quam est Rullus, aut fortasse emptorem ei loco reperire non potuit.

Verum inter hos agros [regios][110] captos veteribus bellis virtute summorum imperatorum adiungit regios agros Mithridatis, qui in Paphlagonia, qui in Ponto, qui in Cappadocia fuerunt, ut eos decemviri vendant. Itane vero? Non legibus datis, non auditis verbis imperatoris, nondum denique bello confecto, cum rex Mithridates amisso exercitu regno expulsus tamen in ultimis terris aliquid etiam nunc moliatur atque ab invicta Cn. Pompei manu Maeote et illis paludibus et itinerum angustiis atque altitudine montium defendatur, cum imperator in bello versetur, in locis autem illis etiam nunc belli nomen reliquum sit, eos agros quorum adhuc penes Cn. Pompeium omne iudicium et potestas more maiorum debet esse decemviri vendent? Et, credo, P. Rullus—is enim sic se gerit ut sibi iam decemvir designatus esse videatur—ad eam auctionem potissimum proficiscetur! Is videlicet antequam veniat in Pontum, litteras ad Cn. Pompeium mittet, quarum ego iam exemplum ab istis compositum esse arbitror: "P. Servilius Rullus tribunus plebis decemvir s. d. ⟨Cn.⟩[111] Pompeio Cn. f." (non credo ascripturum esse "Magno," non enim videtur id quod imminuere lege conatur conces-

---

[109] certarunt $an\chi^2$
[110] *del. Kayser*   [111] *add. Manutius*

---

[77] See on 1.5.   [78] That is, for the administration of the conquered territory, typically handled by the victorious general jointly with a ten-man commission appointed by the senate; see further Manuwald 2018, 306.

DE LEGE AGRARIA 2.51–53

took those who contended with our city for empire.[77] But he was not so careful as Rullus, or perhaps he was unable to find a buyer for that place.

However, to these lands, taken in our ancient wars by the valor of our greatest commanders, he adds the royal lands of Mithridates that were in Paphlagonia, Pontus, and Cappadocia, in order that the Decemvirs may sell them. Really? Before terms have been laid down,[78] the general's report heard, before the war is finished, while King Mithridates, without an army, driven from his kingdom, is nevertheless even now, at the end of the world, engineering some new plot, and is defended from the invincible troops of Pompey by the Maeotis and those marshes, by those narrow defiles and lofty mountains; while our commander is still engaged in war and even now the name of war remains in those districts—shall the Decemvirs sell those lands, over which, according to the custom of our ancestors, Pompey still ought to possess all civil and military authority?[79] And, I suppose, Publius Rullus—for he behaves as if he thinks he were already a Decemvir elect—will take very special care to set out for this sale. Before he reaches Pontus, he will, of course, send a letter to Gnaeus Pompey, of which I think they have already drawn up a copy: "Publius Servilius Rullus, tribune of the people, Decemvir, to Gnaeus Pompey, son of Gnaeus, greetings." (I do not suppose that he will add "Magnus," for he seems unlikely to grant him verbally what he is endeavoring to

52

53

---

[79] On the general's traditional control of plunder seized in war, see on 1.12.

CICERO

surus verbo). "Te volo curare ut mihi Sinopae praesto sis auxiliumque adducas, dum eos agros quos ⟨tu⟩[112] tuo labore cepisti ego mea lege vendam." An Pompeium non adhibebit? In eius provincia vendet manubias imperatoris? Ponite ante oculos vobis Rullum in Ponto inter nostra atque hostium castra hasta posita cum suis formosis fini-
54 toribus auctionantem. Neque in hoc solum inest contumelia, quae vehementer et insignis est et nova, ut ulla res parta bello nondum legibus datis, etiam tum imperatore bellum administrante non modo venierit verum locata sit. Plus spectant homines certe quam contumeliam; sperant, si concessum sit inimicis[113] Cn. Pompei cum imperio, cum iudicio omnium rerum, cum infinita potestate, cum innumerabili pecunia non solum illis[114] in locis vagari verum etiam ad ipsius exercitum pervenire, aliquid illi insidiarum fieri, aliquid de eius exercitu, copiis, gloria detrahi posse. Putant, si quam spem in Cn. Pompeio exercitus habeat aut agrorum aut aliorum commodorum, hanc non habiturum, cum viderit earum rerum omnium potestatem ad de-
55 cemviros esse translatam. Patior non moleste tam stultos esse qui haec sperent, tam impudentes qui conentur; illud queror, tam me ab eis esse contemptum ut haec portenta me consule potissimum cogitarent.

[112] *add. Lauredanus*   [113] inimicis χ^2, *ed. Rom.*: inimici ω
[114] aliis: *corr. Pluygers*

---

[80] A pun on Magnus (the Great) as a cognomen taken by Pompey (*OLD* s.v. *magnus* 7a) and in its literal sense.

[81] Since the reforms of C. Marius, Roman soldiers expected their general to provide them lands to support them when they had completed their service. Cf. Sall. *Iug.* 86.2–3; Weynand, *RE*

diminish by his law.[80]) "I desire you to see that you attend me at Sinope and bring an armed force, while I am selling by my law the lands that you have seized through your efforts." Or will he not invite Pompey? Will he sell the general's spoils in his province? Imagine Rullus in Pontus, between our camp and that of the enemy, with spear stuck in the ground, in the company of his handsome surveyors, holding his auction. Nor is this the only insult, although it is very extraordinary and unprecedented that anything won by war, when terms have not yet been laid down and the commander is still waging war, should be, I do not say sold, but even let. But these men surely have something further in view than mere insult. If the enemies of Pompey are allowed not only to wander about in those districts with military authority, universal jurisdiction, unlimited civil power, and vast sums of money, but even to reach the general's army, they hope that some snare may be laid for him, and that his army, his resources, and his reputation may be diminished. They imagine that, if the army reposes in Pompey any hope of lands or other benefits, it will no longer do so upon seeing that the power of distributing all such favors has been transferred to the Decemvirs.[81] I am not annoyed that they are so foolish as to have such hopes, and so impudent as to attempt to carry them out; what I do complain of is that they had such contempt for me that they would plot such monstrous things in particular during my consulship.

54

55

Suppl. 6.1401.7–1403.41 (s.v. Marius); Schmitthenner 1960, 1–2; Carney 1961, 32–34, with reference to the law of 100; Brunt 1971, 82, 198, and Appendix 12, emphasizing that there is no evidence for extensive grants; Gabba 1976, 14–19, with attached notes.

Atque in omnibus his agris aedificiisque vendendis permittitur decemviris ut vendant quibuscumque in locis videatur. O perturbatam rationem, o libidinem refrenandam, o consilia dissoluta atque perdita! Vectigalia locare nusquam licet nisi in hac urbe, hoc auspicato[115] ex loco, hac vestrum frequentia. Venire nostras res proprias et in perpetuum a nobis abalienari in Paphlagoniae tenebris atque in Cappadociae solitudine licebit? L. Sulla cum bona indemnatorum civium funesta illa auctione sua venderet et se praedam suam diceret vendere, tamen ex hoc loco vendidit nec quorum oculos offendebat eorum ipsorum conspectum fugere ausus est; decemviri vestra vectigalia non modo non vobis, Quirites,[116] arbitris sed ne praecone quidem publico teste vendent?

Sequitur "omnis agros extra Italiam" infinito ex tempore, non, ut antea, ab Sulla et Pompeio consulibus. Cognitio decemvirum, privatus sit an publicus; eique[117] agro pergrande vectigal imponitur. Hoc quantum iudicium, quam intolerandum, quam regium sit, quem praeterit, posse quibuscumque locis velint nulla disceptatione, nullo consilio privata publicare, publica liberare? Excipitur hoc capite ager ⟨in⟩[118] Sicilia Recentoricus; quem ego excipi et propter hominum necessitudinem et propter aequita-

---

115 auspicato *Karsten*: aut illo *VMψεπ (at cf. §56* ex hoc loco; *tradita def. Krostenko 2023, 107 adn. i)*: autem illo *E*
116 non vobis quirites *C. F. W. Müller*: ne vobis quidem *ω*
117 sicque: *corr. Madvig*
118 *add. Naugerius*

DE LEGE AGRARIA 2.55–57

And in selling all these lands and buildings the Decemvirs are allowed to sell them in whatever places they think fit.[82] What perversity! What licentiousness that deserves to be checked! What profligate and abandoned schemes! It is not permitted to farm out the revenues anywhere except in this city, from this inaugurated place, with this full assembly of yours. Shall it be lawful for our property to be sold and alienated from us forever in the obscurity of Paphlagonia or the deserts of Cappadocia? When Lucius Sulla sold the goods of citizens who had not been convicted at that lamentable auction of his and declared that he was selling his plunder, he nevertheless sold it from this place and did not venture to avoid the gaze of those whose eyes he offended.[83] Shall the Decemvirs sell your revenues not only without your presence, Romans, but without even a public crier as a witness?

Next follows: "all the lands outside Italy" with no time limit, not as before, beginning with the consulship of Sulla and Pompeius;[84] an inquiry by the Decemvirs whether the land is private or public; and upon such land a heavy tax is imposed. Who can fail to perceive how extensive, intolerable, and despotic this jurisdiction is—to be able, wherever they choose, without any debate, without a council, to make what is private property public and to exempt public property from taxes? In this section the Recentoric district in Sicily is excepted; and the exception gives me great pleasure, Romans, both on account of my close friendship with the inhabitants and because of the justice

[82] On the probable reason for this provision, see on 1.7.
[83] On this incident, cf. van der Blom 2017.
[84] Cf. §38 with note.

tem rei ipsius, Quirites,[119] vehementer gaudeo. Sed quid hoc impudentius?[120] Qui agrum Recentoricum possident, vetustate possessionis se, non iure, misericordia senatus, non agri condicione defendunt. Nam illum agrum publicum esse fatentur; se moveri possessionibus, antiquissimis[121] sedibus, ac dis penatibus negant oportere. Ac, si est privatus ager Recentoricus, quid eum excipis? Sin autem publicus, quae est ista aequitas ceteros, etiam si privati sint, permittere ut publici iudicentur, hunc excipere nominatim quem publicum esse fatentur?[122] Ergo eorum ager excipitur qui apud Rullum aliqua[123] ratione valuerunt, ceteri agri omnes qui ubique sunt sine ullo dilectu, sine populi Romani notione, sine iudicio senatus decemviris addicentur? Atque etiam est alia superiore capite quo omnia veneunt quaestuosa exceptio, quae teget eos agros de quibus foedere cautum est. Audivit hanc rem non a me, sed ab aliis agitari saepe in senatu, nonnumquam ex hoc loco, possidere agros in ora maritima regem Hiempsalem quos P. Africanus populo Romano adiudicarit; ei[124] tamen postea per C. Cottam consulem cautum esse foedere. Hoc

[119] aequitatem rei ipsius quirites *C. F. W. Müller in app.*: aequitatem quirites saepe ω

[120] hoc impudentius *cod. Torr. (cf. Shackleton Bailey 1979, 256)*: haec impudentia ω

[121] antiquissimis *Lauredanus*: amicissimis *eV¹Mn alii*: a maximis *E*

[122] quem publicum esse fatentur *Coraluppi*: qui publicus esse fateatur ω

[123] alia: *corr. Madvig*

[124] et: *corr. Lambinus*

DE LEGE AGRARIA 2.57–58

of the decision itself. But what could be more impudent than this? Those who occupy the Recentoric district defend themselves on the plea of longstanding occupation, not of right, relying on the sympathy of the senate, not on the status of the land. For they confess that it is public land, but say that they should not be dispossessed and driven from their ancient homes and household gods. And if the Recentoric district is private land, why do you except it? But if it is public, what is the justice in allowing other lands, even if they are private, to be adjudged public, and to except by name this one, which they acknowledge to be public property? Is then an exception made for the land of those men who for some reason had influence with Rullus, while all other lands, wherever they may be, without distinction, without any judicial inquiry by the Roman people, without the verdict of the senate, are to be handed over to the Decemvirs?[85] In addition, there is another 58 lucrative exception in the preceding section that authorizes the general sale, an exception covering those lands that are protected by a treaty. He heard that this matter was often discussed not by me but by others in the senate and sometimes from this place, that King Hiempsal possessed coastal territories that Publius Africanus assigned to the Roman people; but that nonetheless a guarantee was afterward given to him by a treaty through the agency of the consul Gaius Cotta.[86] But because you did not order

---

[85] On the Recentoric district, see 1.10–11, where Cicero likewise suggests that bribery is at play.

[86] For Hiempsal II, who ruled a Numidia reduced in size after Jugurtha's defeat, cf. Lenschau, *RE* s.v. Hiempsal 2. The treaty was concluded by C. Aurelius Cotta, cos. 75: *MRR* 2:96.

CICERO

quia vos foedus non iusseritis, veretur Hiempsal ut satis firmum sit et ratum. Cuicuimodi[125] est illud, tollitur vestrum iudicium, foedus totum accipitur,[126] comprobatur. Quod minuit auctionem decemviralem laudo, quod regi amico cavet non reprehendo, quod non gratis fit indico.

59 Volitat enim ante oculos istorum Iuba,[127] regis filius, adulescens non minus bene nummatus quam bene capillatus.

Vix iam videtur locus esse qui tantos acervos pecuniae capiat; auget, addit, accumulat. "Aurum, argentum ex praeda, ex manubiis, ex coronario ad quoscumque pervenit neque relatum est in publicum neque in monumento consumptum," id profiteri apud decemviros et ad eos referre iubet. Hoc capite etiam quaestionem de clarissimis viris qui populi Romani bella gesserunt, iudiciumque de pecuniis repetundis[128] ad decemviros translatum videtis. Horum erit nunc[129] iudicium quantae cuiusque manubiae fuerint, quid relatum, quid residuum sit; in posterum vero lex haec imperatoribus vestris[130] constituitur, ut quicumque de provincia decesserit, apud eosdem decemviros

---

[125] cuicuimodi *Madvig*: quid? cuiusmodi ω
[126] accipitur *Pluygers*: excipitur ans: excipit VMψ
[127] iubae: *corr. Lauredanus*
[128] residuis *Clark, fort. recte; textum traditum def. Krostenko* 258 *adn.* i
[129] nunc ς *Lauredanus*: nullum ωπ: nunc iam *Pluygers*
[130] nostris VMψ

---

[87] Plural "you": that is, it had not been submitted to the people for ratification. Hiempsal might well be uncertain: in earliest times the senate alone ratified treaties, later important treaties were presented to the people, but popular ratification came to be

DE LEGE AGRARIA 2.58–59

this treaty to be made, Hiempsal is afraid that it is not binding and ratified.[87] However that may be, your judgment is done away with, the entire treaty is accepted and approved. In that it restricts the Decemvirs' auctioning, I approve of it; in that it gives a guarantee to a friendly king, I do not disapprove of it; but I reveal that the transaction is not free of charge. For before those men's eyes flutters the king's son Juba, a young man no less well endowed with money than with hair.[88]

There now hardly seems room to hold such great heaps of money; he amplifies, adds, accumulates. "The gold and silver from plunder, from spoils, from material for making crowns, to whatever people they have passed, and which have never been paid into the public treasury nor spent on a monument," he orders that this be declared before the Decemvirs and be placed at their disposal. According to this section, you see that even an investigation of the most distinguished men who have waged the wars of the Roman people and their trial for extortion is transferred to the Decemvirs. They will now have the power of judging the quantity of the spoils that belonged to each general, what has been paid into the treasury and what is left over. For the future, this law is established for your generals that, when any of them leaves his province, he shall make a declaration before the same Decemvirs as to how

---

disregarded after Sulla. Cf. Mommsen 1887–1888, 3.2:1159–60, 1170–73.

[88] Juba I, son of Hiempsal II, insulted by Caesar during an embassy to Rome (Suet. *Iul.* 71), joined Pompey in the civil war, and committed suicide after the defeat of Pompeian forces at Thapsus; cf. *OCD* s.v. Juba (1).

quantum habeat praedae, manubiarum, auri coronarii,
60 profiteatur. Hic tamen vir optimus eum quem amat excipit, Cn. Pompeium. Unde iste amor tam improvisus ac tam repentinus? Qui honore decemviratus excluditur prope nominatim, cuius iudicium legumque datio, captorum agrorum ipsius virtute cognitio tollitur, cuius non in provinciam, sed in ipsa castra decemviri cum imperio, infinita pecunia, maxima potestate et iudicio rerum omnium mittuntur, cui ius imperatorium, quod semper omnibus imperatoribus est conservatum, soli eripitur, is excipitur unus ne manubias referre debeat. Utrum tandem hoc capite honos haberi homini an invidia quaeri videtur?
61 Remittit hoc Rullo Cn. Pompeius; beneficio isto legis, benignitate decemvirali nihil utitur. Nam si est aequum praedam ac manubias suas imperatores non in monumenta deorum immortalium neque in urbis ornamenta conferre, sed ad decemviros tamquam ad dominos reportare, nihil sibi appetit praecipue[131] Pompeius, nihil; vult se in communi atque in eodem quo ceteri iure versari. Sin est iniquum, Quirites, si turpe, si intolerandum hos decemviros portitores omnibus omnium pecuniis constitui, qui non modo reges atque exterarum nationum homines sed etiam imperatores vestros[132] excutiant, non mihi videntur honoris causa excipere Pompeium, sed metuere ne ille eandem contumeliam quam ceteri ferre non possit.
62 Pompeius autem hoc animo est[133] ut, quicquid vobis pla-

[131] praecipui *Orelli, fort. recte*   [132] vestros *Eπ*: nostros *cett.*   [133] sit: *corr. Garatoni*

---

[89] That is, for administration of the conquered territory; cf. §52 and note.

much plunder, spoils, and crown gold he has. Yet this excellent man has excepted Pompey, the object of his affection. What is the origin of this totally unforeseen and sudden fondness? The man who is almost by name excluded from the honor of the Decemvirate, who is deprived of jurisdiction and the imposition of terms,[89] of investigating the lands captured by his valor, not only into whose province, but even into whose very camp, the Decemvirs are sent with military authority, with unlimited sums of money, with absolute power and jurisdiction over all matters, from whom alone the rights of a general, which have always been preserved for all generals, are snatched away—that one man is exempted from having to return the spoils. Does this section seem to honor the man or to stir envy for him?

Gnaeus Pompeius rejects this offer of Rullus'; he makes no use of that legal favor or the kindness of the Decemvirs. For if it is just for our generals not to devote their plunder and spoils to monuments to the immortal gods or to the embellishment of the city, but to bring them to the Decemvirs as if to their masters, then Pompey wants nothing for himself in particular, nothing; he wishes to live under rights that are common and the same as the rest. But if it is unjust, Romans, if it is disgraceful, if it is intolerable for these Decemvirs to be appointed toll collectors over absolutely everybody's money, for them to examine not only kings and men of foreign nations, but even your generals, it seems to me that Pompey is not excepted to do him honor, but that they are afraid that he may not be able to submit to the same insult as the rest. But Pompey's attitude is that he thinks he must submit to whatever you approve of; but what you cannot submit to, he will cer-

ceat, sibi ferendum putet, quod vos ferre non poteritis, id profecto perficiet[134] ne diutius inviti ferre cogamini. Verum tamen cavet ut, si qua pecunia post nos consules ex novis vectigalibus recipiatur, ea decemviri utantur. Nova porro vectigalia videt ea fore quae Pompeius adiunxerit. Ita remissis manubiis vectigalibus eius virtute partis se frui putat oportere. Parta sit pecunia, Quirites, decemviris tanta quanta sit in terris, nihil praetermissum sit,[135] omnes urbes, agri, regna denique, postremo etiam vectigalia vestra venierint, accesserint in cumulum manubiae vestrorum imperatorum; quantae et quam immanes divitiae decemviris in tantis auctionibus, tot iudiciis, tam infinita potestate rerum omnium quaerantur videtis.

63 Cognoscite nunc alios immensos atque intolerabilis quaestus, ut intellegatis ad certorum hominum importunam avaritiam hoc populare legis agrariae nomen esse quaesitum. Hac pecunia iubet agros emi quo deducamini.[136] Non consuevi homines appellare asperius, Quirites, nisi lacessitus. Vellem[137] fieri posset ut a me sine contumelia nominarentur ei qui se decemviros sperant futuros; iam videretis quibus hominibus omnium rerum et vendendarum et emendarum potestatem permitteretis.

64 Sed quod ego nondum statuo mihi esse dicendum, vos tamen id potestis cum animis vestris cogitare. Unum hoc certe videor mihi verissime posse dicere: tum cum haberet haec res publica Luscinos, Calatinos, Acidinos, homines non solum honoribus populi rebusque gestis verum etiam

---

[134] perficiet *edd. post ed. Ven.*: perficiat ω
[135] sed: *corr. Lauredanus*   [136] quo deducamini *Naugerius*: quo(d) decumani $E\pi VM\psi$: quod decumana $e\epsilon$: quo decumatu $n\chi^2$ [137] velim: *corr. Ernesti*

tainly take care that you are no longer compelled to submit to it against your will. However, the law provides that, if any money is received from any new sources of revenue after our consulship, it shall be at the disposal of the Decemvirs. Moreover, he sees that the new sources of revenue will be those added by Pompey. Accordingly, he forgoes the spoils, but thinks that he ought to enjoy the revenues obtained by his valor. Let the Decemvirs possess all the money that there is in the world, Romans; let nothing be passed over; let all cities, lands, kingdoms, and lastly, even your revenues be sold; let the spoils obtained by your generals be added to the heap. You see what enormous and immense wealth is the object of the Decemvirs in these sales on so large a scale, in so many decisions, in their unbounded power over all things.

Now learn some other enormous and insufferable gains, in order to understand that this name of agrarian law dear to the people has been sought out in order to satisfy certain individuals' insatiable avarice. With this money he orders lands to be bought, on which you may be settled as colonists. I am not in the habit, Romans, of calling men by too harsh a name, unless I am provoked. I would wish it were possible that those men who hope to be Decemvirs could be named by me without insult; you would see at once to what kind of men you would grant the power of buying and selling everything. But what I think I ought not to mention yet, you can nonetheless imagine. There is one thing that I certainly think I can say with perfect truth: at the time when this republic had men like Luscinus, Calatinus, and Acidinus, men not only distinguished by the honors conferred upon them by the people and their own achievements, but also by their en-

CICERO

patientia paupertatis ornatos, et tum cum erant Catones, Phili,[138] Laelii, quorum sapientiam temperantiamque in publicis privatisque, forensibus domesticisque rebus perspexeratis, tamen huiusce modi res commissa nemini est ut idem iudicaret et venderet et hoc faceret per quinquennium toto in orbe terrarum idemque agros vectigalis populi Romani abalienaret et, cum summam tantae pecuniae nullo teste sibi ipse ex sua voluntate fecisset, tum 65 denique emeret a quibus vellet quod videretur. Committite vos nunc, Quirites, his hominibus haec omnia quos odorari hunc decemviratum suspicamini; reperietis partem esse eorum quibus ad habendum, partem quibus ad consumendum nihil satis esse videatur. Hic ego iam illud quod expeditissimum est[139] ne disputo quidem, Quirites, non esse hanc nobis a maioribus relictam consuetudinem ut emantur agri a privatis quo plebes publice deducatur; omnibus legibus agris publicis privatos esse deiectos.[140] Huiusce modi me aliquid ab hoc horrido ac truce tribuno plebis fateor[141] exspectasse; hanc vero emendi et vendendi quaestuosissimam ac turpissimam mercaturam alienam actione tribunicia, alienam dignitate populi Romani sem- 66 per putavi. Iubet[142] agros emi. Primum quaero, quos agros

[138] philippi: *corr. Sigonius*   [139] sit: *corr. Wesenberg*
[140] deiectos *Clark in app.*: deductos ω
[141] fateor V^c *in marg., Lag.9: om. cett.*   [142] iubet α: lubet π

[90] A series of heroes from earlier Roman history: C. Fabricius Luscinus (cos. 282 and 278, cens. 275); A. Atilius Calatinus (cos. 258 and 254, dictator 249, cens. 247); L. Manlius Acidinus (pr. urb. 210) or L. Manlius Acidinus Fulvianus (cos. 179); M. Porcius Cato (cos. 195, cens. 184); L. Furius Philus (cos. 136); C. Laelius

DE LEGE AGRARIA 2.64–66

durance of poverty; also during the lifetime of the Catos, the Phili, and the Laelii, with whose wisdom and moderation in public, private, forensic, and domestic affairs you were well acquainted, no such power as this was ever given to anyone:[90] to act both as judge and seller, and that for a term of five years, throughout the world; to alienate the revenue lands of the Roman people and then, after having amassed so large a sum of money for himself, without any witness and according to his pleasure, finally to buy whatever seemed good to him from anyone whom he chose. Entrust now, Romans, all these powers to these men whom you suspect of sniffing after this Decemvirate; you will find some of them who never think they have enough to keep, and others who never think they have enough to squander. Here I do not even argue a point which is absolutely clear, Romans—that our ancestors left us no such custom as that of buying lands from private persons, on which the common people might be settled as colonists; that by all laws it was from public lands that private persons were dislodged.[91] I confess that I expected some plan of this kind from this bristling and gruff tribune of the plebs,[92] but I have always considered this most lucrative and most disgraceful traffic in buying and selling inconsistent with the functions of a tribune, inconsistent with the dignity of the Roman people. He orders lands to be bought. I first ask, what lands and in what places? I do not

(cos. 140). The *a fortiori* argument is that if these men received no such powers, Rullus and his supporters can hardly be worthy of them.   [91] Manuwald 2018, xiii–xvii, surveys previous Roman agrarian laws.   [92] For Rullus' demeanor and turnout as plebeian tribune, see §13 with note.

et quibus in locis? Nolo suspensam et incertam plebem Romanam obscura spe et caeca exspectatione pendere. Albanus ager est, Setinus, Privernas, Fundanus, Vescinus,[143] Falernus, Literninus,[144] Cumanus, †ancasianas.[145] Audio. Ab alia porta Capenas, Faliscus, Sabinus ager, Reatinus; ⟨ab alia⟩[146] Venafranus,[147] Allifanus, Trebulanus. Habes tantam pecuniam qua hosce omnis agros et ceteros horum similis non modo emere verum etiam coacervare possis; cur eos non definis neque nominas, ut saltem deliberare plebes Romana possit quid intersit sua, quid expediat, quantum tibi in emendis et in vendendis rebus committendum putet? "Definio," inquit, "Italiam." Satis certa regio! Etenim quantulum interest utrum in Massici radices, an in Silam silvam[148] aliove deducamini? Age, non definis locum. Quid? Naturam agri? "Vero," inquit, "qui arari aut coli possit." "Qui possit arari," inquit, "aut coli," non qui aratus aut cultus sit. Utrum haec lex est, an tabula Vera-

67

---

[143] vescinus *ed. Ven.*: festivus *Ee*: festinus π: fescinus ε: vestinus *cett.*

[144] Literninus *Gebhard*: liternius *E*: licernus ε: liternus *cett.*

[145] ancasianas: casinas ς, *alii alia*

[146] *add. Kayser*

[147] Venafranus *Lag.9*: veneranus ω

[148] Silam silvam *C. F. W. Müller in app.*: italiam ω

---

93 A list of names moving from north to south down the Appian Way, the last item corrupt; cf. Vasaly 1988, 416.

94 The two gates will be, respectively, the Porta Flaminia at the Via Flaminia, going north from Rome, and the Porta Latina at the Via Latina, going southeast from Rome. Cicero's lists comprise some of the richest farmland of Italy; Trebula is less than

wish the Roman plebs to be in suspense and uncertainty and dependent upon obscure hopes and blind expectation. There are the lands of Alba, Setia, Privernum, Fundi, Vescia, Falernum, Liternum, Cumae, . . .[93] I hear. Going out by one gate, we have the territory of Capena, the Falisci, the Sabine country, Reate, by the other Venafrum, Allifae, and Trebula.[94] You have so much wealth that you can not only buy all these lands and others like them, but heap them all together; why do you not define and name them, that the Roman plebs may at least be able to consider what its interest is, what is to its advantage, how much discretion it thinks ought to be given to you in buying and selling things? "I do define Italy," he says. A very clearly marked district![95] For how little difference does it make to you, gentlemen, whether you are settled at the foot of the Massic mountain, in the Silan forest, or somewhere else?[96] Well then, you do not define the spot. What of the nature of the soil? "But," he says, "land that can be plowed or cultivated." "That can be plowed or cultivated," he says, not that has been plowed or cultivated. Is this a law, or an advertisement of a sale by Veratius,[97] where they

five Roman miles from Capua, which is being held in reserve. Cf. Vasaly 1988, 417–18.

[95] Whether Italy should be taken in a political or a geographical sense is ambiguous; cf. Manuwald 2018, 127.

[96] The Massic mountain, located near the Appian Way between Campania and Latium, was noted for its wines. The Silan forest was a mountainous area in Bruttium (in the toe of Italy).

[97] Possibly the P. Fulvius Veratius mentioned as the guarantor of a loan at *Flac.* 46, otherwise unknown. In both passages Neratius is a less well-attested variant reading.

tianae auctionis? In qua scriptum fuisse aiunt: "Iugera cc in quibus olivetum fieri potest, iugera ccc ubi institui vineae possunt." Hoc tu emes ista innumerabili pecunia quod arari aut coli possit? Quod solum tam exile et[149] macrum est quod aratro perstringi non possit, aut quod est tam asperum saxetum in quo agricolarum cultus non elaboret? "Idcirco," inquit, "agros nominare non possum quia tangam nullum ab invito." Hoc, Quirites, multo est quaestuosius quam si ab invito sumeret; inibitur[150] enim ratio quaestus de vestra pecunia, et tum denique ager emetur cum idem expediet emptori et venditori.

68 Sed videte vim legis agrariae. Ne ei quidem qui agros publicos possident decedent de possessione, nisi erunt deducti optima condicione et pecunia maxima. Conversa ratio. Antea, cum erat a tribuno plebis mentio legis agrariae facta, continuo qui agros publicos aut qui possessiones invidiosas tenebant extimescebant;[151] haec lex eos homines fortunis locupletat, invidia liberat. Quam multos enim, Quirites, existimatis esse qui latitudinem possessionum tueri, qui invidiam Sullanorum agrorum ferre non possint, qui vendere cupiant, emptorem non reperiant, perdere iam denique illos agros ratione aliqua velint? Qui paulo ante diem noctemque tribunicium nomen horrebant, vestram vim metuebant, mentionem legis agrariae pertimescebant, ei nunc etiam ultro rogabuntur atque

[149] aut *VMṣck*
[150] inibitur *in marg. Ascens.*: inhibetur *aLag.8,13*: inietur *cett.*
[151] expertimescebant: *corr. R. Klotz*

---

[98] The Roman measure of land, the *iugerum*, was actually about two-thirds of an acre: *OLD* s.v.

DE LEGE AGRARIA 2.67–68

say it was written, "Two hundred acres in which an olive grove may be planted, three hundred acres where a vineyard can be established"?[98] Is this what you intend to buy with such an enormous amount of money—land that can be plowed or cultivated? What soil is so poor and thin that it cannot be broken up by the plow, or what stony ground is so rough that a man cannot spend his labor in cultivating it? "The reason," he says, "why I cannot name the lands is that I shall not touch any land belonging to one who does not want to sell." This, Romans, is far more lucrative than if he took it from one who did not want to sell. For they will reckon up the profit (to be made) from your money, gentlemen; and then and only then will the land be bought when the same price shall be advantageous to both purchaser and seller.

But consider the force of the agrarian law. Even those who possess public lands will not give up possession unless they are induced by very advantageous terms and a large sum of money. But the system is changed. Formerly, when a tribune suggested an agrarian law, those who occupied public lands, or had possessions that made them unpopular, immediately began to be alarmed. This law makes them wealthy and frees them from unpopularity. For how many people, Romans, do you think there are who cannot defend the extent of their possessions, or cannot endure the unpopularity attached to the lands given by Sulla; who want to sell them but fail to find a purchaser and would by now finally want to get rid of those fields on any terms whatever? Those who a little while ago shuddered at the name of tribune day and night, who dreaded your violence, who trembled at the suggestion of an agrarian law, will now be themselves asked and entreated to hand over

orabuntur ut agros partim publicos, partim plenos invidiae, plenos periculi quanti ipsi velint decemviris tradant. Atque hoc carmen hic tribunus plebis non vobis, sed sibi intus canit. Habet socerum, virum optimum, qui tantum agri in illis rei publicae tenebris occupavit quantum concupivit. Huic subvenire vult succumbenti iam et oppresso, Sullanis oneribus gravi, sua lege, ut liceat illi invidiam deponere, pecuniam condere. Et vos non dubitatis quin vectigalia vestra vendatis plurimo maiorum vestrorum sanguine et sudore quaesita, ut Sullanos possessores divitiis augeatis, periculo liberetis? Nam ad hanc emptionem decemviralem duo genera agrorum spectant, Quirites. Eorum unum propter invidiam domini fugiunt, alterum propter vastitatem. Sullanus ager a certis hominibus latissime continuatus tantam habet invidiam ut veri ac fortis tribuni plebis stridorem unum perferre non possit.[152] Hic ager omnis, quoquo pretio coemptus erit, tamen ingenti pecunia nobis inducetur. Alterum genus agrorum propter sterilitatem incultum, propter pestilentiam vastum atque desertum emetur ab eis qui eos vident sibi esse, si non vendiderint, relinquendos. Et nimirum illud[153] est quod

[152] posset: *corr. Naugerius*   [153] idem: *corr. C. F. W. Müller*

[99] A proverbial phrase that suggests acting in self-interest; cf. Otto 1890 s.v. Aspendius; *OLD* s.v. *intus* 4b; Krostenko 2023, 233–34 and nn. 57–58, 60.   [100] For Rullus' father-in-law see on 1.14.   [101] For *stridor* denoting a witch's shriek, cf. Krostenko 2023, 235–36.

[102] At a subsequent assembly called by himself, Rullus flung back this charge, claiming that Cicero was the one acting in the interests of the Sullan possessors (3.1 and 3). Though Cicero

to the Decemvirs, at whatever price they like, lands some of which are public, others which make the owners very unpopular and are full of danger to them. And this tribune of the plebs is singing this song, not for you, but for himself.[99] He has a father-in-law, an excellent man, who in those dark days of the republic laid his hands upon as much land as he coveted.[100] By means of his law Rullus wishes to help this man, now that he is giving way and crushed, weighed down by his Sullan burdens, so that he may be allowed to lay down his unpopularity and to lay up his cash. And do you not hesitate to sell your revenues acquired by your ancestors at the cost of so much blood and sweat, in order to increase the wealth of the owners of Sullan allotments and to free them from danger? For two kinds of lands, Romans, are concerned in these purchases of the Decemvirs. The owners of one of them shun it because of the odium attached to it; they shun the other because of its desolate condition. The lands that come from Sulla, widely extended by certain persons, excite such indignation that they cannot endure it, if a genuine and courageous tribune of the plebs utters one shriek.[101] All this land, at whatever price it is bought, will be charged to us at a huge price.[102] The other kind of lands, uncultivated owing to their barrenness, wasted and abandoned owing to their pestilential unhealthiness, will be purchased from those who see that they must abandon them if they have not sold them. And of course this is the point

69

70

raises the specter of Sulla repeatedly before the people, he hardly does so at all before the senate (1.3 and 1.21); cf. Classen 1985, 313.

ab hoc tribuno plebis dictum est in senatu, urbanam plebem nimium in re publica posse; exhauriendam esse; hoc enim ⟨verbo⟩[154] est usus, quasi de aliqua sentina ac non de optimorum civium genere loqueretur!

71 Vos vero, Quirites, si me audire vultis, retinete istam possessionem gratiae, libertatis, suffragiorum, dignitatis, urbis, fori, ludorum, festorum dierum, ceterorum omnium commodorum, nisi forte mavultis relictis his rebus atque hac luce rei publicae in Sipontina siccitate aut in Salpinorum pestilentia[155] Rullo duce collocari. Aut[156] dicat quos agros empturus sit; ostendat et quid et quibus daturus sit. Ut vero, cum omnes urbes, agros, vectigalia, regna vendiderit, tum harenam aliquam aut paludes emat, id vos potestis, quaeso, concedere? Quamquam illud est egregium quod hac lege ante omnia veneunt, ante pecuniae coguntur et coacervantur quam gleba una ematur.

72 Deinde emi iubet, ab invito vetat. Quaero, si qui velint vendere non fuerint, quid pecuniae fiet? [Et][157] Referre in aerarium lex vetat, exigi prohibet. Igitur pecuniam omnem decemviri tenebunt, vobis ager non emetur: vectigalibus abalienatis, sociis vexatis, regibus atque omnibus gentibus exinanitis illi pecunias habebunt, vos agros non

---

[154] *add. ed. Hervagiana*

[155] pestilentia *Boulanger (cf. 1.15; OLD s.v. pestilentia 2)*: pestilentiae finibus ω: plenis pestilentiae finibus *Clark*

[156] aut *Turnebus*: atsi *e*ϵ: at *cett.*

[157] *del. Angelius*

---

[103] Seeking to stir outrage by pointing to Rullus' hypocrisy in promoting his land bill with one argument in the senate but a different one before the general public. Cicero himself used

DE LEGE AGRARIA 2.70–72

that was made by this plebeian tribune in the senate, that the urban plebs has too much power in the republic; that they ought to be drained off. For this is the word that he used, as if he were speaking of sewage instead of a class of excellent citizens![103]

But you, Romans, if you are willing to be guided by me, keep that possession of influence, liberty, votes, standing, the city, the forum, the games, the festivals, and all the other benefits; unless perhaps you prefer to abandon these privileges and this brilliant republic,[104] and settle in the dry sands of Sipontum or in the pestilential swamps of the Salapians, with Rullus as your leader. Or let him tell us what lands he intends to purchase; let him declare what he is going to give, and to whom. But after he has sold all your cities, lands, revenues, and kingdoms, I ask you, can you then allow him to buy some tract of sand or marshes? And yet it is an extraordinary thing that by this law everything is sold, the money got together first and heaped up before a single clod of earth is bought. Then the law orders land to be bought, but forbids anyone being forced to sell. I ask, if there are none who want to sell, what is to be done with the money? The law forbids its being paid in to the treasury; it prohibits its being demanded [from the Decemvirs]. So then the Decemvirs will hold all the money, and no land will be bought for you; your revenues will be transferred, your allies annoyed, kings and all nations exhausted; they will have the money, you will have no lands.

71

72

similar language in private correspondence in discussing the later land bill of L. Flavius: *Att.* 1.19[19].4; cf. Kühnert 1989.

[104] Literally, "the light of the republic"; cf. Pieper 2020, 211 and n. 6; Krostenko 2023, 176.

habebitis. "Facile," inquit, "adducentur pecuniae magnitudine ut velint vendere." Ergo ea lex est qua nostra vendamus quanti possimus, aliena emamus quanti possessores velint.

73 Atque in hos agros qui hac lege empti sint colonias ab his decemviris deduci iubet. Quid? Omnisne locus eius modi est ut nihil intersit rei publicae, colonia deducatur in eum locum necne, an est locus qui coloniam postulet, est ⟨qui⟩ plane recuset?[158] Quo in genere sicut in ceteris rei publicae partibus est operae pretium diligentiam maiorum recordari, qui colonias sic idoneis in locis contra suspicionem periculi collocarunt ut esse non oppida Italiae, sed propugnacula imperi viderentur. Hi deducent colonias in eos agros quos emerint. Etiamne si rei publicae non
74 expediat? "Et in quae loca praeterea videbitur." Quid igitur est causae quin coloniam in Ianiculum possint deducere et suum praesidium in capite atque cervicibus nostris collocare? Tu non definias quo⟨t⟩[159] colonias, in quae loca, quo numero colonorum deduci velis, tu occupes locum quem idoneum ad vim tuam iudicaris, compleas numero, confirmes praesidio quo velis, populi Romani vectigalibus atque omnibus copiis ipsum populum Romanum coerceas, opprimas, redigas in istam decemviralem dicionem
75 ac potestatem? Ut vero totam Italiam suis praesidiis obsidere atque occupare cogitet, quaeso, Quirites, cognoscite. Permittit decemviris ut in omnia municipia, in omnis colo-

---

158 est qui plane recuset *Lauredanus*: est plane rectius et ω
159 *corr. Lauredanus*

---

105 See on 1.16.

DE LEGE AGRARIA 2.72–75

"It will be easy," he says, "to induce them to be willing to sell by offering a large price." So then this is a law by which we are to sell our property for as much as we can, and to buy other people's property at whatever price the owners choose to ask for it.

And he orders colonies to be established by these Decemvirs in the lands that are bought under this law. Tell me: Is every place of such a kind that it makes no difference to the republic whether a colony is established there or not, or is there a place which asks for a colony or which absolutely refuses it? In this type of thing, as in other departments of the republic, it is worthwhile to remember the mindfulness of our ancestors, who established colonies in suitable places to guard against the suspicion of danger in such a way that they appeared to be not so much towns of Italy as bulwarks of an empire. These men will settle colonies in the lands that they have bought. Will they do so even if it is not to the interest of the republic? "And in whatever places besides it shall seem good to them." What, then, is to prevent them from being able to settle a colony on the Janiculum and place their garrison on our heads and necks?[105] Should you not specify how many colonies you wish to be established, in what places, and with how many colonists? Are you going to seize any place that you have judged convenient for your deeds of violence, to fill it with such numbers, to strengthen it with such garrisons as you wish, to use the revenues and all the resources of the Roman people to coerce and crush the Roman people itself and bring it under that Decemviral sway and power? I beg you, Romans, take note of how he designs to besiege and occupy the whole of Italy with his garrisons. He authorizes the Decemvirs to lead any colo-

73

74

75

CICERO

nias totius Italiae colonos deducant quos velint, eisque colonis agros dari iubet. Num obscure maiores opes quam libertas vestra pati potest et maiora praesidia quaeruntur, num obscure regnum constituitur, num obscure libertas vestra tollitur? Nam cum idem omnem pecuniam, maximam multitudinem ‹. . .›,[160] idem totam Italiam suis opibus obsidebunt, idem vestram libertatem suis praesidiis et coloniis interclusam tenebunt, quae spes tandem, quae facultas recuperandae vestrae libertatis relinquetur?

76 "At enim ager Campanus hac lege dividetur orbi[161] terrae pulcherrimus et Capuam colonia deducetur, urbem amplissimam atque ornatissimam."[162] Quid ad haec possumus dicere? De commodo prius vestro dicam, Quirites; deinde ad amplitudinem et dignitatem revertar, ut, si quis agri aut oppidi bonitate delectetur,[163] ne quid exspectet, si quem rei indignitas[164] commovet, ut huic simulatae largitioni resistat. Ac primum de oppido dicam, si quis est forte quem Capua magis quam Roma delectet. Quinque milia colonorum Capuam scribi iubet; ad hunc numerum quin-

[160] *lac. indicavit Boulanger; possis e.g.* opportunissima loca comparaverint
[161] orbe $a\pi n\chi^2$
[162] *post* ornatissimam *hab.* VMψ atque: *del.* Ernesti
[163] delectatur *Lambinus*: delectentur E
[164] indignitas VMψ: dignitas $an\chi^2$

DE LEGE AGRARIA 2.75–76

nists they choose into all the municipalities and all colonies of the whole of Italy, and he orders lands to be assigned to those colonists. Is it not evident that greater resources than your liberty can tolerate and larger garrisons are what he is looking for? Is it not clear that royal power is being set up, is it not clear that your liberty is being destroyed? For when the same men ... all wealth[106] and a vast population, the same men shall by their resources hold all Italy under siege, and the same men shall also have your liberty hemmed in by their garrisons and colonies, what hope, what means of recovering your liberty will be left?[107]

"But the land of Campania, the most beautiful in the world, will be divided by this law, and a colony will be brought to Capua, a very large and magnificent city." What can we say to this? In the first place, I will speak of your interest, Romans; then I will return to the question of your grandeur and standing, so that if anyone is charmed by the excellence of the soil or town, he may not expect anything, but if someone is roused by the outrageousness of the matter, he may resist this pretended largesse. And first I will speak about the town, if perchance there is anyone for whom Capua has a greater charm than Rome. He orders five thousand colonists to be enrolled for Capua; to make up this number they [the Decemvirs] each choose five

---

[106] The lacuna will contain a verb meaning "gather."

[107] For the "militarization" of the Rullan colonists, which continues in the sequel, cf. Vasaly 1988, 418–19; Krostenko 2023, 294 and n. 11. For the argument that the accumulation of power was a danger to Romans' liberty, cf. Arena 2012, 239–40; Krostenko 2023, ch. 4.

77 genos[165] sibi singuli sumunt. Quaeso, nolite vosmet ipsos consolari; vere et diligenter considerate. Num vobis aut vestri similibus, integris, quietis, otiosis hominibus[166] in hoc numero locum fore putatis? Si est omnibus vobis maiori‹ve›[167] vestrum parti, quam‹quam›[168] me vester honos vigilare dies atque noctes et intentis oculis omnis rei publicae partis intueri iubet, tamen paulisper, si ita commodum vestrum fert, conivebo.[169] Sed si quinque hominum milibus ad vim, facinus caedemque delectis locus atque urbs quae bellum facere atque instruere possit quaeritur, tamenne patiemini vestro nomine contra vos firmari opes, armari praesidia, urbes, agros, copias com-
78 parari? Nam agrum quidem Campanum, quem vobis ostentant, ipsi concupiverunt. Deducent suos, quorum nomine ipsi teneant et fruantur; coement[170] praeterea; ista dena iugera continuabunt. Nam si dicent per legem id non licere, ne per Corneliam quidem licet; at videmus, ut longinqua mittamus, agrum Praenestinum a paucis possideri.

[165] quinquagenos: *corr. Lauredanus*
[166] omnibus: *corr. Angelius*
[167] *corr. Richter*
[168] *corr. Angelius*
[169] conivebo *Angelius*: commovebo $α π M^1$: commonebo VM^c *cett.*
[170] coemant: *corr. Manutius*

---

[108] If places were not specified in Rullus' bill (§66), what was Cicero's source? Vasaly 1988, 412n7, suspects that Rullus may have mentioned this plan before the senate on January 1st (cf. §79). Cicero thought that five thousand colonists receiving ten

DE LEGE AGRARIA 2.76–78

hundred.[108] I beg you, do not deceive yourselves;[109] consider the proposal carefully and realistically. Do you think that there will be room among this number for you or those like you, people honorable, peaceful, fond of quiet? If there is room for all of you or the majority of you, although the office that I owe to you bids me keep watch day and night and keep my eyes focused on all departments of the republic,[110] yet I am ready, if it is to your advantage, to wink at it for a while. But if a place and city that is able to organize and make war is being sought for five thousand men, chosen with a view to violence, crime, and murder, will you nevertheless allow, in your name, resources to be strengthened, garrisons to be armed, cities, lands, and troops to be readied to oppose you? For they themselves have coveted the territory of Campania, which they dangle before you. They will settle their own people, in order that in their name they may hold and enjoy it themselves. They will buy up in addition; they will make their ten acres continuous. If they say this is forbidden by their law, it is even forbidden by the Cornelian Law;[111] and yet we see (to set aside the distant past) that the whole district of Praeneste is owned by a few individuals.[112] And I fail to see that these gentlemen lack any

77

78

iugera (ca. seven acres) each was the maximum the Campanian district could accommodate: *Att.* 2.16[36].1.

[109] Literally, "comfort yourselves," that is, with false hopes.

[110] For this self-presentation, cf. Pieper 2020, 221–25.

[111] The Cornelian Agrarian Law of 81, by which the dictator settled forty-seven legions on lands confiscated from victims of the proscriptions: *LPPR* 354; Livy, *per.* 89.12.

[112] Arguing the ineffectiveness of such prohibitions.

CICERO

Neque istorum pecuniis quicquam aliud deesse video nisi eius modi fundos quorum subsidio familiarum magnitudines et Cumanorum ac Puteolanorum praediorum sumptus sustentare possint. Quodsi vestrum commodum spectat, veniat et coram mecum de agri Campani divisione disputet.

79 Quaesivi ex eo Kalendis Ianuariis quibus hominibus et quem ad modum illum agrum esset distributurus. Respondit a Romilia tribu se initium esse facturum. Primum, quae est ista superbia et contumelia, ut populi pars amputetur, ordo tribuum neglegatur, ante rusticis detur ager, qui habent, quam urbanis, quibus ista agri spes et iucunditas ostenditur? Aut, si hoc ab se dictum negat et satisfacere omnibus vobis cogitat, proferat; in[171] iugera dena discribat,[172] a Suburana[173] usque ad Arniensem nomina vestra proponat. Si non modo dena iugera dari vobis sed ne constipari quidem tantum numerum hominum posse in agrum Campanum intellegetis, tamenne vexari rem publicam, contemni maiestatem populi Romani, deludi vosmet ipsos diutius a tribuno plebis patiemini?

80 Quodsi posset ager iste ad vos pervenire, nonne eum tamen in patrimonio vestro remanere malletis? Unumne fundum pulcherrimum populi Romani, caput vestrae pecuniae, pacis ornamentum, subsidium belli, fundamen-

[171] in: *del. Marek (at cf. OLD s.v. discribo 2)*
[172] describat: *corr. Kayser*
[173] a suburana *Lauredanus*: ab usura nam ωπ

---

[113] Compare the similar challenge at 1.23 and 3.16.
[114] Referring to the session of the senate at which he delivered *Leg. agr.* 1, but no such exchange is reflected in our text. The

DE LEGE AGRARIA 2.78–80

wealth except farms of such a kind that with their aid they can support the large households and the expenses of their estates at Cumae and Puteoli. But if Rullus has your interest in view, let him come and debate with me face to face about the division of the territory of Campania.[113]

I asked him on January 1st, to whom, and how, he intended to distribute that land. He replied that he would begin with the Romilian tribe.[114] In the first place, what kind of arrogance and insult is this, to cut off part of the Roman people and flout the order of the tribes; to assign land to the country people, who have it, before the city people, to whom the hope of the enjoyment of land is being held out? Or, if he denies that he said this and intends to satisfy all of you, let him bring forward his plan; let him divide his allotments into ten acres each and put forward your names from the Suburana[115] to the Arniensis.[116] If you recognize not only that ten acres apiece cannot be allotted to you, but that such a large number of people could not even be packed into Campanian territory, will you still allow the republic to be harassed, the majesty of the Roman people to be disdained, and yourselves to be deluded any longer by a tribune of the plebs?

But if this territory could be allotted to you, would you not prefer that it nonetheless remain a part of your patrimony? The Roman people's one most beautiful estate, the source of your wealth, the ornament of peace, the support

79

80

Romilian tribe was the first of the rural tribes, normally called after the four urban tribes; see Manuwald 2018, 357–58.

[115] The first of the urban tribes.

[116] The name is best attested thus (also at Livy 6.5.8). The organizing principle underlying Cicero's names is unclear; see Manuwald 2018, 359.

tum vectigalium, horreum legionum, solacium annonae disperire patiemini? An obliti estis Italico bello amissis ceteris vectigalibus quantos agri Campani fructibus exercitus alueritis? An ignoratis cetera illa magnifica populi Romani vectigalia perlevi saepe momento fortunae inclinatione temporis pendere? Quid nos Asiae portus, quid scriptura,[174] quid omnia transmarina vectigalia iuvabunt

81 tenuissima suspicione praedonum aut hostium iniecta? At vero hoc agri Campani vectigal cum eius modi sit ut cum domi sit et omnibus praesidiis oppidorum tegatur, tum neque bellis infestum nec fructibus varium nec caelo ac loco calamitosum esse soleat, maiores nostri non solum id quod ‹de›[175] Campanis ceperant non imminuerunt verum etiam quod ei[176] tenebant quibus adimi iure non poterat coemerunt. Qua de causa nec duo Gracchi, qui de plebis Romanae commodis plurimum cogitaverunt, nec L. Sulla, qui omnia sine ulla religione quibus voluit est dilargitus, agrum Campanum attingere ausus est. Rullus exstitit, qui ex ea possessione rem publicam demoveret ex qua nec Gracchorum benignitas eam nec Sullae dominatio deiecisset. Quem agrum nunc praetereuntes vestrum esse dicitis et quem per iter[177] qui faciunt externi homines vestrum esse audiunt, is, cum erit divisus, ‹neque erit›[178] ‹ve-

[174] scriptura *Gebhard*: syriae rura α: syriae cura *cett.*
[175] *add. Lauredanus*
[176] et: *corr. Lauredanus*
[177] per iter *E*: pariter *cett.*
[178] *suppl. ed. Hervagiana*

DE LEGE AGRARIA 2.80–81

in war, the basis of your revenues, the granary of the legions, the relief of the grain supply—will you allow it to perish? During the Italian war, when all your other revenues failed, have you forgotten how many armies you supported by the produce from the Campanian territory?[117] Or do you not know that the other splendid revenues of the Roman people often depend upon a slight change of fortune or alteration of circumstances? What will the harbors of Asia avail us, the grazing tax, and all the revenues overseas, if the slightest hint of pirates or enemies has been dropped? But since the revenues derived from the Campanian territory are such that they not only are domestic and are protected by all the garrisons of our towns but also are not threatened by wars, and their produce is not variable,[118] and is not liable to damage from weather or location, our ancestors not only refrained from diminishing what they had taken from the Campanians, but even bought up lands that were held by those who could not justly be deprived of it. For this reason neither the two Gracchi, who took most thought for the interests of the Roman plebs, nor Lucius Sulla, who without any scruples lavished everything on those whom he wished, dared to lay hands on the Campanian territory. Rullus came forward to expel the republic from that ownership of which neither the generosity of the Gracchi nor the absolute power of Sulla had dispossessed it! That land which you now say is yours when you pass by it, which foreigners, who travel through it, hear belongs to you, that land, when

---

[117] Referring to the Social War of 91 to 87, which led to the enfranchising of all Italy south of the Po.

[118] That is, the crop yield is consistently high; cf. §§82–83.

ster⟩[179] neque vester esse dicetur. At qui homines possidebunt? Primo quidem acres, ad vim prompti, ad seditionem parati, qui, simul ac decemviri concrepuerint, armati in civis et expediti ad caedem esse possint; deinde ad paucos opibus et copiis adfluentes totum agrum Campanum perferri[180] videbitis. Vobis interea, qui illas a maioribus pulcherrimas vectigalium sedis armis captas accepistis, gleba nulla de paternis atque avitis possessionibus relinquetur.

At quantum[181] intererit inter vestram et privatorum diligentiam! Quid?[182] Cum a maioribus nostris P. Lentulus, qui princeps senatus ⟨fuit⟩,[183] in ea loca missus esset ut privatos agros qui in publicum Campanum incurrebant pecunia publica coemeret, dicitur renuntiasse nulla se pecunia fundum cuiusdam emere potuisse, eumque qui nollet vendere ideo negasse se adduci posse uti venderet quod, cum pluris fundos haberet, ex illo solo fundo numquam malum nuntium audisset. Itane vero? Privatum haec causa commovit;[184] populum Romanum, ne agrum Campanum privatis gratis Rullo rogante tradat, non commovebit? At idem populus Romanus de hoc vectigali potest dicere quod ille de suo fundo dixisse dicitur. Asia mul-

[179] *suppl. Clark*
[180] perferri *EV^cLag.9*: preferri *cett.*
[181] tantum: *corr. Halm*
[182] quod: *corr. Richter*
[183] *add. Lauredanus*
[184] commovet: *corr. Naugerius*

DE LEGE AGRARIA 2.81–83

it has been divided will neither be nor be said to be yours. But what sort of men will be the owners? In the first place, fierce men ready for violence, prepared for revolution, who, as soon as the Decemvirs have snapped their fingers, can take up arms against the citizens and be ready for murder; next, you will see the whole of the Campanian territory transferred to a few people abounding in wealth and resources. In the meantime, to you, who have received from your ancestors those fairest seats of your revenues won by their arms, not a clod of earth will be left from your paternal and ancestral possessions.

But how great will be the difference between the care you exercise and that of private individuals! Well then, when Publius Lentulus, who was the leader of the senate, had been sent by our ancestors into those regions to purchase, with public money, private lands that jutted into the public Campanian territory,[119] he is said to have reported that he had been unable to buy a certain man's estate at any price, and that the owner who was unwilling to sell said that he could not be induced to do so because, although he had several estates, this was the only one from which he had never heard a bad report. Really? This reason influenced a private individual; shall it not move the Roman people not to hand over the Campanian territory to private individuals for nothing at the bidding of Rullus? But the Roman people can give the same answer concerning this revenue that this individual is reported to have given concerning his estate. For many years Asia brought

---

[119] P. Cornelius Lentulus (cos. suff. 162, princeps senatus from 125); this mission occurred during his praetorship, in 165. Cf. *MRR* 1:438; Manuwald 2018, 365–66.

tos annos vobis fructum Mithridatico bello non tulit, Hispaniarum vectigal temporibus Sertorianis nullum fuit, Siciliae civitatibus bello fugitivorum M'. Aquilius[185] etiam mutuum frumentum dedit; at ex hoc vectigali numquam malus nuntius auditus est. Cetera vectigalia belli difficultatibus[186] adfliguntur; hoc vectigali etiam belli difficultates[187] sustentantur.

84 Deinde in hac adsignatione agrorum ne illud quidem dici potest quod in ceteris, agros desertos a plebe atque a cultura hominum liberorum esse non oportere. Sic enim dico, si Campanus ager dividatur, exturbari et expelli plebem ex agris, non constitui et collocari. Totus enim ager Campanus colitur et possidetur a plebe, et a plebe optima et modestissima; quod genus hominum optime moratum, optimorum et aratorum et militum, ab hoc plebicola tribuno plebis funditus eicitur. Atque illi miseri, nati in illis agris et educati, glebis subigendis exercitati, quo se subito conferant non habebunt; his robustis et valentibus et audacibus decemvirum satellitibus agri Campani possessio tota tradetur,[188] et, ut vos nunc de vestris maioribus praedicatis: "hunc agrum nobis maiores nostri reliquerunt," sic vestri posteri de vobis praedicabunt: "hunc agrum patres

[185] M'. Aquilius *Lauredanus*: m. atilius ωπ
[186] difficultatibus απ: facultatibus *cett.*
[187] difficultates απ: facultates *cett.*
[188] tradetur *k Naugerius*: tradatur ω

[120] Cicero dilates on the subject at *Leg. Man.* 14–19. The three Mithridatic Wars are dated 89–85, 83–81, and 73–63; see *OCD* s.v. Mithradates.
[121] Q. Sertorius (qu. 91, pr. 85 or 83) gathered an anti-Sullan

DE LEGE AGRARIA 2.83–84

you no income at the time of the Mithridatic War;[120] the revenue of the Spanish provinces was nonexistent during the Sertorian crisis;[121] during the war of the fugitive slaves, Manius Aquilius even lent grain to the communities of Sicily;[122] but a bad report has never been heard from this revenue source [i.e., Campania]. The other revenues are weakened by the hardships of war; these even lend support for such hardships.

Besides, in this allotment of lands, it cannot be said, as it can in other cases, that lands ought not to be bereft of the plebs or of cultivation by free men. For I say that, if the Campanian territory is divided, the plebs will be driven out and expelled from the lands, not established and settled in them. For the whole Campanian territory is being cultivated and possessed by the plebs, of an excellent and moderate kind; and this class of men of fine character, excellent as both farmers and soldiers, is being entirely driven out by this "plebs-cultivating" tribune of the plebs! And those unfortunates, born and brought up in these lands, skilled in tilling the soil, will suddenly have nowhere to take refuge; the possession of the Campanian territory will be entirely handed over to these robust, sturdy, and audacious henchmen of the Decemvirs; and, as you now say of your ancestors, "Our ancestors left us this land," so your descendants will say of you, "Our

84

---

force in Spain, where he put up stubborn resistance from 80 to his death in 73; cf. *OCD* s.v.

[122] Remarkable because Sicily ordinarily exported grain and was the mainstay of Rome's supply. This will have occurred during Aquilius' proconsulate (100–99), during which he put down a slave revolt: *MRR* 1:577, 2:2–3.

85 nostri acceptum a patribus suis perdiderunt." Equidem existimo: si iam campus Martius dividatur et uni cuique vestrum ubi consistat bini pedes adsignentur, tamen promiscue toto quam proprie parva frui parte malitis.[189] Quare etiamsi ad vos esset singulos aliquid ex hoc agro perventurum qui vobis ostenditur, aliis comparatur, tamen honestius eum vos universi quam singuli possideretis. Nunc vero cum ad vos nihil pertineat, sed paretur aliis, eripiatur vobis, nonne acerrime, tamquam armato hosti, sic huic legi pro vestris agris resistetis?

Adiungit Stellatem campum agro Campano et in eo duodena discribit[190] in singulos homines iugera. Quasi 86 vero paulum differat ager Campanus a Stellati! Sed[191] multitudo, Quirites, quaeritur qua illa omnia oppida compleantur. Nam dixi antea lege permitti ut quae velint municipia, quas velint veteres colonias colonis suis occupent. Calenum municipium complebunt, Teanum opprimentur, Atellam, Cumas, Neapolim, Pompeios, Nuceriam suis praesidiis devincient, Puteolos vero, qui nunc in sua potestate sunt, suo iure libertateque utuntur, totos novo populo atque adventiciis copiis occupabunt. Tunc illud vexillum[192] Campanae coloniae, vehementer huic imperio timendum, Capuam a decemviris inferetur, tunc

[189] malitis *E*: maletis *VMψ*
[190] describit: *corr. Kayser*
[191] a Stellati; sed *Turnebus*: ac stellatis et ω
[192] vexillum *Lauredanus*: auxilium *E*: exilium *cett.*

---

[123] For the "Stellatian plain," see on 1.20.
[124] A *vexillum* is "a military standard consisting usu. of a piece of cloth suspended from a cross-piece," but also "a banner set up

DE LEGE AGRARIA 2.84–86

fathers received this land from their fathers but lost it." I for one think that, if the Campus Martius were now divided up and two feet of standing room were assigned to each of you, you would still prefer to have the enjoyment of the whole in common than to have a small share as your own. Therefore, even if some of this territory, which is promised to you but is being made ready for others, should come to each of you, it would still be more honorable for you to possess it in common than for each of you to have a portion. But as things stand, since nothing is coming to you but it is meant for others and is being robbed from you, will you not most energetically resist this law, as if it were an armed enemy, in defense of your lands?

Rullus adds the Stellatian plain to the Campanian territory and assigns twelve acres apiece in it to each individual, as if indeed there were so little difference between the Campanian and Stellatian territory![123] But, Romans, a large number of men is being sought to fill all those towns. For I have said before that the law allows them to occupy with their own colonists whatever towns and old colonies they please. They will fill the town of Cales, they will overwhelm Teanum, they will bind Atella, Cumae, Naples, Pompeii, and Nuceria with garrisons, but Puteoli, which is now self-governing and enjoys its liberty and its own jurisdiction, will be occupied entirely by a new population and newly arrived troops. Then that standard of a Campanian colony, greatly to be feared by our empire, will be brought forward to Capua by the Decemvirs,[124] then a

symbolically at the founding of a colony": *OLD* s.v. 1a and c; *vexillum inferre* plays on *signa inferre* = "march (usu. to the attack)": ibid. *infero* 2a.

contra hanc Romam, communem patriam omnium nostrum, illa altera Roma quaeretur. In id oppidum homines nefarii[193] rem publicam vestram transferre conantur, quo in oppido maiores nostri nullam omnino rem publicam esse voluerunt, qui tres solum urbes in terris omnibus, Carthaginem, Corinthum, Capuam, statuerunt posse imperi gravitatem ac nomen sustinere. Deleta Carthago est, quod cum hominum copiis, tum ipsa natura ac loco, succincta portibus, armata muris, excurrere ex Africa, imminere iam[194] fructuosissimis insulis populi Romani videbatur. Corinthi vestigium vix relictum est. Erat enim posita in angustiis atque in faucibus Graeciae sic ut terra claustra locorum teneret et duo maria maxime navigationi diversa paene coniungeret, cum pertenui discrimine separentur. Haec, quae procul erant a conspectu imperi, non solum adflixerunt sed etiam, ne quando recreata exsurgere atque erigere se possent, funditus, ut dixi, sustulerunt. De Capua multum est et diu consultum; exstant litterae, Quirites, publicae, sunt senatus consulta complura. Statuerunt homines sapientes, si agrum Campanis ademissent, magistratus, senatum, publicum ex illa urbe consilium sustulissent, imaginem rei publicae nullam reliquissent, nihil fore quod Capuam timeremus. Itaque hoc perscriptum in monumentis veteribus reperietis, ut esset urbs quae res eas quibus ager Campanus coleretur suppeditare posset, ut esset locus comportandis condendisque fructibus, ut aratores cultu agrorum defessi urbis domiciliis

---

[193] nefarii *Lag.9 Naugerius*: nefarie ωπ
[194] ita: *corr. R. Klotz*

---

[125] Namely, Sicily and Sardinia.

second Rome will be sought to oppose this Rome of ours, the common homeland of us all. It is to that town that the wicked men are endeavoring to transfer your republic, that town in which our ancestors wanted there to be no republic at all. They decided that only three cities in the world—Carthage, Corinth, and Capua—could support the weight and name of an empire. Carthage has been destroyed, because, from the vast number of its people, and its natural strategic position, surrounded by harbors and fortified with walls, it seemed to jut out from Africa and already threaten the most productive islands of the Roman people.[125] Scarcely a trace of Corinth is left. For it was positioned on the straits and the entrance to Greece in such a way that it held the keys to strategic places by land and almost united two seas completely different in terms of navigation, and they were separated by a very small space. These cities, which were far out of sight of our empire, were not only overthrown but also, to prevent them from ever recovering, rearing up, and rising again, were, as I said, utterly destroyed. About Capua there was long and intense discussion; there exist, Romans, public records and several decrees of the senate. In their wisdom they decided that if they deprived the Campanians of their land and removed magistrates, senate, and public council from that city and left no semblance of a republic, there would be no reason to fear Capua. Accordingly, you will find it written in ancient records that there should be a city to be able to supply the means for the cultivation of the Campanian territory, a place for collecting and storing the crops, and in order that the plowmen, fatigued by working the fields, might make use of houses in the city; that was the reason why those

89 uterentur, idcirco illa aedificia non esse deleta. Videte quantum intervallum sit interiectum inter maiorum nostrorum consilia et inter istorum hominum dementiam: illi Capuam receptaculum aratorum, nundinas rusticorum, cellam atque horreum Campani agri esse voluerunt; hi expulsis aratoribus, effusis ac dissipatis fructibus vestris eandem Capuam sedem novae rei publicae constituunt, molem contra veterem rem publicam comparant. Quodsi maiores nostri existimassent quemquam in tam illustri imperio et tam praeclara populi Romani disciplina ‹M.›[195] Bruti aut P. Rulli similem futurum (hos enim nos duos adhuc vidimus qui hanc rem publicam Capuam totam transferre vellent), profecto nomen illius urbis non re-
90 liquissent. Verum arbitrabantur Corinthi et Carthagini, etiamsi senatum et magistratus[196] sustulissent agrumque civibus ademissent, tamen non defore qui illa restituerent atque qui ante omnia commutarent quam nos audire possemus; hic vero, in oculis senatus populique Romani, nihil posse exsistere quod non ante extingui atque opprimi posset quam plane exortum ‹esset› ac natum.[197] Neque vero ea res fefellit homines divina mente et consilio praeditos. Nam post Q. Fulvium Q. Fabium consules, quibus consulibus Capua devicta atque capta est, nihil est in illa urbe contra hanc rem publicam non dico factum, sed nihil

---

[195] *add. Lauredanus*

[196] magistratum: *corr. Graevius*

[197] exortum esset ac natum *Clark*: exortum ac natum *ω*: exortum ac natum esset *ck Angelius*

buildings were not destroyed. See what a great gulf there is between the counsels of our ancestors and the madness of these men: the former wished Capua to be a retreat for the plowmen, a market for the country people, a storeroom and granary for the Campanian territory; the latter, after the plowmen have been driven out, after your profits have been wasted and squandered, are establishing the same Capua as the seat of a new republic, and are preparing a siege work against the old one. But if our ancestors had thought that, in so glorious an empire and in a people so admirably disciplined as the Romans, there would be anyone like Marcus Brutus or Publius Rullus (for these are the two men we have seen so far who desired to transfer this republic entirely to Capua),[126] they would certainly not have left behind the name of that city. But they thought that at Corinth and Carthage, even if they removed the senate and magistrates and deprived the citizens of their lands, there would be no lack of men to restore them and to change everything before we could hear of it; but here [in Campania], under the eyes of the senate and Roman people, no sedition could emerge that could not be put down and crushed before it clearly arose and was born. And in this those men, endowed with superb intelligence and counsel, were not mistaken. For, after the consulship of Quintus Fulvius and Quintus Fabius, during which Capua was conquered and captured, nothing at all has been plotted in that city against our republic, much less

[126] As plebeian tribune of 83, M. Iunius Brutus, the father of Caesar's assassin, carried a law for colonizing Capua (cf. *MRR* 2:63), but Sulla's advance forced the abandonment of the project.

CICERO

omnino est cogitatum. Multa postea bella gesta cum regibus, Philippo, Antiocho, Persa, Pseudophilippo, Aristonico, Mithridate et ceteris; multa praeterea bella gravia, Carthaginiense,[198] Corinthium, Numantinum; multae in hac re publica seditiones domesticae quas praetermitto; bella cum sociis, Fregellanum, Marsicum; quibus omnibus domesticis externisque bellis Capua non modo non obfuit, sed opportunissimam se nobis praebuit et ad bellum instruendum et ad exercitus ornandos et tectis ac sedibus suis recipiendis. Homines non inerant in urbe qui malis contionibus, turbulentis senatus consultis, iniquis imperiis rem publicam miscerent et rerum novarum causam aliquam quaererent. Neque enim contionandi potestas erat cuiquam nec consili capiendi publici; non gloriae cupiditate efferebantur, propterea quod, ubi honos publice non est, ibi gloriae cupiditas esse non potest; non contentione, non ambitione discordes. Nihil enim supere-

91

---

[198] Carthaginiense *Lambinus*: carthaginense $V^c Lag.9$: carthaginiensium ω

---

[127] Misdating the capture of Capua, giving the consuls of 209 not 211 (Cn. Fulvius and P. Servilius Galba); cf. *MRR* 1:272 and 285.

[128] For the Macedonian kings Philip V and Perses (or Perseus), see 1.5n. Antiochus III the Great was a Seleucid king defeated in 191–90 by P. and L. Scipio. Pseudo-Philip, whose real name was Andriscus, claimed to be the son of Perses and ascended the Macedonian throne in 149 as Philip VI but was defeated in 148 by Q. Caecilius Metellus. Aristonicus, illegitimate son of Eumenes II of Pergamum, led an uprising after Rome took possession of the kingdom under the will of Attalus III in 133; he

DE LEGE AGRARIA 2.90–91

acted upon.[127] In the aftermath many wars have been waged with kings—Philip, Antiochus, Perses, Pseudo-Philip, Aristonicus, Mithridates, and others[128]—and many serious wars besides—the Carthaginian, Corinthian, and Numantine wars;[129] there have been many internal dissensions in this republic, which I pass over; wars with our allies, the Fregellan and the Marsic.[130] In all these internal and foreign wars Capua not only did not thwart us, but showed herself most serviceable to us in providing matériel for war, equipping our armies, and billeting them in their buildings and homes. There were no men in the city who, by seditious speeches in assemblies, disorderly decrees of the senate, or unjust exercise of authority, would throw the government into confusion and seek some excuse for revolution. For no one had the power of addressing a meeting of the people or of holding an official consultation; people were not carried away by a desire for glory because, where no office is publicly conferred, there a desire for glory cannot exist. They were not set at odds by rivalry or ambition; for there was nothing left to com- 91

was defeated in 130/29 by M'. Aquillius and M. Perperna (or Perpenna). Mithridates VI of Pontus fought three wars with the Romans; see on §83.

[129] For the three Punic Wars of 264–241, 218–201, and 149–146, see *OCD* s.v. Punic Wars. For Corinth, see 1.5n. Numantia was a center of Celtiberian resistance to Rome in Spain until it was forced to capitulate by the Younger Scipio in 133: *MRR* 1:494.

[130] Fregellae, a city in the Liris Valley, revolted against Rome in 125 and was largely destroyed: *MRR* 1:510. The Social War (see on §80) was sometimes called the Marsic War because the Marsi took a prominent role in the revolt; cf. Rosenberger 1992, 35–37.

rat de quo certarent, nihil quod contra peterent, nihil ubi dissiderent. Itaque illam Campanam arrogantiam atque intolerandam ferociam ratione et consilio maiores nostri ad inertissimum ac desidiosissimum otium perduxerunt. Sic et crudelitatis infamiam effugerunt quod urbem ex Italia pulcherrimam non sustulerunt, et multum in posterum providerunt quod nervis urbis omnibus electis[199] urbem ipsam solutam ac debilitatam reliquerunt.

92   Haec consilia maiorum M. Bruto, ut antea dixi, reprehendenda [et P. Rullo][200] visa sunt; neque te, P. Rulle, omina illa M. Bruti atque auspicia a simili furore deterrent. Nam et ipse qui deduxit et qui magistratum Capuae illo creante[201] ceperunt et qui aliquam partem illius deductionis,[202] honoris, muneris attigerunt, omnes acerbissimas impiorum poenas pertulerunt. Et quoniam ⟨M.⟩[203] Bruti atque illius temporis feci mentionem, commemorabo id quod egomet vidi, cum venissem Capuam colonia modo deducta[204] L. Considio[205] et Sex. Saltio, quem ad modum ipsi loquebantur, "praetoribus," ut intellegatis quantam locus ipse adferat superbiam, quae paucis diebus quibus illo colonia deducta est[206] perspici atque intellegi potuit.

93   Nam primum, id quod dixi, cum ceteris in coloniis duum-

---

[199] electis *Madvig (cf. Liv. 7.39.6 una cum Oakley 1997–2005, 2:369–70)*: eiectis ωπ: exectis ς: exsectis *edd.*

[200] *om. Lag.9, del. Baiter*

[201] Capuae illo creante *Turnebus*: capua et locreanti *e∈VMψn*: capuae et locreariti *n*: capua locare ante *E*

[202] deditionis: *corr. Naugerius*   [203] *add. Baiter*

[204] colonia modo deducta *C. F. W. Müller*: coloniam deductam ω   [205] Considio *edd.*: consio απ *(def. Shackleton Bailey)*

[206] est *Wesenberg*: sit *E*: sint *en*χ^2: fuit *cett.*

pete for, nothing they could aim at in opposition to each other, no room for disagreement. Therefore our ancestors, by their rational policy, converted that Campanian arrogance[131] and intolerable fierceness to the most indolent and slothful ease. Thus they avoided a reputation for cruelty by not wiping a most beautiful city off the face of Italy, and they made provision far into the future by leaving the city itself, after all its sinews had been pulled out, impaired and weakened.

These policies of our ancestors appeared to Marcus Brutus, as I stated before, deserving of blame;[132] nor do those omens and auspices that were given to Marcus Brutus deter you, Publius Rullus, from a similar madness. For both he who conducted the colony and those who received a magistracy at Capua by his appointment, as well as those who had anything to do with that colonization, any office or task, endured all the most terrible punishments of the impious. And since I have mentioned Marcus Brutus and that time, I will relate what I saw myself when I had come to Capua, when the colony had just been founded by Lucius Considius and Sextus Saltius, "praetors" (as they called themselves), so that you may understand what great haughtiness the very place inspires, as could be seen and understood within a few days of the colony being established in that place.[133] Now in the first place, as I have said,

[131] A proverbial trait; cf. on 1.20.
[132] §89, where see note.
[133] In 83, shortly after Brutus enacted his law. Nothing more is known of Considius and Saltius; cf. Münzer, *RE* s.v. Considius 4 and Saltius.

viri appellentur, hi se praetores appellari volebant. Quibus primus annus hanc cupiditatem attulisset, nonne arbitramini paucis annis fuisse consulum nomen appetituros? Deinde anteibant lictores non cum bacillis, sed, ut hic praetoribus urbanis anteeunt, cum fascibus bini.[207] Erant hostiae maiores in foro constitutae, quae ab his praetoribus de tribunali, sicut a nobis consulibus, de consili sententia probatae[208] ad praeconem et ad tibicinem immolabantur. Deinde patres conscripti vocabantur. Iam vero vultum Considi[209] videre ferendum vix erat. Quem hominem "vegrandi[210] macie torridum" Romae contemptum, abiectum videbamus, hunc Capuae Campano fastidio[211] ac regio spiritu cum videremus, Blossios mihi videbar illos videre ac Vibellios.[212] Iam vero qui metus erat tunicatorum illorum, et in Albana et Seplasia quae concursatio percontantium[213] quid praetor edixisset, ubi cenaret, quo denuntiasset![214] Nos autem hinc Roma qui veneramus iam non hospites, sed peregrini atque advenae nominabamur.

[207] fascibus bini *Zumpt*: fascibus duabus *E*: facibus duabus ω
[208] probatis: *corr. Lauredanus*
[209] Considi *ed. Rom.*: consilii ωπ: Consii *Shackleton Bailey*
[210] vegrandi *k Lauredanus*: ut (et, aut) grandi ω
[211] praesidio: *corr. Richter*
[212] Vibellios ς: iubellios *VM*ψ: iubellos απχ: imbellos ς
[213] percontantium *vulgo*: percun(c)tantium ω
[214] quo denuntiasset *R. Klotz*: quod enuntiasset ωπ

---

[134] Praetor was, however, the traditional translation of the Oscan magisterial title *meddix*; cf. Harvey 1982, 156.

[135] That is, calling upon the people to observe silence.

[136] The diction points to a possible poetic quotation.

whereas in other colonies they are called duumviri, these wanted to be called praetors. If their first year had created this desire in them, do you not think that in a few years they would have been eager for the title of consuls?[134] Next, they were preceded by two lictors each, not with staves, but with fasces, like those who precede the urban praetors here. The greater victims stood in the forum and were being sacrificed upon approval by these praetors from the tribunal, as they would be by us consuls, in accordance with the recommendation of a council, with the crier making announcement[135] and a flutist playing. Afterward the members of the senate were summoned. Moreover, the sight of Considius' face was all but intolerable. When the man whom we saw in Rome "dried up with extreme leanness,"[136] despised and abject, appeared to us in Capua with Campanian haughtiness and kingly arrogance, I thought I was looking at one of the Blossii or Vibellii.[137] And how frightened the common people were! What a running to and fro of people on the Alban and Seplasian roads,[138] wanting to know the terms of the praetor's edict, where he was dining, to what place he had issued a summons![139] But we, who had arrived from Rome, were no longer called guests, but strangers and foreigners.

---

[137] Two Blossii brothers organized a revolt after the Roman conquest of Capua in the Second Punic War (Liv. 27.3.4–5). Carrinus Vibellius Taurea was a distinguished Capuan who took Hannibal's side during the Second Punic War; cf. Gundel, *RE* s.v. Vibellius 2.

[138] Roads or districts in Capua; see Manuwald 2018, 393.

[139] That is, a summons to appear.

95 Haec qui prospexerunt,[215] maiores nostros dico, Quirites, non eos in deorum immortalium numero venerandos a nobis et colendos putatis? Quid enim viderunt? Hoc quod nunc vos, quaeso, perspicite atque cognoscite. Non ingenerantur hominibus mores tam a stirpe generis ac seminis quam ex iis rebus quae ab ipsa natura nobis[216] ad vitae consuetudinem[217] suppeditantur, quibus alimur et vivimus. Carthaginienses fraudulenti et mendaces non genere, sed natura loci, quod propter portus suos multis et variis mercatorum et advenarum sermonibus ad studium fallendi studio quaestus vocabantur. Ligures[218] duri atque agrestes; docuit ager ipse nihil ferendo nisi multa cultura et magno labore quaesitum. Campani semper superbi bonitate agrorum et fructuum magnitudine, urbis salubritate, descriptione, pulchritudine. Ex hac copia atque omnium rerum adfluentia primum illa nata[219] est[220] arrogantia qua[221] a maioribus nostris alterum Capua consulem postulavit,[222] deinde ea luxuries quae ipsum Hannibalem armis etiam tunc invictum voluptate vicit. Huc[223]
96 isti decemviri cum IↃↃ[224] colonorum ex lege Rulli deduxerint, centum decuriones, decem augures, sex ponti-

[215] prospexerunt *Zumpt*: prospexerint *eϵ*: perspexerint *EVM ψm*

[216] bonis: *corr. Lauredanus*

[217] ad vitae consuetudinem *k*: a vita consuetudine *ω*

[218] Ligures *απ*: ligures montani *cett.*

[219] nata ς: capta *απ*: apta *cett.*

[220] est *Wesenberg*: fuit *k*: sunt *ω*

[221] qua *Lag.*9: quae *ω*

[222] postulavit *VMψmLag.9*: postularunt *απ*

[223] huic: *corr. Naugerius*

[224] modo: *corr. Lauredanus*

DE LEGE AGRARIA 2.95–96

Do you not think that those who foresaw these things—I mean our ancestors, Romans—should be venerated and worshipped by us among the immortal gods? For what did they see? This point—please now observe and understand it yourselves: Manners are not engendered in human beings so much by lineage and descent as by the elements supplied to us by nature herself for our way of life, the elements by which we are nurtured and live. The Carthaginians were cheats and liars, not by race but by the nature of the place, because owing to their harbors, they were moved by much and varied talk of merchants and strangers to cultivate deceit in pursuit of gain.[140] The Ligurians are hardy rustics; the land itself has taught them, since it produces nothing that is not gained by dint of intensive cultivation and much toil. The Campanians have always been haughty, owing to the fertility of their lands, the abundance of their crops, the healthiness, the plan, and the beauty of their city. It is out of this abundance, this affluence of all things, that first arose Campanian arrogance, by which Capua demanded from our ancestors one of the consuls, then that luxury that vanquished Hannibal himself with pleasure, even though he was still undefeated by arms.[141] When those Decemvirs have settled five hundred colonists there according to the law of Rullus, when they have set up one hundred decurions, ten augurs, and

95

96

---

[140] Similarly in discussing the location of Rome at *Rep.* 2.7–8; but for rhetorical advantage against Sardinian witnesses, at *Scaur.* 42 the influence of heredity is emphasized.

[141] The price Capua demanded from Rome in 216, in the aftermath of Cannae, for its continued support; cf. Livy 23.6.6. For the alleged corruption of Hannibal, see 1.20n.

fices constituerint, quos illorum animos, quos impetus, quam ferociam fore putatis! Romam in montibus positam et convallibus, cenaculis sublatam atque suspensam, non optimis viis,[225] angustissimis semitis, prae sua Capua planissimo in loco explicata ac †prae illis semitis†[226] irridebunt atque contemnent: agros vero Vaticanum et Pupiniam cum suis opimis atque uberrimis[227] campis conferendos scilicet non putabunt. Oppidorum autem finitimorum illam copiam cum hac per risum ac iocum contendent;[228] Veios,[229] Fidenas, Collatiam, ipsum hercle Lanuvium,[230] Ariciam, Tusculum cum Calibus, Teano, Neapoli, Puteolis, Cumis, Pompeiis, Nuceria comparabunt. Quibus illi rebus elati et inflati, fortasse non continuo, sed certe si paululum[231] adsumpserint vetustatis[232] ac roboris, non continebuntur; progredientur, cuncta secum ferent.[233] Singularis homo privatus, nisi magna sapientia praeditus, vix cancellis et[234] regionibus offici magnis in fortunis et copiis continetur, nedum isti ab Rullo et Rulli similibus conquisiti atque electi coloni Capuae in domicilio superbiae atque in sedibus luxuriosis collocati non statim conquisituri sint aliquid sceleris et flagiti, immo vero etiam hoc magis quam illi veteres germanique

---

[225] suis: *corr. Angelius* [226] prae illis semitis *locus conclamatus*: praeclarissime sita *Baiter, alii alia* [227] uberrimis α: uberibus *cett.* [228] contendent *Lag.9, Manutius*: contemnent ω [229] Veios Zumpt: vicos VMψm: fucos eϵ

[230] Lanuvium VMψ: lanuvinum nχ²

[231] paululum E: paulum ω [232] venustatis απnχ²

[233] progredientur cuncta secum ferent *Orelli*: progredientur cuncti secum ferentur π: progrediuntur iuncti secum feruntur α: progredientur longius efferent VM

DE LEGE AGRARIA 2.96–97

six priests, what do you think their arrogance, their attacks, their ferocity will be! They will laugh at and despise Rome, located on mountains and valleys, raised and suspended with garrets, its roads not the best, its alleyways narrow, in comparison with their own Capua, spread out in an open plain and . . . They will certainly not think our Vatican and Pupinian fields fit to be compared with their rich and fertile plains.[142] They will derisively pit the number of their neighboring towns against ours: they will compare Veii, Fidenae, Collatia, Lanuvium itself—for heaven's sake!—Aricia, and Tusculum with Cales, Teanum, Naples, Puteoli, Cumae, Pompeii, and Nuceria. Elated and puffed up by these facts, perhaps not at once, but certainly once they have taken on a little bit of age and vigor, there will be no restraining them; they will advance and sweep everything before them. A private individual, unless he is endowed with great wisdom, can hardly confine himself within the limits and boundaries set by duty in the midst of great wealth and resources, let alone that these colonists, chosen and gathered by Rullus and men like Rullus, once settled in Capua in the abode of arrogance and the seats of luxury, will not at once seek to commit some scandalous crime, indeed, even more so than those old genuine Cam-

---

[142] The Vatican district extended northward from Rome on the west bank of the Tiber; the Pupinian district bordered Rome on the southeast. The soil of both was regarded as inferior; see further Manuwald 2018, 398.

---

234 cancellis et *Richter*: facili(s) esset $a\pi\chi$: facili sese *cett.*

Campani, quod in vetere fortuna illos natos et educatos nimiae tamen rerum omnium copiae depravabant, hi ex summa egestate in eandem[235] rerum abundantiam traducti non solum copia verum etiam insolentia commovebuntur.

98 Haec tu, P. Rulle, M. Bruti sceleris vestigia quam monumenta maiorum sapientiae sequi maluisti, haec tu cum istis tuis auctoribus excogitasti, ut vetera vectigalia nostra ⟨expilaretis⟩,[236] exploraretis[237] nova, ⟨urbem novam huic⟩ urbi[238] ad certamen dignitatis opponeretis; ut sub vestrum ius, dicionem,[239] potestatem urbes, nationes, provincias, liberos populos, reges, terrarum denique orbem subiungeretis; ut, cum omnem pecuniam ex aerario exhausissetis, ex vectigalibus redegissetis, ab omnibus regibus, gentibus, ab imperatoribus nostris coegissetis, tamen omnes vobis pecunias ad nutum vestrum penderent; ut idem partim invidiosos agros a Sullanis possessoribus, partim desertos ac pestilentis a vestris necessariis et a vobismet ipsis emptos quanti velletis populo Romano induceretis; ut omnia municipia coloniasque Italiae novis colonis occuparetis; ut quibuscumque in locis vobis videretur ac quam multis

99 videretur colonias collocaretis; ut omnem rem publicam vestris militibus, vestris urbibus, vestris praesidiis cingeretis atque oppressam teneretis; ut ipsum Cn. Pompeium, cuius praesidio saepissime res publica contra acerrimos hostes et contra improbissimos civis ⟨munita est, exercitu⟩

---

[235] eandemque *eVMψm*

[236] nostra expilaretis *Lauredanus*: ea ω

[237] exploraretis *cod. Turnebi*: expleretis ω

[238] nova urbem novam huic urbi *Clark*: novo urbi ω

[239] ius dicionem *Pluygers*: iurisdicionem ω

panians, because if they, born and brought up in established wealth, were nevertheless corrupted by an excessive supply of all things, these newcomers, transferred from extreme poverty to the same abundance of goods, will be excited not only by its quantity but also by its novelty.

You, Publius Rullus, have preferred to follow these footsteps of the wicked Marcus Brutus rather than the records of our wise ancestors. You and your sponsors have thought out this plan to plunder our old revenues, to seek out new ones, and to set a new city against this city to rival her dignity, to bring beneath your law, sway, and power cities, nations, provinces, free peoples, kings, in fact, the whole world; so that, when you have drained all the money from the treasury, collected it from the revenues, and exacted it from all kings, peoples, and our generals, they may all still pay you money at your nod; so that, after buying lands, some with odium attached from the Sullan occupiers, others desolate and plague-ridden from your kinsmen and yourselves, you may charge them to the Roman people at whatever price you like; that you may occupy all the towns and colonies of Italy with new colonists; that you may found colonies in whatever and as many places as you please; that you may surround the entire republic with your soldiers, your cities, and your garrisons, and keep it cowed; that you may be able to deprive Gnaeus Pompey himself, by whose protection the state has very often been fortified against fierce enemies and nefarious citizens, of

victore[240] atque horum conspectu privare possetis; ut nihil auro et argento violari, nihil numero et suffragiis depravari,[241] nihil vi et[242] manu perfringi posset quod non vos oppressum atque ereptum teneretis; ut volitaretis interea per gentis, per regna omnia cum imperio summo, cum iudicio infinito, cum omni pecunia; ut veniretis in castra Cn. Pompei atque ipsa castra, si commodum vobis esset, venderetis; ut interea magistratus reliquos legibus omnibus soluti, sine metu iudiciorum, sine periculo petere possetis; ut nemo ad populum Romanum vos adducere, nemo producere, nemo[243] in senatum cogere, non consul coercere, non tribunus plebis retinere posset.

100 Haec ego vos concupisse pro vestra stultitia atque intemperantia non miror, sperasse me consule adsequi posse demiror. Nam cum omnium consulum gravis in re publica[244] custodienda cura ac diligentia debet esse, tum eorum maxime qui non in cunabulis, sed in campo sunt consules facti. Nulli populo Romano pro me maiores mei spoponderunt; mihi creditum est; a me petere quod debeo, me ipsum appellare debetis. Quem ad modum, cum petebam, nulli me vobis auctores generis mei commenda-

[240] civis munita est, exercitu victore *Clark*: civis victorem ω
[241] declarari: *corr. Madvig*
[242] vi et *Lag.7,8*: vel laeta α: velata *cett.*
[243] non: *corr. Richter*   [244] p(ublica) Vχck: *om. cett.*

---

143 For this claim, see *Leg. agr.* 1 F 4.
144 Krostenko 2023, 240n75, thinks that here Cicero reconfigures a clause in the bill "limiting nullification of its [the Decemvirate's] decisions" as "a general personal right," since there would be no point in trying to bring the Decemvirs to book.

DE LEGE AGRARIA 2.99–100

his victorious army and the sight of these men; that there may be nothing that can be defiled by gold and silver, corrupted by numbers of votes, or smashed by force and violence that you had not seized and kept under your power; that you may in the meantime roam over nations and all kingdoms with supreme military authority, unlimited jurisdiction, and all money; that you may enter the camp of Gnaeus Pompey and sell the camp itself, if it were convenient for you;[143] that in the meantime, immunized against all laws, without fear of the courts, without any risk, you may be able to canvass for other offices; that no one should be able to bring you before the Roman people, summon you to court, compel you to attend the senate, and that no consul should be able to restrain you, no plebeian tribune to check you.[144]

I am not surprised, considering your folly and lack of restraint, that you have desired these privileges, but I am amazed that you should have hoped to attain them as long as I was consul. For as careful attention in guarding the republic ought to be a serious matter for every consul, so it is especially incumbent upon those who have been made consuls, not in their cradles but in the Campus.[145] None of my ancestors stood surety for me to the Roman people;[146] credit was given to me; it is from me that you ought to claim what I owe you, and to call upon me. Just as, when I was a candidate, no sponsors from my family recom-

---

[145] For "in their cradles," cf. L. Domitius Ahenobarbus (cos. 54), who, according to *Att.* 4.8a[82].2, was consul designate from birth. The Campus Martius was where the *comitia centuriata* met to elect the higher magistrates; cf. *OLD* s.v.

[146] That is, provided a guarantee of high character.

runt, sic,[245] si quid deliquero, nullae sunt imagines quae me a vobis deprecentur.[246] Quare, modo mihi[247] vita suppetat, quam ego summis ⟨viribus⟩[248] ab istorum scelere insidiisque defendere ⟨paro⟩,[249] polliceor hoc vobis, Quirites, bona fide: rem publicam vigilanti homini, non timido, diligenti, ⟨non inerti⟩,[250] commisistis. Ergo ⟨non sum⟩ ego[251] is consul qui contionem metuam, qui tribunum plebis perhorrescam, qui saepe et sine causa tumultuer, qui timeam ne mihi in carcere habitandum sit, si tribunus plebis duci iusserit.[252] Ego cum vestris armis armatus sim insignibusque[253] amplissimis exornatus,[254] imperio, auctoritate, non horreo in hunc locum progredi, possum[255] vobis, Quirites,[256] auctoribus improbitati hominis resistere, nec vereor ne res publica tantis munita praesidiis ab istis vinci aut opprimi possit. Si antea timuissem, tamen hac contione, hoc populo certe non vererer. Quis enim umquam tam secunda contione legem agrariam suasit quam ego dissuasi—si hoc dissuadere est ac non disturbare atque pervertere?

102   Ex quo intellegi, Quirites, potest nihil esse tam populare quam id quod ego vobis in hunc annum consul popularis adfero, pacem, tranquillitatem, otium. Quae nobis

[245] *om. aπ*

[246] deprecentur *V Gell. 7.16.7*: deprecent *cett.*

[247] mihi *Clark*: si *a*: ut *cett.*

[248] *add. Dyck 2019*: *lac. statuit C. F. W. Müller in app.*: *alii alia*   [249] *add. Dyck 2019*   [250] *suppl. Marek*

[251] ergo non sum ego *Dyck*: ergo ero *E*: ergo *eϵ*: ego *cett.*

[252] iusserit *E*: iussisset *cett.*

[253] armatus sim insignibusque *Zumpt*: armatus sim signisque *Lag.9*: armatus signisque *cett.*

DE LEGE AGRARIA 2.100–102

mended me to you, so, if I am at fault, there are no images to intercede with you on my behalf.[147] Therefore, provided that my life lasts long enough, which I intend to defend with all my strength from these men's wickedness and snares, I promise you this, Romans, in good faith: you have entrusted the republic to a man who is watchful and not timid, attentive and not idle. Accordingly, I am not a consul to fear a public assembly, to dread a plebeian tribune, to be often and needlessly perturbed, to be afraid of having to live in prison, if a plebeian tribune gives the order for me to be taken there. Since I have been equipped with your arms and adorned with the most honorable insignia of office, with command and authority, I am not afraid to come forward to this place;[148] I can, with you to support me, Romans, resist a man's wickedness, and I have no fear that the republic, fortified by such strong guardians, can be conquered or crushed by men like these. If I might have been afraid before, I would certainly have no fear in light of this assembly, this populace. For who ever found an assembly so favorable in arguing for an agrarian law as I in arguing against it—if this is "to argue against" and not rather to demolish and overthrow it?

From this you can understand, Romans, that nothing can be so pleasing to the people as that which I, a consul who is a friend of the people, offer you for this year—peace, tranquility, and quiet. By my reasoned policy

---

[147] See on §1.   [148] The Rostra; see on §6.

---

254 exornatus *a*: ornatus *cett.*
255 posse: *corr. Zumpt*
256 vobis, Quirites *C. F. W. Müller in app.*: vobisque *ω*

CICERO

designatis timebatis, ea ne accidere possent consilio meo ac ratione provisa sunt. Non modo vos eritis in otio, qui semper esse volueratis, verum etiam istos quibus odio est otium quietissimos atque otiosissimos[257] reddam. Etenim illis honores, potestates, divitiae ex tumultu atque ex dissensione civium comparari solent; vos, quorum gratia in suffragiis consistit, libertas in legibus, ius[258] in iudiciis et aequitate magistratuum, res familiaris[259] in pace, omni ratione otium retinere debetis. Nam si ii[260] qui propter desidiam in otio vivunt, tamen in sua turpi inertia capiunt voluptatem ex ipso otio, quam[261] vos fortunati eritis,[262] si hunc statum quem habetis vestra[263] non ignavia quaesitum, sed virtute[264] partum [otium][265] tenueritis, Quirites! Ego[266] ea[267] concordia quam mihi constitui cum collega, invitissimis eis hominibus qui nos[268] in consulatu inimicos esse et fore iactabant,[269] providi omnibus, prospexi

---

[257] quibus ... otiosissimos *Madvig*: quibus ociosi ocium fecissemus atque ociosos $a\pi n\chi^2$: quibus otiosi otium fecissemus otiosissimos *cett.*

[258] hos: *corr. Kayser*

[259] magistratuum, res familiaris *Lauredanus*: magnos timores familiares ω

[260] nam si ii *Lambinus*: nam etsi ii V^c *in marg.* $M^c\psi n\chi^2$: tam etsi ii EV^lM^l

[261] quo: *corr. Madvig*

[262] fortunati eritis *Madvig*: fortunam regitis ω

[263] vestra *C. F. W. Müller*: esse ω   [264] ignavia quaesitum sed virtute *Madvig*: ignoravi non quaesitum sed vita ωπ

[265] *del. Boulanger*   [266] Quirites. ego *Clark*: quod ego ω

[267] ea *Madvig*: et ω: ex *ed. Adam. 1472*

[268] qui nos *Madvig*: quos vos ωπ

[269] inimicos esse et fore iactabant *Kasten*: inimico esse et corpus actibus *EeM*ψ: inimico esse et corporis iactibus *V*: *alii alia*

DE LEGE AGRARIA 2.102–3

I have seen to it that the things you feared when I was consul designate could not occur. You will not only enjoy tranquility as you have always wished, but I will also cause those who hate quiet to be most peaceful and full of ease. For it is out of disturbance and civil dissension that such men usually acquire offices, positions of power, and wealth. You, whose influence is based on your votes, your liberty on the laws, your rights on the courts and the justice of the magistrates, and your property on peace, ought to preserve your tranquility by all possible means. For if those who live in tranquility owing to idleness, in spite of their disgraceful laziness, still take pleasure in that tranquility itself, how fortunate will you be, if you hold fast this condition that you enjoy, not gained by sloth but achieved by your own valor, Romans! Owing to the harmony that I have established with my colleague, to the great displeasure of those men who bruited it about that we were and would be enemies during our consulship,[149] I have made provision for all contingencies: I have taken thought for the

103

---

[149] Cicero and Antonius could be thought to be enemies and a reconciliation unlikely; cf. the insulting references to Antonius as a "charioteer" in the speech *In a White Toga* (9 F 10 and 25 Cr.-D.); but when Cicero drew the lucrative province of Macedonia and agreed to an exchange of provinces with his colleague (perhaps with an under-the-table profit-sharing agreement: Shatzman 1975, 133; Buongiorno 2010; Scheuermann 2015, 230–36.), Antonius agreed to cooperate with, or at least not to oppose him. Cicero thus outbid Rullus, who had offered Antonius a place among his Decemvirs; cf. Plut. *Vit. Cic.* 12.3.

CICERO

annonae, revocavi fidem,[270] tribunis plebis denuntiavi[271] ⟨ne⟩[272] quid turbulenti[273] me consule conflarent. Summum et firmissimum est illud communibus fortunis praesidium, Quirites, ut, qualis vos hodierno[274] die maxima contione mihi pro salute vestra praebuistis, talis reliquis temporibus rei publicae[275] praebeatis. Pro certo[276] polliceor hoc vobis atque confirmo, me esse perfecturum ut iam tandem illi qui honori inviderunt meo tamen vos universos in consule deligendo plurimum vidisse fateantur.

[270] annonae revocavi fidem *Clark*: sane revocavi idem ω
[271] om. *VMψ*
[272] *add. Turnebus*
[273] turbulenti *anχ^{2}*: -um *cett.*
[274] hodierno *ed. Ven.*: hodierna ω
[275] rei publicae *Angelius*: p.r. ω
[276] *post* pro certo *hab. Eeπnχ^{2}* repe(r)to: *om. cett., del. Kasten*

DE LEGE AGRARIA 2.103

grain supply; I have restored credit;[150] I have put the plebeian tribunes on notice that they should not engineer any disorder during my consulship. But the greatest and strongest protection for our common fortunes, Romans, is for you to show yourselves in future crises of state such as you have shown yourselves to me today for your own safety in this well-attended assembly. I promise you for sure and confirm[151] that I will cause those who were jealous of my office now finally to confess that all of you showed the greatest wisdom in your choice of a consul.

[150] That is, by strict enforcement of the terms of contracts. Some of the resulting social tension apparently spilled over when mob violence threatened at the Games of Apollo; see further Ramsey 2021, 19–26. On Cicero's policy on credit and debt, see also his comments at *Off.* 2.84.

[151] A formula used in solemn and dramatic vows; cf. Krostenko 2023, 245.

DE LEGE AGRARIA
ORATIO TERTIA CONTRA
P. SERVILIUM RULLUM
TR. PLEB. AD POPULUM

Commodius fecissent tribuni plebis, Quirites, si, quae apud vos de me deferunt, ea coram potius me praesente dixissent; nam et aequitatem vestrae disceptationis et consuetudinem superiorum et ius suae potestatis retinuissent. Sed quoniam adhuc praesens certamen contentionemque fugerunt, nunc, si videtur eis, in meam contionem prodeant et, quo provocati a me venire noluerunt, revocati saltem revertantur. Video quosdam, Quirites, strepitu significare nescio quid et non eosdem vultus quos proxima mea contione praebuerunt in hanc contionem mihi rettulisse. Quare a vobis, qui nihil de me credidistis, ut eam voluntatem quam semper habuistis erga me retineatis peto; a vobis autem, quos leviter immutatos esse sentio, parvam exigui temporis usuram bonae de me opinionis

---

[1] Cf. 1.23: "I desire to employ the Roman people as our judge"; Livy 41.23.13: "to the judgment of the Roman people." Cf. Manuwald 2018, 97; for a different view, cf. *TLL* 5.1:1290.55.

[2] That is, Rullus had gained some traction in his own assembly speech (absent from *FRLO*).

ON THE AGRARIAN LAW III
AGAINST THE PLEBEIAN
TRIBUNE PUBLIUS SERVILIUS
RULLUS TO THE PEOPLE

The plebeian tribunes would have acted more appropriately, Romans, if they had said in my presence the things they reported about me before you; for they would have maintained the fairness of your judgment,[1] the custom of their predecessors, and the rights of their authority. But since so far they have shrunk from a face-to-face contest and debate, let them now, if they please, come forward to join the assembly called by me, and although, when challenged by me, they refused to come, let them at least return now that I have asked them again. I see, Romans, that some men indicate something by their murmurs, and have not brought back to this meeting the same expression they showed at my last one.[2] Therefore I ask of you who have not believed anything about me,[3] to retain the goodwill that you have always shown toward me; but of you, who I perceive are slightly changed, I request the exercise for a brief time of a good opinion of me, on the terms that you

[3] Namely, anything said by Rullus.

postulo, ut eam, si quae dixero vobis probabo, perpetuo retineatis; sin aliter, hoc ipso in loco depositam atque abiectam relinquatis. Completi sunt animi auresque vestrae, Quirites, me gratificantem Septimiis, Turraniis[1] ceterisque Sullanarum adsignationum possessoribus agrariae legi et commodis vestris[2] obsistere. Hoc si qui crediderunt, illud prius crediderint necesse est, hac lege agraria quae promulgata est[3] adimi Sullanos agros vobisque dividi aut denique minui privatorum possessiones ut in eas vos deducamini. Si ostendo non modo non adimi cuiquam glebam de Sullanis agris, sed etiam genus id agrorum certo capite legis impudentissime confirmari atque sanciri, si doceo agris iis qui a Sulla sunt dati sic diligenter Rullum sua lege consulere ut facile appareat eam legem non a vestrorum commodorum patrono, sed a Valgi[4] genero esse conscriptam, num quid est causae, Quirites, quin illa criminatione qua in me absentem usus est non solum meam sed etiam vestram diligentiam prudentiamque despexerit?

Caput est legis quadrigesimum de quo ego consulto, Quirites, neque apud vos ante feci mentionem, ne aut refricare obductam iam rei publicae cicatricem viderer aut aliquid alienissimo tempore novae dissensionis com-

---

[1] Septimiis Turraniis *Madvig:* septem tyrannis ω
[2] commodis vestris *an:* commodo vestro *cett.*
[3] sit: *corr. R. Klotz*
[4] vulgi: *corr. Beroaldus*

---

[4] For mss. *septem tyranni* (seven tyrants), Madvig suggested "Septimii, Turranii," as plausible names of Sulla's beneficiaries.

DE LEGE AGRARIA 3.2–4

keep it forever if I prove to you what I am going to say; but otherwise, that here on this very spot you drop it, fling it away, and abandon it. It has been dinned into your ears and minds, Romans, that I opposed the agrarian law and your interests to gratify the Septimii, the Turranii, and the other possessors of Sulla's allotments.[4] If any did believe this, they must first have believed that by this agrarian law that has been promulgated[5] the Sullan allotments of land are being taken away and divided among you, or that at least the possessions of private persons are being diminished so that you may be settled upon them. If I prove that not only is no clod of earth being removed from anyone's Sullan lands but even that this category of lands is shamelessly confirmed and guaranteed by a particular section of the law; if I show that by his law Rullus provides so carefully for the lands assigned by Sulla that it is easy to see that the law has been drawn up, not by a defender of your interests, but by the son-in-law of Valgus;[6] is there any reason, Romans, why, by that accusation that he has brought against me in my absence, he should not have displayed his contempt, not only for my carefulness and foresight, but also for yours?

It is the fortieth section of the law that I am discussing, Romans; I did not mention it to you before so that I might not seem to be reopening an old wound of the state that is now healed or to be stirring up any new disagreement

---

[5] By the proposing magistrate's public announcement of the text; twenty-four days had to intervene between the promulgation and the assembly that would vote on the law. Cf. Berger 1953 s.v. Promulgare. Cicero describes the promulgation of Rullus' law at 2.13.   [6] Or Valg(i)us; see on 1.14.

CICERO

movere, neque vero nunc ideo disputabo quod hunc statum rei publicae non magno opere defendendum putem, praesertim qui oti et concordiae patronum me in hunc annum populo Romano[5] professus[6] sim, sed ut doceam Rullum posthac in iis saltem tacere rebus in quibus de se
5 et de suis factis taceri velit. Omnium legum iniquissimam dissimillimamque legis esse arbitror eam quam L. Flaccus interrex de Sulla tulit, ut omnia quaecumque ille fecisset essent rata. Nam cum ceteris in civitatibus tyrannis institutis leges omnes exstinguantur atque tollantur, hic rei publicae tyrannum lege constituit. Est invidiosa lex, sicuti dixi, verum tamen habet excusationem; non enim videtur
6 hominis lex esse, sed temporis. Quid si est haec multo impudentior? Nam Valeria lege Corneliisque legibus cum eripitur,[7] datur, coniungitur impudens gratificatio cum acerba iniuria; sed tamen habet in[8] illis legibus spem non nullam cui ademptum est, aliquem scrupulum cui datum[9] est. Rulli cautio est haec: "qui post C. Marium Cn. Papirium consules." Quam procul a suspicione fugit, quod eos consules qui adversarii Sullae maxime fuerunt potissimum nominavit! Si enim Sullam dictatorem nominasset, perspicuum fore et invidiosum arbitratus est. Sed quem vestrum

---

5 populo Romano *Lauredanus*: rei p. *ack*: r. p. *cett.*
6 confessus: *corr. Manutius*   7 cum eripitur *ed. P. Rami 1580*: eripitur cum *M*: eripitur civi *Eπ*: eripitur cui *cett.*
8 habet in *Naugerius, ed. Hervagiana*: inhibet *ωπ*
9 ademptum . . . datum *Puteanus*: ademptus . . . datus *ω*

---

7 Cf. 2.102–3.   8 A law enacted in 82 by L. Valerius Flaccus as interrex naming Sulla as dictator and ratifying his previous acts: *LPPR* 348–49; *MRR* 2:66–67.

at a most inopportune moment. And I do not discuss it now because I think the current state of the republic should not be vigorously defended, especially since I have declared myself to the Roman people the defender of tranquility and harmony for the present year,[7] but to teach Rullus to keep silent in the future at least on those matters on which he would wish silence to be observed concerning himself and his actions. Of all laws, I think the most unjust 5 and least like a law is the one that Lucius Flaccus as interrex enacted in regard to Sulla—that whatever acts he had performed should be ratified.[8] For, while in all other states, when tyrants are set up, all laws are annulled and abolished, this man, by a law, established a tyrant for the republic. It is a hateful law, as I have said, but there is an excuse for it; for it seems to be not the law of the man, but of the time. But what if this law is far more shameless? For 6 by the Valerian and Cornelian laws, when something is taken away, it is given; a shameless favor is combined with a grievous wrong; but still in these laws he allows some hope to the man from whom something has been taken and some worry to him to whom it has been given.[9] This is Rullus' stipulation: "he who after the consulship of Gaius Marius and Gnaeus Papirius."[10] How far he has kept clear of suspicion, by naming in particular those consuls who were especially opponents of Sulla! For if he had named the dictator Sulla, he thought that would be obvi-

[9] For the Valerian law, see the previous note; the Cornelian law will be the one authorizing the proscriptions (also dated to 82): *LPPR* 349.

[10] Consuls of 82: *MRR* 2:65; this Marius was the son of the man elected consul seven times.

CICERO

tam tardo ingenio fore putavit cui post eos consules Sullam dictatorem fuisse in mentem venire non posset?

7 Quid ergo ait Marianus tribunus plebis, qui nos "Sullanos" in invidiam rapit? "Qui post Marium et Carbonem consules agri, aedificia, lacus, stagna, loca, possessiones" (caelum et mare praetermisit, cetera complexus est) "publice data, adsignata, vendita, concessa sunt" (a quo, Rulle? Post Marium et Carbonem consules quis adsignavit, quis dedit, quis concessit praeter Sullam?) "ea omnia eo iure sint" (quo iure? Labefactat videlicet nescio quid; nimium acer, nimium vehemens tribunus plebis Sullana[10] rescindit) "ut quae optimo iure privata sunt."[11]
8 Etiamne meliore quam paterna et avita? Meliore. At hoc Valeria lex non dicit, Corneliae leges non sanciunt, Sulla ipse non postulat. Si isti agri partem aliquam iuris, aliquam similitudinem propriae possessionis, aliquam spem diuturnitatis attingunt, nemo est tam impudens[12] istorum quin agi secum praeclare arbitretur. Tu vero, Rulle, quid quaeris? Quod habent ut habeant? Quis vetat? Ut privatum sit? Ita latum est. Ut meliore ⟨iure⟩[13] tui soceri fundus Hirpinus sit sive ager Hirpinus—totum enim possidet—quam meus paternus avitusque fundus Arpinas? Id
9 enim caves. Optimo enim iure ea sunt profecto praedia

[10] Sullana *VMψm*: sullanus *Eπ*: sullanis *eϵ*
[11] sunt *c, Lag.9, Turnebus*: sint *ω*
[12] imprudens: *corr. Naugerius*
[13] meliore iure *Pluygers*: melior *ω*

---

[11] That is, the possessors of Sullan grants.

DE LEGE AGRARIA 3.6–9

ous and odious. But which of you did he think would be so slow-witted as not to remember that Sulla was dictator after those consuls?

What then does this "Marian" tribune of the plebs say, who is whisking us "Sullans" off into infamy? "Let all the lands, buildings, lakes, marshes, sites, possessions"—he has omitted the sky and sea, but has included everything else—"that have been publicly given, assigned, sold, and granted"—by whom, Rullus? After the consulship of Marius and Carbo, who assigned, gave, or granted except Sulla?—"let them all be under the same title"—what title? Evidently he is going to weaken something; the fierce and vehement plebeian tribune is abolishing acts of Sulla—"as those things that are private property with the best title." By a better title than paternal and ancestral properties? Yes. But the Valerian law does not say this, the Cornelian laws do not sanction this, Sulla himself does not demand it. If those lands have any share of legality, any resemblance to private ownership, any hope of permanence, none of those men[11] is so impudent as not to consider himself extremely well treated. But as for you, Rullus, what are you seeking? That they may keep what they have? Who forbids it? That it may be private property? So it has been enacted. That your father-in-law's farm in the Hirpine district, or rather the territory of Hirpinum—for he possesses it all—be held by a better title than my paternal and ancestral farm at Arpinum?[12] Yes, that is what you stipulate. For those lands are certainly held by the

7

8

9

---

[12] The Hirpine district was in the Apennine area of central Italy between Latium, Campania, and Apulia. Arpinum was a town some sixty miles southeast of Rome.

CICERO

quae optima condicione sunt. Libera meliore iure sunt quam serva; capite hoc omnia quae serviebant non servient. Soluta meliore in causa sunt quam obligata; eodem capite subsignata omnia, si modo Sullana sunt, liberantur. Immunia commodiore condicione sunt quam illa quae pensitant; ego Tusculanis pro aqua Crabra[14] vectigal pendam, quia mancipio fundum accepi; si a Sulla mihi datus esset, Rulli lege non penderem.

10 Video vos, Quirites, sicuti res ipsa cogit, commoveri vel legis vel orationis impudentia, legis, quae ius melius Sullanis praediis constituat quam paternis, orationis, quae eius modi ⟨in⟩[15] causa insimulare quemquam audeat rationes Sullae nimium vehementer defendere. At si illa solum sanciret quae a Sulla essent data, tacerem, modo ipse se Sullanum esse confiteretur. Sed non modo illis cavet verum etiam aliud quoddam genus donationis inducit; et is qui a me Sullanas possessiones defendi criminatur non eas solum sancit verum ipse novas adsignationes instituit 11 et repentinus Sulla nobis exoritur. Nam attendite quantas concessiones agrorum hic noster obiurgator uno verbo facere conetur: "quae data, donata, concessa, vendita." Patior, audio. Quid deinde? "Possessa." Hoc tribunus plebis promulgare ausus est ut, quod quisque post Marium et Carbonem consules possidet, id eo iure teneret quo quod[16]

---

[14] crebra: *corr. Manutius*   [15] *add. Baiter*
[16] quo quod *ed. Ascens.*: quo qui *k*: quod *ω*

---

[13] Tusculum was a city in the Alban Hills some fifteen miles southeast of Rome, near modern Frascati; on Cicero's estate there, cf. Coarelli 1981, 116–19; Marzano 2007, 616–17. The Aqua Crabra was a small stream nearby.

best title which are held on the best terms. Lands that are free from easements are held by a better title than those under an easement; according to this section, all under easement will cease to be so. Those that are unmortgaged are in a better case than those that are mortgaged; by the same section, all those that are encumbered, if only they were assigned by Sulla, are released from encumbrances. Those that are tax-free are in a more advantageous position than those that are taxable. At my Tusculan estate, I will pay a tax for the use of the Aqua Crabra,[13] because I obtained my farm by purchase; if it had been given to me by Sulla, under Rullus' law I would not pay.

I see, Romans, that, as the matter itself requires, you 10 are stirred to indignation by the impudence either of the law or of his speech: of the law, since it establishes a better title to Sullan estates than to paternal ones, of the speech since, in such a case, he dares to accuse anyone of defending Sulla's policies too strongly. But if he only ratified the Sullan allotments, I would say nothing, provided that he confessed that he was himself a Sullan. But he does not only make a stipulation for them but even introduces another kind of donation; and the man who charges me with defending the Sullan possessions not only ratifies them, but initiates fresh allotments himself, and suddenly rises up among us as a Sulla. For listen carefully to what vast 11 grants of land this critic of ours endeavors to make by a single word: "the lands that have been given, donated, granted, sold." Very well, I hear. What next? "Possessed." Did a tribune of the plebs venture to promulgate this: that what anyone has possessed since the consulship of Marius and Carbo he may hold by the best title by which anyone can hold private property? Even if he has thrown out the

CICERO

optimo privatum ⟨est⟩?[17] Etiamne si vi deiecit,[18] etiamne si clam, si precario venit in possessionem? Ergo hac lege ius civile, causae possessionum, praetorum interdicta tol-
12 lentur. Non mediocris res neque parvum sub hoc verbo furtum, Quirites, latet. Sunt enim multi agri lege Cornelia publicati nec cuiquam adsignati neque venditi qui a paucis hominibus impudentissime possidentur. His cavet, hos defendit, hos privatos facit; hos, inquam, agros, quos Sulla nemini dedit, Rullus non vobis adsignare vult, sed eis condonare qui possident. Causam quaero cur ea quae maiores vobis in Italia, Sicilia, Africa,[19] duabus Hispaniis, Macedonia, Asia reliquerunt[20] venire patiamini, cum ea quae vestra sunt condonari possessoribus eadem lege videatis.
13 Iam totam legem intellegetis cum ad paucorum dominationem scriptam,[21] tum ad Sullanae adsignationis rationes esse accommodatissimam. Nam socer huius vir multum bonus est, neque ego nunc de illius bonitate, sed de generi impudentia disputo. Ille enim quod habet retinere vult neque se Sullanum esse dissimulat; hic, ut ipse habeat quod non habet, quae dubia sunt per vos sancire vult et, cum plus appetat quam ipse Sulla, quibus rebus resisto,

[17] add. Baiter   [18] deiecit Lambinus: eiecit ωπ
[19] Africa απ: om. cett.: del. Kayser
[20] reliquerunt nχ: quaesiverunt VMψ: om. απ
[21] scriptam cod. Torr.: scripta sit ωπ

[14] An interdict was an official order issued at the request of a claimant enjoining another person to do or not to do a specific act. Most relevant here would be the *interdictum uti possidetis* maintaining existing possessory relations pending judicial resolu-

DE LEGE AGRARIA 3.11–13

owner by violence, has obtained possession of it by stealth or on sufferance? So then this law will annul civil law, the titles to possessions, and the interdicts of the praetors.[14] This is not an unimportant matter, Romans, nor is it a petty larceny that is hidden under this expression. For many lands have been confiscated under the Cornelian law that have neither been assigned nor sold to anyone, and are shamelessly occupied by a few men. He looks out for them, defends them, and makes them private property; these lands, I say, that Sulla gave to no one, Rullus does not mean to assign to you, but to present them as a gift to those who possess them. I ask why you would allow the properties that your ancestors bequeathed to you in Italy, Sicily, Africa, the two Spains, Macedonia, and Asia, to be sold, when you see property that is yours presented as a gift to the possessors by the same law.

You will now understand that the whole law has been drafted not only to secure the domination of a few, but is also most perfectly adapted to the system of Sulla's allotments. Now his father-in-law is a fine gentlemen, and I am not now speaking about his character, but I am discussing the impudence of his son-in-law.[15] The former desires to keep what he has and makes no bones about being a Sullan;[16] the latter, in order to have what he does not have, desires through your agency to ratify the titles that are uncertain; and although he craves more than Sulla him-

---

tion of a dispute over ownership; see further Berger 1953 s.vv. Interdictum and Interdictum uti possidetis.

[15] On Rullus' father-in-law, Valg(i)us, see on 1.14.

[16] On the term "Sullan" and its usage, cf. Santangelo 2012, esp. 188–89.

CICERO

14 Sullanas res defendere ⟨me⟩ criminatur.[22] "Habet agros non nullos," inquit, "socer meus desertos atque longinquos; vendet eos mea lege quanti volet. Habet incertos ac nullo iure possessos; confirmabuntur optimo iure. Habet publicos; reddam privatos. Denique eos fundos quos in agro Casinati optimos fructuosissimosque continuavit—cum usque eo vicinos proscriberet quoad oculis conformando[23] ex multis praediis unam fundi regionem formamque perfecerit—quos nunc cum aliquo metu tenet, sine ulla cura possidebit."

15 Et quoniam qua de causa et quorum causa ille hoc promulgarit[24] ostendi, doceat ipse nunc[25] ego quem possessorem defendam cum agrariae legi resisto. Silvam Scantiam vendis; populus Romanus[26] possidet; defendo. Campanum agrum dividis; vos estis in possessione; non cedo. Deinde Italiae, Siciliae ceterarumque provinciarum possessiones venalis ac proscriptas hac lege video; vestra sunt praedia, vestrae possessiones; resistam atque repugnabo neque patiar a quoquam populum Romanum de suis possessionibus me consule demoveri, praesertim,
16 Quirites, cum[27] vobis nihil quaeratur. Hoc enim vos ⟨in⟩[28] errore versari diutius non oportet. Num quis vestrum ad vim, ad facinus, ad caedem accommodatus est? Nemo. Atqui ei generi hominum, mihi credite, Campanus ager et

[22] me criminatur *Lambinus*: criminor ωπ   [23] oculis conformando *Gulielmius*: oculis confirmando απVMψ: oculos confirmando $n\chi^2$ [24] promulgavit: *corr. Graevius*

[25] num: *corr. Mommsen*

[26] p(opulus) R(omanus) k, *Lauredanus*: r(es) p(ublica) ω

[27] praesertim, Quiritus, cum *R. Klotz*: praesertimque cum απ: praesertim quom *cett.*   [28] *add. Naugerius*

self, he accuses me of defending the acts of Sulla, which I am resisting.[17] "My father-in-law has some lands that are desolate and far away," he says; "by my law he will sell them for whatever price he likes. He has lands of uncertain status and with no title; they will be confirmed with the best title. He holds public lands; I will make them private. Finally, as to the rich and productive estates that he connected one to another in the district of Casinum, when he announced the enforced sale of the neighboring lands until such time as he created out of many estates a single area and plan of an estate by modeling it with his eyes—these lands, which he now holds with some apprehension, he will possess without any anxiety."

And since I have shown for what reason and for whose sake he has made this promulgation, let him now inform you what occupier I am defending when I resist the agrarian law. You are selling the Scantian forest; the Roman people possess it. I am defending it. You are dividing the Campanian territory; you [plural] are in possession of it. I refuse to give it up. Next, I see that possessions in Italy, Sicily, and the other provinces are for sale and proscribed by this law: they are your estates, your possessions. I shall resist and fight back, and while I am consul, I will not allow the Roman people to be turned out of its possessions by anyone, especially, Romans, since nothing is being sought for you. For you must not be subject to this error any longer. Is there any one of you inclined to violence, crime, or murder? No one. And yet, believe me, it

---

[17] On the exploitation of the hatred of Sulla and his beneficiaries as an important factor in the debate on the agrarian law, see Eckert 2016, 139–40.

praeclara illa Capua servatur; exercitus contra vos, contra libertatem vestram, contra Cn. Pompeium constituitur; contra hanc urbem Capua, contra vos manus hominum audacissimorum, contra Cn. Pompeium decem duces comparantur. Veniant et coram,[29] quoniam me in vestram contionem vobis flagitantibus non vocaverunt,[30] disserant.

[29] et coram *Richter*: coram απ: coram et *cett.*
[30] non vocaverunt *Morstein-Marx 2004, 192–93 adn. 133*: convocaverunt ω

is for that kind of men that the Campanian territory and that splendid Capua are reserved. An army is being raised against you, against your liberty, against Gnaeus Pompey; against this city, Capua is being prepared; against you, bands of criminals; against Gnaeus Pompey, ten generals.[18] Let them come and, since they have not summoned me before your assembly, though you eagerly demanded it, let them debate face to face.[19]

[18] Resuming the characterological contrast between the urban plebs and the supposedly intended beneficiaries of Rullus' law from 2.77.

[19] Evidently a challenge that Rullus was not keen to take up; cf. 1.23 and 2.78.

INDEX OF PERSONAL NAMES

This index lists the names of (ancient) persons mentioned in the introductions to the speeches by page number (in italics) and in Cicero's Latin text by section number; fictive characters are excluded. No separate reference is given for a footnote if it is on the same page as a page reference. In the forensic speeches, references to Cicero's client in the given speech are excluded. A passage where the person is clearly identified but not named is enclosed in parentheses. The speeches are abbreviated as follows:

Q = Pro Quinctio
RA = Pro Roscio Amerino
RC = Pro Roscio Comoedo
T = Pro Tullio
A = De lege agraria

Acerronius, Cn., *331*; T 16, 17, 20
Acidinus. *See* Manlius Acidinus
Aemilius Lepidus, M. (cos. 78), *330n11*
Aemilius Paullus, L. (cos. I 182), A 1.5
Albius, L., Q 24, 58
Alexa (or Alexas). *See* Ptolemy X Alexander I
Alfenus, Sex. (eques; Quinctius' agent), *3*; Q 21, 27, 29, 61, 68–70, 73, 76, 83

Antiochus III the Great (Seleucid king), A 2.90
Antistius, P. (professional prosecutor), RA 90
Antonius, C. (cos. 63), *393*
Antonius, M. (cos. 99), Q 80
Apion. *See* Ptolemy Apion
Aquilius, C. (pr. 66; jurist), *5*, *6*; Q 1, 3–5, 8, 10, 17, 22, 28, 32, 33, 35, 36, 43, 44, 46–48, 53, 54, 60, 64, 68, 77, 79, 81, 84, 91, 96, 99
Aquilius, M'. (cos. 101), A 2.83

571

INDEX OF PERSONAL NAMES

Aristonicus of Pergamum, *A* 2.90
Atilius Calatinus, A. (cos. I 258), *A* 2.64
Atilius Saranus (?), *RA* 50
Aurelius Cotta, C. (cos. 75), *A* 2.58
Aurelius Cotta, L. (cos. 65), *A* 2.44
Automedon, *RA* 98

Blossii, *A* 2.93
Burrenus, P. (pr. 83), *3*; *Q* 25, 30, 69

Caecilia Metella, *116*; *RA* 27, 147, 149
(Caecilii) Metelli, *RA* 15
Caecilius Metellus, L. (pr. 71, cos. 68), *328n1*, *329*, *332*; *T* 39
Caecilius Metellus, M. (pr. 69), *RA* 77
Caecilius Metellus Balearicus, Q. (cos. 123), *116n10*; *RA* 27, 147
Caecilius Metellus Nepos, Q. (cos. 98), *RA* 27, 147
Caecilius Rufus, L. (tr. pl. 63), *387n15*, *395*
Calatinus. *See* Atilius Calatinus, A.
Calpurnius Piso, C. (cos. 67), *264*, *265*; *RC* 7, 12, 15, 18, 21, 22, 37, 38, 45, 51
Cassius Longinus Ravilla, L. (cos. 127), *RA* 84
Catius Aemilianus, Q., *T* 19
Cato. *See* Porcius Cato, M.

Claudius, C. (a senator), *T* 14
Claudius Marcellus, M. (leg. 102?), *Q* 54
Claudius Pulcher, App. (cos. 79), *116n10*
Clodia Metelli, *116n10*
Clodius Pulcher, P. (tr. pl. 58, aed. cur. 56), *116n10*
Cloelius, T., of Tarracina, *RA* 64
Cluentius Habitus, A. (Cicero's client), *272*
Cluvius, C. (eques), *270*, *271n20*; *RC* 42, 43, 47–51
Considius, L., *A* 2.92, 2.93
(Cornelii) Scipiones, *RA* 15. *See also* Cornelius Scipio, P.; Cornelius Scipio Calvus, Cn.
Cornelius Chrysogonus, L. (freedman), *111*, *112*, *113*, *115–17*; *RA* 6, 7, 20, 21, 23, 25, 28, 34, 35, 49, 58, 60, 72, 77, 105–8, 110, 114, 120–22, 125, 127, 130, 132, 138, 140–42, 144, 146, 150
Cornelius Dolabella, Cn. (cos. 81), *A* 2.35
Cornelius Dolabella, Cn. (pr. 81), *Q* 30, 31
Cornelius Lentulus, P. (cos. suff. 162), *A* 2.82
Cornelius Scipio, L. (cos. 83), *Q* 24
Cornelius Scipio, P. (cos. 218), *A* 1.5 ("two Scipios")
Cornelius Scipio Africanus Aemilianus, P. (cos. I 147), *RA* 103; *A* 1.5, 2.51, 2.58

INDEX OF PERSONAL NAMES

Cornelius Scipio Asiagenus, L. (cos. 83), *Q* 24

Cornelius Scipio Calvus, Cn. (cos. 222), *A* 1.5 ("two Scipios")

Cornelius Scipio Nasica, P. (pr. 93), *RA* 77

Cornelius Sulla, Faustus, *385*; *A* 1.12

Cornelius Sulla Felix, L. (dict. 82–80), *111*, *115*, *116*, *331*, *385*, *390*, *391*, *393*; *Q* 76; *RA* 6, 20, 21, 25, 26, 105, 110, 126, 127, 130, 131, 136, 143, 146; *A* 1.10, 1.21, 2.38, 2.39, 2.56, 2.81, 3.3, 3.5–10, 3.12, 3.13

Cornelius Tacitus, *328*, 329n3

Curtii, *RA* 90

Dionysia (dancer), *RC* 23

Domitius Ahenobarbus, Cn. (tr. pl. 104, cos. 96), *A* 2.18, 2.19

Eros (comic actor), *RC* 30

Erucius, C. (professional prosecutor), *113*, *114*, *117*; *RA* 35, 38, 39, 42, 43, 44, 45, 50, 52, 55, 58, 61, 62, 72, 73, 78, 79, 80, 82, 83, 89, 91, 93, 101, 104, 122, 127, 132

Fabius, P. (former Sullan officer; landowner), *328–34*; *T* 3, 5, 7, 14, 20, 21, 24, 31, 35, 48, 55, F 1a–c

Fabius Maximus Verrucosus, Q. (cos. V 209), *A* 2.90

Fabricius Luscinus, C. (cos. I 282), *A* 2.64

Fannius, M. (pr. 80), *RA* 11, 12, (85)

Fannius Chaerea, C., *264–67*, *269*, *270*, *271*; *RC* 1–3, 8, 9, 14, 16, 19–22, 24, 27, 28, 35, 36–39, 40–42, 45, 48–52, 55, 56

Fimbria. *See* Flavius Fimbria, C.

Flaccus. *See* Valerius Flaccus

Flavius of Tarquinia, Q., *265–67*, *271*; *RC* 32, 34, 35, 37–39, 40–42, 51, 52, 54–56

Flavius, L. (tr. pl. 60), *390*n20

Flavius Fimbria, C. (leg. 82), *RA* 33

Fulvius Flaccus, Q. (cos. IV 209), *A* 2.90

Fulvius Veratius, P. (?), *A* 2.67

Furius Philus, L. (cos. 136), *A* 2.64

Gallonius, *Q* 94

Glaucippus, *A* 1.13

Gracchi. *See* (Sempronii) Gracchi

Hannibal, *383*; *A* 1.20, 2.95

Hiempsal II (king of Numidia), *A* 1.10, 1.11, 2.58

Hortensius Hortalus, Q. (cos. 69), *Q* 1, 8, 34, 35, 44, 45, 63, 68, 72, 77, 78, 80

Iuba I (king of Numidia), *A* 2.59

573

INDEX OF PERSONAL NAMES

Iulius Caesar, C. (cos. I 59), *390n20*
Iunius, M. (advocate), *3*; *Q* 3
Iunius Brutus, M. (tr. pl. 83), *392*; *Q* 65, 69; *A* 2.89, 2.92, 2.98

Laelius Sapiens, C. (cos. 140), *A* 2.64
Licinius Crassus, L. (cos. 95), *2*; *Q* 80
Licinius Crassus, M. (cos. I 70), *328n1*
Lucilius Balbus, L. (jurist), *Q* 53, 54
Lucullus, M. *See* Terentius Varro Lucullus, M.
Luscius Ocrea, C. (senator), *RC* 43–46

Mallius Glaucia (freedman), *112*, *114*, *115*; *RA* 19, 96, 97, 98
Manilius, T. (senator), *RC* 43–46
Manlius Acidinus, L. (pr. urb. 210) (?), *A* 2.64
Manlius Acidinus Fulvianus, L. (cos. 179) (?), *A* 2.64
Manlius Torquatus, L. (cos. 65), *A* 2.44
Marcius Philippus, L. (cos. 91), *Q* 72, 77, 80; *A* 2.42
Marii, *RA* 90
Marius, C. (cos. I 107), *390*; *RA* 33
Marius C. (son of preceding; cos. 82), *A* 3.6, 3.7, 3.11
Metelli. *See* (Caecilii) Metelli
Mithridates VI Eupator (king of Pontus), *389*; *A* 1.6, 2.51, 2.52, 2.90
Mucius Scaevola, Q. ("the Augur"; cos. 117), *2*
Mucius Scaevola, Q. ("the Pontifex"; cos. 95), *2*; *RA* 33, 34
Mummius, L. (cos. 146), *A* 1.5

Naevius, Sex. (auctioneer), *3–6*; *Q* 1, 7, 9, 11, 12, 14–16, 18, 20, 22, 24, 25, 27, 28, 36–38, 40–42, 45, 48, 53, 55, 59, 60, 62, 63, 65, 67, 68, 70, 74–76, 79, 80, 84, 85, 87–90, 93, 94, 96, 97, 99
Norbanus, C. (cos. 83), *Q* 24

Panurgus (slave), *264–65*; *RC* 27–29, 31, 32, 35, 39, 41, 42, 49, 54
Papirius Carbo, Cn. (cos. III 82), *A* 3.6, 3.7, 3.11
Perpenna (or Perperna), M. (cos. 92), *RC* 3, 22
Perses (or Perseus; king of Macedonia), *A* 1.5, 2.50, 2.90
Philinus (slave), *T* 19, 22
Philip V (king of Macedonia), *A* 2.50, 2.90
Plautus, T. Maccius, *270*
Pompeius Magnus, Cn. ("Pompey"; cos. I 70), *388*, *390–92*, *396*; *A* F 4, 1.5, 1.6, 1.13, 2.23–25, 2.46, 2.49, 2.52–54, 2.60–2.62, 2.99, 3.16
Pompeius Rufus, Q. (cos. 88), *A* 1.10, 2.38, 2.56
Porcius Cato, M. (cos. 195), *A* 2.64

INDEX OF PERSONAL NAMES

Pseudo-Philip (Andriscus), *A* 2.90
Ptolemy X Alexander I (King Alexa or Alexas), *A* 2.41
Ptolemy XII Auletes, *A* (2.42), 2.44
Ptolemy Apion, *A* 2.51
Publicius, L., *Q* 24

Quinctii Scapulae (sons of P. Quinctius Scapula), *Q* 17, 18, 20
Quinctius, C. (brother of P. Quinctius), *3*; *Q* 11, 12, 14, 15, 17, 37, 38, 41, 73
Quinctius, L. (tr. pl. 74, pr. 68), *328n1*, *329–30*, *332–35*; *T* 1, 3, 6, 35, 37
Quinctius, P. (Cicero's client), *264*
Quinctius Flamininus, T. (cos. 192), *A* 1.5
Quinctius Scapula, P., *Q* 17
Quinctius Valgus, C. (?), *391*, *394–95*; *A* (1.15), 3.3, (3.13)
Quin(c)tilius (Varus?), P., *Q* 54

Roscii (i.e., Capito and Magnus), *RA* 35
Roscius, Sex. of Ameria (father of Cicero's client), *110*, *112*, *114*, *116*; *RA* 15, 18, 19–21, 24–26, 43, 76, 78, 87, 88, 92, 94, 95, 96, 105, 120, 145
Roscius Capito, T., *112–15*; *RA* 17, 19, 21, 26, 84, 96, 98, 100, 108, 109, 115, 117
Roscius Gallus, Q. (comic actor), *2*; *Q* 77

Roscius Magnus, T., *112–15*; *RA* 17, 18, 19, 21, 23, 24, 30, 77, 84, 92, 95, 98, 108, 119
Rullus. *See* Servilius Rullus, P.

Saltius, Sex., *A* 2.92
Saturius, P. (advocate), *264*, *269*, *270*; *RC* 3, 18, 22, 27, 28, 40, 51, 56
Scipiones. *See* (Cornelii) Scipiones
(Sempronii) Gracchi (i.e., C. and Ti.), *385*, *387*; *A* 1.21, 2.10, 2.81
Sempronius Gracchus, C. (tr. pl. 123–122), *A* 2.10
Sempronius Gracchus, Ti. (tr. pl. 133), *A* 2.10, 2.31
Septimii (?), *A* 3.3
Sertorius, Q. (qu. 91, pr. 85 or 83), *A* 2.83
Servilii, *RA* 15
Servilius Rullus, P. (tr. pl. 63), *382–83*, *385–90*, *392–97*; *A* 1.14, 1.16, 1.21–23, 2.13, 2.19–24, 2.31, 2.43, 2.51, 2.53, 2.57, 2.61, 2.71, 2.81, 2.83, 2.89, 2.92, 2.96–98, 3.3, 3.4, 3.6–9, 3.12
Servilius Vatia Isauricus, P. (cos. 79), *A* 1.5, 2.50
Solon, *RA* 70
Spartacus, *328*, *331*
Statilius (actor), *RC* 30

Tacitus. *See* Cornelius Tacitus
Terentius Varro Lucullus, M. (cos. 73), *329–30*; *T* 8

575

INDEX OF PERSONAL NAMES

Trebellius, M., *Q* 21
Turranii (?), *A* 3.3

Valerius Flaccus, C. (cos. 93), *Q* 28
Valerius Flaccus, L. (cos. 100, interrex 82), *393*; *A* 3.5
Valerius Messalla Niger, M. (cos. 61) (?), *110*, *116*; *RA* 149
Valerius Messalla Rufus, M. (cos. 53) (?), *110*, *116*; *RA* 149
Valgus (or Valgius). *See* Quinctius Valgus, C.
Veratius. *See* Fulvius Veratius, P.
Vibellius Taurea, Carrinus, *A* 2.93